16th Edition

Law *for* Business

John D. Ashcroft, J.D.
Member of the District of Columbia and Missouri Bars

Janet E. Ashcroft, J.D.
Member of the District of Columbia and Missouri Bars

SOUTH-WESTERN
CENGAGE Learning

Australia • Brazil • Japan • Korea • Mexico • Singapore • Spain • United Kingdom • United States

SOUTH-WESTERN
CENGAGE Learning™

Law for Business, 16th edition
John D. Ashcroft • Janet E. Ashcroft

VP/Editorial Director:
Jack W. Calhoun

Publisher:
Rob Dewey

Acquisitions Editor:
Steve Silverstein, Esq.

Developmental Editor:
John Abner

Editorial Assistant:
Krista Kellman

Executive Marketing Manager:
Lisa Lysne

Marketing Manager:
Jennifer Garamy

Sr. Production Editor:
Cliff Kallemeyn

Manager of Technology, Editorial:
John Barans

Technology Project Editor:
Pam Wallace

Sr. Manufacturing Coordinator:
Charlene Taylor

Art Director:
Michelle Kunkler

Production House:
ICC Macmillan Inc.

Printer:
China Translation & Printing
Services Ltd.

Cover and Internal Designer:
Red Hanger Design, LLC

Cover Images:
Frank Herholdt/Stone/Getty Images

Library of Congress Control Number:
2007928359

For more information about our products,
contact us at:

Cengage Learning
Customer & Sales Support
1-800-354-9706

South-Western
5191 Natorp Boulevard
Mason, OH 45040
USA

Brief Contents

Contents

v

Preface

WHY STUDY BUSINESS LAW?

Newspapers, magazines, television, radio—and even our computers—relate business information to us almost by the minute. Behind the scenes of business activity—from startups of new businesses to corporate mergers, marketing, advertising, technology, and employment—laws governing business play a vital role. The study of business law is necessary to provide students with an overview of the law of commercial transactions and other business legal issues. *Law for Business, Sixteenth Edition,* focuses on these laws to prepare students to conduct business in our dynamic world marketplace.

PURPOSE OF THE TEXT

Law for Business, Sixteenth Edition, is a practical approach to law that emphasizes current and relevant topics students need to understand about business transactions and issues, such as contracts, property, employer/employee relations, and insurance. The basic concepts of business law are covered without the excessive theory that often makes law seem incomprehensible. Practical coverage of law pertaining to business, without the detailed treatment of a law school text, is the hallmark of this text. The substantial breadth of this text, complete with examples and cases, is an effective introduction to a variety of legal topics.

NEW AND SUCCESSFUL FEATURES

Integrated Learning Objectives

Each chapter begins with learning objectives that outline what the students will accomplish after reading the chapter. Margin icons indicate where learning objectives are first discussed in the text. Each objective is briefly restated as reinforcement, so students need not refer to the beginning of each chapter. These learning objective icons create a natural outline to help students easily comprehend the information.

Actual U.S. Court Cases with Citations

This book contains no make-believe cases. Every case example, problem, and summary is an actual U.S. court case, transferring theory into reality. These exciting actual cases help students relate to the subject as they learn about real world legal situations that can occur in business. Case citations are included in the text for each case example, to further clarify these resources and inspire further research and reading.

Ethical Points

In order to give greater focus to ethical considerations in various business situations, the text contains ethical point questions and comments interspersed in the margins. These questions highlight pertinent ethical issues, show the relationships between law and ethics, and serve as a basis for class discussion.

Ethics in Practice

Ethics in Practice bullets appear at the end of each Part, just before the Part Summary Cases. Ethics in Practice poses a hypothetical business situation and asks students to consider the ethical implications. In conjunction with the Ethical Points scattered throughout the chapters, the new Ethics in Practice feature reinforces the importance of ethical responsibility in today's climate of corporate scandal and recrimination.

ENHANCED CONTENT AND OTHER IMPORTANT FEATURES

In the Sixteenth Edition, we have maintained the format of the previous edition, but of course, have updated the content as needed throughout. This edition reflects the recent major changes in the federal bankruptcy law. It also contains many new cases, some of which are listed here:

- *Green v. Racing Ass'n of Cent. Iowa,* 713 N.W.2d 234 (Iowa)
- *McCalla v. Stuckey,* 504 S.E.2d 269 (Ga.)
- *Audio Visual Associates, Inc. v. Sharp Electronics Corp.,* 210 F.3d 254 (4th Cir.)
- *Fisher v. Schefers,* 656 N.W.2d 592 (Minn. App.)
- *In re Estate of Hollett,* 834 A.2d 348 (N.H.)
- *Ureneck v. Cui,* 798 N.E.2d 305 (Mass. App.Ct.)
- *St Clair Medical, P.C. v. Borgiel,* 715 N.W.2d 914 (Mich. App.)
- *Metro-Goldwyn-Mayer Studios Inc. v. Grokster, Ltd.,* 545 U.S. 913
- *Cloud Corp. v. Hasbro, Inc.,* 314 F.3d 289 (7th Cir.)
- *Mitsch v. General Motors Corp.,* 833 N.E.2d 936 (Ill. App.)
- *Buckeye Check Cashing, Inc. v. Camp,* 825 N.E.2d 644 (Ohio App.)
- *In re Estate of Ferrara,* 852 N.E.2d 138 (N.Y.)
- *Riser v. Target Corp.,* 458 F3d 817 (8th Cir.)

In addition, in response to suggestions from our users and reviewers, we have made significant revisions to the chapters, such as coverage of intellectual property in Chapter 14 and the addition of a section on ethics in practice in Chapter 1.

Ample Questions and Cases

The end-of-chapter materials include questions and case problems. This gives the teacher and the student the opportunity to check how well the student understands the material.

Key Terms and Definitions

Key terms and their definitions, critical to students' understanding of business law, are printed in the margins for easy identification and mastery. The terms are also compiled into a glossary at the end of the text.

Improved Readability

In *Law for Business*, special attention has been given to improving the readability of the text and cases by using such techniques as shortened sentences, active voice, and more information presented in list format rather than in paragraph form.

Short Chapters

Long chapters tend to dilute the critical points and confuse the reader. *Law for Business* is set up in short, easy-to-understand chapters so that critical points stand out.

Chapter Opening Preview Case and Preview Case Revisited

After two introductory chapters, each chapter begins with a "Preview Case" to involve students in the issues to be discussed in the chapter. Each preview case ends with a question that is answered by the court's decision in the "Preview Case Revisited."

FOR THE INSTRUCTOR

Law for Business comes with a complete and integrated teaching package. The following supplements are available to aid the instructor:

Instructor's Resource CD (IRCD)

The IRCD contains the Instructor's Manual in Microsoft Word files. This manual, by the text authors, acts as a guide to the text and course, providing teaching suggestions, lesson outlines, explanations and citations for the example cases, and answers to the problems contained in the text. It also contains answers to the achievement tests and exams, and transparency masters. This edition also adds a suggestion for group projects at the beginning of each part.

In addition the IRCD includes the ExamView testing software files, the test bank in Microsoft Word files, and the Microsoft PowerPoint lecture slides.

ISBN: 0-324-38161-1

Achievement Tests and Exams

These tests provide an assessment opportunity for the instructor to show what students have learned by using this text.

ISBN: 0-324-38158-1

ExamView Testing Software—Computerized Testing Software

This testing software contains all of the questions in the traditional test bank. This easy-to-use test creation software program is compatible with Microsoft Windows. Instructors can add or edit questions, instructions, and answers; and select questions by previewing them on the screen, selecting them randomly, or selecting them by number. Instructors can also create and administer quizzes online, whether over the Internet, a local area network (LAN), or a wide area network (WAN). The ExamView testing software is available on the Instructor's Resource CD.

Test Bank

Written by Janet Ashcroft, this supplement provides more than 900 objective and case questions by chapter, giving the instructor additional assignments and questions for student testing. The test bank may be obtained on the IRCD or downloaded at academic.cengage.com/blaw/ashcroft.

PowerPoint Presentation Slides

A PowerPoint presentation package, prepared by Jimidene Murphey of South Plains College, provides enhanced lecture materials for the instructor, as well as study aids for students. Available online at academic.cengage.com/blaw/ashcroft or on the Instructor's Resource CD-ROM.

SOUTH-WESTERN LEGAL STUDIES IN BUSINESS MULTIMEDIA SUPPLEMENTS

South-Western is committed to providing you, our educational partners, with the finest educational resources available, including the full complement of South-Western resources. Because we prepare our instructor resources with a variety of teaching environments in mind, it is likely that you will need only a portion of these for your course. Before you request an item, we ask that you please read thoroughly the description of each resource. If you still need more information about resources, we urge you to contact your local sales representative or visit our web site at academic.cengage.com/blaw. Many teaching and learning resources can be downloaded directly from this site.

Business Law Digital Video Library

Featuring 60+ segments on the most important topics in Business Law, Business Law Digital Video Library helps students make the connection between their textbook and the business world. Access to Business Law Digital Video Library is free when bundled with a new text, and students with used book can purchase access to the video clips online. New to this edition are LawFlix, twelve scenes from Hollywood movies with instructor materials for each film clip. The accompanying instructor materials include elements such as goals for the clips, questions for students (with answers for the instructor), background on the film and the scene, and fascinating trivia about the film, its actors, and its history. For more information about Business Law Digital Video Library, visit: academic.cengage.com/blaw.

South-Western Legal Studies in Business Resource Center

This Web site offers a unique, rich and robust online resource for instructors and students. The address academic.cengage.com/blaw provides customer service and product information, links to all text-supporting Web sites, and other cutting-edge resources such as **NewsEdge** and **Court Case Updates.**

Cengage Learning Custom Solutions

Whether you need print, digital, or hybrid course materials, Cengage Learning Custom Solutions can help you create your perfect learning solution. Draw from Cengage Learning's extensive library of texts and collections, add or create your own original work, and create customized media and technology to match your learning and course objectives. Our editorial team will work with you through each step, allowing you to concentrate on the most important thing—your students. Learn more about all our services at www.custom.cengage.com.

CaseNet

CaseNet is Cengage Learning's legal and business case collection featuring selections from the South-Western Legal Studies in Business case database and other prestigious partners. Using TextChoice you can search, preview, arrange cases, and add your original material or legal cases from your state to create the perfect case resource for your course. To start building your casebook, visit CaseNet at http://academic.cengage.com/casenet or contact your local South-Western Legal Studies sales representative.

FOR THE STUDENT

Also available are supplementary materials for the student that provide further opportunities to learn and review business law. Some of the supplements are specific to this text, while others are part of the extensive offering of the multimedia supplements. These materials include

Study Guide and Workbook

Written by Ronald L. Taylor, from Metropolitan State College in Denver, the *Study Guide* provides chapter outlines, general rules and limitations on the rules, examples, and study hints. In addition, objective questions and case problems assist students in reviewing terms and applying concepts learned in each chapter. Students' comprehension is reinforced by reviewing the concepts and applying them to factual situations and through a variety of learning exercises including true/false questions, fill-in-the-blank statements, yes/no questions, questions referring to fact situations, and definition exercises. The *Study Guide* includes all answers.

ISBN: 0-324-38156-5

A Handbook of Basic Law Terms: Black's Dictionary Series

A *Handbook of Basic Law Terms* is a guide to the most important and most common words and phrases used in the law today. This supplement is available at an additional cost when bundled with the text. Students can keep this comprehensive and helpful dictionary for both their professional and personal lives.

ISBN: 0-324-03737-6

ACKNOWLEDGMENTS

We would like to thank the following reviewers who helped with the revision of this and other editions of the text, as well as the many reviewers whose assistance was invaluable throughout numerous past editions. It is your suggestions and comments that have helped make this text what it is today.

James E. Bailey, Jr.
*Arkansas State University—
    Mountain Home*

Gretchen Carroll
Owens Community College

Marilyn S. Chernoff
Sawyer School

Robert D. Colestock
Indiana Vocational Technical College

Elizabeth Cummings
Mississippi Delta Community College

Linda B. Davis
Vance-Granville Community College

Paul Davis
Cincinnati Technical College

Jennie Dehn
Bryant and Stratton Business Institute

Gamewell Gantt
Idaho State University

Julie A. Goodwin
Heald Business College

Tamara Griffin
*University of Arkansas Community
    College at Batesville*

Timothy R. Hart
College of the Sequoias

James P. Hess
Ivy Tech State College

Jay S. Hollowell
Commonwealth College, Virginia Beach

Jeff Holt
Tulsa Community College

Roxanne Jackson
Vance-Granville Community College

Catherine R. Johns
Genesee Community College

Susan Johnson
Central Wesleyan College

Joanna Jones
Vance-Granville Community College

Mary Ellen Keith
*New Mexico State University—
    Alamogordo*

J. Franklin Lee
Pitt Community College

Louie J. Michelli
Belmont Technical College

Lee Miller
Indiana Business College

Karen S. Mozingo
Pitt Community College

Jimidene Murphey
South Plains College

John M. Newcome
Renton Technical College

Barb Portzen
Mid-State Technical College

Clovie C. Quick
Columbus Technical Institute

Michael L. Ramsey
Sanford Brown Business College

Margaret O'Toole Rogers
*Wayland Baptist University /
    University of Alaska Fairbanks*

John Sedensky
Newbury College

Alan L. Sheets
Indiana Business College

Esther M. Tremblay
Duff's Business Institute

Charlotte A. Weybright
Brown Mackie College

Timothy G. Wiedman
Thomas Nelson Community College

Hugh L. Wink
Kilgore College

Allen Young
Bessemer State Technical College

Clint Wolf
Brown Mackie College

Betty Young
Washington State Community College

John Zahar, Jr.
Heald Business College

We would also like to thank Ronald L. Taylor of Metropolitan State College, preparer of the *Study Guide,* and Jimidene Murphey of South Plains College, preparer of the PowerPoint Presentation Package and online quizzes, for their assistance with these supplements to the text.

John D. Ashcroft

Janet E. Ashcroft

ABOUT THE AUTHORS

JOHN ASHCROFT served as the 79th attorney general of the United States from February, 2001 to February, 2005. He served one term in the United States Senate from 1995 to 2001, and previously served as governor of Missouri for two terms. As governor, Ashcroft balanced eight consecutive budgets during his terms, and *Fortune* magazine rated him one of the top 10 education governors.

In the Senate, Ashcroft took a leading role on key issues such as welfare reform, juvenile crime, and reform of the civil justice system, while authoring significant changes to federal law. He served on the Judiciary, the Commerce, Science, and Transportation, and the Foreign Relations committees and was also the chairman of subcommittees on the Constitution, consumer affairs, and Africa, respectively.

Ashcroft, widely recognized for his innovative use of technology and the Internet, has taught students in Missouri and across the country about using the Internet and on-line information as a tool of citizenship. Ashcroft is currently the Attorney General of the United States.

Prior to entering public service, Ashcroft taught business law at what is now Missouri State University in Springfield. He graduated with honors from Yale University in 1964, met his wife, Janet, at the Law School of the University of Chicago where they each received law degrees in 1967, and later co-authored two college textbooks together. Both have been admitted to practice law in the U.S. Court for the Western District of Missouri.

JANET ASHCROFT has been a full-time faculty member at Howard University, teaching business law, taxation, and accounting, and serving on the Judiciary Committee at the university. She has taught at what is now Missouri State University and Central Bible College in Springfield, Missouri, and at Stephens College in Columbia, Missouri. She is a member of the Board of Trustees of Patrick Henry College and has served on the Visiting Committee of the University of Chicago, chair of the Alzheimer's disease Task Force for the State of Missouri and as state liaison for the National Alzheimer's Association. In these capacities, Janet Ashcroft has authored numerous reports and articles relating to Alzheimer's disease. In addition, she has been the general counsel for the Missouri Department of Revenue.

The Legal System and the Legal Environment of Business

PART 1

Copyrights and trademarks are covered in Chapter 3, "Business Torts and Crimes." You can learn more about copyright laws, registration, fees, international issues and regulations, and the latest on digital transmissions at the Web site of the U.S. Copyright Office. A similar Web site at the U.S. Patent Office provides many links to information about trademarks and patents, fees, laws, how to apply, and more. For more information, see http://www.uspto.gov and http://www.copyright.gov

Introduction to Law

LEARNING OBJECTIVES

1. Define law.
2. Explain why we have laws.
3. List four sources of law.
4. Distinguish among crimes, torts, and ethics.

LO 1
Define law

Law
Governmental rule prescribing conduct and carrying a penalty for violation

Damages
A sum of money a wrongdoer must pay to an injured party

Business Law
Rules of conduct for the performance of business transactions

Many authors have tried to define law. Blackstone's definition is famous: "**Law** is a rule of civil conduct, commanding what is right and prohibiting what is wrong." Many rules of civil conduct commend what is right and condemn what is wrong, but rules are not necessarily laws. Only when a sovereign state issues rules prescribing what is right and what is wrong can a rule be called a law. Even then rules are not effective unless penalties are applied when the rules are broken. Thus, a law is a rule that prescribes conduct and that is enacted and enforced by a government.

Religious teachings, social mores, habit, and peer pressure all contribute to social control of conduct, but only the rules of law apply with equal force to every member of society. A breach of some of these rules is a crime, for which the penalty is a fine, a jail sentence, or possibly both. A breach of other rules is a civil wrong, for which the penalty most often is the payment of a sum of money called **damages**.

Business law is that class of laws that are concerned primarily with rules of conduct prescribed by government for the performance of business transactions.

The laws governing business transactions in the United States did not come into existence overnight. Laws result from society's changing concepts of what is right and what is wrong. They may be created or modified to deal with new technology or circumstances. For example, for several centuries in England and America, an individual who owned land owned the soil and minerals below the topsoil and the air above the land "all the way to heaven." The law prohibited trespassing on a person's land or air. A telephone company that wanted to string a telephone wire through the air had to buy a right of way. When airplanes were invented, this law became a millstone around society's neck. Under this law, a transcontinental airline would have to buy a right of way through the air of every property owner in its path from New York to San Francisco. The modification of this rule by judicial decree shows how the law changes when circumstances change.

OBJECTIVES OF LAW

We live in a complex society. Every time we have business dealings with others—working, making a purchase, starting a business, traveling, renting an apartment, or trying to insure against loss—we have the potential for a dispute. The law seeks to establish rules so that we will be able to resolve those disputes that arise.

LO 2
Why we have laws

The law also sets the rules of conduct for many transactions so that we will know how to avoid disputes. The law thus tries to establish a stable framework to keep society operating as smoothly as possible.

ROOTS OF OUR LEGAL SYSTEM

When the European colonists settled in this country, they instituted legal systems similar to what they had in their native lands. Therefore, English, French, and Spanish colonists set up legal systems similar to those in England, France, and Spain. The 13 colonies that originally became the United States were all English colonies, so they adopted a legal system like England's. Although additional territory was added and the influence of other legal systems was felt, the system we have today is still based heavily on the English legal system of common law and equity.

THE COMMON LAW

Common law is custom that has come to be recognized by the courts as binding on the community and therefore law. In medieval England, there were no laws prescribing the proper rule of conduct in hundreds of situations. When a dispute came before a judge, the court prescribed a rule of its own based on the customs of the time. Over a period of several centuries, these court decisions developed into a body of law. The colonists brought this body of law from England to America. After the United States became a sovereign nation, most of these common laws, including legal maxims developed here, were either enacted as statutory laws or continued as judge-made laws. Much of our current law is based on this common law.

Common Law
English custom recognized by courts as binding

COURT CASE

Facts: When Mabel Ruth Budd died, she bequeathed her home to her husband, George. There was a mortgage on the home and George asked the court to rule that the estate pay the mortgage so he would get the property freed of it. There was no statute covering this question.

Outcome: The court looked to the state constitution that said the common law continued as a part of state law. Because the common law was that a person willed real estate had a right to have a mortgage paid, George got the property freed of the mortgage.

—*In re Budd's Estate*, 105 N.W.2d 358 (Wis.)

EQUITY

Uniformity in the common law spread throughout England because judges tended to decide cases the same way other judges had decided them. But some wrongs occurred for which the law provided no remedy except for money damages.

In some cases, money was not an appropriate remedy. To obtain suitable relief, people began to petition the king for justice. The king delegated these matters

Equity
Justice system based on fairness; provides relief other than merely money damages

to the chancellor, who did not decide the cases on the basis of recognized legal principles, but on the basis of *equity*—what in good conscience ought to be done. Eventually, an additional system of justice evolved that granted judicial relief when no adequate remedy at law existed. This system is called **equity**.

Courts of equity, although they sometimes recognized legal rights, also provided new types of relief. For example, instead of merely ordering a person who had breached a contract agreeing to sell real estate to pay money damages, they would order "specific performance"—that is, require the seller to comply with the terms of the contract and sell the real estate. They also provided for preventive action to protect individuals from likely harm. In this type of case, a court with equity powers might initially issue a **restraining order**, a temporary order forbidding a certain action. Upon a complete hearing, the court might issue an **injunction**, a permanent order forbidding activities that would be detrimental to others. Today, only a few states maintain separate equity courts or, as they are also called, *chancery courts*. In most states, courts apply legal and equitable principles to each case as the facts justify, without making any formal distinction between law and equity.

Restraining Order
Court's temporary order forbidding an action

Injunction
Court's permanent order forbidding an action

SOURCES OF LAW

LO ❸
Sources of law

Our laws come from several sources. They include judges' decisions, federal and state constitutions, statutes, and administrative agency orders.

Judicial Decisions

Judicial interpretation is an important element of the legal process. Because courts can interpret laws differently, the same law might have somewhat different consequences in different states. Interpretations by the highest courts have the effect of setting **precedents**. A precedent is a decided case or court decision that determines the decision in a subsequent case because the cases are so similar.

Precedent
Court decision that determines the decision in a subsequent, similar case

Under the doctrine of *stare decisis* (stand by the decision), these precedents bind the lower courts. These interpretations may concern a situation not previously brought before the court, or the court may decide to reverse a previous decision.

Any state supreme court or the Supreme Court of the United States can reverse a decision of a lower court. For legal stability and so that we can know our rights before we undertake a transaction, courts must generally adhere to the judicial precedents set by earlier decisions. However, changing situations or practices sometimes make it necessary for the previous case law to be overturned and a new rule or practice to be established.

Stare Decisis
Principle that a court decision controls the decision of a similar future case

C O U R T   C A S E

Facts: An accident involving a power lawnmower operated by his father, Alan Clark, injured Paul Clark, age five. Paul sued the lawnmower's manufacturer and Alan and his insurer. Alan said the doctrine of "parental immunity" prevented him from being sued by his dependent son. The state supreme court had held in a case two years previously that parental immunity was abolished; thus, a child could sue a parent.

Outcome: The state supreme court said that it was the policy of courts to stand by previous decisions because judges, lawyers, and citizens have a right to rely on previous holdings. Thus, stare decisis required that parental immunity not prevent the suit.

—*Clark v. Snapper Power Equipment, Inc.*,
488 N.E.2d 138 (Ohio)

Constitutions

A **constitution** is the document that defines the relationships of the parts of the government to each other and the relationship of the government to its citizens or subjects. The U.S. Constitution is the supreme law of the land. State constitutions, as well as all other laws, must agree with the U.S. Constitution. The Supreme Court of the United States is the final arbiter in disputes about whether a state or federal law violates the U.S. Constitution. A state supreme court is the final judge as to whether a state law violates the constitution of that state.

In 1791, after the U.S. Constitution had been adopted, it was amended by the addition of the Bill of Rights. The Constitution contained no specific guarantees of individual liberty. The **Bill of Rights** consists of ten amendments specifically designed to protect the civil rights and liberties of the citizens and the states. It is a part of the U.S. Constitution. Rights protected by the Bill of Rights are frequently referred to by the number of the amendment in which they can be found. Most people have heard of First Amendment rights to free speech or Fifth Amendment rights against self-incrimination.

Constitution
Document that contains fundamental principles of a government

Bill of Rights
First ten amendments to U.S. Constitution

Statutes

Statutes are laws enacted by legislative bodies. The federal Congress, state legislatures, and city councils, all composed of persons elected by the voters, comprise the three chief classes of legislative bodies in the United States. Cities and other municipalities make laws usually called **ordinances**, a specific type of statutory law.

Sometimes, statutes enacted by one legislative body conflict with statutes enacted by another legislative body. Statutes enacted by a higher legislative body prevail over those of lower legislative bodies. Thus, a state law prevails over conflicting county or municipal legislation. A constitutional federal statute prevails over a conflicting state statute.

Unlike constitutions, which are difficult to amend and are designed to be general rather than specific, statutes may be enacted, repealed, or amended at any regular or special session of the lawmaking body. Thus, statutes respond more to the changing demands of the people.

In the field of business law, the most important statute is the Uniform Commercial Code (UCC).[1] The UCC regulates sales and leases of goods; negotiable instruments, such as checks; secured transactions; and particular aspects of banking and fund transfers, letters of credit, warehouse receipts, bills of lading, and investment securities. Although all 50 states have enacted at least some portions of the UCC, individual states have made some changes. Therefore, variations in the UCC exist from state to state.

Statute
Law enacted by legislative bodies

Ordinance
Law enacted by cities

Administrative Agency Orders

Administrative agencies set up by legislative bodies carry on many governmental functions today. **Administrative agencies** are commissions or boards that have the power to regulate particular matters or implement laws. At the federal level alone, almost 60 agencies are involved in regulatory activity. The legislative branch of government enacts laws that prescribe the powers that administrative agencies may exercise, the principles that guide the agencies in exercising those powers,

Administrative Agency
Governmental board or commission with authority to regulate matters or implement laws

[1]The UCC has been adopted at least in part in every state. The UCC also has been adopted in the Virgin Islands and for the District of Columbia.

and the legal remedies available to those who want to question the legality of some administrative action.

Administrative agencies may be given practically the same power to make law as the legislature and almost the same power to decide cases as the courts. However, agencies are created by laws and have the power to enact law only if that power has been delegated to them by the legislature.

The president of the United States, with the consent of the Senate, appoints the heads of federal administrative agencies. The governor appoints heads of state administrative agencies. Administrative agencies are given wide latitude in setting up rules of procedure. They issue orders and decrees that have the force of law unless set aside by the courts after being challenged. If an agency rule conflicts with a statute, the statute takes precedence.

COURT CASE

Facts: State law required a year of apprenticeship under "the supervision of a licensed barber" before a person could take the barber examination. The Board of Barbers issued a rule requiring every person who wanted to take the examination to have worked for one year in a commercial barbershop setting. Big Sky College asked the board if Clare Delaney's teaching at the college could qualify as the required apprenticeship before examination.

Outcome: The court found that the requirement of serving the apprenticeship in a commercial barbershop was an additional requirement not found in the statute. The rule was invalid.

—*Board of Barbers of Professional and Occupational Licensing v. Big Sky College of Barber-Styling, Inc., 626 P.2d 1269 (Mont.)*

LO ④
Distinguish among crimes, torts, ethics

Civil Law
Law dealing with enforcement or protection of private rights

Criminal Law
Law dealing with offenses against society

Crime
Offense against society

Prosecutor or District Attorney
Government employee who brings criminal actions

Felony
A more serious crime

Misdemeanor
A less serious crime

CIVIL VERSUS CRIMINAL LAW

Law may be classified as either civil or criminal. A person may file a lawsuit in order to enforce or protect a private right by requesting compensation for damage suffered or other action for restoration of his or her property. This action in **civil law** is concerned with private or purely personal rights.

Criminal law is that branch of the law dealing with crimes and the punishment of wrongdoers. A **crime** is an offense that tends to injure society as a whole. A criminal action differs from a civil action in that an employee of the government—usually called the **prosecutor** or **district attorney**—brings a criminal action. The standard of proof required is greater than in a civil case. A person can be convicted of a crime only if proven guilty "beyond a reasonable doubt." If a person accused of a crime is subject to the penalty of imprisonment, the accused has a right to an attorney even if he or she cannot pay for one. In addition, the constitutional prohibition against double jeopardy means that a person can only be tried for a crime once. This protection is not absolute because it allows for retrial, for example, if a conviction is overturned or if there is no decision in a first trial.

Historically, crimes are usually classified, according to the nature of the punishment provided, as felonies or misdemeanors. Generally speaking, **felonies** are the more serious crimes and are usually punishable by death or by imprisonment in a penitentiary or state prison for more than one year. **Misdemeanors** are offenses of a less serious character and are punishable by a fine or imprisonment in a county or local jail. Forgery is a felony, but disorderly conduct and unauthorized entry of a dwelling are misdemeanors.

COURT CASE

Facts: Roosevelt Terry reached into an empty car and stole a purse. This petty theft was normally a misdemeanor punishable by a fine and/or imprisonment in the county jail for at most six months. However, Terry had two prior felony convictions. In that case, state law provided that the penalty for petty theft was one year in the county jail or the state prison. The judge sentenced Terry to the state prison. The state had a "three strikes" sentencing law. Terry was sentenced to 25 years to life for the petty theft as if it were a third felony. Terry argued he should not get such a severe penalty.

Outcome: The punishment imposed determines whether an offense is a felony or a misdemeanor. Because Terry had been sentenced to state prison for the petty theft, that offense was a felony, making it his third felony under the "three strikes" law.

—*People v. Terry*, 54 Cal. Rptr. 2d 769 (Cal.)

Some offenses carry penalties that can be either misdemeanor penalties or felony penalties. These offenses are called **wobblers**. In the case of wobblers, if the punishment imposed is more than a year of imprisonment, the offense is a felony. If the punishment is less than a year of imprisonment, the offense is a misdemeanor.

Because there are some offenses punished by government that are not considered serious offenses and therefore do not carry severe penalties, a number of states have established a third level of offense. These offenses are at a level below that of misdemeanors and might be called violations or infractions. An infraction could be speeding or making an illegal U-turn while driving. In some states, **violations** or **infractions** might not even be considered criminal offenses. They would carry penalties of a fine or imprisonment, but only in a local jail for a few days. Obviously, criminal statutes vary somewhat from state to state.

Wobbler
An offense that can be either a felony or a misdemeanor

Violation or **Infraction**
Offense less serious than a misdemeanor

COURT CASE

Facts: After being convicted in a nonjury trial of violating West Almond's "Junkyard-Landfill Law," Jack Brown and Michael Rochester appealed because they had requested a jury trial. They were charged with a violation, but the local law permitted a punishment of imprisonment for 30 days. State law defined a violation as an offense for which the penalty was imprisonment for no more than 15 days. It also gave a right to a jury trial for misdemeanors.

Outcome: Because violating the "Junkyard-Landfill Law" could result in 30 days' imprisonment, the offense was a misdemeanor. Brown and Rochester were entitled to a jury trial.

—*People v. Brown*, 648 N.Y. S.2d 283 (N.Y.)

TORT LAW

A **tort** is a private or civil wrong or injury for which there may be an action for damages. A tort may be intentional or it may be caused by negligence. **Negligence** is the failure to exercise reasonable care toward someone. It is tort law that allows an innocent motorist who is the victim of a careless or negligent driver to sue the

Tort
Private wrong f... damages may... recovered

Negli... *...rcise ...are*
Fai...

negligent driver for damages. Other torts include fraud, trespass, assault, slander, and interference with contracts. A tort action must be brought by the injured person against the person alleged to be negligent.

ETHICS

This chapter has discussed the basis for laws. One of the most important ideas mentioned is that "laws are the result of society's changing concepts of what is right and what is wrong." That means laws are based on our judgment regarding what human conduct is right, and therefore should be encouraged, and what conduct is wrong, and therefore should be discouraged. We thus base our laws on our morals. Those principles that help a person determine the morality of conduct, its motives, and its duties are called our **ethics**.

Ethics
Principles that determine the morality of conduct, its motives, and its duties

Bases for Ethical Judgment

Everyone has opinions on what behavior and thinking is right and what is wrong, basing these ethical judgments on personal values. We develop our values from our religious beliefs, our experience, our cultural background, and our scientific knowledge. Because people have differing backgrounds, our judgments as to what is right and wrong vary somewhat.

Ethical Principles

In considering how ethics relates to the law, several principles regarding the application of ethics emerge. These principles include:

1. Seriousness of consequences
2. Consensus of the majority
3. Change in ethical standards

Seriousness of Consequences. Although law is based on what we believe is right and wrong, our laws do not reflect everything we believe is right or wrong. Our laws set a minimum standard for behavior. Ethics sets a higher standard of behavior.

When unethical behavior can harm others—when the matter is of serious consequence to people—laws are usually enacted to regulate that behavior. Less serious matters can be considered wrong, but laws do not address them. For example, rules of etiquette frequently reflect our ethical judgments about behavior, but they do not have serious enough consequences that we pass laws to enforce them.

Consensus of the Majority. Our laws cannot express every individual's ethical principles since everyone does not agree on what is moral. There may be no law reflecting a judgment on a particular matter, or the laws might reflect the judgment of some. For example, vegetarians and nondrinkers may not believe laws permitting the eating of meat or the consumption of alcoholic beverages are ethical. Their morality may not be reflected in law. In a democratic society such as ours, the laws are designed to reflect the ethical view of the majority.

Change in Ethical Standards. Ethical standards change over time. Behavior believed ethical in the past becomes unethical, and behavior previously viewed as immoral becomes acceptable. Consider the matter of cigarette smoking on airplanes.

Many years ago airline passengers could smoke no matter where they were seated. Then the law mandated smoking and nonsmoking sections on planes. Now all commercial airlines in the United States prohibit smoking in all sections and the federal government uses the force of law to enforce this rule.

This change in government rules reflects the change in the view of most people about the harmful effects of cigarette smoking. Our ethical standards have changed, and this is reflected in the law.

Business Ethics

Our ethical standards apply to every aspect of life. For businesspeople, this means that ethical standards help determine their business practices. In our competitive economic system, the standard people in business have been expected to follow in determining behavior is "the bottom line." Is the behavior something that will help the business financially? When studying ethics as applied to business, we ask, does a business have obligations other than simply to make a profit or maximize "the bottom line"?

Many types of businesses or professional organizations have adopted codes of ethics to guide the behavior of their members. Variety occurs not only in the types of businesses that have adopted such codes but also in the impact of the codes on business. Some codes are legally enforceable, technically making them laws, not ethical rules. Other codes are strictly voluntary and are thus truly rules of ethics.

Legally Enforceable. A number of professions have codes of ethics, usually called *codes of professional responsibility,* which when violated provide the basis for penalties against members of the profession. For example, the American Bar Association has produced a model code and model rules for ethical behavior by lawyers. Although these particular models have not been adopted by every state, each state has adopted an ethical code for lawyers. A violation of the ethical code subjects a lawyer to discipline, including suspension from practicing law or even disbarment.

Voluntary. Some businesses have adopted codes of ethics for themselves as guides for individuals employed in these businesses. Because government has not imposed the codes, they do not carry legal penalties for violation. However, employees who violate ethical codes subject themselves to discipline by their employers. The codes recognize that ethical business conduct is a higher standard than that required by law and encourage behavior that is fair, honest, and, if disclosed, not embarrassing to the individual or the business.

The need for ethical practices, particularly in business, is greater than ever. The demand for such ethical behavior is so great that we often see it reflected in new legislation. If the public is not confident that businesses will comply with their ethical responsibilities, we will undoubtedly see more and more legislation asking business to rise to ethical, rather than just the previously legal, standards. Chapter 36 discusses new requirements for ethical behavior by corporate officers.

Ethics In Practice

The law seeks to make business behavior conform to society's standards of what is appropriate behavior by punishing those who do not live up to the standards. In reality, businesspeople find that there is a positive incentive to be ethical in business. In the long run, it is a good business practice to be ethical. Businesses find that customers are more likely to want to do business with ethical establishments.

Customers who deal with unethical businesses are much more likely to have problems with the business, causing additional time and expense.

QUESTIONS

1. Discuss whether a business may enact a law.
2. What are the objectives of law?
3. Explain what common law and equity are and how they differ.
4. Why do courts generally adhere to the judicial precedents set by earlier decisions?
5. When the statutes of two legislative bodies conflict, which statutes prevail? Give an example.
6. Why was the Bill of Rights enacted?
7. How does the enactment of statutes differ from the issuance of administrative agency orders?
8. What determines whether an offense is a felony or a misdemeanor? Are there offenses less serious than misdemeanors?
9. Are all persons' ethical judgments the same? Why or why not?
10. Discuss whether businesspersons have a positive incentive to behave ethically. When the statutes of two legislative bodies conflict, which statutes prevail? Give an example.

Courts and Court Procedure

LEARNING OBJECTIVES

1 Explain the function of the courts.
2 Explain the relationships of the various courts in our society.
3 Describe the procedure for filing a lawsuit.
4 Describe the basic procedure for a jury trial.

Each state has two distinct court systems—federal and state. Federal courts are part of the federal government headquartered in Washington, D.C. There are 50 different state court systems, each part of a state government head-quartered at its state capital. Although the federal and state court systems are largely independent of each other, they have similar functions.

FUNCTION OF THE COURTS

A court declares and applies judicial precedents, or case law, and applies laws passed by the legislative arm of government. However, this is not the whole story. Constitutions by their very nature must be couched in generalities. Statutes are less general than constitutions, but they could not possibly be worded to apply to every situation that may arise. Thus, the chief function of the courts is to interpret and apply the law from whatever source to a given situation. For example, the U.S. Constitution gives Congress power to regulate commerce "among the several states." This is the power to regulate interstate commerce. Under this power, Congress passes a law requiring safety devices on trains. If the law is challenged, the court must decide whether this is a regulation of interstate commerce.

Similarly, an act of Congress regulates minimum wages for the vast majority of workers. A question may arise as to whether this applies to the wages paid in a sawmill located in a rural section of the country. The court must decide whether or not the sawmill owner engages in interstate commerce. The court's decision may become a judicial precedent that will be followed in the future unless the court changes its decision in a subsequent case.

LO 1
Function of courts

JURISDICTION OF COURTS

Jurisdiction
Authority of a court to hear a case

The power or authority of a court to hear cases is called its **jurisdiction**. Courts must have jurisdiction over both the subject matter of the case and the persons involved. If a claim is made for damages as a result of an automobile accident, a probate court does not have jurisdiction over the subject matter because a probate court deals with wills and the distribution of deceased persons' property. The damage action would have to be brought in a court of general jurisdiction. A court may have jurisdiction over the subject matter but not over the person. If a resident of Ohio is charged with trespassing on a neighbor's property in that state, the courts in Indiana do not have jurisdiction over the person of the accused. Nor does the Ohio court system have jurisdiction over the person of the accused if the accused has not been properly served with notice of the trial. Before any court can try a case, it must be established that the court has jurisdiction over both the subject matter and the person in the case at issue.

COURT CASE

Facts: For several years, Walter Cole, Cleveland Hughes, Richard Johnson, and James Weeks, all residents of North Carolina, had pooled money to buy Virginia Lotto tickets. They would agree on the numbers for the tickets, and one member of the group would purchase them. They understood that any winnings would be shared. Cole bought six tickets for the group and then one for himself using a number the group had previously agreed on and used. The ticket Cole bought was a $9 million winner. Cole delivered the ticket to the Virginia Lottery Department and told the others he was keeping the money.

The others got a Virginia court to prevent the lottery from paying Cole. He then sued the others in North Carolina, asking the court there to declare him the sole owner of the ticket.

Outcome: The North Carolina court said that determining the ownership of the ticket required the court to have jurisdiction over the ticket. Because the ticket was located in Virginia, the North Carolina court did not have jurisdiction over the subject matter of this case.

—Cole v. Hughes, 442 S.E.2d 86 (N.C.)

Venue

Venue
Location where a case is to be tried

Once it is determined what court system has jurisdiction to decide a case, it must be decided at what location the case should be tried. Determining the location where a case is to be tried means determining the proper **venue**. Each state has trial courts throughout the state. Proper venue requires choosing the proper one of these courts. For example, if two citizens of San Diego have a controversy, proper venue would be in San Diego, not Sacramento. However, the right to a particular venue can be surrendered. In criminal cases, the court frequently changes venue to try to give the defendant a fairer trial.

CLASSIFICATION OF COURTS

LO ❷
Relationships of various courts

Courts are classified for the purpose of determining their jurisdiction. This classification can be made in a variety of ways. One classification can be made according to the governmental unit setting up the court. Under this classification system, courts are divided into (1) federal courts, (2) state courts, and (3) municipal courts.

The same courts may be classified according to the method of hearing cases. Under this system, they are classified as trial courts and appellate courts. **Trial courts** conduct the original trial of cases. **Appellate courts** review cases appealed from the decisions of lower courts. A losing party appeals to the higher court to review the lower court's decision by claiming the lower court made a mistake that caused the party to lose. Appellate courts include courts of appeals and supreme courts. Appellate courts exercise considerable authority over the courts under them. Lower courts are bound by the decisions of their appellate courts.

Trial Court
Court that conducts original trial of a case

Appellate Court
Court that reviews decision of another court

Federal Courts

The federal courts have exclusive jurisdiction over such matters as bankruptcy, claims against the United States, and patent and copyright cases. Federal courts (see Illustration 2–1) include:

1. Special federal courts
2. Federal district courts
3. Federal courts of appeals
4. United States Supreme Court

Special Federal Courts. The **special federal courts** are limited in their jurisdiction by the laws of Congress creating them. For example, the Court of International Trade hears cases involving the rates of duty on various classes of imported goods, the collection of the revenues, and similar controversies. The U.S. Court of Federal Claims hears cases involving claims against the U.S. government. The Tax Court hears only cases involving tax controversies. Bankruptcy courts decide bankruptcy cases. Most bankruptcy appeals are to a three-judge appellate panel of bankruptcy judges.

Special Federal Court
Federal trial court with limited jurisdiction

Federal District Courts. By far the largest class of federal courts consists of the almost 100 **federal district courts**. There is at least one district court in each state, and in some states there are as many as four. These courts are strictly trial courts in which all criminal cases involving a violation of the federal law are tried. The district courts also have jurisdiction over civil suits that: (1) are brought by the United States; (2) arise under the U.S. Constitution, federal laws, or treaties; or (3) are brought by citizens of different states—called **diversity jurisdiction**—or between citizens of one state and a foreign nation or one of its citizens where the amount in controversy is $75,000 or more.

Federal District Court
Trial court of federal court system

Diversity Jurisdiction
Federal jurisdiction based on parties being from different states

COURT CASE

Facts: Eric Bischoff was a member of a N.Y. company called Frank Brunkhorst Co. Bischoff sued the other members of the company in state court in New York and named Brunkhorst as a nominal defendant. He claimed that the others had diverted profits from Brunkhorst to a related corporation in which they held a greater interest than Bischoff. Bischoff was a resident of New York and the other members were residents of Florida. The others had the case removed to federal court on the basis of diversity.

Outcome: Because Bischoff was a N.Y. resident and Brunkhorst was a N.Y. company, there was not complete diversity between the plaintiff and all the defendants. The court did not have jurisdiction.

—*Bischoff v. Boar's Head Provisions Co, Inc.*,
2006 Westlaw 1793653 (N.Y.)

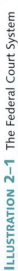

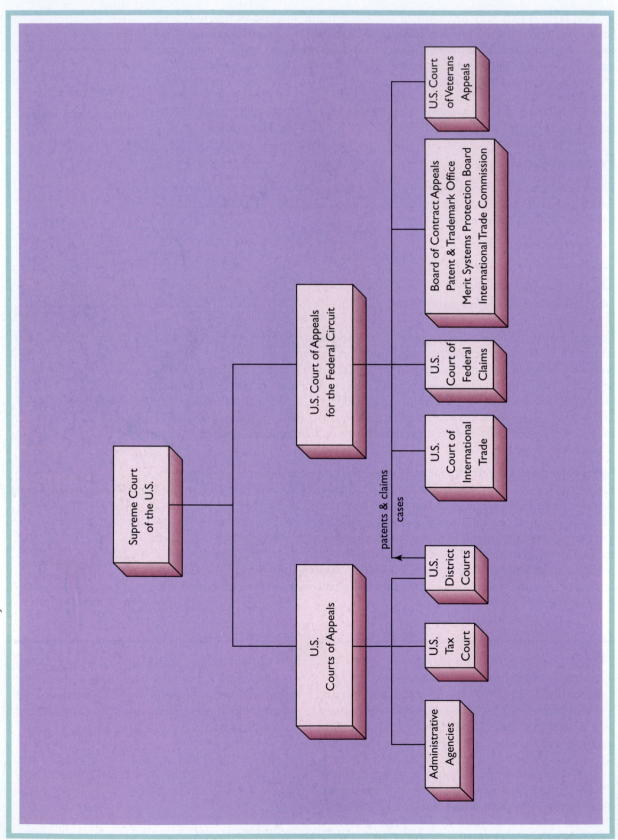

ILLUSTRATION 2–1 The Federal Court System

Federal Courts of Appeals. The United States is divided geographically into 12 federal judicial circuits. Each circuit has a court of appeals, which hears appeals from cases arising in its circuit. The **federal courts of appeals** hear appeals from federal district courts and from federal administrative agencies and departments. A decision of a federal court of appeals is binding on all lower courts within the jurisdiction of that circuit.

It is possible that one court of appeals could decide an issue one way and another court of appeals could decide it in another way. Because the lower courts within each court of appeals' jurisdiction must follow the decision of its court of appeals, courts in different circuits might decide similar cases differently. When this occurs, there is a conflict between the circuits. The conflict lasts until one circuit changes its decision or the U.S. Supreme Court rules on the issue.

There is also another court of appeals called the Court of Appeals for the Federal Circuit. It reviews decisions of special federal courts (such as the Court of International Trade and the U.S. Court of Federal Claims), decisions of four administrative agencies, and appeals from district courts in patent and claims cases.

United States Supreme Court. The **Supreme Court of the United States** has original jurisdiction in cases affecting ambassadors, public ministers, and consuls, and in cases in which a state is a party. It has appellate jurisdiction in cases based on the U.S. Constitution, a federal law, or a treaty.

The majority of cases heard by the U.S. Supreme Court are cases appealed from the federal courts of appeals. Under certain circumstances, a decision of a federal district court may be appealed directly to the Supreme Court. A state supreme court decision also may be reviewed by the U.S. Supreme Court if the case involves a federal constitutional question or if a federal law or treaty has been held invalid by the state court. Unlike the courts of appeals, the Supreme Court does not have to take all cases appealed. It chooses which appealed cases it will hear.

The normal way a case gets to the Supreme Court is by application for a **writ of certiorari**. The party asking for the Supreme Court review of a case asks the court to issue a writ of *certiorari,* which requires the lower court that has decided the case to produce the record of the case for the Supreme Court's review. The court issues a writ for only a small number of the requests.

The U.S. Supreme Court is the highest tribunal in the land, and its decisions are binding on all other courts. Its decisions are final until the Court reverses its own decision or until the effect of a given decision is changed by a constitutional amendment or an enactment by Congress. The Constitution created the Supreme Court and gave Congress the power to establish inferior courts.

State Courts

State courts (see Illustration 2–2) can best be classified into the following groups:

1. Inferior courts
2. Courts of original general jurisdiction
3. Appellate courts
4. Special courts

Inferior Courts. Most states have **inferior courts** that hear cases involving minor criminal offenses and minor disputes between citizens. The names of inferior courts vary greatly from state to state. These courts are most frequently called district, magistrate, county, municipal, small claims, justice, or even taxi courts.

Federal Court of Appeals
Court that hears appeals in federal court system

Supreme Court of the United States
The highest court in the United States

Writ of *Certiorari*
Order to produce record of a case

Inferior Court
Trial court that hears only cases involving minor offenses and disputes

ILLUSTRATION 2–2 Typical State Court System

State
Supreme Court

State Courts
of Appeals

State Courts of
Original General
Jurisdiction (Trial Courts)

Inferior Courts
(Small Claims,
limited jurisdiction)

Some states have more than one of these named courts. Civil jurisdiction is limited to controversies involving a maximum amount of money, which generally varies from $1,000 to $25,000, or to a particular type of controversy. In addition, these courts may try all criminal cases involving misdemeanors. The loser in any of these courts may normally appeal to a court of original general jurisdiction.

Courts of Original General Jurisdiction. The most important courts of a state for the average citizen are called **courts of original general jurisdiction**. These courts have broad jurisdiction over disputes between two or more parties as well as criminal offenses against the state. They are called courts of original general jurisdiction because the case is first instituted in them. On occasion, they hear appeals from inferior courts, but this does not make them true appellate bodies because the entire case is retried at this level. Thus, such an appeal is actually treated as a case of original jurisdiction. These courts are also called trial courts because they hear witnesses, receive evidence, and try the case.

An official, permanent record is kept of the trial showing the testimony, evidence, statements of counsel and the judge, the judgment, and the findings of the court. For this reason, these courts are referred to as **courts of record**. The official

Court of Original General Jurisdiction
Court of record in which case is first tried

Court of Record
Court in which an official record of the proceedings is kept

name of such a court of original general jurisdiction varies from state to state, but in almost every state is one of the following: circuit court, district court, or superior court.[1]

Appellate Courts. All states provide for an appeal to an appellate court by the party dissatisfied with the final judgment of the trial court or any of its rulings and instructions. Most states have a system of intermediate appellate courts, usually called **courts of appeals**, as well as one final appellate court. Decisions of the appellate courts bind lower courts. The **state supreme court** is usually the title of the highest appellate court of a state.

State Court of Appeals
Intermediate appellate court

State Supreme Court
Highest court in most states

Probate Court
Court that handles estates

C O U R T   C A S E

Facts: Robert and Margaret Rohde had an insurance policy that protected against loss from vandalism or malicious mischief. A motor was damaged when stored oil used to service it was contaminated with water. In county court, the Rohdes sued their insurance carrier, Farmers Alliance Mutual, when it denied coverage for the damage under the vandalism and malicious mischief coverage.

Outcome: The court found in favor of Farmers, saying the Rohdes had not proved their case. The Rohdes appealed to the district court. The district court found for the Rohdes, so Farmers appealed to the court of appeals. The court of appeals dismissed the case and Farmers appealed to the state supreme court. After the three appeals, the highest court found the Rohdes had proven their case.

—Rohde v. Farmers Alliance Mutual Ins. Co.,
509 N.W.2d 618 (Neb.)

Special Courts. Many states have additional special courts, such as **probate courts** that handle wills and estates; **juvenile courts** that are concerned with delinquent, dependent, and neglected children; and **domestic relations courts** that handle divorce and child custody cases. These are not courts of general jurisdiction but of special jurisdiction. In some states, these courts are on the same level as the trial courts. When this is the case, they are properly called *trial courts* and are courts of record. In other states, they are on the same level as the inferior courts and are not courts of record.

Juvenile Court
Court that handles delinquent, dependent, and neglected children

Domestic Relations Court
Court that handles divorce and related cases

COURT OFFICERS

The chief officer of an inferior court is the **judge, justice of the peace, magistrate, trial justice,** or similar officer. The executive officer is the constable or bailiff. In a state court of record, the chief officer is the judge, the executive officer is the **sheriff**, and the recorder is the clerk of the court. These titles are the same in the federal courts, except that the executive officer is called a **marshal**.

Persons educated in the profession of the law and licensed to practice law, which means they may represent others in legal matters, are known as **lawyers** or **attorneys**. They are officers of the court and are subject to punishment for a

Judge, Justice of the Peace, Magistrate, or **Trial Justice**
Chief officer of court

Sheriff
Court of record executive officer

Marshal
Executive officer of federal court

Lawyer or **Attorney**
Person licensed to represent others in court

---

[1]In New York, this court is known as a Supreme Court, and in Ohio it is known as a Court of Common Pleas.

breach of duty. Lawyers ordinarily represent the parties in a civil or a criminal action, although many states permit the parties to represent themselves. The practice of presenting one's own case, however, is usually not advisable because a disinterested person is normally better able to assess and present the case rationally.

PROCEDURE IN COURTS OF RECORD

Procedural Law
Law specifying how actions are filed and what trial procedure to follow

Procedural laws are laws that specify how parties are to go forward with filing civil actions and how these actions are to be tried. They must be followed if the parties wish to have the case settled by a court.

Filing Suit in a Civil Action

LO ❸
Lawsuit procedure

Complaint or **Petition**
Written request to a court to settle a dispute

Plaintiff
Person who begins a civil lawsuit

Defendant
Person against whom a case is filed

Summons or **Process**
Notice of suit

Answer or **Motion**
Response of defendant to a complaint

Discovery
Means of obtaining information from other party before a trial

With few exceptions, courts are powerless to settle disputes between individuals unless one of the parties so requests the court. The written request, called a **complaint** or **petition**, begins a civil suit. The individual who institutes a civil action is called the **plaintiff**, and the individual against whom action is brought is called the **defendant**. The order of events in bringing an action is generally as follows:

1. *Filing suit.* The first step in a lawsuit is the filing of the complaint or petition with the clerk of the court by the plaintiff. This petition sets forth the jurisdiction of the court, the nature of the claim, and the remedy sought.

2. *Notice of suit.* As soon as the petition is filed, the clerk issues a **summons** or, as it is sometimes called, a **process**. This gives the defendant notice of the complaint and informs the defendant of the time in which to respond.

3. *Response.* The defendant has a specified number of days available in which to file an **answer** or a **motion**. The answer admits or denies the facts alleged in the complaint. A motion is an application to the judge for an order requiring an act be done in favor of the moving party. The complaint and answer constitute the first pleadings.

4. *Discovery.* To obtain information relevant to the subject matter of the action, the parties may request unprivileged information from another party in a number of ways, called **discovery**, including:
   a. Interrogatories: Written questions to be answered in writing
   b. Deposition: Examination of a party or potential witness outside court and under oath
   c. Admissions: Requests to agree that a certain fact is true or a matter of law is decided
   d. Medical examination by a physician
   e. Access to real and personal property
   If a court issues an order compelling discovery, failure to comply can result in punishment. The party who does not comply may be found in contempt of court or the judge may dismiss the case.
   The parties may take other actions after a case has been instituted and before it goes to trial. A party may file a wide variety of motions, including a motion to dismiss the case, a motion for a judgment based solely on the pleadings, and a motion to obtain a ruling on the admissibility of certain evidence or to suppress evidence prior to trial.

5. *Fact finding.* If disagreements occur about facts of the case, a jury may be impaneled to decide these facts. If neither party requests a jury, the case may be tried before a judge alone, who would act as both judge and jury.

Trial Procedure

A typical jury trial proceeds in the following order:

LO ❹
Jury trial procedure

1. The jury is selected and sworn in.

2. The attorney for the plaintiff makes an opening statement to the jury indicating the nature of the action and what the plaintiff expects to prove. This is usually followed by the defendant's attorney's opening statement.

3. The plaintiff presents evidence in the form of testimony of witnesses and exhibits designed to prove the allegations made in the plaintiff's petition. The plaintiff has the burden of proving facts adequate to support the petition's allegations. If this burden is not met, the case can be dismissed and the lawsuit ends. The plaintiff's evidence is followed by the defendant's evidence. The defendant tries to disprove the plaintiff's allegations. The defendant also may present evidence excusing the behavior complained of by the plaintiff.

4. The attorneys for each side summarize the evidence and argue their points in an attempt to win the jury to their version of the case.

5. The judge instructs the jury as to the points of law that govern the case. The judge has the sole power to determine the points of law, and the jury decides what weight is to be given to each point of evidence.

6. The jury adjourns to the jury room and in secret arrives at its decision, called the **verdict**. The judge may set aside this verdict if it is contrary to the law and the evidence. Unless this is done, the judge enters a judgment in accordance with the verdict.

Verdict
Decision of a jury

Appeals

If either the plaintiff or the defendant is dissatisfied with the judgment and can cite an error of law by the court, an appeal generally may be taken to a higher court. When an appeal is taken, a complete transcript or written record of the trial is given to the appellate court. Rather than hear testimony from witnesses, the appellate court reviews the entire proceedings from the transcript. The attorney for each side files a brief, setting forth the reasons that warrant the appellate court to either affirm or reverse the judgment of the lower court. The decision of the appellate court becomes judicial precedent and is binding on lower courts. The appellate court may, however, reverse itself in a future case, although this seldom occurs.

PROCEDURE IN SMALL CLAIMS COURT

Filing and trying a suit in an inferior court like a small claims court is a much simpler matter than filing and trying a suit in a court of record. A form for the complaint may be obtained from the court and filled out by the plaintiff without help from a lawyer. Frequently, court employees will assist in filling out the forms. The defendant is then served with the complaint.

When the case is tried, the procedure is much more informal than in a court of record. A judge tries the case, so there is no jury. Because neither party has to be represented by an attorney, and in some courts may not be so represented, the judge asks the parties to state their positions. Witnesses and evidence may be presented, but the questioning is more informal. The judge is likely to ask questions in order to assist in ascertaining the facts. The judge then renders the verdict and judgment of the court. Normally, either party may appeal the judgment to a court of record, in which case the matter is retried there.

QUESTIONS

1. Explain why each state has two court systems.
2. What types of jurisdiction must a court have in order to hear a case?
3. Over what types of cases do federal courts have exclusive jurisdiction?
4. Is it ever possible for cases involving the same issue to be decided differently in different courts of a court system? Explain.
5. Name the court in which the following disputes would be settled:
    a. A claim for an unpaid bill of $100
    b. A case involving the tariff on imported caviar
    c. A controversy among cousins regarding their share of a deceased grandparent's estate
    d. An allegation that a child has been neglected
    e. A child custody case
    f. A damage suit for $7,500
6. Must a party to a lawsuit be represented by a lawyer? Explain.
7. Who are the officers of
    a. An inferior court?
    b. A state court of record?
    c. A federal court?
8. What is the purpose of discovery?
9. How does trying a case in a small claims court differ from trying a case in a court of record?
10. May the verdict of a jury ever be set aside by anyone?

Business Torts and Crimes

LEARNING OBJECTIVES

❶ Discuss the basis for intentional and negligent tort liability.

❷ List and explain the generally recognized business torts.

❸ Explain what business crimes are.

❹ Describe what computer crimes are and the three types that affect business.

PREVIEW CASE

→ At a supermarket, a police officer observed Victor Balboni remove two cartons of cigarettes from their rack and place them in an opened bag in his shopping cart. Balboni then put more cartons of cigarettes in the opened bag. The officer walked down the aisle to Balboni's shopping cart and looked into the bag. He saw several cartons of cigarettes in it. The officer arrested Balboni because state law specified that concealing merchandise with the intention of depriving the merchant of its use without payment constituted shoplifting. Balboni was searched and found to have no money. Is he guilty of shoplifting? Do you think he intended to pay for the cigarettes?

How do businesses relate to society and to other businesses? Can the activity of a business unfairly damage another business or even violate a criminal law? With some variations from state to state, courts have found some activities by businesses and some activities against businesses actionable.

TORTS

Chapter 1 defined a tort as a private wrong or injury. The law permits people to sue for injuries caused by the intentional or negligent acts of others. The person who causes the injury is called a **tortfeasor**.

LO ❶
Basis for tort liability

Tortfeasor
Person whose action causes injury

Intentional Torts

To recover for an intentional tort, the injured person must show three things:

1. An act by the defendant
2. An intention to cause the consequences of the act
3. Causation—the injury was caused by the defendant's act or something set in motion by the act

Intentional torts include such actions as assault (putting a person in fear of a wrongful touching), battery (a wrongful touching), trespass (invading someone's property), and false imprisonment (improperly confining a person). Although a business could be involved in these torts, parties involved in these types of cases come from every sector of the community.

COURT   CASE

Facts: Security personnel of Liz Claiborne, Inc. questioned Andria Arrington, a clerical employee, about her time sheet. She admitted in writing that she had falsified it. After being fired, Arrington sued Liz Claiborne for false imprisonment. She alleged she "thought" the door to the office in which she had been questioned was locked. She also did not "feel" free to leave because she had been told if she did not cooperate, the police would be called. Questioning Arrington was clearly an intentional act, so she claimed there had been an intentional tort.

Outcome: To find the intentional tort of false imprisonment the court said Arrington had to prove the Claiborne personnel intended to confine her, not just question her. She did not do this.

—*Arrington v. Liz Claiborne, Inc.,*
688 N.Y.S.2d 544 (N.Y. App. Div.)

Negligence Torts

To recover for a tort based on negligence, the injured party must show:

1. A duty of the tortfeasor
2. Breach of that duty
3. The breach was the actual and proximate cause of the injury
4. Injury or damage

A person may recover in tort for negligence whenever these four elements occur. Courts frequently hear such cases involving automobile accidents, medical malpractice, injuries from products, and injuries resulting from the condition of a landowner's property.

Business Torts

LO ❷
General business torts

The type of tort caused by a business or involving a business is a **business tort**. Businesses become involved in a tort action in several common ways.

Business Tort
Tort caused by or involving a business

Product Liability. Manufacturers of products incur potential liability in tort for injuries caused by the products. A person injured through the use or condition of a product could sue on the basis of the manufacturer's negligence in the preparation or manufacture of the article. The plaintiff must go (figuratively) into the defendant's plant or factory, learn how the article was made, and prove negligence.

Unless the plaintiff can show negligence in the design of the manufacturer's product or the general method of manufacture, it is unlikely the plaintiff will be able to prove negligence.

COURT CASE

Facts: An overhead guard on a forklift fell and hit John Harper on the head. Harper sued Clark Equipment Co., the manufacturer of the forklift, for negligence in its design. Experts testified that the guard met all the industry standards. It had been tested at the equivalent of 10,000 hours of use for endurance and passed.

Outcome: The court said Harper had not shown negligence in the design so he could not recover.

—Harper v. Clark Equipment Co.,
779 S.W.2d 175 (Ark.)

Whenever a manufacturer, as a reasonable person, should foresee that a particular class of persons would be injured by the product, the manufacturer is liable to an injured member of that class without regard to whether such member purchased from the manufacturer or from anyone else.

The difficulty of proving negligence has helped lead the courts to expand a doctrine called **strict tort liability**. This doctrine makes a manufacturer liable without proof of negligence. It applies to anyone injured because of a defect in the manufacture of a product when such defect makes the use of the product dangerous to the user or persons in the vicinity of the product. The person injured or killed must be a user or person in the vicinity.

Strict Tort Liability
Manufacturer of product liable without proof of negligence for dangerous product

Business Activity. Several other business activities have been widely recognized as tortious. They are intentional torts and may be based on state law, federal law, or common law. Although some variation exists among the states, an injured party may recover damages on the basis of conduct that causes two general types of harm:

1. Interference with a contract or economic advantage
2. Confusion about a product

Interference with a Contract Or Economic Advantage

Although contracts are not discussed until Chapter 5, the tort of interference with a contract or economic advantage basically occurs when a business relationship has been formed, and in some way a third party causes one party to end that business relationship. If injured, the other party to the business relationship may have a cause of action against the party causing the breakup. This tort also could be the result of unjustified interference with a person's reasonable expectation of future economic advantage.

Traditionally, proof of this tort only required showing that the defendant knowingly interfered with a business relationship. However, more and more states require that the intentional interference be improper. Improper interference can occur because of an improper motive, an improper means, or by acting other than in the legitimate exercise of the defendant's own rights. Defendants who protect their economic or safety interests or assert honest claims are not acting improperly.

In a free market economy, competitors inevitably injure one another. Courts do not hold such injury tortious, even when intentional, if the action was taken to advance a person's economic interest and results from the competitive economic system.

However, if a person unjustifiably interferes with another's business relationship or reasonable expectation of future economic advantage, there is a tort. Interference with leasing opportunities, with the opportunity of buying and selling goods or services, and with the hiring of employees are examples of the types of interference that can be actionable.

COURT CASE

Facts: An employee of the Racing Association of Central Iowa (RACI), Ray Famous, alleged that four jockeys racially harassed him in an extremely offensive and threatening manner. The RACI excluded the jockeys from the racetrack. After an investigation, RACI allowed one jockey to reenter the racetrack and another to reenter after apologizing to Famous. The jockeys sued RACI for interference with their contracts.

Outcome: The court stated there was a legitimate reason for an employer to investigate charges of harassment in the workplace. This was a proper purpose for the exclusion of the jockeys.

—*Green v. Racing Ass'n of Cent. Iowa,*
713 NW2d 234 (Iowa)

Confusion about a Product

A person may commit a tort by intentionally causing confusion about another's product. This could be done by making false statements about another's product or by representing goods or services as being the goods or services of someone else.

Injurious Falsehood. When a person makes false statements of fact that degrade the quality of another's goods or services, the tort of **injurious falsehood** occurs. Courts also call this tort by other names such as **commercial disparagement** or **trade libel**. The false statement must be made to a third person. This is called **communication**. The hearer must understand the statement to refer to the plaintiff's goods or services and to degrade their quality. The injured party also must show that the statement was a substantial element in causing damage. In some states, the plaintiff must identify specific customers lost as a result of the statement.

Finally, the statement normally must have been made maliciously. Malice can always be shown by proving that the statement was made as a result of ill will, spite, or hostility with the intention of causing harm to the plaintiff. In some jurisdictions, the plaintiff need only show that the false statement was made knowing it was false or with reckless disregard as to its truth or falsity.

Injurious Falsehood, Commercial Disparagement or **Trade Libel**
False statement of fact that degrades quality of another's goods or services

Communication
Telling a third person

COURT CASE

Facts: In a book, Time-Life Books, Inc. reproduced Charles Atlas, Ltd.'s classic ad about a "97-pound weakling" who becomes a "real man" after using the Atlas exercise system. The caption above the reproduced ad described the Atlas system as isometric. The text of the book warned readers of the extreme dangers of isometric exercises. Atlas sued Time-Life, alleging product disparagement.

Outcome: The court found that reading the caption in conjunction with the text, a reasonable reader could conclude that Atlas marketed an isometric exercise program, isometric exercises are dangerous, and, therefore, Atlas's exercise program was dangerous. Time-Life falsely described the Atlas system as isometric, so Atlas stated a claim for injurious falsehood.

—*Charles Atlas, Ltd. v. Time-Life Books, Inc.,*
570 F. Supp. 150 (S.D.N.Y.)

Confusion of Source. The tort that occurs when a person attempts to represent goods or services as being the goods or services of someone else is **confusion of source**. The law assumes customers would be confused as to the source of the goods or services. Actual confusion need not be shown. This tort occurs from trademark or trade name infringement or unfair competition.

Confusion of Source
Representing goods or services as those of another

Trademarks. Federal law defines a **trademark** as a word, name, symbol, device, or any combination adopted and used by a person to identify and distinguish goods, including a unique product, from another's goods and to indicate the source of the goods. A trademark indicates that goods carrying that mark all come from one source. A trademark or trade name gives the owner the exclusive right to use a word or device to distinguish a product or a service.

Trademark
Word, symbol, device, or combination of them used to identify and distinguish goods

Not all words or symbols qualify for protection as trademarks. Only those marks used by a business in a way that identifies its goods or services and differentiates them from others are entitled to protection. The mark normally must be inherently distinctive, which means that the mark is unique, arbitrary, and nondescriptive.

A mark that is not so distinctive may be a trademark if it has acquired a **secondary meaning**. A secondary meaning is a special or trade meaning developed by usage that distinguishes the goods or services in such a way as to warrant trademark protection. A generic term can be protected if it has acquired a secondary meaning. If the right to trademark protection is based on the doctrine of secondary meaning, the geographical area of protection will be limited to the area in which the mark has such a secondary meaning.

Secondary Meaning
Special meaning of a mark that distinguishes goods

Marks that are fanciful, arbitrary, or subtly suggest something about the product can be protected. Protected marks include words such as *Ivory* for soap, the letters *S* and *ECI*, abbreviations and nicknames such as *Coke,* made-up words such as *Exxon* and *Rolex,* and the shapes of packages and products. Generic terms such as *superglue* and *soft soap* cannot be trademarks.

A trademark may be registered or unregistered. A trademark registered under the federal trademark law provides the holder with all the rights and remedies of that law. The holder of an unregistered trademark also has some rights under the federal law and rights provided by the common law. Many states also have trademark laws; however, they vary greatly. In some states the holder of a mark may not get greater protection by registering than the common law affords an unregistered mark.

Trademark or **trade name infringement** is the unauthorized use or confusingly similar imitation of another person's mark or name. If the imitation is likely to cause confusion or mistake or deceive people, courts will halt use of the imitation. Courts examine a number of factors when deciding whether a likelihood of confusion between two marks exists. Although the various courts do not always use the same factors, those factors most commonly considered include:

Trademark or **Trade Name Infringement**
Unauthorized use or imitation of another's mark or name

1. The similarity of the two marks
2. The similarity of the products represented by the marks
3. The similarity of marketing and customers
4. The similarity and amount of advertising used
5. The area of overlapping use
6. The intent of the parties in adopting the marks
7. The strength of the marks
8. Actual confusion by the public

The imitation of another's trademark is not always done to cause confusion and does not always lead to infringement. However, where the imitation is for the purpose of jest or commentary, the parody is successful only when there is no confusion and therefore no infringement.

COURT CASE

Facts: Jim Henson Productions planned to release a movie, *Muppet Treasure Island,* which featured a wild boar puppet called "Spa'am." Spa'am, the high priest of a tribe of wild boars that worshipped Miss Piggy, was intended to poke fun at the luncheon meat, SPAM. Henson also planned to market movie-related merchandise displaying the words "Muppet Treasure Island" with a likeness of Spa'am and the name "Spa'am." Hormel Foods had a distinctive, widely recognized trademark on the name "SPAM" for its luncheon meat. Hormel also merchandised products featuring SPAM and sued for trademark infringement.

Outcome: In recognizing that the two marks were superficially similar, the court also found that the two marks would appear in very different contexts, be very dissimilar visually, and be used in different merchandising markets. Because the SPAM trademark was such a strong mark, the court held there would be no confusion.

—*Hormel Foods Corp. v. Jim Henson Productions, Inc.,* **73 F.3d 497 (2d Cir.)**

When infringement is a tort, rather than a crime, the holder of the trademark or name has the duty of bringing any legal action to stop the alleged infringement and recover damages.

Trademarks identify and distinguish tangible goods; service marks identify and distinguish services. However, the same legal principles govern trademark infringement and service mark infringement.

Trademark or Trade Name Dilution
Lessening the capacity of a famous mark to identify and distinguish goods

The owner of a trademark is protected from unauthorized use of the trademark even when confusion might not result. **Trademark** or **trade name dilution** is "the lessening of the capacity of a famous mark to identify and distinguish goods or services." This could be done either by what is called *blurring* or by tarnishing a trademark. Blurring means to diminish the selling power of a trademark by unauthorized use on noncompeting products. A blurring use would occur if someone produced McDonald's light bulbs or Chrysler tires, for example. Tarnishing a trademark occurs when the mark is used in a disparaging manner or on low-quality goods. The owner of a trademark or name may get an injunction against anyone's commercial use of the trademark or name. A federal law, the Anticybersquatting Consumer Protection Act, gives trademark owners the right to sue people who register Internet domain names of well-known trademarks and then try to profit from them. The trademark owner needs to show ownership of the mark, that the defendant registered or trafficked in identical or confusingly similar domain names, and that the defendant in bad faith intended to profit from the mark.

Unfair Competition
Total impression of product results in confusion as to its origin

Unfair Competition. Unfair competition exists when the total impression a product gives to the consumer results in confusion as to the origin of the product. The impression of a product includes its packaging, size, color, shape, design, wording, any decorative indicia, and name. When unfair competition is claimed, the total physical image conveyed by the product and its name are considered together.

COURT CASE

Facts: Intermatic, Inc. was the exclusive owner of the famous trade name *intermatic*. Dennis Toeppen operated an Internet service provider business. He registered 240 Internet domain names, including *intermatic.com*, without permission from anyone who had previously used the names registered. He hoped to sell companies the right to use domain names he had registered. At a Web page at intermatic.com, he used a map of Champaign-Urbana, Illinois. When Intermatic could not register *intermatic.com* as its domain name, it asked Toeppen to give up the domain name. He refused, so Intermatic sued him for trade name dilution.

Outcome: The court held that Toeppen's registration lessened the ability of Intermatic to identify its goods on the Internet since it could not use its own name as its domain name. The Trademark Dilution Act protected Intermatic from having its federally registered trade name used as a domain name by Toeppen.

—*Intermatic, Inc. v. Toeppen*, 947 F. Supp. 1227 (N.D. Ill.)

CRIMES

The news media report on crimes every day, so everyone hears about murders, robberies, assaults, and break-ins. Some of these crimes involve businesses or businesspeople.

Business Crimes

Certain criminal offenses, such as arson, forgery, fraudulent conveyances, shoplifting, and embezzlement, closely relate to business activities. **Business crimes** are crimes committed against a business or in which the perpetrator uses a business to commit the crime.

LO **3**
What business crimes are

Business Crime
Crime against a business or committed by using a business

TYPES OF BUSINESS CRIMES

The types of crimes committed by and against businesses appear to be limited only by the ingenuity of the human mind. Many crimes include stealing from the business. In this age of computers, wire transfers, and organized crime, the range of crime has been growing. Today, crimes affecting business include:

1. Theft
2. RICO cases
3. Computer crimes

Theft. **Theft** is the crime of stealing. It involves taking or appropriating another's property without the owner's consent and with the intention of depriving the owner of it. This definition includes taking and depriving another of property even when the thief initially obtains the property lawfully.

Some states use different terms to identify the various possible types of theft. As it relates to business, types of theft include such crimes as shoplifting, embezzlement, and larceny. The elements of each of these offenses differ somewhat from state to state, but the crimes generally consist of the following:

1. **Shoplifting**: Taking possession of goods in a store with the intent to use as the taker's own without paying the purchase price. In some states, merely

Theft
Taking another's property without consent

Shoplifting
Taking unpurchased goods from a store

concealing unpurchased goods while in a store constitutes shoplifting. The intent required for shoplifting is the intent to use the property as the taker's. This crime must be committed in a store by taking store merchandise, so it is always a business crime.

PREVIEW CASE REVISITED

Facts: At a supermarket, a police officer observed Victor Balboni remove two cartons of cigarettes from their rack and place them in an opened bag in his shopping cart. Balboni then put more cartons of cigarettes in the opened bag. The officer walked down the aisle to Balboni's shopping cart and looked into the bag. He saw several cartons of cigarettes in it. The officer arrested Balboni because state law specified that concealing merchandise with the intention of depriving the merchant of its use without payment constituted shoplifting. Balboni was searched and found to have no money.

Outcome: The court held that he was guilty of shoplifting because he concealed the cartons and had no money to pay for them.

—*Com. v. Balboni*, 532 N.E.2d 706 (Mass. App. Ct.)

Embezzlement
Fraudulent conversion of property lawfully possessed

2. **Embezzlement**: Fraudulent conversion of another's property by someone in lawful possession of the property. Embezzlement requires the intent to defraud the owner of the property. Conversion here means that the defendant handles the property inconsistently with the arrangement by which he or she has possession of it. Because many businesses rely on employees to receive payments and make disbursements, embezzlement is often a crime against a business.

COURT CASE

Facts: Philip F. Wieler II was the owner of NW Group, Inc. NW Group supplied property management for condominium associations. When several condominiums Wieler owned did not generate enough income to pay their bills, funds from condos he did not own were used to pay those bills. The checks used to pay these bills were treated as loans; however, the properties managed by NW but not owned by Wieler had not authorized the payments or any loans to Wieler. Wieler was convicted of embezzlement.

Outcome: The disposal of others' property without the intent to permanently deprive them of the property was sufficient to prove embezzlement. Weiler's conviction was upheld.

—*State v. Wieler*, 660 A.2d 740 (Conn.)

Larceny
Taking and carrying away of property without consent

3. **Larceny**: Taking and carrying away the property of another without the consent of the person in possession and with the intention of depriving the possessor of the property. The intent to deprive the person in possession of the property must exist at the time the property is taken. For larceny to exist, the taker need not take the property from the owner—merely from the person in possession of it. Larceny can relate to business whenever someone takes any business property, whether inventory, tools, or even office supplies.

COURT CASE

Facts: Stephen Murray made false entries in his corporate employer's books and forged 180 of his employer's checks, making them payable to himself. The amounts of the checks ranged from $2,000 to $60,000, and over five years Murray stole more than $4 million.

Outcome: The court found him guilty of 180 larcenies because he had taken his employer's property 180 times without consent and with the intention of depriving the employer of the money.

—*Com. v. Murray*, 519 N.E.2d 1293 (Mass.)

RICO Cases. The Racketeer Influenced and Corrupt Organizations Act, called RICO for short, is a federal law designed to prevent the infiltration of legitimate businesses by organized crime. It prohibits investing income from racketeering to obtain a business, using racketeering to obtain a business (through conspiracy, extortion, and so on), using a business to conduct racketeering, and conspiring to do any of these. The conspirators do not have to do the acts themselves. If they direct the action, they are responsible. The law includes stiff criminal penalties for violation.

However, RICO includes civil sanctions as well as criminal ones. As a result, it has been used by one business against another in cases not involving organized crime. The injured party brings the action under RICO based on the perpetration of criminal activity and requests damages. In criminal cases a government brings the action. To find a business violation of RICO, a plaintiff must show all of the following:

1. Conduct
2. Of an enterprise (at least two people)
3. Through a pattern (at least two related acts within 10 years)
4. Of racketeering activity

Racketeering activity means acts specified in the law that are labeled criminal under state or federal laws. Examples of the specified crimes include murder, kidnapping, arson, robbery, bribery, extortion, distribution of illegal narcotics, prostitution, obstruction of justice, and the white-collar crimes of mail or wire fraud, money laundering, forgery, and securities fraud. The defendant does not have to have been convicted; it is enough just to have engaged in activity for which a conviction could be obtained. This makes it easier to win a civil RICO case than a criminal case.

COURT CASE

Facts: Harvey Robbins owned a cattle and guest ranch. He had permits to use federal Bureau of Land Management (BLM) land for grazing his cattle and for some recreation. The BLM asked Robbins for a right-of-way across the ranch. After Robbins refused, he claimed BLM employees tried to extort the right-of-way from him by refusing to maintain the road to his property, threatening to cancel and then canceling Robbins's right-of-way across federal land, canceling his recreation permit and grazing privileges, bringing false criminal charges against him, trespassing and interfering with cattle drives. Robbins sued the employees under RICO.

Outcome: The court held that if the BLM employees acted with the intent to extort the right-of-way from Robbins it was wrongful. That would then state a cause of action under RICO.

—*Robbins v. Wilkie*, 433 F.3d 755 (10th Cir)

Civil suits under RICO have been very popular because of the liberal damages available. Rather than allowing merely compensatory damages, RICO provides recovery of three times the damages suffered as a result of the RICO violation. It also allows the recovery of attorneys' fees, which can be a substantial sum.

In addition to the federal RICO, many states have passed so-called *Baby RICO* laws. Similar to the federal law, these laws apply to activities in intrastate (within a state) commerce. The federal law has jurisdiction over interstate (between states) commerce.

LO ④
What computer crimes are

Computer Crime
Crime that is committed with aid of computers or because computers are involved

Computer Crimes. Computer crimes are crimes committed with the aid of a computer or because computers are involved. Under this definition, computers can be involved in crimes in various ways:

1. They can be the objects of the crimes—such as when a computer is stolen or damaged.
2. They can be the method of committing a crime—such as when a computer is used to take money from an account.
3. They can represent where the crime is committed—such as when copyrights are infringed on the Internet.

Today, more and more businesses rely on computers, computer systems have become more interconnected, and an increasing number of businesses and private individuals use the Internet and the information on the Internet. As a result, more opportunities exist for criminal behavior. Frequently, prosecutors can successfully prosecute computer offenses by using existing criminal laws prohibiting theft, mail fraud, wire fraud, and the transportation of stolen property.

Some courts have refused to apply traditional criminal laws to computer offenses. Both the federal government and the states have responded to the need for laws that clearly apply to computer crimes by enacting specific computer crime legislation.

One federal law is called the Computer Fraud and Abuse Act. This act makes it an offense to, without authorization, access a computer or exceed authorized access of a computer used by or for the U.S. government or a financial institution and to (1) fraudulently obtain anything of value; (2) intentionally and without authorization obtain or destroy information; (3) affect the use of the computer; or (4) cause damage. It is also an offense to (1) deal in computer passwords and thereby affect interstate commerce; (2) knowingly access a computer, obtain national defense information, and disclose, attempt to disclose, or retain that information; and (3) transmit a threat to damage a U.S. government or financial institution computer in order to extort money from anyone. The punishment is a fine and/or up to 10 years' imprisonment for the first offense and up to 20 years' imprisonment for the second offense.

The federal government has also enacted a law called the *Electronic Communications Privacy Act*. This law prohibits the interception of computer communications, such as e-mail, or obtaining and divulging without permission data stored electronically.

The laws enacted by the states vary considerably. However, they generally prohibit alteration of a computer program or intentional, unauthorized access to a computer regardless of the reason for the access and the disclosure of any information gained by such access.

COURT CASE

Facts: Eastman Kodak Corp. employed Robert Versaggi as a computer technician. To perform his job, Kodak supplied him with a security device that allowed him to access the Kodak computer systems. Versaggi accessed the computer system that controlled the telephone system at Kodak and entered specific commands that activated a series of instructions directing the computer system off its existing operation. The result shut down 3,000 phone lines at Kodak for 1½ hours. Versaggi was charged with computer tampering by altering computer programs.

Outcome: Finding that a program's function is to control the computer's activities, the court stated that by disconnecting the normal application programs and ordering the computer to shut down, Versaggi had altered the programs. He was guilty of computer tampering.

—People v. Versaggi,
608 N.Y.S.2d 155 (Ct. App.)

Criminal activity relating to computers can be classified as three types: trespass, fraud, and criminal copyright infringement.

Trespass. As applied to business crime, **computer trespass** means unauthorized use of or access to a computer. A trespass can range from being harmless to being a threat to national security. Such activities as merely using a business computer to play games or prepare personal documents constitute computer trespass. More serious trespasses include learning trade secrets, gaining customer lists, and obtaining classified defense information. Computer trespass has been the focus of state computer crime laws.

A computer trespass may be committed in a number of ways, depending on who gains unauthorized access and the use made of the computer. The access might be by:

1. An employee not authorized to use a computer in the business
2. An employee authorized to use a computer who uses it for nonbusiness purposes
3. An unauthorized outsider who gains access to the business's computer system—called a **hacker**

Because all computer trespass involves the use of computer time without permission, all trespass technically can be classified as theft of computer time. However, computer trespass causes even more serious problems. It ties up computers and prevents employees from doing their jobs and may reveal trade secrets, customers' personal financial records, or confidential medical information. Because computers house so much information, it is helpful that the computer crime laws of the majority of jurisdictions protect the confidentiality of all information stored in computers.

One of the most highly publicized methods of trespass involves damaging computer record systems by using rogue programs. A **rogue program** is a set of software instructions that produces abnormal or unexpected behavior in a computer. Various kinds of rogue programs have such colorful names as viruses, bacteria, worms, Trojan horses, and time bombs. They may cause computer users difficulty, inhibit normal use, or impose injury. The programs can be introduced to a computer by being attached to a useful program or even e-mail; they spread to other computers through modems, disks, or network connections. Once introduced, a rogue program can alter the operations of a program, destroy data or screen displays, create false information, display a message, or even damage the computer.

Computer Trespass
Unauthorized use of or access to a computer

Hacker
Unauthorized outsider who gains access to another's computer system

Rogue Program
Set of software instructions that produces abnormal computer behavior; see http: //www.copyright .gov

COURT CASE

Facts: Robert Morris, a graduate student at Cornell University, had authorization to use computers at Cornell. He wanted to demonstrate that security measures on computer networks were inadequate. Morris released a worm into the Internet from a computer at MIT. The worm was supposed to take up little computer time and be difficult to detect. The worm duplicated and infected computers much faster than Morris expected. An estimated 6,200 computers at universities, military sites, and medical research facilities all over the country crashed or would not work.

Outcome: The court found Morris guilty of violation of the Computer Fraud and Abuse Act.

—*United States v. Morris*, 928 F.2d 504 (2d Cir.)

Rogue programs may not show up for some time, so they can spread without alerting operators to their presence and damage all files in a computer system. One large computer software company inadvertently sent out copies of a software program containing a virus. The product had been accidentally infected after being loaded onto a computer that had received the virus from another program. In this case, the virus merely caused a message to flash on computer users' screens. However, the software company had the expense of recalling thousands of copies of its software program.

Fraud. As applied to computer crime, fraud encompasses larceny and embezzlement. It includes causing bank deposits to be credited to just one individual's account. Such an action might be prosecuted under traditional crime statutes or new computer crime statutes.

The use of the Internet has made it possible for a wide variety of frauds to be perpetrated on unsuspecting businesses and individuals. Sometimes the Internet provides an easy and inexpensive way to advertise a scam because so many people "surf the Web." A fraud can be easily advertised on the Internet, such as the one in which a 15-year-old advertised computer parts for sale. Customers were required to pay cash on delivery or by a check on which payment could not be stopped. The box supposedly containing the computer parts would be empty and the perpetrator had the customers' money.

Other Internet fraud has included a long-distance telephone company employee selling more than 50,000 calling card numbers. The employee was convicted and sent to prison. The Federal Trade Commission stopped an illegal pyramid arrangement after it scammed participants of $6 million.

Computer criminals frequently target businesses, particularly large banks. Citibank lost $10 million, but recovered all but $400,000, when some Russians broke into its computer system and engaged in fraudulent transactions. Businesses frequently suffer losses quietly in preference to advertising to customers, stockholders, and clients that they are vulnerable to hackers, so it is impossible to accurately measure the dollar amount of loss to business from computer fraud.

Criminal Copyright Infringement. In addition to civil copyright infringement, there exists the crime of criminal copyright infringement. In order to establish the criminal offense, the prosecutor needs to prove that (1) there has been copyright infringement, (2) the infringement was willful, and (3) the infringement was done for business advantage or financial gain.

As anyone who has used the Internet knows, it is relatively easy to copy material found on the Net. The most serious problems for business occur when software is copied. Software that is copied illegally is called **pirated software**. Pirating software is a worldwide industry because the Internet links people all over the world. Software is sometimes copied without the owner's knowledge and stored in someone else's computer located anywhere else in the world. Within a relatively short time, people all over the world can make numerous illegal copies. If the owner of the computer used for storage finds out, the pirated software can be removed from the computer, but the copying has already taken place. Hundreds or thousands of copies of the pirated software could have already been made.

Pirated Software
Software copied illegally

COURT CASE

Facts: Robin Rothberg, Christian Morley, and perhaps hundreds of others were members of a computer software piracy group called "Pirates with Attitudes." The group stored huge numbers of pirated software programs at file transfer protocol (called FTP) sites. Members of the group could download the pirated software to their own computers. When the FBI seized computer hardware at the University of Sherbrooke in Canada, there were still 5,000 programs on it; however, at trial, an FBI computer specialist testified that more than 54,000 programs had been uploaded to the hardware. Rothberg, Morley, and others were charged with conspiracy to commit copyright infringement.

Outcome: All the defendants either pled guilty or were found guilty after trial of the conspiracy charge. The pirated software was clearly on the computer hardware and available for downloading.

—*United States v. Rothberg*, **2002 WL 171963 (N.D. Ill.)**

Finding software pirates can be extremely difficult, if not impossible. They could have used fake identification and nicknames or used an anonymous remailer. An **anonymous remailer** is a device that permits a person who has access to a computer and an e-mail account to send messages and software to an e-mail address or a group without the recipient knowing the source of the communication. The person who wants to send an anonymous communication sends it to the anonymous remailer. The remailer removes the identity and address of the sender and then sends, or "remails," the communication to the address indicated by the sender. The recipient receives the communication with the remailer's address on it. Because some remailers keep a record showing the sender's identity, some communications can be traced. However, if the sender uses a remailer that does not keep such a record or uses several anonymous remailers, the communication could be impossible to trace. As a result, computer copyright infringement is, in dollar terms, the most serious crime on the Internet. It has been estimated to cost copyright holders billions of dollars a year.

Anonymous Remailer
Device that permits sending anonymous e-mail messages

QUESTIONS

1. What must an injured person show in order to recover for an intentional tort?
2. Explain the benefit to plaintiffs of the doctrine of strict tort liability.
3. Is it inevitably a tort when competitors intentionally injure one another? Explain.
4. What is a trademark, and what does it indicate?

5. What does RICO prohibit?

6. Why is it that civil RICO cases have been so popular?

7. What existing criminal laws have been used to successfully prosecute computer offenses?

8. What is a rogue program, and what effects might it cause?

CASE PROBLEMS

When the concluding question in a case problem can be answered simply yes or no, state the legal principle or rule of law that supports your answer.

LO ❸   1. Teleline, Inc. ran a telephone gambling game called "Let's Make a Deal" using a 900-phone number. Playing the game cost $3.88 a minute. People who called were not charged for the phone calls, but only for the ability to gamble provided by Teleline. AT&T carried the calls over its long distance lines and Teleline paid AT&T for the cost of the calls. Felix Kemp's grandson called the 900-number. AT&T listed Teleline's charges under the heading, "direct dialed calls," as long distance charges mixed in with charges for long distance calls on phone bills mailed to Kemp. AT&T's name and logo were displayed on the pages showing the LMD charges. The LMD charges were illegal gambling debts not collectable under state law. Kemp's local phone company told him he had to pay the charges or his phone would be disconnected. He paid the phone bill and sued AT&T for violating RICO claiming mail fraud. Were the bills so misleading that they constituted fraud?

LO ❶   2. Heather Gamble entered a Dollar General store to buy a shirt. Not finding one, she left and went to another store. She noticed a Dollar General employee (Sherry Thornton) had followed her by car, and parked blocking Gamble's car. Gamble asked Thornton why she had followed her. Thornton asked Gamble what she had in her pants. Gamble found nothing in her pocket, but Thornton grabbed at Gamble's panties from behind and tugged on them. Gamble realized Thornton was accusing her of shoplifting. Thornton left because it was clear that Gamble had not shoplifted. Gamble recited all this when she sued Dollar General for assault. Did she state adequate facts to raise the issue of whether there had been an assault?

LO ❷   3. Microsoft Corp. holds copyrights on many software programs. V3 Solutions, Inc. sold and distributed computer software. Microsoft had two investigators order Microsoft copyrighted software from V3. Also, one of V3's customers ordered 38 copies of a Microsoft copyrighted software program from V3 and sent one copy to Microsoft. All the software sent to Microsoft was missing manufacturing codes present on genuine Microsoft software. The Microsoft logo on that software also varied from genuine Microsoft logos. Microsoft sued V3 for copyright infringement, alleging V3 had infringed its right to reproduce its software. Was there copyright infringement?

LO ❸, ❹   4. Anaheim police detective Stockwell asked Diane Terry to help in a sting investigation of wrongful computer access. Terry worked for Trans Union, a credit reporting agency. She created a phony file in her company's credit data bank using the name Diane T. Wolfe, but without supplying any data. She phoned National Credit Service, which advertised as a service to help people with bad credit. Lelas Gentry told her he could create a new credit file for her with false information. She and Stockwell met with Gentry, who gave Stockwell a full credit report on Diane T. Wolfe from Trans Union. Gentry did not have authorization for access to Trans Union's files, and only Gentry, Stockwell, and Terry knew of the fictitious Diane T. Wolfe. Gentry was charged with gaining access to a computer system and obtaining services with fraudulent intent. Was he guilty?

5. Knaack Manufacturing Co. registered the trademark WEATHER GUARD to identify toolboxes and other truck and van equipment (not car covers), which it sold through contractors and industrial supply houses. Rally Accessories, Inc. sold two car covers called SILVERGUARD and GOLDGUARD through mass retailers. It produced a car cover in a weather-resistant fabric and chose the name WeatherGUARD for it. Both Rally's attorney and the U.S. trademark office advised that the name was registerable for car covers. There were 12 registrations and approved applications using "weather guard." Knaack sued Rally for infringement and dilution of its mark. Knaack used its mark in red and Rally used its mark on a four-color box. None of Knaack's distributors carried any Rally car covers, and there was no evidence of confusion by customers. Since Knaack's and Rally's products differed in function, price, packaging, method of installation, and use, was Rally guilty of infringement or dilution?   **LO ❷**

6. As a contact representative in an IRS office, Richard Czubinski, for use in his official duties, had a password that allowed him to access information from IRS computers. He used the password with his office computer to get information about the tax returns of, among others: a prosecutor who had charged Czubinski's father with a felony, a city councillor who had defeated him in an election, and a woman he had dated. Czubinski did nothing more than observe the confidential information he had obtained. He was charged with violating the Computer Fraud and Abuse Act. To be guilty he must have exceeded authorized access of a federal computer and obtained something of value. Is he guilty?   **LO ❹**

7. Teilhaber Manufacturing Co. produced an industrial storage rack called the *Cue-Rack*. It competed with one sold by Unarco Materials Storage, Inc. Unarco conducted tests on a hybrid rack composed of uprights manufactured by Teilhaber for the Cue-Rack and beams manufactured by another company. Unarco distributed a report on these tests written by Unarco's chief engineer. It stated that the tests were performed on a Cue-Rack "furnished by Teilhaber." Teilhaber sued Unarco for product disparagement. Was the report false?   **LO ❶, ❷**

8. Hawkeye Bank & Trust and affiliated banks agreed to refer bank customers to Financial Marketing Services, Inc. (FMS) for the purchase of life insurance. Hawkeye and FMS shared the commissions. Hawkeye employees and some independent agents licensed through FMS made the actual sales; however, all insurance business was FMS's property. Because of concern about the confidentiality of bank customer information, Hawkeye decided to terminate its contract with FMS and sell insurance directly to its customers. The independent agents claimed Hawkeye terminating the contract with FMS constituted intentional interference with the agents' contracts and prospective business relations. Was it?   **LO ❷**

9. Intending to operate a commercial Internet site, Netfire, Inc. acquired the Internet domain name "marchmadness.com." It developed content for the site related to the NCAA basketball tournament and operated the site for several years. The Illinois High School Association (IHSA) had previously licensed the term "March Madness" and sued Netfire for trademark infringement. Had   **LO ❷**

the term "March Madness" acquired a secondary meaning and was it likely that "marchmadness.com" would be confused with it?

LO ❷ 　**10.** Highland Enterprises, Inc. agreed to build roads for Shearer Lumber to transport timber it purchased from the U.S. Forest Service. The Service issued an order restricting public access to the area where the roads were being built. A group of environmental protesters engaged in activities to slow the road construction, and they were arrested. Billy Jo Barker and John Kreilick were buried in the road. Jennifer Prichard was chained to an access gate. Peter Leusch and Beatrix Jenness interfered with Highland's efforts to remove slash piles from the road. Boards with nails protruding and sharpened rebar were put in the road and construction equipment was damaged. Highland sued the protesters for intentional interference with economic advantage. Should it succeed?

Government Regulation of Business

LEARNING OBJECTIVES

1. Explain why government regulates business.
2. Discuss the types and powers of administrative agencies.
3. List the major antitrust laws.
4. Summarize the areas in which the federal government has enacted legislation for environmental protection.

PREVIEW CASE

→ Federal law stated the Bureau of Prisons (BOP) may reduce "the period a prisoner convicted of a nonviolent offense remain[ed] in custody" after successfully completing a substance abuse program. The BOP issued a regulation denying early release to felons who carried, possessed, or used a firearm during their crimes. Christopher Lopez, convicted of possession with intent to distribute methamphetamine, had possessed a gun in connection with his offense. Lopez challenged the regulation saying, as the law identified violent offenders as ineligible for early release, the BOP was barred from identifying further classes of ineligible inmates. The BOP argued that it *may* grant sentence reduction, but under the law it also may *not*. It further argued that because offenders who possessed a gun during their crimes indicated a readiness to endanger others, they should not receive early release. What did the use of a gun in commission of a crime imply? Did it make sense to try to classify prisoners as more violent if they used a gun? Did the language of the law imply discretion on the part of the BOP?

G overnment rules and regulations affect the operation of every business, no matter what type. Government regulations, both state and federal, affect areas of business operation ranging from prices and product safety to the relationship of the business to its employees. This chapter discusses some ways in which government regulates the operation of business. Some other aspects of governmental regulation of business are discussed in Chapter 19 (consumer protection) and in Chapters 28 and 29 (employers and employees).

PURPOSE OF REGULATION

LO ❶
Why government
regulates

Government regulates business in order to eliminate abuses and to control conduct considered to be unreasonable. The goal is to enhance the quality of life for society as a whole by setting the rules under which all businesses compete.

ADMINISTRATIVE AGENCIES

Chapter 1 defined administrative agencies as governmental boards or commissions with the authority to regulate or implement laws. Most governmental regulation of business is done by administrative agencies.

Most administrative agency regulation occurs because of the complex nature of the area of regulation. Each administrative agency can become a specialist in its particular area of regulation. Agencies can hire scientists and researchers to study industries or problems and set standards that businesses must follow. Agencies conduct research on proposed drugs (the Food and Drug Administration), examine the safety of nuclear power facilities (the Nuclear Regulatory Commission), certify the wholesomeness of meat and poultry (the Food Safety and Inspection Service), and set standards for aircraft maintenance (the Federal Aviation Administration). In all these areas, research has been necessary to determine a safe level for the public.

Some agencies investigate industries and propose rules designed to promote fairness to the businesses involved and the public. This occurs in the area of trading in stocks (the Securities and Exchange Commission), the granting of radio and television licenses (the Federal Communications Commission), and the regulation of banks (the Federal Deposit Insurance Corporation). The legislature thus can set up the guidelines and specify the research to be done by specialists in the field.

Structure of Administrative Agencies

Agencies may be run by a single administrator who serves at the pleasure of the executive, either the president of the United States in the case of federal agencies or the governor in the case of state agencies. Alternatively, a commission, the members of which are appointed for staggered terms, frequently of five years, may run agencies.

Types of Agencies

LO ❷
Types and powers of
agencies

The two types of administrative agencies are usually referred to as regulatory and nonregulatory. Regulatory agencies govern the economic activity of businesses. They prescribe rules stating what should or should not be done in particular situations. They decide whether a law has been violated and then proceed against those violating the law by imposing fines and, in some cases, ordering that the activity be stopped. Regulatory-type agencies include agencies such as the Environmental Protection Agency, the Securities and Exchange Commission, and the Federal Trade Commission.

Regulatory agencies also regulate a wide variety of professions that serve the public. Those supervised by governmental agencies in an effort to protect the interests of consumers include barbers, doctors, insurance agents, morticians, cosmetologists, fitters of hearing aids, and restaurateurs. In order to be licensed to practice a regulated profession, an individual must meet the requirements set by the appropriate regulatory agency.

Public utility companies, which are granted monopoly status, are regulated to ensure that they charge fair rates and render adequate service. Such businesses include natural gas, electric, and water companies. A Public Service Commission or Public Utilities Commission regulates these companies in most states.

Nonregulatory agencies, also called social regulatory agencies, dispense benefits for social and economic welfare and issue regulations governing the distribution of benefits. Such agencies include the Railroad Retirement Board, the Farm Credit Administration, and the Department of Health and Human Services.

Powers of Agencies

Different regulatory agencies have different powers. However, the three major areas of regulations include:

1. Licensing power: Allowing a business to enter the field being regulated
2. Rate-making power: Fixing the prices that a business may charge
3. Power over business practices: Determining whether the activity of the entity regulated is acceptable or not

Agencies such as the Federal Communications Commission, the Nuclear Regulatory Commission, and the Securities and Exchange Commission have licensing power. The Civil Aeronautics Board, the Federal Power Commission, and the Interstate Commerce Commission all have rate-making power. The primary powers of the Federal Trade Commission and the National Labor Relations Board are to control business practices.

Rule Making

Administrative agencies primarily set policy through the issuance of rules and regulations. When an agency's rule is challenged, the courts primarily focus on the procedures followed by the agency in exercising its rule-making power. The rule-making procedure followed by state agencies resembles that which must be used by federal agencies.

After investigating a problem, an agency will develop a proposed rule. A federal agency must publish a notice of the proposed rule in the *Federal Register*. This allows interested parties the opportunity to comment on the proposed rule. The agency might hold formal hearings, but informal **notice and comment rule making** has been more and more common. When an agency uses notice and comment rule making, it publishes a proposed rule, but does not hold formal hearings. After time for comments, the proposed rule could be published as proposed, changed, or entirely abandoned by the agency. Once a rule or regulation is adopted, it has the force of a statute; however, persons affected by it may challenge it in court.

Notice and Comment Rule Making
Enacting administrative rules by publishing the proposed rule and then the final rule without holding formal hearings

State Agencies

Whereas federal administrative agencies affect businesses throughout the country, state administrative agencies affect businesses operated in their states. The most common state agencies include public service commissions, state labor relations boards or commissions, and workers' compensation boards.

PREVIEW CASE REVISITED

Facts: Federal law stated the Bureau of Prisons (BOP) may reduce "the period a prisoner convicted of a nonviolent offense remain[ed] in custody" after successfully completing a substance abuse program. The BOP issued a regulation denying early release to felons who carried, possessed, or used a firearm during their crimes. Christopher Lopez, convicted of possession with intent to distribute methamphetamine, had possessed a gun in connection with his offense. Lopez challenged the regulation saying, as the law identified violent offenders as ineligible for early release, the BOP was barred from identifying further classes of ineligible inmates. The BOP argued that it *may* grant sentence reduction, but under the law it also may *not*. Because offenders who possessed a gun during their crimes indicated a readiness to endanger others they should not receive early release.

Outcome: The U.S. Supreme Court held that the law gave the BOP discretion because it used the word *may*. If Congress had meant to order the BOP to reduce all sentences of nonviolent offenders it would have used the word *shall*. The BOP's determination that an inmate's involvement with a gun while committing a felony implied a readiness to use life-threatening violence properly decided the question of early release. The regulation was valid.

—*Lopez v. Davis*, 121 S. Ct. 714

ANTITRUST

LO ❸
Major antitrust laws

Antitrust Law
Statute that seeks to promote competition among businesses

Government also regulates business by means of **antitrust laws** that seek to promote competition among businesses.

The most important antitrust law, the federal Sherman Antitrust Act, declares that, "Every contract, combination in the form of trust or otherwise, or conspiracy, in restraint of trade or commerce among the several states, or with foreign nations is . . . illegal."[1] It further provides that anyone who monopolizes or tries to obtain a monopoly in interstate commerce is guilty of a felony.

The Sherman Act applies to commerce or trade between two or more states and to buyers and sellers. Most states also have antitrust laws, very similar to the Sherman Act, which prohibit restraint of trade within their states.

In interpreting the Sherman Act, the federal courts have said it prohibits only those activities that *unreasonably* restrain trade. The *rule of reason* approach means that the courts examine and rule on the anticompetitive effect of a particular activity on a case-by-case basis. The effect of the activity, not the activity itself, is the most important element in deciding whether the Sherman Act has been violated.

Per Se **Violation**
Activity illegal regardless of its effect

However, some activities are illegal under the Sherman Act without regard to their effect. Called *per se* **violations**, they include price fixing, group boycotts, and horizontal territorial restraints.

Many activities may lessen competition. Obviously, every business firm seeks to have cooperation within its firm. This is the basis of economic productivity, and this is lawful under the antitrust laws. Only when separate businesses make a commitment to a common plan or some type of joint action to restrain trade does an antitrust violation occur.

In addition to the Sherman Act, the federal government has enacted three other important antitrust laws. These include the Clayton Act, the Robinson-Patman Act, and the Federal Trade Commission Act.

---

[1]15 USC § 1.

The Clayton Act amends the Sherman Act by prohibiting certain practices if their effect may be to substantially lessen competition or to tend to create a monopoly. The Clayton Act prohibits price discrimination to different purchasers where price difference does not result from differences in selling or transportation cost. The Clayton Act also prohibits agreements to sell on the condition that the purchaser shall not use goods of the seller's competitors, ownership of stock or assets in a competing business where the effect may be to substantially lessen competition, and interlocking directorates between boards of directors of competing firms.

COURT CASE

Facts: The Brown Shoe Co. and the G. R. Kinney Co., which together would have controlled 5 percent of the U.S. shoe market, attempted to merge. The federal government sought to stop the merger on the grounds that it violated the Clayton Act, which prohibits corporations from acquiring other corporations where the effect of the acquisition might substantially lessen competition or tend to create a monopoly.

Outcome: The U.S. Supreme Court prohibited the merger, holding that the proposed merger would tend to lessen competition.

—*Brown Shoe Co. v. United States*, 370 U.S. 294

The Robinson-Patman Act, an amendment to the Clayton Act, prohibits price discrimination generally and geographically for the purpose of eliminating competition. It also prohibits sales at unreasonably low prices in order to eliminate competition.

The Federal Trade Commission Act prohibits "unfair methods of competition in commerce and unfair or deceptive acts or practices in commerce."[2] In addition, this law prohibits false advertising. To prevent these unfair and deceptive practices, a federal administrative agency, the Federal Trade Commission, was established.

ENVIRONMENTAL PROTECTION

In recognition of the fact that the environment is the property of everyone, the federal government and many states have enacted a number of laws to protect our environment. A federal agency, the Environmental Protection Agency (EPA), administers many of these federal laws. The laws the EPA administers include the following:

LO 4
Federal environmental protection legislation

1. Clean Air Act
2. Water Pollution and Control Act
3. Resource Conservation and Recovery Act
4. Comprehensive Environmental Response, Compensation, and Liability Act

Clean Air Act

The Clean Air Act was the first national environmental law. Under this law, the EPA sets minimum national standards for air quality and regulates hazardous air pollutants. These standards protect public health and welfare. The states apply

[2]15 USC § 45 (a) (1).

and enforce these standards under state implementation plans setting limits on pollutants and approved by the EPA. The law provides civil and criminal penalties for its violation.

Water Pollution and Control Act

Congress enacted the Water Pollution and Control Act (also referred to simply as the Clean Water Act—or CWA) to restore and maintain the proper chemistry of U.S. waters, including adjacent wetlands. The law seeks to prevent the discharge of pollutants into navigable waters. The EPA has the primary administration and enforcement responsibility under the law. It sets limits on discharges, including pollutants into sewer systems; has the responsibility for wetlands protection; and can block or overrule the issuance of permits under the law. The EPA or private citizens may sue on the basis of the act, which even includes criminal liability for violation.

COURT CASE

Facts: Cherokee Resources, Inc. had a wastewater treatment and oil reclamation business. It accepted oil and industrial wastewater and processed the oil for reuse and treated the wastewater. Cherokee accepted more oil and wastewater than it could treat and often dumped untreated oil and water into the sewer system, which ultimately discharged into rivers and the ocean. Cherokee, its president, and its vice president were charged with conspiracy to violate the CWA. They argued the CWA applied only to navigable waters and their discharges were into the sewer system, not a navigable waterway.

Outcome: The court said that the CWA regulates discharges into sewer systems and Congress has the authority to regulate such discharges. The defendants were convicted.

—*United States v. Hartsell*,
127 F. 3d 343 (4th Cir.)

Resource Conservation and Recovery Act

The Resource Conservation and Recovery Act regulates the generation, storage, transportation, treatment, and disposal of hazardous waste. The law lists certain wastes defined as hazardous, but the term includes ignitable, corrosive, reactive, or toxic waste.

The law gives the EPA the duty of setting standards for individuals who own or operate hazardous waste disposal facilities. Anyone who generates or transports hazardous waste, and owners and operators of facilities for the treatment, storage, or disposal of such waste, must obtain a permit and must comply with the requirements of the permit. The law requires individuals handling hazardous waste to keep extensive records in order to track it from generation to disposal. The law provides large civil and criminal penalties for its violation. This law also permits suits by private citizens.

Comprehensive Environmental Response, Compensation, and Liability Act

Perhaps the most discussed federal environmental legislation, the Comprehensive Environmental Response, Compensation, and Liability Act (CERCLA), also called the "superfund" law, seeks the cleanup of waste from previous activities and requires notification of the release of hazardous substances. CERCLA imposes liability for cleanup on past and current owners or operators of facilities where hazardous substances have been released, on anyone who arranged for disposal of substances where released, and on anyone who transported them. CERCLA imposes liability retroactively—acts that occurred before enactment of this law and were not negligent or illegal then can be the basis of liability.

Multiple Party Liability. Because CERCLA imposes liability on four groups of people—owners, operators, disposers, and transporters—several parties could be liable for one site. A liable party may take legal action to require other responsible or potentially responsible parties to pay a share of cleanup costs. Courts have stated that when several defendants are responsible under CERCLA, liability should be apportioned according to their contribution to the problem. However, if liability cannot be apportioned or only one liable party has any funds, one party could be liable for the entire cleanup cost. These costs can run into millions of dollars.

Business Costs. These provisions of CERCLA concern businesses and potential business owners because of the possibility of courts imposing huge cleanup costs on them as new owners of facilities who never released hazardous wastes there. A past owner of a facility could have released a hazardous substance 20 years ago. There could have been a series of sales of the facility so that the current owner did not know about the release. Yet the current owner might still have to pay for or help pay for the cleanup. Some courts have found everyone in the chain of ownership of contaminated property, from disposal of the substance to the current owner, liable for cleanup. Thus, anyone buying contaminated land is potentially liable for cleanup costs. This can have serious repercussions for all landowners but particularly for businesses, since business or manufacturing sites are the most likely to have been the site of a release of hazardous substances.

Business costs could include not only large cleanup costs but also legal fees. Litigation under the superfund law can be extremely expensive. A party responsible for cleanup costs can sue to require other "potentially" liable parties to share in the costs. Just the cost of defending against such a lawsuit can be very expensive. Legal fees have been reported to be 30 percent to 60 percent of superfund costs.

In addition to owners of facilities, courts have imposed CERCLA liability on business employees who had control over disposal decisions. Even lenders have been found liable for cleanup costs if the court found them adequately involved in running the business.

State Laws

A number of states have enacted state superfund laws. They also impose liability for cleanup costs and may require notification of release of hazardous substances to state environmental agencies.

Protection from Liability

A person can take some steps to help reduce the potential of liability under CERCLA and state superfund statutes. Banks and other lending institutions should require environmental assessments of properties before making a loan and before foreclosing on property. Before anyone buys or invests in property, an investigation should be made to identify any environmental risks and determine expected costs. Cleanup costs that run in the millions of dollars can be much greater than the value of the property involved.

QUESTIONS

1. Explain why most administrative agency regulation occurs.

2. By whom are administrative agencies run? How long do these individuals serve?

3. What do regulatory agencies do and how do they do it?

4. What do nonregulatory agencies do?

5. What are the three types of powers possessed by regulatory agencies?

6. Explain what an agency does when it uses notice and comment rule-making.

7. What is the effect of an administrative regulation? Is there any way to challenge a regulation?

8. What is the difference between the rule of reason approach to antitrust and *per se* violations?

9. How are standards for air quality set under the authority of the Clean Air Act enforced?

10. What can a person do to help reduce the potential of liability under CERCLA and state superfund statutes?

Ethics in Practice

Is it ethical for the law to impose liability retroactively? Should government force a person to pay for doing something that was legal and carried no penalty at the time it was done?

Contracts

Nature and Classes of Contracts

LEARNING OBJECTIVES

1 State the five requirements for a valid contract.

2 Describe the types of contracts and how they differ from agreements.

3 Explain the difference between a contract and a quasi contract.

PREVIEW CASE

→ Brooklyn Union Gas Co. (BUG) discovered that gas was being consumed at 369 Euclid Avenue although there was no record of an account or meter at that address. The last account at that address had been closed 14 years before. John Diggs was in possession of the premises at 369 Euclid. BUG sued him for the gas consumed at that location on the basis of a quasi contract for his unjust enrichment. Had BUG suffered any detriment? Had Diggs received any benefit for which he had not paid? Do you think it was ethical for Diggs to use the gas when there was no account for his address?

Contract
Legally enforceable agreement

A **contract** can be defined as a legally enforceable agreement between two or more competent persons. At first glance this seems like a very simple definition. Notice that this definition does not even require a written document. Chapters 5 through 13 are devoted exclusively to explaining and clarifying this definition.

Making contracts is such an everyday occurrence that we often overlook their importance, except when the contracts are of a substantial nature. When one buys a cup of coffee during a coffee break, a contract has been made. When the purchaser agrees to pay 50¢ for the coffee, the seller agrees not only to supply one cup of coffee but also agrees by implication of law that it is safe to drink. If the coffee contains a harmful substance that makes the purchaser ill, a breach of contract has occurred that may call for the payment of damages. A **breach of contract** is the failure of one of the parties to perform the obligations assumed under the contract.

Breach of Contract
Failure to perform contractual obligations

Business transactions result from agreements. Every time a person makes a purchase, buys a theater ticket, or boards a bus, an agreement is made. Each party to the agreement obtains certain rights and assumes certain duties and obligations. When such an agreement meets all the legal requirements of a contract, the law recognizes it as binding on all parties. If one of the parties to the contract fails or refuses to perform, the law allows the other party an appropriate action for obtaining damages or enforcing performance by the party breaking the contract.

Contracts are extremely important in business because they form the very foundation upon which all modern business rests. Business consists almost entirely of the making and performing of contracts. A contract that is a sale of goods is governed by the Uniform Commercial Code (see Chapter 16).

REQUIREMENTS FOR A CONTRACT

A **valid contract** is an agreement that courts will enforce against all parties. Such a contract must fulfill the following definite requirements:

1. It must be based on a mutual agreement by the parties to do or not to do a specific thing.

2. It must be made by parties who are competent to enter into a contract that will be enforceable against both parties.

3. The promise or obligation of each party must be supported by consideration (such as the payment of money, the delivery of goods, or the promise to do or refrain from doing some lawful future act) given by each party to the contract.

4. It must be for a lawful purpose; that is, the purpose of the contract must not be illegal, such as the unauthorized buying and selling of narcotics.

5. In some cases, the contract must meet certain formal requirements, such as being in writing or under seal.

You may test the validity of any contract using these five requirements.

LO ❶
Requirements for valid contract

Valid Contract
Contract enforceable by law

CONTRACTS CONTRASTED WITH AGREEMENTS

A contract must be an agreement, but an agreement need not be a contract. An agreement results whenever two or more persons' minds meet on any subject, no matter how trivial. Only when the parties intend to be legally obligated by the terms of the agreement will a contract come into existence. Chapter 6 explains how such agreements are formed. Ordinarily, the subject matter of the contract must involve a business transaction as distinguished from a purely social transaction.

If Mary and John promise to meet at a certain place at 6 P.M. and have dinner together, this is an agreement, not a contract, as neither intends to be legally bound to carry out the terms of the agreement.

If Alice says to David, "I will pay you $25 to be my escort for the Spring Ball," and David replies, "I accept your offer," the agreement results in a contract. David is legally obligated to provide escort service, and Alice is legally bound to pay him $25.

LO ❷
Types of contracts and differences from agreements

CLASSIFICATION OF CONTRACTS

Contracts are classified by many names or terms. Unless you understand these terms, you cannot understand the law of contracts. For example, the law may state that executory contracts made on Sunday are void. You cannot understand this law unless you understand the words *executory* and *void*. Every contract may be placed in one of the following classifications:

1. Valid contracts, void agreements, and voidable contracts
2. Express and implied contracts
3. Formal and simple contracts
4. Executory and executed contracts
5. Unilateral and bilateral contracts

Valid Contracts, Void Agreements, and Voidable Contracts

Void
Of no legal effect

Unenforceable Contract
Agreement that is not currently binding

Voidable Contract
Enforceable agreement that may be set aside by one party

Agreements classified according to their enforceability include valid contracts (defined earlier), void agreements, and voidable contracts.

An agreement with no legal effect is **void**. An agreement not enforceable in a court of law does not come within the definition of a contract. A void agreement (sometimes referred to as a void contract) must be distinguished from an **unenforceable contract**. If the law requires a certain contract to be in a particular form, such as a deed to be in writing, and it is not in that form, it is merely unenforceable, not void. It can be made enforceable by changing the form to meet the requirements of the law. An agreement between two parties to perform an illegal act is void. Nothing the parties can do will make this agreement an enforceable contract.

A **voidable contract** would be an enforceable agreement but, because of circumstances or the capacity of a party, one or both of the parties may set it aside. The distinguishing factor of a voidable contract is the existence of a choice by one party to abide by or to reject the contract. A contract made by an adult with a person not of lawful age (legally known as a minor or infant) is often voidable by the minor. Such a contract is enforceable against the adult but not against the minor. If both parties to an agreement are minors, either one may avoid the agreement. Until the party having the choice to avoid the contract exercises the right to set the contract aside, the contract remains in full force and effect. An agreement that does not meet all five of the requirements for a valid contract might be void or it might be a voidable contract.

Express and Implied Contracts

Express Contract
Contract with the terms of the agreement specified in words

Implied Contract (Implied in Fact Contract)
Contract with major terms implied by the parties' conduct

Contracts classified according to the manner of their formation fall into two groups: express and implied contracts. In an **express contract**, the parties express their intentions by words, whether in writing or orally, at the time they make the agreement. Both their intention to contract and the terms of the agreement are expressly stated or written. Customary business terms, however, do not need to be stated in an express contract in order to be binding.

An **implied contract** (also called a **contract implied in fact**) is one in which the duties and the obligations that the parties assume are not expressed but are

COURT CASE

Facts: Sean Smith and others were indicted for the capital murder of Hilton Merriman. Smith and District Attorney Randall Sherrod entered into an oral immunity agreement by which Smith agreed to give a videotaped statement and testify against a co-defendant. Smith gave the statement and although not called to testify was available to do so. When the other defendants' cases were disposed of, the indictment as to Smith was dismissed. Two years later, James Farren was elected district attorney. Farren got a second indictment against Smith. Smith asked the court to enforce the immunity agreement saying that he had complied with it. Sherrod testified that when he dismissed the first indictment against Smith he had considered the immunity agreement a "done deal."

Outcome: Although the immunity agreement was oral, Smith had complied with it. An oral agreement is enforceable, so Smith was acquitted.

—Smith v. State, **96 S.W.3d 377 (Tex.)**

implied by their acts or conduct. The adage "actions speak louder than words" very appropriately describes this class of contracts. The facts of a situation imply that a contract exists. The parties indicate so clearly by their conduct that they have a mutual agreement and what they intend to do that there is no need to express the agreement in words to make it binding.

COURT CASE

Facts: William Shoemake of Texas insured his home with Hochheim Prairie Farm Mutual Insurance Co. through Live Oak Insurance Agency. After he died, his son, Billy Dan of Louisiana, told Live Oak's customer representative of the death and to switch the insurance to his name. For two years Hochheim sent renewal notices to Texas. When they were returned undelivered, Live Oak sent them to Billy Dan, who paid them. Live Oak included a note with the second renewal notice asking if he still wanted the policy and where to send it. Billy Dan's wife called Live Oak and said to send the policy to Louisiana. Hochheim asked Live Oak to forward the next renewal notice to Shoemake and requested his address. The renewal was not paid so Hochheim sent a notice of policy lapse to Live Oak and asked it to send that notice to Shoemake. Live Oak did not. A few months later fire destroyed the home. When Hochheim denied the claim because the policy had lapsed, Billy Dan sued Live Oak for failing to perform an implied contract. The jury found for Billy Dan, and Live Oak appealed.

Outcome: The appellate court found that although there was no express contract with Live Oak, its actions were adequate to find that it had agreed to provide an insurance policy on the house.

—Live Oak Insurance Agency v. Shoemake, **2003 WL 21982237 (Tex.)**

Formal and Simple Contracts

A **formal contract** must be in a special form or be created in a certain way. Formal contracts include contracts under seal, recognizances, and negotiable instruments.

When very few people could write, contracts were signed by means of an impression in wax attached to the paper. As time passed, a small wafer pasted on the contract replaced the use of wax. The wafer seal was in addition to the written signature. This practice is still used occasionally,

Formal Contract
Contract with special form or manner of creation

but the more common practice is to sign formal contracts in using the word "Seal" or the letters "L.S." after the signatures:

Jane Doe (Seal); Jane Doe [L.S.]

Today, it is immaterial whether these substitutes for a seal are printed on the document, typewritten before signing, or the persons signing write them after their respective names. However, in some states, the document itself also must recite that it is under seal. In jurisdictions where the use of the seal has not been abolished, the seal implies consideration.

In some states, the presence of a seal on a contract allows a party a longer time in which to bring suit if the contract is broken. Other states make no distinction between contracts under seal and other written contracts. The Uniform Commercial Code abolishes the distinction with respect to contracts for the sale of goods.

COURT CASE

Facts: Charles Stuckey signed an agreement to purchase an interest in a condominium. The agreement recited that it was executed under seal. The word "seal" appeared after Stuckey's signature and the signatures of the sellers, but not after the signature of the escrow agent, Phillip Johns. Eleven years after the sale of the property, Stuckey sued the escrow agent. The agent asked the court to dismiss the suit because a suit on a written contract had to be brought within six years. Stuckey alleged the contract was under seal so a suit could be brought up to 20 years after its execution.

Outcome: Because there was no indication that the escrow agent's signature was under seal, the agreement was not a sealed contract as to him. The six year requirement applied and the case was dismissed.

—*McCalla v. Stuckey*, 504 S.E.2d 269 (Ga.)

Recognizance
Obligation entered into before a court to do an act required by law

Recognizances, a second type of formal contract, are obligations entered into before a court whereby persons acknowledge that they will do a specified act that is required by law. The persons acknowledge that they will be indebted for a specific amount if they do not perform as they agreed, such as the obligation undertaken by a criminal defendant to appear in court on a particular day.

Negotiable Instrument
Document of payment, such as a check

Negotiable instruments, discussed in later chapters, are a third type of formal contract. They include checks, notes, drafts, and certificates of deposit.

All contracts other than formal contracts are informal and are called **simple contracts**. A few of these, such as an agreement to sell land or to be responsible for the debt of another, must be in writing in order to be enforceable; otherwise they need not be prepared in any particular form. Generally speaking, informal or simple contracts may be in writing, may be oral, or may be implied from the conduct of the parties.

Simple Contract
Contract that is not formal

Written Contract
Contract with terms in writing

A **written contract** is one in which the terms are set forth in writing rather than expressed orally. An **oral contract** is one in which the terms are stated in spoken, not written, words. Such a contract is usually enforceable; however, when a contract is oral, disputes may arise between the parties as to the terms of the agreement. No such disputes need arise about the terms of a written contract if the wording is clear, explicit, and complete. For this reason most

Oral Contract
Contract with terms spoken

businesspeople avoid making oral contracts involving matters of very great importance. Some types of contracts are required to be in writing and are discussed in Chapter 11.

Executory and Executed Contracts

Contracts are classified by the stage of performance as executory contracts and executed contracts. An **executory contract** is one in which the terms have not been fully carried out by all parties. If a person agrees to work for another for one year in return for a salary of $3,500 a month, the contract is executory from the time it is made until the 12 months expire. Even if the employer should prepay the salary, it would still be an executory contract because the other party has not yet worked the entire year, that is, executed that part of the contract.

Executory Contract
Contract not fully carried out

An **executed contract** is one that has been fully performed by all parties to the contract. The Collegiate Shop sells and delivers a dress to Benson for $105, and Benson pays the purchase price at the time of the sale. This is an executed contract because nothing remains to be done on either side; that is, each party has completed performance of each part of the contract.

Executed Contract
Fully performed contract

COURT ☀ CASE

Facts: Lockheed sent M. B. Electronics a written order to repair a shaker-amplifier system. The order contained an indemnity agreement stating M. B. would indemnify Lockheed from injury arising out of the repair work. While working, Wichman, an employee of M. B., was electrocuted. Lockheed paid Wichman's heirs $115,000 and sued M. B. for reimbursement under the purchase order. Under state law, M. B. was not liable unless the order was fully executed before the injury.

Outcome: Because Wichman was killed during the process of repairing the system, the repairs had not been completed nor had they been paid for; therefore, the purchase agreement was not fully executed.

—Lockheed Missiles & Space Co. v. Gilmore Indus., 185 Cal. Rptr. 409

Unilateral and Bilateral Contracts

When an act is done in consideration for a promise, the contract is a **unilateral contract**. If Smith offers to pay $100 to anyone who returns her missing dog and Fink returns the dog, this would be a unilateral contract. It is unilateral (one-sided) in that only one promise is made. A promise is given in exchange for an act. Smith made the only promise, which was to pay anyone for the act of returning the dog. Fink was not obligated to find and return the dog, so only one duty existed.

Unilateral Contract
Contract calling for an act in consideration for a promise

A **bilateral contract** consists of a mutual exchange of promises to perform some future acts. One promise is the consideration for the other promise. If Brown promises to sell a truck to Adams for $5,000, and Adams agrees to pay $5,000, then the parties have exchanged a promise for a promise—a bilateral contract. Most contracts are bilateral because the law states a bilateral contract can be formed when performance is started. This is true unless it is clear from the first promise or the situation that performance must be completed. The test is whether there is only one right and duty or two.

Bilateral Contract
Contract consisting of mutual exchange of promises

Quasi Contract

One may have rights and obligations imposed by law when no real contract exists. This imposition of rights and obligations is called a **quasi contract** or **implied in law contract**. It is not a true contract because the parties have not made an agreement. Rights and obligations will be imposed only when a failure to do so would result in one person unfairly keeping money or otherwise benefiting at the expense of another. This is known as **unjust enrichment**. For example, suppose a tenant is obligated to pay rent of $300 a month but by mistake hands the landlord $400. The law requires the landlord to return the overpayment of $100. The law creates an agreement for repayment even though no actual agreement exists between the parties. For the landlord to keep the money would mean an unjust enrichment at the expense of the tenant. Courts will also invoke the principles of unjust enrichment when there is a contract, but there is no remedy provided under the contract. An unjust enrichment offends our ethical principles, so the law imposes a contractual obligation to right the situation.

PREVIEW CASE REVISITED

Facts: Brooklyn Union Gas Co. (BUG) discovered that gas was being consumed at 369 Euclid Avenue although there was no record of an account or meter at that address. The last account at that address had been closed 14 years before. John Diggs was in possession of the premises at 369 Euclid. BUG sued him for the gas consumed at that location on the basis of quasi contract for his unjust enrichment.
Outcome: The fact that Diggs knew he was receiving gas and BUG was not paid for it established his quasi-contractual liability.

—*Brooklyn Union Gas Co. v. Diggs*, 2003 WL 42106 (N.Y.)

QUESTIONS

1. What is a contract? How does it differ from an agreement?
2. Why are contracts so important to business?
3. How does a voidable contract differ from a valid contract?
4. What two items must be expressed in order to have an express contract?
5. How do parties form an implied contract?
6. How must a sealed contract be executed?
7. What is a recognizance?
8. Are all contracts the result of mutual promises by both parties?
9. Beth tells Alec she will pay him $1,000 to paint her garage. Alec agrees. Beth pays $500 in advance and Alec paints one-quarter of the garage. Explain how this contract could be classified.
10. When will the law impose a contract when no real contract exists?

CASE PROBLEMS

When the concluding question in a case problem can be answered simply yes or no, state the legal principle or rule of law that supports your answer.

1. Rental Management, Inc. demonstrated its computer software to Rent-A-PC, a computer rental business. Rent-A-PC discovered that the software needed to be modified for its business. Rent-A-PC agreed to Rental's charges and paid a deposit of $42,110. Rent-A-PC discovered that the software did not include the modifications it had requested. It informed Rental it was going to stop implementation of the software and requested the deposit back. When Rental did not return the $42,110, Rent-A-PC sued alleging unjust enrichment. Rental claimed that because it had incurred costs in obtaining the software for Rent-A-PC, it was not unjustly enriched. Was it?   LO ❸

2. Nina Parkhurst owned a ranch and asked her son, Doug Boykin, to move to it and manage it for her. Boykin and his wife moved to the ranch and managed it for several years. They talked with Parkhurst many times urging her to transfer 49 percent of the ranch to them. Parkhurst said she had thought and talked about possibly transferring the ranch but had made no decision. The Boykins claimed they were on the ranch under an oral contract with Parkhurst and the oral contract also entitled them to a 49 percent interest in the ranch. She sued them and asked the court to declare that there was no contract. Was there a contract?   LO ❶

3. David and Kimberly Birt met with Richard Gibbs, a loan officer with Wells Fargo Home Mortgage, Inc. After reviewing the Birts' financial documents Gibbs said they were eligible for a home construction loan. He told them to get a builder and design plans. The Birts had plans drawn and gave them to their proposed builder. Gibbs knew from a second credit report that the Birts would not be able to borrow as much as expected, but told them to sign a contract with the builder, which they did. They got a letter welcoming them to Wells Fargo Mortgage Resources and containing lending disclosures but they knew the figures in the disclosures were just an example. Several weeks later when they still had not received a loan commitment letter, the Birts contacted Gibbs's supervisor. He told them the loan was denied. They sued Wells Fargo. Was there an implied in fact contract with Wells Fargo?   LO ❷

4. Alan Kortmeyer and Carolyn Allen owned a lot in Glenhaven, a mobile home park. They lived there for 13 years and got water, sewer, garbage, and snow removal services. For six years, they paid $60 a month for these services, but then concluded that they were only required to pay a proportionate share of the costs of the services. Glenhaven continued to supply the services and bill them $60 a month; they received the services but paid nothing for them. Glenhaven finally sued. Must Kortmeyer and Allen pay for the services and if so, on what basis?   LO ❸

5. Gary P. Fleming asked Stan's Lumber to supply building supplies for a home. Fleming completed Stan's credit application, which required the applicant to pay "attorney's fees, costs, or any other expense of collection." Stan's approved the application. Fleming ordered materials, which Stan's delivered, but he owed $33,000 for them. Stan's sued Fleming for payment and attorney's fees. Attorney's fees were awardable only if there was an enforceable contract providing for them. Was the credit application an enforceable contract?   LO ❶, ❷

LO ❷

6. Aberdeen White was employed full-time by Hugh Chatham Memorial Hospital when she was fired because of a disabling illness. Three years before she left, the hospital had distributed a personnel handbook that stated: "A fulltime employee who becomes disabled during his employment will be able to maintain his group insurance." This statement was not withdrawn before White left. White knew about the statement, but was not allowed to continue the insurance. She sued, saying she had a contract with the hospital requiring it to allow her to continue the insurance. The hospital said that White had not promised to continue her employment after the handbook was issued. Was there a contract between White and the hospital?

LO ❶, ❷

7. After an argument with his wife, Russell Pelo bought a shotgun and made threats of self-harm. In accordance with state law, he was detained in a hospital psychiatric unit for examination after a judge found him seriously mentally impaired. After Pelo was released, he refused to pay the hospital bill or allow his health insurer to pay it. When sued for the hospital bill Pelo said he should not have to pay because he did not want to be hospitalized. Must he pay for services he did not want?

Offer and Acceptance

LEARNING OBJECTIVES

1 Discuss the requirements for a valid contract.
2 Explain the difference between an offer and an invitation to make an offer.
3 Summarize the rules affecting the duration of an offer.
4 Define a counteroffer.
5 State the way to accept an offer made by mail.

PREVIEW CASE

Weldon Hall sponsored a boat race for which the advertised first prize was a 14-foot boat, a trailer, and a 20-horsepower motor. After Gerald Bean called Hall's marina and verified the first prize, he won, but Hall offered a 6-horsepower motor as first prize. Bean sued to recover the advertised first prize. May he recover? Did Hall convey the impression that he would award the 20-horsepower motor?

A valid contract is created by the agreement of the parties. This agreement, vital to the formation of a contract, is frequently called "a meeting of the minds" of the parties. The agreement exists when one party makes an offer and the other party accepts the offer.

LO 1
Valid contracts

The parties may expressly state, either orally or in writing, what they agree to do, or they may indicate their intentions by their actions. If *A*'s conduct reasonably leads *B* to believe that *A* intends to enter into a binding contract, then *A* is bound as effectively as if the contract had been expressed. However, in business, a person seldom indicates every intention solely by acts. In most cases only a part of the contract is expressed, and the other part is implied.

Two essential elements of a contract are: (1) an offer, either expressed or implied; and (2) an acceptance, either expressed or implied.

REQUIREMENTS OF A VALID OFFER

Offer
A proposal to make a contract

Offeror
Person who makes an offer

Offeree
Person to whom offer is made

The proposal to make a contract is the **offer**. The **offeror** is the person who makes the offer; the **offeree** is the person to whom the offer is made. An offer expresses the willingness of the offeror to enter into a contractual agreement. The mutual agreement required for a contract is composed of an offer and an acceptance. A valid offer includes three requirements:

1. The offer must be definite.
2. It must appear to be seriously intended.
3. It must be communicated to the offeree.

The Offer Must Be Definite

A contract will not be enforced unless the court can ascertain what the parties agreed to. The offeror's intentions are ascertained from the offer, and these intentions cannot be ascertained unless the offer is definite. Terms usually required to be stated would include who the offeree is, the subject matter of the offer, and the price, quantity, and time of performance.

COURT CASE

Facts: Douglas & Lomason Co. fired Terry Anderson when a box of company pencils was found in his pickup. Douglas had an employee handbook that outlined a discipline procedure for unauthorized possession of company property. The procedure imposed a warning for a first offense, suspension for a second offense, and firing for the third. However, the handbook also stated that it was not intended to create any contractual rights and could be changed by Douglas at any time. Anderson sued, alleging the handbook created a contract that Douglas breached by firing him for his first offense.

Outcome: The court said a reasonable person could not believe Douglas agreed to be bound to the provisions in the handbook. Because the handbook was not definite enough to create a valid offer, there was no contract.

—*Anderson v. Douglas & Lomason Co.,*
540 N.W.2d 277 (Iowa)

The Uniform Commercial Code modifies this strict rule somewhat as to contracts for the sale of goods. It is not always practical for a businessperson to make an offer for the sale of merchandise that is definite as to price. The offeror may state that the price will be determined by the market price at a future date or by a third party. If the contract does not specify the price, the buyer must ordinarily pay the reasonable value of the goods.

The Offer Must Appear to Be Seriously Intended

One may make an offer in jest, banter, fear, or extreme anger; and if this fact is known or should be known by the offeree because of the surrounding circumstances, no contract is formed. A business transaction is ordinarily not entered into in jest or because of extreme fear or anger, and the offeree has no right to think that the offer is seriously intended when it is made under these circumstances.

There are times when the offer is not seriously intended, but the offeree has no way of knowing this. In that event, if the offer is accepted, a binding contract results.

COURT CASE

Facts: Charles Luebbert and Mary Simmons were dating. Simmons had financial problems and frequently borrowed money from Luebbert. She rented her home and moved into Luebbert's lake home with her daughters. Luebbert kept asking her when she was going to repay him. She insisted she would pay him back. One evening they sat having drinks on Luebbert's deck. Using a form, Simmons sloppily wrote Luebbert a promissory note stating she owed him $12,200 at 10 percent due December 30. Simmons and her daughters moved out, and

Luebbert sued Simmons. She alleged she was drunk and just joking when she filled out the note.

Outcome: Since Luebbert loaned Simmons the money and expected her to pay it back, and since Simmons insisted she would pay him back, the court said she appeared to have the intention to make an agreement to repay. Simmons had to pay the note.

—Luebbert v. Simmons,
98 S.W.3d 72 (Mo.)

The Offer Must Be Communicated to the Offeree

Until the offeror makes the offer known to the offeree, it is not certain that it is intended that the offeree may accept and thereby impose a binding contract. Accordingly, the offeree cannot accept an offer until the offeror has communicated the offer to the offeree. If one writes out an offer and the offer falls into the hands of the offeree without the knowledge or consent of the offeror, it cannot be accepted. Furthermore, an offer directed to a specific individual or firm cannot be accepted by anyone else. This is because people have a right to choose the parties with whom they deal.

COURT CASE

Facts: For 11 years, John Kartheiser was employed by American National Can Co. American's Engineering Office Manual, which was made available for Kartheiser's use, contained an overtime policy. As a supervisor, Kartheiser oversaw payment of employees under the overtime policy. American's Human Resources Manual, of which Kartheiser was not aware, had a disclaimer that any manuals an employee might receive were for informational purposes only. Kartheiser sued American for overtime pay under the

overtime policy. American claimed its disclaimer prevented the overtime policy from being enforceable.

Outcome: Because an offer is not effective until it is communicated to the offeree, the offer of the disclaimer was not effective because it was not communicated to Kartheiser.

—Kartheiser v. American Nat. Can Co.,
84 F.Supp.2d 1008 (S.D. Iowa)

INVITATIONS TO MAKE OFFERS

In business, many apparent offers are not true offers. Instead, they are treated as invitations to the public to make offers at certain terms and prices. If a member of the public accepts the invitation, and an offer is submitted embodying all the terms set out in the invitation, the inviter may refuse to accept the offer. Ordinarily,

LO ❷
Offer versus invitation to make offer

however, as a practical matter and in the interest of maintaining goodwill, such an offer will be accepted. The most common types of general invitations are advertisements, window displays, catalogs, price lists, and circulars. If a merchant displays in a store window a coat for $95, there is no binding requirement to sell at this price. Most businesspeople would consider refusing to sell a very poor business policy, but nevertheless merchants may legally do so. Considering advertisements and window displays as invitations to make offers rather than offers provides protection to businesspeople. Otherwise they might find that they were subjected to many suits for breach of contract if they oversold their stock of goods.

COURT CASE

Facts: Audio Visual Associates, Inc. sued Sharp Electronics Corp. for, among other things, breach of contract. In its complaint, Audio alleged it contacted Sharp about purchasing 1,400 Sharp graphing calculators and that Sharp first quoted a price of $71 per calculator, but later orally quoted Audio a price of $31. Audio faxed a purchase order to Sharp for 1,400 calculators at $31 each. When Audio inquired of its order, a Sharp employee told it the calculators were "sold out." Audio alleged Sharp had more than 30,000 in stock. Sharp did refer Audio to a Sharp distributor from whom Audio purchased the calculators.

Outcome: The court stated that buyers and sellers may exchange price quotations, purchase orders, telephone calls, and faxes concerning a proposed transaction without incurring contractual obligations until there is an offer by one party followed by an acceptance by the other. Unless there is more, a price quote is simply an invitation to negotiate. There was no contract in this case.

—*Audio Visual Associates, Inc. v Sharp Electronics Corp.*, 210 F.3d 254 (4th Cir.)

The general rule is that circulars are not offers but invitations to the recipients to make an offer. However, it is often difficult to distinguish between a general sales letter and a personal sales letter. The fact that the letter is addressed to a particular individual does not necessarily make it a personal sales letter containing an offer. If the wording indicates that the writer is merely trying to evoke an offer on certain terms, it is an invitation to the other party to make an offer.

An advertisement, however, may be an offer when it clearly shows it is intended as an offer. This is primarily true with advertisements that offer rewards.

PREVIEW CASE REVISITED

Facts: Weldon Hall sponsored a boat race for which the advertised first prize was a 14-foot boat, a trailer, and a 20-horsepower motor. After Gerald Bean called Hall's marina and verified the first prize, he won, but Hall offered a 6-horsepower motor as first prize. Bean sued to recover the advertised first prize.
Outcome: The court found that Hall had made an offer to the public, which Bean accepted by winning the race.

—*Hall v. Bean*, 582 S.W.2d 263 (Tex. Civ. App.)

DURATION OF THE OFFER

Several rules affect the duration of an offer:

1. The offeror may revoke an offer at any time before its acceptance. If it has been revoked, the offeree can no longer accept it and create a contract. Normally the offer can be revoked even if the offeror has promised to keep it open.

LO ❸
Rules on duration of offers

COURT CASE

Facts: On April 14, Saint Switch, Inc. offered to sell fuel pumps to Norca Corp. The offer was to be kept open for 15 months. On August 18, Saint made a new offer to Norca with a different price for the fuel pumps. In November, Norca tried to accept the April offer. When Saint did not sell the pumps under the terms of that offer, Norca sued for breach of contract.

Outcome: The court said Saint revoked its April offer when it made an inconsistent offer in August. Even though the offer was to be kept open for 15 months, it could be revoked.

—*Norca Corp. v. Tokheim Corp.,*
643 N.Y.S.2d 139 (N.Y.)

2. An option cannot be revoked at will. If the offeror receives something of value in return for a promise to hold the offer open, it is said to be an **option**, and this type of offer cannot be revoked.

If the offer relates to the sale or purchase of goods by a merchant, a signed written offer to purchase or sell that states that it will be held open cannot be revoked during the time stated. If no time is stated, it cannot be revoked for a reasonable time, not to exceed three months. This type of offer is called a **firm offer**. It is valid even though no payment is made to the offeror.

Option
Binding promise to hold an offer open

Firm Offer
A merchant's signed, written offer to sell or purchase goods saying it will be held open

COURT CASE

Facts: In April, Mid-South Packers, Inc. sent a letter to Shoney's, Inc. listing prices at which Mid-South would supply bacon. The letter, titled "Proposal," stated Shoney's would have 45 days notice of price changes. In July, Shoney's began purchasing meat from Mid-South. In August, Mid-South told Shoney's that the price of bacon would be 7¢ per pound higher. Shoney's next order requested shipment at the old, lower price, but orders were filled and billed at the higher price. Shoney's reduced its payment by what it claimed it was overcharged by the price increase. Mid-South sued for payment.

Shoney's argued that the proposal was an offer, which it accepted by placing orders. As a binding contract, it required 45 day's notice of price increases.

Outcome: The court said that as a firm offer, the proposal was irrevocable for no more than three months, which expired in July, prior to Shoney's acceptance. Mid-South had the right to raise its price in August and collect full payment.

—*Mid-South Packers, Inc. v. Shoney's, Inc.,*
761 F.2d 1117 (5th Cir.)

In states in which the seal has its common-law effect, an offer cannot be revoked when it is contained in a sealed writing that states that it will not be revoked.

3. A revocation of an offer must be communicated to the offeree prior to the acceptance. Mere intention to revoke is not sufficient. This is true even though the intent is clearly shown to persons other than the offeree, as when the offeror dictates a letter of revocation.

    Notice to the offeree that the offeror has behaved in a way that indicates the offer is revoked, such as selling the subject matter of the offer to another party, revokes the offer.

COURT CASE

Facts: Melvin Ingebretson, the major stockholder of the First State Bank of Thornton, sought to employ Glenn Emmons as manager. Ingebretson agreed to give Emmons an option to purchase his and some other stock if Emmons would work for the bank. Ingebretson signed an option agreement and sent it to Emmons. Before Emmons signed it, Ingebretson called and told him to "hold up on the contract" because he could not get all the stock to sell. Four days later,

Emmons signed the contract and returned it to Ingebretson with a check for the first payment.

Outcome: The court held that the obvious implication of Ingebretson's statement was that he would not be able to continue the offer to sell the stock and he therefore revoked the offer.

—*Emmons v. Ingebretson,*
279 F. Supp. 558 (N.D. Iowa)

4. An offer is terminated by the lapse of the time specified in the offer. If no time is specified in the offer, it is terminated by a lapse of a reasonable time after being communicated to the offeree. A reasonable length of time varies with each case depending on the circumstances. It may be 10 minutes in one case and 60 days in another. Important circumstances are whether the price of the goods or services involved are fluctuating rapidly, whether perishable goods are involved, and whether there is keen competition with respect to the subject matter of the contract.

5. Death or insanity of the offeror automatically terminates the offer. This applies even though the offeree is not aware of the death or the insanity of the offeror and communicates an acceptance of the offer. Both parties must be alive and competent to contract at the moment the acceptance is properly communicated to the offeror.

6. Rejection of the offer by the offeree and communication of the rejection to the offeror terminates the offer.

7. If, after an offer has been made, the performance of the contract becomes illegal, the offer is terminated.

THE ACCEPTANCE

Acceptance
Assent to an offer resulting in a contract

When an offer has been properly communicated to the party for whom it is intended and that party or an authorized agent accepts, a binding contract is formed. The offer then can no longer be revoked. **Acceptance** is the assent to an offer that results in a contract. The acceptance must be communicated to the offeror, but no particular procedure is required. The acceptance may be made by words, oral or written, or by some act that clearly shows an intention to accept. Silence does not, except in rare cases, constitute an acceptance; nor is a mental intention to accept sufficient. If the offer stipulates a particular mode of acceptance, the offeree must meet those standards in order for a contract to be formed.

COURT CASE

Facts: The check Michael O'Brien used to apply for auto insurance with Nationwide Mutual bounced. On October 2, he mailed a money order with a copy of his original insurance application to Nationwide. Nationwide sent him a letter saying it was not insuring him because the check bounced. When it received the money order, Nationwide deposited it, but immediately returned the payment saying the original policy was still cancelled. On October 27, O'Brien had an auto accident and sued Nationwide saying he had insurance coverage.

Outcome: Sending the application and check was an offer that Nationwide clearly did not accept because the check bounced. Sending the money order and copy of the application was another offer to purchase insurance from Nationwide. However, Nationwide never accepted this offer, so there was no contract of insurance.

—*O'Brien v. Nationwide Mutual Ins. Co.,* **689 A.2d 254 (Pa. Super.)**

COUNTEROFFERS

An offer must be accepted without any deviation in its terms. If the intended acceptance varies or qualifies the offer, this **counteroffer** rejects the original offer. This rejection terminates the offer. This rule is changed to some extent when the offer relates to the sale or purchase of goods. In any case, a counteroffer may be accepted or rejected by the original offeror.

LO **4**
Define counteroffer

Counteroffer
Offeree's response that rejects offer by varying its terms

COURT CASE

Facts: Duane McDermond and Denise Klimas contracted to buy a house from Ashley Albright. Written notice of unsatisfactory conditions resulting from a home inspection had to be given to Albright by December 16. If she and the buyers had not agreed to a settlement of the unsatisfactory conditions by December 17, the contract stated it would "terminate three calendar days" later. The buyers had an inspection and gave Albright written notice of unsatisfactory conditions requiring they be corrected prior to closing the sale. On December 16, Albright wrote that: she accepted the conditions; the maximum estimate on correction was $3,600; she would put aside $4,500 and have the work done after closing. The buyers bought another house and asked for return of their $4,000 deposit. Albright refused saying the buyers breached the contract, so they sued.

Outcome: The court stated that because the buyers required the repairs before closing while the seller made a counteroffer that the repairs would be done after closing, there was no agreement on a settlement of the inspection problems. Without agreement on the repairs, the sales contract terminated and the deposit had to be returned.

—*Albright v. McDermond,* **14 P.3d 318 (Colo.)**

INQUIRIES NOT CONSTITUTING REJECTION

The offeree may make an inquiry about terms that differ from the offer's terms without rejecting the offer. For example, if the offer is for 1,000 shares of stock for $20,000 cash, the offeree may ask: "Would you be willing to wait 30 days for $10,000 and hold the stock as collateral security?" This mere inquiry about changed terms does not reject the offer. If the offeror says no, the original offer may still be accepted, if it has not been revoked in the meantime.

MANNER OF ACCEPTANCE

LO 5
Acceptance by mail

An offer that does not specify a particular manner of acceptance may be accepted in any manner reasonable under the circumstances. However, the offeror may stipulate that the acceptance must be written and received by the offeror in order to be effective. If there is no requirement of delivery, a properly mailed acceptance is effective when it is posted. This rule is called the "mailbox rule," and it applies even though the offeror never receives the acceptance.

COURT CASE

Facts: Crab House, Inc. leased restaurant property from Morton's of Chicago/Great Neck LLC. Crab House closed its restaurant and located a potential new tenant. In accordance with the terms of its lease, Crab House wrote Morton's that it wanted to transfer the lease and offered to let Morton terminate the lease. On February 18, Morton's mailed Crab House a certified letter confirming acceptance of the offer to terminate the lease. The next day Crab House faxed Morton's a revocation of its offer to terminate. On February 22, Crab House received Morton's letter of acceptance and Morton's received a letter from Crab House attempting to revoke its offer to terminate. Morton's sued for a declaration that the lease was terminated.

Outcome: Morton's letter confirming acceptance of Crab House's offer to terminate the lease was effective on mailing. Because the mailing occurred before Crab House attempted to revoked its offer on February 19, the lease was terminated.

—Morton's of Chicago/Great Neck LLC v. Crab House, Inc., 746 N.Y.S.2d 317 (N.Y.A.D.)

Similarly, the delivery of an acceptance to the telegraph company is effective unless the offeror specifies otherwise or unless custom or prior dealings indicate that acceptance by telegraph is improper. In former years, the courts held that an offer could be accepted only by the same means by which the offer was communicated, called the "mirror-image rule." But this view is being abandoned in favor of the provision of the Uniform Commercial Code, Sec. 2-206(1)(a), relating to sales of goods: "Unless otherwise unambiguously indicated by the language or circumstances, an offer to make a [sales] contract shall be construed as inviting acceptance in any manner and by any medium reasonable in the circumstances." Under this principle, an acceptance can be made by telephone or even by fax. The contract is made on the date and at the place the fax acceptance is sent.

Careful and prudent persons can avoid many difficulties by stipulating in the offer how it must be accepted and when the acceptance is to become effective. For example, the offer may state, "The acceptance must be sent by letter and be received by me in Chicago by 12 noon on June 15 before the contract is complete." The acceptance is not effective unless it is sent by letter and is actually received by the offeror in Chicago by the time specified.

QUESTIONS

1. Explain how a valid contract is created.

2. Under what circumstances can an offer be definite and yet the price is not definite?

3. What are common types of invitations to make an offer?

4. **a.** When may an offer be revoked?

   b. What is the effect of death or insanity of the offeror?

5. Is an offer revoked if the offeror clearly communicates revocation to someone other than the offeree?

6. When may an offeree accept an offer?

7. How is a "reasonable time" after which an offer would "lapse" determined?

8. Does an inquiry about terms that differ from the offer terms reject the offer, thus preventing a contract on the offer's terms?

9. How may an offer received by (a) letter, (b) telegraph, or (c) fax be accepted?

CASE PROBLEMS

1. Knowing of a building project that required boilers, H. B. Smith, a boiler manufacturer, sent a quote for the boilers to Hazelton Manufacturing Co. Although Smith gave a retail price in some other quotes, in this quote Smith gave a "net" price of $131,711 and said there would be no discounts. When given a net price, a distributor normally marks it up to generate its profit. Instead Hazelton thought it was a retail price so followed the industry practice of discounting it. Hazelton wrote $88,200 and "dealer cost" next to the price on the Smith form and added its name, address, and phone number. It sent these unsolicited forms to I & R Mechanical Inc. and a large number of businesses it thought might bid on the project. I & R based its bid on the project on Hazelton's $88,200 figure. I & R got the bid and called Hazelton to order the boilers. Hazelton said there was a mistake and would not sell the boilers for $88,200. I & R bought the boilers elsewhere for $140,000 and sued Hazelton for breach of contract. Did I & R and Hazelton have a contract?   LO ②

2. MLS Construction, LLC asked MD Drilling and Blasting, Inc. to do rock drilling and blasting work required for an excavation project. MD had previously done work for MLS and had not been fully paid. MD agreed to do the new work if MLS made a significant payment on the balance due. MLS agreed and gave MD a check for $15,000. MD began work and the same day faxed an unsigned written agreement to MLS. Two weeks later, MD found out MLS had stopped payment on the check. MD stopped work on the project and sued MLS for breach of contract. MLS argued the unsigned agreement MD faxed revoked the original offer and therefore there was no contract. Did it?   LO ③

LO ❶

3. Cutter Dodge advertised in the Honolulu newspaper, "$0 Cash Down!" and "New . . . GRAND CHEROKEE LAREDO" priced at "$229 Month 24 Mos. $0 Cash Down." The fine print stated sales were "on approved credit." In response, Mary and Thomas Pico went to Cutter's lot. One of the Laredos was on hand, and the Picos drove it. They tried to buy it, but the sales agent told them they would have to put down $1,400. They pointed out that the ad said no cash down for the Laredo. The agent said that offer was only for recent college graduates. The Picos sued. Was the ad an offer that the Picos could accept, forming a contract?

LO ❹

4. Roy Gilbert was an expert witness in a toxic tort lawsuit. When Gilbert sent his final bill to attorneys Akins & Pettiette, they did not pay, so Gilbert's lawyer sent a letter demanding $5,448.25. Akins & Pettiette sent a check for $5,448.25 that stated: "Endorsement of this check constitutes . . . indemnity . . . of any and all claims and/or causes of action that arise or may arise out of" the toxic tort case and the present case. Gilbert rejected the check. The lawyers claimed he breached a contract to settle for $5,448.25. Did he?

LO ❶

5. Gary Neugent leased a gas station and purchased gas from Amoco Oil Co. Walter and Vernice Beroth met with Neugent to discuss buying gasoline from them instead of directly from Amoco. One of the Beroths mentioned a price of "6¢ over Beroth's cost." Neugent thought "cost" meant the "rack price" or the price at which the Beroths bought the fuel, and the Beroths meant rack price plus tax and freight. Three months later, the Beroths took over Amoco's lease, and Neugent starting getting gas from them. He later discovered that they had been charging him rack price plus freight plus 6¢ a gallon and sued for breach of an oral contract. Did he have a contract with the Beroths at rack price?

LO ❺

6. A candidate in the Democratic primary election for the municipal council in Ridgefield, New Jersey, withdrew. A petition nominating Michael Madden was prepared, but because Madden was a student at Purdue University in Indiana he was not in New Jersey to sign the nomination acceptance. He signed the acceptance in Indiana and faxed it to New Jersey where it was properly and timely filed with the borough clerk. The clerk said the acceptance was defective because of the "facsimile" signature and refused to certify Madden as a candidate. Using principles of contract law, what is your opinion about the faxed document?

LO ❶

7. Charles Wohltmann of Executive Recruitment, an employee recruitment company, twice talked with a Boston Scientific Corp. sales representative who had no authority to accept offers for hiring employees. Later, Thomas Schmidt contacted a friend who worked for Boston Scientific and found out that the company had a job opening in Birmingham where he wanted to work. Schmidt applied and eventually was hired by Boston. Executive Recruitment then claimed it had an oral contract for recruiting with Boston and should be paid for Schmidt's hiring. Should it?

Capacity to Contract

LEARNING OBJECTIVES

❶ Identify classifications of individuals who may not have the capacity to contract.

❷ Define disaffirmance.

❸ Explain how a minor's contract can be ratified.

❹ Discuss reasons other than age that may impair a person's ability to contract.

PREVIEW CASE

→ When Susan Shaner was 14 years old, she went to softball camp at Bloomsburg University. While playing in a softball game at the camp, she suffered a severe broken leg. She sued for her injuries. Before going to the camp, she had signed a statement on the camp's registration form that released the university, the director, and everyone connected with the clinic from liability for any injuries incurred at the camp. The defendants alleged that the release prevented Susan from recovering against them. Do you think a 14-year-old understands the language of a release? Is there a good reason to try to protect children from the consequences of signing a release?

For an agreement to be enforceable at law, all parties must have the legal and mental capacity to contract. This means that the parties must have the ability to understand that a contract is being made, have the ability to understand its general nature, and have the legal competence to contract. The general rule is that the law presumes that all parties have this capacity. This means that anyone alleging incapacity must offer proof of incapacity to overcome that presumption.

However, in the eyes of the law, some parties lack such capacity because of age, physical condition, or public policy. Among those whom the law considers to be incompetent, at least to some degree, are minors, mentally incompetent persons, intoxicated persons, and convicts.

LO ❶
Those lacking capacity.

MINORS

The common-law rule that persons under 21 years of age are **minors** has been abolished by most of the states. Most states have enacted statutes making persons competent to contract at 18 years of age, and a few set the age at 19. In some states, all married minors are fully competent to contract. In still other states, minors in business for themselves are bound on all their business contracts.

Contracts of Minors

Almost all of a minor's contracts are voidable at the minor's option. That is, if a minor so desires, the minor can avoid the contract. If a minor wishes to treat a contract made with an adult as valid, the adult is bound by it. An adult cannot avoid a contract on the ground that the minor might avoid it. If a contract is between two minors, each has the right to avoid it. Should the minor die, the personal representative of the minor's estate may avoid the contract that the minor could have avoided.

PREVIEW CASE REVISITED

Facts: When Susan Shaner was 14 years old, she went to softball camp at Bloomsburg University. While playing in a softball game at the camp, she suffered a severe broken leg. She sued for her injuries. Before going to the camp, she had signed a statement on the camp's registration form that released the university, the director, and everyone connected with the clinic from liability for any injuries incurred at the camp. The defendants alleged that the release prevented Susan from recovering against them.

Outcome: Because the release Susan signed was a contract and she was only 14 at the time, the court said that she could avoid it. Filing suit clearly showed her decision to avoid it.

—*Shaner v. State System of Higher Educ.*, 40 Pa.D.&C. 4th 308 (Pa.)

Firms that carry on business transactions in all the states must know the law dealing with minors in each state. Mail-order houses and correspondence schools are particularly susceptible to losses when dealing with minors. The significance of the law is that, with but few exceptions, people deal with minors at their own risk. The purpose of the law is to protect minors from unscrupulous adults, but in general the law affords the other party no more rights in scrupulous contracts than in unscrupulous ones. The minor is the sole judge as to whether a voidable contract will be binding.

Contracts that Cannot Be Avoided

Although most contracts made by minors are voidable, a few are not. These include contracts for necessaries, business contracts, and other specially enforced contracts such as student loan agreements.

Contracts of Minors for Necessaries. If a minor contracts for **necessaries**, the contract is voidable, but the minor is liable for the reasonable value. Necessaries include items required for a minor to have a reasonable standard of living that are not provided by the minor's parents or guardian. The dividing line between necessaries and luxuries is often a fine one. Historically, necessaries included food, clothes, and shelter. With the raising of standards of living, courts now hold that necessaries also include medical services such as surgery, dental work, and medicine; education through high school or trade school, and in some cases through college; working tools for a trade; and other goods that are luxuries to some people but necessaries to others because of peculiar circumstances.

The minor's liability is quasi-contractual in nature. The reasonable value of what is actually received must be paid in order to prevent the minor from being unjustly enriched. The minor is not, however, required to pay the contract price.

COURT CASE

Facts: When Daphne Williams was a minor, she was admitted to Birmingham Baptist Medical Center Princeton. She was hospitalized for various tests and received several units of blood by transfusion. The services were reasonable, necessary, and professionally performed. At the time Daphne did not work, had no income, and was dependent on her mother for support. Daphne's mother did not pay the hospital bill and in fact obtained bankruptcy relief, which prevented the hospital from recovering from the mother. The hospital sued Daphne.

Outcome: Judgment was for the hospital. The court stated that when a parent has failed or refused to provide necessary medical care for a child, the provider of services may enforce liability for payment of the reasonable cost on the minor.

—*Williams v. Baptist Health Systems, Inc.,*
857 So.2d 149 (Ala. Civ. App.)

Disaffirmance. The term **disaffirmance** means the repudiation of a contract; that is, the election to avoid it or set it aside. A minor has the legal right to disaffirm a voidable contract at any time during minority or within a reasonable time after becoming of age. In some states, if the minor has received no benefits under the contract, disaffirmance does not have to be within a reasonable time. If the contract is wholly executory, a disaffirmance completely nullifies the contract.

LO **2**
Define disaffirmance

Disaffirmance
Repudiation of a voidable contract

COURT CASE

Facts: Without misrepresenting his age, Richard Youngblood, aged 17, sold Joe Blankensopp a wrecked car. Later, Blankensopp could not find the car. Without Blankensopp's knowledge, Youngblood had taken the car and sold it for more money to someone else. Youngblood was arrested for unlawfully appropriating the car.

Outcome: The court stated that because Youngblood's contract with Blankensopp was voidable, Youngblood's sale of the car constituted a disaffirmance of the contract. Youngblood was acquitted.

—*Youngblood v. State,*
658 S.W.2d 598 (Tex. App.)

On electing to disaffirm contracts, minors must return whatever they may have received under the contracts, provided they still have possession of it. The fact that the minor does not have possession of the property, however, regardless of the reason, does not prevent the exercise of the right to disaffirm the contract. In most jurisdictions, an adult may not recover compensation from a minor who returns the property in damaged condition.

If an adult purchases personal property from a minor, the adult has only a voidable title to the property. If the property is sold to an innocent third party before the minor disaffirms the contract, the innocent third party obtains good title to the property. However, the minor may recover from the adult the money or the value of property received from the third party. Statutes in some states make minors' contracts void, not merely voidable. In these states, disaffirmance is not necessary.

LO ③
Minor's ratification

Ratification
Adult indicating contract made while a minor is binding

Ratification. A minor may ratify a voidable contract only after attaining majority. **Ratification** means indicating one's willingness to be bound by promises made during minority. It is in substance a new promise and may be oral, written, or merely implied by conduct.

After majority is reached, silence ratifies an executed contract.

COURT CASE

Facts: John Marshall and Kirsten Fletcher rented an apartment for a year. They agreed to each pay one-half of the rent. At the time Marshall was 17. After he turned 18 he moved into the apartment and paid rent for 1½ months. He then moved out and refused to pay any more rent. Fletcher sued him for his share of the rent for the rest of the lease term. Marshall claimed his moving out and refusing to pay any more rent constituted disaffirmance.

Outcome: The court held that Marshall had ratified the contract by moving into the apartment and paying rent after he turned 18. He was liable for the rent for the remainder of the lease.

—Fletcher v. Marshall,
632 N.E.2d 1105 (Ill.App.)

A minor cannot ratify part of a contract and disaffirm another part; all or none of it must be ratified. Ratification must be made within a reasonable time after reaching majority. A reasonable time is a question of fact to be determined in light of all surrounding circumstances.

Minors' Business Contracts. Many states, either by special statutory provision or by court decisions, have made a minor's business contracts fully binding. If a minor engages in a business or employment in the same manner as a person having legal capacity, contracts that arise from such business or employment cannot be set aside.

COURT CASE

Facts: When 17 years old, Kate Michaelis came to Dr. Janet Schori for pregnancy care. Michaelis signed an agreement for binding arbitration of disputes regarding the quality of the medical care. When Michaelis went into labor Schori told her another doctor would meet her at the hospital. The other doctor never showed up and the baby, otherwise normal, was stillborn. Michaelis and Bodie Stroud, the baby's father, sued saying Michaelis disaffirmed the arbitration agreement. State law provided that a minor could give binding consent for medical care related to treatment of pregnancy.

Outcome: The court pointed out that consent to medical treatment necessarily includes the resolution of disputes over the quality of care. Furthermore, a minor who had to have a parent consent to pregnancy treatment might forgo prenatal care. Thus, Michaelis could not disaffirm the arbitration provision entered into as part of the contract for treatment of her pregnancy.

—Michaelis v. Schori,
24 Cal. Rptr. 2d 380 (Cal. App.)

Other Enforceable Contracts. A number of states prevent a minor from avoiding certain specified contracts. These contracts include educational loan agreements, contracts for medical care, contracts made with court approval or in performance of a legal duty, and contracts involving bank accounts.

Contracting Safely with Minors

Because in general it is risky to deal with minors, every businessperson must know how to be protected when contracting with minors. The safest way is to have an adult (usually a parent or guardian) join in the contract as a cosigner with the minor. This gives the other party to the contract the right to sue the adult who cosigned. A merchant must run some risks when dealing with minors. If a sale is made to a minor, the minor may avoid the contract and demand a refund of the purchase price years later. Because few minors exercise this right, businesspersons often run the risk of contracting with minors rather than seeking absolute protection against loss.

Minors' Torts

As a general rule, a minor is liable for torts as fully as an adult is. If minors misrepresent their age, and the adults with whom they contract rely upon the misrepresentation to their detriment, the minors have committed a tort. The law is not uniform throughout the United States as to whether or not minors are bound on contracts induced by misrepresenting their age. In some states, when sued, they cannot avoid their contracts if they fraudulently misrepresented their age. In some states they may be held liable for any damage to or deterioration of the property they received under the contract. If minors sue on the contracts to recover what they paid, they may be denied recovery if they misrepresented their age. However, the rule is not uniform.

COURT CASE

Facts: The Manasquan Savings & Loan Association loaned Lynn Mayer, a minor, and her husband $22,000 based on her sworn statement that she was of age. Mayer and her husband later separated and defaulted on the loan. When Manasquan sued to recover the collateral, Mayer asserted her minority and demanded that Manasquan return all her funds used to make payments on the note.

Outcome: The court held that minority was no defense to Manasquan's action because Mayer misrepresented her age.

—Manasquan Savings & Loan Assn. v. Mayer, 236 A.2d 407 (Super. Ct. of N.J.)

MENTALLY INCOMPETENT PERSONS

A number of reasons beyond a person's control result in mental incompetence. These include insanity or incompetence as a result of stroke, senile dementia, and retardation. In determining a mentally incompetent person's capacity to contract, the intensity and duration of the incompetency must be determined. In most states, if a person has been formally adjudicated incompetent, contracts made by the person are void without regard to whether they are reasonable or for necessaries. Such a person is considered incapable of making a valid acceptance of an offer no matter how fair the offer is. When a person has been judicially declared insane and sanity is later regained and a court officially declares the person to be competent, the capacity to contract is the same as that of any other normal person.

LO 4
Impairment other than by reason of age

If a person is incompetent but has not been so declared by the court, then the person's contracts are voidable, not void. Like a minor, the person must pay the reasonable value of necessaries that have been supplied. On disaffirmance, anything of value received under the contracts and which the person still has must be returned.

COURT CASE

Facts: A court found Kathy Hauer incompetent from a brain injury and appointed a guardian. Her monthly income was $900 from social security and interest from a mutual fund worth $80,000. Based on a letter from Hauer's doctor, the guardianship was terminated. Ben Eilbes, who was in default on a $7,600 business loan from Union State Bank of Wautoma, met Hauer. He learned of her mutual fund and convinced her to "invest" in his business. However, she could only cash in her mutual fund at certain times. Eilbes told Richard Schroeder, an officer of the bank, that Hauer wanted to invest in his business, needed a loan, and would put up the mutual fund as collateral. He said Hauer's loan would either bring his payments current or pay off his loan. Schroeder called Hauer's financial consultant who said she had the mutual fund, but needed the income to live on and should not use it as collateral. He also said she suffered from brain damage. Schroeder told Eilbes the bank would loan Hauer $30,000. Schroeder met Hauer for the first time when she signed the loan documents thinking she was cosigning for Eilbes who would pay the money back. Hauer sued the bank stating she had cognitive disabilities and was very gullible—people could convince her of almost anything.

Outcome: The court held that she clearly lacked capacity to understand the loan. Because the bank failed to act in good faith toward Hauer, she did not have to return the $30,000 which Eilbes had spent.

—*Hauer v. Union State Bank of Wautoma,*
532 N.W.2d 456 (Wis. App.)

A person who has not been declared by a court to be insane and has only intervals of insanity or delusions can make a contract fully as binding as that of a normal person if it is made during a sane or lucid interval. The person must be capable of understanding that a contract is being made at the time the contract is entered into.

COURT CASE

Facts: Kristine Schefers phoned John Lentner at the nursing home where he lived and asked about buying his farm. Lentner subsequently agreed to sell the farm to Schefers. Lentner told Schefers he needed to go to the bank to get the deed. Schefers took Lentner to the bank and to meet Bruce Latterell who prepared the transfer documents. Latterell felt the sales price was appropriate and Lentner seemed quite competent. Lentner and Schefers told Latterell what personal property was to be included and Lentner responded to all of Latterell's questions. After the sale, Lentner phoned Earl Fisher and told him he had sold the farm. Fisher talked to Schefers and was convinced Lentner did not have contractual capacity. Fisher took Lentner to an attorney who sued for recission of the sale. Fisher was appointed Lentner's conservator.

Outcome: The court found that Lentner knew the nature and effect of his actions. To complete the sale, he got the deed and dealt appropriately with Latterell. After the sale he knew what had happened since he told Fisher. The sale was affirmed by the court.

—*Fisher v. Schefers,*
656 N.W.2d 592 (Minn. App.)

INTOXICATED PERSONS

People also may put themselves in a condition that destroys contractual capacity. Contracts made by people who have become so intoxicated that they cannot understand the meaning of their acts are voidable. On becoming sober, such persons may affirm or disaffirm contracts they made when drunk. If one delays unreasonably in disaffirming a contract made while intoxicated, however, the right to have the contract set aside may be lost.

That a contract is foolish and would not have been entered into if the party had been sober does not make the contract voidable.

A person who has been legally declared to be a habitual drunkard cannot make a valid contract but is liable for the reasonable value of necessaries furnished. If a person is purposely caused to become drunk in order to be induced to contract, the agreement will be held invalid.

The rule regarding the capacity of an intoxicated person also applies to people using drugs.

COURT CASE

Facts: Carolyn Williamson had defaulted on her home mortgage and was threatened with foreclosure. She signed a contract to sell the house to the Matthews for $1,800 plus the unpaid mortgage and later deeded the house to them. Hours after the sale, Williamson consulted an attorney who filed suit for relief from the sale on the grounds of incapacity because of intoxication. Williamson's doctor testified that she had early organic brain syndrome due to excessive drinking and her ability to transact business had been impaired. She had a history of drinking and had been drinking the day she signed the contract.

Outcome: The court stated that the combination of Williamson's impaired ability, history of drinking, drinking on the day of the contract coupled with the threat of foreclosure warranted the conclusion that she was not capable of fully and completely understanding the nature and terms of the contract. The court set the transaction aside.

— *Williamson v. Matthews*,
379 So.2d 1245 (Ala.)

CONVICTS

Although many states have repealed their former laws restricting the capacity of a **convict** (one convicted of a major criminal offense, namely, a felony or treason) to contract, some jurisdictions still have limitations. These range from depriving convicts of rights as needed to provide for the security of the penal institutions in which they are confined and for reasonable protection of the public, to classifying convicts as under a disability, as are minors and insane persons. In these instances, the disability lasts only as long as the person is imprisoned or supervised by parole authorities.

Convict
Person found guilty by court of major criminal offense

QUESTIONS

1. What is the legal and mental capacity to contract?
2. What is the legal presumption regarding capacity to contract, and what is the effect of this presumption?

3. What is the obligation of a minor on disaffirming a contract?

4. With regard to contracts of minors, what are necessaries?

5. When and how may a minor ratify a voidable contract?

6. Can silence ever constitute ratification of a contract? Explain.

7. What is the safest way for a businessperson to be protected when contracting with minors?

8. If Gordon, a minor, lies about his age to induce an adult to enter a contract, is he guilty of a tort? Can any resulting contract be enforced?

9. What is the effect in most states of a person being formally adjudicated incompetent?

10. Can a person who has not been judicially declared insane and has only intervals of insanity or delusions make a binding contract?

CASE PROBLEMS

LO ❸

1. Tina Muller applied for a loan with CES Credit Union so that she could buy a car from her brother, Joseph Muller. They both signed the loan contract, Joseph signing as a co-signor. It was two months before Joseph's 18th birthday. The loan was approved, so Joseph transferred the car to Tina. When she defaulted on the loan, CES repossessed the car and sold it for less than the loan amount. More than ten years after Joseph co-signed the note, CES sued him for the deficiency. He tried to disaffirm the contract. Could he?

LO ❷

2. When 15, Hilda Villalobos suffered cuts to her head and face when the car in which she was riding collided with another vehicle. The vehicles were insured, but a year after the accident, Shirley Smith, an insurance adjuster, discovered Hilda's claims had not been finally resolved. Smith phoned Hilda's father, Antonio, and told him Hilda was entitled to compensation. Antonio described Hilda's scars, but was in a hurry to leave for Mexico. Hilda was already there for the next year. Smith explained that without seeing Hilda's scars her estimate of the value of Hilda's claim could be inaccurate, but offered $3,000. Antonio wanted the money for Hilda right away. Smith paid him $3,000 and he and Hilda's mother, as Hilda's parents, signed releases for Hilda's injuries. Eight months later, when Hilda was 17, Antonio sued on behalf of Hilda. Did the suit constitute disaffirmance by Hilda?

LO ❸

3. Howard Wilcox was the president of Superior Automation Co. On behalf of Superior, Wilcox signed a lease with Marketing Services of Indiana, Inc., which included a personal guarantee from Wilcox. Superior made payments for about two and a half years after executing the lease. Six months before executing the lease, Wilcox had complained he had problems with concentration and functioning at work. His psychiatrist said he had lithium toxicity, which lasted at most ten months after execution of the lease. During this time, he had impaired cognitive function that limited his ability to appreciate and understand the nature and quality of his actions and judgments. Superior stopped making payments and MSI sued. Is the lease enforceable?

LO ❶

4. When Macarita Sanchez died, she owned some real estate. She had five children who orally agreed to divide the property. The two youngest children, Evilia and Cinesio, were minors at the time. An older brother of Sanchez's, Salome Duran, took possession of the part assigned to them and paid the

taxes on it until his death 60 years later. He left a will giving everything to Grace Rodriguez. Evilia and Cinesio claimed an interest in his estate saying the agreement was voidable as to them, and because they had never ratified it they could now disaffirm it. Could they?

5. Zula Dowdy had made a will leaving all her property to her nephew, Tommy Smith. She had certificates of deposit, made payable at her death to Smith, and her checking account was held jointly with Smith's wife, Dorothy. On October 19, her brother, J. T. Malone, had Dowdy admitted to a nursing home. On October 30, Malone and his lawyer had Dowdy sign a power of attorney to Malone. They did not explain the document to her. Dowdy's doctor had examined her the day before and several days later. He said she was confused, heavily medicated, unresponsive to questions, and thought she was talking with dead relatives. Under the authority of the power of attorney Malone removed Smith's name from the certificates of deposit and Dorothy's from the checking account. After Dowdy's death who owned the certificates of deposit and checking account?   LO ❹

6. When Jennifer Cohen was 17 she was seriously injured in an automobile collision and had to be taken to the hospital by helicopter. The total charged was $221,274. After Jennifer reached majority the hospital sued her for payment. Is Jennifer liable on this contract? Explain.   LO ❶

7. Todd Hannegan sold a used truck to Larry Swalberg for $2,500. The fact that Swalberg was a minor never came up. He paid $640 at the sale and agreed to pay the rest three months later. Instead of paying the balance, Swalberg disaffirmed the contract because of his minority. Hannegan sued for return of the truck and asked that Swalberg be accountable for the value of his use of the truck or its depreciation while he had it since the truck was only worth $700 at disaffirmance. Analyze and decide the case.   LO ❷

8. Before their marriage, Alicia and Albert Goldberg signed an agreement giving up their rights to inherit from each other (an antenuptial agreement). Albert was more than 30 years older than Alicia. He continued to live with his sister, Ethel, and did not tell her he had married. Four years later Albert had two heart attacks and a stroke. While Albert was at Rusk Rehabilitation Hospital, Alicia called Mr. Velardi, an attorney, and told him her husband wanted to revoke an antenuptial agreement. Albert telephoned Velardi several times. Velardi told Albert to talk to his own lawyer, but Albert finally persuaded Velardi to visit at Rusk. With Alicia out of the room, Albert told him he wanted to cancel the agreement because it was unfair to Alicia. Velardi again told Albert to get his own lawyer. Albert called Velardi and persuaded him to visit again. When Albert said he did not know how long he would last and he wanted Alicia to share in his estate, Velardi wrote out a revocation which Albert and Alicia signed. After Albert died Ethel challenged Albert's capacity to revoke the antenuptial agreement. Did Albert have contractual capacity?   LO ❶, ❹

CHAPTER 8

Consideration

LEARNING OBJECTIVES

1 Define consideration.

2 Explain when part payment constitutes consideration.

3 Give three examples of insufficient or invalid consideration.

4 Recognize when consideration is not required.

PREVIEW CASE

Gina Bono and Matthew McCutcheon signed a contract for the sale of a puppy named Doozie to Bono. Bono agreed to show Doozie, breed her, and give McCutcheon second pick of Doozie's first litter. McCutcheon gave Bono possession of Doozie. Sometime later, McCutcheon got Doozie back and refused to return her to Bono. Bono sued for breach of contract. The contract did not specify a price, and Bono had not paid for Doozie, so McCutcheon alleged lack of consideration. Must consideration always be expressed in dollars? Did Bono agree to do anything that could help McCutcheon?

LO 1
Define consideration

Consideration
What promisor requires as the price for a promise

Courts will compel compliance with an agreement only when it is supported by consideration. Consideration distinguishes mere agreements from legally enforceable obligations. **Consideration** is whatever the promisor demands and receives as the price for a promise. This could be money, personal or real property, a service, a promise regarding behavior, or any of these items.

NATURE OF CONSIDERATION

In most contracts, the parties require and are content with a promise by the other party as the price for their own promises. For example, a homeowner may promise to pay a painter $1,000 in return for the promise of the painter to paint the house. Correspondingly, the painter makes the promise to paint in return for the promise of the homeowner to make such payment. By its nature, this exchange of a promise for a promise occurs at the one time and creates a contract.

For a promise to constitute consideration, the promise must impose an obligation on the person making it. If a merchant promises to sell a businessperson all of the computer paper ordered at a specific price in return for the businessperson's promise to pay that price for any computer paper ordered, there is no contract. There is no certainty that any computer paper will be needed.

COURT CASE

Facts: The Indiana-American Water Co. had a contract with the town of Seelyville to supply water. The contract stated the company would sell and the town would buy " . . . such quantities of water as the Town may hereafter from time to time need . . . " The town announced it was going to make the improvements needed to get water from land it owned and the water company sued to stop it. The company alleged that the contract was a valid requirements contract and the town had to buy all the water it needed from the company.

Outcome: The court found that a requirements contract is one in which the buyer promises to buy all its needs of a product solely from the seller who agrees to fill those needs. Because the Seelyville contract did not permit the town to shop around for water, it was a valid requirements contract.

—*Indiana-American Water Co. v. Seelyville,*
698 N.E.2d 1255 (Ind.)

A promise that is conditional can still be consideration for a contract. Such a promise is consideration even if the condition is unlikely to occur. If *A* promises to sell *B* paint if the paint shipment arrives, the promise is consideration.

Consideration may also be the doing of an act or the making of a promise to refrain from doing an act that can be lawfully done. Thus, a promise to give up smoking or drinking can be consideration for a promise to make a certain payment in return.

In contrast, a promise to stop driving an automobile in excess of the speed limit is not consideration because a person does not have a right to drive illegally. The promise to drive lawfully does not add anything to that already required.

ADEQUACY OF CONSIDERATION

As a general rule, the adequacy of the consideration is irrelevant. The law does not prohibit bargains. Except in cases where the contract calls for a performance or the sale of goods that have a standard or recognized market value, it is impossible

PREVIEW CASE REVISITED

Facts: Gina Bono and Matthew McCutcheon signed a contract for the sale of a puppy named Doozie to Bono. Bono agreed to show Doozie, breed her, and give McCutcheon second pick of Doozie's first litter. McCutcheon gave Bono possession of Doozie. Sometime later, McCutcheon got Doozie back and refused to return her to Bono. Bono sued for breach of contract. The contract did not specify a price, and Bono had not paid for Doozie, so McCutcheon alleged lack of consideration.
Outcome: Bono, the court held, had given consideration when she agreed to give McCutcheon the second pick of Doozie's first litter. The agreement to provide a puppy to McCutcheon resulted in a benefit to him, so there was consideration.

—*Bono v. McCutcheon,* 824 N.E.2d 1013 (Ohio App.)

to fix the money value of each promise. If the consideration given by one party is grossly inadequate, this is a relevant fact in proving fraud, undue influence, duress, or mistake.

Part Payment

A partial payment of a past-due debt is not consideration to support the creditor's promise to cancel the balance of the debt. The creditor is already entitled to the part payment. Promising to give something to which the other party is already entitled is not consideration.

Several exceptions apply to this rule:

1. If the amount of the debt is in dispute, the debt is canceled if a lesser sum than that claimed is accepted in full settlement.

COURT CASE

Facts: Woodrow Wilson Construction Co., Inc. contracted to remodel a building. Wilson awarded the drywall/painting portion of the job to Precision Drywall & Painting, Inc. Wilson alleged it had problems with Precision's performance and logged the expenses caused by Precision. Wilson deducted the expenses from its final check to Precision and indicated that it was full payment for the job. Precision's lawyer informed Wilson that Precision rejected the final check but offered to settle. Then Precision deposited the check. Precision then sued Wilson for the expenses deducted from the payment.

Outcome: The court stated that since the amount of the debt was in dispute and a lesser sum than that claimed by Precision was accepted by Precision, it could not now sue for more.

—*Precision Drywall & Painting, Inc. v.
Woodrow Wilson Constr. Co. Inc.,*
843 So. 2d 1286 (La. App.)

**Composition of
Creditors**
*When all of multiple
creditors settle in full
for a fraction of the
amount owed*

2. If there is more than one creditor, and each one agrees, in consideration of the others' agreement, to accept in full settlement a percentage of the amount due, this agreement will cancel the unpaid balance due these creditors. This arrangement is known as a **composition of creditors**.

3. If the debt is evidenced by a note or other written evidence, cancellation and return of the written evidence cancels the debt.

COURT CASE

Facts: The Henry B. Gilpin Co. agreed to pay David Moxley $56,390 and signed a note to Moxley in that amount. When interest came due, Gilpin could not make the payment. It proposed a composition of creditors by which it would pay 60 percent of all debts owed in full settlement. Moxley and a majority of the creditors agreed. Two months later, Gilpin offered a new plan to ensure that it continued in business. This offer stated it superseded the previous offer, which Gilpin withdrew. This offer also precluded Gilpin from paying any creditor under the previous offer. All creditors except Moxley accepted the second offer. Moxley demanded payment of the whole amount due including interest. Gilpin paid only interest, and Moxley sued, claiming Gilpin had breached its agreement.

Outcome: The court found that the first composition was a binding contract, and Moxley was entitled to sue on it.

—*Henry B. Gilpin Co. v. Moxley,*
434 N.E.2d 914 (Ind. Ct. App.)

4. If the payment of the lesser sum is accompanied by a receipt in full and some indication that a gift is made of the balance, the debt may be cancelled.

5. If a secured note for a lesser amount is given and accepted in discharge of an unsecured note for a greater amount, the difference between the two notes is discharged. The security is the consideration to support the contract to settle for a lesser sum.

Insufficient or Invalid Consideration

Many apparent considerations lack the full force and effect necessary to make enforceable agreements. Consideration of the following classes is either insufficient or invalid:

LO ③
Insufficient and invalid consideration

1. Performing or promising to perform what one is already obligated to do
2. Refraining or promising to refrain from doing what one has no right to do
3. Past performance

Performing or Promising to Perform What One Is Already Obligated to Do. If the supposed consideration consists merely of a promise to do what one is already legally obligated to do, consideration is invalid. If the consideration is invalid, the contract is invalid. In such case, the promise gives nothing new to the other contracting party.

COURT CASE

Facts: Brenda Brown lived in an apartment run by the Philadelphia Housing Authority (PHA). The property was in terrible condition, so she paid her rent to an account held by the Urban League of Philadelphia. PHA got a judgment against her for unpaid rent. Employees of PHA told her she would not be evicted if the Urban League sent a letter giving the amount it held and saying it would promptly pay the PHA. The letter was sent, but the PHA had Brown evicted. She sued the PHA and several employees for breaching the agreement not to evict her if the Urban League sent the letter.

Outcome: The court stated that payment of the valid judgment against Brown was not consideration for the later agreement because Brown was already required to pay the judgment.

—Brown v. Philadelphia Housing Authority,
19 F. Supp. 2d 23 (E.D. Pa.)

Parties to a contract may at any time mutually agree to cancel an old contract and replace it with a new one. For this new contract to be enforceable, there must be some added features that benefit both parties, although not necessarily to an equal extent. If a contractor agrees to build a house of certain specifications for $80,000, a contract of the homeowner to pay an additional $1,000 is not binding unless the contractor concurrently agrees to do something the original contract did not require as a consideration for the $1,000. The value of the additional act by the contractor need not be $1,000. It merely must have a monetary value.

If unforeseen difficulties arise that make it impossible for the contractor to complete the house for $80,000, these unforeseen difficulties may, in rare cases, be consideration. Unforeseen difficulties include underground rock formations or a change in the law relative to the building codes and zoning laws. The homeowner is not bound to agree to pay more because of unforeseen difficulties; but if such an agreement is made, these difficulties will constitute a consideration even though the contractor does not agree to do anything additional. Strikes, bad weather, and a change in prices are examples of foreseeable difficulties, which would not be consideration.

Refraining or Promising to Refrain from Doing What One Has No Right to Do.
When one refrains or promises to refrain from doing something, this conduct is called **forbearance**. If the promisor had a right to do the act, forbearance is a valid consideration. Consideration is invalid when it consists of a promise to forbear doing something that one has no right to do, such as to commit an unlawful act.

Forbearance
Refraining from doing something

Often the forbearance consists of promising to refrain from suing the other party. Promising to refrain from suing another constitutes consideration if the promisor has a reasonable right to demand damages and intends to file a suit. Such a promise is even valid when a suit lacks merit if the promisor mistakenly, but honestly and reasonably, believes a suit would be valid.

COURT CASE

Facts: Union Oil Co. of California (Unocal) bought a service station from Terrible Herbst, Inc. with the condition that Herbst would clean up the site. Seven years later, the site remained polluted. Thinking Unocal was going to immediately file suit and to keep it from doing so, Herbst signed an agreement that the statute of limitations would not run and that it would waive its statute of limitations defenses to any claims Unocal asserted against Herbst. A year later Unocal sued Herbst who argued that there was no consideration for its statute of limitations waiver.

Outcome: There was consideration for the waiver. The court said that even if Unocal asserted a doubtful claim, its forbearance was adequate consideration.

—*Union Oil Co. of California v. Terrible Herbst, Inc.*, 331 F.3d 735 (9th Cir.)

Past Performance.
An act performed prior to the promise does not constitute valid consideration. If a carpenter gratuitously helps a neighbor build a house with no promise of pay, a promise to pay made after the house is completed cannot be enforced. The promise to pay must induce the carpenter to do the work, and this cannot be done if the promise is made after the work is completed.

A debt that is discharged by bankruptcy may be revived under certain circumstances, usually by the debtor's agreeing, with approval from the bankruptcy

COURT CASE

Facts: After Donald Lovekamp died, Louise Serrato, his former wife, filed a claim for $60,000 alleging an oral contract. Shortly after they had divorced, Donald and Louise began living together again. After about six years, Donald gave Louise a check for $60,000 and told her it was for returning and staying with him after the divorce. He told her to cash the check if he sold his ranch or something happened to him. Louise had not cashed the check, so she filed the claim.

Outcome: The claim was disallowed. The fact that the check was given after Louise returned and stayed with Donald for six years meant that it was past consideration.

—*Estate of Lovekamp v. Lovekamp*, 24 P.3d 894 (Okla. Civ. App.)

court, to pay it. Such promises are enforceable even though the creditor, the promisee, gives no new consideration to support the promise. The debtor is said to have waived the defense of discharge in bankruptcy; the original debt, therefore, is deemed to remain in force.

EXCEPTIONS TO REQUIREMENT OF CONSIDERATION

As a general rule, a promise must be supported by consideration. Certain exceptions to the rule involve voluntary subscriptions, debts of record, promissory estoppel, and modification of sales contracts.

LO ④
When consideration is not required

Voluntary Subscriptions

When charitable enterprises are financed by voluntary subscriptions of many persons, the promise of each person is generally held to be enforceable. When a number of people make pledges to or subscribe to a charitable association or to a church, for example, the pledges or subscriptions are binding. One theory for enforcing the promise is that each subscriber's promise is supported by the promises of other subscribers. Another theory is that a subscription is an offer of a unilateral contract that is accepted by the charity creating liabilities or making expenditures—by relying on the promise. Despite the fact that such promises lack the technical requirements of ordinary contracts, the courts in most states will enforce the promises as a matter of public policy.

COURT CASE

Facts: Boston University (BU) planned to build a library to house special collections. It asked Dr. Martin Luther King Jr., who had received a graduate degree from BU, to deposit his papers with the library. King deposited some of his papers with BU in July 1964, pursuant to a letter. The letter stated the papers were King's property, but he intended make future deposits and to transfer title to the papers in installments until they all became the property of BU. He further stated that in the event of his death all the papers deposited would become the absolute property of BU.

BU indexed the papers, made them available to researchers, and provided trained staff to care for them and assist researchers. Many years later, Coretta King, as executrix of her husband's estate, sued for possession of the papers.

Outcome: The activities of BU constituted reliance on King's promise to give it the papers, so the charitable pledge was enforced.

—*King v. Trustees of Boston University,*
647 N.E.2d 1196 (Mass.)

Debts of Record

Consideration is not necessary to support an obligation of record, such as a judgment, on the basis that such an obligation is enforceable as a matter of public policy.

Promissory Estoppel

Although not supported by considerations, courts enforce some promises on the basis of **promissory estoppel**. According to this doctrine, if one person makes a promise to another and that other person acts in reliance upon the promise, the

Promissory Estoppel
Substitute for consideration when another acts in reliance on promisor's promise

promisor will not be permitted to claim lack of consideration. Enforcement is held to be proper when the promisor should reasonably expect to cause and does cause action by the promisee and the promisee would be harmed substantially if the promise is not enforced. The theory has gained support as a means of realizing justice. The elements of promissory estoppel include:

1. A promise is made.
2. The promisor reasonably expects the promise to induce action by the promisee.
3. The promisee does act.
4. Justice requires enforcement of the promise.

Courts will find that justice requires enforcement of the promise when the promisee would be substantially harmed if it were not enforced.

COURT CASE

Facts: McNeill and Associates was a general agent for ITT Life Insurance. Insurance Marketing, Inc. (IMI) owed ITT a large amount of money and was failing. ITT asked McNeill to purchase IMI's business. McNeill refused. IMI had ten times as many accounts as McNeill. Later ITT again asked McNeill to purchase IMI's business. McNeill, IMI, and ITT signed a written agreement of sale. ITT separately promised McNeill it would not terminate its general agency with McNeill if the agent purchased IMI. McNeill purchased IMI's business for $510,000.

ITT later terminated the agency. McNeill sued and alleged that promisory estoppel required enforcement of the promise not to terminate the agency.

Outcome: The court said justice required enforcing the promise because of liabilities McNeill incurred by purchasing a much larger business in reliance on ITT's promise.

—*McNeill & Associates v. ITT Life Ins.,*
446 N.W.2d 181 (Minn. Ct. App.)

Modification of Sales Contracts

Sales of goods are regulated by the Uniform Commercial Code (see Chapter 16). The Code provides that when a contract for the sale of goods is modified by agreement of the parties, no consideration is necessary to make it enforceable.

QUESTIONS

1. What is the importance of consideration?
2. May a promise that is conditional constitute consideration?
3. What is the relevance of a grossly inadequate consideration given by one party to a contract?
4. Why is partial payment of a past-due debt not consideration to support a creditor's promise to cancel the whole debt?
5. If a boy promises his father that he will not own and operate an automobile until he is 18 in exchange for his father's promise to pay him $2,000, is this a valid contract?
6. If Davis owes Dennis $10,000, and Dennis offers to settle for $7,000, what must be done to make the contract binding?

7. When will courts apply the doctrine of promissory estoppel?

8. What is the effect of the giving and acceptance of a secured note in return for an unsecured note for a greater amount? Why?

9. Is a promise to pay a debt discharged by bankruptcy enforceable? Explain.

10. Under what theory will courts enforce a promise to pay a voluntary subscription?

CASE PROBLEMS

1. Dominic Costanzo and other agents selling insurance exclusively for Nationwide Mutual Insurance Company sued Nationwide for a court determination of their rights to the ownership of the names and other information of Nationwide's policyholders. Nationwide had instituted a new computer system which allowed its agents to remotely access files. Nationwide required the agents to sign an agreement stating policyholder information belonged to Nationwide and that the agents would not copy or disclose it. Nationwide provided servers, routers, and software for the system, and the agents were billed $100 a month. Was the agreement supported by consideration?

LO ❶

2. Brian Center Nursing Care/Austell, Inc. leased five nursing homes from William Foster. The leases expired and Brian kept possession of the nursing homes while it negotiated a new lease with Foster. No new lease was agreed upon, and Foster leased the homes to another company. Brian would not give up possession, so Foster sued. Brian alleged Foster had promised that the terms of the lease would continue as long as Brian paid the rent and continued to negotiate. Brian claimed it was injured by relying on this promise because it continued to occupy the premises, paid the rent, and negotiated for a new lease. Did promissory estoppel apply to these facts?

LO ❹

3. When Sandra Watson and Charles Givens were divorced, the court ordered a division of their property and awarded Sandra $64,721. This award was a judgment against Charles, who failed to pay it. Sandra asked the court to find him in contempt. Their lawyers had a conference with the judge, and they agreed that Charles would pay $2,400 immediately and $300 a month until the judgment was paid in full. Charles alleged this agreement was a binding contract since Sandra had accepted his offer of payments. Was it?

LO ❸

4. Carl Evans Boyd and Luther Claud Boyd died, leaving two sets of wills. The beneficiaries of the earlier wills contested the later wills, claiming the Boyds did not have the testamentary capacity to make them. While the will contest was pending, all the parties entered into written agreements resolving all the questions regarding the distribution of the estates of the Boyds. They then asked the judge to enter an order confirming the agreements and disposing of the will contest in accordance with the agreements. The judge claimed he could not enter a judgment declaring the later wills void without finding that the Boyds lacked capacity to make them. Was there sufficient consideration for the agreements?

LO ❷

5. The Orleans Parish School Board employed Mary Ellen Carter as a Secretary I. Later Carter performed the responsibilities of an Executive Secretary, then an Administrative Assistant and finally a Software Resources Coordinator without a change in title or increase in pay. She was continuously assured by her

LO ❹

supervisors that her position and pay grade would be reclassified and she would be paid retroactively for her greater duties. The request was submitted to the budget committee. For five years, she performed the duties and responsibilities of higher levels than her pay grade. When she was not compensated for the higher level duties, she sued the school board. Did Carter demonstrate a case of promissory estoppel?

LO ❶   6. After Prudential Bache Securities signed a confidentiality agreement, Robert Apfel allowed it to review a system he proposed to permit bonds to be traded and held solely by means of computerized book entries. Prudential then contracted with Apfel to pay him to use the system even if the technique became public knowledge. The first year Prudential was the only underwriter using such a system. After paying Apfel for several years, Prudential stopped. By this time investment banks were using computerized systems more and more. Apfel sued. Prudential said no contract existed because Apfel gave no consideration. Had he?

LO ❸   7. After forming a partnership with Lloyd Lyons, James Fafoutis and Lyons dissolved the partnership. Lyons told Fafoutis he was entitled to $16,000. Fafoutis sued for the $16,000 more than six years later. The law did not allow a suit to be brought that long after the obligation arose, but Fafoutis alleged that Lyons had made a promise to pay him the $16,000 if Fafoutis forbore suing for three more years. Fafoutis argued his right to sue arose at the end of the three years. Did the promise to pay if Fafoutis did not sue constitute a valid contract on which Fafoutis could maintain a suit against Lyons?

LO ❷   8. William Coester had a beer distributorship agreement with H.H.B. Co. The parties entered into a Termination of Business Agreement, which included a full release of H.H.B. from Coester. H.H.B. agreed to purchase all Coester's inventory at retail price and pay off a $44,164.10 mortgage on a warehouse rented by Coester from his mother for use in his business. H.H.B. performed all its obligations under the agreement. Coester sued H.H.B., arguing that the release was invalid because it was not supported by adequate consideration because the retail price of the beer was not much and he did not receive the benefit of the $44,164.10 paid on the mortgage. Was the release valid?

Defective Agreements

LEARNING OBJECTIVES

1 Describe the mistakes that invalidate a contract.

2 State what types of mistakes normally do not invalidate contracts.

3 Identify the situations in which fraud, duress, or undue influence is present.

PREVIEW CASE

Easy Parking, through its president, Vincent Smith, contracted with John Bachman to lease a parking lot at 1102 Dodge Street without meeting Bachman at the property. The legal description of the property was " . . . the south 54 feet of Lot 1 and all of Lot 8 . . . ," even though a building occupied most of Lot 8. Smith did not check the location of the described lot and had flyers announcing new management of the lot put on cars in a parking lot on Lot 7. Smith was told the next day that Bachman did not own the parking lot on Lot 7, but had the parking lot just north of the building on Lot 8. Easy Parking then claimed the lease was void because of mutual mistake and a lawsuit ensued. Who was mistaken about the parking lot? What could Smith have done to avoid making a mistake about the parking lot location? How much effort would it have taken?

Even when an offer and an acceptance have been made, situations exist in which the resulting contract is defective. Some mistakes make contracts defective. In addition, fraud, duress, or undue influence makes contracts voidable because they are defective. A victim of an act rendering a contract defective has a choice of remedies.

MISTAKES

Whether a mistake affects the validity of a contract normally depends on whether just one of the parties or both parties have made a mistake. A **unilateral mistake** occurs when only one party makes a mistake regarding the contract. When both parties to a contract make the same mistake, a **mutual mistake** occurs.

Unilateral Mistake
Mistake by one party to a contract

Mutual Mistake
Mistake by both parties to a contract

MISTAKES THAT INVALIDATE CONTRACTS

LO ①
Invalidating mistakes

For a mistake to invalidate a contract the mistake ordinarily must be a mutual one about a material fact. However, there are some very limited cases in which a unilateral mistake will invalidate a contract.

Mutual Mistakes

When a mutual mistake concerns a material fact, some courts say such a contract is void because no genuine assent by the parties existed. Other courts say the contract is voidable. Some courts are not precise about whether the contract is void or voidable. However they classify a mutual-mistake contract, courts do not find them enforceable.

COURT CASE

Facts: Mark Wallace filed a workers' compensation claim against Summerhill Nursing Home for injuries suffered in a work related accident. While the claim was pending, Summerhill's workers' compensation carrier voluntarily paid Wallace partial disability of $8,784. A settlement agreement was eventually reached by which Summerhill agreed to pay Wallace $7,938 representing 17.5 percent partial permanent disability. Neither the attorneys negotiating the agreement nor the judge who approved it knew of the voluntary payments when they agreed on $7,938. Wallace sued for payment under the settlement agreement.

Outcome: Since Wallace had already received an amount greater than the amount of the settlement agreement, there was a mutual mistake regarding Wallace's entitlement to further payments. The agreement was not enforceable.

— *Wallace v. Summerhill Nursing Home*, 883 A.2d 384 (N.J. Super. A.D.)

The area of mistake is one in which significant variations exist among the states and also where exceptions to the general rules have been established by courts in order to avoid harsh results. In some states, it is much easier than in other states to get the courts to agree with a party that a contract should not be enforced when there has been a mistake.

Unilateral Mistakes

As a general rule, a unilateral mistake made at the time of contracting has no effect on the validity of a contract. However, when there has been a unilateral mistake of a fact, the mistaken party sometimes receives relief. Courts will generally allow a unilateral mistake of fact to impair the enforceability of a contract if the nonmistaken party has caused the mistake or knew or should have known of the other party's mistake, and the mistaken party exercised ordinary care. Courts show extreme unwillingness to allow one party to hold the other to a contract if the first party knows that the other one has made a mistake.

COURT CASE

Facts: DSP Venture Group, Inc. contracted to buy real property owned by Minnie Allen from Richard Allen, Minnie's grandson and the beneficiary of her will. The contract provided for closing in 30 days, subject to probate of the will so that Richard had title. The contract also provided that if there were any defects in the title, DSP had seven days to notify Richard. He then had 30 days to cure the defects, and closing would be within 10 days of that. Within seven days of signing the contract, DSP notified Richard of a title defect, and it was cured. Shortly thereafter, Richard contracted to sell the property to a third party for $25,000 more. DSP sued to enforce its contract. Richard alleged he could avoid the contract with DSP because he was mistaken in thinking the contract required closing in seven days no matter what. He had not read the contract.

Outcome: Richard was mistaken about the closing requirement, but DSP was not. This was a unilateral mistake caused by Richard's failure to read the contract, so this unilateral mistake did not invalidate the contract with DSP.

—*DSP Venture Group, Inc. v. Allen,*
830 A.2d 850 (D.C.)

A small number of states allow a party who has made a unilateral mistake of fact to raise the mistake as a defense when sued on the contract. This is allowed when the party has not been inexcusably negligent in making the mistake, and the other, nonmistaken, party has not taken actions in reliance on the contract so that failure to enforce it would be unconscionable.

To entitle a party to relief, the mistake must be one of fact, not mere opinion. If *A* buys a painting from *B* for $10 and it is actually worth $5,000, even if *A* knows *B* is mistaken as to its value, there is a valid contract. *B*'s opinion as to its value is erroneous, but there is no mistake as to a fact.

Because there are few exceptions to the rule that a unilateral mistake does not affect a contract, it is clear that the law does not save us from the consequences of all mistakes. The exceptions cover a very small percentage of mistakes made in business transactions. Knowledge and diligence, not law, protect businesses against losses caused by mistakes.

Contract Terms Govern

It is important to remember that no matter what the law provides when a mistake occurs, the parties may specify a different outcome in their contract. And when the contract specifies what is to happen in the case of a mistake, the contract

COURT CASE

Facts: A. Cushman and Beresha Atkins purchased a residential lot from E. F. and Janice Kirkpatrick. Their contract stated: "This property is purchased 'as is.'" The Atkinses tried to have a house built on the lot, but when the contractor dug footings, ground water seeped into the holes making it impossible to use them. The Atkinses sued the Kirkpatricks claiming mutual mistake as to the suitability of the lot for use as a residential building lot.

Outcome: The court found mutual mistake of fact, but said the contract clearly allocated the burden of loss to the purchasers, and the contract terms governed.

—*Atkins v. Kirkpatrick,*
823 S.W.2d 547 (Tenn. App.)

provision will apply even if the law would be otherwise. The contract also could indicate which party assumes the risk that the facts are not as believed. The law as to mistake applies only in the absence of a governing provision in the contract, so long as that governing provision is not unconscionable.

A contract could specify that it will be void if a specified fact is not as believed. *A*, owning a stone, could believe it to be worth very little money. However, if *A* wants to sell the stone to *B* for $100, the contract could recite that it is void if the stone is actually a valuable diamond. This applies in spite of the general rule outlined previously that a unilateral mistake does not invalidate a contract.

The contract also could make the realization of certain expectations a condition of the contract. If those expectations were not realized, even if only one party was mistaken about them, the contract would not be binding.

Frequently, contracts are entered into orally and then reduced to writing. If, through an error in typing, the written form does not conform to the oral form, the written form does not bind the parties. The contract is what the parties agreed to orally.

MISTAKES THAT DO NOT INVALIDATE CONTRACTS

LO ❷
Noninvalidating mistakes

It is said that every rule has an exception, and the rules regarding the impact of mistake on contract validity also have exceptions. Most states recognize the exceptions to the rule on mutual mistake; however, significant variation occurs among the states regarding whether exceptions to the unilateral-mistake rule are recognized.

Unilateral Mistakes

The rule is that a unilateral mistake has no effect on a contract. Such a mistake will not, for example, invalidate a contract if a unilateral mistake occurs as to price or quantity. Even if the unilateral mistake as to price results from an error in typing or in misunderstanding an oral quotation of the price, the contract is valid.

PREVIEW CASE REVISITED

Facts: Easy Parking, through its president, Vincent Smith, contracted with John Bachman to lease a parking lot at 1102 Dodge Street without meeting Bachman at the property. The legal description of the property was " . . . the south 54 feet of Lot 1 and all of Lot 8 . . . ," even though a building occupied most of Lot 8. Smith did not check the location of the described lot and had flyers announcing new management of the lot put on cars in a parking lot on Lot 7. Smith was told the next day that Bachman did not own the parking lot on Lot 7, but had the parking lot just north of the building on Lot 8. Easy Parking then claimed the lease was void because of mutual mistake and a lawsuit ensued.

Outcome: It was apparent to the court that the only mistake was made by Easy Parking. As a unilateral mistake, it did not void the contract.

—*Bachman v. Easy Parking of America, Inc.*, 562 N.W.2d 369 (Neb.)

Mutual Mistakes

The rule given previously is that a mutual mistake will normally make a contract defective. However, this is not true in the case of mistake as to:

1. Value, quality, or price
2. The terms of the contract
3. The law
4. Expectations

Mistakes as to Value, Quality, or Price. A contract is not affected by the fact that the parties made mistaken assumptions as to the value, quality, or price of the subject matter of the contract. Normally, the parties assume the risk that their assumptions regarding these matters can be incorrect. If buyers do not trust their judgment, they have the right to demand a warranty from the seller as to the quality or value of the articles they are buying. Their ability to contract wisely is their chief protection against a bad bargain. If Snead sells Robinson a television set for $350, Robinson cannot rescind the contract merely because the set proved to be worth only $150. This is a mistake as to value and quality. Robinson should obtain as a part of the contract an express warranty as to the set's quality. Conversely, if the seller parts with a jewel for $50, thinking it is a cheap stone, a complaint cannot later be made if the jewel proves to be worth $2,500.

Mistakes as to the Terms of the Contract. A mistake as to the terms of the contract usually results from failure to understand a contract's meaning or significance or from failure to read a written contract. Such mistakes in both written and oral contracts do not affect their validity; otherwise, anyone could avoid a contract merely by claiming a mistake as to its terms.

Mistakes of Law. Ordinarily, when the parties make a mutual mistake of law, the contract is fully binding. The parties are expected to have knowledge of the law when making a contract.

COURT CASE

Facts: George Bruner was paid $32,000 in settlement of a lung disease claim against Illinois Central Gulf Railroad. He signed a release that forever discharged the railroad "from any and all claims, demands, damages, actions, . . . or suits of any kind" which he had or might later have from his employment with the railroad. The release specifically included damages arising from any hearing loss. Nine months later, Bruner sued Illinois Central for hearing loss from working for the railroad. He said he did not intend the release he signed to release the railroad from a hearing loss claim. He just wanted to release it from his lung disease claim.

Outcome: The court held that Bruner's mistake was one of law, not of fact. He could not avoid the contract because of a mistaken opinion as to its legal effect.

—*Bruner v. Illinois Cent. R. Co.,* **578 N.E.2d 1385 (Ill. App.)**

Mistakes as to Expectations. When the parties to a contract are mutually mistaken as to their expectations, the contract is binding.

FRAUD

LO **3**
Situations of fraud, duress, or undue influence

Fraud
Inducing another to contract as a result of an intentionally or recklessly false statement of a material fact

Fraud in the Inducement
Defrauded party intended to make a contract

Fraud in the Execution
Defrauded party did not intend to enter into a contract

Active Fraud
Party engages in action that causes the fraud

One who intends to and does induce another to enter into a contract as a result of an intentionally or recklessly false statement of a material fact commits **fraud**. The courts recognize two kinds of fraud relating to contracts. These are fraud in the inducement and fraud in the execution.

Fraud in the Inducement

When the party defrauded intended to make the contract, **fraud in the inducement** occurs. Fraud in the inducement involves a false statement regarding the terms or obligations of the transaction between the parties and not the nature of the document signed. The false statement might relate to the terms of the agreement, the quality of the goods sold, or the seller's intention to deliver goods. A contract so induced is voidable.

Fraud in the Execution

The defrauded party might also be tricked into signing a contract under circumstances in which the nature of the writing could not be understood. The law calls this **fraud in the execution** or fraud in the *factum*. In this case, the victim unknowingly signs a contract. A person who cannot read or who cannot read the language in which the contract is written could be a victim of this type of fraud. When fraud in the execution occurs, the contract is void.

Fraud also may be classified according to whether a party engages in some activity that causes the fraud or does nothing. A party who actually does something or takes steps to cause a fraud commits **active fraud**. Sometimes a party may be

COURT CASE

Facts: Thomas Webb severely injured his back and was awarded lifetime medical benefits from Industrial Indemnity Insurance Co. His chiropractor notified Industrial that Webb needed in-home attendant care to help with showering, cooking, cleaning, walking, and so on. For two years, Industrial paid the woman Webb was living with for providing such care and then had Webb examined by Dr. Daniel Ovadia. Webb told Ovadia he suffered severe pain and could not take care of himself. Ovadia could not find a basis for the pain and disability Webb reported, so Industrial stopped paying for the in-home care. Industrial hired a private detective to watch Webb. The detective videotaped Webb piloting a 26-foot boat to a pier, climbing over the side of the boat, and scaling a steep 12-foot vertical ladder onto the dock. With a winch, Webb lifted baskets of fish from the boat, then bent at the waist and dragged the baskets 70 feet. He lifted the baskets waist high to tables, sorted the fish, and dumped them into tanks. Another time, the detective videotaped him hosing down the boat, towing it home with his pickup, and uncoupling the boat trailer. The next day he arrived at a hearing regarding his need for in-home care using a walker. Several neighbors testified they had never seen him use a walker. Webb was charged with making a fraudulent statement to obtain benefits.

Outcome: Webb had knowingly made a false, material statement in order to obtain workers' compensation benefits. Because the action Webb sought to induce occurred, the payment of benefits, he had committed fraud.

—*People v. Webb*,
88 Cal. Rptr.2d 259 (Ct. App.)

guilty of fraud without engaging in any activity at all. **Passive fraud** results from the failure to disclose information when there is a duty to do so.

Passive Fraud
Failure to disclose information when there is duty to do so

Active Fraud

Active fraud may occur either by express misrepresentation or by concealment of material facts.

Express Misrepresentation. Fraud, as a result of express misrepresentation, consists of four elements, each of which must be present to constitute fraud:

1. **Misrepresentation**: a false statement of a material fact.
2. Must be made by one who knew it to be false or made it in reckless disregard of its truth or falsity.
3. Must be made with intent to induce the innocent party to act.
4. The innocent party justifiably relies on the false statement and makes a contract.

Misrepresentation
False statement of a material fact

   If these four elements are present, a party who has been harmed is entitled to relief in court.

Concealment of Material Facts. If one actively conceals material facts for the purpose of preventing the other contracting party from discovering them, such concealment results in fraud even without false statements.

COURT CASE

Facts: Michael and Kathy Gregg contracted to buy a house from Silvio and Judy DiPaulo. The DiPaulos supplied a disclosure report stating they knew of no termite infestation or structural defects caused by previous termite infestation. During a home inspection, they denied any past or current termite problems. Three months after buying the home, the Greggs found it was infested with termites and found patchwork on the drywall and other efforts to hide the termite infestation.

Outcome: The court said that sellers had a duty to disclose defects that could not be discovered on an inspection. Failure to do so in order to induce the Greggs to buy the house was fraud.

—CNA Ins. Co. v. DiPaulo,
794 N.E.2d 965 (Ill. App.)

   Merely refraining from disclosing pertinent facts unknown to the other party is not fraud in some states. In those states, there must be an active concealment. However, in other states, refraining from disclosing relevant facts does constitute fraud.

Passive Fraud

If one's relationship with another relies on trust and confidence, then silence may constitute passive fraud. Such a relationship exists between partners in a business firm, an agent and principal, a lawyer and client, a guardian and ward, a physician and patient, and in many other trust relationships. In the case of an attorney-client relationship, for example, the attorney has a duty to reveal anything material to the client's interests, and silence has the same effect as making a false statement

ETHICAL POINT
Refraining from disclosing pertinent facts may not be fraud, but is it ethical behavior?

that there was no material fact to be told to the client. The client could, in such a case, avoid the contract.

Silence, when one has no duty to speak, is not fraud. If Lawrence offers to sell Marconi, a diamond merchant, a gem for $500 that is actually worth $15,000, Marconi's superior knowledge of value does not, in itself, impose a duty to speak.

Innocent Misrepresentation

Innocent Misrepresentation
False statement made in belief it is true

When a contract is being negotiated, one party could easily make a statement believing it to be true when it is in fact false. Such a statement, made in the belief that it is true, is called an **innocent misrepresentation**. Courts generally hold that if it was reasonable for the misled party to have relied on the innocent misrepresentation, the contract is voidable.

Statements of Opinion

Statements of opinion, as contrasted with statements of fact, do not, as a rule, constitute fraud. The person hearing the statement realizes or ought to realize that the other party is merely stating a view and not a fact. But if the speaker is an expert or has special knowledge not available to the other party and should realize that the other party relies on this expert opinion, then a misstatement of opinion or value, intentionally made, would amount to fraud.

Such expressions as "This is the best buy in town," "The price of this stock will double in the next 12 months," "This business will net you $25,000 a year" are all statements of opinion, not statements of fact. However, the statement "This business has netted the owner $25,000" is not an opinion or a prophecy, but a historical fact.

DURESS

Duress
Obtaining consent by means of a threat

For a contract to be valid, all parties must enter into it of their own free wills. **Duress** is a means of destroying another's free will by one party obtaining consent to a contract as a result of a wrongful threat to do the other person or family members some harm. Duress causes a person to agree to a contract he or she would not otherwise agree to. Normally, to constitute duress, the threat must be made by the other party and must be illegal or wrongful. A contract made because of duress is voidable.

COURT CASE

Facts: Amy Maida was employed by RLS Legal Solutions, LLC. RLS told her to sign an employment agreement containing an arbitration provision. Maida initially refused to sign the agreement because she did not agree to the arbitration provision. RLS withheld her pay for work already performed because she did not sign the agreement. Maida was afraid she would not be able to pay her mortgage, car loan, and insurance without her compensation. She finally signed the agreement but told RLS she was signing under duress. Maida sued RLS.

Outcome: RLS was not entitled to withhold pay to which Maida was entitled on condition that she sign an agreement to arbitrate. This was duress.

—In re RLS Legal Solutions, LLC,
156 S.W.3d 160 (Tex. App.)

Duress is classified according to the nature of the threat as physical, emotional, or economic.

Physical Duress

When one party makes a threat of violence to another person who then agrees to a contract to avoid injury, physical duress occurs. Holding a gun to another's head or threatening to beat a person clearly risks injury to a human being and is unlawful.

Emotional Duress

Emotional duress occurs when one party's threats of something less than physical violence result in such psychological pressure that the victim does not act under free will. Courts will consider the age, health, and experience of the victim in determining whether emotional duress occurred.

COURT CASE

Facts: John Hollett was 30 years older than Erin and a successful businessman. Two days before their scheduled wedding, Erin learned he wanted her to sign a prenuptial agreement. John's lawyers had hired a recent law school graduate to counsel Erin, who had dropped out of high school. The lawyer arranged to meet Erin at John's lawyers' office the next day, one day before the scheduled wedding. All the arrangements for an elaborate 200-guest wedding had been made and paid for, and Erin's parents had flown in from Thailand. During the meeting with the lawyer and negotiations with John's lawyers, Erin sobbed for three or four hours and was frequently unable to speak with her lawyer. Her lawyer got some provisions of the agreement changed in her favor but she remembered almost nothing about the conference. The agreement was signed the morning of the wedding. Erin and John were married until John died 11 years later. Erin asked the court to invalidate the agreement on the basis of emotional duress.

Outcome: The court found that Erin's signing of the prenuptial agreement was involuntary as a result of duress. It was invalid.

—In re Estate of Hollett, **834 A.2d 348 (N.H.)**

Economic Duress

When one party wrongly threatens to injure another person financially in order to get agreement to a contract, economic duress occurs. However, duress does not exist when a person agrees to a contract merely because of difficult financial circumstances that are not the fault of the other party. Also, duress does not exist when a person drives a hard bargain and takes advantage of the other's urgent need to make the contract.

UNDUE INFLUENCE

One person may exercise such influence over the mind of another that the latter does not exercise free will. Although there is no force or threat of harm (which would be duress), a contract between two such people is nevertheless regarded as voidable. If a party in a confidential or fiduciary relationship to another induces

Undue Influence
*Person in special
relationship causing
another's action
contrary to free will*

the execution of a contract against the other person's free will, the agreement is voidable because of **undue influence**. If, under any relationship, one is in a position to take undue advantage of another, undue influence may render the contract voidable. Relationships that may result in undue influence are family relationships, a guardian and ward, an attorney and client, a physician and patient, and any other relationship in which confidence reposed on one side results in domination by the other. Undue influence may result also from sickness, infirmity, or serious distress.

In undue influence, there are no threats to harm the person or property of another as in duress. The relationship of the two parties must be such that one relies on the other so much that he or she yields because it is not possible to hold out against the superior position, intelligence, or personality of the other party. Whether undue influence exists is a question for the court (usually the jury) to determine. Not every influence is regarded as undue; for example, a nagging spouse is ordinarily not regarded as exercising undue influence. In addition, persuasion and argument are not per se undue influence. The key element is that the dominated party is helpless in the hands of the other.

C O U R T C A S E

Facts: When Agnes Seals was 80 years old, she was in declining health and had recently had to move out of her apartment because of a fire next door. She sold her building to David Aviles. Seals had met Aviles at the bank, and he had promised to take care of her for life if she transferred the building to him. He paid $10,000 down and executed a $40,000 mortgage. Aviles's lawyer brought the lawyer with whom he shared office space to represent Seals at the closing. She had never seen him, and he did not recommend that Seals get an appraisal before the sale or prepare any documents assuring Seals's right to live in the building. Aviles's mortgage payments were never deposited into Seals's account, but were redeposited into Aviles's account. He ran up $30,000 in charges on Seals's credit cards. After Seals's death, the beneficiaries under her will sued Aviles. A doctor testified that Seals suffered from severe Alzheimer's dementia at the time of the sale. Other witnesses testified that 16 months after the sale Seals was completely homebound and dependent on others, particularly Aviles.

Outcome: Aviles's free use of Seals's money and credit cards coupled with her weakened condition and reliance on him implied he intended to obtain Seals's building through improper means.

—Sepulveda v. Aviles,
762 N.Y.S.2d 358 (1st App. Div.)

REMEDIES FOR BREACH OF CONTRACT BECAUSE OF FRAUD, DURESS, OR UNDUE INFLUENCE

Because some mistakes, such as fraud in the inducement, duress, and undue influence, render contracts voidable, not void, you must know what to do if you are a victim of one of these acts. If you do not take steps to protect your rights, your right to avoid the contract's provisions may be lost. Furthermore, you may ratify the contract by some act or word indicating an intention to be bound. After you affirm or ratify the contract, you are as fully bound by it as if there had been no mistake, fraud, duress, or undue influence. But still you may sue for whatever damages you have sustained.

If the contract is voidable, you might elect to **rescind** it or set it aside. Recission seeks to put the parties in the position they were in before the contract was made. In order to rescind, you must first return or offer to return what you received under the contract. After this is done, you are in a position to take one of four actions, depending upon the circumstances:

1. You may bring a suit to recover any money, goods, or other things of value given up, plus damages.

2. If the contract is executory on your part, you may refuse to perform. If the other party sues, you can plead mistake, fraud, duress, or undue influence as a complete defense.

3. You may bring a suit to have the contract judicially declared void.

4. If a written contract does not accurately express the parties' agreement, you may sue for **reformation**, or correction, of the contract.

In no case can the wrongdoer set the contract aside and thus profit from the wrong. If the agreement is void, neither party may enforce it; no special act is required for setting the agreement aside.

Rescind
To set a contract aside

Reformation
Judicial correction of a contract

QUESTIONS

1. What normally determines whether a mistake affects the validity of a contract?

2. What is the difference between a mutual mistake and a unilateral mistake?

3. How do courts classify a mutual-mistake contract, and what is its effect?

4. What is the general rule regarding the effect of a unilateral mistake made at the time of contracting on the validity of a contract?

5. Is there any way to avoid the law's provisions about the effect of mistake on the validity of a contract?

6. What types of mutual mistakes do not make a contract defective?

7. Explain the difference between fraud in the inducement and fraud in the execution of a contract.

8. What is duress?

9. What is the key element in finding a contract was entered into by undue influence?

10. Why should the victims of acts that make contracts voidable, such as duress or undue influence, take steps to protect their rights?

CASE PROBLEMS

1. Orange County, N.Y., deeded two lots to Josclynne and Harriet Grier. At the time of the execution of the deeds, all the parties believed Orange County owned the property. When it later turned out that the county did not own the lots, the county asked the court to vacate the deeds. How should the court rule on the case?

LO ❶

2. New Horizon Deli, Inc. leased property from 1266 Apartment Corp. After the lease expired, New Horizon continued in possession and paid rent each month. Three years later, Russell Dizon, the president of New Horizon, fell in

LO ❸

front of the property allegedly on ice resulting from an accumulation of inadequately cleared snow. Later, 1266 offered a three-year lease with a $500 increase in monthly rent. A few months later, Dizon sued 1266 for his injuries from his fall. During further negotiations, 1266 said it would not sign a lease as long as Dizon maintained his personal injury action. When New Horizon failed to vacate, 1266 sued for eviction. New Horizon alleged 1266 subjected it to economic duress. Did it?

LO ②

3. Carolina Marble and Tile employed Jimmy Foster to do tile and brick work. He complained of headaches and ringing in his ears after working where jackhammers were in use. Foster and Carolina entered into a workers' compensation agreement, by which Carolina would pay Foster temporary total disability benefits for tinnitus (the perception of ringing, or other sounds when no external sound is present) and hearing loss. Two years later, Carolina tried to stop the benefits because state law provided there were to be no compensation awards for tinnitus. Could Carolina set aside its agreement to pay the benefits?

LO ③

4. When Craig Catrett bought a truck with 4,700 miles on it from Landmark Dodge, it had the manufacturer's new vehicle price sticker inside it. A salesman said it was a "demonstrator." Catrett also bought an extended warranty. The warranty contract said it only applied to new vehicles. However, the tag application, purchase contract, and finance agreement indicated the truck was "used." Later, when Catrett took the truck to Landmark for service, he found out the front end was misaligned and a nonfactory weld had broken, making the truck inoperable and unsafe. He discovered the truck was not a demonstrator but previously had been owned and involved in two wrecks. The prior owner had told Landmark it had been in a collision. Catrett sued for fraud. Landmark argued Catrett did not show justifiable reliance on its false statement. Did he?

LO ②

5. As an employee at the New Hampshire State Prison, Catherine Barney made contributions to the New Hampshire Retirement System (NHRS). Several years later her employment was terminated. Under financial pressure, Barney withdrew her retirement contributions after reading and signing an application which stated that she waived all her rights to any funds from NHRS. When she later believed she would have been eligible for disability benefits, Barney claimed her withdrawal constituted a unilateral mistake. Was it?

LO ①

6. Donna and Clifford Murray, divorced, agreed to a judgment that awarded Clifford their home and custody of the younger of their two sons. The older son attended college in another state. The older son returned home and the two boys fought, so the younger went to live with Donna. She asked the court to set aside the judgment because she had given up her right to the home thinking Clifford would totally support the younger son. Donna claimed the judgment was based on mutual mistake of fact that the younger son would live with Clifford. By law, the judgment was a contract that could only be rescinded on the same grounds as any other contract. Should the judgment be set aside?

LO ②

7. D.R. was a multihandicapped student needing special education. D.R.'s parents and the school board signed an agreement that required the board to pay the placement costs for D.R. at a residential school, the Benedictine School, at the current annual rate of $30,000. The agreement required the

board to pay, for the next year, 90 percent of any increase over the previous rate. The board was to pay no other costs for D.R.'s placement. Several months later the board received an estimate of $62,487 for the next year's cost at Benedictine for D.R. The $62,487 included the services of a one-to-one aide for D.R. during his waking hours. The board refused to pay for the aide. In the proceedings that followed, D.R.'s parents asserted that because the need for the aide was not anticipated when the agreement was signed, there was a mutual mistake of fact and the agreement was defective. Was it?

8. After being fired from her job with Hilton Hotels Corp., Marcia Evans filed charges with government agencies and a grievance with Hilton through her union. Evans claimed she was fired because she refused her supervisor's sexual advances. A hearing was held on the grievance. A lawyer represented Evans, and an agreement was signed. Evans was to get $2,750 and be allowed to quit. She was to withdraw all her filings. Evans then filed suit against Hilton under the Civil Rights Act. Evans could not sue if the agreement she signed was binding. She alleged undue influence by her attorney caused her to sign the agreement. Was the agreement binding?   LO ❸

9. A partnership defaulted on a note given to South Washington Associates for the purchase of a building, so Washington foreclosed. The foreclosure recovered $1.2 million less than was owed, so Washington sued the partners. Before trial, the parties agreed to arbitration. The agreement provided that, for the purpose of any appeal, the arbitrators' award should be reviewed like a trial court's decision. Washington did not like the arbitrators' award and appealed to the state court of appeals. The court stated that the law did not give it jurisdiction to review such an award. Washington argued that the agreement to arbitrate was then based on mutual mistake and was invalid. Was the agreement to arbitrate valid?   LO ❷

Illegal Agreements

LEARNING OBJECTIVES

1 Explain the consequences of a contract for an unlawful purpose or a purpose achieved illegally.

2 Explain what types of contracts are void for illegality.

3 Identify the types of contracts that are contrary to public policy.

PREVIEW CASE

Rainbow International Marriage Services, Inc. advertised as a convenient way for people to meet their marriage partner. Rainbow contracted with Ping Cui to introduce her to suitable prospective marriage partners until she was married. Ping Cui paid a registration fee of $700 and agreed to pay $7,500 following her marriage to a person introduced by Rainbow. She was listed and profiled on Rainbow's website. John Choma expressed an interest in her. Rainbow relayed information Choma gave it about himself to Ping Cui, and they corresponded. She and Choma were later married, but she did not pay the $7,500 fee. Rainbow sued her for breach of contract. Was the agreement to pay someone to find a spouse valid? Is it public policy to treat marriage like a business? Are there possibilities for deception and exploitation associated with matchmaking over the Internet?

LO 1
Unlawful contracts

A contract must be for a lawful purpose, and this purpose must be achieved in a lawful manner. Otherwise the contract is void. If this were not true, the court might force one party to a contract to commit a crime. If the act itself is legal, but the manner of committing the act that is called for in the contract is illegal, the contract is void.

If the parties are not equally guilty, courts may assist the less guilty party. However, courts will not allow a wrongdoer to enforce a contract against an innocent party.

If the contract is indivisible, that is, it cannot be performed except as an entity, then illegality in one part renders the whole contract invalid. If the contract is divisible, so that the legal parts can be performed separately, the legal parts of

COURT CASE

Facts: In a letter to Gerald Horn, Morris Frydman outlined an arrangement for Frydman to be employed as president of Horn's medical corporation. Horn was a physician and Frydman was not. After his employment with Horn was terminated, Frydman sued alleging the terms in the letter constituted a contract. State laws forbid a person who was not a physician from being president of a medical corporation.

Outcome: The court held that the alleged contract violated state law and was therefore illegal and unenforceable.

—Frydman v. Horn Eye Center, Ltd.,
676 N.E.2d 1355 (Ill. App.)

the contract are enforceable. For example, when one purchases several articles, each priced separately, and the sale of one article is illegal because the price was illegally set by price-fixing, the whole contract will not fall because of the one article.

COURT CASE

Facts: None of Birbrower, Montalbano, Condon & Frank's (a New York law firm) attorneys were licensed to practice law in California. Birbrower contracted to represent ESQ Business Services in a dispute with Tandem Computers. California law governed ESQ and Tandem's contract. Birbrower sent its attorneys to California to discuss the dispute with ESQ and strategies for settling it. They met with Tandem and demanded it pay ESQ $15 million, alleging, that damages from litigation would be greater than that. The dispute was settled, but ESQ did not pay Birbrower's fee. ESQ argued that by practicing law in California without a license Birbrower had violated the law; therefore, the contract between ESQ and Birbrower was unenforceable for illegality.

Outcome: The court would not enforce the part of the contract requiring payment for the unauthorized practice of law in California. However, if that portion of the fee could be severed from the rest of the agreement Birbrower could collect for law practice outside California.

—Birbrower v. Superior Court,
949 P.2d 1 (Cal.)

A contract that is void because of illegality does not necessarily involve the commission of a crime. It may consist merely of a private wrong—the commission of a tort—such as an agreement by two persons to slander a third. A contract contrary to public policy is also illegal.

LO ❷
Contracts void for illegality

CONTRACTS PROHIBITED BY STATUTE

There are many types of contracts declared illegal by statute. Some common ones include:

1. Gambling contracts
2. Sunday contracts
3. Usurious contracts
4. Contracts of an unlicensed operator
5. Contracts for the sale of prohibited articles
6. Contracts in unreasonable restraint of trade

Gambling Contracts

Gambling Contract
Agreement in which parties win or lose by chance

A **gambling contract** is a transaction wherein the parties stand to win or to lose based on pure chance. What one gains, the other must lose. Under the early common law, private wagering contracts were enforceable, but they are now generally prohibited in all states by statute. In recent years, certain classes of gambling contracts regulated by the state, such as state lotteries and pari-mutuel systems of betting on horse races and dog races, have been legalized in many states.

In general, the courts will leave the parties to a private gambling contract where it finds them and will not allow one party to recover damages from the other for the breach of a gambling debt. If two parties to a gambling contract give money to a stakeholder with instructions to pay the money to the winner, the parties can demand a return of their money. If the stakeholder pays the money to the winner, then the loser may sue either the winner or the stakeholder for reimbursement. No state will permit the stakeholder, who is considered merely a trustee of the funds, to keep the money. The court in this event requires the stakeholder to return each wagerer's deposit.

COURT CASE

Facts: After borrowing $50,000 from Carnival Leisure Industries, Ltd. with which to legally gamble at Carnival's casino in the Bahamas, Phil Froug lost it all. He did not repay the loan. Carnival sued him to collect in a Florida court. Froug argued recovery was barred by law. Florida law provided that "all promises . . . for the repayment of money lent . . . for the purpose of being . . . wagered, are void . . ."

Outcome: Although the gambling debt may have been legally incurred in the Bahamas, the court said Florida law prohibited recovering it there.

—Froug v. Carnival Leisure Industries, Ltd., 627 So. 2d 538 (Fla. Ct. App.)

Closely akin to gambling debts are loans made to enable one to gamble. If *A* loans *B* $100 and then wins it back in a poker game, is this a gambling debt? Most courts hold that it is not. If *A* and *B* bet $100 on a football game and *B* wins, and if *A* pays *B* by giving a promissory note for the $100, such a note may be declared void.

Trading on the stock exchange or the grain market represents legitimate business transactions. But the distinction between such trading and gambling contracts is sometimes very fine.

Alewine and Goodnoe could form a contract whereby Alewine agrees to sell Goodnoe 10,000 shares of stock one month from the date at $42 a share. If they do not actually intend to buy and sell the stock, but agree to settle for the difference between $42 a share and the closing price on the date fixed in the contract, this is a gambling contract.

However, Ripetto could agree to sell Bolde 10,000 bushels of wheat to be delivered six months later at $1.70 a bushel. Ripetto does not own any wheat, but intends to buy it for delivery in six months. They agree that at the end of the six-month period the seller does not actually have to deliver the wheat. If the price of wheat has gone up, the seller may pay the buyer the difference between the current price and the contract price. If the price of wheat has gone down, the buyer may pay the seller the difference. Such a contract is legal because the intention was to deliver. The primary difference between the Alewine case and the Ripetto case is the intention to deliver. In the case of trading, the seller (Ripetto) intended at the time of the contract to deliver the wheat and the buyer to accept it. In the gambling case, the seller (Alewine) did not intend to deliver.

Sunday Contracts

The laws pertaining to Sunday contracts resulted from statutes and judicial interpretation. They vary considerably from state to state. Most states have repealed their statutes that had made Sunday contracts illegal. The violators of Sunday acts are seldom prosecuted. For this reason, the types of transactions one observes being carried on Sunday do not necessarily indicate restrictions imposed by these laws.

Usurious Contracts

State laws that limit the rate of interest that may be charged for the use of money are called **usury** laws. Frequently there are two rates: the maximum contract rate and the legal rate. The **maximum contract rate** is the highest rate that may be charged; any rate above that is usurious. In some states this rate fluctuates depending on the prime rate. The **legal rate**, which is a rate somewhat lower than the contract rate, applies to all situations in which interest may be charged but in which the parties were silent as to the rate. If merchandise is sold on 30 days' credit, the seller may collect interest from the time the 30 days expire until the debt is paid. If no rate is agreed on in a situation of this kind, the legal rate may be charged.

The courts will treat transactions as usurious when there is in fact a lending of money at a usurious rate even though disguised. Such activities as requiring the borrower to execute a note for an amount in excess of the actual loan and requiring the borrower to antedate the note so as to charge interest for a longer period than that agreed on could make a loan usurious.

Usury
Charging higher rate of interest than law allows

Maximum Contract Rate
Highest legal rate of interest

Legal Rate
Interest rate applied when no rate specified

COURT CASE

Facts: In an attempt to evade the official exchange rate of Nigerian currency for dollars, Christopher Ekwunife contracted to loan Emmanuel Erike $3,000. Within a few weeks, Erike was to give Ekwunife's relative in Nigeria 66,000 Nira. At the official exchange rate, the relative should have received only 27,000 Nira. When a lawsuit was brought, Erike argued the loan was usurious because at the official exchange rate he was paying 200 percent interest.

Outcome: Such a huge profit in interest was found by the court to be usurious.

—*Ekwunife v. Erike,*
658 N.Y.S.2d 166 (N.Y.)

The penalty for usury varies from state to state. In most states, the only penalty might prohibit the lender from collecting the excess interest. In other states, the entire contract is void, and in still others, the borrower need not pay any interest but must repay the principal. If the borrower has already paid the usurious interest, the court will require the lender to refund to the borrower any money collected in excess of the contract rate.

In all states, special statutes govern consumer loans by pawnbrokers, small loan companies, and finance companies. In some states, these firms may charge much higher rates of interest.

Contracts of an Unlicensed Operator

Statutes make it illegal to operate certain types of businesses or professions without a license. Most of these statutes are made to protect the public from incompetent operators. The most common types of professional persons who must be licensed to operate include doctors, lawyers, certified and licensed public accountants, dentists, and insurance and real estate salespeople. A person who performs these services without license not only cannot sue to collect for the services but also may be guilty of a crime.

COURT CASE

Facts: Meteor Motors, Inc. owned Palm Beach Acura, an auto dealership in Florida. It agreed to pay Thompson Halbach & Associates a commission of 5 percent of the sales price if Thompson found a buyer for the stock of the dealership. Neither Halbach nor any of its principals was a licensed broker in Florida. Halbach gave Craig Zinn Automotive Group, a Florida-based automotive group, information about Meteor so Zinn could evaluate the possibility of purchasing Meteor. Halbach did not participate in negotiations between Meteor and Zinn. Zinn purchased Meteor's stock for $5,000,000, and Halbach was not paid a commission. Halbach sued Meteor for breach of contract.

Outcome: Since Halbach was not registered in Florida, the court held the contract was invalid.

—Meteor Motors, Inc. v. Thompson Halbach & Associates, **914 So.2d 479 (Fla. App.)**

A licensing law may be designed solely as a revenue measure by requiring payment of a fee for a license. Contracts made by an unlicensed person operating in one of the fields or businesses covered by such a law are normally held valid. However, the unlicensed operator may still be subject to fine or imprisonment for violating the law.

Contracts for the Sale of Prohibited Articles

If a druggist sells morphine or a similar drug to one who does not have a prescription, a suit to collect the price would not be successful. One who sells cigarettes or alcoholic beverages to a minor when such a sale is prohibited cannot recover on the contract. In such cases, the court will not interfere to protect either party.

Contracts in Unreasonable Restraint of Trade

Government policy encourages competition. Any contract, therefore, intended to unreasonably restrain trade is null and void. The dividing line between reasonable and unreasonable restraint of trade is often dim, but certain acts have become well established by judicial decision as being an unreasonable restraint of trade. The most common acts in this class include:

1. Contracts not to compete
2. Contracts to restrain trade
3. Contracts to fix the resale price
4. Unfair competitive practices

Contracts Not to Compete. Normally, a contract not to compete is illegal; however, it can be valid when buying a business or making an employment contract.

When one buys a going business, not only are the physical assets acquired but also the goodwill, which is often the most valuable asset of the firm. In the absence of a contract prohibiting the seller from attempting to retake the asset *goodwill,* the seller may engage in the same business again and seek to retain former customers. It is customary and highly desirable when purchasing a business to include in the contract a provision prohibiting the seller from entering the same business again in the trade territory for a specified length of time. Such a contract not to compete is legal if the restriction is reasonable as to both time and place.

The restriction as to territory should not go beyond the trade area of the business. Because the restriction is sustained to protect the buyer of the business from competition of the seller, it follows that the restriction should not reach out into areas where the buyer's reputation has not reached, nor should the seller be subjected to the restriction longer than is reasonably necessary for the buyer to become established in the new business. When the restriction goes further or longer than necessary to protect the buyer of the business, it is unlawful not only because it burdens the seller but also because it deprives the business community and society in general of the benefit of the activities of the seller.

Closely allied to this type of contract is one whereby an employee, as a part of the employment contract, agrees not to work for a competing firm for a certain period of time after terminating employment. These contracts must be reasonable as to time and place.

COURT CASE

Facts: Bruce Graham, a colorectal surgeon, recruited William Cirocco to join his practice in the Kansas City area. At the time, there were six colorectal surgeons in the metropolitan Kansas City area: four in Missouri, and Graham and Cirocco on the Kansas side. They signed an employment contract which provided that for two years after leaving Graham's employment, Cirocco would not open an office within 25 miles of, or provide services at, hospitals listed in the agreement. The restriction included the entire Kansas City metropolitan area. Six years later, Cirocco resigned and opened an office next door to Graham, within the restricted area. Graham sued alleging Cirocco breached the noncompete agreement.

Outcome: The court found that the two-year restriction was reasonable, but that the area covered was unreasonable.

—*Bruce D. Graham, M.D., P.A. v. Cirocco,*
69 P.3d 194 (Kan. App.)

Contracts to Restrain Trade. Contracts to fix prices, divide up the trade territory, limit production so as to reduce the supply, or otherwise limit competition are void. The Sherman Antitrust Act and the Clayton Act specifically declare illegal such contracts that affect interstate commerce and are therefore subject to regulation by the federal government. Most of the states have similar laws applicable to intrastate commerce.

Contracts to Fix the Resale Price. An agreement between a seller and a buyer that the buyer shall not resell below a stated price is generally illegal as a price-fixing agreement. The original seller (manufacturer) can, of course, control the price by selling directly to the public through outlet stores.

Unfair Competitive Practices. The Robinson-Patman Act attempted to eliminate certain unfair competitive practices in interstate commerce. Under this act it is unlawful to discriminate in price between competing buyers if the goods are of like grade, quantity, and quality. Most states have passed similar laws for intrastate commerce. Some state statutes go further and prohibit the resale of goods at a loss or below cost for the purpose of harming competition.

Administrative Agency Orders

As was mentioned in Chapter 4, many government administrative agencies have the authority to issue rules and regulations that have the force of law. A contract that violates such a rule is illegal.

CONTRACTS CONTRARY TO PUBLIC POLICY

LO **3**
Contracts against
public policy

Contracts contrary to public policy are unenforceable. The courts must determine from the nature of the contract whether or not it is contrary to public policy.

One court, in attempting to classify contracts contrary to public policy, defined them thus: "Whatever tends to injustice, restraint of liberty, restraint of a legal right, whatever tends to the obstruction of justice, a violation of a statute, or the obstruction or perversion of the administration of the law as to executive, legislative, or other official action, whenever embodied in and made the subject of a contract, the contract is against public policy and therefore void and not susceptible to enforcement." (*Brooks v. Cooper,* 50 N.J. Eq. 761, 26 A. 978.)

The most common types of contracts contrary to public policy include:

1. Contracts limiting the freedom of marriage
2. Contracts obstructing the administration of justice
3. Contracts injuring the public service

Contracts Limiting the Freedom of Marriage

It is contrary to public policy to enter into any contract the effect of which is to limit freedom of marriage. Such contracts are void. The following provisions in contracts have been held to render the contract a nullity: (1) an agreement whereby one party promises never to marry; (2) an agreement to refrain from marrying for a definite period of time (an agreement not to marry during minority, however, is valid); (3) an agreement not to marry certain named individuals.

Similarly, marriage brokerage contracts are unenforceable as against public policy. A marriage brokerage contract is one in which a person agrees to pay another for negotiating, procuring, or bringing about a marriage.

Also, in order to preserve and protect marriages, it is held that an agreement to seek a divorce for a consideration is void as against public policy. However, property settlement agreements made in contemplation of divorces are valid.

Contracts Obstructing the Administration of Justice

Any contract that may obstruct our legal processes is null and void. It is not necessary that justice actually be obstructed. If the contract has the tendency to do so, the courts will not enforce it.

PREVIEW CASE REVISITED

Facts: Rainbow International Marriage Services, Inc. advertised as a convenient way for people to meet their marriage partner. Rainbow contracted with Ping Cui to introduce her to suitable prospective marriage partners until she was married. Ping Cui paid a registration fee of $700 and agreed to pay $7,500 following her marriage to a person introduced by Rainbow. She was listed and profiled on Rainbow's website. John Choma expressed an interest in her. Rainbow relayed information Choma gave it about himself to Ping Cui, and they corresponded. She and Choma were later married, but she did not pay the $7,500 fee. Rainbow sued her for breach of contract.

Outcome: The court found that the contract was clearly a marriage brokerage contract and void as against public policy.

—Ureneck v. Cui, **798 N.E.2d 305 (Mass. App. Ct.)**

The following provisions have been held to render contracts void: (1) an agreement to pay a witness a larger fee than that allowed by law, provided the promisor wins the case; (2) an agreement by a candidate for sheriff that a certain individual will be appointed deputy sheriff in return for aid in bringing about the promisor's election; (3) an agreement to pay a prospective witness a sum of money to leave the state until the trial is over; (4) an agreement not to prosecute a thief if the stolen goods will be returned.

COURT CASE

Facts: While employed as the credit manager of Smithfield Ford, Alfred Coats embezzled $54,000. Alfred and his mother and stepfather, Ann and William Adams, contracted to pay Smithfield $25,000 over time, and Smithfield agreed to "abstain from pursuing any legal remedies . . . including criminal prosecution." After making payments for several years, Ann and William sued to invalidate the contract.

Outcome: The court found that a contract made in consideration of refraining to prosecute a crime was void as against public policy.

—Adams v. Jones, **441 S.E.2d 699 (N.C. App.)**

Contracts Injuring the Public Service

Any contract that may, from its very nature, injure public service is void. A person may contract as an attorney to appear before any public authority to obtain or oppose the passage of any bill. But a contract to use improper influence such as bribery to obtain the desired results is void.

Contracts to use one's influence in obtaining a public contract that by statute must be let to the lowest responsible bidder, to obtain pardons and paroles, or to pay a public official more or less than the statutory salary are also void.

QUESTIONS

1. With regard to illegality of a contract, what is the difference between a divisible and an indivisible contract?

2. Does a contract that is void for illegality necessarily involve the commission of a crime?

3. What is the rule regarding the enforceability of gambling contracts?

4. Is the penalty for usury the same in all states?

5. What is the difference between the maximum contract rate of interest and the legal rate of interest?

6. Are all contracts entered into by an unlicensed person unenforceable?

7. Why are noncompete contracts that have restrictions that go further or longer than necessary to protect the buyer of the business unlawful?

8. May manufacturers control the prices at which their products are sold to the public?

9. What is the effect of a contract to divide up trade territory that affects interstate commerce?

10. What are the consequences of a contract to seek a divorce for a consideration?

CASE PROBLEMS

LO ❷ 1. The Thomas Lakes Owners Association sued some owners of cabins and lots at Thomas Lakes for unpaid assessments and dues with interest. The Association's bylaws prescribed that a late charge would accrue on delinquent dues at the rate of 1.5 percent per 30 days. That amounted to 18 percent per year. The owners alleged that the interest rate was usurious, as state law set the maximum amount of interest at 16 percent. How would you decide the case?

LO ❸ 2. Robert Lawlor was an officer of K-Brew, Inc. K-Brew owed money to Allen Foods, Inc. Lawlor wrote out four personal checks to Allen, but they bounced. Timothy Mahoney, credit manager for Allen, dealt with the police in seeking to arrest Lawlor for passing the bad checks. Lawlor signed a note to pay K-Brew's debt over time, so in return for the note, Allen dismissed the criminal charges with the police. When Lawlor did not continue to make payments on the note Allen sued him for payment. Is this agreement to pay enforceable?

LO ❷ 3. The town of Lunenburg asked for bids on a multimillion dollar construction project to be financed by the state. State law required the town to publish a notice for bids in a newspaper of general circulation in the locality. Lunenburg failed to advertise for bids in a local newspaper. Baltazar Contractors, Inc. was the low bidder, and Lunenburg signed a contract with it. The state Department of Environmental Protection questioned the bid award and told Lunenburg its state financing was in jeopardy. Lunenburg told Baltazar it was ending the contract. It re-advertised for bids, this time publishing a notice in the local newspaper. Baltazar bid again but MDR Construction Co., Inc., who had not bid the first time, was the low bidder and got the contract. Baltazar sued Lunenburg for damages. Should Baltazar recover?

LO ❶ 4. Martin McMahon, a practicing attorney, signed a lease of office space from Anderson, Hibey & Blair. The lease required the office to be occupied by McMahon or his clients, Louis Zadi and Ibrahim Metzer. Only the clients used the space and paid rent. Rent was paid for two months although the space was occupied for five months. When AH&B could not recover the unpaid rent from the clients, it sued McMahon. McMahon argued the lease was illegal because it was executed to evade local zoning laws that limited the tenants to professionals such as he. Zadi and Metzer could not have leased the property themselves, so AH&B's administrator had come up with the plan for McMahon to sign the lease. Did McMahon allege adequate facts to show the contract was illegal and unenforceable?

5. After being injured in an auto accident, Robert Harris saw Dr. Greg Swafford for treatment of his injuries. Harris and Swafford agreed that Swafford would act as a medical/legal consultant and assist in preparing a personal injury lawsuit by Harris in return for 151.2 percent of any recovery. Swafford testified at a deposition and supplied medical consultation and treatment. Harris's personal injury claim was settled for $625,000 and Swafford sued for 151.2 percent. The American Medical Association's (AMA) code of ethics condemns contingency fees for medical services or as payment for a medical witness. The state board that denies, suspends, or revokes doctors' licenses for, among other things, unethical conduct adopted the AMA code as a regulatory policy. Was the agreement a violation of public policy?   LO ❸

6. Local 369 Building Fund, Inc. operated a function hall business. By written lease, it leased the hall to Hastings Associates. The primary source of revenue for the hall was the sale of alcoholic beverages. Hastings applied for a liquor license, but it was denied, so Hastings used Local 369's license. Several years later, Local 369 terminated the lease and Hastings sued for breach of contract. The law required everyone who sold alcoholic beverages to have a license and did not permit licensees to transfer their licenses to others. May Hastings recover for breach of contract?   LO ❷

7. When preparing a bid on managing and selling homes for the government for the Re/Max real estate agency he worked for, Tom Gibbons asked George Vessell to estimate how much he would charge for upkeep and lawn maintenance on the properties. When Gibbons bid the yard work at much less, Vessell refused to do the lawns. Gibbons told him to make up the difference by bid-rigging and stealing appliances. Vessell decided to turn Gibbons in to the FBI and cooperated with a sting operation. After the sting was conducted, Re/Max still had the government contract, but did not ask Vessell to do the lawn work. Vessell sued alleging he had a contract with Re/Max for the lawn work. Did he?   LO ❶

8. Gina Marie Hoffman and Brian Boyd, while both married to others, signed an agreement by which Boyd agreed to marry Hoffman within 12 months or support her indefinitely. Hoffman agreed to give up her job and leave a secure home and marriage. When Boyd stopped supporting her and did not marry her, Hoffman sued. Was this agreement contrary to public policy and therefore void?   LO ❸

Written Contracts

LEARNING OBJECTIVES

❶ Identify which contracts the Statute of Frauds requires to be in writing.

❷ Distinguish adequate from inadequate writings when a written contract is required.

❸ Explain the parol evidence rule.

PREVIEW CASE

→ Milton Blankenship bought land from Ella Mae Henry with a ten year option to purchase an additional 28 acres. At the same time, Ella Mae and her husband, Clifford, entered into an oral agreement with Blankenship that he would operate a car skeleton processing plant on the land within six to fifteen months. Blankenship never operated the car skeleton processing plant. Several years later, Blankenship exercised his option to purchase the additional 28 acres. Ella Mae had died but her heirs, Clifford and Richard Henry, refused to sell. Blankenship sued to force the sale. Clifford alleged Blankenship breached their oral agreement. Blankenship argued that the oral agreement was unenforceable because it was for more than a year. Was this contract enforceable? How long would it take to fully perform this contract?

LO ❶
Requirement of writing

Contracts may be in written or oral form. All contracts of importance ought to be in writing, but only a few must be written in order to be enforceable. An oral contract is just as effective and enforceable as a written contract unless it is one of the few types specifically required by statute to be in writing.

REASONS FOR WRITTEN CONTRACTS

A written contract has advantages over an oral contract, provided it includes all the terms and provisions of the agreement. In the first place, the existence of a contract cannot be denied if it is in writing. If there were no witnesses when an oral contract was formed, one of the parties might successfully deny that any contract was made. In the second place, one of the parties might die or become incompetent and therefore be unable to testify as to the terms of an oral contract. The administrator or executor of an estate in case of death, or the committee or guardian in case of incapacity, is tremendously handicapped in enforcing an oral agreement that the deceased or incompetent person made. Even when there are witnesses present at the time an oral contract is formed, their testimony may vary considerably as to the actual terms of the contract. Written evidence, composed in clear and unambiguous language, is more reliable than oral evidence.

For these reasons most businesspeople prefer to have contracts pertaining to matters of importance put in writing, even when the law does not require them to do so.

STATUTE OF FRAUDS

In the year 1677, the English Parliament enacted a law known as the **Statute of Frauds**. This statute listed certain classes of contracts that could not be enforced unless their terms were evidenced by a written document. Most of our states have adopted this list with but slight variations.

The Statute of Frauds applies only to executory contracts. If two parties enter into an oral contract that falls under the Statute of Frauds and both parties have fully performed according to its terms, neither party can seek to set aside the transaction on the ground that there was no writing.

The Statute of Frauds provides that the following types of agreements must be in writing:

1. An agreement to sell land or any interest in or concerning land
2. An agreement the terms of which cannot be performed within one year from the time it is made
3. An agreement to become responsible for the debts or default of another
4. An agreement of an executor or administrator to pay the debts of the estate from the executor's or the administrator's personal funds
5. An agreement containing a promise in consideration of marriage
6. An agreement to sell goods for $500 or more (discussed in detail in Chapter 17)

An Agreement to Sell Land or Any Interest in or Concerning Land

An agreement to sell any interest in land comes under the Statute of Frauds. The required writing differs from the deed, which will be executed later and by which the seller makes the actual transfer of title to the buyer.

One may wish to sell not the land itself, but only an interest in the land. This type of contract also must be in writing. These sales usually involve rights of way, joint use of driveways, mineral rights, or timber. A lease of real property for more than one year must be in writing in order to be binding.

Frequently, oral contracts relative to land are performed before any question of their validity is raised. For example, one leases a building by oral contract for two years. The building is occupied for that period, and then the rent is not paid on the ground that the oral contract is invalid. The law will compel payment of the rent orally agreed to for the time that the premises were occupied. If one has paid money or performed a service under an oral contract, the money or the value of the service may be recovered even though the executory part of the contract cannot be enforced. If one party has made part performance of an oral contract and would be hurt if the contract is not enforced, courts will allow enforcement of it. These outcomes are based on equitable principles of preventing the unjust enrichment of one party.

Statute of Frauds
Law requiring certain contracts to be in writing

COURT CASE

Facts: Bill and Jeff Kuntz submitted a written offer to purchase the farming assets of their uncle, George Kuntz. George orally accepted. On the basis of this oral acceptance, Bill and Jeff took out a loan and rented more pasture land for the additional cattle. They operated George's farm with no input from him and paid all the expenses. Bill and Jeff sued to complete the sale.

Outcome: Since the nephews partially performed the oral contract to their detriment, the contract was binding.

—Kuntz v. Kuntz,
595 N.W.2d 292 (N.D.)

An Agreement the Terms of Which Cannot Be Performed within One Year from the Time It Is Made

The terms of a contract that cannot be performed in one year might easily be forgotten before the contract is completed. To minimize the need to resort to the courts because the parties do not remember the terms of a contract, the law requires all contracts that cannot be performed within one year to be in writing.

This provision of the Statute of Frauds means that if the terms of the contract are such that, by their nature, they cannot be performed within one year from the date of the contract, then the contract must be in writing. The contract can be so worded that it may not be completed for 50 years, yet if it is physically possible to complete it within one year, it need not be in writing. If John agrees in consideration of $50,000 to care for Chen for "as long as he (Chen) lives," this contract need not be in writing because there is no certainty Chen will live one year. But an agreement to manage a motel for five years will, by its terms, require more than one year for performance; therefore, it comes under the Statute of Frauds.

PREVIEW CASE REVISITED

Facts: Milton Blankenship bought land from Ella Mae Henry with a ten year option to purchase an additional 28 acres. At the same time, Ella Mae and her husband, Clifford, entered into an oral agreement with Blankenship that he would operate a car skeleton processing plant on the land within six to fifteen months. Blankenship never operated the car skeleton processing plant. Several years later, Blankenship exercised his option to purchase the additional 28 acres. Ella Mae had died but her heirs, Clifford and Richard Henry, refused to sell. Blankenship sued to force the sale. Clifford alleged Blankenship breached their oral agreement. Blankenship argued that the oral agreement was unenforceable because it was for more than a year.
Outcome: Blankenship's agreement to operate a car skeleton processing plant in six to fifteen months was clearly capable of being performed within a year. The Statute of Frauds did not make the oral agreement unenforceable.

—Henry v. Blankenship, **621 S.E.2d 601 (Ga. App.)**

An Agreement to Become Responsible for the Debts or Default of Another

Debt
Obligation to pay money

The term **debt** refers to an obligation to pay money; **default** refers to a breach of contractual obligations other than money, such as failure to build a house. An agreement to be responsible for the debts or default of another occurs when the promisor undertakes to make good the loss that the promisee would sustain if another person does not pay the promisee a debt owed or fails to perform a duty imposed by contract or by law. If Allen promises Charlotte to pay Betty's debt to Charlotte if Betty fails to pay, the Statute of Frauds requires Allen's promise to be in writing. Allen's promise is to be responsible for the debt of another. This provision of the Statute of Frauds was designed especially for those situations where one promises to answer for the debt of another person purely as an accommodation to that person.

An exception to the Statute of Frauds occurs if in fact a promise is an original promise by the promisor rather than a promise to pay the debt of another. For example, if Andy buys goods on credit from Betsy and tells Betsy to deliver the goods to Cindy, Andy is not promising to pay the debt of another; the promise is to pay Andy's own debt. Andy's promise does not have to be in writing.

The Statute of Frauds requirement of a writing does not apply if the main purpose of the promise is to gain some advantage for the promisor. Sometimes one person promises to answer for the debt or default of another because it is in the promisor's personal financial interest to do so. In such a case the promise does not need to be in writing.

Default
Breach of contractual obligation other than money

COURT CASE

Facts: When the commonwealth of Pennsylvania contracted with A&L, Inc. to resurface a road, A&L got a bond from Safeco Insurance and retained Boss Construction, Inc. as a subcontractor. Boss bought material from Trumbull Corp. but failed to pay the bill. At a meeting of A&L and Trumbull, Louis Ruscitto, president of A&L, promised A&L would pay the bill at the end of the fiscal year if Trumbull would not pursue a claim on the bond. Trumbull did not proceed on the bond claim until after the end of A&L's fiscal year when the bill was still unpaid. Ruscitto and his wife, who was a co-owner of Boss, had personally guaranteed the bond. A&L alleged its oral promise to pay another's debt was unenforceable.

Outcome: The fact that Ruscitto and his wife had guaranteed the bond and she was a co-owner of Boss meant that Ruscitto's oral promise was for his financial advantage. The oral promise was enforceable.

—*Trumbull Corp. v. Boss Constr., Inc.,* **801 A.2d 1289 (Pa. Commw. Ct.)**

The Statute of Frauds does not apply when the promisor promises the debtor that the promisor will pay the debt owed to the third person.

COURT CASE

Facts: Sharon Steinberger sued her husband, Chaim, for divorce. Chaim sued his father-in-law, Marton Grossman, seeking a declaration that Grossman was primarily liable for payment of the mortgage on the Steinberger's house. The oral promise allegedly made by Grossman to be primarily liable on the mortgage was made to Chaim. Grossman alleged such a promise was not enforceable under the Statute of Frauds.

Outcome: Because the promise was made to Grossman and not to the lender bank, it did not fall under the prohibitions of the Statute of Frauds.

—*Steinberger v Steinberger,* **676 N.Y.S.2d 210 (N.Y. A.D.)**

An Agreement of an Executor or Administrator to Personally Pay the Debts of the Estate

When a person dies, an executor or administrator takes over all the deceased's assets. From these assets the executor or administrator pays all the debts of the deceased before distributing the remainder according to the terms of the decedent's will or, in the absence of a will, to the decedent's heirs. The executor or the administrator is not obligated to pay the debts of the deceased out of the executor's personal funds. For this reason, a promise to pay the debts of the estate from personal funds is in reality a contract to become responsible for the debts of another and must be in writing to be enforceable.

An Agreement Containing a Promise in Consideration of Marriage

An agreement by which one person promises to pay a sum of money or to transfer property to another in consideration of marriage or a promise to marry must be in writing. This requirement of the Statute of Frauds does not apply to mutual promises to marry.

COURT CASE

Facts: Before Miles Dutton and Patricia Black were married, they signed an agreement in which Black relinquished any rights to Dutton's estate. Dutton agreed to purchase a house that would go to Black upon his death. After Dutton died, his daughter from a previous marriage sued to enforce the agreement.

Outcome: The court found that the agreement was one made in consideration of marriage and was required by the Statute of Frauds to be in writing. Because it was in writing, it was enforceable.

—*Lemaster v. Dutton*, 694 So.2d 1360 (Ala. Civ. App.)

NOTE OR MEMORANDUM

LO 2
Adequacy of written contract

The Statute of Frauds requires either that the agreement be in writing and signed by both parties, or that there be a note or memorandum in writing signed by the party against whom the claim for breach of promise is made. With the enactment of the federal Electronic Signatures in Global and National Commerce Act, that signature no longer has to be on paper. This law makes electronic signatures legally enforceable.

With the exception of the case of the sale of goods (Chapter 17), the contract and the note or memorandum required by the Statute of Frauds must set forth all the material terms of the transaction. For example, in the case of the sale of an interest in real estate, the memorandum must contain the names of the parties, the subject matter of the contract, the basic terms of the contract, including the price and the manner of delivery, and it must be signed by the one to be charged.

The law states that the memorandum must contain all the essential terms of the contract; yet the memorandum differs materially from a written contract.

Probably the chief difference is that one may introduce oral testimony to explain or complete the memorandum. A court held that the following receipt was an adequate memorandum: "Received of Sholowitz $25 to bind the bargain for the sale of Moorigan's brick store and land at 46 Blackstone Street to Sholowitz. Balance due $1,975."

C O U R T ★ C A S E

Facts: Peoples Bank offered land for sale. William Whatley, a real estate broker, showed the property to James Barnes, who signed a check for $5,500 as a deposit. On the check, Whatley filled in the name of the payee and wrote a notation that it was "earnest money" on the land. He sent a real estate sales agreement to the bank, which the vice president signed. The agreement provided for a real estate commission to Whatley "when the sale is consummated." It also stated it was "an offer by the [person] who first signs . . . and is open for acceptance by the other." Barnes never signed the agreement. The bank sold the land to someone else and Whatley sued Barnes to recover the commission he would have received if Barnes had bought the land.

Outcome: The court said there must be a writing signed by the party to be charged in order to have a binding contract for the sale of land. Barnes did not sign the agreement, so he was not liable.

—Barnes v. Whatley,
470 S.E.2d 498 (Ga. App.)

The memorandum need not be made at the time the contract is executed. It only needs to be in existence at the time suit is brought. The one who signs the memorandum need not sign with the intention of being bound. If Jones writes to Smith, "Since my agreement to pay you the $500 Jacobson owes you was oral, I am not bound by it," there is a sufficient memorandum that removes the objection based on the Statute of Frauds.

OTHER WRITTEN CONTRACTS

The five classes of contracts listed by the Statute of Frauds are not the only contracts required by law to be in writing in order to be enforceable. Every state has a few additional types of contracts that must be in writing to be enforceable. The more common ones are contracts for the sale of securities, agreements to pay a commission to real estate brokers, and a new promise to extend the statute of limitations.

PAROL EVIDENCE RULE

Spoken words, or **parol evidence**, will not be permitted to add to, modify, or contradict the terms of a written contract that appears to be complete unless evidence of fraud, accident, or mistake exists so that the writing is in fact not a contract or is incomplete. This is known as the **parol evidence rule**.

If a written contract appears to be complete, the parol evidence rule will not permit modification by oral testimony or other writing made before or at the time of executing the agreement. However, an exception is made when the contract refers to other writings and indicates they are considered as incorporated into the contract.

LO ③
Parol evidence rule

Parol Evidence
Oral testimony

Parol Evidence Rule
Complete, written contract may not be modified by oral testimony unless evidence of fraud, accident, or mistake

COURT CASE

Facts: Thomas leased a farm from Clark. The lease contained this uncompleted provision: "Lessor does hereby rent and lease to the Lessee the following described property . . . for a term commencing on the __ day of __, 19 __, and ending on the __ day of __, 19 __." Clark later sued to regain possession. Thomas wanted to prove an oral agreement that the lease was to run as long as a note, but the maturity date of the note had not been known when the lease was signed.

Outcome: The court found that the written contract (the lease) was clearly incomplete, so parol evidence was permitted to establish the term of the lease.

—*Thomas v. Clark*, 344 S.E.2d 754 (Ga. App.)

The parol evidence rule assumes that a written contract represents the complete agreement. If, however, the contract is not complete, the courts will admit parol evidence to clear up ambiguity or to show the existence of trade customs that are to be regarded as forming part of the contract. If the contract is ambiguous and there is no oral evidence that can clear up the ambiguity, the contract is construed against the party who wrote it.

A contract that appears to be complete may, in fact, have omitted a provision that ought to have been included. If the omission is due to fraud, alteration, typographical errors, duress, or other similar conduct, oral testimony may be produced to show such conduct.

QUESTIONS

1. Must all contracts be in writing in order to be enforceable?

2. If an oral contract to lease land is performed by the owner of the property allowing the other party to occupy the land, may the owner recover any rent?

3. Why must a contract that cannot be performed in one year be in writing to be enforceable?

4. Under what circumstances is the Statute of Frauds requirement of a writing unnecessary when a person agrees to be responsible for the debt of another?

5. Why does the Statute of Frauds require the agreement of an executor to personally pay the debts of the estate to be in writing?

6. What must be included in a note or memorandum required by the Statute of Frauds?

7. Must the note or memorandum required by the Statute of Frauds be made at the time of the contract?

8. What is the impact of the parol evidence rule on a written contract that appears to be complete?

9. If a contract is ambiguous and there is no oral evidence to clear up the ambiguity, how is it construed?

10. When does the parol evidence rule allow oral testimony when a written contract appears complete?

CASE PROBLEMS

1. Medical Associates of Bristol County, Inc.'s property separated Anthony Nunes's property from Hope Street. Nunes asked Medical's officers for an easement across its property to Hope Street and offered to construct a road over the easement, relocate a traffic light, and install utilities along the road. Nunes presented a site plan that showed a straight road across the property. Medical sent a letter saying it agreed to Nunes's concepts, making three additional stipulations, and asking him to work with its administrator "in clarifying and solidifying these details." Nunes later transferred his property to the Rhode Island Five (RI5) partnership, which met with Medical's administrator and presented the same site plan. Medical sent a letter saying "it confirmed its commitment made in its" previous letter. Several years later, RI5 presented a plan to the administrator that showed a curving road. Medical denied the easement. RI5 sued alleging a contract that gave it a right-of-way across Medical's land. Was there an enforceable contract?   LO ❷

2. Glenn Page began borrowing money from Gulf Coast Motors. He had a gambling problem. One of the owners of Gulf Coast, Jerry Sellers, became concerned about Page's debt to Gulf Coast. He testified that he phoned Page's wife, Mary, who orally promised to pay the debt. There was no evidence that Mary received any benefit from the money Glenn borrowed. Gulf Coast sued both Glenn and Mary for the debt. Must Mary pay it?   LO ❶

3. In order to construct, operate, and maintain a "floodwater retarding structure," the Lincoln County Conservation District purchased a written easement from Eddie Fowler and others. The easement permitted storing "any waters impounded, stored, or detained by such structure" (a lake). Fowler used the lake to water his cattle. A dozen years later he noticed a greenish substance on the lake. When the District did nothing about it and 46 head of cattle died, Fowler sued for breach of contract. He alleged the floodwater retaining structure included the lake. There was evidence at trial that the lake could be a floodwater-retarding structure, but the District argued that in this case, it was just the dam. Fowler testified that in return for the easement the District had orally promised to make a nice lake and "take care of it." Should this oral testimony be admitted?   LO ❸

4. Newell and Carol Simons owned a house with 60 acres plus an interest with DeLila and Joel Simons in 1,500 to 1,800 acres of farmland. The Federal Land Bank mortgage on all the property was greater than its value. To avoid sharing in bankruptcy proceedings, Newell and Carol agreed to and did deed their interest in the property to DeLila and Joel. DeLila and Joel agreed to reconvey the house and 60 acres to Newell and Carol when the debt was satisfied. The debt could not be satisfied without Newell and Carol's interest in the property. Joel died, and after the debt was satisfied, DeLila refused to reconvey the house property to Newell and Carol. Did the Statute of Frauds prevent enforcement of this agreement?   LO ❶

LO ❷   **5.** After negotiating about the sale of her cottage to Betty Jean Sprague, Laura Johnson signed a piece of notepaper on which was written:

Check 7414 is for down payment on cottage

$$
\begin{array}{r}
42,000.00 \\
-1,000.00 \\
\hline
41,000.00
\end{array}
$$

I will relinquish if I don't buy or finish in one month—Aug. 13

Johnson received a check for $1,000 from Sprague on which was written "down payment on cottage." Johnson later tried to return the check, claiming that under the Statute of Frauds they did not make an enforceable contract to sell the cottage. Sprague sued to enforce the sale. Should she win?

LO ❸   **6.** Lobo, Inc. and Carr Construction Co., Inc. used Frost Construction's proposal for the paving work in bidding on a highway construction project. They were awarded the contract and issued a subcontract to Frost incorporating all the terms and conditions in Frost's proposal. Months later, Frost sent a different subcontract to Lobo and Carr that imposed liability on them for consequential damages for delays to Frost's work. They rejected it and insisted Frost adhere to the original proposal. Frost claimed there was an oral condition precedent that it would be able to start the paving by May 1. Lobo and Carr subcontracted the work to someone else. Frost sued alleging its original proposal was a contract that was modified by a later oral condition. Was it?

LO ❶   **7.** When Frank Workland was managing a Genuine Parts Co. (GPC) store, Roger Fitzgerald of GPC offered to let him buy two auto parts stores, named General Auto, in Boise, Idaho. GPC distributed NAPA parts, and Fitzgerald promised Workland if he bought the stores he would have the exclusive right to run NAPA stores in Boise "as long as there was a Workland running General Auto." Workland bought the stores. Twenty years later, GPC bought six competing stores in Boise and sold NAPA parts in them. Workland sued alleging breach of the oral agreement. GPC argued the Statute of Frauds prevented enforcement of the exclusive dealer promise since it could not be performed within a year. Decide the case.

LO ❸   **8.** Limited partners sued their former law firm. The parties agreed to a written partial settlement that dismissed some of their claims and agreed to further negotiations on the remaining claims. It also stated, "This agreement . . . constitute[s] the entire agreement of the parties. There are no additional promises . . . except those expressly set forth in this agreement." The law firm finally offered to settle for $80,000 when the partners had expected $275,000 to $550,000. The higher amount expected resulted from an oral promise made by the law firm before the signing of the agreement. Should the promise modify the settlement agreement?

Third Parties and Contracts

LEARNING OBJECTIVES

1 Discuss the difference between a third-party beneficiary contract and a novation.

2 Explain the difference between assignment of a contract and delegation of duties under it.

3 Describe the different types of contracts involving more than two people.

PREVIEW CASE

After being injured in an auto accident, Elaine Parker retained attorney Joseph Ohlin to pursue a personal injury action and consulted with Dr. Wi Hsu for treatment. Parker and Ohlin signed a document that authorized Hsu to furnish Ohlin with complete reports of the medical services and directed Ohlin to withhold and pay funds due Hsu from any settlement, judgment, or verdict. Hsu treated Parker, operated on her knee, and furnished Ohlin with the reports. After Parker settled her personal injury claim, she told Ohlin not to pay Hsu's medical fee. Hsu sued Ohlin. Can he recover? Did Parker make an assignment? Did Ohlin know Hsu had a right to part of the settlement?

A contract creates both rights and obligations. Ordinarily, one who is not a signer of the contract has no right to the benefits to be derived from the contract or responsibility for any of the duties or obligations. However, parties may intend to benefit a third person when they make a contract. Also, third parties may acquire rights or assume duties.

INVOLVING A THIRD PARTY

A third party can become involved in a contract in several common ways. These include as a third-party beneficiary, by novation, by assignment, and by delegation.

Third-Party Beneficiary

LO ❶
Third-party beneficiary
versus novation

Third-Party Beneficiary
*Person not party to
contract but whom
parties intended to
benefit*

Creditor Beneficiary
*Person to whom
promisee owes
obligation, which is
discharged if promisor
performs*

Donee Beneficiary
*Third-party beneficiary
for whom performance
is a gift*

Incidental Beneficiary
*Person who
unintentionally benefits
from performance of
contract*

At common law, only the parties to a contract could sue upon or seek to enforce the contract. Courts held that strangers to a contract had no rights under it. But courts began to make exceptions to the rule when it seemed evident that the contracting parties intended to benefit a third person, called a **third-party beneficiary**.

The rule today specifies that a third person expressly benefited by the performance of the contract may enforce it against the promisor if the contracting parties intended benefit to the third party. The third person may be either a creditor beneficiary or a donee beneficiary. A **creditor beneficiary** is a person to whom the promisee owes an obligation or duty that will be discharged to the extent that the promisor performs the promise. If *A* makes a contract to pay *B*'s debt to *C*, *C* is the creditor beneficiary of the contract between *A* and *B*. A **donee beneficiary** is one to whom the promisee owes no legal duty but to whom performance is a gift, such as the beneficiary named in a life insurance contract. When an event must occur before the donee beneficiary is benefited, the contracting parties may change the beneficiary.

Not everyone who benefits by the performance of a contract between others is properly considered a third-party beneficiary with rights under the contract. If a person merely incidentally benefits by the performance of a contract, suit for breach or for performance will not be successful. For example, a town contracts with a contractor for the paving of a certain street and the contractor fails to perform. The property owners whose property would have been improved by the paving are not entitled to sue for damages for nonperformance because they were to be only incidentally benefited. The contract for the paving of the street was designed essentially to further the public interest, not to benefit individual property owners. The property owners are merely **incidental beneficiaries**.

COURT CASE

Facts: For tax reasons, Paul and Lydia Kalmanovitz executed similar wills and a will agreement binding the survivor to leave everything to a charitable foundation. The agreement did not mention any specific bequests, although the wills had bequests of $100,000 each to Alma, Karol, and Stanley Kalmanovitz, and to Ronald Weibelt. Paul died and his $100,000 bequests were paid. Lydia deleted the bequests from her will. After Lydia died, Alma, Karol, Stanley, and Ronald sued for $100,000 each as third-party beneficiaries of the will agreement.

Outcome: The claimants were never intended to be beneficiaries of the agreement and could not recover.

—*Kalmanovitz v. Bitting,*
50 Cal. Rptr. 2d 332 (Cal. App. 1st Dist.)

Novation

Novation
*Termination of a
contract and
substitution of a new
one with same terms
but new party*

The party entitled to receive performance under a contract may agree to release the party who is bound to perform and to permit another party to render performance. When this occurs, it is not just a matter of delegating the duties under the contract; rather, it is a matter of abandoning the old contract and substituting a new one in its place. The change of contract and parties is called a **novation**. To be more precise, a novation substitutes a new party for one of the original parties at the mutual agreement of the original parties, such that the prior contract terminates and a new one substitutes for it. The terms of the contract remain the same but with different parties. For example, if Koslov and Burnham have a contract, they, together with Caldwell, may agree that Caldwell shall take Koslov's place, and a novation occurs. Koslov is discharged from the contract, and Burnham and Caldwell are bound. It must be shown that a novation was intended. However, a novation does not need to be in writing nor must it be expressed. It can be implied from the parties' actions. When a novation occurs, the original obligor drops out of the picture. The new party takes the original obligor's place and is alone liable for the performance.

COURT CASE

Facts: Cincinnati Insurance Co. issued a bond for payment of motor fuel taxes by Dixie Management Group, Inc. Dixie officers Timothy Leighton and Mark and Kathy Beeler signed the bond application as guarantors. Leighton was fired, and a year later Cincinnati requested execution of a new bond application. Cincinnati insisted on updated financial information from the Beelers because it knew Leighton no longer worked at Dixie, and it had relied on his personal financial statement when issuing the initial bond. The Beelers executed a new bond application and guarantee. The state asked Cincinnati to pay the amount of the bond to cover unpaid taxes. Cincinnati demanded Dixie and the Beelers create a cash reserve to cover its loss under their guarantee. Two years later, Dixie and the Beelers declared bankruptcy and Cincinnati paid the amount of the bond to the state. Cincinnati then sued Leighton. He argued that the second bond application was a novation of the first and released him from his guarantee.

Outcome: The court found a novation. Leighton was released as a guarantor by the creation of the substitute agreement.

—*Cincinnati Ins. Co. v. Leighton*, **403 F.3d 879 (7th Cir.)**

Assignment

A party to a contract may wish to assign the rights or to delegate the duties under the contract or to do both. If one party transfers the contract in its entirety, it is "an assignment of rights and a delegation of duties." An **assignment** means that one party conveys rights in a contract to another who is not a party to the original undertaking.

As a general rule, a party's rights under a contract may be assigned. One's rights under a contract may be transferred almost as freely as property. The party making the assignment is known as the **assignor**; the one to whom the right is transferred is the **assignee**.

Statutes may impose some restrictions on the assignment of rights. Statutes in a number of states prohibit employees from assigning their wages. Statutes also prohibit the assignment of future pay by soldiers, sailors, and marines. Many states and cities also prohibit the assignment of the pay of public officials. In many states, the law prohibits public works employees from assigning a certain minimum percentage of their wages. This protects wage earners and their families from hard-pressing creditors.

Often one's right under a contract is to receive the services of the other party, such as a bookkeeper, salesperson, or other employee. A right to personal services cannot be assigned because an employee cannot be required to work for a new employer without the employee's consent.

LO ❷
Assignment versus delegation

Assignment
Conveyance of rights in a contract to a person not a party

Assignor
Person making an assignment

Assignee
Person to whom contract right is assigned

COURT CASE

Facts: Robin Sims stopped working at J.H. Renarde, Inc.'s beauty shop and two weeks later opened a shop three miles away. Renarde was the assignee of an employment contract Sims had signed with Renarde's predecessor. The contract prohibited a former employee from competing within nine miles of Renarde's business for nine months. When Renarde sued to enforce the contract, Sims claimed enforcing it would be compelling specific performance of a personal services contract against an employee in violation of the 13th Amendment.

Outcome: The court stated that Renarde was not asking for the enforcement of a personal services contract. It was not asking Sims to continue working for it. Renarde was simply asking to enforce rights under an assignment.

—*J.H. Renarde, Inc. v. Sims,*
711 A.2d 410 (N.J. Super. Ct.)

The parties may include in the original contract a prohibition of the assignment of rights thereunder. Such a prohibition, however, is not effective in some states when only the right to money has been assigned.

Thus, whether rights may be assigned depends upon their nature and the terms of the contract.

Delegation

Delegation
Transfer of duties

The term **delegation** describes a transfer of the duties alone without a transfer of rights. Neither party can delegate the duties under a contract as readily as the rights can be assigned because a "personal" element more frequently exists in the performance aspect of a contract. It would change the obligation thereof if another performed it. If Allen retains Bentley, an attorney, to obtain a divorce for a fee of $350, Bentley can assign the right to receive the $350 to anyone, and Allen must pay. The duty to represent Allen in the divorce proceeding, however, may not be delegated. In those contracts that involve trust and confidence, one may not delegate the duties. If one employs the Local Wonder Band to play for a dance, the contract cannot be assigned, even to a nationally known band. Taste, confidence, and trust cannot be scientifically measured. It is not material that a reasonable person would be satisfied or content with the substitution.

But if one hires Horne to paint a house for $900, whether or not the house has been painted properly can readily be determined by recognized standards in the trade. Therefore, this task could be delegated.

COURT CASE

Facts: At the time the United Auto Workers (UAW) contracted to use the Doral Resort and Country Club for a convention, a union represented Doral employees. However, the contract did not require that a union represent Doral employees. KSL Recreation Corp. bought the Doral and replaced the resort's employees with nonunion employees. When the UAW found out the Doral no longer had union employees, it canceled the contract and sued for a return of its deposit.

Outcome: Because the provision of hotel facilities for a convention, including maintenance of rooms, preparation of meals, and supplying of bellhop or valet services, did not contemplate personal performance, the contract could be delegated. The UAW could not get back the deposit.

—*UAW-GM Human Resource Center v.*
KSL Recreation Corp.,
579 N.W.2d 411 (Mich. App.)

Only when the performance is standardized may one delegate its performance to another. In the construction industry, for example, many instances of delegation of duties occur because the correct performance can be easily ascertained. Contracts calling for unskilled work or labor may in most instances be delegated.

In all cases of delegation, the delegating party remains fully liable under the contract. Suit may be brought for any breach of contract even though another party actually performed. In such an event, the delegating party may in turn sue the party who performed inadequately.

The parties to the original contract may expressly prohibit the delegation of duties thereunder.

The assignment or transfer cannot modify rights transferred by assignment and duties transferred by delegation. They remain the same as though only the original parties to the contract were involved.

TECHNICALITIES OF AN ASSIGNMENT

Even if a contract may be assigned, there may be some technical requirements that must be met to make sure the assignment is effective. It is also important to understand the legal position of the three parties as a result of the assignment.

Notice of an Assignment

Notice need not be given to the other party in order to make the assignment effective as between the assignor and the assignee. Business prudence demands that the original promisor be notified, however. The assignee may not receive payment if notification of the assignment is not given to the original promisor. The promisor has a right to assume that the claim has not been assigned unless otherwise notified. For example, Gonzales promised to pay Hodges $500 in 30 days. When the account came due, as no notice of assignment had been given, Gonzales was safe in paying Hodges. But if Hodges had assigned the account to Wilson and Wilson had not given Gonzales notice, then Wilson would not have been able to collect from Gonzales.

PREVIEW CASE REVISITED

Facts: After being injured in an auto accident, Elaine Parker retained attorney Joseph Ohlin to pursue a personal injury action and consulted with Dr. Wi Hsu for treatment. Parker and Ohlin signed a document that authorized Hsu to furnish Ohlin with complete reports of the medical services and directed Ohlin to withhold and pay funds due Hsu from any settlement, judgment, or verdict. Hsu treated Parker, operated on her knee, and furnished Ohlin with the reports. After Parker settled her personal injury claim, she told Ohlin not to pay Hsu's medical fee. Hsu sued Ohlin.
Outcome: The court stated that the document Parker signed constituted an assignment. Because Ohlin signed the document, he had notice of the assignment.

—*Hsu v. Parker,* **688 N.E.2d 1099 (Ohio App.)**

In most jurisdictions, if a party to a contract makes more than one assignment and the assignees all give notice, the law gives priority in the order in which the assignments were made.

In the event the assignor assigns a larger sum than the debtor owes, the debtor has no obligation to pay the entire assignment. When the creditor assigns only part of a claim, the debtor has no obligation to make payment thereof to the assignee, although such payment may be made, and it reduces the debtor's liability to the creditor to the extent of such payment.

Form of the Assignment

An assignment may be made either by operation of law or by the act of the parties. In the event of death, the law assigns the rights and duties (except for personal services) of the deceased to the executor or administrator of the estate. In the event of bankruptcy, the law assigns the rights and duties of the debtor to the trustee in bankruptcy. These two types of assignments are effective without any act of the parties.

When the assignment is made by act of the parties, it may be either written or oral; however, it must be clear that a present assignment of an interest held by the assignor is intended. If the original contract must be in writing, the assignment must be in writing; otherwise, it may be made orally. It is always preferable to make an assignment in writing. This may be done in the case of written contracts by writing the terms of the assignment on the back of the written contract. Any contract may be assigned by executing an informal written assignment. The following written assignment is adequate in most cases:

> In consideration of the Local Finance Company's canceling my debt of $500 to it, I hereby assign to the Local Finance Company $500 owed to me by the Dale Sand and Gravel Company.
> Signed at noon, Friday, December 16, 1995, at Benson, Iowa.
> (Signed) Harold Locke

Although an assignment may be made for consideration, consideration is not necessary.

Effect of an Assignment

An assignment transfers to the assignee all the rights, title, or interest held by the assignor in whatever is being assigned. The assignee does not receive any greater right or interest than the assignor held.

COURT CASE

Facts: Linda and Louis Crispino both owned their home. Louis, as if he were the sole owner, mortgaged the property to Royal Mortgage Bankers, of which he was vice president. Royal assigned the mortgage to Greenpoint Mortgage Corp. After Louis died, Linda sued to set aside the mortgage. Because Louis acted for Royal in mortgaging the home, Linda could have had the mortgage set aside if Royal still held it.

Outcome: Because Greenpoint was the assignee of Royal, it was subject to the same defense as Royal. The court cancelled the mortgage.

—Crispino v. Greenpoint Mortgage Corp., **758 N.Y.S.2d 367 (N.Y. App. Div.)**

The nonassigning party retains all rights and defenses as though there had never been an assignment. For example, if the nonassigning party lacked competence to contract or entered into the contract under duress, undue influence, fraud, or misrepresentation, the nonassigning party may raise these defenses against the assignee as effectively as they could have been raised against the assignor.

Warranties of the Assignor

When one assigns rights under a contract to an assignee for value, the assignor makes three implied warranties:

1. That the assignor is the true owner of the right.
2. That the right is valid and subsisting at the time the assignment is made.
3. That there are no defenses available to the debtor that have not been disclosed to the assignee.

If the assignor commits a breach of warranty, the assignee may seek to recover any loss from the assignor.

Most assignments involve claims for money. The Fair Deal Grocery Company assigned $10,000 worth of its accounts receivable to the First National Bank. The assignor warranted that the accounts were genuine. If a customer, therefore, refused to pay the bank and proved that no money was owed, the grocery company would be liable. If payment was not made merely because of insolvency, most courts would hold that the assignor was not liable.

In the absence of an express guarantee, an assignor does not warrant that the other party will perform the duties under the contract, that the other party will make payment, or that the other party is solvent.

If the Harbottle Distributing Company owes the Norfolk Brewery $10,000, it could assign $10,000 of its accounts receivable to the Norfolk Brewery in full satisfaction of the debt. If the assignee is able to collect only $7,000 of these accounts because the debtors were insolvent, the brewery would have no recourse against Harbottle. If the $3,000 is uncollectible because the debtors had valid defenses to the claims, the Harbottle Distributing Company would have to make good the loss.

The Norfolk Brewery Company should not take these accounts receivable by assignment. An assignment allows Harbottle Distributing Company to pay its debt, not with cash, but by a transfer of title to its accounts receivable. From the brewery company's standpoint, the same result can be obtained not by taking title to these accounts but by taking them merely as collateral security for the debt with a provision that the brewery is to collect the accounts and apply the proceeds to the $10,000. Under this arrangement, the brewery can look to the distributing company for the balance of $3,000.

JOINT, SEVERAL, AND JOINT AND SEVERAL CONTRACTS

When two or more persons enter into a contract with one or more other persons, the contract may be joint, several, or joint and several. The intention of the parties determines the type of contract.

Joint Contracts

A **joint contract** is a contract in which two or more persons have all promised the entire performance, which is the subject of the contract. Each obligor is bound for the performance of the entire obligation. A joint contract is also a contract in which two or more persons are jointly entitled to the performance of another party or parties. If Sands and Cole sign a contract stating "We jointly promise . . . ," the obligation is the joint obligation of Sands and Cole. If the promise is not carried out, both Sands and Cole must be joined in any lawsuit. The aggrieved party may not sue just one of them. Unless otherwise expressed, a promise by two or more persons is generally presumed to be joint and not several.

Several Contracts

A **several contract** arises when two or more persons individually agree to perform the same obligation even though the individual agreements are contained in the same document. Express words must be used to show that a several contract is intended.

If Anne and Cathy sign a contract stating "We severally promise" or "Each of us promises" to do a particular thing, the two signers are individually bound to perform. If the contract is not performed, either Anne or Cathy may be sued alone for the obligation she assumed.

Joint and Several Contracts

A **joint and several contract** is one in which two or more persons are bound both jointly and severally. If Sands and Cole sign a contract stating "We, and each of us, promise" or "I promise" to perform a particular act, they are jointly and severally obligated.

The other party to the contract may treat the obligation as either a joint obligation or as a group of individual obligations and may bring suit against all or any one or more of them at one time. Statutes in some states interpret a joint contract to be a joint and several contract.

COURT CASE

Facts: Robert Schubert sued Trailmobile Trailer, LLC for injuries from an accident. Lawyers for Trailmobile, its primary insurer, Zurich Insurance Co., and National Union Fire Insurance Co., Trailmobile's excess insurance carrier, orally agreed to settle with Clifton Smart, Schubert's lawyer. During negotiations the parties stated Zurich was to pay $1,500,000. Mike Oliver, Trailmobile's lawyer, sent Smart a letter stating, "[o]n behalf of [Trailmobile] and [Zurich] and [National Union] we will pay the amount of [$4,250,000] to settle the claims of [Schubert]." Zurich's portion was to be paid first. Smart responded by letter that the $2,750,000 to be

paid by Trailmobile and National Union "will be paid regardless of the financial ability of Trailmobile." The second payment was $800,000 short. Schubert moved to enforce the settlement claiming it was joint and several. Trailmobile was in bankruptcy and National Union claimed the agreement was several.

Outcome: The court found that Trailmobile and National Union were jointly and severally liable for the $2,750,000.

—Schubert v. Trailmobile Trailer, LLC,
111 S.W.3d 897 (Mo. App.)

QUESTIONS

1. Ordinarily, what are the rights of a party who is not a signer of a contract?
2. How can a third party become involved in a contract?
3. May everyone who benefits by the performance of a contract between others successfully sue for breach or performance of the contract?
4. What is a novation?
5. May a right to personal services be assigned? Explain.
6. What is the difference between an assignment of a contract and the delegation of duties under it?
7. In what way does an assignment or transfer modify rights or duties transferred?
8. Normally, if a party to a contract makes more than one assignment and the assignees all give notice, in what order do the assignees take priority?
9. May a several contract be formed merely by two or more persons making a promise?
10. If Rich jointly promises to pay $10,000 with Sharon, and Andrew severally promises to pay $10,000, who will have to pay more?

CASE PROBLEMS

1. Former asbestos companies signed an agreement forming the Center for Claims Resolution (CCR) to administer and resolve asbestos related claims. The agreement included a formula for calculating the share of liability payments of each member. The CCR negotiated a settlement agreement for 19 member companies with the law firm of Kelley & Ferraro LLP, resolving 15,000 claims. The settlement was to be paid to Kelley in biannual installments. The agreement stated that, "each CCR member shall be liable . . . only for its individual share." An installment was $1 million short because GAF Corp. disputed CCR's calculation of its share. Kelley sued alleging the agreement was joint and several so that the other companies had to make up the full installment even if one company withheld its contribution. Was the agreement joint and several or merely several? LO ❸

2. A contract by which Carroll Kennedy sold his dental practice to his nephew, Jeffrey Kennedy, contained an agreement not to compete within 15 miles for three years after leaving Jeffrey's employment. Carroll and Jeffrey later could not agree on work hours so they agreed Carroll would leave. Jeffrey wrote him a letter saying "there is no alternative to ending our association." Carroll moved out of Jeffrey's offices and the next month opened an office in Hillsborough, within 15 miles. Jeffrey sued Carroll for breach of contract. Carroll claimed Jeffrey orally agreed he could open a practice in Hillsborough. Carroll claimed by agreeing to his leaving and saying there was no alternative, he and Jeffrey had agreed to a novation of their agreement. Had there been a novation? LO ❶

3. The Federal Deposit Insurance Corp. (FDIC) assigned a note executed by Donald Gerard to Federal Financial Company (FFC). FFC sued Gerard on the note more than six years after it was due. The statute of limitations on notes was six years. By federal law, the FDIC had a longer statute of limitations, and the suit was LO ❷

brought within that time. FFC argued that as the assignee of the FDIC, it had the FDIC's rights including the longer statute of limitations. Does it?

LO **3**

4. Ti-Well International Corp. contracted with Quindao First Textile Co. to import corduroy fabric. Wujin Nanxaishu Secant Factory contracted to supply the fabric to Quindao. Wujin delivered the fabric to Ti-Well through Quindao, but Ti-Well did not pay Quindao, who did not pay Wujin. After negotiations, Juntai Li, the sole shareholder, director, officer, and employee of Ti-Well, executed a note agreeing to make payments to Wujin. The note did not mention Ti-Well. Li also signed an agreement stating that Ti-Well and Li would assume responsibility for Quindao's debt to Wujin. When the debt was not paid, Wujin sued Li. Was his obligation joint with Ti-Well's?

LO **1**

5. Shortly before 9 P.M., when the stores closed, Jill Marker was beaten severely while working at a store in the Silas Creek Crossing Shopping Center. She suffered permanent injuries. ZT-Winston-Salem Associates owned Silas Creek and had contracted with Wackenhut Corp. to furnish security guard services. The contract required Wackenhut to maintain high visibility by providing vehicular and foot patrol from 8 P.M. to 4 A.M. Marker sued Wackenhut, alleging she was a third-party beneficiary of the contract. Was she?

LO **2**

6. After making purchases, Caldor, Inc. received invoices which were stamped: "PAYABLE TO: CAPITAL FACTORS, INC. . . . REMITTANCE IS TO BE MADE ONLY TO THEM . . . ANY OBJECTION TO THIS BILL, OR ITS TERMS, MUST BE REPORTED TO THEM WITHIN TEN DAYS AFTER ITS RECEIPT." When Caldor did not make payment to Capital, it sued. Had Caldor been notified of the assignment to Capital?

LO **1**

7. When Mary Ann and Richard Healey divorced, they agreed on Richard's child support responsibility. Richard voluntarily continued to make maintenance payments to Mary Ann for seven years after his duty to make them stopped. When Mary Ann later tried to get the child support obligation changed, she claimed that Richard's continuation of maintenance payments when they were not required constituted a novation. Richard said he made the payments because he thought it was "fair" and the children would benefit. Was there a novation?

Termination of Contracts

LEARNING OBJECTIVES

1 Describe the requirements for terminating a contract by performance.

2 Recognize the circumstances that discharge a contract by operation of law.

3 Explain what breach of contract is and the potential remedies for breach.

PREVIEW CASE

Harris Corp. contracted to deliver eight orders of radio spare parts to Harriscom Svenska for distribution to Iran. The U.S. government later prohibited all sales of goods it categorized as military equipment to Iran. The customs service detained a shipment, and Harris negotiated with the government for more than six months. The government did not allow Harris to fill any of the other orders. The U.S. State Department and Harris finally reached a compromise, but it only allowed Harris to fill three of the eight orders. Harriscom sued Harris for breach of contract. Was there a breach of contract? Was there any way that Harris could have filled the other five orders?

Although it is important to know how a contract is formed and who is bound on it, it is also important to know when it is ended, or terminated, and when the parties are no longer bound.

METHODS BY WHICH CONTRACTS ARE TERMINATED

Five common methods by which contracts may be terminated include: (1) by performance of the contract, (2) by operation of law, (3) by voluntary agreement of the parties, (4) by impossibility of performance, and (5) by acceptance of a breach of contract.

Performance

When all the terms of a contract have been fulfilled, the contract is discharged by performance. Not all the parties need to perform simultaneously, however. Parties

LO 1
Terminating contract by performance

are discharged from further liability as soon as they have done all that they have agreed to do. The other party or parties are not discharged, nor is the contract, if any material thing remains to be done by them.

Several factors determine whether there has been performance:

1. Time of performance
2. Tender of performance
3. Tender of payment
4. Satisfactory performance
5. Substantial performance

Time of Performance. If the contract states when performance is to be rendered, the contract provisions must be followed unless under all the circumstances performance on the exact date specified is not vital. When performance on the exact date is deemed vital, it is said that "time is of the essence." If the contract states no time for performance, then performance must ordinarily be rendered within a reasonable time.

Tender of Performance
Offer to perform in satisfaction of terms of contract

Tender of Performance. An offer to perform an obligation in satisfaction of the terms of a contract is called a **tender of performance**. If a contract calls for the performance of an act at a specified time, a tender of performance will discharge the obligation of the one making the tender so long as the tender conforms to the agreement.

Tender of Payment
Offer and ability to pay money owed

Tender of Payment. An offer to pay money in satisfaction of a debt or claim when one has the ability to pay is a **tender of payment**. The debtor must offer the exact amount due, including interest, costs, and attorneys' fees, if any are required. If the debtor says, "I am now ready to pay you," a sufficient tender has not been made. The debtor must pay or offer the creditor the amount due.

Legal Tender
Any form of lawful money

A tender in the form of a check is not a proper tender. The payment must be made in **legal tender**. With but few minor exceptions, this is any form of U.S. money. If a check is accepted, the contract is performed as soon as the bank on which it is drawn honors the check.

If the tender is refused, the debt is not discharged. However, proper tender does stop the running of interest. In addition, if the creditor should bring suit, the person who has tendered the correct amount is not liable for court costs after the date of the tender. The debtor must, however, be in readiness to pay at any time. If a tender is made after a suit, the debtor frequently pays the money over to the court.

Satisfactory Performance. It frequently happens that contracts specifically state that the performance must be "satisfactory to" or "to the satisfaction of" a certain person. What constitutes satisfactory performance is frequently a disputed question. The courts generally have adopted the rule—especially when a definite, objective measure of satisfaction exists—that if the contract is performed in a manner that would satisfy an ordinary, reasonable person, the terms of the contract have been met sufficiently to discharge it. If the performance is clearly intended to be subject to the personal taste or judgment of one of the parties, however, it may be rejected on the ground that it is not satisfactory to that particular party.

Substantial Performance. Under the early common law, each party to a contract had to perform to the last letter of the contract before a demand for the party's rights under the contract could be made. Such a rule was often extremely inequitable. If a contractor built a $50 million office building, it might be grossly

COURT CASE

Facts: The contract under which Optus Software hired Michael Silvestri to supervise the support services staff gave Optus the right to fire him for failure to perform to Optus's satisfaction. Nine months later, Optus had received numerous complaints from clients and other employees about the performance and attitude of the support services staff. A big customer complained about Silvestri's lack of cooperation and dour, condescending attitude. Optus fired him. Silvestri sued for breach of contract.

Outcome: The court said that as long as Optus's dissatisfaction was genuine, the satisfaction clause in the contract gave the company the right to fire Silvestri. The complaints made Optus's dissatisfaction genuine.

—Silvestri v. Optus Software, Inc.,
814 A.2d 602 (N.J.)

unfair to say that none of the $50 million could be collected because of a relatively minor breach.

The law today can be stated as follows: If a construction contract is substantially performed, the party performing may demand the full price under the contract less the damages suffered by the other party. In the case of the office building, if the contract price is $50 million and the damages are $5,000, the contractor will be allowed to collect $49,995,000. Suppose, however, that the contractor completed the excavation and then quit. The contractor would be entitled to collect nothing.

Just how far the contractor must proceed toward full performance before there has been substantial performance is often difficult to determine. The performance must be so nearly complete that it would be a great injustice to deny the contractor any compensation for the work and there must have been an honest attempt to perform. A court will weigh all the circumstances surrounding the deviation, including the significance of and reasons for it, the ease of correction, the extent to which the purpose of the contract is defeated, and the use or benefit to the owners of the work completed. For construction contracts, some statutes prescribe substantial performance as being that stage of progress of the project at which the project is sufficiently complete in accordance with the contract that the owner can occupy or utilize the project for its intended use.

COURT CASE

Facts: All Seasons Construction, Inc. (ASC) agreed to re-roof and replace the fascia and soffit on 28 buildings for the Mansfield Housing Authority (MHA) by April 28. On April 18, ASC told MHA the work was complete other than the "punch list"—an itemized list of items needed to be corrected. However, the buildings were totally re-roofed, all siding on the fascia and soffits was completely attached, and the buildings were occupied by tenants at all times. MHA had not given ASC the punch list. On May 2, MHA sent ASC the punch list which included caulking, cleaning debris, reconfiguring where the soffit met the eave, and tucking the J-mold into the fascia on most buildings. It said the project was not substantially complete. MDA withheld $22,200 as damages for failure to substantially complete by April 28. ASC sued MHA for the $22,200.

Outcome: The court said that the majority of the work had been completed on time. The work was substantially completed by April 28 so the damages should not have been withheld.

—All Seasons Const., Inc. v. Mansfield Housing Authority, **920 So.2d 413 (La. App.)**

Discharge by Operation of Law

Under certain circumstances the law will cause a discharge of the contract, or at least the law will bar all right of action. The most common conditions under which the law operates to discharge contracts include:

1. Discharge in bankruptcy
2. Running of the statute of limitations
3. Alteration of written contract
4. Impossibility of performance

Bankruptcy. Individuals and business firms overwhelmed with financial obligations may petition the court for a decree of voluntary bankruptcy. Creditors may, under certain circumstances, force one into involuntary bankruptcy. In either event, after a discharge in bankruptcy, creditors' rights of action to enforce most of the contracts of the debtor are barred.

Statute of Limitations
Time within which right to sue must be exercised or lost

Statute of Limitations. A person's right to sue must be exercised within the time fixed by a statute called the **statute of limitations**. This time varies from state to state, for different types of suits and for different types of debts. For open accounts, accounts receivable, and ordinary loans, the time varies from 2 to 8 years, whereas for notes it varies from 4 to 20 years.

After a person has brought suit and obtained judgment, the judgment must be enforced by having the property of the debtor levied upon and sold. If this is not done, in some states a statute of limitations operates even against judgments. In those states where a statute applies to judgments, the time varies from 5 to 21 years from date of judgment. If a payment is made on a judgment, the payment constitutes an acknowledgment of the debt and the statute starts to run again from the date of payment.

The time is calculated from the date the obligation is due. In the case of running accounts, such as purchases from department stores, the time starts from the date of the last purchase. If a part payment is made, the statute begins to run again from the date of such payment. If the promisor leaves the state, the statute ceases to run while the promisor is beyond the jurisdiction of the court.

COURT CASE

Facts: Dean Drake borrowed money from Willa Tyner several times. When he then bought some land from her, he executed a mortgage for $44,000. Drake made payments 1 year, 3 years, 6 years, and 10 years after this purchase. He did not specify to which debt the payments were to be applied. Three years after the last payment, Tyner recorded the mortgage. Drake sued for a declaration that the debt was barred by the six-year statute of limitations.

Outcome: Because Drake did not specify to which debt the payments should apply, Tyner could apply the 3-, 6-, and 10-year payments to the mortgage, starting the 6-year statute of limitations anew with each payment. The mortgage debt was not barred by the statute of limitations.

—*Drake v. Tyner,* 914 P.2d 519 (Colo. App.)

A debt that has been outlawed by a statute of limitations may be revived. Some states do this by a written acknowledgment of or a promise to pay the debt, others by part payment after the debt has been outlawed, and still others by the mere payment of the interest. After the debt is revived, the period of the statute of limitations begins to run again from the time of the revival.

Alteration of Written Contract. If one of the parties intentionally and without the consent of the other party alters the written contract, the other innocent party is discharged. However, the altering party can be held to either the original contract terms or the terms as altered. In most states the alteration must also be material or important. If a contractor who has undertaken to build a house by January 15 realizes that because of winter conditions it cannot be finished by that date, erases and changes the date to March 15, there is a material alteration that will discharge the other party to the contract.

Impossibility of Performance. If the act called for in a contract is impossible to perform at the time the contract is made, no contract ever comes into existence. Frequently, impossibility of performance arises after a valid contract is formed. This type of impossibility discharges the contract under certain circumstances. The fact that performance has merely become more difficult does not discharge the contract. However, if, in a practical sense, the contract is impossible to perform, it is discharged.

PREVIEW CASE REVISITED

Facts: Harris Corp. contracted to deliver eight orders of radio spare parts to Harriscom Svenska for distribution to Iran. The U.S. government later prohibited all sales of goods it categorized as military equipment to Iran. The customs service detained one shipment, and Harris negotiated with the government for more than six months. Meanwhile, the government did not allow Harris to fill any of the other orders. The U.S. State Department and Harris finally reached a compromise, but it only allowed Harris to fill three of the eight orders. Harriscom sued Harris for breach of contract.

Outcome: The court stated that because the U.S. government would not allow Harris to go ahead with sales to Iran, Harris had proved the defense of commercial impracticability. Harris had acted in good faith, but simply could not carry out the contract.

—*Harriscom Svenska, AB v. Harris Corp.*, 3 F.3d 576 (2d Cir.)

The most common causes of discharge by impossibility of performance occurring after the contract is made include:

1. Destruction of the subject matter
2. New laws making the contract illegal
3. Death or physical incapacity of person to render personal services
4. Act of other party

Destruction of the Subject Matter. If the contract involves specific subject matter, the destruction of this specific subject matter without the fault of the parties discharges the contract because of impossibility of performance. This rule applies only when the performance of the contract depends on the continued existence of a specified person, animal, or thing. The contract is not discharged if an event occurs that it is reasonable to anticipate. Any payment made in advance must be returned when performance of the contract is excused.

Facts: Farmers' Electric Cooperative contracted with the state department of corrections to supply electricity to a tract of land. Because the land was not in a municipality, Farmers' was the legal supplier of electricity. The department requested that the city of Cameron annex the land and the city did so. The department then decided to build a prison on part of the land. Because the land was then in a city, it was illegal for Farmer's to supply electricity, and the department obtained electricity from the city. Farmers' sued.

Outcome: The court stated a party may not put itself in a position to be unable to perform a contract and then use that inability to perform as an excuse for nonperformance. Because the department voluntarily took the action to make the contract illegal, it violated its contract.

—*Farmers' Elec. v. Missouri Dept. of Corrections*, 977 S.W.2d 266 (Mo.)

In some states, a contract is discharged by impracticability of performance rather than strict impossibility. In such states, extreme and unreasonable difficulty, expense, injury, or loss would discharge a contract.

New Laws Making the Contract Illegal. If an act is legal at the time of the contract but is subsequently made illegal, the contract is discharged. However, if one of the parties takes deliberate action to render the contract illegal, that party will be liable in damages.

Death or Physical Incapacity. If the contract calls for personal services, death or physical incapacity of the person to perform such services discharges the contract. The personal services must be such that they cannot readily be performed by another or by the personal representative of the promisor.

Death or incapacity discharges such acts as painting a portrait, representing a client in a legal proceeding, and other services of a highly personal nature. In general, if the performance is too personal to be delegated, the death or disability of the party bound to perform will discharge the contract.

Facts: When River Phoenix died from an apparent overdose of illegal drugs, an uncompleted film he had contracted to appear in was delayed. The insurance companies that had supplied entertainment package insurance policies covering the film sued Phoenix's estate for breach of contract. The estate claimed the personal services contract was impossible to perform after Phoenix's death. The insurance companies argued the defense of impossibility of performance only applied when the impossibility was accidental, unavoidable, and through no fault of either party.

Outcome: The court stated the rule was that death makes a personal services contract impossible to perform and therefore dissolves the contract. The insurance companies could not collect.

—*CAN Intl. Reinsurance Co., Ltd. v. Phoenix*, 678 So. 2d 378 (Fla. App.)

Act of Other Party. When performance of a contract by a party is made impossible by the wrongful act of the other party, the performance is excused. The party who cannot perform has not breached the contract by the failure to perform.

Voluntary Agreement of the Parties

A contract is a mutual agreement. The parties are as free to change their minds by mutual agreement as they are to agree in the first place. Consequently, whenever the parties to a contract agree not to carry out its terms, the contract is discharged. The contract itself may recite events or circumstances that will automatically terminate the agreement. The release of one party to the contract constitutes the consideration for the release of the other.

Acceptance of Breach of the Contract by One of the Parties

When one of the parties fails or refuses to perform the obligations assumed under the contract, there is a **breach** of the contract. This does not terminate the contract. Only if the innocent party accepts the breach of the contract is the contract discharged.

   If one party, prior to the time the other party is entitled to performance, announces an intention not to perform, **anticipatory breach** occurs. When there has been anticipatory breach, the innocent party may sue immediately for breach of contract and is released from any obligations under the contract.

Breach
Failure or refusal to perform contractual obligations

Anticipatory Breach
One party announces intention not to perform prior to time to perform

COURT CASE

Facts: Crest Construction, Inc. hired James Murray as the subcontractor on a construction project. During construction, the parties had a disagreement, and Murray quit the job. Murray agreed to waive his right to get payment from a forced sale of the project, and Crest agreed to sign a promise to pay Murray. Crest finished the job and told Murray it would not pay as agreed. Murray then sought to get paid from a sale of the project. In the lawsuit that followed, Murray claimed he did not have to comply with his agreement because Crest had announced it was not going to comply.

Outcome: The court said that once Crest repudiated its agreement, Murray was not required to honor his agreement.

—*Murray v. Crest Constr., Inc.,*
900 S.W.2d 342 (Tex.)

REMEDIES FOR BREACH OF CONTRACT

If a breach of contract occurs, the innocent party has three courses of action that may be followed:

1. Sue for damages

2. Rescind the contract

3. Sue for specific performance

LO ❸
Breach of contract and remedies

Sue for Damages

The usual remedy for breach of contract is to sue for **damages** or a sum of money to compensate for the breach. A suit for damages really consists of two suits in one. The first requires proving breach of contract. The second requires proving damages. Four kinds of damages include: (1) nominal, (2) compensatory, (3) punitive, and (4) liquidated.

Damages
Sum of money awarded to injured party

Nominal Damages
Small amount awarded when there is technical breach but no injury

Nominal Damages. If the plaintiff in a breach of contract suit can prove that the defendant broke the contract but cannot prove any loss was sustained because of the breach, then the court will award **nominal damages**, generally one dollar, to symbolize vindication of the wrong done to the plaintiff. Although very low damages are frequently awarded, the award also can be substantial.

COURT CASE

Facts: MTW Investment Co. was a limited partner in Regency Forrest Association. Regency sold some land to Alcovy Properties, Inc. MTW sued Alcovy, alleging that Regency did not have authority to sell the land. Alcovy alleged that MTW's action clouded the title to the land and it lost a substantial profit it could have made by subdividing the land. When MTW alleged the loss of profits was too speculative, the jury awarded Alcovy $625,000 in nominal damages. MTW appealed, saying the amount was excessive.

Outcome: The court held that although nominal damages are normally a trivial amount when no serious loss is shown, it is not restricted to a very small amount. The award was not excessive.

—MTW Inv. Co. v. Alcovy Properties, Inc.,
616 S.E.2d 166 (Ga. App.)

Compensatory Damages
Amount equal to the loss sustained

Compensatory Damages. The theory of the law of damages is that an injured party should be compensated for any loss that may have been sustained but should not be permitted to profit from the other party's wrongdoing. When a breach of contract occurs, the law entitles the injured party to compensation for the exact amount of loss, but no more. Such damages are called **compensatory damages.** Sometimes the actual loss is easily determined, but at other times it is very difficult to determine. As a general rule, the amount of damages is a question for the jury to decide.

Punitive Damages
Amount paid to one party to punish the other

Punitive, or Exemplary, Damages. In most breach-of-contract cases, the awarding of compensatory damages fully meets the ends of justice. Cases occur, however, where compensatory damages are not adequate. In these instances, the law may permit the plaintiff to receive **punitive damages**. Punitive damages are damages paid to the plaintiff in order to punish the defendant, not to compensate the plaintiff. Punitive damages are more common in tort than contract actions. For example, if a tenant maliciously damages rented property, the landlord may frequently recover as damages the actual cost of repairs plus additional damages as punitive damages.

Liquidated Damages
Sum fixed by contract for breach where actual damages are difficult to measure

Liquidated Damages. When two parties enter into a contract, in order to avoid the problems involved in proving actual damages, they may include a provision fixing the amount of damages to be paid in the event one party breaches the contract. Such a provision is called **liquidated damages**. Such a clause in the contract specifies recoverable damages in the event that the plaintiff establishes a breach by the defendant. Liquidated damages must be reasonable and should be provided only in those cases in which actual damages are difficult or impossible to prove. If the amount of damages fixed by the contract is unreasonable and in effect the damages are punitive, the court will not enforce this provision of the contract.

COURT CASE

Facts: A physician, Christopher Borgiel, contracted with St. Clair Medical, PC, agreeing that he would not practice medicine within seven miles of either of Medical's two offices for the first year after leaving St. Clair's employment. The contract set St. Clair's damages for Borgiel's breach of this provision at $40,000. After working for St. Clair for almost two years, he resigned to work at a location within seven miles of one of Medical's offices. St. Clair sued him for $40,000 for breach of contract.

Outcome: Because the court found the actual damages would be difficult to calculate and the amount was reasonable, it enforced the liquidated damages provision.

—*St Clair Medical, P.C. v. Borgiel,*
715 N.W.2d 914 (Mich. App.)

Rescind the Contract

When a contract is breached, the aggrieved party may elect to **rescind** the contract, which releases this party from all obligations not yet performed. If this party has executed the contract, the remedy is to sue for recovery of what was parted with. If the aggrieved party rescinds a contract for the sale of goods, damages for the breach also may be requested.

Rescind
Set aside or cancel

Sue for Specific Performance

In some cases neither a suit for damages nor rescission will constitute an adequate remedy. The injured party's remedy under these circumstances is a suit in equity to compel **specific performance**; that is, the carrying out of the specific terms of the contract.

This remedy is available in limited cases. This includes most contracts for the sale of real estate or any interest in real estate and for the sale of rare articles of personal property, such as a painting or an heirloom, the value of which cannot readily be determined. There is no way to measure sentimental value attached to a relic. Under such circumstances mere money damages may be inadequate to compensate the injured party. The court may compel specific performance under such circumstances.

As a general rule, contracts for the performance of personal services will not be specifically ordered. This is both because of the difficulty of supervision by the courts and because of the Constitution's prohibition of involuntary servitude except as a criminal punishment.

Specific Performance
Carrying out the terms of contract

MALPRACTICE

A professional person, such as a lawyer, accountant, or doctor, who makes a contract to perform professional services has a duty to perform with the ability and care normally exercised by others in the profession. A contract not so performed is breached because of **malpractice**. An accountant is liable to a client who suffers a loss because the accountant has not complied with accepted accounting practices.

In some cases, a person other than a party to the contract may sue a professional person for malpractice. In the case of a contract for accounting services, a third party may, under certain circumstances, recover when the negligence or fraud by the accountant causes a loss to that party.

Malpractice
Failure to perform with ability and care normally exercised by people in the profession

COURT ⚡ CASE

Facts: For five years, Boris Elieff had done all the accounting and tax work for Jerry Clark Equipment. Elieff sold the business to Roger Hibbits, a CPA and tax attorney, and Clark agreed to have him continue to do the accounting work. Three years later, Clark ended Hibbits's services because Hibbits had failed to prepare Clark's last three corporate income tax returns. Interest and penalties for that failure were $8,033, so Clark sued Hibbits.

Outcome: The court held that Hibbits was negligent and awarded damages.

—*Jerry Clark Equipment, Inc. v. Hibbits,*
612 N.E.2d 858 (Ill. App. Ct.)

QUESTIONS

1. Must all the parties to a contract perform simultaneously in order to discharge the contract by performance?

2. What is the effect of a tender of performance?

3. Does refusal of a tender of payment discharge a debt?

4. May the performance of a contract ever be refused on the ground that the performance is not satisfactory to the particular contracting party?

5. What is the modern rule on substantial performance?

6. What is the effect of a discharge in bankruptcy on a creditor's right to collect a debt?

7. May a debt that has been outlawed by the statute of limitations ever be revived?

8. What is the effect of an intentional alteration by one party without the consent of the other?

9. If a singer contracts to sing at a party, is the contract released if the singer develops laryngitis just before the party starts?

10. May the parties to a contract mutually agree not to carry it out?

11. What is the theory that the law applies in determining compensatory damages?

12. Why will a court normally deny an order of specific performance of a contact for personal services?

CASE PROBLEMS

LO ❶

1. Jack Shewmake and Jim Kelly contracted to add a playroom, hobby room, and concrete deck to Al and Lisa DelGreco's home. After the new concrete deck was poured, rain leaked into the new playroom and hobby room. Shewmake and Kelly tried to correct this, but three months later the leak was not corrected. Al told Shewmake and Kelly he would not make any more payments until the leak was corrected. They did not perform any more work on the house, so the DelGrecos paid an architect $1,500 to determine what needed to be done to correct the defects in the work. They paid another contractor $18,500 correct the job. To eliminate the leak the second contractor demolished the concrete deck installed by Shewmake and Kelly. The DelGrecos sued Shewmake and Kelly for breach of contract. They claimed they had spent $19,100 in labor and materials to work on the house for which they had not been paid. What if anything should the DelGrecos recover?

2. Kathryn and Ronald Frazier signed a note to pay Philip O'Malley $27,000 with 14% interest in 90 days. The Fraziers made some interest payments and Ronald frequently told O'Malley he would pay the principal. Thirteen years after the last interest payment, Ronald delivered a check for $5,000 signed by Kathryn to O'Malley. A few months later, Ronald offered to pay O'Malley $22,000 for a release acknowledging no further obligation on the debt. O'Malley refused and sued the Fraziers. At the time Ronald paid the $5,000, the five-year statute of limitations had run on the debt. Decide the case.

LO ❷

3. On June 14, Ronald and Barbara Ouellette applied for a loan at Park Square Credit Union. Park denied a loan because a real estate mortgage of the Ouellettes had been foreclosed, and Park could not find out if they still owed any money. On July 6, the Ouellettes contracted to buy Bruce Filippone's house, making a down payment of $8,400. The contract stated: "If, despite Buyers' diligent efforts to obtain . . . a loan commitment, they are unable to do so by August 1 . . . Buyers may terminate this Agreement." Without any formal applications, Ronald attempted to get loans from three other banks but was denied for the same reason. Filippone extended the deadline to September 1. Ronald did not file any loan applications during the extension. On September 9, the Ouellettes requested return of their down payment and included a copy of a mortgage rejection notice from Park dated September 7. Do the Ouellettes get the $8,400 back?

LO ❸

4. Mills Construction, Inc. contracted with Double Diamond Construction to erect a steel arena. Mills was to provide the parts for the building and Double Diamond was to provide the labor and equipment. Double Diamond began construction, the materials were delivered late, and many of the steel components did not fit together properly. Some of the mainframes were twisted and other parts were missing or the wrong length. Double Diamond reported the problems to Mills and its supplier, but nothing was done. Double Diamond stopped work on the project and three days later the structure collapsed. Double Diamond billed Mills for the work it had completed up to the collapse and said it would not continue work until the bill was paid. When it was not paid, Double Diamond sued Mills. Had Mills made it impossible for Double Diamond to complete the contract?

LO ❷

5. Lightmotive Fatman, Inc. offered Joist Brandis the job of gaffer on a film for 14 weeks at $2,000 a week. Brandis told Lightmotive he accepted and moved to North Carolina. He began work on the film, but two days later Lightmotive told him someone else had been given the job and there was no work for him. Had Lightmotive breached a contract?

LO ❸

6. Ed Jenkins and Lynn Jones contracted to acquire a Subway sandwich shop franchises. Jenkins agreed to put up the money, and Jones agreed to attend any training and manage the business. They formed a corporation, and once the business repaid Jenkins's investment, he would transfer 25 percent of the stock to Jones. They acquired franchises in Jones's name so Jenkins would not have to attend Subway's training school. After Jenkins died, his widow Rose inherited his share. Jones used Rose's funds to purchase a 50 percent interest in a partnership running a Subway franchise in a hospital. The partnership agreement prohibited participation by Rose. Jones supplied Rose with monthly financial data on the hospital Subway. It was successful, and he repaid Rose's investment. Jones then claimed he and not the corporation owned the 50 percent interest in the hospital Subway. Rose sued Jones for breach of contract. Jones claimed impossibility of performance saying the partnership agreement made it impossible to perform his contract. Who owns the 50 percent interest?

LO ❷

LO **1**

7. Farrell Smith contested his father's will. He settled the contest with an agreement with his mother, Mavis. Mavis was to deed 150 acres of land to Farrell. He was to pay for a survey, build a fence on the boundary of the 150 acres, and sign all documents necessary to settle the dispute. Mavis's attorney hired and instructed the surveyor. They changed the boundary several times. When the survey was completed, Farrell built a fence that exceeded the specifications in the agreement, paid for the survey, and signed all necessary documents. Mavis died and Farrell's sister, Carol, inherited Mavis's acreage. Another survey determined the fence included 13 acres of Carol's land with Farrell's. She sued him. Farrell defended saying he had substantially performed the agreement. Did he?

LO **3**

8. After paying First National Bank of Glenwood a fee for processing a loan, the bank made a loan to James and Laurie Goossen to purchase a home. The Goossens wanted a low interest, low down payment loan, so the loan was processed through the Wisconsin Housing and Economic Development Authority (WHEDA). WHEDA required lenders to have any septic systems inspected. The bank normally did not require such inspection and neither the Goossens nor the bank knew it was required by WHEDA. After the Goossens moved in, the county required them to replace the improper system at their house. The Goossens sued the bank for breach of contract. Had the bank breached its contract with the Goossens?

LO **1**

9. Florida Federal held a mortgage on property owned by Summa Investing Corp. Florida Federal told Summa if it did not pay the $2,505 it owed by April 2 by certified or cashier's check, the entire debt plus collection costs and additional interest would be due. No funds were received by April 2, so Florida Federal began foreclosure proceedings. Summa then tendered an ordinary check for $3,032. Florida Federal returned the check, saying the amount was now $4,373 and the funds must be certified. Summa sent another ordinary check, which was returned. Did Florida Federal reject a valid tender?

LO **3**

10. The parents of Lance Nelson, a minor, hired Challoner McBride to represent Lance in a lawsuit against his school. Lance's mother signed a contingent fee agreement giving McBride a 33⅓ percent fee. Two and a half years later, McBride filed suit. There was a series of dismissed suits because McBride did not follow proper procedure. Five years after being hired, McBride filed a fourth complaint which the trial court dismissed, but a year later the appellate court upheld it. Lance, then of age, fired McBride and hired Daniel Whetter who eight months later settled Lance's claim for $47,400. McBride sued claiming a contractual right to one-third of the settlement. Did she have such a right?

Ethics in Practice

You have learned what a contract is and the consequences for failing to live up to the provisions of a contract. The usual remedy for breach of contract is money damages. But can money truly compensate the nonbreaching party for all the loss suffered? How accurately can loss of potential profit be estimated? What about the stress and inconvenience caused the nonbreaching party by the breach? Would this be difficult to measure in monetary terms? What about the example failing to live up to a promise sets? If an employee finds out that the company is manufacturing appliances with substandard parts so that the appliances will fail much sooner, does the employee have an ethical obligation to do anything?

Summary Cases

CONTRACTS

1. Tim Beverick, an attorney for Koch Power, Inc., was negotiating a contract for the purchase of electricity over a ten year period. He alleged that Koch orally promised that he and another attorney would split a bonus of 10 to 15 percent of the expected savings when the contract was executed. It took Beverick two years to get the contract signed. Koch did not pay the bonus, and Beverick sued for breach of contract and promissory estoppel. He testified there would have had to be a lot of things fall in place to get the contract signed within one year. Did the statute of frauds ban the suit based on an oral promise which could not be completed within one year? [*Beverick v. Koch Power, Inc.,* 186 SW2d 145 (Tex. App.)]

2. Velma Lee Robinson executed a will by which she left most of her property to the Velma Lee and John Harvey Robinson Charitable Foundation. Twelve years later, she executed new estate planning documents which left her estate to her nieces and nephews. Nine months after executing the later will, she suffered the first of a series of strokes. After she died, there was a contest between the two wills. Friends and caregivers testified that Robinson would have been unable to read the later documents and would not have understood them at the time she signed them. She was unable to handle her business and became confused. A physician testified from her medical records that there was a progression of pathological disease processes that was causing her to lose brain cells. Did Robinson have the necessary capacity to execute the later will? [*In re Estate of Robinson,* 140 S.W.3d 782 (Tex. App.)]

3. Jerry Worley worked for Wyoming Bottling. He wanted to get a loan to buy a new car and appliances for his home. He asked Joe DeCora, Wyoming's president, about job security. DeCora told him his job was secure and to take out the loan. Worley checked with his supervisor, Butch Gibson, to make sure his job performance was satisfactory. Gibson told him everything was fine and "to go on about my affairs." Worley took out the loan and the next month Wyoming demoted Worley so he lost the use of a company car and $11,000 in annual pay. Worley sued alleging promissory estoppel. Did these facts state a case for it? [*Worley v. Wyoming Bottling Co., Inc.,* 1 P.3d 615 (Wyo.)]

4. Rodin Properties-Shore Mall loaned Shore Mall Associates, L.P. (SMA) $49 million to refinance the Shore Mall shopping center. A condition of the loan was that SMA get an appraisal that showed the value of the mall was at least $60 million. SMA hired Cushman & Wakefield (C&W) to appraise the property with the agreement that the appraisal was to help SMA get financing and it would be shown to lenders. C&W appraised the mall at $65.5 million, an inflated value. The appraisal understated the mall's competition and overstated its cash flow. Rodin sued C&W for breach of its professional

duty. Was C&W guilty of such a breach? [*Rodin Properties-Shore Mall v. Ullman*, 694 N.Y.S.2d 374 (A.D.)]

5. Big Red Keno, Inc. operated Keno games at its main location and at a satellite location, Brothers Lounge, through a computer link. The computer link to Brothers went down, but an audio link broadcast the winning numbers. Dewey Houghton was at Brothers and heard the winning numbers. He filled out betting slips marked with these numbers. The computer started working, and Houghton placed bets. He received a ticket that listed a game already played even though he had not intended to play that game. The computer reported the ticket as a $200,000 winner. Big Red refused to pay on it, and Houghton sued claiming he had a contract. Did he? [*Houghton v. Big Red Keno, Inc.*, 574 N.W.2d 494 (Neb.)]

6. General Tire decided to terminate Horst Mehlfeldt's employment and through its employee, Ross Bailey, made several proposals to Mehlfeldt in lieu of the benefits provided in his employment contract. Bailey thought Mehlfeldt had accepted a proposal, while Mehlfeldt expected a larger final figure. In drafting a separation agreement, Bailey made a mistake so that General Tire had to pay $494,000—the total Bailey had offered—plus what the employment contract specified. Mehlfeldt thought the larger amount was a result of his request for more money and signed the agreement. General Tire paid him $494,000. When Mehlfeldt asked when he would get the rest, General Tire realized the mistake. It sued alleging mutual mistake. Was it? [*Gen. Tire Inc. v. Mehlfeldt*, 691 N.E.2d 1132 (Ohio App.)]

7. Eggers Consulting Co. employed Brad Moore as a personnel recruiter under an employment contract with a noncompete clause. Moore agreed not to compete in hiring data processing personnel in the continental United States for one year after leaving Eggers. Moore had concentrated on placements in the Midwest. Within a year after leaving Eggers, Moore did compete in that field in South Dakota. When Moore sued Eggers for unpaid wages, Eggers alleged breach of the noncompete clause. Was the noncompete clause valid? [*Moore v. Eggers Consulting Co., Inc.*, 562 N.W.2d 534 (Neb.)]

8. After a divorce decree was entered, Richard Pressley was ordered to pay $20-per-week child support. He made payments directly to his ex-wife. A year later she applied for public assistance and was required to assign her right to support to the Commonwealth of Pennsylvania, Department of Public Welfare. Pressley was never notified of the assignment and continued to make payments to his ex-wife. Four years later the Department of Public Welfare sought to collect the support payments from Pressley. Was Pressley bound on the assignment? [*Commonwealth v. Pressley*, 479 A.2d 1069 (Pa. Super. Ct.)]

9. Babylon Associates contracted to build a water pollution control plant for Suffolk County. It hired Lizza Industries, Inc. as subcontractor to install reinforced "102-inch" pipe. Lizza subcontracted with Clearview Concrete Products Corp. to manufacture the 102-inch pipe. Clearview was convicted of making defective pipe used in the water pollution control plant. The EPA's reduction in its grant for the project and test to determine the soundness of the pipes delayed construction. The contract with Suffolk County provided that the contractor agreed "to be fully and directly responsible . . . for all acts and omissions of his Subcontractors and of any other person employed directly or indirectly by the . . . Subcontractors." In claiming breach of contract, the county alleged it was entitled to recission of the whole contract and

all the money it had paid Babylon. Is it? [*Babylon Associates v. County of Suffolk*, 475 N.Y.S.2d 869 (N.Y. App. Div.)]

10. An underinsured driver injured Sandell and Alan Mostow. They requested arbitration under the underinsured motorist provisions of their policy written by State Farm. Those provisions set limits of "$100,000 each person, $300,000 each accident." "Each Person" meant coverage for bodily injury to one person. "Each Accident" meant "the total amount . . . for all damages due to bodily injury to two or more persons in the same accident." Arbitrators awarded Sandell $190,000 and Alan $100,000. State Farm argued the $300,000 limit was subject to the $100,000 per person limit, so neither could receive more than $100,000. The Mostows argued $100,000 was the limit if one person was injured, but when two or more were injured, $300,000 was the limit. How should the court decide? [*Mostow v. State Farm Ins. Companies*, 645 N.Y.S.2d 421 (Ct. App.)]

11. Ristorante Toscano applied for a license to sell beer and wine. Representatives of the Beacon Hill Civic Association told the restaurant they would oppose the application unless it signed an agreement not to apply for an all-alcohol license in the future. Toscano signed the contract. Nine years later it applied for an all-alcohol license. The association sued for breach of contract. Should it succeed? [*Beacon Hill Civic v. Ristorante Toscano*, 662 N.E.2d 1015 (Mass.)]

12. McLeish Ranch signed an agreement to list land for sale with Reinhold Schauer. The agreement stated the terms would be "cash upon delivery of deed. Sale includes one-half of the mineral rights, oil, gas." Erwin Grossman signed a "contract for sale" to purchase the land for the full price in the listing agreement, subject to financing, and stating coal and gravel were included minerals. The ranch would not sell the land. Grossman sued for specific performance alleging the listing agreement constituted an offer to sell that was accepted by Grossman's signing of the "contract for sale." Was there a contract? [*Grossman v. McLeish Ranch*, 291 N.W.2d 427 (N.D.)]

Personal Property

PART

3

Intangible personal property is covered in Chapter 14. The most personal kind of intangible personal property is your identity, and its theft, through use of your social security number, bank account, or credit card numbers, is not only frightening, but also difficult to solve. Federal and state governments are addressing the problem through various laws and regulations. For information on this issue, visit http://www.consumer.gov/idtheft

Nature of Personal Property

LEARNING OBJECTIVES

1 Discuss the types of personal property and how it can be acquired.

2 Explain the difference between lost and abandoned property.

3 Define and give examples of a bailment.

4 Distinguish the three types of bailments.

PREVIEW CASE

A van had gone through two fences to the middle of a privately owned field. A police officer arrived five hours later. The van was unlocked and the officer looked for someone inside. Although no one was inside, there was a purse, briefcase, and partially consumed bottle of vodka. Opening the purse, the officer found a wallet, Tanja Rynhart's driver's license and a small bag with a white powdery substance in it. The owner of the field asked to have the van removed so the fences could be repaired. The van was towed, and when Rynhart came to pick it up, she was arrested for possession of cocaine. Rynhart alleged the evidence found as a result of the warrantless search of her van should be excluded. The state argued the search was legal because Rynhart had abandoned her property. Was the van abandoned in the field? Did Rynhart have a right to park her van in the field?

Property
Anything that may be owned

Anything that may be owned is **property**. A person may enter into a contract with another to use property without becoming the owner of the property. The law protects not only the right to own property but also the right to use it. Property includes not only physical things but also such things as bank deposits, notes, and bonds that give the right to acquire physical property or to use such property.

PERSONAL PROPERTY

Personal Property
Movable property; interests less than complete ownership in land or rights to money

Property is frequently classified according to its movability. If it is movable property, it is **personal property**. Thus, clothing, food, TVs, theater tickets, and even house trailers are personal property.

Land is not personal property, but an interest in land less than complete ownership, such as a leasehold, is normally classified as personal property.

LO ❶
Types of personal property

COURT CASE

Facts: When Michael and Judy Kimm were divorced, the court awarded Judy the house subject to Michael's right to 25 percent of the equity, called a lien, when the children became adults or Judy remarried or sold the house. Later, Granse & Associates got a judgment against Michael and filed a notice that it was going to have the sheriff sell the house to pay the judgment. If Michael's interest in the house was personal property, Granse could do that.

Outcome: The court held that even though Michael's lien was on real property, it was not an interest in the land itself. The lien was a claim on the property and personal property.

—Granse & Associates, Inc. v. Kimm,
529 N.W.2d 6 (Minn. App.)

In addition to movable physical property, personal property includes rights to money such as notes, bonds, and all written evidences of debt. Personal property is divided into two classes:

1. Tangible
2. Intangible

Tangible Personal Property

Tangible personal property is personal property that can be seen, touched, and possessed. Tangible personal property includes animals, merchandise, furniture, annual growing crops, clothing, jewelry, and similar items.

Tangible Personal Property
Personal property that can be seen, touched, and possessed

Intangible Personal Property

Intangible personal property consists of evidences of ownership of rights or value. The property itself cannot be touched or seen. Some common forms of intangible personal property include checks, stocks, contracts, copyrights, and savings account certificates.

Intangible Personal Property
Evidences of ownership of rights or value

COURT CASE

Facts: When Elizabeth H. Plummer died, her will left her tangible personal property to her brother, Paul Higgins, and sister-in-law, Adelaide Higgins. All property not left to specific persons was left to eight charities. In her safe deposit box were found 240 gold coins—57 Kruggerands and 183 Canadian maple leaf coins. The executors believed the coins were intangible personal property because they were purchased for investment.

Outcome: The court said the coins could be felt and touched, thus they were tangible property. They went to the Higginses, not the charities.

—Prince v. Higgins, 572 So. 2d 1217 (Ala.)

METHODS OF ACQUIRING PERSONAL PROPERTY

The title to personal property may be acquired by purchase, will, descent, gift, accession, confusion, and creation.

Purchase

Purchase
Ownership by payment

Ownership most commonly occurs through **purchase**. The buyer pays the seller, and the seller conveys the property to the buyer.

Will

The owner of property may convey title to another by will. Title does not transfer by will until the person who made the will dies and appropriate judicial proceedings have taken place.

Descent

When a person dies without leaving a will, that person dies intestate. The person's heirs acquire title to the personal property according to the laws existing in the decedent's state of residence.

Gift
Transfer without consideration

Donor
Person who makes a gift

Donee
Person who receives a gift

Gift

A **gift** is a transfer made without consideration in return. The person making a gift is called the **donor**. The person receiving the gift is called the **donee**. In order to have a valid gift, the donor must have the intention to make the gift, and there must be a delivery of the property being given to the donee.

COURT CASE

Facts: David Chiaro sued his wife, Thecia, for divorce. She claimed the apartment in which they lived during their marriage was a gift to them from David's parents. No stock certificates for the apartment were delivered to David and Thecia, but they voted the unit's stock shares at co-op board meetings, and at some meetings, David's father had voted the shares by proxies signed by David and Thecia. They had made expensive renovations with the parent's knowledge.

Outcome: The court stated that there was an intent to make a gift and delivery.

—*Chiaro v. Chiaro*, 623 N.Y.S.2d 312 (A.D.)

Accession

Accession
Adding property of another

Accession is the acquiring of property by means of the addition of personal property of another. If materials owned by two people are combined to form one product, the person who owned the major part of the materials owns the product.

Confusion

Confusion
Inseparable mixing of goods of different owners

Confusion is the mixing of the personal property of different owners so that the parts belonging to each owner cannot be identified and separated. Grain, lumber, oil, and coal are examples of the kinds of property susceptible to confusion. The property, belonging to different owners, may be mixed by common consent, by accident, or by the willful act of some wrongdoer.

When confusion of the property occurs by common consent or by accident, each party will be deemed the owner of a proportionate part of the mass. If the confusion is willful, the title to the total mass passes to the innocent party, unless it can be clearly proven how much of the property of the one causing the confusion was mingled with that of the other person.

ETHICAL POINT

Why do you suppose a willful confusion results in title passing to the innocent party? Is this result based on the principles of ethics?

COURT CASE

Facts: ANR agreed with Coteau Properties Company to buy coal reserves for a royalty of 40 cents per ton of mined coal. Eight years later, this agreement was amended so that Dakota Coal Company agreed to buy future coal reserves and limited ANR's royalty to coal reserves already acquired. As a result, the Freedom Mine contained coal on which ANR was entitled to a royalty and coal on which it was not entitled to a royalty. Coteau would record the amount of royalty coal and non-royalty coal mined and commingle this identical coal in handling it. The coal was sold to four end users including Basin Electric Power Cooperative. Prior to the agreement limiting ANR's royalty, Basin had prepaid ANR $40 million as royalty on coal from ANR's reserves delivered to Basin. Because Coteau commingled the coal, the parties needed to determine how much royalty

coal was delivered to Basin and was therefore exempt from royalty payments. Coteau figured all coal in the mixture sold to Basin was royalty coal. ANR alleged because of the confusion, royalty coal should be proportioned to each of the four end users.

Outcome: The court held that a consequence of the confusion was that the contributors of the commingled mass were tenants in common. A tenancy in common implied the royalty coal was an undivided proportion of the commingled coal delivered to each of the end users. The royalty was proportioned.

—*Basin Elec. Power Co-op. v. ANR Western Coal Development Co.,* **105 F.3d 417 (8th Cir.)**

Creation

One may acquire personal property by **creation**. This applies to inventions, paintings, musical compositions, books, artwork, trade secrets, and other intellectual productions. This novel and unique property is called **intellectual property** because it is produced by human innovation and creativity. The law recognizes the value of this property and gives its creator title for a period of years through patents and copyrights. This property also can be protected by trademark and trade secret protection.

The one who first applies for and obtains a patent gets title to the invention. Creation does not give absolute title; it gives only the right to obtain absolute title by means of a patent, which protects the creator for 17 years.

Songs, books, and other compositions fixed in any tangible medium of expression are protected by copyright from their creation. A copyright gives the owner the exclusive right to reproduce, copy, perform, or display the work or authorize another to do so. The only exceptions involve teaching, research, or scholarship. Although the copyright provides protection from the time of creation of the work, the copyright must be registered for the owner to sue for infringement. Copyrights protect authors for their lifetime plus 70 years, as of January 1, 1978.

The Internet has allowed the sharing of huge amounts of information, but it also allows individuals to violate copyright law by quickly and easily copying and

Creation
Bringing property into being

Intellectual Property
Property produced by human innovation and creativity

distributing huge amounts intellectual property illegally. This is a serious problem for owners of intellectual property as billions of computer files have been shared each month, and many of these are copyrighted files. Recording companies and artists as well as movie companies have sued to try to stop the illegal sharing of copyrighted material, but the problem is a global one.

C O U R T   C A S E

Facts: Grokster, Ltd. and StreamCast Networks, Inc. distributed free software that allowed computer users to share files by means of peer-to-peer networks allowing users' computers to communicate directly with each other. Because almost 90 percent of the files available for sharing were copyrighted, software users mainly employed it to share copyrighted music and video files without permission of the copyright owners. Grokster and StreamCast knew their software was used to download copyrighted material and encouraged that use. The companies sold advertising that appeared on the computer screens of users of the software while downloading. Thus, the more downloading that occurred, the greater the companies' revenue. A group of movie studios and other copyright holders sued them.

Outcome: Grokster and StreamCast aimed to cause third-party copyright infringement and profit from it by distributing their software. The court held they could be held liable for the infringement of third parties.

—Metro-Goldwyn-Mayer Studios Inc. v. Grokster, Ltd., 545 U.S. 913

Lost and Abandoned Property

The difference between abandoned and lost property lies in the intention of the owner to part with title to it. Property becomes **abandoned** when the owner actually discards it with no intention of reclaiming it.

A person who discovers and takes possession of property that has been abandoned and that has never been reclaimed by the owner acquires a right thereto. The finder of abandoned goods has title to them and thus has an absolute right to possession. The prior owner, however, must have relinquished ownership completely.

PREVIEW CASE REVISITED

Facts: A van had gone through two fences to the middle of a privately owned field. A police officer arrived five hours later. The van was unlocked and the officer looked for someone inside. While no one was inside, there was a purse, briefcase, and partially consumed bottle of vodka. Opening the purse, the officer found a wallet, Tanja Rynhart's driver's license and a small bag with a white powdery substance in it. The owner of the field asked to have the van removed so the fences could be repaired. The van was towed, and when Rynhart came to pick it up, she was arrested for possession of cocaine. Rynhart alleged the evidence found as a result of the warrantless search of her van should be excluded. The state argued the search was legal because Rynhart had abandoned her property.

Outcome: By leaving her van and purse at an accident scene without any indication she intended to return, Rynhart had abandoned them, and the search was legal.

—State v. Rynhart, 125 P.3d 938 (Utah)

A number of states have enacted the Uniform Disposition of Unclaimed Property Act. This law provides that holders of property that the law presumes is abandoned must turn over the property to the state.

Property is considered to be **lost** when the owner, through negligence or accident, unintentionally leaves it somewhere.

The finder of lost property has a right of possession against all but the true owner as long as the finder has not committed a wrong of some kind. No right of possession exists against the true owner except in instances when the owner cannot be found through reasonable diligence on the part of the finder and certain statutory requirements are fulfilled.

Lost Property
Property unintentionally left with no intention to discard

COURT CASE

Facts: Charles and Rosa Nelson and then their only child, Opal, lived in a house for 60 years. After Opal died, the representative of her estate abandoned the property because of problems with its title. The county bought it at a tax sale and sold it to Selma United Methodist Church. The church tore down the house and garage and found $24,500 in paper money and coins buried in tin cans and glass jars. Ruth Ritz and other heirs of Charles, Rosa, and Opal claimed the money. The court had to decide whether the money was lost or abandoned.

Outcome: While the real estate had been abandoned, the court said the representative would not have meant to abandon the money. A desire to preserve rather than abandon the money could be inferred from the fact that it was found in tins and jars.

—*Ritz v. Selma United Methodist Church,*
467 N.W.2d 266 (Iowa)

In a few cases, the courts have held that if any employee finds property in the course of employment, the property belongs to the employer. Also, if property is mislaid, not lost, then the owner of the premises has first claim against all but the true owner. This especially applies to property left on trains, airplanes, in restaurants, and in hotels.

BAILMENTS

The transfer of possession, but not the title, of personal property by one party, usually the owner, to another party is called a **bailment**. The transfer is on condition that the same property will be returned or appropriately accounted for either to the owner or to a designated person at a future date. The person who gives up possession, the **bailor**, is usually the owner of the property. The **bailee** accepts possession of the property but not the title.

Some typical transactions resulting in a bailment include:

1. A motorist leaving a car with the garage for repairs.
2. A family storing its furniture in a warehouse.
3. A student borrowing a tuxedo to wear to a formal dance.
4. A hunter leaving a pet with a friend for safekeeping while going on an extended hunting trip.

LO ❸
Nature and examples of bailment

Bailment
Transfer of possession of personal property on condition property will be returned

Bailor
Person who gives up possession of bailed property

Bailee
Person in possession of bailed property

C O U R T   C A S E

Facts: At an amusement park operated by Sports Complex, Inc., Tabitha Golt bought and used tickets to drive a go-cart. The driver of another go-cart drove into Tabitha's. She was severely injured. She sued Sports alleging it had a mutual-benefit bailment with her.

Outcome: The court stated that the arrangement constituted a bailment. Once the driver began to drive a go-cart, Sports had no mechanism to stop the cart, so it was in the possession of the driver.

—*Golt by Golt v. Sports Complex, Inc.,*
644 A.2d 989 (Super. Ct. Del.)

THE BAILMENT AGREEMENT

A true bailment is based on and governed by a contract, express or implied, between the bailor and the bailee. When a person checks a coat upon entering a restaurant, nothing may be said, but the bailment is implied by the acts of the two parties. A bailment can be created by the conduct of the parties, whether spoken or written.

C O U R T   C A S E

Facts: To obtain information for a divorce action, Aegis Investigative Group put an electronic tracking device on a client's wife's car. When the wife found the device she had the Nashville police remove it as part of a staking investigation. The police held the device as potential evidence. Aegis sued the police for failure to return the device.

Outcome: The court said that the police department was a bailee under an implied bailment.

—*Aegis Investigative Group v. Metropolitan Govt. of Nashville and Davidson County,*
98 S.W.3d 159 (Tenn. Ct. App.)

DELIVERY AND ACCEPTANCE

A bailment can be established only if delivery occurs accompanied by acceptance of personal property. The delivery and acceptance may be actual or constructive. Actual delivery and acceptance results when the goods themselves are delivered and accepted. When no physical delivery of the goods occurs, constructive delivery and acceptance results when control over the goods is delivered and accepted.

C O U R T   C A S E

Facts: Roger Eddy contracted with Lear, Inc. to transport some equipment in two shipments. After the first shipment was delivered, Eddy asked Lear to deliver the second shipment to a different city. He also asked Lear to store the equipment until he decided on a destination for it. Eddy never gave Lear a destination, and eight months later Lear sued for storing the equipment. Eddy examined the equipment and found it was demolished. He alleged breach of a bailment.

Outcome: The judge ruled that Eddy made a valid claim of a bailment. Although Lear did not normally store equipment, once it accepted custody of the second shipment and agreed to store it, the requirements for a bailment were met.

—*Lear, Inc. v. Eddy,* 749 A.2d 971 (Pa. Super.)

A **constructive bailment** arises when someone finds and takes possession of lost property. The owner does not actually deliver the property to the finder, but the law holds this to be a bailment. A constructive bailment also can occur when property of one person is washed ashore. The finder becomes a bailee if some overt act of control over the property occurs.

Constructive Bailment
Bailment imposed when a person controls lost property

RETURN OF THE BAILED PROPERTY

In some cases, a bailment may exist when the recipient does not return the actual goods.

In the case of fungible goods, such as wheat, a bailment exists if the owner expects to receive a like quantity and quality of goods. If the goods are to be processed in some way, a bailment arises if the product made from the original goods is to be returned.

When a consignment exists, the property may be sold by the consignee and not returned to the consignor. Finally, when property is left for repair, the property returned should be repaired and therefore not be identical to the property left. In each case, a bailment arises although the identical property is not returned.

COURT CASE

Facts: Fred Peterson asked Nathan Shay to sell some jewelry. Shay was in business as a jeweler and picked up the jewelry at Peterson's house. He gave Peterson a receipt listing the items and an estimated value for each. He wrote at the bottom of the receipt, "To be sold at the agreed prices above." Two days later, Peterson told Shay to return the jewelry, but one item had been stolen. Peterson sued his insurance company for the loss. The company denied liability claiming the jewelry had been sold to Shay and was not owned by Peterson when it was stolen.

Outcome: The court held that the transaction was a bailment because any unsold jewelry was to be returned to Peterson.

—Employers Casualty Co. v. Peterson,
609 S.W.2d 579 (Tex. Civ. App.)

TYPES OF BAILMENTS

The three types of bailments include:

LO ❹
Types of bailments

1. Bailments for the sole benefit of the bailor.
2. Bailments for the sole benefit of the bailee.
3. Mutual-benefit bailments.

Bailments for the Sole Benefit of the Bailor

If one holds another's personal property only for the benefit of the owner, a bailment for the sole benefit of the bailor exists. This occurs when a person takes care of a pet for a vacationing friend. The bailee receives no benefits or compensation.

Such a bailment arises when a person asks a friend to store some personal property. For example, a friend may keep a piano until the owner finds a larger apartment. The friend may not play the piano or otherwise receive any benefits of ownership during the bailment. The bailee may only use the property if the use will benefit or preserve it.

A constructive bailment is a bailment for the sole benefit of the bailor. The loser is the bailor, and the finder is the bailee. In a bailment for the sole benefit of the bailor, most states hold that the bailee need exercise slight care and is liable only for gross negligence with respect to the property.

COURT CASE

Facts: When Jerry and Susan Moore were divorced, the court awarded Susan 10 horses and all the sheep and lambs on their ranch. Jerry got the ranch, and because Susan had no place to keep the livestock, she left it there. Seven months later, Jerry sued for feed and storage costs. Although Jerry fed, watered, and cared for Susan's livestock as well as he did his own, Susan alleged her livestock did not receive proper care and asked for damages.

Outcome: Because Susan left her livestock on Jerry's ranch without his consent, the arrangement was a bailment for the sole benefit of the bailor. Jerry exercised reasonable care and was not liable.

—*Moore v. Moore*, 835 P.2d 1148 (Wyo.)

Bailments for the Sole Benefit of the Bailee

If the bailee holds and uses another's personal property, and the owner of the property receives no benefit or compensation, a bailment for the sole benefit of the bailee exists. This type of bailment arises when someone's personal property is borrowed.

COURT CASE

Facts: Wendy Jeeninga let Laura Dado borrow her car so that Dado could drive to her home and check to see that her home was locked. While driving the car, Dado was involved in an accident and the car was damaged. When Dado did not pay for the damage to the car, Jeeninga sued her.

Outcome: The court said the arrangement between Dado and Jeeninga was a bailment, and Dado was liable for her negligence with regard to the bailed property.

—*Dado v. Jeeninga*, 743 N.E.2d 291(Ind. App.)

The bailee must exercise great care over the property. However, any loss or damage due to no fault of the bailee falls upon the owner. If Petras borrows Walker's diamond ring to wear to a dance and is robbed on the way to the dance, the loss falls on Walker, the owner, as long as Petras was not negligent.

The bailee must be informed of any known defects in the bailed property. If the bailee is injured by reason of such a defect, the bailor who failed to inform the bailee is liable for damages.

Mutual-Benefit Bailments

Most bailments exist for the mutual benefit of both the bailor and the bailee. Some common bailments of this type include: a TV left to be repaired; laundry and dry cleaning contracts; and the rental of personal property, such as an automobile or furniture. The bailor of rented property must furnish safe property, not just inform the bailee of known defects.

In mutual-benefit bailments, the bailee renders a service and charges for the service. This applies to all repair jobs, laundry, dry cleaning, and storage bailments. The bailee has a lien against the bailed property for the charges. If these charges are not paid after a reasonable time, the bailee may advertise and sell the property for the charges. Any money remaining after paying expenses and the charges must be turned over to the bailor.

A bailee rendering services may receive a benefit other than a fee or monetary payment. For example, a skating rink may offer to check shoes for its customers without charging for the service. A mutual-benefit bailment exists. The customer (bailor) receives storage service and the skating rink (bailee) gains the benefit of a neater, safer customer area.

In mutual-benefit bailments, the standard of care required of the bailee for the property is reasonable care under the circumstances. Such care means the degree of care that a reasonable person would exercise in order to protect the property from harm. The bailee is liable for negligence.

COURT CASE

Facts: Felice Jasphy took three fur coats to Cedar Lane Furs for cleaning and storage. Three years earlier the coats had been appraised at $18,995. Above the signature line on the receipt Jasphy signed was the statement, "I . . . agree that Cedar Lane Furs liability for loss or damage from any cause whatsoever, including their own negligence . . . is limited to the declared valuation." Jasphy was not told of the limitation, asked for a value for the furs, or given room on the receipt to indicate a valuation. The next day a fire caused by an iron left plugged in overnight at Cedar destroyed all the coats that had not been put in the vault. When she was not reimbursed for her loss, Jasphy sued.

Outcome: The court said Cedar was liable for its negligence in failing to put the coats in the vault and unplug the iron.

—Jasphy v. Osinsky,
834 A.2d 426 (N.J. Super. A.D.)

Special Mutual-Benefit Bailments

A mutual-benefit bailment includes the deposit of personal property as security for some debt or obligation. Tangible property left as security, such as livestock, a radio, or an automobile, is a **pawn**. Intangible property left as security, such as notes, bonds, or stock certificates, is a **pledge**.

CONVERSION OF BAILED PROPERTY BY THE BAILEE

Not being the owner of the property, a bailee normally has no right to convert the property. **Conversion** is the unauthorized exercise of ownership rights over another's property. Thus, the bailee may not sell, lease, or even use the bailed property as security for a loan, and one who purchases such property from a bailee ordinarily does not get good title to it.

Pawn
Tangible personal property left as security for a debt

Pledge
Intangible property serving as security for a debt

Conversion
Unauthorized exercise of ownership rights

However, when the purpose of the bailment is to have the property sold and the proceeds remitted to the bailor, the bailee has the power to sell all goods regardless of any restriction upon the right to sell, unless the buyer knows of the restriction.

A bailor may mislead an innocent third person into believing that the bailee owns the bailed property. In this situation, the bailee may convey good title.

QUESTIONS

1. How does tangible personal property differ from intangible personal property?
2. **a.** What is a gift?
   b. What is necessary to make a valid gift?
3. Who owns the product formed by the combination of materials owned by two people?
4. How has the Internet made problems for owners of intellectual property?
5. What is the difference between lost and abandoned property?
6. When does a bailment occur?
7. Can a bailment exist when the recipient of the property does not return the actual goods? Explain.
8. What standard of care is required of a bailee in a bailment for the sole benefit of the bailor?
9. Explain the types of special mutual-benefit bailments in which property is left as security.
10. Under what circumstances does a bailee have the power to sell bailed goods?

CASE PROBLEMS

LO ❷

1. While staying at a Comfort Inn, Alex Franks found $14,200 in a dresser drawer in his room. The bills were wrapped tightly with masking tape, like a brick, with some bills showing. There were 46 $100 bills and 480 $20 bills. All the bills faced in the same direction. Franks notified the hotel manager who notified police. The city held the money. Franks sued claiming ownership of it. Should he recover the money?

LO ❸, ❹

2. After investigating Darrell Pelvit for several months, agents of the Eastern Montana Drug Task Force (EMDTF) without a warrant searched the trash in garbage cans along a public alley behind Pelvit's house. The agents removed an opaque trash bag from one of the unlocked cans and found pseudoephedrine boxes and empty naptha cans inside. Naptha is a solvent used in the manufacture of methamphetamine. Finding these items was the basis for the issuance of a search warrant covering Pelvit's home, pickup, and boat. Drug related evidence was found during the resulting search. Pelvit argued the evidence should be excluded because the search of his garbage cans was illegal. The state claimed Pelvit abandoned his trash so he had no expectation of privacy in it and the search of it was therefore legal. Was the trash abandoned?

LO ❸

3. Mark Hadfield's car was parked on private property without permission of the owner of the property. Gilchrist Towing Company had towed the car to its storage facility. There was a chain link fence around the facility and an employee

present, but at some distance from the storage area. When Hadfield came to pick up his car, he paid towing and storage fees and went to find his car. It had been extensively vandalized. The car never functioned properly afterward. Hadfield sued Gilchrist for the damages. Should Gilchrist be liable?

4. Prior to selling a piece of real estate, Mary Campbell reviewed the documents presented by the real estate agent with her daughter and son-in-law, Trula and Randall Walker. Campbell signed the deed and handed all the documents, including a promissory note to be signed by the buyer, to Trula and said, "Here, these are yours." After the buyer signed everything, he mailed them to a post office box in Campbell's and Trula's names. Walker handed the signed promissory note to Trula and said, "Here, this is yours." The buyer's payments were sent to the post office box and deposited in a bank account in Campbell's and Trula's names. The account was the only one Trula had and she wrote all her checks out of it. After Campbell died, Trula's sister alleged Campbell had not given Trula the note. Was there a gift?   LO ❶

5. Richard Gray bought a ticket for an "Alpine Slide" ride owned by Snow King. The ride involved routing a wheeled bobsled down a winding, trough-shaped slide. Gray was directed to choose a sled. As he went down the slide the sled hit a dip in the slide and became airborne. Gray suffered back injuries from the force of the landing. Gray sued alleging that the transaction was a bailment. Was it?   LO ❸

6. The city of St. Peters leased restaurant space to Art and Greg Scarato. They assigned the lease to John and Thelma Hill who assigned it to Joe Vallero. Each assignee purchased equipment and inventory from the assignor by means of a note and agreed to assume the responsibilities of the original lease. Vallero defaulted on his note to the Hills. He closed the restaurant and gave the keys to the city. He was $21,000 in default on rent. The lease provided that before surrendering the premises the "tenant had to remove all its personal property." Any personal property left would be deemed abandoned. The city sued the lessees and all the assignees. The Hills claimed the personal property, and the city alleged it was abandoned. Decide the case.   LO ❷

7. The Elliott System, Inc. hired Fred Adams and promised he would be enrolled in its health insurance plan when he completed three months' work. Adams worked for the required time, but Elliott failed to enroll him. A year later Adams suffered kidney failure requiring hospitalization. Aetna, Elliott's health insurer, refused to cover Adams's expenses; the expenses would have been covered if Adams had been enrolled. Elliott had an insurance policy covering liability for injury to tangible property. Adams sued Elliott, saying loss of the health insurance policy was loss of tangible property. Is health insurance tangible or intangible property?   LO ❶

8. Amoco Oil Co. manufactured oil for Ford Tractor, Nissan, and Massey-Ferguson and packaged it in cans with the labels of those companies. Amoco contracted with American Fuel & Supply Co., Inc. (AFSCO) to warehouse these oils and deliver them at Amoco's direction. The contract prohibited AFSCO from borrowing or selling any of this oil. Under the contract, Amoco delivered oil to AFSCO. Amoco took orders; directed AFSCO to deliver the oil and paid it for storage and delivery; and the recipients of the oil paid Amoco. AFSCO filed for bankruptcy and its creditors claimed the arrangement with Amoco was a consignment, and thus they could claim the oil. Amoco claimed it was a bailment. What was it?   LO ❸

LO ❶

9. When Gabriel Schlosser pled guilty to a crime, he agreed to make restitution of $55,000 to Phyllis Timmins. Three years later, Timmins asked the department of corrections to seize any money in Schlosser's prison account and pay it toward the restitution. The law exempted personal property to the value of $1,000. Should any of Schlosser's account be exempt?

LO ❸

10. By written agreement, Clifton Taylor took possession of a Buick from Buick dealer Mark Singleton Buick, Inc. for 48 months. The agreement obligated Taylor to make monthly payments, pay the taxes and insurance, make all necessary repairs, and return the car at the expiration of the agreement. The agreement preserved the warranties made by the manufacturer "or its dealers." Singleton repaired and serviced the car numerous times, but after 15 months refused to make any further repairs. The court had to decide if the transaction was a sale or a lease and whether Singleton had any obligation to repair the car. You decide.

Special Bailments

LEARNING OBJECTIVES

❶ Explain what a carrier does and name the two categories of carriers.

❷ Identify the exceptions to the normal rule of a common carrier being an insurer of the safety of goods.

❸ Discuss the difference between hotelkeepers and boardinghouse keepers, explaining the special duties and liabilities of hotelkeepers.

PREVIEW CASE

→ When a bar closed at 2 A.M., Maurice Gardin told his brother, Alfred, he was going out with a woman with whom he had been dancing. She said she had to pick up something and asked the brothers to follow her to the University Inn parking lot. She seemed to go into a motel room. Two men told the brothers to leave. An argument began and when Alfred tried to walk home, several men from the bar blocked his way. Alfred ran to the locked motel lobby and asked the night manager, Mike Patel, to let him in. Patel refused, but called the police. One of the men stabbed Alfred several times. What was Alfred doing at the motel? Did he intend to register? Does everyone have a duty to help in this situation?

There are several types of mutual-benefit bailments in which the bailor, under the common law, is held to a higher than normal standard of care for the bailed property. These bailments, sometimes called *extraordinary bailments*, include common carriers and hotelkeepers.

CARRIERS

A **carrier** engages in the business of transporting either goods or persons, or both. A carrier of goods is a bailee. Because a carrier charges a fee for such service, the bailment exists for the mutual benefit of both parties.

Carrier
Transporter of goods, people, or both

Classification of Carriers

LO ❶
Categories of carriers

Carriers are usually classified into two groups:

1. Private carriers
2. Common carriers

Private Carriers

Private Carrier
Carrier that transports under special arrangements for a fee

A **private carrier**, for a fee, undertakes to transport goods or persons. It transports only under special instances and special arrangements and may refuse service that is unprofitable. The usual types of private carriers are trucks, moving vans, ships, and delivery services. A carrier owned by the shipper, such as a truck from a fleet owned and operated by an industrial firm for transporting its own products, is a private carrier.

Private carriers' contracts for transporting goods are mutual-benefit bailments, and the general law of bailments governs them. They are liable only for loss from the failure to exercise ordinary care. By contract, a private carrier may further limit liability for loss to the goods.

COURT CASE

Facts: Cook Tractor Co., Inc. bought, sold, and transported large farm and construction equipment. Every month except July it held a public equipment auction that about 500 people attended. During the auctions, Cook announced that it could be hired to transport equipment for buyers. It had a fleet of trucks it used for hauling purchased and other equipment for its customers. It negotiated its contracts, charging per mile for hauling and sometimes per hour for loading. It had no hauling income in July. It did not advertise as a hauler of goods, but its employees regularly hauled equipment, using trucks with the company's name and phone number on the side. Cook bought motor vehicle parts and did not pay sales tax on them because state law exempted parts used on motor vehicles engaged as common carriers. The state director of revenue alleged Cook was not a common carrier and assessed sales tax.

Outcome: The court held that Cook was not a common carrier since it did not advertise itself to the general public as a carrier or offer its services without discrimination at an approved rate.

—*Cook Tractor Co., Inc. v. Director of Revenue*,
187 S.W.3d 870 (Mo.)

Common Carriers

Common Carrier
One that undertakes to transport without discrimination all who apply for service

Consignor
One who ships by common carrier

Consignee
One to whom goods are shipped

Bill of Lading
Receipt and contract between consignor and carrier

A **common carrier** undertakes to transport goods or persons, without discrimination, for all who apply for that service. The goods to be transported must be proper, and facilities must be available for transport. One who ships goods by a common carrier is called the **consignor**; the one to whom the goods are shipped is called the **consignee**; and the receipt and contract between the carrier and the consignor is called a **bill of lading**.

A common carrier must serve without discrimination all who apply. If it fails to do so, it is liable for any damages resulting from such a refusal. A common carrier may, however, refuse service because the service is not one for which it is properly equipped. For example, an express company does not have to accept lumber for transportation. Also, a common carrier may refuse service if its equipment is inadequate to accommodate customers in excess of the normal demands. A common carrier of persons is not required to transport (1) any person who requires unusual attention, such as an invalid, unless that person is accompanied by an attendant; (2) any person who intends or is likely to cause harm to the carrier or the passengers; or (3) any person who is likely to be offensive to passengers, such as an intoxicated person.

The usual types of common carriers of persons are trains, buses, airplanes, ships, and subways. Common carriers are public monopolies and are subject to regulations as to their prices, services, equipment, and other operational policies. This public regulation is in lieu of competition as a determinant of their prices and services.

LIABILITY OF COMMON CARRIERS OF GOODS

LO **2**
When common carrier is not an insurer

Although common carriers of goods and common carriers of persons are alike in that they must serve all who apply, they differ sharply in their liability for loss. Common carriers of goods are insurers of the safety of the transported goods and are liable for loss or damage regardless of fault, unless the carrier can prove the loss arises from:

1. Acts of God
2. Acts of a public authority
3. Inherent nature of the goods
4. Acts of the shipper
5. Acts of a public enemy

These exceptions do not excuse the carrier if the carrier failed to safeguard the goods from harm.

Acts of God

The carrier is not liable for unusual natural occurrences such as floods, snowstorms, tornadoes, lightning, or fire caused by lightning, as these are considered acts of God. Normal weather such as a rainstorm is not.

Acts of a Public Authority

An act of a public authority occurs if public officials seize illicit goods, or if health officials seize goods that are a menace to health. The carrier is not liable for such loss.

Inherent Nature of the Goods

The carrier is not liable for damage due to the inherent nature of the goods, such as decay of vegetables, fermentation or evaporation of liquids, and death of livestock as a result of natural causes or the fault of other animals.

Acts of the Shipper

Acts of the shipper that can cause loss include misdirection of the merchandise, failure to indicate fragile contents, and improper packing. If improper packing is noticeable, the carrier should refuse to accept the goods because it is still liable for damage. If improper packing is latent and cannot be noticed on ordinary observation, the shipper, not the carrier, will be liable because of the improper packing.

COURT CASE

Facts: American Welding & Tank Co. employees loaded propane tanks of various sizes on a Thom's Transport Co. (TTC) flatbed trailer. They put two 1,000-gallon tanks in indentations in the floor of the trailer; they put boards across the top of the tanks and put two more 1,000-gallon ones onto the boards. The outsides of the top tanks were "chocked" and a board was nailed along the outside of each of them. All the tanks were strapped in place. TTC's driver, Jimmy Willis, inspected and accepted the load. While driving he stopped several times to check the load. When he arrived at the Dead River Co. he met an employee, John Smart, who offered to help unload. Willis told Smart to secure boom straps to a tank and get out of the way for unloading. As Willis lowered the first tank, the next tank rolled toward Smart. In avoiding it, Smart fell off the flatbed. He died from the injuries. His widow, Joan, sued both American and TTC.

Outcome: The court held that American would be liable if the defect in loading was latent and concealed and could not be discovered by ordinary observation.

—Smart v. American Welding & Tank Co., Inc.,
836 A.2d 570 (N.H.)

Acts of a Public Enemy

Organized warfare or border excursions of foreign bandits constitute acts of a public enemy. Mobs, strikers, and rioters are not classified as public enemies in interpreting this exclusion.

Contractual Limitations on Liability

A common carrier may attempt to limit or escape the extraordinary liability imposed upon it by law, often by a contract between the shipper and the carrier. As the written evidence of the contract, the bill of lading sets out the limitations on the carriers' liability. Because the shipper does not have any direct voice in the preparation of the bill of lading, the law requires every carrier to have its printed bill of lading form approved by a government agency before adoption. This restricts the way in which liability can be limited by the bill of lading.

In addition to uniform limitations set out in the printed form of a bill of lading, additional limitations may be added that the shipper and the carrier may agree upon. The Federal Bills of Lading Act governs this matter as to interstate shipments, and the Uniform Commercial Code controls with respect to intrastate shipments. In general, the limitations upon the carrier's liability permitted by these acts fall into the following classes:

1. A carrier may limit its loss by agreement to a specified sum or to a specified percentage of the value of the goods. However, a carrier must give the shipper the choice of shipping at lower rates subject to the limited liability or at a higher rate without limitation of liability.

2. Most states permit carriers to exempt themselves from liability because of certain named hazards. The most common named hazards include fire, leakage, breakage, spoilage, and losses due to riots, strikes, mobs, and robbers. Some states specifically prohibit an exemption for loss by fire. These exemptions must be specifically enumerated in the bill of lading or shipper's receipt. The exemptions are not effective if the loss is due to carrier negligence.

COURT ✴ CASE

Facts: Rational Software hired Sterling Corporation to move a computer disk array. The "computer" weighed 1,540 pounds and was worth $250,000. During the previous four years, Rational had hired Sterling to move items more than 200 times. Each time Sterling had issued a bill of lading that a Rational employee had signed. The bills of lading contained a limitation of liability of $.60 per pound immediately followed by a space for Rational to declare a higher value. The limitation also was in Sterling's rate tariff filed with the appropriate state agency. Sterling orally informed Rational of the limitation. The Rational employee in charge of the move acknowledged he knew of the limitation. Sterling broke the computer during the move prior to issuing a bill of lading. Rational sued Sterling for the value of the computer.

Outcome: The court held that the parties, through their prior course of dealing, understood and agreed that Sterling's liability would be limited to sixty cents per pound unless Rational declared a higher value.

—Rational Software Corp. v. Sterling Corp., **393 F.3d 276 (1st Cir.)**

3. Delay in transportation of livestock may result in serious losses or extra expense for feed. Most states allow some form of limitation on the carrier's liability if the loss is due to a delay over which the carrier has no control.

In those cases in which the carrier is held liable only for loss due to negligence, the Uniform Commercial Code provides for liability only for ordinary negligence.

Duration of the Special Liability

The carrier's high degree of liability lasts only during transportation. If the goods are delivered to the carrier ready for shipment and are received from the carrier promptly on arrival, the goods are regarded as being transported during the entire transaction.

Carrier as Bailee Before Transportation

Frequently, goods are delivered to the carrier before they are ready for transportation. The carrier is liable only as a mutual-benefit bailee until the goods are ready for transportation.

Carrier as Bailee After Transportation

When the goods arrive at their destination, the consignee has a reasonable time to accept delivery of the goods. Railroads need only place the goods in the freight depot, or, in the case of car lots, set the car on a siding where the consignee can unload the goods. If the consignee does not call for the goods within a reasonable time after being notified by the carrier that the goods have arrived, the carrier is liable only as a mutual-benefit bailee.

Connecting Carriers

The initial carrier and the final, or terminal, carrier are each liable for a common carrier loss occurring on the line of a connecting carrier. Whichever of these carriers has been held liable may then compel the connecting carrier to reimburse it.

Bills of Lading

The bill of lading not only sets forth the contract between the shipper and the carrier, it is a document of title. Transferring a bill of lading may transfer title to the goods described in it to the purchaser. There are two types of bills of lading:

1. Straight, or nonnegotiable, bills of lading
2. Order, or negotiable, bills of lading

Straight Bill of Lading
Contract requiring delivery of shipped goods to consignee only

Straight Bills of Lading. Under a **straight bill of lading** (see Illustration 15–1), the consignee alone is designated as the one to whom the goods are to be delivered. The consignee's rights may be transferred to another, but the third party normally obtains no greater rights than the shipper or the consignee had. However, if the bill of lading contains a recital as to the contents, quantity, or weight of the goods, the carrier is bound to a bona fide transferee as to the accuracy of these descriptions unless the bill of lading itself indicates that the contents of packages are unknown to the carrier.

The assignee should notify the carrier of the assignment when the original consignee sells the goods before receipt. The carrier is justified in delivering goods to the consignee if it has not received notice of assignment.

ILLUSTRATION 15–1 Bill of Lading

21040

ALWAYS LIST HAZARDOUS MATERIALS FIRST IN DESCRIPTION OF ARTICLES COLUMN.

STRAIGHT BILL OF LADING - SHORT FORM - Original-Not Negotiable
RECEIVED, subject to the classification and tariffs in effect on the date of issue of this Original Bill of Lading

NOT to be used for ORDER NOTIFY SHIPMENTS. DATE

BIG BEAR Transfer Company

BIG BEAR TRANSFER COMPANY

NOTE: DRIVER AFIX PRO NUMBER LABEL HERE

(NAME OF CARRIER) (SCAC)

CUSTOMER P.O. NO. ROUTE SHIPPER'S NUMBER

TO: CONSIGNEE on COD Shipments the letters "COD" must appear before consignee's name. FROM: SHIPPER

STREET STREET

(DESTINATION) CITY, STATE, ZIP (ORIGIN) CITY, STATE, ZIP

C.O.D. AMT $ FEE PPD ☐ COL ☐ IS CUSTOMER'S CHECK ACCEPTABLE FOR C.O.D.? YES ☐ NO ☐

NO. SHIPPING UNITS	(X) HM	RATE AND CLASS	KIND OF PACKAGING, DESCRIPTION OF ARTICLES, SPECIAL MARKS AND EXCEPTIONS (LIST HAZARDOUS MATERIALS FIRST)	WEIGHT LBS (Subject to Correcitons)
	◄ TOTAL		TOTAL ►	

NOTE: Where the rate is dependent on value, shippers are required to state specifically in writing the agreed or declared value of the property.
The agreed or declared value of the property is hereby specifically stated by the shipper to be not exceeding
$ ______
per ______

Subject to Section 7 of the conditions, if this shipment is to be delivered to the consignee without recourse on the consignor, the consignor shall sign the following statement:
The carrier shall not make delivery of this shipment without payment of freight and all other lawful charges.

______
(Signature of Consignor

FREIGHT CHARGES
WRITE IN PREPAID OR COLLECT

RECEIVED, subject to the classifications and tariffs in effect on the date of the issue of this Bill of Lading, the property described above in apparent good order, except as noted (contents and condition of contents of packages unknown), marked, consigned and destined as indicated above which said carrier (the word carrier being understood throughout this contract as meaning any person or corporation in possession of the property under the contract) agrees to carry to its usual place of delivery at said destination, if on its route, otherwise to deliver to another carrier on the route to said destination. It is mutally agreed as to each carrier of all or any of, said property over all or any to all the bill of lading terms and conditions in the governing classification on the date of shipment.

Shipper hereby certifies that he is familiar with all the bill of lading terms and conditions in the governing classification and the said terms and conditions are hereby agreed to by the shipper and accepted for himself and his assigns.

This is to certify that the above-named materials are properly classified, described, packaged, marked and labeled, and are in proper condition for transportation according to the applicable regulations of the Department of Transportation	SHIPPER:	BIG BEAR TRANSFER COMPANY	
	PER:	DRIVER	TRAILER
		PIECES	DATE

MARK "X" IN "HM" COLUMN FOR HAZARDOUS MATERIALS.

COURT CASE

Facts: Italian Leather Italy sent shipments of leather skins in a locked, sealed, multi-modal shipping container from Italy to the United States. When the container was unloaded from the ship, Marine Freight issued a receipt/bill of lading specifying the weight and trucked the container from Virginia to North Carolina. When Italian Leather opened the container, 20 percent of the skins were missing.

Outcome: Because a common carrier is liable unless damage is caused by one of the recognized exceptions, the court found Marine Freight liable. It was bound by the weight specified on the bill of lading.

—AIG Europe, S.A. v. M/V MSC Lauren,
940 F. Supp. 925 (E.D. Va.)

Order Bills of Lading. The bill of lading may set forth that the goods are shipped to a designated consignee or order, or merely "to the bearer" of the bill of lading. In such case, the bill of lading is an **order**, or negotiable, **bill of lading** and must be presented to the carrier before the carrier can safely deliver the goods. If the goods are delivered to the named consignee and later a bona fide innocent purchaser of the order bill of lading demands the goods, the carrier is liable to the holder of the bill of lading.

Order Bill of Lading
Contract allowing delivery of shipped goods to bearer

COURT CASE

Facts: Nissho Pacific Corp., a Japanese corporation, ordered hog grease from Amkor Corp. in the United States. Nissho reserved space on Iino Kaiun Kaisha, Ltd.'s ship bound for Kobe, Japan, and Amkor purchased the grease from Swift and Co. Amkor asked Chase Manhattan Bank to finance the sale. Chase agreed if it got a signed mate's receipt issued in its name. Grease was pumped aboard Iino's ship, and on May 8 an order bill of lading was issued showing Nissho as owner. While the ship was en route to Japan, Chase was working on the details of financing,

including receiving a receipt from Swift. It was not until May 26 that Chase wrote Iino claiming to own the goods. Iino replied that upon delivery of the order bill of lading, Iino had released the grease to Nissho. Chase sued.

Outcome: The court said the carrier, Iino, properly delivered the merchandise to the holder when the order bill of lading was presented.

—Chase Manhattan Bank v. Nissho Pacific Corp.,
254 N.Y.S.2d 571 (N.Y. App. Div.)

Common Carriers of Persons

Common carriers of persons have the right to prescribe the place and time of the payment of fares, usually before boarding the plane, train, bus, or other vehicle. They also have the right to prescribe reasonable rules of conduct for transporting passengers. They may stop the vehicle and remove any passenger who refuses to pay the fare or whose conduct offends the other passengers. They also have the right to reserve certain coaches, seats, or space for special classes of passengers, as in the case of first-class seats in the forward cabin of aircraft.

Liability of Common Carriers of Persons

The liability of a carrier for the passengers' safety begins as soon as passengers enter the terminal or waiting platform and does not end until they have left the terminal at the end of the journey. Unlike a common carrier of goods, a common carrier of persons is not an insurer. In most states, a carrier must provide only ordinary care while passengers are in the terminal; however, some states have modified this rule. When passengers board the bus, train, plane, or other vehicle, the highest degree of care consistent with practical operation is required. However, even when the highest degree of care is required, a carrier of persons is only liable if it has been negligent.

COURT CASE

Facts: At around 1 A.M. Joseph Skelton entered the train platform at a Chicago Transit Authority (CTA) station intending to catch the next train. No ticket agent was on duty and a sign stated, "Board Here, Please Pay on Train." He sat and waited. A train passed through without stopping so when he heard a second train he got up to flag it down to make sure it stopped. Standing at the edge of the platform, he leaned over and waved to get the driver's attention. He lost his balance and fell onto the tracks. He was run over by the train and his right arm had to be amputated. Skelton sued the CTA.

Outcome: In this case, the court held that the CTA owed Skelton the highest degree of care because he was a passenger when hit by the train.

—*Skelton v. Chicago Transit Authority,*
573 N.E.2d 1315 (Ill. App.)

Duties of Common Carriers of Persons

A carrier's duties to its passengers consist of:

1. Duty to provide reasonable accommodations and services
2. Duty to provide reasonable protection to its passengers

Duty to Provide Reasonable Accommodations and Services. A carrier is required to furnish adequate and reasonable service. A passenger is not necessarily entitled to a seat; however, the carrier must make a reasonable effort to provide sufficient facilities so that the public can be accommodated, which may be merely standing room. A passenger may make an express reservation that requires the carrier to provide a seat. The carrier must notify the passenger of the arrival of the train, bus, or airplane at the destination and stop long enough to permit the passenger to disembark.

Duty to Provide Reasonable Protection to Its Passengers. Common carriers of passengers need not insure the absolute safety of passengers but must exercise extraordinary care to protect them. Any injury to the passenger by an employee or fellow passengers subjects the carrier to liability for damages, provided the injured passenger is without blame. The vehicle must stop at a safe place for alighting, and passengers must be assisted when necessary for alighting.

Baggage

Baggage
Articles necessary for personal convenience while traveling

Baggage consists of those articles of personal convenience or necessity usually carried by passengers for their personal use at some time during the trip. Articles carried by travelers on similar missions and destinations constitute the test. For example, fishing paraphernalia is baggage for a person who expects to go fishing while away, but not for the ordinary traveler. Any article carried for one who is not a passenger is not baggage. A reasonable amount of baggage may be carried as a part of the cost of the passenger's fare. The carrier may charge extra for baggage in excess of a reasonable amount.

The liability of a common carrier for checked baggage historically was the same as that of a common carrier of goods—an insurer of the baggage with the five exceptions previously mentioned. The liability for baggage retained in the possession of the traveler was only for lack of reasonable care or for willful misconduct of its agents or employees. However, today carriers are allowed to limit their liability for loss of baggage to a fixed maximum amount. This amount will be stated on the ticket. Such limitations are binding on passengers.

COURT CASE

Facts: On the way to her Delta Airlines flight, Felice Lippert took a handbag containing $431,000 worth of jewelry through a Palm Beach International Airport security checkpoint. She placed the bag on the conveyor belt and walked through the archway magnetometer. The alarm sounded and security personnel briefly inspected her. Lippert then discovered her handbag was missing. She sued Delta and Wackenhut, which operated the security checkpoint for Delta. They asserted that the $1,250 limitation of liability, printed on the back of Lippert's ticket,

should apply. It covered "baggage or other property (including carry-on baggage . . . delivered into the custody of [Delta])."

Outcome: The court held that the $1,250 limitation applied because the handbag clearly was delivered into the custody of Delta at the security checkpoint.

—*Wackenhut Corp. v. Lippert*,
609 So. 2d 1304 (Fla.)

HOTELKEEPERS

A **hotelkeeper** regularly engages in the business of offering lodging to all transient persons. The hotelkeeper also may supply food or entertainment, but providing lodging to transients is the primary business.

A person who provides rooms or room and board to permanent lodgers but does not behave as able and willing to accommodate transients is not a hotelkeeper. Such persons are **boardinghouse keepers**, and the laws of hotelkeepers do not apply to them. The owner of a tourist home is not a hotelkeeper if the establishment does not advertise as willing to accommodate all transients who apply. Most people who run hotels and motels are hotelkeepers. A hotel that caters to both permanent residents and transients is a hotelkeeper only with respect to the transients.

Who Are Guests?

To be a **guest** one must be a transient obtaining lodging, not a permanent resident or visitor. One who enters the hotel to attend a ball or other social function, to visit a guest, or to eat dinner is not a guest. A guest need not be a traveler nor come from a distance. A guest might be a person living within a short distance of the hotel who rents a room and remains there overnight.

The relationship of guest and hotelkeeper does not begin until the hotelkeeper receives the person seeking lodging as a guest. The relationship terminates when the guest leaves or makes arrangements for permanent residence at the hotel.

LO ❸
Boardinghouse keeper versus hotelkeeper and special duties of hotelkeeper

Hotelkeeper
One engaged in business of offering lodging to transients

Boardinghouse Keeper
Person in business to supply accommodations to permanent lodgers

Guest
Transient received by hotel for accommodations

PREVIEW CASE REVISITED

Facts: When a bar closed at 2 A.M., Maurice Gardin told his brother, Alfred, he was going out with a woman with whom he had been dancing. She said she had to pick up something and asked the brothers to follow her to the University Inn parking lot. She seemed to go into a motel room. Two men appeared and told the brothers to leave. An argument began and when Alfred tried to walk home, several men from the bar blocked his way. Alfred ran to the locked motel lobby and asked the night manager, Mike Patel, to let him in. Patel refused, but called the police. One of the men stabbed Alfred several times. Alfred sued the motel.

Outcome: Although a hotelkeeper has a duty to protect guests, Alfred was not a guest of the motel. The motel had no duty to protect Alfred.

—*Gardin v. Emporia Hotels, Inc.*, 61 P.3d 732 (Kan. App.)

Duties of a Hotelkeeper

The duties of a hotelkeeper include:

1. To serve all who apply
2. To protect a guest's person
3. To care for the guest's property

Duty to Serve All Who Apply

The basic test of hotelkeepers is that they hold themselves out as willing to serve without discrimination all who request lodging. However, this does not require hotelkeepers to serve someone who is drunk, someone who is criminally violent, someone who is not dressed in a manner required by reasonable hotel regulations applied to all, or when no rooms are available. If a hotel refuses lodging for an improper reason, it is liable for damages, including exemplary damages, to the person rejected.

In addition, a hotel may be liable for discrimination under a civil rights or similar statutory provision and may also be guilty of a crime if a court has issued an injunction prohibiting such discrimination. By virtue of the Federal Civil Rights Act of 1964, neither a hotel nor its concessionaire can discriminate against patrons nor segregate them on the basis of race, color, religion, or national origin. When there has been improper discrimination or segregation, or it is reasonably believed that such action may occur, the federal act authorizes the institution of proceedings in the federal courts for an order to stop such practices.

Duty to Protect a Guest's Person

A hotelkeeper must use reasonable care for the guests' personal safety. The same standard applies to the personal safety of a visitor or a patron of a newsstand or lunchroom.

Reasonable care requires that a hotelkeeper provide fire escapes and also have conspicuous notices indicating directions to the fire escapes. If a fire starts due to no negligence of the hotelkeeper or employees, there is no liability to the guests for their personal injuries unless they can show that the fire was not contained because of a failure to install required fire safety features. In one case, the court held that the hotelkeeper was not liable for the loss of life on the floor where the fire started but was liable for all personal injuries on the four floors to which the fire spread because of the negligence of the hotel.

If a hotelkeeper knows of prior criminal acts on or near the hotel premises, additional security measures may be required. However, the hotelkeeper is not liable if the guest's behavior increases the risk of criminal attack.

COURT CASE

Facts: Merle Fritts, the estranged husband of Erma, an on-duty motel employee, came to the motel and threatened to kill her. Merle had been drinking and had a history of beating Erma and threatening her with a gun. Merle got a shotgun from his truck and returned to the motel. The manager of the business next door saw Merle and asked a customer, Stewart, to help him stop Merle. Merle started shooting in the motel lobby and severely injured Stewart. Stewart sued the motel.

Outcome: The court stated that the motel had a duty to take all precautions for the protection of its guests that reasonable prudence and ordinary care would suggest. Since a reasonable person would have foreseen a risk of harm as a result of Merle's conduct, the motel was liable.

—*Catlett v. Stewart*, 804 S.W.2d 699 (Ark.)

Duty to Care for the Guest's Property

Traditionally, the hotelkeeper had a very high duty and was an insurer of the guest's property except for losses occurring from:

1. An act of God
2. The act of a public enemy
3. An act of a public authority
4. An act of the guest
5. The inherent nature of the property

In every state this liability has been modified to some extent. The statutes vary greatly but most limit a hotel's liability to a designated sum or simply declare that the law of mutual-benefit bailments applies.

Some states permit the hotelkeeper to limit liability by posting a notice in the guest's room. Some of the statutes require that the hotelkeeper, in order to escape full liability, provide a vault or other safe place of deposit for valuables such as furs and jewelry. If a guest fails to deposit valuable articles when proper notice required by state law, such as the availability of a safe, has been posted, the hotelkeeper is released from liability as an insurer.

Hotelkeeper's Lien

A hotelkeeper has a lien on the baggage of guests for the value of the services rendered. This lien extends to all wearing apparel not actually being worn, such as an overcoat or an extra suit.

If hotel charges are not paid within a reasonable time, the hotelkeeper may sell the baggage to pay the charges. Any residue must be returned to the guest. The lien terminates if the property is returned to the guest even though the charges are unpaid.

Facts: Thelma and Christina Paraskevaides, guests at the Four Seasons Washington hotel, put jewelry worth $1.2 million in their bedroom closet safes accessible with keys supplied by the hotel. They left their rooms, and when they returned the rooms had been entered, but not forcibly, and the safes were empty. The rooms and safes could be opened only with one of two master keys or their guest keys. One master key ring had been missing for six months and the locks had not been changed. The Paraskevaideses sued the Four Seasons. The law limited a hotel's

liability for guests' property if the hotel conspicuously displayed in guest and public rooms a copy of the limiting law. The Four Seasons posted disclaimers near the safes on the closet walls and on the door of each safe.

Outcome: The court held that the Four Seasons had not followed the law since it had posted disclaimers only in guest rooms and not in public rooms.

—Paraskevaides v. Four Seasons Washington,
292 F.3d 886 (D.C. Cir.)

The lien usually attaches only to baggage. It does not apply to an automobile, for example, in most states. If a hotelkeeper charges separately for car storage, this charge (but not the room charge) must be paid before the car can be removed.

QUESTIONS

1. What law governs private carriers' contracts for transporting goods, and what is their liability?
2. When may a common carrier refuse service?
3. What is the liability of a common carrier of goods?
4. If a carrier wants to limit its loss by agreement to a specified sum, what must it do?
5. Does a carrier's high degree of liability last until the consignee picks up the goods?
6. What is the difference between a straight bill of lading and an order bill of lading?
7. What rights do common carriers of persons have with respect to prescribing rules for transportation?
8. Is a common carrier of persons always liable for any injury to a passenger by an employee?
9. What constitutes baggage, and what is the liability of a common carrier for baggage carried by a passenger?
10. Who is a guest?
11. What is the liability of a hotel for refusing lodging for an improper reason?
12. What are the duties and liabilities of a hotelkeeper to guests?

CASE PROBLEMS

LO **1**, **2**

1. T.T. Dunphy, Inc. was a carrier who was to deliver steel industrial filters approximately 11 feet by 11 feet and weighing 2,000 pounds from Castine Energy Construction, Inc.'s factory in Maine to Virginia. To help load the filters onto

trailers, Castine welded iron cross bars on them. Castine then loaded them onto a flatbed trailer. Castine did not intend the cross bars to be used to secure the filters to the trailers. However, Dunphy's driver arrived and secured the filters to the trailer by attaching chains to the iron cross bars. While driving to Virginia, the driver drove over a bump in the highway. The filters came loose, fell onto the highway and were irreparably damaged. Castine sued Dunphy. Who suffers the loss?

2. While traveling, Joseph and Marie Ippolito checked in to a Holiday Inn. The registration card Joseph signed and the pouch enclosing his key-card stated the hotel was not responsible for valuables outside the hotel's safe deposit boxes. The Ippolitos put their luggage containing jewelry and cash worth $500,000 in their room and left for 40 minutes. They did not see a notice on the back of their room door stating safe deposit boxes were available. When the Ippolitos returned the jewelry and money were gone. State law excused innkeepers from liability for loss of money and jewels if they posted notice in a conspicuous manner requiring guests to leave such items in the innkeeper's safe deposit box. Had the hotel complied with the law and thus limited its liability for the loss? **LO ❸**

3. U-States Forwarding Services Corp., issued bills of lading for goods from Shineworld Industrial Limited of Hong Kong. The goods were consigned "To order" without listing a name or person, but were to be shipped to Jacobs & Turner, Ltd. in Scotland who had agreed to pay $200,000 for them. Shineworld assigned the bills of lading to BII Finance Company Ltd. as collateral for a loan. While the shipment was in transit, BII sent the bills of lading to Jacobs' bank for payment. The bank found discrepancies in the documents and would not pay until Jacobs agreed. However, at Shineworld's direction, U-States released the goods to Jacobs without surrender of the bills of lading. U-States did not know Shineworld had assigned the bills of lading to BII. Shineworld had no assets, but BII recovered 65 percent from Jacobs. BII then sued U-States for the remainder. Is U-States liable for delivery of the goods without surrender of the bill of lading? **LO ❶, ❷**

4. Holiday Inn St. Louis Airport North advertised a "Park and Fly" package by which the hotel supplied one night of lodging and shuttle service to and from the airport, and permitted people to leave a vehicle on the hotel's parking lot for up to two weeks. Jack Garrett spent a night at the hotel, checked out, took the shuttle to the airport, and left on a trip. He came back 18 days later, took the shuttle to the hotel, and found out his truck had been stolen. Is the hotel liable for the stolen truck? **LO ❸**

5. While working for Railway Switching Services (RSS), Darrell Loveless was injured. He sought compensation from RSS under a law that applied only to common carriers. RSS performed in-plant rail switching for clients at the clients' facilities. RSS moved cars between holding yards and various points all on a client's property. It did this under separately negotiated contracts and did not transport people or property from place to place. Was RSS a common carrier? **LO ❶**

6. Paul and Wendy Carter rented a room at a Travelodge. While in the room, they heard bumping and scratching sounds that seemed to come from behind a wall covered by a mirror. Later, Paul noticed two scratches in the mirror at eye level. He took off the mirror and found scratches on the back of the mirror through which a person could easily see and a large hole in the wall behind where the scratches would be. There was a 1½-foot hollow space between the **LO ❸**

wall and the wall of the adjoining room. There was also a hole in the adjoining room wall covered by a mirror with scratches. If the mirror in that room was removed, one could see into the Carters' room. The Carters sued the hotel. Was the hotel negligent?

LO ❷

7. SCA Graphic Sundsvall AB shipped reels of printing paper from Sweden to World Color Press (WCP) in Tennessee in containers on Star Shipping AS ships. The containers arrived at Mobile, Alabama, and were put in the container yard at the Alabama State Docks. A hurricane caused flooding of the container yard. In the ensuing lawsuit, Star claimed the hurricane was an "act of God," and it should not be liable. The container yard had never been flooded in a hurricane before and prior to the flooding the hurricane's path had changed numerous times. There was no prediction that the area of the State Docks might suffer flooding until very shortly before the hurricane hit. Should Star escape liability?

LO ❶, ❷

8. Accura Systems, Inc. delivered 12 wrapped packages of specially coated aluminum panels to Watkins Motor Lines, Inc. for shipping. Watkins issued a bill of lading that stated the goods were "in apparent good order, except as noted (contents and conditions of contents of packages unknown)." At destination, most of the panels had scratches, gouges, and dents. Accura sued Watkins. Does the statement "good condition" in the bill of lading bind Watkins?

LO ❸

9. Timothy Augustine attended a seminar at a Marriott hotel. The seminar sponsor, who had rented the meeting room, requested a movable coat rack, which Marriott put outside the room. Augustine hung his coat on the rack and at the noon break found the coat rack had been moved around a corner. His cashmere coat was missing. Augustine sued Marriott as a hotelkeeper for the loss of the coat. Is Marriott liable as a hotelkeeper?

LO ❷

10. After Antoinette Sebastian was seriously injured in an automobile accident, a District of Columbia ambulance transported her to the hospital. During the ride the ambulance attendant sexually molested her. She sued the district. Should Sebastian recover from the district?

Ethics in Practice

Since a hotelkeeper has a higher degree of liability to guests if there has been criminal activity on the hotel's premises or even in the area of the hotel, would it be ethical for a hotel owner to instruct employees not to report crimes such a car break-ins or assaults committed at the hotel? What would the likely result of such failure to report crime be?

Summary Cases

PERSONAL PROPERTY

1. Robert Kulovany was injured while working when he fell through the floor of a trailer. Kulovany's employer leased the trailer from Cerco Products, Inc. and had had the trailer in its possession for 20 months. At the time of the injury there was a visible defect in the floor of the trailer. Under the lease agreement, Kulovany's employer had a duty to inspect the trailer for defects. Kulovany sued Cerco. As the bailor in a mutual benefit bailment, was Cerco liable for Kulovany's injuries? [*Kulovany v. Cerco Products, Inc.*, 809 N.Y.S.2d 48 (N.Y. A.D.)]

2. FMC Corporation hired Quality Carriers, Inc. to transport a hazardous material, lithium butoxide, in containers called "isotainers" from Optima Chemical Group, LLC's plant in Georgia to FMC's plant in North Carolina. FMC leased the isotainers and the chasses on which they were hauled and provided them to Quality. After delivering a load of lithium butoxide to NC, the driver drove the isotainer, described as empty in FMC's bill of lading, back to Optima's plant. About six hours after the isotainer was delivered to Optima, its employees Alvin Booth and Kenneth Wilson prepared to connect a hose to re-load the isotainer with lithium butoxide. Booth accidentally made contact with a liquid discharge relief valve. It hissed and then exploded spraying Booth with lithium butoxide and causing disabling injuries. Booth sued Quality alleging that as a common carrier it was required to keep the isotainer in safe condition. Was it? [*Booth v. Quality Carriers, Inc.*, 623 S.E.2d 244 (Ga. App.)]

3. Viola Waterton rented a room at Linden Motor Inn. She had parked her car in the below ground garage on the inn's premises. There was no separate charge for parking the car, and Waterton did not register it with the inn. There was nothing to control entry or exit from the garage and no attendant in it. The next morning Waterton discovered the car had been vandalized and several items stolen from it. Waterton sued Linden for the loss. Was the inn the bailee of the car? [*Waterton v. Linden Motor Inc.*, 810 N.Y.S.2d 319 (N.Y. City Civ. Ct.)]

4. When Thomas Stafford sold some real estate, the purchasers gave him notes made out to him and June Zink (his daughter) "or the survivor." Payments on the notes were put into a bank account in the names of both Stafford and Zink with right of survivorship. The money in the account was spent as Stafford directed. After Stafford died, Zink claimed the notes were a gift to her. Were they? [*Zink v. Stafford*, 509 S.E.2d 833 (Va.)]

5. Carroll Decker drove for R.D. Roy Transport, Inc. He had driven a load of paper pulp bales from New England Public Warehouse (NEPW) to the S.D. Warren mill. Warren asked that the bales be stacked in a contiguous configuration that meant four high and placed side by side at the ends of the trailer

169

and single file down the center. Decker had asked NEPW to use a spaced configuration for his load that meant the bales were side by side at the ends but no bales were between the stacked bales at the front and back. A Roy driver picked up another load at NEPW. He watched NEPW load using a continuous configuration and drove the load to Roy's terminal. Decker inspected the load from the ground because it looked the same as his prior load. He could not see which configuration was used. Decker drove to an entrance ramp of the turnpike. He heard several thumps and then the trailer rolled over and crashed. He sued NEPW. Is NEPW, the shipper, liable? [*Decker v. New England Public Warehouse, Inc.*, 749 A.2d 762 (Me.)]

6. State law provided that all intangible property remaining unclaimed by the owner for more than seven years after it was payable was presumed abandoned. Such intangible property could be claimed by the state. Blue Cross and Blue Shield (BC/BS) held $125,000 in uncashed checks issued by it to pay benefits and premium refunds. The state demanded the funds. Were they intangible property? [*Revenue Cabinet v. Blue Cross and Blue Shield*, 702 S.W.2d 433 (Ky.)]

7. Two young men pounded on the door as a bus started and the driver stopped for them. They smelled of alcohol and were stumbling and boisterous. They argued with the driver about the fare, and one did not pay. The driver demanded the nonpayer come forward, and after an argument, he paid. He walked erratically, grabbing poles to balance, and tripped over a woman's leg. The man yelled at her and threatened to kill her. For at least 10 minutes he walked up and down shouting obscenities. An elderly man, William O'Neill, asked the driver to do something, but he refused. The man threatened O'Neill for a minute. When O'Neill got up the man grabbed him. The driver hit the brakes causing them both to fall. The two young men beat O'Neill, caving in his face, breaking his nose and jaw, and causing brain and spinal cord injuries. O'Neill sued the bus company. Should the bus company be liable for O'Neill's injuries? [*Washington Metropolitan Area Transit Authority v. O'Neill*, 633 A.2d 834 (D.C. App.)]

8. The painter Alphonse Mucha had more than 20 of his paintings, including a large one called "Quo Vadis," delivered to the Newcomb-Macklin gallery for the gallery to try to sell for him. Mucha had occasional contact by letter with the gallery, but died 19 years after the delivery. His son, Jiri, thought he had recovered all the remaining paintings after Alphonse's death. Fifty-nine years after receiving the paintings, the gallery was liquidating and a dealer named Rupprecht asked the owner for the rolled-up paintings in the basement. One of the paintings was "Quo Vadis," which Rupprecht sold to an art dealer who sold it to Charles King. A year later a friend of King's wrote to Jiri, asking about the symbolism in the painting. Jiri found out King had it and sued for its return, claiming a conversion by the gallery. Was there a 59-year bailment and a conversion of "Quo Vadis"? [*Mucha v. King*, 792 F.2d 602 (7th Cir.)]

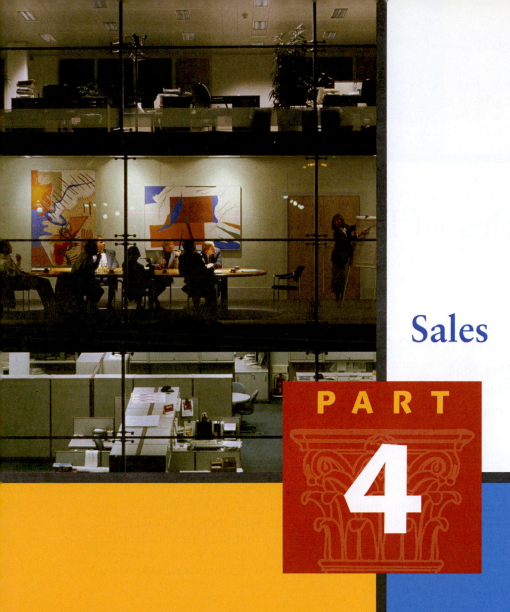

Sales

This part covers topics in sales, including what is required for a sale, warranties, product liability, and consumer protection. If you buy a used computer through a newspaper ad, will you have a warranty with it? If you purchase used goods through the Internet—for example through an auction site such as eBay—you may or may not have protection for some aspects of your purchase. As recourse to fraud, trading offenses, illegally auctioned items, and other Internet sales offenses, the Internet Fraud Complaint Center, through the FBI and the National White Collar Crime Center, acts on complaints. Visit eBay to examine its safety measures and then visit the IFCC to see how complaints are handled.

http://www.ebay.com

http://www.ic3.gov/

Sales of Personal Property

LEARNING OBJECTIVES

1 Define goods.

2 Define a sale of goods and distinguish it from a contract to sell.

3 Distinguish between existing and future goods.

PREVIEW CASE

Frank Sabia agreed to purchase a boat from Mattituck Inlet Marina & Shipyard, Inc. Although Mattituck was the true seller, title was transferred to Sabia through R. Gil Liepold & Associates in a scheme to avoid $23,000 in sales tax. Sabia alleged that the boat was defective and sued Mattituck for breach of contract and fraud. Would a court consider a scheme to avoid sales tax an appropriate activity and one that should be encouraged? Do you think it would be legal to engage in such a scheme?

LO 1
Define goods

Goods
Movable personal property

In terms of the number of contracts as well as the dollar volume, contracts for the sale of **goods**—movable personal property—constitute the largest class of contracts in our economic system. Every time one purchases an ice cream bar, one makes a sales contract. If the ice cream bar contained some harmful substance, the sale could be the basis of a suit for thousands of dollars in damages. Article 2 of the Uniform Commercial Code (UCC), effective in all states except Louisiana, governs sales of movable personal property.

A sales contract that does not meet the requirements of the UCC is unenforceable. However, if both parties—the buyer and the seller—choose to abide by its terms even if they are not legally bound to do so, neither one can later avoid the contract. Both parties must honor the contract.

PROPERTY SUBJECT TO SALE

Movable Personal Property
All physical items except real estate

As used in the UCC and in these chapters, *sale* applies only to the sale of movable personal property (discussed in chapter 14). Thus, it does not apply to (1) real property or (2) intangible personal property. **Movable personal property** consists of all physical items that are not real estate. Examples include food, vehicles, clothing, and furniture. **Real property** is land, interests in land, and things permanently attached to land. **Intangible personal property** consists of evidences of ownership of personal property, such as contracts, copyrights, certificates of stock, accounts receivable, notes receivable, and similar assets.

Sales contracts must have all the essentials of any other contract, but they also have some additional features. Many rules pertaining to sales of personal property have no significance to any other type of contract, such as a contract of employment.

SALES AND CONTRACTS TO SELL

A sale differs from a contract to sell, and it is important to know the differences.

A **sale** of goods involves the transfer of title, or ownership, to identified goods from the seller to the buyer for a consideration called the *price*. The ownership changes from the seller to the buyer at the moment the bargain is made, regardless of who has possession of the goods.

A **contract to sell** goods is a contract whereby the seller agrees to transfer ownership of goods to the buyer in the future for a consideration called the *price*. In this type of contract individuals promise to buy and to sell in the future. The party seeking to purchase the goods does not have the right to possess them unless the contract specifically so provides.

An important distinction exists between a sale and a contract to sell. In a sale, the actual **title**, or the ownership of the subject matter, is transferred at once. Title can be transferred as soon as there is agreement on the goods and the price is fixed. The goods need not be delivered nor the price paid. In a contract to sell, the title will be transferred at a later time. A contract to sell is not in the true sense of the word a sale; it is merely an agreement to sell.

Real Property
Land and things permanently attached to land

Intangible Personal Property
Evidences of ownership of personal property

LO ❷
Sale versus contract to sell

Sale
Transfer of title to goods for a price

Contract to Sell
Agreement to transfer title to goods for a price

Title
Ownership

COURT CASE

Facts: Production Credit Association (PCA) loaned McGraw Farms money. To secure payment of the loan, McGraw gave PCA an interest in all its crops growing or later planted. A year later, Farm & Town Industries, Inc. (FTI) entered into a contract with McGraw to buy 20,000 bushels of corn then growing. McGraw was to deliver the corn in two months. After McGraw went into bankruptcy, a dispute arose between PCA and FTI as to their rights to the corn. If FTI's contract with McGraw was a present sale of the growing corn, PCA had no interest in the corn. If FTI's contract with McGraw was a contract to sell the corn in the future, PCA had an interest in the corn, and FTI's payment for the corn would have to go to PCA.

Outcome: The court stated that because the contract simply said "20,000 bushels of corn" without identifying the corn or even the land on which it was growing, there could not have been a transfer of ownership. The transaction was a contract to sell, not a sale.

—*Production Credit Assn. v. Farm & Town Industries, Inc.*, **518 N.W.2d 339 (Iowa)**

In order to determine who owns goods, a sale must be distinguished from a contract to sell. Ownership always rests with either the seller or the buyer. Because the owner normally bears the risk of loss, the question of whether the seller or buyer has ownership must be answered. Also, any increase in the value of the property belongs to the one who owns it. It is essential, therefore, to have definite rules to aid the courts in determining when ownership and risk of loss pass from one party to another if the parties to the contract have not specified these matters. If the parties specify when title or risk of loss passes, the courts will enforce that agreement.

SALES OF GOODS AND CONTRACTS FOR SERVICES

An agreement to perform some type of service must be distinguished from a sale of goods because Article 2 of the UCC governs sales of goods but not agreements to perform services. When a contract includes the supplying of both services and articles of movable personal property, the contract is not necessarily considered a contract for the sale of goods. Whether it is a sale or service is determined by which factor is predominant. If the predominant factor is supplying a service, with the goods being incidental, the contract is considered a service contract and is not covered by Article 2. For example, the repair of a television set is not a sale even though new parts are supplied.

COURT CASE

Facts: Cold Spring Egg Farm, Inc.'s chicken barn had several fans, each with its own control. Cold Spring purchased a fan control unit from Aerotech, Inc. to control all the fans. Cease Electric, Inc. installed the fan control and a backup thermostat following a one page wiring schematic. The fan system failed and 18,000 chickens died. Cease had improperly wired the fan control to the same power circuit as the backup thermostat and had failed to test the system. Testing would have shown the backup thermostat was not working. Cease had supplied conduit and wiring and billed Cold Spring for its time on an hourly basis. Cold Spring sued Cease alleging Cease had provided a service rather than a sale of goods.

Outcome: The court held that Cease had supplied the service of installing the new ventilation system and had not made a sale.

—*Insurance Co. of North America v. Cease Elect., Inc.*, 688 N.W.2d 462 (Wis.)

PRICE

Price
Consideration in a sales contract

The consideration in a sales contract is generally expressed in terms of money or money's worth and is known as the **price**. The price may be payable in money, goods, or services.

The chapters on contracts explained that an express contract is one in which all the terms are stated in words either orally or in writing. An implied contract is one in which some of the terms are understood without being stated. A sales contract is ordinarily an express contract, but some of its terms may be implied. If the sales contract does not state the price, it will be held to be the reasonable price for the same goods in the market. For goods sold on a regulated market, such as a commodity exchange, the price on that market will be deemed the reasonable price. If the parties indicate that the price must be fixed by them or by a third person at a later date, no binding contract arises if the price is not thus fixed. If the price can be computed from the terms of the contract, the contract is valid.

COURT CASE

Facts: Howard Leight Industries (HLI) made foam earplugs. When purchasing HLI, Bacou Dalloz USA, Inc. offered by letter to purchase all its requirements for polyurethane prepolymer, the raw material for foam earplugs, from Continental Polymers, a corporation owned by HLI executives. The letter stated Bacou would purchase the material if the price of the prepolymer was "equivalent to that which is then used by HLI and available from third parties." Continental built a plant to manufacture prepolymer. Its market price was about $2 per pound, but Bacou had requested a price reduction from its supplier, Dow.

Dow knew of the letter agreement and reduced its price only to Bacou to $1.56 per pound. Bacou then said the "then available" price was $1.56. A lawsuit ensued in which Bacou claimed the letter agreement was unenforceable because it omitted the price.

Outcome: Because the letter gave the price term as the price then available from others, it was discoverable by getting price quotes from other sellers. The price was not too vague.

—*Bacou Dalloz USA, Inc. v. Continental Polymers, Inc.*, 344 F.3d 22 (1st Cir.)

EXISTING GOODS

In order to be the subject of a sale, the goods must be existing. **Existing goods** are those both in existence (as contrasted with goods not yet manufactured) and then owned by the seller. If these conditions are not met, the goods are not existing and the only transaction that can be made between the seller and the buyer will be a contract to sell goods.

Identified goods are a type of existing goods. They are goods that the seller and buyer have agreed are to be received by the buyer or have been picked out by the seller. When the seller specially manufactures the goods to the buyer's order, identification occurs at the time when manufacture begins.

LO ❸
Existing versus future goods

Existing Goods
Goods that are in being and owned by the seller

Identified Goods
Goods picked to be delivered to the buyer

COURT CASE

Facts: Matthew Serra agreed to buy a Lincoln Continental Mark V from Suburban Ford Lincoln Mercury. Serra paid a portion of the price, got a title certificate, registered the car, and paid the necessary sales tax. Serra wanted to store the Lincoln for several years because it was in a collectors' series. Because he had no room in his garage, Suburban agreed to keep it on its lot. Suburban had stored the car for more than a year when the car Serra drove was damaged in an

accident, and he went to Suburban to get the Lincoln. The car was not there because Suburban was in financial trouble and its main creditor had repossessed all the cars. Serra sued for possession of the Lincoln.

Outcome: Serra was successful because the court said the Lincoln was identified goods.

—*Serra v. Ford Motor Credit Co.*, 463 A.2d 142 (R.I.)

FUTURE GOODS

Goods that are not existing goods are **future goods**. The seller expects to acquire the goods in the future either by purchase or by manufacture. For example, if Arnold contracts to buy an antique dresser, he might then contract to sell the dresser to Biff. Since Arnold does not yet own the dresser, he cannot now sell the dresser to Biff. He can only make a contract to sell it in the future, after he

Future Goods
Goods not both existing and identified

acquires title to it. Any contract purporting to sell future goods is a contract to sell and not a sale, because the seller does not have title to the goods. Thus, future goods are goods that are not yet owned by the seller or not in physical existence. However, title to future goods does not pass immediately to the buyer when the goods come into existence. The seller must first take some further action, such as shipment or delivery.

BILL OF SALE

Bill of Sale
Written evidence of title to tangible personal property

A **bill of sale** provides written evidence of one's title to tangible personal property (see Illustration 16–1). No particular form is required for a bill of sale. It can simply state that title to the described property has been transferred to the buyer.

Generally, a buyer does not need a bill of sale as evidence of ownership; but if a person's title is questioned, such evidence is highly desirable. If an individual buys a stock of merchandise in bulk, livestock, jewelry, furs, or any other relatively expensive items, the buyer should demand a bill of sale from the seller. The bill of sale serves two purposes:

1. If the buyer wishes to resell the goods and the prospective buyer demands proof of ownership, the bill of sale can be produced.

2. If any question arises as to whether or not the buyer came into possession of the goods legally, the bill of sale is proof.

ILLUSTRATION 16–1 Bill of Sale

BILL OF SALE OF CATTLE

Purchaser Mickey Bedrosian

Address Bedrosian Farms

Rt. 3 Box 1246-A

Miller, KS

Date March 26 20—

Animals	Tattoo#	Sex	Price
Simmental cow with heifer by side	6783	F	$950
Simmental heavy heifer	17302	F	$725

By receipt of above, which is hereby acknowledged, the undersigned grants, bargains, sells and assigns all its rights, title and interest in and to the cattle described above; if check or draft is given in full or part payment of said described animal(s), title and ownership shall remain with Seller until check is cleared by the bank on which drawn.

Seller Cadaret & Co.

Address Rt. 1 Box 1793-C

Wichita, KS

Signed Curt McCaskill

COURT CASE

Facts: State Farm issued auto insurance to Don Crowley covering loss to Crowley's vehicle by theft. The coverage included a car newly owned by him. Crowley bought a Jaguar XJ6 and received a bill of sale for it instead of a title. When Crowley sold the Jaguar to Al Locke, Locke paid with checks returned for insufficient funds. Crowley filed criminal charges against Locke for theft and made a theft claim with State Farm. State Farm claimed since Crowley did not have a title, he had not owned the Jaguar; thus it was not covered by the policy.

Outcome: The bill of sale established ownership of the Jaguar by Crowley.

—*Crowley v. State Farm Mut. Auto. Ins. Co.,*
591 So.2d 53 (Ala.)

ILLEGAL SALES

Many difficulties arise over illegal sales; that is, the sale of goods prohibited by law, such as stolen property. If the sale is fully executed, the court will not intervene to aid either party. If one party is completely innocent and enters into an illegal sale, the court will compel a restoration of any goods or money the innocent party has transferred.

PREVIEW CASE REVISITED

Facts: Frank Sabia agreed to purchase a boat from Mattituck Inlet Marina & Shipyard, Inc. Although Mattituck was the true seller, title was transferred to Sabia through R. Gil Liepold & Associates in a scheme to avoid $23,000 in sales tax. Sabia alleged that the boat was defective and sued Mattituck for breach of contract and fraud.

Outcome: Since the arrangement was for the purpose of improper tax avoidance, the contract for the purchase of the boat was illegal. Sabia was barred from suing on the contract.

—*Sabia v. Mattituck Inlet Marina & Shipyard,* **805 N.Y.S.2d 346 (N.Y. A.D.)**

If the illegal sale is wholly executory, that is, has not yet been completed, the transaction is a contract to sell and will not be enforced. If it is only partially executory, the court will leave the parties where it finds them unless the one who has fulfilled his part of the contract is an innocent victim of a fraud.

If the sale is divisible with a legal part and an illegal part, the court will enforce the legal part. If the individual goods are separately priced, the sale is divisible. If the sale involves several separate and independent items but is a lump-sum sale, then the sale is indivisible. An indivisible sale with an illegal part makes the entire sale illegal.

INTERNATIONAL SALES CONTRACTS

Questions may arise about what law governs an international contract for the sale of goods. These questions could present major problems to the parties if any litigation arises on the contract. Of course, the parties may specify in the contract what law governs. However, many international sales contracts are made without such a specification. To help in this type of situation, the United States has ratified the United Nations Convention on Contracts for the International Sale of Goods (CISG). This convention, or agreement, applies to contracts for the sale of goods if the buyer and seller have places of business in different countries that agree to the convention. Several dozen countries have ratified or acceded to the convention.

Businesses may choose to indicate in their international contracts that they will not be governed by the convention. However, unless the parties state that the contract will not be governed by the convention, it will be. The convention does not cover contracts between two parties unless their places of business are in countries that have adopted the convention. It also does not cover personal consumer transactions but is intended to apply in business-to-business situations. Some provisions of the CISG are similar to the UCC, but many are not.

QUESTIONS

1. What property can be the subject of a sale? Give some examples

2. **a.** What is the difference between a sale and a contract to sell?

   b. Why is it important to make a distinction between a sale and a contract to sell?

3. What determines whether a contract is for the sale of goods or the providing of a service?

4. If a sales contract does not state the price, can the price be determined?

5. What are identified goods?

6. Can a buyer and a seller make a sale of future goods? Explain.

7. Can a completely innocent party to an illegal sale get any assistance from a court?

8. When an international sales contract does not specify what law governs its interpretation, what law could be applied?

CASE PROBLEMS

LO ❶

1. Jack Kasper bought several thousand gallons of jet fuel and stored it without permission in Robert Praegitzer's underground tank beneath Praegitzer's airplane hangar. Praegitzer sold the hangar and tank to William Curtright. Curtright would not let Kasper remove the fuel insisting he had bought it along with the tank and hangar. Kasper sued Curtright. Curtright argued that the UCC applied to the fuel because it was "goods." Was it?

LO ❷

2. Thirteen-year-old Teasha Wilkerson was injured in an accident while a passenger in a pickup. State Farm Insurance had issued a liability policy covering the pickup to Catherine Bordelon. Bordelon held record title to the pickup but had entered into an agreement with Debra Hewitt, Teasha's mother. The agreement simply stated Bordelon did "lease purchase one . . . Isuzu Hombre pickup . . . to Debra S. Hewitt" for a set monthly payment for 60 months. Hewitt took immediate possession of the pickup and treated it as her own. She sued State Farm on behalf of Teasha arguing that the arrangement was a contract to sell so State Farm's insurance policy still applied to the pickup. Was this a sale or a contract to sell?

3. From Electrodyne, Champion Manufacturing Industries ordered four 104-foot, 210,000-pound masts used in the oil and gas industry. Three masts were completed and accepted by Champion and the fourth was 60 percent complete when Champion canceled the order. The fourth mast was never completed, accepted, or even shipped. Electrodyne sued for the order price of the mast. Under state law, Electrodyne could not recover on its suit unless the mast had been sold to Champion. Analyze the situation and explain whether Electrodyne could recover.

LO ❸

4. Hilton Contract Carpet Co. agreed to install carpet in Jane Pittsley's home for $4,402. Hilton paid the installers $700. Pittsley complained about the installation, and Hilton tried to correct it, but Pittsley was not satisfied and refused to pay the balance due on the contract. Pittsley sued for rescission of the contract and return of the money she had paid. The case hinged on whether the transaction was a sale of goods or the supplying of a service. Which was it?

LO ❷

5. Dakota Pork Industries contracted with the city of Huron to give the city its water rights in the James River in exchange for the city providing Dakota's water. Three years later, Dakota noticed a foreign substance on the meat at Dakota. Dakota sued Huron for breaching warranties in the sale of the water. The court had to decide if the sale of water was a sale of goods and thus governed by the UCC. Was this sale of water a sale of goods?

LO ❶

6. The Plantation Shutter Co. contracted with Ricky Ezell to sell and install interior shutters in Ezell's home for $6,000. They signed a written document titled "Terms of Sale." After the shutters were installed, Ezell was dissatisfied with 12 of the 37 panels. Plantation remade and installed the panels, but Ezell still had complaints and did not like the exposed hinges. Plantation agreed to provide side strips to hide the hinges and reduced the price of the shutters. Plantation made the strips and tried to schedule installation but Ezell would not permit completion of the work. Plantation sued for the balance due on the contract alleging it was a sale of goods. Was it a sale of goods or a services contract?

LO ❷

Formalities of a Sale

LEARNING OBJECTIVES

❶ List the requirements of the Statute of Frauds for sales, and explain the exceptions to it.

❷ Define an auction sale, and describe its peculiarities compared to the law of sales.

❸ Describe the nature of the writing required by the Statute of Frauds.

PREVIEW CASE

→ Homer Buffaloe orally contracted to buy five tobacco barns he rented from Patricia and Lowell Hart. Buffaloe was to pay $20,000 in $5,000 annual installments. Under the rental agreement, the Harts had paid the insurance on the barns, but after the purchase contract, Buffaloe paid the insurance. He paid for improvements on the barns. A year after Buffaloe contracted to buy the barns, he found three people who were willing to buy them for $8,000 each. He delivered a check for $5,000 to Patricia. The next day, Patricia told Buffaloe she did not want to sell the barns to him. Two days later, Hart mailed Buffaloe a letter containing the check that had been torn up. When do you think Patricia decided she did not want to sell to Buffaloe? What do you think Buffaloe believed when Patricia took the check? What are the exceptions to the Statute of Frauds requirements of a written contract?

LO ❶
Application of Statute of Frauds to sales

All contracts for the sale of goods must exist in writing when the sale price is $500 or more. This Statute of Frauds' requirement has been included in the Uniform Commercial Code (UCC). If the sale price is less than $500, the contract may be oral, written, implied from conduct, or a combination of any of these.

COURT CASE

Facts: Robert and Virginia Hartley sold irrigation equipment to Robert Cummins, who paid all but $1,000 of the sale price. The Hartleys claimed they orally agreed to repurchase some of the equipment from Cummins in exchange for canceling his debt and therefore claimed ownership of that equipment. A lawsuit ensued to determine the ownership of that equipment. The decision depended on whether the contract to repurchase was valid.

Outcome: The court held that because the alleged contract to repurchase some of the equipment was oral and the price exceeded $500, it was barred by the Statute of Frauds.

—*Cummins v. Hartley,*
600 P.2d 463 (Or. App.)

MULTIPLE PURCHASES AND THE STATUTE OF FRAUDS

Frequently, one makes several purchases from the same seller on the same day. The question may then be raised whether there is one sale or several sales. If one contracts to purchase five items from the same seller in one day, each item having a sale price of less than $500 but, when combined, the total exceeds $500, must this contract meet the requirement of the Statute of Frauds? If the several items are part of the same sales transaction, it is one sale and must meet the requirement of the statute. If all the items are selected during the same shopping tour and with the same salesperson who merely adds up the different items and charges the customer with a grand total, the several items are considered to be part of the same transaction. However, if a separate sales slip is written for each purchase as an individual shops in a store, each transaction is a separate sale.

WHEN PROOF OF ORAL CONTRACT IS PERMITTED

In some instances, the absence of a writing does not bar the proof of a sales contract for $500 or more.

Receipt and Acceptance of Goods

An oral sales contract may be enforced if it can be shown that the goods were delivered by the seller and were received and accepted by the buyer. Both a receipt and an acceptance by the buyer must be shown. **Receipt** is taking possession of the goods. **Acceptance** is the assent of the buyer to become the owner of specific goods. The contract may be enforced only as it relates to the goods received and accepted.

Receipt
Taking possession of goods

Acceptance
Assent of buyer to become owner of goods

Payment

An oral contract may be enforced if the buyer has made full payment on the contract. In the case of part payment, a contract may be enforced only with respect to goods for which payment has been made and accepted.

COURT ✦ CASE

Facts: Norwick Adams ran the Whataburger franchise for two cities in Mexico. He would order meat products from H&H Meat Products and tell it to invoice the meat to Proveedora de Alimentos Contratados (PAC) because PAC had a permit to import meat into Mexico. Three shipments (for $7,172, $6,614, and $2,232) delivered to Whataburger Mexico were not paid for. H&H sued for breach of contract. Adams claimed the Statute of Frauds barred collection since it was an oral contract for a sale of goods for more than $500.

Outcome: Because Whataburger received the meat, this was a receipt and acceptance by Whataburger. It had to pay for the meat.

—Adams v. H&H Meat Products, Inc.,
41 S.W.3d 762 (Tex. App.)

Some uncertainty occurs under this rule as to the effectiveness of payment by check or a promissory note executed by the buyer. Under the law of commercial paper, a check, draft, or note is conditional payment when delivered. It does not become final and complete until a financial intermediary, such as a bank, pays the check, draft, or note. However, since businesspeople ordinarily regard the delivery of a check or note as payment, in most states the delivery of such an instrument is sufficient to make the oral contract enforceable. A check or promissory note tendered as payment but refused by the seller does not constitute a payment under the Statute of Frauds.

PREVIEW CASE REVISITED

Facts: Homer Buffaloe orally contracted to buy five tobacco barns he rented from Patricia and Lowell Hart. Buffaloe was to pay $20,000 in $5,000 annual installments. Under the rental agreement, the Harts had paid the insurance on the barns, but after the purchase contract, Buffaloe paid the insurance. He also paid for improvements. A year after Buffaloe contracted to buy the barns he found three people who were willing to buy them for $8,000 each. He delivered a check for $5,000 to Patricia. The next day Patricia told Buffaloe she did not want to sell him the barns. Two days later Hart mailed Buffaloe a letter containing the check that had been torn up.

Outcome: The court held that the check was an accepted payment for the barns under the contract to sell them. The Harts were liable to Buffaloe.

—Buffaloe v. Hart, 441 S.E.2d 172 (N.C. App.)

When the buyer has negotiated or assigned to the seller a negotiable instrument executed by a third person, and the seller has accepted the instrument, a payment has been made within the meaning of the Statute of Frauds.

Judicial Admission

When a person voluntarily acknowledges a fact during the course of some legal proceedings, this is a **judicial admission**. No writing is required when the person against whom enforcement of the contract is sought voluntarily admits, in the course of legal proceedings, to having made the contract.

Judicial Admission
Fact acknowledged in course of legal proceeding

Nonresellable Goods

Goods that are specifically made for the buyer and are of such an unusual nature that they are not suitable for sale in the ordinary course of the seller's business are called **nonresellable goods**. No writing is required in such cases. For this exception to apply, however, the seller must have made a substantial beginning in manufacturing the goods or, if a middleman, in procuring them, before receiving notice of rejection by the buyer.

Nonresellable Goods
Specially made goods not easily resellable

COURT CASE

Facts: P. N. Hirsch & Co. Stores, Inc. had bought its paper bags from Smith-Scharff Paper Co. for 36 years. The bags were imprinted with the P. N. Hirsch logo. Smith-Scharff kept a supply of the bags in stock so it could promptly fill Hirsch's purchase orders. Hirsch was aware of this practice and even provided a generalized profile of its business forecasts to Smith-Scharff to help it judge how many bags to have on hand. After Hirsch was sold it refused to purchase $20,000 worth of bags left in Smith-Scharff's inventory. Smith-Scharff sued Hirsch for breach of contract. Hirsch argued that it was not liable because there was no written contract.

Outcome: The court held that the bags were nonresellable goods, so the contract did not have to be in writing.

—*Smith-Scharff Paper Co. v. P.N. Hirsch & Co., 754 S.W.2d 928 (Mo. Ct. App.)*

Auction Sales

An **auction** is a sale in which a seller or an agent of the seller orally asks for bids on goods and orally accepts the highest bid. A sale by auction for any amount is valid even though it is, by necessity, oral. In most states, the auctioneer is the special agent for both the owner and the bidder. When the auctioneer, or the clerk of the auction, makes a memorandum of the sale and signs it, this binds both parties. The **bidder** is the one who makes the offer. There is no contract until the auctioneer accepts the offer, which may be done in several ways. The most common way is the fall of the hammer, with the auctioneer saying, "Sold" or "Sold to (a certain person)." In most auctions several lower bids precede the final bid. When a person makes a bid to start the sale, the auctioneer may refuse to accept this as a starting bid. If the bid is accepted and a higher bid is requested, the auctioneer can later refuse to accept this starting bid as the selling price.

If a bid is made while the hammer is falling in acceptance of a prior bid, the auctioneer has the choice of reopening the bid or declaring the goods sold. The auctioneer's decision is binding.

Goods may be offered for sale with reserve or without reserve. If they are **without reserve**, then the goods cannot be withdrawn after the bidding starts unless no bid is received within a reasonable time after the auctioneer calls for bids. It is presumed that goods are offered **with reserve**; that is, they may be withdrawn, unless the goods are explicitly put up without reserve.

LO ❷
Auctions and the law of sales

Auction
Sale of property to the highest bidder

Bidder
Person who makes offer at auction

Without Reserve
Auction goods may not be withdrawn after bidding starts

With Reserve
Auction goods may be withdrawn after bidding starts

LO ❸
Requirements of the writing

NATURE OF THE WRITING REQUIRED

The UCC does not have stringent requirements that indicate what in a written contract or other writing is adequate to satisfy the Statute of Frauds for sales contracts.

Terms

The writing need only give assurance that a transaction existed. Specifically, it must indicate that a sale or contract to sell has been made and state the quantity of goods involved. Any other missing terms may be shown by parol evidence in the event of a dispute.

Signature

When a suit is brought against an individual on the basis of a transaction, the terms of which must be in writing, either the person being sued or an authorized agent of that person must have signed the writing. The signature must be placed on the writing with the intention of authenticating the writing, or indicating an intent to form a contract. It may consist of initials; it may be printed, stamped, or typewritten, and the signature can be electronic as on an e-mail. The important thing is that it was made with the necessary intent.

COURT CASE

Facts: Cloud Corporation supplied Hasbro, Inc. with packets of powder for a toy. Hasbro would issue purchase orders to Cloud for a quantity of packets. Hasbro had sent Cloud a form stating that Cloud could not deviate from a purchase order without Hasbro's written consent. As requested, Cloud signed the form and sent it to Hasbro. Demand for the toy later decreased. With the supplies it had, Cloud figured it could fill Hasbro's existing purchase orders plus 1.8 million more packets. It sent an acknowledgment to purchase orders for this larger amount. Hasbro sent a number of e-mails to Cloud referencing quantities greater than in its purchase orders and consistent with Cloud's acknowledgment. When Hasbro did not purchase all of the packets, Cloud sued.

Outcome: The court found that the sender's name on an e-mail satisfied the signature requirement of the Statute of Frauds. Hasbro was liable for the purchase of all the packets.

—*Cloud Corp. v. Hasbro, Inc.,*
314 F.3d 289 (7th Cir.)

The UCC makes an exception to the requirement of signing regarding a transaction between merchants. It provides that the failure of a merchant to refuse to accept within 10 days a confirming letter sent by another merchant is binding just as though the letter or other writing had been signed. This ends the possibility of a situation under which the sender of the letter was bound, but the receiver could safely ignore the transaction or could hold the sender as desired, depending upon which alternative gave the better financial advantage.

Time of Execution

To satisfy the Statute of Frauds, a writing may be made at, or any time after, the making of the sale. It may even be made after the contract has been broken or a suit brought on it. The essential element is the existence—at the time the trial is held—of written proof of the transaction.

Particular Writings

The writing that satisfies the Statute of Frauds may be a single writing or it may be several writings considered as a group. Formal contracts, bills of sale, letters, and telegrams are common forms of writings that satisfy the Statute of Frauds.

Purchase orders, cash register receipts, sales tickets, invoices, and similar papers generally do not satisfy the requirements as to a signature, and sometimes they do not specify any quantity or commodity.

QUESTIONS

1. Discuss the difference in form required of contracts for the sale of goods when the sale price is $500 or more and when the price is less than $500.

2. What factors help determine whether the purchase of several items from the same seller on the same day constitute one sale or several sales?

3. Explain the receipt and acceptance exception to the Statute of Frauds.

4. Does part payment make an oral contract for goods worth more than $500 enforceable?

5. Does payment by check or promissory note constitute payment for purposes of enforcing an oral contract?

6. Why is an auction sale of goods for more than $500 enforceable when it is oral?

7. In order to satisfy the Statute of Frauds for sales, what must a writing include?

8. What can the signature required on a writing by the Statute of Frauds consist of?

CASE PROBLEMS

1. Charles Lohman wanted to convert his pig operation (raising them to 50 pounds) to a weaner pig facility (raising pigs only to 7 to 14 pounds). John Wagner was putting together a network of pork producers and buyers. Lohman began selling weaner pigs to Wagner although Lohman still needed a loan to remodel his building. Lohman asked Wagner for a sample of a weaner pig purchase agreement the pork network might use to show his banker. Wagner made one up and even signed it though there were blanks including the quantity of pigs. He faxed it to Lohman saying he hoped it would help Lohman get a loan. Lohman put in 300 per week for the quantity; he signed it but never sent it to Wagner. He supplied weaner pigs to Wagner at $28 per pig consistent with the price in the sample agreement, until Wagner paid only $18 because the price for pork had dropped. Months later, Lohman sued Wagner for breach of contract. Was there an enforceable contract? **LO ③**

2. The Small Business Administration auctioned the assets of a business. The auction was conducted in two phases, first auctioning the property in bulk, and then piecemeal. If the piecemeal auction did not produce as much as the highest bulk bid, the bulk bidder took the property. Jack Conrad bid $20,000, the highest bulk bid. At the fall of the hammer the clerk made a memorandum of sale showing Conrad's bid. After the piecemeal auction began, Conrad told the auctioneer he wanted to withdraw his bid, but the auctioneer refused. The piecemeal auction did not produce $20,000, so the auctioneer announced the winner of the bulk bid had bought the property. Conrad refused to pay for the property, so the SBA sued him. Was there an enforceable contract? **LO ②**

3. For years, under an oral agreement, Barbara Kalas printed and delivered written materials to Adelma Simmons. Simmons had designed the materials to sell at her herb farm, Caprilands, so they included that name. Since Simmons **LO ①**

had limited space, Kalas stored them until Simmons requested some. Tolland, Connecticut, acquired the farm and Simmons had to vacate by the end of the year. In December Simmons died. Kalas made a $24,000 claim against Simmons's estate for unpaid deliveries of materials including two made after Simmons's death. The estate claimed the materials were goods printed under an oral contract in violation of the Statute of Frauds. Was the oral contract enforceable?

LO ❸   **4.** Abhe & Sxoboda, Inc. and Rainbow, Inc., a joint venture, made a bid to the State of Minnesota to sandblast, repair, and repaint a bridge. Simplex Supplies, Inc. faxed the joint venture an offer to provide an abrasive agent for removing the paint. The offer contained the project number and the contract amount of $362,500. The joint venture submitted to the state a Description of Work, an affidavit signed by Rainbow's president, and a Request to Sublet, all saying Rainbow would subcontract to Simplex and listing the project number and the contract amount. After the state awarded the contract to the joint venture, it denied that it had a contract with Simplex. Simplex sued and the joint venture alleged since there was no written contract, the Statute of Frauds barred enforcement of the oral contract. Was there a writing sufficient to satisfy the Statute of Frauds?

LO ❶, ❸   **5.** Joseph Kiser agreed to sell James Casazza his sailboat. On separate pieces of paper, each wrote down the details of their discussions that led to their agreement. Casazza typed up an agreement that had a sale price of $200,000 and required a marine survey, sea trial, and replacement of the mast step. Kiser did not sign this agreement. They both executed a software license transfer contract for navigational software. This contract did not refer to the boat. After Casazza arranged for a marine survey and got an estimate for mast step repair, Kiser told him he would not sell him the boat. Casazza sued. Was there an agreement sufficient to satisfy the Statute of Frauds?

LO ❶   **6.** Bernard Stanfield orally agreed to give Glenn Grove a 1936 car in exchange for Grove doing reupholstering on Stanfield's 1953 car. Grove received the 1936 car, but not its title, and the reupholstering was never done. Eight years later Stanfield sued Grove alleging Grove owed $8,000 for the car. Because the contract was oral and came within the Statute of Frauds, the court had to address the question of whether there had been receipt and acceptance of the goods. Had there?

LO ❸   **7.** Quality Oil Co. sent a letter to Pee Dee Oil Co. saying, "We propose to purchase your Shell contract for $75,000.00 and the Fastway station . . . for $140,000.00. . . . [W]e would pay you a reasonable market value for the equipment located at the Rockingham Self Service and Holiday Shell. We would . . . assume the leases on these locations. . . . Please contact us as soon as you have made your decision on our proposal." Quality prepared a written contract, which Pee Dee signed and returned to Quality. Four months later, Quality had not signed the contract and Pee Dee had to sell some of the assets at a loss. When Pee Dee sued for breach of contract, Quality said the contract was not binding because Quality had not signed it. Was there an enforceable contract?

Transfer of Title and Risk in Sales Contracts

LEARNING OBJECTIVES

① Explain the importance of determining when ownership and risk of loss pass.

② Distinguish between a sale on approval, a sale or return, and a consignment.

③ Discuss the rule regarding attempted sales by people who do not have title to the goods, and list exceptions to the rule.

PREVIEW CASE

→ Brawn of California sold clothing by mail-order. It required customers to pay a $1.48 "insurance fee" on all orders. This covered its costs to replace items lost or damaged in transit. Customers were entitled to return any items with which they were not satisfied for a full refund. Jacq Wilson bought items from Brawn and paid the insurance fee. He sued Brawn on behalf of himself and all other similarly situated persons claiming Brawn's sales were sales on approval. As such sales, he alleged Brawn bore the risk of loss until buyers accepted the merchandise. What were the terms of the contracts between Brawn and Wilson? Can the parties to a sales contract determine when risk of loss passes?

The right of ownership of property or evidence of ownership is called **title**. When a person owns a television set, for example, that owner holds all the power to control the set. If desired, the set may be kept or sold. When sold, title to—and, normally, physical possession of—the set passes to the buyer, who then has control over it. Normally, if the TV set is damaged or lost, the owner bears any loss. In business transactions some problems may arise regarding title to goods and risk of loss. This is because businesses deal in large volumes of goods and often must arrange the sale of goods before they may even exist, both of which may make physical possession of the goods difficult or impossible.

LO ①
When title and risk pass

Title
Evidence of ownership of property

POTENTIAL PROBLEMS IN SALES TRANSACTIONS

In the vast majority of sales transactions, the buyer receives the proper goods and makes payment, which completes the transaction. However, several types of problems may arise that, for the most part, can be avoided if the parties expressly state their intentions in their sales contract. When the parties have not specified the results they desire, however, the rules in this chapter apply. Some of the potential issues are ownership, insurance, and damage to goods.

Ownership

Creditors of the seller may seize the goods in the belief that the seller owns them, or the buyer's creditors may seize them on the theory that they belong to the buyer. In such a case, ownership of the goods must be determined. The question of ownership is also important in connection with resale by the buyer, liability for or computation of certain kinds of taxes, and liability under certain registration and criminal statutes.

Insurable Interest

Until the buyer has received the goods and the seller has been paid, both the seller and buyer have an economic interest in the sales transaction. The question arises as to whether either or both have enough interest to entitle them to insure the property involved; that is, whether they have an insurable interest.

Risk of Loss

If the goods are damaged or totally destroyed through no fault of either the buyer or the seller, must the seller bear the loss and supply new goods to the buyer? Or must the buyer pay the seller the purchase price even though the buyer now has no goods or has only damaged goods? The essential element in determining who bears the risk of loss is identifying the party who has control over the goods.

CLASSIFICATION OF SALES TRANSACTIONS

The nature of the transaction between the seller and the buyer determines the answer to be given to each question in the preceding section. However, sales transactions may be classified according to

1. The nature of the goods
2. The terms of the transaction

Nature of the Goods

As explained in Chapter 16, goods may be existing goods, identified goods, or future goods. Goods are existing goods even if the sellers must do some act or complete the manufacture of the goods before they satisfy the terms of the contract.

Terms of the Transaction

The terms of the contract may require that the goods be sent or shipped to the buyer; that is, that the seller make shipment. In that case, the seller's part is performed when the goods are handed over to a carrier, such as a truck line, for shipment.

Instead of calling for actual delivery of goods, the transaction may involve a transfer of the document of title representing the goods. For example, the goods may be stored in a warehouse with the seller and the buyer having no intention of moving the goods, but intending that there should be a sale and a delivery of the **warehouse receipt** that stands for the goods. In this case the seller must produce the proper paper as distinguished from the goods themselves. The same is true when the goods are represented by a bill of lading issued by a carrier, or by any other document of title.

Warehouse Receipt
Document of title issued by storage company for goods stored

OWNERSHIP, INSURABLE INTERESTS, AND RISK OF LOSS IN PARTICULAR TRANSACTIONS

The kinds of goods and transaction terms may be combined in a number of ways. Only the more common types of transactions will be considered here. The following rules of law apply only in the absence of a contrary agreement by the parties concerning these matters.

Existing Goods Identified at Time of Contracting

The title to existing goods, identified at the time of contracting and not to be transported, passes to the buyer at the time and place of contracting.

If existing goods require transporting, title to the goods passes to the buyer when the seller has completed delivery. If the seller is a merchant, the risk of loss passes to the buyer when the goods are received from the merchant. If the seller is a nonmerchant, the risk passes when the seller tenders or makes available the goods to the buyer. Thus, the risk of loss remains longer on the merchant seller on the ground that the merchant seller, being in the business, can more readily arrange to be protected against such continued risk.

The buyer, who becomes the owner of the goods, has an insurable interest in them against risk of loss when title passes. Conversely, the seller no longer has an insurable interest unless by agreement a security interest has been reserved to protect the right to payment.

The buyer of a motor vehicle bears the risk of loss when the transaction between the buyer and seller is completed even though the state may not yet have issued a new title in the buyer's name.

Negotiable Documents Representing Existing Goods Identified at Time of Contracting

When documents that can transfer title, or ownership, represent existing, identified goods, the buyer has a property interest, but not title, and an insurable interest in such goods at the time and place of contracting for their sale. The buyer does not ordinarily acquire the title nor become subject to the risk of loss until delivery of the documents is made. Conversely, the seller has an insurable interest and title up to that time.

Future Goods Marking and Shipment

A buyer may send an order for goods to be manufactured by the seller or to be filled from inventory or by purchases from third persons. If so, one step in the process of filling the order is the seller's act of marking, tagging, labeling, or otherwise indicating to the shipping department or the seller that certain goods are the ones to be sent or delivered to the buyer under contract. This act gives the buyer a property interest in the goods and the right to insure them. However, neither title nor risk of loss passes to the buyer until shipment or delivery occurs. The seller, as continuing owner, also has an insurable interest in the goods until shipment or delivery.

Shipment Contract
Seller liable until goods delivered to carrier

When the contract is a **shipment contract**, the seller completes performance of the contract when the goods are delivered to a carrier for shipment to the buyer. Under such a contract, the title and risk of loss pass to the buyer when the goods are delivered to the carrier; that is, title and risk of loss pass to the buyer at the time and place of shipment.

Destination Contract
Seller liable until goods delivered to destination

When the seller is required to deliver goods to a particular destination, the contract is a **destination contract**, and the seller's performance is not completed until the goods are delivered to the destination. Title and risk of loss do not pass to the buyer until such delivery is made.

COURT CASE

Facts: After Payless Cashways filed for bankruptcy protection, its large supplier of wood products, Canfor Corp., received only Payless stock for its claim. Canfor continued to supply Payless with lumber but met with Payless to try to set up payment terms that would limit its risk of nonpayment. All the contracts were destination contracts to Payless facilities. Payless agreed to make all payments by electronic fund transfer (EFT) based on the average delivery time by rail or truck. After Payless again filed for bankruptcy protection, the bankruptcy trustee asked the court to order Canfor to return large payments. The outcome hinged on whether the sales were cash on delivery or credit transactions.

Outcome: Since the contracts were destination contracts, Canfor retained risk of loss, title to, and control of the lumber until it was delivered. Since Canfor retained title, they were not credit sales.

—*In re Payless Cashways,*
306 B.R. 243 (8th Cir. BAP)

Normally, the contract will specify whether it is a shipment contract or a destination contract. If the contract does not expressly specify that the seller must deliver to a particular destination, the Uniform Commercial Code (UCC) presumes it is a shipment contract.

COURT CASE

Facts: When Jordan Panel Systems Corp. contracted to install window wall panels at Kennedy Airport, it ordered custom-made windows from Windows, Inc. The contract stated the windows were "to be shipped properly crated . . . for . . . motor freight transit and delivered to New York City." Windows built the window panels and delivered them to Consolidated Freightways intact and properly packaged. They were extensively damaged during shipment. Jordan did not pay for them, and Windows sued.

Outcome: Because the court said there was not an express agreement for a destination contract, this was a shipping contract and risk of loss passed to Jordan when Windows delivered the windows to the shipper. Jordan had to pay for the windows.

—*Windows, Inc. v. Jordan Panel Systems Corp.,*
177 F.3d 114 (2d Cir.)

COD Shipment

In the absence of an extension of credit, a seller has the right to keep the goods until the buyer pays for them. The seller loses this right if possession of the goods is delivered to anyone for the buyer. However, where the goods are delivered to a carrier, the seller may keep the right to possession by making the shipment COD (cash on delivery), or by the addition of any other terms indicating that the carrier is not to surrender the goods to the buyer until the buyer has paid for them. The COD provision does not affect when title or risk of loss passes.

Auction Sales

When goods are sold at an auction in separate lots, each lot is a separate transaction, and title to each passes independently of the other lots. Title to each lot passes when the auctioneer announces by the fall of the hammer or in any other customary manner that the auction is completed as to that lot.

Free on Board

A contract may call for goods to be sold **FOB (free on board)** a designated point. Goods may be sold FOB the seller's plant, the buyer's plant, an intermediate point, or a specified carrier. The seller bears the risk and expense until the goods are delivered at the FOB point designated.

FOB (Free on Board)
Designated point to which seller bears risk and expense

COURT CASE

Facts: Saul Boyman contracted to buy a boat. The contract required the boat to be delivered "FOB Stuart, Florida." The boat was manufactured in North Carolina and shipped by ocean freight to Stuart, Florida. A dispute about the sale resulted in a lawsuit in which the seller of the boat alleged that Boyman was required to pay the freight charge.

Outcome: The court held that the term "FOB Stuart" required the seller to pay freight charges until the boat reached its destination of Stuart, Florida.

— *Boyman v. Stuart Hatteras, Inc.,*
527 So. 2d 853 (Fla. Dist. Ct. App.)

International Sales Terms

Sales in the United States are governed by the foregoing rules regarding commercial shipping terms and how they relate to when title and risk of loss pass. The situation can differ in the case of international sales. In Chapter 16, the Convention on Contracts for the International Sale of Goods (CISG) was mentioned because it could apply to parties whose countries have ratified it. The CISG incorporates 13 International Commercial Terms, called **Incoterms**, to supply international rules to interpret sales terms widely used in international trade. For example, CFR, which is short for Cost and Freight, when used in an international sales contract means the seller pays the costs and freight to the delivery port, but title and risk of loss pass to the buyer once the goods are on board the ship at the port of shipment. Because these Incoterms are incorporated into the CISG, parties whose contracts might be subject to the CISG should know what they mean before entering into an international sales contract.

Incoterms
International commercial terms

Sales of Fungible Goods

Fungible Goods
Goods of a homogeneous nature sold by weight or measure

Fungible goods are goods of a homogeneous or like nature that may be sold by weight or measure. They include goods of which any unit is treated as the equivalent of any other unit, due to its nature or its commercial use. Fungible goods include wheat, oil, coal, and similar bulk commodities, as any one bushel or other unit of the whole will be the same as any other bushel or similar unit within the same grade.

The UCC provides that title to an undivided share or quantity of an identified mass of fungible goods may pass to the buyer at the time of the transaction. This makes the buyer an owner in common with the seller. For example, when one person sells to another 600 bushels of wheat from a bin that contains 1,000 bushels, title to 600 bushels passes to the buyer at the time of the transaction. This gives the buyer a six-tenths undivided interest in the mass as an owner in common with the seller. The courts in some states, however, have held that the title does not pass until a separation has been made.

The passage of title to a part of a larger mass of fungible goods differs from the passage of title of a fractional interest with no intent to make a later separation. In the former case, the buyer will become the exclusive owner of a separated portion, such as half a herd of cattle. In the latter case, the buyer will become a co-owner of the entire mass. Thus, there can be a sale of a part interest in a radio, an automobile, or a flock of sheep. The right to make a sale of a fractional interest is recognized by statute.

DAMAGE TO OR DESTRUCTION OF GOODS

Damage to or the destruction of the goods affects the transaction.

Damage to Identified Goods Before Risk of Loss Passes

When goods identified at the time of contracting suffer some damage, or are destroyed through no fault of either party before the risk of loss has passed, the contract is avoided—or annulled—if the loss is total. If the loss is partial, or if the goods have so deteriorated that they do not conform to the contract, the buyer has the option, after inspecting the goods, (1) to treat the contract as avoided, or (2) to accept the goods subject to an allowance or deduction from the contract price. In either case, the buyer cannot assert any claims against the seller for breach of contract.

Damage to Identified Goods After Risk of Loss Passes

If partial damage or total destruction occurs after the risk of loss has passed, it is the buyer's loss. However, the buyer may be able to recover the amount of the damages from the person in possession of the goods or from a third person causing the loss. For example, in many instances, the risk of loss passes at the time of the transaction even though the seller will deliver the goods later. During the period from the transfer of the risk of loss to the transfer of possession to the buyer, the seller has possession of the goods and is liable to the buyer for failure to exercise reasonable care.

Damage to Unidentified Goods

As long as the goods are unidentified, no risk of loss has passed to the buyer. If a buyer contracts, for example, to sell wheat without specifying whether it is growing, to be grown, or the land on which it is to be grown, the contract is for unidentified goods. If they are damaged or destroyed during this period, the seller bears the loss. The buyer may still enforce the contract and require the seller to deliver the goods according to the contract. A seller who fails to deliver the goods is liable to the buyer for breach of the contract. The only exceptions arise when the parties have specified in the contract that destruction of the seller's supply shall release the seller from liability, or when the parties clearly contracted for the purchase and sale of part of the seller's supply to the exclusion of any other possible source of such goods.

COURT CASE

Facts: Expecting to produce 360,000 bushels of corn, the Bartlett Partnership contracted to sell four shipments of corn amounting to 300,000 bushels to ConAgra at specified times in the future. A hailstorm severely damaged Bartlett's crop in August, and it only delivered 108,000 bushels. ConAgra sued, and Bartlett alleged its performance was excused because the goods were identified at the time of contracting, and therefore the law allowed it to avoid a contract if the goods were damaged without fault of either party before risk of loss passed.

Outcome: The court stated that there was nothing in the contract that identified the corn to be sold by Bartlett except by kind and amount. Since corn is fungible, it was not identified to the contract, and Bartlett was not excused from performing.

—*ConAgra, Inc. v. Bartlett Partnership,*
540 N.W.2d 333 (Neb.)

Reservation of Title or Possession

When the seller reserves title or possession solely as security to make certain that payment will be made, the buyer bears the risk of loss if he would bear the loss without such a reservation.

SALES ON APPROVAL AND WITH RIGHT TO RETURN

A sales transaction may give the buyer the privilege of returning the goods even though they conform to the contract. In a **sale on approval**, the sale is not complete until the buyer approves the goods. A **sale or return** is a completed sale with the right of the buyer to return the goods and thereby set aside the sale. The contract the parties have made determines whether the sale is a sale on approval or a sale or return. If the parties fail to indicate their intention, a returnable-goods transaction is deemed a sale on approval if a consumer purchases the goods for use. It is deemed a sale or return if a merchant purchases the goods for resale.

LO **2**
Distinguish sale on approval, sale or return, consignment

Sale on Approval
Sale that is not completed until buyer approves goods

Sale or Return
Completed sale with right to return goods

PREVIEW CASE REVISITED

Facts: Brawn of California sold clothing by mail-order. It required customers to pay a $1.48 "insurance fee" on all orders. This covered its costs to replace items lost or damaged in transit. Customers were entitled to return any items with which they were not satisfied for a full refund. Jacq Wilson bought items from Brawn and paid the insurance fee. He sued Brawn on behalf of himself and all other similarly situated persons claiming Brawn's sales were sales on approval. As such sales, he alleged Brawn bore the risk of loss until buyers accepted the merchandise.

Outcome: The court held that since Brawn's contracts required buyers to pay for insurance, the risk of loss in transit was on buyers.

—*Wilson v. Brawn of California, Inc.,* 33 Cal. Rptr.3d 769 (Cal. App.)

Consequence of Sale on Approval

Unless agreed otherwise, title and risk of loss remain with the seller under a sale on approval. Use of the goods by the buyer for the purpose of trial does not mean approval. However, an approval occurs if the buyer acts in a manner inconsistent with a reasonable trial, or if the buyer fails to express a choice within the time specified (or within a reasonable time if no time is specified). For example, a "ten-day home trial" of a set of encyclopedias allows a consumer to use the books for ten days. If the consumer does not return the encyclopedias by the tenth day, the books are considered approved. If the buyer returns the goods, the seller bears the risk and the expense involved. Since the buyer is not the "owner" of the goods while they are on approval, the buyer's creditors may not claim the goods.

Consequence of Sale or Return

Commercial Unit
Quantity regarded as separate unit

In a sale or return, title and risk of loss pass to the buyer as in the case of an ordinary sale. In the absence of a contrary agreement, the buyer under a sale or return may return all of the goods or any commercial unit thereof. A **commercial unit** includes any article, group of articles, or quantity commercially regarded as a separate unit or item, such as a particular machine, a suite of furniture, or a carload lot. The goods must still be in substantially their original condition, and the option to return must be exercised within the time specified by the contract or within a reasonable time if not specified. The return under such a contract is at the buyer's risk and expense. As long as the goods are in the buyer's possession, the buyer's creditors may treat the goods as belonging to the buyer.

SPECIAL RULES ON TRANSFER OF TITLE

LO ❸
Attempted sales without title

Bailment
Temporary transfer of possession of personal property

As a general rule, people can sell only such interest or title in goods as they possess. For example, if property is subject to a **bailment** (personal property temporarily in the custody of another person), a sale by the owner is subject to the bailment. Thus, if the owner of a rented car sells the car to another person, the person who has rented the car, the bailee, may still use the car according to the terms of the bailment. Similarly, bailees can only transfer their individual rights under the bailments, assuming that the bailment agreements permit the rights to be assigned or transferred.

A thief or finder generally cannot transfer legal title to property. Only the actual property in possession (in the case of a thief or finder) can be passed. In fact, the purchaser from the thief not only fails to obtain title but also becomes liable to the owner as a converter of the property. Liability occurs even though the property may have been purchased in good faith.

COURT CASE

Facts: Steve Sitton obtained a gold Rolex watch from Nowlin Jewelry by forging a check for $9,000. He asked Eddie Kotis, a car salesman who owned a Rolex, if he wanted to buy one. Kotis was interested so Sitton came to the car lot and sold him the watch for $3,500. Kotis called Nowlin's and, although initially refusing to identify himself, was told Sitton had purchased the watch the previous day with a check that had not yet cleared. Kotis would not say how much Sitton was asking for the watch and claimed he did not have it and did not want it. Nowlin's found out the check was bad and tried to talk to Kotis, who said to talk to his lawyer. When Nowlin sued, Kotis claimed to be a good faith purchaser and entitled to the watch.

Outcome: The court said that Kotis was not a good faith purchaser. He knew the price was exorbitantly low, which was evidence the watch was stolen. Kotis could not willfully disregard suspicious facts that would make a reasonable person believe the deal was illegal.

—Kotis v. Nowlin Jewelry, Inc.,
844 S.W.2d 920 (Tex. App.)

Certain instances occur, however, when because of the conduct of the owner or the desire of society to protect the bona fide purchaser for value, the law permits a greater title to be transferred than the seller possesses. It is important to note that the purchaser must act in good faith, which means be unaware the seller does not have title. These situations include:

1. A sale by an entrustee
2. Consignment sales
3. Estoppel
4. When documents of title transfer ownership
5. When documents must be recorded or filed
6. Voidable title

Sale by Entrustee

If the owner entrusts goods to a merchant who deals in goods of that kind, the merchant has the power to transfer the entruster's title to anyone who buys in the ordinary course of business. This is true as long as the merchant is not doing business in the entrusting owner's name. Similarly, the goods are subject to the claims of the merchant's creditors.

It is immaterial why the goods were entrusted to the merchant. Hence the leaving of a watch for repairs with a jeweler who sells new and secondhand watches would give the jeweler the power to pass the title to a buyer in the ordinary course of business. The entrustee is, of course, liable to the owner for damages caused by the sale of the goods and may be guilty of a statutory offense such as embezzlement.

If the entrustee is not a merchant, but merely a prospective customer, no transfer of title occurs if the entrustee sells to a third person.

Consignment Sales

Consignment
Transfer of possession of goods for purpose of sale

A manufacturer, distributor, or other person may send goods to a dealer for sale to the public with the understanding that the manufacturer, distributor, or other person is to remain the owner and the dealer is, in effect, to act as an agent. This is a **consignment.** Title does not normally pass to the consignee. However, when the dealer maintains a place of business at which dealings are made in goods of the kind in question under a name other than that of the person consigning the goods, the creditors of the dealer may reach the goods as though the dealer owned them. Also, the dealer will pass good title to goods sold to a buyer in the ordinary course of business.

COURT CASE

Facts: Chilla Mitchell left her car for sale at Tommy Thrash's car dealership, called "Repo City." Thrash agreed to pay her $16,500 when her car sold. Roosevelt Jones bought the car from Repo City, but Thrash did not pay Mitchell. Mitchell went to where she had left her car, but the car lot was gone, and she was not able to find Thrash. She learned that Jones had her car and sued him for its return.

Outcome: Because Jones was a buyer in the ordinary course of Thrash's business, and Jones bought the car in good faith, he had title to the car.

—Jones v. Mitchell,
816 So. 2d 68 (Ala. Civ. App.)

A consignment differs from a sale on approval or a sale with right to return. In the absence of any contrary provision, it is an agency and means that property is in the possession of the consignee for sale. Normally the consignor may revoke the agency at will and retake possession of the property. Whether goods are sent to a person as buyer or on consignment to sell for the owner depends upon the intention of the parties.

Estoppel

ETHICAL POINT

How is the doctrine of estoppel based on ethical considerations?

The owner of property may be estopped (barred) from asserting ownership and denying the right of another person to sell the property to a good-faith purchaser. A person may purchase a product and have the bill of sale made out in the name of a friend who receives possession of the product and the bill of sale. This might be done in order to deceive creditors or to keep other persons from knowing that the purchase had been made. If the friend should sell the product to a bona fide purchaser who relies on the bill of sale, the true owner is estopped or barred from denying the friend's apparent ownership.

Documents of Title

Document of Title
Document that shows ownership

Documents that show ownership are called **documents of title.** They include bills of lading and warehouse receipts. By statute, certain documents of title, when executed in the proper form, may transfer title. The holder of such a document may convey the title of the person who left the property with the issuer of the document if all of the following conditions are met:

1. The document indicates it may be transferred.
2. The transferee does not know of any wrongdoing.
3. The transferee has purchased the document by giving up something of value.

In such cases, it is immaterial that the transferor had not acquired the documents in a lawful manner.

Recording or Filing Documents

In order to protect subsequent purchasers and creditors, statutes may require that certain transactions be recorded or filed. The statutes may provide that a transaction not recorded or filed has no effect against a purchaser who thereafter buys the goods in good faith from the person who appears to be the owner or against creditors who have lawfully seized the goods of such an apparent owner.

Suppose a seller makes a credit sale and wants to be able to seize and sell the goods if the buyer does not make payment. The UCC requires the seller to file certain papers. If they are not filed, the buyer will appear to own the goods free from any interest of the seller. Subsequent bona fide purchasers or creditors of the buyer can acquire title, and the seller will lose the right to repossess the goods.

Voidable Title

If the buyer has a voidable title, as when the goods were obtained by fraud, the seller can rescind the sale while the buyer is still the owner. If, however, the buyer resells the property to a bona fide purchaser before the seller has rescinded the transaction, the subsequent purchaser acquires valid title. It is immaterial whether the buyer having the voidable title had obtained title by fraud as to identity, or by larceny by trick, or that payment for the goods had been made with a bad check, or that the transaction was a cash sale and the purchase price had not been paid.

QUESTIONS

1. Normally, what right and what liability does a person who holds title to goods have?
2. When does title to existing, identified goods that are not to be transported pass?
3. What interests does a buyer have at the time of contracting when documents that can transfer title represent existing, identified goods?
4. When does the buyer of a motor vehicle bear the risk of loss?
5. When a seller must deliver goods to a specified destination, when do title and risk of loss pass to the buyer?
6. What is the difference between a shipment contract and a destination contract?
7. Why might a party to an international sales contract have to be knowledgeable about Incoterms?
8. Distinguish among a sale on approval, a sale or return, and a consignment.
9. Normally, can a thief or finder transfer title to property to a purchaser? Explain.
10. If a buyer obtains goods by means of fraud, may the seller always recover the property?

CASE PROBLEMS

LO **1**   1. Steve Hammer and Ron Howe gave Kevin Thompson possession of 150 heifers for grazing. Thompson was an order buyer—he bought cattle for people who wanted to buy them and tried to help people who wanted to sell cattle sell them. Thompson sold the 150 heifers to Roger Morris. Hammer and Howe sued. Thompson had purchased cattle in 25 transactions but made only six sales during the year prior to selling Hammer and Howe's heifers. During the five months after that sale, Thompson made many purchases but only one sale. Morris alleged the sale to him was by a merchant who dealt in goods of the kind. Was it?

LO **3**   2. Robert Murphy owned a Cadillac and agreed to let Rickwood Auto, a used car dealer, display the car for sale on its lot. Murphy was to receive any proceeds greater than $18,500. Rickwood got an advance on its line of credit from SouthTrust Bank of Alabama, N.A. to pay for the Cadillac. Rickwood later defaulted and SouthTrust went to Rickwood to repossess all its cars. Elizabeth Howard had agreed to buy the Cadillac from Rickwood. A lawsuit ensued, and the court had to decide whether the transaction between Murphy and Rickwood was a sale or a consignment. Which was it?

LO **2**   3. Sam and Mac, Inc. (SMI) ordered kitchen cabinets from Gruda Enterprises for a house it was building. Gruda was to deliver and install the cabinets. Gruda ordered them from a manufacturer, and SMI paid Gruda for them. Gruda received the cabinets and called SMI to say it was ready to deliver and install them. SMI asked Gruda to keep the cabinets at the warehouse until the house was ready for them. The owners of Gruda went bankrupt and Gruda closed. SMI asked James Treat, Gruda's landlord, to open the business and let SMI get the cabinets. Treat refused. SMI sued Treat alleging it had title to the cabinets. Did it?

LO **1**   4. Revco Drug Stores, Inc. ordered skin care products from Stevens Skin Softener, Inc. on a sale or return basis. Revco did not pay for them. About 30,000 units were purchased, but Revco sold fewer than 1,000 units. In February, Revco asked to return the products and Stevens agreed. Normal industry practice is that 60 to 90 days would be a suitable time for the returns. Stevens received returns starting in March and going through October. Stevens sued Revco for payment of the goods. Does Revco have to pay anything?

LO **2**   5. After Automaster Motor Co. bought a Honda from a private owner, it sold the car to Carey's Auto Sales. A Carey's employee went to Automaster, delivered a check in payment for the car, put Carey's dealer's plates on it, and drove it away. While returning to Carey's lot, the employee had an accident. Automaster assigned the title to Carey's several days later. Automaster's and Carey's insurance companies argued the other was liable for the injuries suffered by Carey's employee. Their liability hinged on which auto dealer owned the Honda. Did Automaster or Carey own the car?

LO **1**   6. Kenneth Stevenson, a car dealer doing business as T & S Enterprises, asked Peter Pan Motors if it could find a certain kind of white BMW. Peter Pan said it could and located and bought one. T & S picked up the car. The parties had made previous deals in which Peter Pan would sell T & S cars, and T & S would resell them. T & S deposited payment for the BMW in Peter Pan's bank account, but stopped payment on the check and told Peter Pan it did not want the car. While T & S had the BMW, a creditor, Wayne Minor, claimed it. He said the transaction was a sale or return, so the BMW's title passed to T & S, and Minor had a valid claim against it. Was there a sale or return?

7. Stephen Snider bought and paid for an "as is" used car from Berea Kar Co. Snider had trouble with the car and ceased using it a month later. It sat in his driveway for several months and was then stolen. The certificate of title had never been transferred to Snider, so he sued Berea for return of his purchase money. He argued he did not bear the risk of loss since he did not have the certificate of title. Did Snider bear the risk of loss?   LO ❸

8. Vernon Crum was a merchant in the business of selling used cars to used car dealers. By means of a sight draft, J&T Auto Sales bought some cars for resale from Crum. While keeping the certificates of title for the cars, Crum transferred possession of the cars to J&T. J&T transferred the cars to By-Pass Auto Sales, another used car dealer, which resold the cars in the course of its business to buyers who gave notes for them. By-Pass sold the notes to SouthTrust Bank of Alabama. By-Pass did not pay J&T for the cars, and J&T's draft was not paid. The people who had bought the cars from By-Pass applied for certificates of title, but the state would not issue them without the current title certificates, which Crum had. SouthTrust sued Crum and J&T for the title certificates. Did ownership of the cars pass to By-Pass's customers?   LO ❷

Warranties, Product Liability, and Consumer Protection

LEARNING OBJECTIVES

❶ Define a warranty, and distinguish between express and implied warranties.

❷ Specify the warranties that apply to all sellers and those that apply only to merchants.

❸ Explain how warranties may be excluded or surrendered.

❹ Explain the various means the law uses to provide consumer protection.

PREVIEW CASE

Amy and Joseph Mitsch bought a used GMC Yukon from Rockenbach Chevrolet. The purchase contract stated: "THIS USED MOTOR VEHICLE IS SOLD AS IS WITHOUT ANY WARRANTY EITHER EXPRESSED OR IMPLIED. THE PURCHASER WILL BEAR THE ENTIRE EXPENSE OF REPAIRING OR CORRECTING ANY DEFECTS THAT PRESENTLY EXIST OR MAY OCCUR." Joseph signed his name directly below this statement. For 18 months, the Mitschs took the Yukon to be repaired on a number of occasions, according to them without success. Because of the frequency of repairs, they lost confidence in the vehicle. They sought to revoke acceptance of it and sued for breach of warranty, alleging Rockenbach's disclaimer failed because it did not contain the word "merchantability." Was the language in the contract easy to read? Would words in all capital letters be very noticeable when the rest of the contract was not in all capitals?

LO ❶
Warranties, express and implied

Warranty
Assurance article conforms to a standard

In making a sale, a seller often makes a **warranty**. A warranty is an assurance that the article sold will conform to a certain standard or will operate in a certain manner. By the warranty, the seller agrees to make good any loss or damages that the purchaser may suffer if the goods are not as represented.

A warranty made at the time of the sale is considered to be a part of the contract and is therefore binding. A warranty made after a sale has been completed is binding even though not supported by any consideration; it is regarded as a modification of the sales contract.

EXPRESS WARRANTIES

The statement of the seller in which the article sold is warranted or guaranteed is known as an **express warranty**. The UCC specifically provides that any affirmation of fact or promise made by the seller to the buyer that relates to the goods and becomes part of the basis of the bargain creates an express warranty. The seller actually and definitely states an express warranty either orally or in writing. For example, the statement, "The whopper pizza contains one pound of cheese," is an express warranty as to the amount of cheese on the pizza.

However, the seller needs no particular words to constitute an express warranty. The words "warranty" or "guarantee" need not be used. If a reasonable interpretation of the language of a statement or a promise leads the buyer to believe a warranty exists, the courts will construe it as such. A seller is bound by the ordinary meaning of the words used, not by any unexpressed intentions.

The seller can use the word "warrant" or "guarantee" and still not be bound by it if an ordinary, prudent person would not interpret it to constitute a warranty. If the seller of a car says, "I'll guarantee that you will not be sorry if you buy the car at this price," no warranty exists. This is mere sales talk, even though the seller used the word "guarantee."

Express Warranty
Statement of guarantee by seller

Seller's Opinion

Sellers may praise their wares, even extravagantly, without being obligated on their statements or representations. A person should not be misled by "puffing." Such borderline expressions as "Best on the market for the money," "These goods are worth $10 if they are worth a dime," "Experts have estimated that one ought to be able to sell a thousand a month of these," and many others, which sound very convincing, are mere expressions of opinion, not warranties.

Although an expression by the seller of what is clearly an opinion does not normally constitute either a warranty or a basis for fraud liability, the seller may be liable for fraud if, in fact, the seller does not believe the opinion. Also, a statement of opinion by the seller is a warranty if the seller asserts an opinion on a matter of which the buyer is ignorant so that the buyer has to rely on the seller for information on the matter. If the seller merely states an opinion on a matter of which the seller has no special knowledge and on which the buyer may be expected also to have an opinion and exercise judgment, it is not a warranty.

ETHICAL POINT

The law may not define statements of opinion as warranties, but is it ethical for a seller to make such statements when they are not true?

ETHICAL POINT

Is it ethical for a seller to make extravagant claims about merchandise?

COURT ✦ CASE

Facts: Charmaine Schreib and Dale Worker bought Walt Disney Co. movies on VHS videotape. The videos were described as part of a "Gold Collection" and "Masterpiece Collection" and marketed with the statement, "Give Your Children The Memories Of A Lifetime—Collect Each Timeless Masterpiece." After a few years, the videotapes deteriorated, and Schreib and Worker sued Disney alleging breach of express warranty. They alleged the statements constituted an express warranty that the tapes would last for generations.

Outcome: The court stated that the word "collection" meant a group of objects so that none of the statements promised the videotapes would last a lifetime. Even if the advertising had stated the tapes would last a lifetime, that statement would have been simply opinion or puffery.

—*Schreib v. Walt Disney Co.*, **2006 WL 573008 (Ill. App.)**

Defective Goods

If defects are actually known to the buyer, or defects are so apparent that no special skill or ability is required to detect them, an express warranty may not cover them. The determining factor is whether the statement becomes a part of the basis of the bargain. If it does, an express warranty results. This would not be true if the seller used any scheme or artifice to conceal the defect, such as covering the defect with an item of decoration.

IMPLIED WARRANTIES

Implied Warranty
Warranty imposed by law

An **implied warranty** is one that the seller did not make but that is imposed by the law. The implied warranty arises automatically from the fact that a sale has been made. For example, every seller implies that he or she owns the goods being sold and has the right to sell them. Express warranties arise because they form part of the basis on which the sale has been made.

Express warranties do not exclude implied warranties. When both express and implied warranties exist, they should be construed as consistent with each other. When not construed as consistent, an express warranty prevails over an implied warranty as to the same subject matter, except in the case of an implied warranty of fitness for a particular purpose.

FULL OR LIMITED WARRANTIES

Full Warranty
Warranty with unlimited duration of implied warranties

Limited Warranty
Written warranty, not a full warranty

A written warranty made for a consumer product may be either a **full warranty** or a **limited warranty**. The seller of a product with a full warranty must remedy any defects in the product in a reasonable time without charge, place no limit on the duration of implied warranties, not limit consequential damages for breach of warranty unless done conspicuously on the warranty's face, and permit the purchaser to choose a refund or replacement without charge if the product contains a defect after a reasonable number of attempts by the warrantor to remedy the defects. All other written warranties for consumer products are limited warranties (see Illustration 19–1).

WARRANTIES OF ALL SELLERS

The following warranties apply to all sellers.

Warranty of Title

LO ❷
Warranties of all sellers

All sellers, by the mere act of selling, make a warranty that they have good titles and make rightful transfers. This means that the seller is confirming ownership of the goods and that ownership is being transferred to the buyer.

A warranty of title may be excluded or modified by the specific language or the circumstances of the transaction. The latter situation occurs when the buyer has reason to know that the seller does not claim title or that the seller is purporting to sell only such right or title as the seller or a third person may have. For example, no warranty of title arises when the seller makes the sale in a representative capacity, such as a sheriff or an administrator. In another example, there is no warranty of title when a country singer's possessions are sold to pay an income tax lien. Likewise, no warranty arises when the seller makes the sale by virtue of a power of sale possessed as a pledgee or mortgagee.

ILLUSTRATION 19–1 Limited Warranty

ONE YEAR LIMITED WARRANTY

ABC Company warrants this product, to original owner, for one year from purchase date to be free of defects in material and workmanship.

Defective product may be brought or sent (freight prepaid) to an authorized service center listed in the phone book, or to Service Department, ABC Company, Main and First Streets, Riverdale, MO 65000, for free repair or replacement at our option.

Warranty does not include: cost of inconvenience, damage due to product failure, transportation damages, misuse, abuse, accident or the like, or commercial use. IN NO EVENT SHALL THE ABC COMPANY BE LIABLE FOR INCIDENTAL OR CONSEQUENTIAL DAMAGES. Some states do not allow exclusion or limitation of incidental or consequential damages, so above exclusion may not apply.

This warranty is the only written or express warranty given by The ABC Company. This warranty gives specific legal rights. You may have other rights which vary from state to state.

For information, write Consumer Claims Manager, at the Riverdale address. Send name, address, zip, model, serial number, and purchase date.

Keep this booklet. Record the following for reference:

Data purchased _____

Model Number_____

Serial Number_____

C O U R T   C A S E

Facts: ITT Industrial Credit Co. made a loan to Edward McGinn General Contractors, Inc., so McGinn gave ITT a lien on a hydraulic excavator. After McGinn had severe financial problems, Vilsmeier Auction Co. sold the excavator at auction. Before the auction, Vilsmeier declared that all the equipment being sold had no liens on it. Frank Arnold Contractors bought the excavator at the auction. Later, ITT sued Arnold on the basis of its lien on the excavator. Arnold sued Vilsmeier for breach of the warranty of title.

Outcome: The court held that disturbing the buyer's quiet possession of goods is one way in which a breach of the warranty of title can be established. Buyers should not have to participate in a contest over the validity of their ownership.

—*Frank Arnold Contractors, Inc.*
v. Vilsmeier Auction Co., Inc.,
806 F.2d 462 (3d Cir.)

Warranty Against Encumbrances

Every seller also makes a warranty that the goods shall be delivered free from any security interest or any other lien or encumbrance of which the buyer at the time of making the sales contract had no knowledge. Thus, a breach of warranty exists when the automobile sold to the buyer is already subject to an outstanding claim that had been placed against it by the original owner and which was unknown to the buyer at the time of the sale.

The warranty against encumbrances applies to the goods only at the time they are delivered to the buyer. It is not concerned with an encumbrance that existed before or at the time the sale was made. For example, a seller may not have paid in full for the goods being resold, and the original supplier may have a lien on the goods. The seller may resell the goods while that lien is still on them. The seller's only duty is to pay off the lien before the goods are delivered to the buyer.

A warranty against encumbrances does not arise if the buyer knows of the existence of the encumbrance in question. Knowledge must be actual knowledge as contrasted with constructive notice. **Constructive notice** is information that the law presumes everyone knows by virtue of the fact that it is filed or recorded on the public record.

Constructive Notice
Information or knowledge imputed by law

Warranty of Conformity to Description, Sample, or Model

Any description of the goods, sample, or model made part of the basis of the sales contract creates an express warranty that the goods shall conform in kind and quality to the description, sample, or model. Ordinarily, a **sample** is a portion of a whole mass that is the subject of the transaction, whereas a **model** is a replica of the article in question. The mere fact that a sample is exhibited during negotiation of the contract does not make the sale a sale by sample. There must be an intent shown that the sample is part of the basis of contracting. For example, a sample may be exhibited not as a promise or warranty that the goods will conform to it but just to allow the buyer to make a judgment on its quality. A small piece of molded plastic shown to a boat buyer to illustrate the materials and methods used in the construction of boats does not create a sale by sample.

Sample
Portion of whole mass of transaction

Model
Replica of an article

Warranty of Fitness for a Particular Purpose

When the seller has reason to know at the time of contracting that the buyer intends to use the goods for a particular or unusual purpose, the seller may make an implied warranty that the goods will be fit for that purpose. Such an implied warranty arises when the buyer relies on the seller's skill or judgment to select or furnish suitable goods and when the seller has reason to know of the buyer's reliance. For example, where a government representative inquired of the seller whether the seller had a tape suitable for use on a particular government computer system, there arose an implied warranty, unless otherwise excluded, that the tape furnished by the seller was fit for that purpose. This warranty of fitness for a particular purpose does not arise when the goods are to be used for the purpose for which they are customarily sold or when the buyer orders goods on particular specifications and does not disclose the purpose.

The fact that a seller does not intend to make a warranty of fitness for a particular purpose is immaterial. Parol evidence is admissible to show that the seller had knowledge of the buyer's intended use.

ADDITIONAL WARRANTIES OF MERCHANT

A seller who deals in goods of the kind involved in the sales contract, or who is considered because of occupation to have particular knowledge or skill regarding the goods involved, is a **merchant**. Such a seller makes additional implied warranties.

Merchant
Person who deals in goods of the kind or by occupation is considered to have particular knowledge or skill regarding goods involved

Warranty Against Infringement

Unless otherwise agreed, a merchant warrants that goods shall be delivered free of the rightful claim of any third person by way of patent or trademark infringement. However, this is not true when a buyer supplies the seller with exact specifications for the preparation or manufacture of goods. In such cases, the merchant seller makes no implied warranty against infringement. The buyer in substance makes a warranty to protect the seller from liability should the seller be held liable for patent violation by following the specifications of the buyer. For example, a business that orders the manufacture of a machine from blueprints and specifications supplied by the buyer must defend the manufacturer if it is later sued for patent infringement by someone holding a patent on a similar machine.

When the buyer furnishes the seller with specifications, the same warranties arise as in the case of any other sale of such goods by that seller. However, no warranty of fitness for a particular purpose can arise since the buyer is clearly purchasing on the basis of a decision made without relying on the seller's skill and judgment.

Warranty of Merchantability or Fitness for Normal Use

Unless excluded or modified, merchant sellers make an implied warranty of merchantability (or salability) which results in a group of warranties. The most important is that the goods are fit for the ordinary purposes for which they are sold.

The implied warranty of merchantability relates to the condition of the goods at the time the seller is to perform under the contract by selling the goods. Once the risk of loss has passed to the buyer, no warranty exists as to the continuing merchantability of the goods unless such subsequent deterioration or condition is proof that the goods were in fact not merchantable when the seller made delivery.

C O U R T   C A S E

Facts: Gina and Douglas Felde bought a new car from Schaumburg Dodge and signed a contract to make 48 monthly payments to Chrysler Credit Corp. Three weeks later, Gina noticed the car occasionally surged forward and accelerated by itself. She took it to the dealer, who replaced the throttle sensor. The problem continued, and Gina took the car back two or three times more, but the acceleration continued. Gina took the car to another dealer five times for the problem. The throttle sensor was replaced three times, but the sudden acceleration was not corrected. A year after buying the car, it lurched forward from a stop when Gina took her foot off the brake, and it hit a truck. Gina had the car towed to Schaumburg Dodge. The manager called her the next day and told her she would be charged for storage. Gina told him to keep the car. The Feldes sued for breach of the implied warranty of merchantability. At trial, a certified mechanic testified that the car was not safe to drive.

Outcome: The court said the warranty of merchantability was breached.

—Felde v. Chrysler Credit Corp.,
580 N.E.2d 191 (Ill. App. Ct.)

Warranty of merchantability relates only to the fitness of the product made or sold. It does not impose upon the manufacturer or seller the duty to employ any particular design or to sell one product rather than another because another might be safer.

WARRANTIES IN PARTICULAR SALES

As discussed in the following sections, particular types of sales may involve special considerations.

Sale of Food or Drink

The sale of food or drink, whether to be consumed on or off the seller's premises, is a sale. When made by a merchant, the sale carries the implied warranty that the food is fit for its ordinary purpose of human consumption. Some courts find no breach of warranty when a harmful object found in food was natural to the particular kind of food, such as an oyster shell in oysters, a chicken bone in chicken, and so on.

COURT CASE

Facts: In good health, William Simpson ate tuna at the Hatteras Island Gallery Restaurant. When he returned home from dinner, Simpson was flushed, short of breath, had rapid pulse, diarrhea, and was vomiting. He subsequently died from scombroid fish poisoning. Such poisoning results from an elevated histamine level in fish from mishandling. Simpson's widow sued the restaurant and the supplier of the tuna.

Outcome: The appellate court held that the warranty of merchantability was breached and Mrs. Simpson could recover.

—*Simpson v. Hatteras Island Gallery Restaurant,*
427 S.E.2d 131 (N.C. App.)

Other courts regard the warranty as breached when the presence of the harm-causing substance in the food could not be reasonably expected, without regard to whether the substance was natural or foreign, as in the case of a nail or piece of glass. In these cases, a determination of fact must be made, ordinarily by the jury, to determine whether the buyer could reasonably expect the object in the food.

It is, of course, necessary to distinguish the foregoing situations from those in which the preparation of the foods involves the continued presence of some element such as prune pits in cooked prunes or shells of shellfish.

Sale of Article with Patent or Trade Name

The sale of a patent- or trade-name article does not bar the existence of a warranty of fitness for a particular purpose, or of merchantability, when the circumstances giving rise to such a warranty otherwise exist. It is a question of fact whether the buyer relied on the seller's skill and judgment when making the purchase. If the buyer asked for a patent- or trade-name article and insisted on it, the buyer clearly did not rely on the seller's skill and judgment. Therefore, the sale lacks the factual basis for an implied warranty of fitness for the particular purpose. If the necessary reliance upon the seller's skill and judgment is shown, however, the warranty arises in that situation.

The seller of automobile parts, for example, is not liable for breach of the implied warranty of their fitness when the parts, for example, oil filters, were ordered by catalog number for use in a specified vehicle and the seller did not know that the lubrication system of the automobile had been changed so as to make the parts ordered unfit for use.

Sale of Secondhand or Used Goods

No warranty arises as to fitness of used property for ordinary use from a sale made by a casual seller. If made by a merchant seller, such a warranty may exist. A number of states follow the rule that implied warranties apply in connection with the sale of used or secondhand goods, particularly automobiles and equipment.

Leased Goods

Rather than purchase expensive goods, many people and businesses lease them. The users of the goods could suffer personal injury or property damage from the use or condition of leased property. Most states have adopted Article 2A of the UCC, which applies to personal property leasing. Article 2A treats lease transactions similarly to the way Article 2 treats sales, which includes express and implied warranty provisions. However, a warranty of possession without interference replaces the warranty of title.

EXCLUSION AND SURRENDER OF WARRANTIES

Warranties can be excluded or modified by the agreement of the parties, subject to the limitation that such a provision must not be unconscionable. If a warranty of fitness is to be excluded, the exclusion must be in writing and so conspicuous as to ensure that the buyer will be aware of its presence. If the implied warranty of merchantability is excluded or modified, the exclusion clause must expressly mention the word "merchantability" and if in writing, must be conspicuous.

LO ❸
Warranty exclusion and surrender

Particular Provisions

A statement such as, "There are no warranties that extend beyond the description on the face hereof" excludes all implied warranties of fitness. Normally, implied warranties are excluded by the statements "as is," "with all faults," or other language that in normal common speech calls attention to the warranty exclusion and makes it clear that no implied warranty exists. For example, an implied warranty that a steam heater would work properly in the buyer's dry cleaning plant is effectively excluded by provisions that "the warranties and guarantees herein set forth are made by us and accepted by you in lieu of all statutory or implied warranties or guarantees, other than title. . . . This contract contains all agreements between the parties, and there is no agreement, verbal or otherwise, that is not set down herein," and the contract has only a "one-year warranty on labor and material supplied by seller."

PREVIEW CASE REVISITED

Facts: Amy and Joseph Mitsch bought a used GMC Yukon from Rockenbach Chevrolet. The purchase contract stated: "THIS USED MOTOR VEHICLE IS SOLD AS IS <u>WITHOUT</u> ANY WARRANTY EITHER EXPRESSED OR IMPLIED. THE PURCHASER WILL BEAR THE <u>ENTIRE</u> <u>EXPENSE</u> OF REPAIRING OR CORRECTING ANY DEFECTS THAT PRESENTLY EXIST OR MAY OCCUR." Joseph signed his name directly below this statement. For 18 months, the Mitschs took the Yukon to be repaired on a number of occasions, according to them without success. Because of the frequency of repairs, they lost confidence in the vehicle. They sought to revoke acceptance of it and sued for breach of warranty, alleging Rockenbach's disclaimer failed because it did not contain the word "merchantability."

Outcome: The court held that the words "as is" in the contract were sufficient to disclaim the implied warranty of merchantability. It found that the prominent placement and size of the disclaimer were effective to give notice of it.

—*Mitsch v. General Motors Corp.*, 833 N.E.2d 936 (Ill. App.)

In order for a disclaimer of warranties to be a binding part of an oral sales contract, the disclaimer must be called to the attention of the buyer. When the contract as made does not disclaim warranties, a disclaimer of warranties accompanying goods delivered later is not effective because it is a unilateral, or one-sided, attempt to modify the contract.

Examination by the Buyer

No implied warranty exists with respect to defects in goods that an examination should have revealed when, before making the final contract, the buyer has examined the goods, or a model or sample, as fully as desired. No implied warranty exists if the buyer has refused to make such examination.

Dealings and Customs

An implied warranty can be excluded or modified by the course of dealings, the course of performance, or usage of trade. For example, if in the trade engaged in by the parties the words "no adjustment" meant "as is," the words "no adjustment" would exclude implied warranties.

Caveat Emptor

Caveat Emptor
Let the buyer beware

In the absence of fraud on the part of the seller, or in circumstances in which the law imposes a warranty, the relationship of the seller and the buyer is described by the maxim *caveat emptor* (let the buyer beware). Common-law courts rigidly applied this rule, requiring purchasers in ordinary sales to act on their own judgment except when sellers gave express warranties. The trend of the earlier statutes, the UCC, and decisions of modern courts has been to soften the harshness of this rule, primarily by establishing implied warranties for the protection of the buyer. Consumer protection statutes have also greatly softened this rule. The rule of caveat emptor still applies, however, when the buyer has full opportunity to make an examination of the goods that would disclose the existence of any defect, and the seller has not committed fraud.

PRODUCT LIABILITY

When harm to person or property results from the use or condition of an article of personal property, the person injured may be entitled to recover damages. This right may be based on the theory of breach of warranty.

Privity of Contract in Breach of Warranty

In the past, in common law there could be no suit for breach of warranty unless **privity of contract** (a contract relationship) existed between the plaintiff and the defendant. Now, however, a "stranger," one who does not have a contractual relationship, can sue on the theory of breach of warranty. For example, it has been held that a mechanic injured because of a defect in an automobile being fixed may sue the manufacturer for breach of implied warranty of fitness.

Privity of Contract
Relationship between contracting parties

In most states, an exception to the privity rule allows members of the buyer's family and various other persons not in privity of contract with the seller or manufacturer to sue for breach of warranty when injured by the harmful condition of food, beverages, or drugs.

The UCC expressly abolished the requirement of privity against the seller by members of the buyer's family, household, and guests in actions for personal injury. Apart from the express provision made by the UCC, a conflict of authority exists as to whether other cases require privity of contract. Some states lean toward the abolition of the privity requirement, while many states flatly reject the doctrine when a buyer sues the manufacturer or a prior seller. In many instances, recovery by the buyer against a remote manufacturer or seller is based on the fact that the defendant had advertised directly to the public and, therefore, made a warranty to the purchasing consumer of the truth of the advertising. Although advertising by the manufacturer to the consumer is a reason for not requiring privity when the consumer sues the manufacturer, the absence of advertising by the manufacturer frequently does not bar such action by the buyer. Although most jurisdictions have modified the privity requirement beyond the exceptions specified in the UCC, each state has retained limited applications of the doctrine.

COURT CASE

Facts: While William Bernick was playing hockey for Georgia Tech, he was struck in the face by a hockey stick. His mouthguard was shattered, his upper jaw was fractured, three teeth were knocked out, and a part of a fourth tooth was broken off. The manufacturer of the mouthguard, Cooper of Canada, Ltd., had promoted it through hockey catalog advertisements and parent guides as giving "maximum protection to the lips and teeth."

Outcome: The language was such as to induce the purchase of the mouthguard by Bernick's mother for his use while playing. Bernick did rely on an express warranty.

—Bernick v. Jurden,
293 S.E.2d 405 (N.C.)

Recovery also may be allowed when the consumer mails to the manufacturer a warranty registration card that the manufacturer had packed with the purchased article.

Warranty Protection

The Magnuson-Moss Warranty and Federal Trade Commission Improvement Act requires that written warranties for consumer goods meet certain requirements. Clear disclosure of all warranty provisions and a statement of the legal remedies of the consumer, including informal dispute settlement, under the warranty must be a part of the warranty. According to the act, the consumer must be informed of the warranty prior to the sale. In order to satisfy the law, the language of warranties of goods costing more than $15 must not be misleading to a "reasonable, average consumer."

C O U R T   C A S E

Facts: Roxanne Sadat bought a new car covered by a full written warranty. Unfortunately, the brakes faded or were hard to engage, the steering column vibrated excessively, the transmission slipped from park to reverse, the car leaked oil and diesel fuel after the engine was turned off, and the passenger compartment smelled of exhaust. Sadat took the car in to the dealer seven times for repair of these problems, but they were never cured. Sadat asked to have her car replaced at no cost. American Motors refused, so Sadat sued for relief under the Magnuson-Moss Act.

Outcome: The court said the law gave Sadat a right to sue for breach of warranty.

—Sadat v. American Motors Corp.,
448 N.E.2d 900 (Ill. App. Ct.)

The warranty time can be extended if repairs require that the product be out of service for an unreasonable length of time. When this occurs, the consumer may recover incidental expenses. If, after a reasonable number of opportunities, the manufacturer is unable to remedy the defect in a product, the consumer must be permitted to elect to receive a refund or a replacement when the product has been sold with a full warranty.

A significant aspect of the act requires that no written warranty may waive the implied warranties of merchantability and fitness for a particular purpose during the term of the written warranty, or unreasonably soon thereafter. Thus, the previously common practice of replacing the implied warranties of fitness and merchantability with substandard written warranties has been significantly limited. The act also curtails the limitation of implied warranties on items for which a service or maintenance contract is offered within 90 days after the initial sale. In addition, the act extends the coverage of a warranty to those who purchase consumer goods secondhand during the term of the warranty.

Effect of Reprocessing by Distributor

Frequently, a manufacturer produces a product or a supplier distributes it but believes or expects additonal processing or changes by the ultimate distributor or retailer. Such a manufacturer or supplier is not liable to the ultimate consumer for breach of warranty or negligence if the retailer does not complete the additional processing. For example, a supplier of pork sausage to a delicatessen might advise the delicatessen it would no longer heat the sausage to destroy trichinae. If the delicatessen advises the supplier that it will heat the sausage and does not, a person who becomes ill from eating the sausage can sue the delicatessen but not the supplier.

IDENTITY OF PARTIES

The existence of product liability may be affected by the identity of the claimant or of the defendant.

Third Persons

Although the UCC permits recovery for breach of warranty by the guests of the buyer, it makes no provision for recovery by employees or strangers.

A conflict of authority exists as to whether an employee of the buyer may sue the seller or manufacturer for breach of warranty. Some jurisdictions deny recovery on the ground that the employee is outside of the distributive chain, not being a buyer. Others allow recovery in such a case. By the latter view, an employee of a construction contractor may recover for breach of the implied warranty of fitness made by the manufacturer of the structural steel that proved defective and fell, injuring the employee. Because the UCC is a state law, some states have extended recovery in areas in which others have not.

COURT CASE

Facts: After J. C. Reed was arrested, he attempted suicide, so police officers removed his clothing and dressed him in a paper isolation gown. Reed's mother sued the manufacturer for breach of warranty when the gown did not tear away when he tried to hang himself.

Outcome: The court pointed out that the person who would benefit from any warranty by the manufacturer of the gown is a potentially suicidal prisoner such as Reed. The court allowed recovery by Reed's mother.

—*Reed v. City of Chicago,*
263 F. Supp. 2d 1123 (N.D. Ill.)

Manufacturer of Component Part

Many items of goods in today's marketplace were not made entirely by one manufacturer. Thus, the harm caused may result from a defect in a component part of the finished product. Because the manufacturer of the total article was the buyer from the component-part manufacturer, the privity rule barred suit against the component-part manufacturer for breach of warranty by anyone injured. In jurisdictions in which privity of contract is not recognized as a bar to recovery, it is not material that the defendant manufactured merely a component part. In these cases, the manufacturer of a component part cannot defend a lawsuit by the final purchaser on the ground of absence of privity. Thus, the purchasers of a tractor trailer may recover from the manufacturer of the brake system of the trailer for damages sustained when the brake system failed to work.

NATURE AND CAUSE OF HARM

The law is more concerned in cases where the plaintiff has been personally injured rather than economically harmed. Thus, the law places protection of the person of the individual above protection of property rights. The harm sustained must have been "caused" by the defendant.

To prove a case for breach of warranty, only facts of which the plaintiff has direct knowledge, or about which information can readily be learned, need be proven. Thus, the plaintiff must only show that a sale and a warranty existed, that the goods did not conform to the warranty, and that injury resulted from the goods.

By the terms of a contract, a manufacturer or seller may always assume a liability broader than would arise from a mere warranty.

CONSUMER PROTECTION

Consumer protection laws are designed to protect the parties to a contract from abuse, sharp dealing, and fraud. They also strengthen legitimate business interests. Laws requiring fairness and full disclosure of business dealings make it more difficult for unscrupulous businesspeople to operate and thus infringe on the trade of those with sound business practices.

Product Safety

The range of products affected by safety standards includes toys, television sets, insecticides, and drugs. The federal government has set safety standards for bumpers, tires, and glass. Substandard products are often subject to recall at the instigation of federal agencies. In some instances fines and imprisonment may be imposed on corporate executives whose businesses have distributed clearly hazardous, substandard goods.

The federal government enacted the Consumer Product Safety Act, which established the Consumer Product Safety Commission (CPSC). The CPSC has broad power to promulgate safety standards for many products. Federal courts have the power to review these standards to make sure they are necessary to abolish or decrease the risk of injury and that they do so at a reasonable cost. The CPSC may order a halt to the manufacture of unsafe products. It may ban certain inherently dangerous or hazardous products, if there appears to be no way to make the product safe. The law requires manufacturers, distributors, and retailers of consumer products to immediately notify the CPSC if a product fails to comply with an applicable safety standard or contains a defect that creates a substantial risk of injury to the public.

C O U R T ✴ C A S E

Facts: Mirama Enterprises distributed a juice extractor. In February, a consumer reported to Mirama that his juicer had exploded, throwing pieces of plastic and shreds of razor-sharp metal as far as eight feet. Two weeks later, a consumer reported her juicer had shattered and a piece of it had cut her arm. Two weeks after that a consumer reported the juicer blade had penetrated the plastic top and cut his palm, requiring 16 stitches. By November, Mirama had been told of 23 juicers that had shattered, injuring 22 people. Seven people required medical treatment. Mirama filed a report with the CPSC on November 16. The government sued Mirama for failing to report alleged defects to the CPSC.

Outcome: The court said that in February, Mirama had information that implied the juicer could have a dangerous defect. Waiting to report the problems until November was not immediate notification.

—United States v. Mirama Enterprises, Inc.,
185 F. Supp. 2d 1148 (S.D. Cal.)

Truth in Advertising

The Federal Trade Commission (FTC) has been active in demanding that advertisements be limited to statements about products that can be substantiated. The FTC may seek voluntary agreement from a business to stop false or deceptive advertising and, in some instances, to agree to corrective advertising. Such agreement is obtained by a business's signing a consent order. The FTC also has the power to order businesses to "cease and desist" from unfair trade practices. The business has the right to contest an FTC order in court.

The FTC has the authority to require that the name of a product be changed if it misleads or tends to mislead the public regarding the nature or quality of the product. If an advertisement actually misstates the quality of a product or makes the product appear to be what it is not, the FTC can prohibit the advertising.

COURT CASE

Facts: Pantron I Corp. marketed a product called the Helsinki Formula. It advertised that the Helsinki Formula stopped hair loss and stimulated the regrowth of hair in persons suffering from baldness. The FTC sued Pantron for false advertising since scientific evidence showed that the Helsinki Formula did not stop hair loss or stimulate regrowth, and that the only beneficial effect was its placebo effect (the psychosomatic effect produced by advertising and marketing the product). Hair growth studies generally showed that the placebo effect was very high.

Outcome: Because the product's effectiveness was solely the result of the placebo effect, an advertisement saying it was effective constituted false advertising. The claim was misleading because the product was not inherently effective in stopping baldness or regrowing hair.

—*F.T.C. v. Pantron I Corp.,*
33 F.3d 1088 (9th Cir.)

Product Uniformity

A number of required practices give consumers the ability to make intelligent choices when comparing competing products. For years, some states have required certain products to be packaged in specifically comparable quantities.

Some local governments require **unit pricing**. In unit pricing, the price for goods sold by weight is stated as the price per ounce or other unit of measurement of the product as well as a total price for the total weight. Thus, all products sold by the ounce would be marked with not only a total price but also a price per ounce that could be compared to competing products even if the competing products were not packaged in an equal number of ounces.

Unit Pricing
Price stated per unit of measurement

Usury Laws

Laws that fix the maximum rate of interest that may be charged on loans are called *usury laws*. They recognize that the borrower is frequently in a weak position and therefore unable to bargain effectively for the best possible rates of interest.

Most states provide for several rates of interest. The legal rate, which varies from state to state from about 5 percent to 15 percent, applies when interest must be paid but no rate has been specified. The maximum contract rate is the highest rate that can be demanded of a debtor. This rate varies from about 8 percent to as much as 45 percent. Some states allow the parties to set any rate of interest. A number of jurisdictions have recently adopted a fluctuating maximum rate of interest based on such rates as the Federal Reserve discount rate, the prime rate, or the rate on U.S. Treasury bills. Statutes usually permit a higher rate to be charged on small loans on the theory that the risks and costs per dollar loaned are greater in making small loans.

The laws vary regarding the damages awarded to a person charged a usurious rate of interest. Some laws allow recovery of the total interest charged and others allow recovery of several times the amount charged.

Truth in Lending

The federal Truth in Lending Act (TILA) requires lenders to make certain written disclosures to borrowers before extending credit. These disclosures include:

1. The finance charge
2. The annual percentage rate
3. The number, amount, and due dates of all payments, including any **balloon payments**—payments that are more than twice the normal installment payments

Balloon Payment
Payment more than twice the normal one

Finance Charge
Total amount paid for credit

Annual Percentage Rate (APR)
Amount charged for loan as percentage of loan

The **finance charge** is the total dollar amount the borrower will pay for the loan. The finance charge includes all interest and any other fees or charges the customer must pay in order to get the loan.

The **annual percentage rate (APR)** is the dollar amount charged for the loan expressed as a percentage of the amount borrowed. The APR must be on a yearly rate. This helps a borrower "comparison shop" among different lenders when seeking credit.

When a company solicits an application for a credit card, the required disclosures must be made in the solicitation literature. The company may not wait until the card is issued to make required TILA disclosures.

Advertisements indicating any credit terms also must meet substantially the same requirements regarding disclosure. The law provides that when a mortgage on the debtor's principal dwelling finances the purchase of consumer products, the debtor has three days in which to rescind the mortgage agreement. Both criminal penalties and civil recovery are available against those who fail to comply with the Truth in Lending Act.

COURT CASE

Facts: After Albert Delaney contracted to buy a five year old car from Garden State Auto Park, Garden State tried to sell him a service contract for $1,100. Delaney declined the service contract as too expensive. He signed a retail installment sales contract that did not enumerate any pre-delivery servicing. After Delaney made all the payments, he got a copy of the installment contract. It showed he had paid $2,200 more for the car than he had agreed. The $2,200 was the cost for rust proofing, undercoating, paint sealer, and fabric guard. These items had not been discussed with Delaney and there was no breakdown of their pricing in any document. They were included in vehicle cleaning for which

Garden State paid a detailer a flat fee of $85. Delaney sued Garden State under state law allowing recovery of triple damages for unconscionable charges.

Outcome: The court found the contract unconscionable because Garden State made an enormous profit by charging Delaney for items he had explicitly rejected and were not disclosed in the final sales agreement. It awarded Delaney three times the $2,200, plus the interest and sales tax he paid on that amount.

—Delaney v. Garden State Auto Park,
722 A.2d 967 (N.J. Super. A.D.)

Statutes Prohibiting Unconscionable Contracts

Section 2-302 of the UCC provides courts with authority to refuse to enforce a sales contract or a part of it because it is "unconscionable." If the terms of the contract are so harsh or the price so unreasonably high as to shock the conscience of the community, the courts may rule the contract to be unconscionable.

[handwritten margin note: can reform / refuse to enforce / enforce half]

Fair Credit Reporting

The Fair Credit Reporting Act requires creditors to notify a potential recipient of credit whenever any adverse action or denial of credit was based on a credit report. It permits the consumer about whom a credit report is written to obtain from a credit agency the substance of the credit report (see Illustrations 19–2 and 19–3 for sample forms). An incorrect credit report must be corrected by the credit agency. In some cases, if the consumer disagrees with a creditor about the report the consumer may be permitted to add an explanation of the dispute to the report. Certain types of adverse information may not be maintained in the reports for more than seven years. The reports may only be used for legitimate business purposes such as for the extension of credit, employment, to get insurance, or for the collection of an account.

Individuals whose rights under the act have been violated may sue and recover ordinary damages if the harm resulted from negligent noncompliance. If the injury resulted from willful noncompliance with the Fair Credit Reporting Act, the aggrieved party may seek punitive damages.

COURT CASE

Facts: When Saleh Hasbun and his wife divorced, he was ordered to pay child support. He made few payments, and his former wife got a $62,000 judgment against him. The district attorney's office requested a copy of his credit report in order to enforce the judgment. When Hasbun found out he sued the county claiming it had violated the Fair Credit Reporting Act by wrongfully obtaining his credit report.

Outcome: Collecting a debt against the subject of a credit report the court said was like the collection of an account. The Fair Credit Reporting Act allows obtaining a credit report for that purpose.

—*Hasbun v. County of Los Angeles.*, 323 F.3d 801 (9th Cir.)

State Consumer Protection Agencies

A number of states have enacted laws giving either the state attorney general or a special consumer affairs office the authority to compel fairness in advertising, sales presentations, and other consumer transactions. State officials will investigate complaints received from consumers. If the complaint appears valid, efforts will be made to secure voluntary corrective action by the seller. Frequently these agencies have **injunctive powers**. That means they may issue cease-and-desist orders similar to those of the FTC. In a limited number of jurisdictions, the agencies may prosecute the offending business, and significant criminal penalties may be imposed that substantially augment the operation of these efforts.

Injunctive Powers
Power to issue cease-and-desist orders

ILLUSTRATION 19–2   Challenge to a Denial of Credit

S A M P L E

_____
_____
_____   _____   _____

December 05, 2008

_____
_____
_____   _____   _____

Dear Sir or Madam:

I applied for credit with you on _____, for _____._____
I was notified on _____, that my application had been denied.

Please advise if the adverse action was based in whole or in part on information contained in a consumer credit report or on information obtained from a source other than a consumer reporting agency. If the adverse action was based on information from a source other than a consumer reporting agency, please indicate the nature of the adverse information, such as my credit worthiness, credit standing, credit capacity, character, general reputation, or personal characteristics.

If you have requested an investigative report, please provide me with a complete and accurate description of the nature and scope of the investigation.

Your review of this matter is greatly appreciated. Please respond as soon as possible regarding the results of your review.

Please contact me if you have any questions or need additional information.

Sincerely,

_____

ILLUSTRATION 19–3 Request for a Credit Report

S A M P L E

_____
_____
_____

December 05, 2008

_____
_____
_____

Re: Credit Report Request

Dear Sir or Madam:

I would like to request a copy of my credit report file. I am providing the following information to obtain the report.

Current address:

_____
_____,_____ _____

Previous name or address within the last five (5) years:

Other Information:
      Telephone number: _____

As proof of identity, enclosed _____.

Enclosed is a copy of a letter from _____,
denying me credit within the last sixty (60) days. Therefore, the credit report should be provided to me free of charge.

Please contact me if you have any questions or need additional information.

Sincerely,

_____

Enclosure

QUESTIONS

1. What is it that a seller agrees to do by making a warranty?

2. Does the statement, "I guarantee you will love to wear these shoes," constitute a warranty? Explain.

3. When can the expression of an opinion by a seller constitute a warranty?

4. How does an implied warranty differ from an express warranty?

5. If a sample is exhibited during negotiation of a sales contract, is the sale a sale by sample? Explain.

6. When does an implied warranty of fitness for a particular purpose arise?

7. Explain the difference in the "foreign/natural" test and the "reasonable expectation" test as applied to the sale of food or drink.

8. When will the warranty of fitness for a particular purpose arise in the sale of a patent- or trade-name article?

9. How may warranties be excluded or surrendered?

10. Does the rule requiring privity of contract keep everyone except the purchaser of goods from suing the seller or manufacturer for breach of warranty?

11. What authority does the FTC have when a business has engaged in false or deceptive advertising?

12. When will a court find a sales contract unconscionable?

CASE PROBLEMS

LO ❸

1. Robert and Mariah Davis bought a new Daewoo car from LaFontaine Motors, Inc., an authorized Daewoo service provider. The vehicle purchase order the Davises signed stated that if the car was subject to a manufacturer's warranty, LaFontaine "DISCLAIMS ALL WARRANTIES, EXPRESS AND IMPLIED (INCLUDING ANY IMPLIED WARRANTY OF MERCHANTABILITY)." It expressly stated LaFontaine was not an agent of Daewoo. LaFontaine did minor repairs under Daewoo's warranty, but ended its service agreement with Daewoo. After Daewoo went bankrupt, Mariah was told by every service facility she contacted that she would have to pay for any repairs. The Davises sued LaFontaine for breach of express and implied warranties. Should LaFontaine be liable?

LO ❹

2. Cars 4 Causes was a nonprofit corporation that solicited donations of cars that it sold from its lot. It kept half the sales proceeds and after deducting towing costs distributed the remainder to charities. Cars 4 Causes advertised that it provided "free towing" of a vehicle from the donor's residence. Its advertising did not disclose that in fact it paid a fee to a towing company and deducted that fee from the portion of the sales proceeds it gave to charities. The state of California and its Department of Motor Vehicles sued Cars 4 Causes alleging it engaged in false advertising. Did it?

LO ❷

3. George Saber bought a used, red Corvette with automatic transmission from Dan Angelone Chevrolet, Inc. During the next two years, Saber had a number of mechanical problems with the Corvette and researched the car's history. He found that a title application for the car described it as black with a manual transmission. Saber contacted the police who discovered discrepancies

involving the vehicle identification number (VIN) and major components. VIN's on the frame, engine, and transmission were not the same as the VIN on the window downpost. The police believed some of the parts were stolen and impounded the car. They told Saber he could not have it back. Later investigation revealed that the parts were not stolen. The car had been in a fire and rebuilt using parts from various cars. Saber sued Angelone. The car was still impounded at the time of trial. Did the impoundment constitute breach of the warranty of title?

4. When James River Equipment Co. bought an implement dealership from Beadle County Equipment, Inc., a separate schedule attached to the sales agreement and incorporated by reference listed each piece of used equipment included in the sale. Five combines listed on the schedule had significantly more use than indicated, which reduced their value. The sales agreement stated the implements were purchased "in an AS IS condition" and that Beadle made no representations about them "except as specifically provided in this Agreement." James River sued for breach of express warranty alleging that the hours of use in the schedule constituted an express warranty. Beadle alleged "as is" disclaimed any description of the implements. You decide.   LO ❶, ❸

5. Fleet Bank sent Paula Rossman an invitation to get a "Fleet Platinum Master-Card" with "no annual fee." To accept, Rossman was to check a box next to which was printed, ". . . the no-annual-fee Platinum MasterCard." On the required chart of the card's terms, under the column headed "Annual Fee," was the word "None." The interest rate was 7.99 percent but would go up to 24.99 percent upon closure of the account. Rossman accepted the offer and got a "no-annual fee Platinum MasterCard" along with a cardholder agreement that stated there was no annual fee. Five months later Fleet announced a $35 annual fee. Rossman sued Fleet alleging the description of the card as one with no annual fee violated the TILA conditions of honest disclosure. What is the purpose of the TILA disclosures? Why might it matter if a company can change to an annual fee a few months after issuing a card?   LO ❹

6. John Crow took a ride on a new model sport fishing boat manufactured by Bayliner Marine Corp. There was no equipment on the boat for determining the speed. The salesman told Crow he had no information about the speed but did have two documents called "prop matrixes" from Bayliner's dealer's manual that listed the maximum speed for each boat model. When equipped with a size "20 × 20" propeller the boat's maximum speed was listed as 30 MPH. At the bottom of the prop matrix was the statement: "All testing . . . at full fuel and water tanks and . . . 600 pounds passenger and gear weight." Crow bought the boat, but it had a "20 × 17" propeller. He added equipment weighing 2,000 pounds. The boat only went 13 MPH. The dealer's repairs and adjustments got the speed up to 17 MPH. Crow sued Bayliner for breach of an express warranty. Did the statements in the prop matrixes create an express warranty?   LO ❶

7. Ray Vickers owned an automobile pawn business. When a person pawned a car, Vickers issued a standard pawn ticket and required the customer to leave the pawned vehicle at his business. Vickers required each customer to pay a "storage fee" while he kept the vehicle. Wilfred Yazzie pawned his car at Vickers, and Vickers charged him a $30 "storage fee." Yazzie later filed suit alleging the "storage fee" was a finance charge under the Truth in Lending Act and therefore Vickers understated the annual percentage rate and the finance charge. Was the "storage fee" a finance charge?   LO ❹

LO ❸

8. By means of long-distance telephone conversations, Ace, Inc. agreed to buy an airplane from Unified Technologies of Texas, Inc. subject to a test flight by Thompson Comerford, the sole shareholder of Ace. Comerford arrived in Dallas where the plane was, but he did not have time to test fly the plane. He and Ken Gedney, the broker for the plane, agreed Comerford's flight back home would constitute the test flight. In order to take the plane, Gedney required Comerford to sign a "Purchase Agreement" which stated, "the aircraft . . . and accessories, are being sold 'As Is,'" and "there are no representations or warranties, express or implied . . . including . . . merchantability." Comerford found brake, steering, climb, and cruise performance problems with the plane. When Unified refused to repair the problems, Ace sued for breach of warranty including merchantability. Were warranties properly excluded?

LO ❶

9. Fuqua Chrysler-Plymouth bought a used Chevrolet from Alfred Dirico, and Fuqua then sold the car at retail. The car odometer showed 50,864 miles, but it had more than 128,000. After being sued by the buyer, Fuqua sued Dirico for breach of express warranty, contending that the odometer mileage statement received when it purchased the car from Dirico formed an express warranty. Since the mileage was incorrect, Fuqua claimed it was a breach of the warranty. After giving the mileage, a box was checked on the mileage statement form by the statement, "I hereby certify to the best of my knowledge the odometer reading . . . reflects the actual mileage." Did the mileage statement create an express warranty?

Ethics in Practice

Consider the ethical implications of a seller who decides to make his product in a less expensive way. The less expensive way will shorten the life of the product. So, instead of giving a two-year written warranty that the seller has been giving, the seller no longer provides a warranty on the product. The seller cuts costs, reduces the likelihood of returns and lawsuits because of breached warranty, and is much happier. What about the consumer?

Summary Cases

SALES

1. Pamela Lee purchased a car from Mercedes-Benz USA, LLC (MBUSA). The car needed to be repaired an excessive number of times, so Lee lost the use of it. She also paid $7,300 for repairs not covered by the car's warranty. That warranty included the statement "NO PAYMENT OR OTHER COMPENSATION WILL BE MADE FOR INDIRECT OR CONSEQUENTIAL DAMAGE SUCH AS, DAMAGE OR INJURY TO . . . PROPERTY OR LOSS OF REVENUE." Lee sued and at trial the judge instructed the jury that Lee could recover consequential damages even though MBUSA' warranty excluded them. Was the exclusion of consequential damages unconscionable? [*Lee v. Mercedes-Benz USA, LLC,* 622 S.E.2d 361 (Ga. App.)]

2. Anthony and Sharon Gruda operated a kitchen supply business. They contracted to sell, deliver, and install cabinets to Sam and Mac, Inc. (SMI). Gruda ordered the cabinets from a manufacturer, and SMI paid Gruda for the cabinets. Before the cabinets were delivered and installed, the Grudas filed for bankruptcy and stopped operating their business. SMI asked James Treat, the Grudas' landlord, to open the business premises and let him remove the cabinets. Treat refused so SMI sued him. Did SMI have title to the cabinets? [*Sam and Mac, Inc. v. Treat,* 783 N.E.2d 760 (Ind. App.)]

3. Peck Industries ordered 210,000 custom-manufactured decals from Weisz Graphics to be stored by Weisz and released in increments of 500 decals as requested by Peck. Weisz's acknowledgment of the order stated, "On Releases over 12 months." Weisz manufactured the entire order and over the next 12 months released seven shipments as requested by Peck. Weisz then refused to make any more releases until Peck paid the full amount of the remaining balance of the order. When Peck refused to pay, Weisz sued alleging it was entitled to recover the price of the goods since they were identified to the contract. Were the goods identified? [*Weisz Graphics Division of Fred B. Johnson Co., Inc., v. Peck Industries, Inc.,* 403 S.E.2d 146 (Ct. App. S.C.)]

4. Songbird Jet Ltd., Inc. and Jet Leasing Corp., acting together, negotiated with Amax Inc. for the purchase of a jet airplane. Songbird and Jet Leasing claimed that an oral agreement was reached by which they would purchase the jet for $8,850,000. Jet Leasing sent Amax a check for $250,000, which it claimed was a deposit on the sale. Amax later notified Jet Leasing the jet was not for sale and that no contract had been made. Songbird and Jet Leasing sued Amax claiming the $250,000 check was partial performance of the alleged contract. Amax alleged that the claim was barred by the Statute of Frauds. Was it? [*Songbird Jet Ltd., Inc. v. Amax, Inc.,* 581 F. Supp. 912 (S.D. N.Y.)]

5. The FTC ordered Bristol-Myers not to make any claims regarding "thera-peutic performance or freedom-from-side-effects" of Bufferin or Excedrin unless it had competent and reliable scientific evidence to support the claim. Bristol alleged that order violated its First Amendment right to free speech. The FTC had found that statements made by Bristol that Bufferin and Excedrin relieved tension and that doctors recommended Bufferin more often than any other over-the-counter analgesic had been deceptive. Should Bristol have to obey the order? [*Bristol-Myers Co. v. F.T.C.*, 738 F.2d 554 (2d Cir.)]

6. After Timothy Garcia was convicted for unlawful distribution of a con-trolled substance, the state sued him for return of the "buy money" used to buy narcotics from him. The state could compel repayment if there was a valid civil basis for recovery. Since the sale of a controlled substance is an il-legal sale, does the state have a legal basis for recovery? [*State v. Garcia*, 866 P.2d 5 (Ct. App. Utah)]

7. At an auction, Gaylen Bennett bought 55 head of cattle from Tony Jansma. The next day some of the cattle were sick. Eventually, 19 of the 55 cattle died. Jansma regularly dealt in the buying and selling of cattle and held him-self out as having knowledge peculiar to cattle transactions. Bennett sued for breach of the warranty of merchantability. Was Jansma a merchant? [*Bennett v. Jansma*, 392 N.W.2d 134 (S.D.)]

8. Conida Warehouses sold light red kidney bean seed to Larry Mallory. After Mallory planted the seeds, the beans developed halo blight, a disease. Mallory sued Conida for breach of warranty. Conida claimed it had effectively dis-claimed the warranty of merchantability by attaching a tag to the bag of seed. That tag showed the word *warranty* in capital letters at the top and the rest of the letters were in standard-size type. The disclaimer tag contained no con-trasting color or other emphasis. That tag was attached with two other tags at the bottom of the bag and under the other two tags. Was this an effective disclaimer? [*Mallory v. Conida Warehouses, Inc.*, 350 N.W.2d 825 (Mich. Ct. App.)]

Negotiable Instruments

PART

5

Information on bad checks and duties of a bank regarding negotiable instruments can be found in Chapter 22. Chapter 25 covers recourse, or defenses, to nonpayment of commercial paper. One recourse to checks not paid by a bank due to insufficient funds is a debt collection service. See the Web site of AllBusiness, a company dedicated to assisting small businesses with collections.
http://www.allbusiness.com

Nature of Negotiable Instruments

LEARNING OBJECTIVES

❶ Discuss how negotiable instruments are transferred.
❷ Differentiate between bearer paper and order paper.
❸ Describe an electronic fund transfer.

PREVIEW CASE

When Abbott Development Co. (ADCO) defaulted on a note, the FDIC allowed it to refinance by issuing a new note payable to the FDIC. The FDIC made a sale of many notes, including the ADCO note, to SMS Financial, L.L.C. The FDIC indorsed the ADCO note to SMS but failed to deliver it. Under the sale agreement, SMS had the right to ask for a refund of this note, which it later did. The FDIC refunded SMS's payment for the note and requested SMS deliver it. Because SMS did not have the note, it could not return it. Later, the FDIC inadvertently sent the note to SMS in a box with other documents. After receiving the note, SMS sued ADCO for payment. ADCO alleged SMS was not the holder of the note. Was SMS in possession of the note? To whom was the note payable?

Commercial Paper or Negotiable Instrument
Writing drawn in special form that can be transferred as substitute for money or as instrument of credit

Negotiable instruments or commercial paper are writings drawn in a special form that can be transferred from person to person as a substitute for money or as an instrument of credit. Such an instrument must meet certain definite requirements in regard to its form and the manner in which it is transferred. Two types of negotiable instruments include checks and notes. Since a negotiable instrument is not money, the law does not require a person to accept one in payment of a debt.

HISTORY AND DEVELOPMENT

The need for instruments of credit that would permit the settlement of claims between distant cities without the transfer of money has existed as long as trade has existed. Negotiable instruments were developed to meet that need. References to bills of exchange or instruments of credit appeared as early as 50 B.C. Their wide-spread usage, however, began about A.D. 1200 as international trade began to flourish in the wake of the Crusades. At first, these credit instruments were used only in international trade, but they gradually became common in domestic trade.

In England, before about A.D. 1400, special courts set up on the spot by the merchants settled all disputes between merchants. The rules applied by these courts became known as the **law merchant**. Later the common-law courts took over the adjudication of all disputes, including those between merchants. However, these courts retained most of the customs developed by the merchants and incorporated the law merchant into the common law. Most, but by no means all, of the law merchant dealt with bills of exchange or credit instruments.

In the United States, each state modified the common law dealing with credit instruments so that eventually the various states had different laws regarding them. The American Bar Association and the American Banks Association appointed a commission to draw up a Uniform Negotiable Instruments Law. In 1896, the commission proposed a uniform act. This act was adopted in all the states, but Article 3 of the Uniform Commercial Code (UCC) then displaced it.

In 1990, a commission that writes uniform laws issued a revised Article 3. This text explains the law according to the changes made by the revision. The revision uses the term *negotiable instruments,* whereas the original Article 3 uses the term *commercial paper.* Although states adopt uniform laws, it is important to note that the states do not necessarily adopt the uniform laws exactly as written. Frequently they make minor changes that do not significantly affect the impact of the law. We say that a state has adopted a uniform law when it has adopted the law with but minor changes.

NEGOTIATION

Negotiation is the act of transferring ownership of a negotiable instrument to another party. The owner may negotiate a negotiable instrument owned by and payable to such owner. The owner negotiates it by signing the back of it and delivering it to another party. The signature of the owner made on the back of a negotiable instrument before delivery is called an *indorsement.*[1]

When a negotiable instrument is transferred by negotiation to one or more parties, these parties may acquire rights superior to those of the original owner. Parties who acquire rights superior to those of the original owner are known as **holders in due course**. It is mainly this feature of the transfer of superior rights that gives negotiable instruments a special classification all their own.

ORDER PAPER AND BEARER PAPER

If commercial paper is made payable to the order of a named person, it is called **order paper**. If commercial paper is made payable to whoever has possession of it, the bearer, it is called **bearer paper**. Bearer paper may be made payable to bearer, cash, or any other indication that does not purport to designate a specific person. Order paper must use the word *order,* as in the phrase, "pay to the order of John Doe," or some other word to indicate it may be paid to a

Law Merchant
Rules applied by courts set up by merchants in early England

LO ❶
Transfer of negotiable instruments

Negotiation
Act of transferring ownership of negotiable instrument

Holder in Due Course
Person who acquires rights superior to original owner

LO ❷
Bearer paper versus order paper

Order Paper
Commercial paper payable to order

Bearer Paper
Commercial paper payable to bearer

---

[1] Indorsement is the spelling used in the UCC, although endorsement is commonly used in business.

transferee. Order paper is negotiated only by indorsement of the person to whom it is then payable and by delivery of the paper to another person. In the case of bearer paper, merely handing the paper to another person may make the transfer.

Payment is made on a different basis with order paper than with bearer paper. Order paper may be paid only to the person to whom it is made payable on its face or the person to whom it has been properly indorsed. However, bearer paper may be paid to any person in possession of the paper.

C O U R T   C A S E

Facts: Doseung Chung purchased a voucher for use in SAMS machines at Belmont Park Racetrack. The SAMS allow a bettor to enter a bet by inserting money, vouchers, or credit cards, and selecting the number or combination desired. The SAMS issue betting tickets and, when a voucher is used, a new voucher showing the balance left. Chung left the SAMS, taking his betting tickets but not the new voucher that showed he had thousands of dollars in value left. Chung noticed his mistake within minutes, but the new voucher was gone. The track issued a stop order on it, but it had already been cashed out. Each voucher was marked "Cash Voucher" and "Bet Against the Value or Exchange for Cash." Chung sued the racetrack.

Outcome: The terms of the vouchers indicated they were bearer paper. As such, a finder could negotiate them by transfer of possession even if it was involuntary.

—*Chung v. New York Racing Assn.,*
714 N.Y.S.2d 429 (N.Y. Dist. Ct.)

CLASSIFICATION OF COMMERCIAL PAPER

The basic negotiable instruments are:

1. Drafts
2. Promissory notes

Drafts

Draft or **Bill of Exchange**
Written order by one person directing another to pay sum of money to third person

A **draft** is also called a **bill of exchange**. It is a written order signed by one person and requiring the person to whom it is addressed to pay on demand or at a particular time a fixed amount of money to order or to bearer. Checks and trade acceptances are special types of drafts. When you make out a check on your bank account you are actually writing out a type of draft. (See Chapter 22.)

Promissory Notes

Promissory Note
Unconditional written promise to pay sum of money to another

A **promissory note** is an unconditional promise in writing made by one person to another, signed by the promisor, engaging to pay on demand of the holder, or, at a definite time, a fixed amount of money to order or to bearer (see Illustration 20–1). If the note is a demand instrument, the holder may demand payment or sue for payment at any time and for any reason.

ILLUSTRATION 20–1   Promissory Note   Parties: maker, Jan L. Hendricks; payee, Ana Nieves

NOTE

$ _7,000.00_   Greenfield, Missouri   _April 1,_   20 -- _____

_____One (1) year_____ after date, for value received _____I_____ promise

to pay to the order of _____Ana Nieves_____

the sum of _____Seven Thousand Dollars ($7,000.00)_____

with interest thereon from date at the rate of _____fifteen percent (15%)_____

per annum, interest payable _____semiannually_____ and if interest

is not paid _____semiannually_____ to become as principal and bear

the same rate of interest.

Payable at _Northside Bank_____

_____Jan L. Hendricks_____

PARTIES TO NEGOTIABLE INSTRUMENTS

Each party to a negotiable instrument is designated by a certain term, depending on the type of instrument. Some of these terms apply to all types of negotiable instruments, whereas others are restricted to one type only. The same individual may be designated by one term at one stage and by another at a later stage through which the instrument passes before it is collected. These terms include *payee, drawer, drawee, acceptor, maker, bearer, holder, indorser,* and *indorsee.*

Payee

The person or persons to whom any negotiable instrument is made payable is called the **payee**.

Payee
Party to whom instrument is payable

Drawer

The person who executes or signs any draft is called the **drawer** (see Illustration 20–2).

Drawer
Person who executes a draft

ILLUSTRATION 20–2   Draft   Parties: drawer, Lee W. Richardson; drawee, Walter Evans; payee, Community Bank

$ _450.00_____   _December 22,_   20 -- _____

_____Six months after date_____   PAY TO THE

ORDER OF_____Community Bank_____

_Four hundred fifty dollars and no/100_____

VALUE RECEIVED AND CHARGE TO ACCOUNT OF   FOR CLASSROOM USE ONLY   DOLLARS

TO   _Walter Evans_____

No. _27 Walden, Virginia_____   _Lee W. Richardson_____

Drawee

The person who is ordered to pay a draft is called the **drawee**.

Acceptor

A drawee who accepts a draft, thus indicating a willingness to assume responsibility for its payment, is called the **acceptor**. A person accepts drafts not immediately payable by writing on the face of the instruments these or similar words: *Accepted, Jane Daws*. This indicates that Jane Daws will perform the contract according to its terms.

Maker

The person who executes a promissory note is called the **maker**. The maker contracts to pay the amount due on the note. This obligation resembles that of the acceptor of a draft.

Bearer

Any negotiable instrument may be made payable to whoever possesses it. The payee of such an instrument is the **bearer**. If the instrument is made payable to the order of *Myself, Cash,* or another similar name, it is payable to the bearer.

Holder

Any person who possesses an instrument is the **holder** if it has been delivered to the person and it is either bearer paper or it is payable to that person as the payee or by indorsement. The payee is the original holder of an instrument.

PREVIEW CASE REVISITED

Facts: When Abbott Development Co. (ADCO) defaulted on a note, the FDIC allowed it to refinance by issuing a new note payable to the FDIC. The FDIC made a sale of many notes, including the ADCO note, to SMS Financial, L.L.C. The FDIC indorsed the ADCO note to SMS but failed to deliver it. Under the sale agreement, SMS had the right to ask for a refund of this note, which it later did. The FDIC refunded SMS's payment for the note and requested SMS deliver it. Because SMS did not have the note, it could not return it. Later, the FDIC inadvertently sent the note to SMS in a box with other documents. After receiving the note, SMS sued ADCO for payment. ADCO alleged SMS was not the holder of the note.
Outcome: The court found that because SMS had possession of the note payable to itself, SMS was the holder.

—*SMS Financial, L.L.C. v. ABCO Homes, Inc.*, 167 F.3d 235 (5th Cir.)

Holder in Due Course

A holder who takes a negotiable instrument in good faith and for value is a holder in due course.

Indorser

When the payee of a draft or a note wishes to transfer the instrument to another party, it must be indorsed. The payee is then called the **indorser**. The payee makes the indorsement by signing on the back of the instrument.

Indorser
Payee or holder who signs back of instrument

Indorsee

A person who becomes the holder of a negotiable instrument by an indorsement that names him or her as the person to whom the instrument is negotiated is called the **indorsee**.

Indorsee
Named holder of indorsed negotiable instrument

NEGOTIATION AND ASSIGNMENT

The right to receive payment of instruments may be transferred by either negotiation or assignment. Nonnegotiable paper cannot be transferred by negotiation. The rights to it are transferred by assignment. Negotiable instruments may be transferred by negotiation or assignment. The rights given the original parties are alike in the cases of negotiation and assignment. In the case of a promissory note, for example, the original parties are the maker (the one who promises to pay) and the payee (the one to whom the money is to be paid). Between the original parties, both a nonnegotiable and a negotiable instrument are equally enforceable. Also, the same defenses against fulfilling the terms of the instrument may be set up. For example, if one party to the instrument is a minor, the incapacity to contract may be set up as a defense against carrying out the agreement.

C O U R T   C A S E

Facts: Brian and Penny Grieme bought a house financed by a loan from the North Dakota Housing Finance Agency (NDHFA). The home was insured by Center Mutual Insurance Co. Sometime later, the house was damaged by hail. Center issued a check for the damage payable jointly to Brian and NDHFA and mailed it to Brian. He presented the check for payment at a bank. The check bore Brian's indorsement signature and below in hand-printed block letters the words "ND Housing Finance." The check was paid to Brian. Center refused to pay NDHFA.

The Griemes had defaulted on the mortgage and filed for bankruptcy. NDHFA sued Center.

Outcome: Because the check was order paper, the indorsement of NDHFA was necessary to negotiate it. The unauthorized writing of "ND Housing Finance" did not negotiate the check. NDHFA recovered the amount of the check.

—*State ex rel. North Dakota Housing Finance Agency v. Center Mut. Ins. Co.,* **720 N.W.2d 425 (N.D.)**

However, the rights given to subsequent parties differ depending on whether an instrument is transferred by negotiation or assignment. When an instrument is transferred by assignment, the assignee receives only the rights of the assignor and no more. (See Chapter 12.) If one of the original parties to the instrument has a defense that is valid against the assignor, it is also valid against the assignee.

When an instrument is transferred by negotiation, however, the party who receives the instrument in good faith and for value may obtain rights that are superior to the rights of the original holder. Defenses that may be valid against the original holder may not be valid against a holder who has received an instrument by negotiation.

CREDIT AND COLLECTION

Negotiable instruments are called *instruments of credit* and *instruments of collection*. If *A* sells *B* merchandise on 60 days' credit, the buyer may at the time of the sale execute a negotiable note or draft due in 60 days in payment of the merchandise. This note or draft then is an instrument of credit.

If the seller in the transaction above will not extend the original credit to 60 days, a draft may be drawn on the buyer, who would be the drawee. In this case, the drawer may make a bank the payee, the bank being a mere agent of the drawer, or one of the seller's creditors may be made the payee so that an account receivable will be collected and an account payable will be paid all in one transaction. When the account receivable comes due, the buyer will mail a check to the seller. In this example, the draft is an instrument of collection.

ELECTRONIC FUND TRANSFERS

LO ❸
Electronic fund
transfers

**Electronic Fund
Transfer**
*Fund transfer initiated
electronically,
telephonically, or by
computer*

More and more transfers of funds occur today in which a paper instrument is not actually transferred and the parties do not have face-to-face, personal contact. An **electronic fund transfer** (EFT) is any transfer of funds initiated by means of an electronic terminal, telephonic instrument, or computer or magnetic tape that instructs or authorizes a financial institution to debit or credit an account. An EFT does not include a transfer of funds begun by a check, draft, or similar paper instrument.

EFTs are popular because they are faster and less expensive than the transfer of paper instruments. EFTs can reduce the risk of problems resulting from lost instruments. If a check, for example, does not have to make the entire trip from the payee to the drawee bank to the drawer customer, costs and delays can be reduced.

A federal law, the Electronic Fund Transfer Act (EFTA), regulates EFTs and defines them as carried out primarily by electronic means. A transfer initiated by a telephone call between a bank employee and a customer is not an EFT unless it is in accordance with a prearranged plan.

The EFTA requires disclosure of the terms and conditions of the EFTs involving a customer's account at the time the customer contracts for an EFT service. This notification must include:

1. What liability could be imposed for unauthorized EFTs
2. The type of EFTs the customer may make
3. The charges for EFTs

Under the EFTA, a customer's liability for an unauthorized EFT can be limited to $50; however, the customer must give the bank very prompt notice of circumstances that lead to the belief that an unauthorized EFT has been or may be made. Also, a bank does not need to reimburse a customer who fails to notify a bank of an unauthorized EFT within 60 days of receiving a bank statement on which the unauthorized EFT appears.

Several widely used types of EFTs include check truncation, preauthorized debits and credits, automated teller machines, and point-of-sale systems.

Check Truncation

Check Truncation
*Shortening check's trip
from payee to drawer*

A system of shortening the trip a check makes from the payee to the drawee bank and then to the drawer is called **check truncation**. It used to be that all banks returned cancelled checks to customers with their monthly bank statement. However, most banks no longer return the actual cancelled checks to their customers with the monthly statements. Instead, the statements to customers list the check numbers. The dollar amount on the checks is shown, and the transactions are printed in numerical order. The customer can easily reconcile the account without having the cancelled checks. However, banks must be able to supply legible copies of the checks at the customers' request for seven years. This is a type of check truncation.

Preauthorized Debits and Credits

Checking account customers may authorize that recurring bills, such as home mortgage payments, insurance premiums, or utility bills, be automatically deducted from their checking accounts each month. This is called a **preauthorized debit**. It allows a person to avoid the inconvenience and cost of writing out and mailing checks for these bills.

A **preauthorized credit** allows the amount of regular payments to be automatically deposited in the payee's account. This type of EFT is frequently used for depositing salaries and government benefits, such as Social Security payments. It benefits the payor, who does not have to issue and mail the checks. The payee does not have to bother depositing a check and normally has access to the funds sooner.

Preauthorized Debit
Automatic deduction of bill payment from checking account

Preauthorized Credit
Automatic deposit of funds to account

Automated Teller Machines

An **automated teller machine** (ATM) is an EFT terminal capable of performing routine banking services. Many thousands of such machines exist at locations designed to be accessible to customers. The capabilities of the machines vary; however, some ATMs do such things as dispense cash and account information and allow customers to make deposits, transfer funds between accounts, and pay bills. ATMs are conveniently found at many locations, even in foreign countries, and are open when banks are not.

Automated Teller Machine
EFT terminal that performs routine banking services

Point-of-Sale Systems

Electronic fund transfers that begin at retailers when consumers want to pay for goods or services with debit cards are called **point-of-sale systems** (POS). These transactions occur when the person operating the POS terminal enters information regarding the payment into a computer system. The entry debits the consumer's bank account and credits the retailer's account by the amount of the transaction.

Point-of-Sale System
EFTs begun at retailers when customers pay for goods or services

QUESTIONS

1. What need did the development of negotiable instruments meet?
2. Is the law exactly the same in all states that have adopted Article 3 of the UCC? Explain.
3. What is the feature that gives negotiable instruments a special classification of their own?
4. To whom may order paper and bearer paper be paid?
5. What does it mean for a promissory note to be a demand instrument?
6. What does it mean for a drawee to accept a draft, and how is it done?

7. Are the rights given to parties subsequent to the original payee the same whether the instrument is transferred by assignment or negotiation? Explain.

8. Why are EFT's popular?

9. What is the limit of a customer's liability for an unauthorized EFT, and what is the customer's responsibility in order to so limit the liability?

10. What happens when an electronic fund transfer is begun at a retailer by a consumer paying for goods with a debit card?

CASE PROBLEMS

LO **2**
1. Cathy and Ray Vigneri authorized Nationwide Credit, Inc., a debt collector, to withdraw $100 per month from their checking account to pay a debt to American Express. For four months, Nationwide initiated $100 debits on the Vigneri's account at U.S. Bank National Association. Nationwide initiated the transfers by depositing a paper draft at its bank. The drafts contained the bank's routing number, the bank's stamp, and other coding and symbols indicating they had been processed through the Federal Reserve. In August, Nationwide told the Vigneris that American Express wanted the debt paid off and without the Vigneri's consent withdrew $1,075. As it had done previously, this withdrawal was done by means of a paper draft. The Vigneris sued U.S. Bank, alleging it had violated the EFTA by making an unauthorized withdrawal from their account. Had U.S. Bank violated the EFTA?

LO **1**
2. Charles Risner owned Metro Electric & Maintenance, Inc. and Computer Power and Technology, Inc., which both had checking accounts with Bank One Corp. Metro had customers and frequent deposits, but Computer was dormant. Risner's daughter Janece was the office manager and bookkeeper for both corporations. She deposited checks payable to Metro into Computer's account. The checks had no indorsement. Janece would then write checks to herself from Computer's account. When Charles discovered the embezzlement, he sued Bank One and Janece. Were the funds validly negotiated to Computer?

LO **3**
3. Gary and Clara Delffs signed a note to Joe Waldron that read, "_____ after date _____ promise to pay to the order of." After the word "of" was a long blank line on which was handwritten, "one hundred and fifty-three thousand and four hundred and forty dollars." Following this was printed, "Dollars." The parties agreed the document was not order paper. A lawsuit ensued, and the court had to decide whether the note was bearer paper. Decide the case.

LO **2**
4. While the head of a department at the *Charlotte Observer*, Oren Johnson submitted phony invoices from Graphic Image, Inc. (GII). Knight Publishing Co., the owner of the *Observer*, would issue checks in payment payable to GII. Johnson and others used this scheme to steal from the newspaper. They had the checks indorsed by Graphic Color Prep, a business they owned, and deposited in its account. About 55 checks were deposited this way for a total of $1.5 million. When Knight found out, it sued its bank for paying the checks on allegedly improper indorsements. May Knight recover?

LO **1, 2**
5. Lawrence and Georgene Kruser had a joint checking account with Bank of America. The bank had issued each of them ATM cards. The Krusers thought

Lawrence's card had been destroyed in September, but their December bank statement showed an unauthorized withdrawal of $20 by someone using Lawrence's card. The next year, the Krusers discovered in September that the statements for July and August showed 47 unauthorized withdrawals totaling $9,020. When the bank refused to reimburse them, the Krusers sued. Does the bank have to reimburse them the $9,020?

6. Miller Furs, Inc. executed a note that stated it "promised to pay, on demand" to the Shawmut Bank an amount not more than $1 million. The note also specified that upon the occurrence of certain events the bank could decide that the note "shall become and be due and payable forthwith without demand, notice of nonpayment, presentment. . . . " Two years later Shawmut demanded payment of the note. In the lawsuit that followed, Miller argued that the note was not a demand note due and payable when issued, and the bank could only demand payment in good faith. Was the note a demand note? LO 3

7. Joe Jernigan executed a note payable to Mbank Houston, N.A. Mbank indorsed the note to the Federal Reserve Bank of Dallas. When Mbank became insolvent, the Federal Deposit Insurance Corp. was appointed its receiver. The note and other assets were sold to the Deposit Insurance Bridge Bank, N.A., which changed its name to Bank One, Texas, N.A. Bank One sued Jernigan for the balance due. To recover, Bank One had to show it had received the note by negotiation. Had it? LO 1

Essentials of Negotiability

LEARNING OBJECTIVES

❶ List the seven requirements of negotiability.

❷ Explain the requirements for issuance and delivery of a negotiable instrument.

❸ State whether a negotiable instrument must be dated and whether the location of making payment must be indicated.

PREVIEW CASE

→ Katherine Lenares had a bank issue a check for $8,000 to Michael Miano. A notation on it stated, "Loan from Katherine Lenares." She intended to loan Miano the money, but the loan agreement was oral. When Miano did not repay the $8,000, Lenares sued him. The court had to decide whether there was a negotiable note. What are the essentials of a note? What are the requirements for a negotiable instrument?

An important characteristic of negotiable instruments is their transferability or negotiability. However, instruments must meet certain requirements in order to be negotiable.

REQUIREMENTS

LO ❶
Requirements of negotiability

An instrument must comply with seven requirements in order to be negotiable. If it lacks any one of these requirements, the document is not negotiable. However, even though an instrument is not negotiable it may be, and many are, valid and enforceable between the original parties to it. The seven requirements are:

1. The instrument must be in writing and signed by the party executing it.
2. The instrument must contain either an order to pay or a promise to pay.
3. The order or the promise must be unconditional.
4. The instrument must provide for the payment of a fixed amount of money.
5. The instrument must be payable either on demand or at a fixed or definite time.

6. The instrument must be payable to the order of a payee or to bearer.

7. The payee (unless the instrument is payable to bearer) and the drawee must be designated with reasonable certainty.

A Signed Writing

A negotiable instrument must be written. The law does not, however, require that the writing be in any particular form. The instrument may be written with pen and ink or with pencil; it may be typed or printed; or it may be partly printed and partly typed or handwritten. An instrument executed with a lead pencil meets the legal requirements of **negotiability**. However, a person executing an instrument in pencil takes a risk because of the ease with which the instrument could be altered without detection.

A signature must be placed on a negotiable instrument in order to indicate the intent of the promisor to be bound. The normal place for a signature is in the lower right-hand corner, but the location of the signature and its form are wholly immaterial if it is clear that a signature was intended. The signature may be written, typed, printed, or stamped. It may be a name, a symbol, a mark, or a trade name. The signature, however, must be on the instrument. It cannot be on a separate paper attached to the instrument.

Some odd but valid signatures follow:

1. His
   Richard ✕ Cooper   This type of signature might be made by a person who
   Mark   does not know how to write. The signer makes the ✕ in the center. A witness writes the signer's name, Richard Cooper, and the words *His Mark* to indicate who signed the instrument and that it was intended as a signature.

2. "I, Tammy Morley," written by Morley in the body of the note but with her name typed in the usual place for the signature.

3. "Snowwhite Cleaner," the trade name under which Glendon Sutton operates his business.

The instrument may be signed by an agent, who is another person who has been given authority to perform this act.

Negotiability
Transferability

PREVIEW CASE REVISITED

Facts: Katherine Lenares had a bank issue a check for $8,000 to Michael Miano. A notation on the check stated, "Loan from Katherine Lenares." She intended to loan Miano the money, but the loan agreement was oral. When Miano did not repay the $8,000, Lenares sued him. The court had to decide whether there was a negotiable note.

Outcome: In order to have a negotiable instrument, there must first be a written document. In this case, the only writing was the check by which Lenares made the loan, and a check is not a note.

—*Lenares v. Miano,* 811 A.2d 738 (Conn. App.)

An Order or a Promise to Pay

A draft, such as a trade acceptance or a check, must contain an order to pay. If the request is imperative and unequivocal, it is an order even though the word *order* is not used.

A promissory note must contain a promise to pay. The word *promise* need not be used—any equivalent words will answer the purpose—but the language used must show that a promise is intended. Thus, the words *I will pay, I guarantee to pay,* and *This is to certify that we are bound to pay* were held to be sufficient to constitute a promise. A mere acknowledgment of a debt does not suffice.

Unconditional

The order or the promise must be absolute and unconditional. Neither must be contingent upon any other act or event. If Baron promises to pay Noffke $500 "in 60 days, or sooner if I sell my farm," the instrument is negotiable because the promise itself is unconditional. In any event, a promise to pay the $500 in 60 days exists. The contingency pertains only to the time of payment, and that time cannot exceed 60 days. If the words *or sooner* were omitted, the promise would be conditional, and the note would be nonnegotiable. As stated previously, however, an instrument may be binding on the parties even though nonnegotiable.

If the order to pay is out of a particular fund or account, the instrument is still negotiable. For example, "Pay to the order of Leonard Cohen $5,000 out of my share of my mother's estate," would not be a conditional order to pay. The order or the promise need not commit the entire credit of the one primarily liable for the payment of the instrument.

A reference to the consideration in a note that does not condition the promise does not destroy negotiability. The clause, "This note is given in consideration of a typewriter purchased today," does not condition the maker's promise to pay. If the clause read, "This note is given in consideration for a typewriter guaranteed for 90 days, breach of warranty to constitute cancellation of the note," the instrument would not be negotiable. This promise to pay is not absolute, but conditional. Also, if the recital of the consideration is in such form as to make the instrument subject to another contract, the negotiability of the instrument is destroyed.

COURT CASE

Facts: In order to buy a new Chevrolet Corvette, Cory Babcock and Honest Air Conditioning & Heating, Inc. signed a retail installment sale contract (RISC) and made monthly payments to General Motors Acceptance Corp. (GMAC). In the RISC, Babcock and Honest agreed to buy the vehicle on credit, give GMAC a security interest in it, keep the Corvette in the United States, and reimburse GMAC for any advances for repairs or storage bills. A year later, Babcock and Honest Air traded the Corvette to Florida Auto Brokers for another vehicle. A few months later, Florida sent a check in the correct amount to GMAC, which released the lien on the Corvette and sent Florida the title. Florida's check bounced so GMAC sued Babcock and Honest. They argued the RISC was a negotiable instrument.

Outcome: The court stated that to be negotiable the RISC had to be an unconditional promise. It could not contain any other undertaking by the promisor other than the payment of money. The RISC was not negotiable.

—General Motors Acceptance Corp. v. Honest Air Conditioning and Heating, Inc., **933 So.2d 34 (Fla. App.)**

Thus, a mere reference to a separate agreement or a statement that the instrument arises out of a separate agreement does not make the promise or order conditional. However, if the promise or order states it is subject to or governed by another agreement, it is conditional.

A Fixed Amount of Money

The instrument must call for the payment of money. It need not be American money, but it must be some national medium of exchange that is legal tender at the place payment is to be made. Thus, it could be payable in dollars, yen, euros, pounds, pesos, or rubles. It cannot be in scrip, gold bullion, bonds, or similar assets. However, the instrument may provide for the payment of either money or goods. If the choice lies with the holder, such a provision does not destroy its negotiability.

The sum payable must be a fixed amount, not dependent upon other funds or upon future profits.

COURT CASE

Facts: The firm of Hill, Heard, O'Neal, Gilstrap & Goetz, P.C. executed a promissory note for $50,000 to Commonwealth Bank. The note stated $13,000 was advanced but contemplated additional advances, and $50,000 was the maximum amount that could be borrowed. The note stated the $50,000 could be borrowed more than once as long as the balance was paid off each time. Diversified Financial Systems, Inc. purchased the note and sued the firm for failure to make payments. The firm claimed there was a break in Diversified's chain of title. The court had to determine whether the note was negotiable.

Outcome: The court held that the note was not negotiable, so Diversified's title was good.

—*Diversified Financial Systems, Inc. v. Hill, Heard, O'Neal, Gilstrap & Goetz, P.C., 99 S.W.3d 349 (Tex. App.)*

Not only must the contract be payable in money to be negotiable, but the amount must be determinable from the wording of the instrument itself. If a note for $5,000 provides that all taxes that may be levied on a certain piece of real estate will be paid, it is nonnegotiable. The amount to be paid cannot be determined from the note itself. A provision providing for the payment of interest or exchange charges, however, does not destroy negotiability. Other terms that have been held not to destroy negotiability are provisions for cost of collection, a 10 percent attorney's fee if placed in the hands of an attorney for collection, and installment payments.

A variable rate of interest does not destroy negotiability. Although the Uniform Commercial Code (UCC) requires the instrument to call for payment of a "fixed amount" of money, the fixed amount refers to principal. The Code specifically permits the rate of interest to be a variable one without destroying negotiability.

Sometimes, through error of the party writing the negotiable instrument, the words on the instrument may call for the payment of one amount of money, while the figures call for the payment of another. The amount expressed in words prevails because one is less likely to err in writing this amount. Also, if anyone should attempt to raise the amount, it would be much simpler to alter the figures than the words. By the same token, handwriting prevails over conflicting typewriting, and typewriting prevails over conflicting printed amounts.

Payable on Demand or at a Definite Time

An instrument meets the test of negotiability as to time if it is payable on demand (as in a demand note) or at sight (as in a sight draft). If no time is specified (as in a check), the commercial paper is considered payable on demand.

COURT CASE

Facts: To get financing to construct and operate a grocery store, White City Development, a partnership, asked United Grocers to lease property White owned. United would then sublease the property to Schiffer and Gast, two of the partners. United executed the lease, which required White to pay United $68,800 to purchase lease guarantee insurance. The insurance would indemnify United if Schiffer and Gast defaulted. White's partners signed a note that stated: "We . . . promise to pay to the order of [United] . . . the sum of $68,800 due and payable at such time as [United] under a Lease Agreement . . . is granted possession of the subject property." United failed to collect the $68,800 and the grocery failed. After United asked White for payment, a lawsuit ensued. The decision in the case rested on whether the note was negotiable.

Outcome: Because the note was clearly not payable on demand and there was no way to know just when possession of the property would occur, the note was not negotiable.

—*Schiffer v. United Grocers, Inc.,*
989 P.2d 10 (Ore.)

If the instrument provides for payment at a time in the future, the due date must be fixed.

Promissory notes often include either an acceleration clause or a prepayment clause. An acceleration clause protects the payee, and the prepayment clause benefits the party obligated to pay. A typical acceleration clause provides that in the event one installment is in default, the whole note shall become due and payable at once. This does not destroy its negotiability. Most prepayment clauses give the maker or the drawee the right to prepay the instrument in order to save interest. This also does not affect the negotiability of the instrument.

Payable to Order or Bearer

The two most common words of negotiability are *order* and *bearer*. The instrument is payable to order when some person is made the payee, and the maker or drawer wishes to indicate that the instrument will be paid to the person designated or to anyone else to whom the payee may transfer the instrument by indorsement.

It is not necessary to use the word *order*, but it is strongly recommended. The law looks to the intention of the maker or the drawer. If the words used clearly show an intention to pay either the named payee or anyone else whom the payee designates, the contract is negotiable. A note payable to "Smith and assigns" was held to be nonnegotiable. If it had been payable to "Smith or assigns," it would have been negotiable.

However, there is an exception in the case of checks. Article 3 of the UCC provides that a check reading "Pay to Smith" is negotiable. This applies only to checks and not to other drafts or notes.

The other words of negotiability, *payable to bearer,* indicate that the maker or the acceptor of a draft is willing to pay the person who possesses the instrument at maturity. The usual form in which these words appear is *Pay to bearer* or *Pay to Lydia Lester or bearer.* Other types of wording make an instrument a bearer instrument. For example, *Pay to the order of cash,* and *Pay to the order of bearer,* or any other designation that does not refer to a natural person or a corporation is regarded as payable to bearer.

Payee and Drawee Designated with Reasonable Certainty

When a negotiable instrument is payable "to order," the payee must be so named that the specific party can be identified with reasonable certainty. For example, a check that reads "Pay to the order of the Treasurer of the Virginia Educational Association" is not payable to a specific named individual, but that person can be ascertained with reasonable certainty. Therefore, the check is negotiable. If, on the other hand, the check is payable "to the order of the Treasury of the Y.M.C.A." and the city has three such organizations, it would not be possible to ascertain the payee with reasonable certainty. This check would not be negotiable.

The drawee of a draft must likewise be named or described with reasonable certainty so that the holder will know who will accept or pay it.

ISSUE AND DELIVERY

A negotiable instrument written by the drawer or maker does not have any effect until it is "issued." The UCC defines **issue** as "the first delivery of an instrument by the maker or drawer . . . for the purpose of giving rights on the instrument to any person." **Delivery** means the intentional transfer of possession and control of something. So *issue* ordinarily means that the drawer or maker mails it or hands it over to the payee or does some other act that releases possession and control over it and sends it on its way to the payee. Whenever delivery is made in connection with either the original issue or a subsequent negotiation, the delivery must be absolute, as contrasted with conditional. If it is conditional, the issuing of the instrument or the negotiation does not take effect until the condition is satisfied; although, as against a holder in due course, a defendant will be barred from showing that the condition was not satisfied.

To negotiate order paper, it must be both indorsed by the person to whom the paper is then payable and delivered to the new holder. Bearer payer requires no indorsement, and a physical transfer of the instrument alone effects negotiation.

LO ❷
Issue and delivery requirements

Issue
First delivery of negotiable instrument by maker or drawer to give rights to another

Delivery
Intentional transfer of possession and control of something

DELIVERY OF AN INCOMPLETE INSTRUMENT

If a negotiable instrument is only partially filled in and signed before delivery, the maker or drawer is liable if the blanks are filled in according to instructions. If the holder fills in the blanks contrary to authority, the maker or drawer is liable to the original payee or an ordinary holder for only the amount actually authorized. A holder in due course, however, can enforce the paper according to the filled-in terms even though they were not authorized.

COURT CASE

Facts: Joseph Fasano agreed to an investment that required him to execute a promissory note payable to International Dynergy, Inc. but with the date, principal amount, and dates of payment left blank. Fasano also executed a power of attorney that authorized Dynergy to complete the note if certain conditions occurred. The conditions did not occur, but Dynergy completed the note in the amount of $240,000 and sold it to Equilease Corp. When Fasano did not pay the note, Equilease sued him.

Outcome: The court stated that a holder in due course, Equilease, could enforce the note, even though Dynergy had improperly completed it.

—Equilease v. Indemnity Ins. Co. of N.Am.,
584 N.Y.S.2d 793 (A.D.)

DATE AND PLACE

LO ❸
Requirements of date
and place

Various matters not of commercial significance do not affect the negotiable character of a negotiable instrument.

1. The instrument need not be dated. The negotiability of the instrument is not affected by the fact that it is undated, antedated, or postdated. The omission of a date may cause considerable inconvenience, but the date is not essential. The holder may fill in the correct date if the space for the date is left blank. If an instrument is due 30 days after date and the date is omitted, the instrument is payable 30 days after it was issued or delivered. In case of dispute, the date of issue may be proved.

2. The name of the place where the instrument was drawn or where it is payable need not be specified. For contracts in general, the law where the contract is made or where it is to be performed governs one's rights. This rule makes it advisable for a negotiable instrument to stipulate the place where it is drawn and where it is payable, but neither is essential for its negotiability.

COURT CASE

Facts: By written agreement of May 6, David and Hazel Morrison loaned Shanwick International Corp. $25,000 for 60 days with $2,500 interest. On July 6, a written agreement extended the loan for 60 more days. Shanwick signed the agreement and attached a check for $27,500 postdated to September 6. The Morrisons also received a check for $2,500 postdated to July 12. Both checks were returned for insufficient funds and never paid. Morrison sued under the bad check statutes. Shanwick argued that the postdated checks were simply promises to pay and not negotiable instruments.

Outcome: The court held that postdated checks were fully negotiable instruments that had a demand date in the future.

—Morrison v. Shanwick Intl. Corp.,
804 P.2d 768 (Ariz. Ct. App.)

QUESTIONS

1. State the seven requirements of negotiability.

2. In what form does the law require a writing to be in order to be negotiable? Explain.

3. Must the signature of the promisor required on a negotiable instrument be in a specific location?

4. To be negotiable, must a promissory note contain the word *"promise"*?

5. The state signed a draft for $5,000 payable to Jenkins out of the Highway Trust Fund. Is the draft negotiable? Why or why not?

6. When may an instrument call for payment in goods and yet be negotiable?

7. What is the result if the amount in words on an instrument does not agree with the amount in figures?

8. What is an acceleration clause and how does it affect the negotiability of an instrument?

9. Explain the difference between negotiation of an instrument that is payable to order and one that is payable to bearer.

10. When an incomplete instrument is filled-in without authorization, what is the liability of the maker or drawer?

CASE PROBLEMS

1. Whistler Village Partnership executed notes to Alpine Federal Savings & Loan Association to buy nine condominiums in Colorado. John Burns bought the condos and signed assumption agreements covering the notes and requiring him to pay the taxes on the properties. Several years later, Burns defaulted, so Alpine foreclosed. Foreclosure did not pay off the notes, so Alpine sued Burns to recover the deficiencies. Alpine became insolvent, so the Resolution Trust Corporation (RTC) was substituted for Alpine in the lawsuit. RTC was not subject to some defenses of Burns if the notes were negotiable. Burns alleged the provision to pay the taxes which could vary each year made the documents nonnegotiable because they did not contain an obligation to pay a fixed amount. Were the notes negotiable?   LO ❶

2. Felix Villafuerte filed a complaint that he worked 80 hours for Inter Con Security Systems, Inc. for which he was not paid. Inter Con had issued a check payable to Villafuerte and mailed it, but someone had intercepted the check and cashed it. The indorsement signature misspelled Villafuerte's first and last names and was not in Villafuerte's handwriting. Had Inter Con delivered the check to Villafuerte?   LO ❷

3. On a Thursday, Deborah Wallace went to Morris Murdock Travel to buy airline tickets. Because she did not have a credit card, Wallace had to pay cash. She told Murdock she did not have the money to cover the tickets in her account but would have it the next Tuesday and asked Murdock to take a postdated check. Wallace delivered to Murdock a check that was not postdated, but dated the previous day. Murdock held the check until Tuesday, but it bounced, and Wallace was charged with issuing a bad check. Wallace argued the instrument was not a check. Did predating the check destroy negotiability?   LO ❸

LO ❶

4. Some American Express money orders were stolen. They had the preprinted signature of Louis Gerstner, the then chairman of American Express, but the amount, payee, and date were blank. Chuckie's, a check cashing business, cashed three of them not knowing they were stolen. However, American Express refused to pay Chuckie's for the money orders. In the ensuing lawsuit, the court had to decide whether the money orders were negotiable. Did the preprinted signature make them signed writings?

LO ❷

5. On behalf of Nirmaco Corp., Roger Khemlani ordered chemicals from Isaac Industries, Inc. to be shipped directly to a company in Jamaica. Khemlani gave Isaac two postdated checks in payment. Isaac shipped the chemicals and tried to cash the checks, but payment had been stopped. Isaac discovered, two other checks drawn on Florida National Bank payable to Isaac had been issued, but it never received them. Khemlani had had them and they had been deposited in Nirmaco's account at Southeast Bank. Isaac's indorsement had been forged. Isaac sued Florida National and Southeast claiming to be the payee of the checks. Did it have the rights of a payee?

LO ❶

6. All Ways, Inc. and its president, Gary Ross, purchased two motor vehicles from County Ford Lincoln Mercury by signing two installment contracts. County assigned the contracts to Ford Motor Credit Co. To pay for the vehicles, All Ways and Ross presented Ford with two "certified money orders." They stated that the sums of $20,500 and $25,200 were to be paid "On Demand, Money of Account of the United States, as required by law . . . of Coinage Act of 1792 . . . OR, in U.C.C.1-201(24) Credit Money." They further stated they were "REDEEMABLE AT FULL FACE VALUE WHEN PRESENTED To: O.M.B.; W.D. McCALL; P.O. Box 500-284; VICTORIA, TEXAS." Ford tried to deposit the documents in a bank, but they were returned as nonnegotiable. Are they negotiable? Why or why not?

LO ❶

7. At his accountant's suggestion, Billy Huff invested in a limited partnership, Willow Creek Group, Ltd., as a tax shelter. Willow bought an apartment complex for $3.6 million by means of a $2.7 million mortgage and a $890,000 note. Willow then borrowed $1.05 million from Security Federal Savings & Loan. Security required all the partners to sign an agreement to pay the note and all future obligations of Willow if it defaulted. Willow defaulted, and Security asked the partners to pay under the agreement. Huff refused to pay, claiming he had been fraudulently induced to sign it. The other partners formed a new partnership called Guarantor Partners. Guarantor bought the note and agreement from Security and sued Huff. He could raise the defense of fraudulent inducement if the agreement was not a negotiable instrument. Was it a negotiable instrument?

Promissory Notes and Drafts

LEARNING OBJECTIVES

1 State the accountability of the maker and distinguish among the different types of notes.

2 Identify the two different kinds of drafts.

3 Explain how drafts are accepted and what admissions are made by acceptance.

4 Describe the characteristics of a check.

PREVIEW CASE

→ Decatur Auto Center sent a $30,500 check drawn on its account in Wachovia Bank to Northside Sales & Leasing to be cashed when Northside got title to a Mercedes Decatur wanted. Instead, Northside deposited the check in its account at Colonial Bank, and Colonial immediately paid $30,500 into Northside's account. The check bounced. Decatur paid for the Mercedes another way. However, Colonial kept the check and asked Wachovia almost daily over several months whether there were funds in Decatur's account to pay it. When Colonial learned there were sufficient funds, it sent Gregory Cade to a Wachovia branch where he met Decatur's president, Raimi Sanuse. Sanuse told Cade Northside had been paid for the Mercedes and put a stop-payment order on the check. Wachovia processed and charged Decatur for the stop order, but paid the check to Colonial and would not reimburse Decatur. What is the significance of Wachovia charging Decatur for the stop-payment order? What is a bank's responsibility to its depositors?

Notes and drafts are negotiable instruments widely used in commercial and personal transactions. Each has unique features.

NOTES

Any written promise to pay money at a specified time is a promissory note, but it may not be a negotiable instrument. To be negotiable, a note must contain the essential elements discussed in Chapter 21.

The two original parties to a promissory note are the maker, the one who signs the note and promises to pay, and the payee, the one to whom the promise is made.

Accountability of the Maker

The maker of a promissory note has accountability for (1) expressly agreeing to pay the note according to its terms, (2) admitting the existence of the payee, and (3) warranting that the payee is competent to transfer the instrument by indorsement.

C O U R T ☀ C A S E

Facts: Thomas Sessions bought farm machinery from Charles McCarthy to use on the farms he owned and operated with his wife Dorothy. Thomas and Dorothy signed a promissory note to McCarthy in the amount due on the machinery on February 8. Thomas Sessions died on March 31. McCarthy sued to collect on the note. Dorothy said she was not liable because Thomas purchased the machinery, not her, and Thomas was liable for the underlying debt.

Outcome: The court stated she was a maker of the note. As a maker, Dorothy contracted to pay the note according to its terms at the time she signed it and was liable to McCarthy.

—*McCarthy v. Sessions*, 572 N.Y.S.2d 749 (N.Y. App. Div.)

Types of Notes

LO ❶
Types of notes

Many types of notes known by special names include:

1. Bonds
2. Collateral notes
3. Real estate mortgage notes
4. Debentures
5. Certificates of Deposit

Bond
Sealed, written contract obligation with essentials of note

Bonds. A **bond** is a written contract obligation, usually under seal, generally issued by a corporation, a municipality, or a government, that contains a promise to pay a fixed amount of money at a set or determinable future time. In addition to the promise to pay, it will generally contain certain other conditions and stipulations. A bond issued by a corporation is generally secured by a deed of trust on the property of the corporation. A bond may be a coupon bond or a registered bond.

Coupon Bond
Bond with detachable individual coupons representing interest payments

A **coupon bond** is so called because the interest payments that will become due on the bond are represented by detachable individual coupons to be presented for payment when due. Coupon bonds and the individual coupons are usually payable to the bearer; as a result, they can be negotiated by delivery. There is no registration of the original purchaser or any subsequent holder of the bond.

Registered Bond
Bond payable to specific person, whose name is recorded by issuer

A **registered bond** is a bond payable to a named person. The bond is recorded under that name by the organization issuing it to guard against its loss or destruction. When a registered bond is sold, a record of the transfer to the new bondholder must be made under the name of the new bond-holder.

Collateral Note
Note secured by personal property

Collateral Notes. A **collateral note** is a note secured by personal property. The collateral usually consists of stock, bonds, or other written evidences of debt, or a security interest in tangible personal property given by the debtor to the payee-creditor.

The transaction may vary in terms of whether the creditor keeps possession of the property as long as the debt is unpaid or whether the debtor may keep possession of the property until default. When the creditor receives possession of collateral, reasonable care of it must be taken, and the creditor is liable to the debtor for any loss resulting from lack of reasonable care. If the creditor receives any interest, dividend, or other income from the property while it is held as collateral, such amount must be credited against the debt or returned to the debtor.

Regardless of the form of the transaction, the property is freed from the claim of the creditor if the debt is paid. If not paid, the creditor may sell the property in the manner prescribed by law. The creditor must return to the debtor any excess of the sale proceeds above the debt, interest, and costs. If the sale of the collateral does not provide sufficient proceeds to pay the debt, the debtor is liable for any deficiency.

Real Estate Mortgage Notes. A **real estate mortgage note** is given to evidence a debt that the maker-debtor secures by giving to the payee a mortgage on real estate. As in the case of a real estate mortgage, generally the mortgagor-debtor retains possession of the property. If the real estate is not freed by payment of the debt, the holder may proceed on the mortgage or the mortgage note to enforce the maker-mortgagor's liability. Chapter 43 more thoroughly describes real estate mortgages.

> **Real Estate Mortgage Note**
> *Note secured by mortgage on real estate*

Debentures. An unsecured bond or note issued by a business firm is called a **debenture**. A debenture, like any other bond, is nothing more or less than a promissory note, usually under seal. It may be embellished with gold-colored edges, but this does not in any way indicate its value. A debenture is usually negotiable in form.

> **Debenture**
> *Unsecured bond issued by a business*

COURT CASE

Facts: Moxham National Bank loaned John and Anthony Horbal and Elaine Adams $120,000. The Horbals assigned a $25,000 certificate of deposit (CD) to the bank. The assignment transferred all of the Horbals' right, title, and interest in the CD to the bank. The loan was not repaid, so the bank withdrew the CD and applied the proceeds to the loan balance. The Horbals assigned their causes of action against the bank to Highland Financial Ltd. and James Walsh, who sued the bank. The issue in the case was whether the CD was a negotiable instrument; if it was, the bank was the holder and entitled to payment of it.

Outcome: The court held that the CD was a negotiable instrument because it was payable at an indefinite time and payable "to order."

—*Horbal v. Moxham Natl. Bank,*
657 A.2d 1261 (Pa. Super.)

Certificates of Deposit. The Uniform Commercial Code (UCC) defines a **certificate of deposit** (CD) as "an acknowledgment by a bank that a sum of money has been received by the bank and a promise by the bank to repay the sum of money." The bank repays the sum to the person designated on the CD. Normally the money is repaid with interest. The UCC classifies a certificate of deposit as a note even though it does not contain the word *promise*. A CD is not a draft because it does not contain an order to pay.

> **Certificate of Deposit**
> *Acknowledgment by bank of receipt of money with engagement to repay it*

DRAFTS

The drawer draws or executes a draft in favor of the payee, who has the drawer's authority to collect the amount indicated on the instrument. It must be clear that the signature is intended to be that of a drawer; otherwise the signature will be construed to be that of an indorser. A draft is addressed to the drawee, who is the person ordered by the drawer to pay the amount of the instrument. The drawee pays the amount to the payee or some other party to whom the payee has transferred the instrument by indorsement.

An **inland**, or domestic, **draft** is one that shows on its face that it is both drawn and payable within the United States. A foreign draft shows on its face that it is drawn or payable outside the United States.

Inland Draft
Draft drawn and payable in the United States

Forms of Drafts

Two kinds of drafts exist to meet the different needs of business:

1. Sight drafts
2. Time drafts

LO ❷
Kinds of drafts

Sight Drafts. A **sight draft** is a draft payable at sight or on presentation by the payee or holder. By it, the drawer demands payment at once. Special types of sight drafts include money orders and checks.

Sight Draft
Draft payable on presentation by holder

Time Drafts. A **time draft** has the same form as a sight draft except with respect to the date of payment. The drawer orders the drawee to pay the money a certain number of days or months after the date on the instrument or a certain number of days or months after presenting it for acceptance. **Acceptance** is the drawee's signed agreement to pay a draft, delivered to the holder.

In the case of a time draft, the holder cannot require payment of the paper until it has matured. The holder normally presents the draft to the drawee for acceptance. However, whether or not the draft has been accepted does not affect the time when it matures if it is payable a certain length of time after its date.

A time draft payable a specified number of days after sight must be presented for acceptance. The due date is calculated from the date of the acceptance, not from the date of the draft.

Time Draft
Draft payable certain number of days or months after date or presentation

Acceptance
Drawee's signed agreement to pay draft

Trade Acceptance

A **trade acceptance** is a type of draft used in the sale of goods. It is a draft drawn by the seller on the purchaser of goods sold and accepted by such purchaser. The drawer draws a trade acceptance at the time goods are sold. The seller is the drawer, and the purchaser is the drawee. A trade acceptance orders the purchaser to pay the face of the bill to the order of the named payee, who is frequently the seller.

Trade Acceptance
Draft drawn by seller on purchaser of goods

Presentment for Acceptance

All trade acceptances and all time drafts payable a specified time after sight must be presented for acceptance by the payee to the drawee. In case of other kinds of drafts, presentment for acceptance is optional and is made merely to determine the intention of the drawee and to give the paper the additional credit strength of the acceptance. A qualified acceptance destroys the negotiability of the instrument. An acceptance could be qualified by adding additional terms such as "if presented for payment within 24 hours" or "in 10 days from date." The drawee, after accepting the instrument, that is, after agreeing to pay it, becomes the acceptor.

Place. The holder should present the instrument at the drawee's place of business. If there is no place of business, it may be presented at the drawee's home or wherever the drawee may be found.

Party. A draft must be presented to the drawee or to someone authorized either by law or by contract to accept it. If there are two or more drawees, the draft must be presented to all of them unless one has authority to act for them all.

Form of Acceptance

The usual method of accepting a draft is to write on the face:

> Accepted
> Jane Roe

LO 3
Acceptance procedure
and admissions

The drawee's signature alone on the draft is sufficient to constitute a valid acceptance; however, adding the word *accepted* is advisable to make clear that an acceptance is intended. If an acceptance on a sight draft does not include a date, the holder may supply the date. The drawee may use other words of acceptance, but the words used must indicate an intention to be bound by the terms of the instrument and must be written on the instrument. The instrument or notification of the acceptance must then be delivered to the holder for the purpose of giving rights on the acceptance to the holder.

If the drawee refuses to accept a draft or to accept it in a proper way, the holder of the draft has no claim against the drawee but can return the draft to the drawer. Any credit given the drawer by the delivery of the draft is thereby canceled. If the draft is a trade acceptance, the refusal of the drawee to accept means that the buyer refuses to go through with the financing terms of the transaction; unless some other means of financing or payment is agreed on, the transaction falls through.

COURT CASE

Facts: Jeff Messing, the payee on a check drawn on the Bank of America, handed the check to a teller at the bank. The teller put the check in a computer validation slot. The computer stamped the time, date, account number, and teller number on the back. The teller asked Messing to indorse the check, and he did. When the teller asked him for an ID, he displayed his driver's license and a credit card. Then the teller asked Messing if he was a customer of Bank of America, and he said, "No." The teller gave the check back to him and asked him to put his "thumbprint signature" on the check. Messing refused. The teller would not cash the check. Messing sued the bank alleging it had accepted the check by validating it.

Outcome: Although the bank teller had put the check through a validation slot causing writing to be stamped on it, the bank did not notify Messing that an acceptance had occurred. Returning the check to him was for his thumbprint, not to complete acceptance.

—*Messing v. Bank of America, N.A.,* 792 A.2d 312 (Md. App.)

Admissions of the Acceptor

A draft presented to a drawee for acceptance must be either accepted or returned. If the draft is not returned, the drawee is treated as having stolen the paper from the holder. By accepting the instrument, the drawee assumes liability for the payment of the paper. This liability of the acceptor runs from the due date of the paper until the statute of limitations bars the claim.

When the drawee accepts a draft, two admissions concerning the drawer are made:

1. That the signature of the drawer is genuine
2. That the drawer has both the capacity and the authority to draw the draft

The drawee, by accepting a draft, also admits the payee's capacity to indorse, but not the genuineness of the payee's indorsement.

Having made these admissions, the acceptor cannot later deny them against a holder of the instrument.

Money Orders

Money Order
Instrument issued by business indicating payee may receive indicated amount

A **money order** is an instrument issued by a bank, post office, or express company indicating that the payee may request and receive the amount indicated on the instrument. When paid for, issued, and delivered to the payee, the issuer has made a contract to pay.

CHECKS

LO ❹
Characteristics of checks

Check
Draft drawn on a bank and payable on demand

Chapter 20 mentioned that a **check** is a type of draft. To be a check, the draft must be drawn on a bank and payable on demand. It is a type of sight draft with the drawee, a bank, and the drawer, a depositor—a person who has funds deposited with a bank. Just like other drafts, a check is an order by the drawer, on the drawee, to pay a sum of money to the order of another person, the payee.

The numbers at the bottom of a check (see Illustration 22–1) are printed in magnetic ink. The numbers identify the specific account and the bank that holds the account. Because the numbers are printed in magnetic ink, the check may be sorted by electronic data processing equipment. The Federal Reserve System requires that all checks passing through its clearinghouses be imprinted with such identifying magnetic ink. In most cases, however, the drawee bank will accept checks that do not carry the magnetic ink coding. In fact, the material on which a check is written does not affect the validity of a check.

ILLUSTRATION 22–1 Check

CURTRON HEATING/AIR CONDITIONING 1401 Dixie Highway Newport, Kentucky	No. **83** — 46-0039 / 0420
	May 28, 20 – –
PAY TO THE ORDER OF __Ashland Oil__	$ 243 21
Two hundred forty-three 21/100 ———————————————— DOLLARS	
FOR CLASSROOM USE ONLY	
PROVIDENCE NATIONAL BANK Covington, Kentucky	Jane E.Congdon

⑊0420⑊0392⑊ 2461705⑊

Special Kinds of Checks

Five special types of checks include:

1. Certified checks
2. Cashier's checks
3. Bank drafts
4. Voucher checks
5. Traveler's checks

Certified Checks. A **certified check** is an ordinary check accepted by an official of the drawee bank. The official accepts it by writing across the face of the check the word *certified,* or some similar word, and signing it. Either the drawer or the holder may have a check certified. The certification of the check by the bank has the same effect as an acceptance. It makes the bank liable for the payment of the check and binds it by the warranties made by an acceptor. A certification obtained by a holder releases the drawer from liability.

The drawer of a draft accepted by a bank is relieved of liability on the instrument. It does not matter when or by whom acceptance was obtained.

Certified Check
Check accepted by bank's writing certified on it

Cashier's Checks. A check that a bank draws on its own funds and that the cashier or some other responsible official of the bank signs is called a **cashier's check**. It is accepted for payment when issued and delivered. A bank in paying its own obligations may use such a check, or it may be used by anyone else who wishes to remit money in some form other than cash or a personal check.

Cashier's Check
Check drawn by bank on its own funds

COURT CASE

Facts: From December 22 through 26, Anatoly Rybner deposited checks from Good Guys Auto Sales' account at Commerce Bank, N.A. totaling $424,000 to a Bayway Auto, Inc. account at Commerce Bank's Woodbridge, N.J., branch. There were insufficient funds to cover those checks. Between December 24 and 30, Pierre Parks, president of Bayway, transferred funds from the Bayway Commerce account to a second Bayway account at Commerce and from that account to the account of another company he owned in Fleet Bank. He also obtained four cashier's checks from the Fleet Bank account and one from Bayway's first Commerce account. Because the cashier's checks were issued based on Good Guys now dishonored checks, Commerce issued a stop payment order and asked the other banks to withhold release of the funds. Parks and Bayway sued to compel the banks to honor the cashier's checks.

Outcome: The court held that the banks had a legal obligation to honor the cashier's checks.

—*Parks v. Commerce Bank, N.A.,*
872 A.2d 1116 (N.J. Super. A.D.)

Bank Drafts. A **bank draft** or **teller's check** is a check drawn by one bank on another bank. Banks customarily keep a portion of their funds on deposit with other banks. A bank, then, may draw a check on these funds as freely as any corporation may draw checks. People purchase teller's checks because they rely on the bank's credit, not an individual's. Also, a purchaser of a teller's check has no right to insist that the issuing bank stop payment on a teller's check that is not payable to the purchaser. Thus, teller's checks are more readily accepted by payees than are personal checks.

Bank Draft or **Teller's Check**
Check drawn by one bank on another

Facts: Isabel Gonzales closed her accounts at New Haven Savings Bank and received two teller's checks payable to Isabel Rodriquez. The next day, New Haven received a notice of garnishment that the property of Isabel Gonzales was seized for collection of a debt. The notice did not mention anyone named Rodriquez. The Hospital of St. Raphael obtained a judgment against Gonzales and sued New Haven claiming that at the time of the notice the bank had owed Gonzales money. New Haven claimed it discharged its obligation to Gonzales when it issued the teller's checks, so when it received the notice it no longer owed her anything.

Outcome: The court agreed with New Haven saying that not only did it not owe Gonzales any money, but it could not have stopped payment on the teller's checks without being liable to the payee and possible future holders.

—*Hospital of St. Raphael v. New Haven Savings,* **534 A.2d 1189 (Conn.)**

Voucher Check
Check with voucher attached

Voucher Checks. A **voucher check** is a check with a voucher attached. The voucher lists the items of an invoice for which the check is the means of payment. In business, the drawer of the check customarily writes on the check such words as "In full of account, For invoice No. 1622," or similar notations. These notations make the checks excellent receipts when returned to the drawer. A check on which additional space is provided for the drawer to make a notation for which the check is issued is sometimes referred to as a voucher check. A payee who indorses a check on which a notation has been made agrees to the terms of the check, which include the terms written in the notation by the drawer.

Traveler's Checks. A traveler's check is an instrument much like a cashier's check of the issuer except that it requires signature and countersignature by its purchaser. Traveler's checks, sold by banks and express companies, are payable on demand. The purchaser of traveler's checks signs each check once at the time of purchase and then countersigns it and fills in the name of the payee when the check is to be used.

Postdated Checks

Postdated Check
Check drawn before its date

A check drawn before the time it is dated is a **postdated check**. If it is drawn on June 21, but dated July 1, it is, in effect, a ten-day draft. There is nothing unlawful about a postdated check as long as it was not postdated for an illegal or fraudulent purpose. A bank on which such a check is drawn may pay it before its date without liability unless the customer/drawer has properly notified the bank of the postdated check.

Bad Checks

Bad Check
Check the drawee bank refuses to pay

If a check is drawn with intent to defraud the payee, the drawer is civilly liable as well as subject to criminal prosecution in most states under so-called bad check laws. A **bad check** is a check that the holder sends to the drawee bank and the bank refuses to pay, normally for insufficient funds. Usually these statutes state that if the check is not made good within a specific period, such as ten days, a presumption arises that the drawer originally issued the check with the intent to defraud.

COURT CASE

Facts: John McFadden presented a check for $395 drawn on United Bank and Trust to Midland Financial Services. McFadden had written his Midland savings account number on it and had crossed out the printed telephone number and written in a different number. Midland's teller did not notice the check was postdated, and McFadden did not tell her it was postdated. The teller gave McFadden $395 for the check. After McFadden left, the teller checked his savings account and found it had $3 in it. She called United and found out McFadden's account had been closed five months before. Midland presented the check to United, which refused to pay it. The police arrested McFadden for theft for unlawfully giving a check in exchange for property while knowing the check would not be paid. McFadden argued the postdated check was not a check.

Outcome: The court held that a postdated check was a check, and therefore McFadden had violated the theft law.

—*State v. McFadden*, 467 N.W.2d 578 (Iowa)

COURT CASE

Facts: When Lor-Mar/Toto, Inc. opened an account at 1st Constitution Bank, it authorized the bank to honor checks bearing the actual signature of one of four named officers and employees. Later, Lor-Mar told the bank that two of the persons' signatures would be "stamped" on the checks and provided samples of their stamped facsimile signatures. Years later, unauthorized checks totaling $24,000 were drawn on the account. They appeared to have one of the stamped facsimile signatures but were a different color and on different stock than Lor-Mar's genuine checks. Lor-Mar discovered the unauthorized checks from its statement and promptly notified the bank. When the bank would not recredit Lor-Mar's account, it sued.

Outcome: The court stated the bank had a duty to charge Lor-Mar's account only for properly payable items. Although Lor-Mar authorized checks with stamped signatures, it did not approve unauthorized use of an officer's facsimile signature. The bank had to reimburse Lor-Mar.

—*Lor-Mar/Toto, Inc. v. 1st Constitution Bank*, 871 A.2d 110 (N.J. Super. A.D.)

Duties of the Bank

The bank owes several duties to its customer, the depositor-drawer. It must maintain secrecy regarding information acquired by it in connection with the depositor-bank relationship.

The bank also has the duty of comparing the signature on the depositor's checks with the signature of the depositor in the bank's files to make certain the signatures on the checks are valid. If the bank pays a check that does not have the drawer's signature, it is liable to the drawer for the loss.

Refusal of Bank to Pay. The bank is under a general contractual duty to its depositors to pay on demand all of their checks to the extent of the funds deposited to their credit. When the bank breaches this contract, it is liable to the drawer for damages. A bank may pay a properly payable check even when an overdraft will result, and it must pay checks that exceed the amount on deposit if there is an agreement that the bank will pay overdrafts. In the case of a draft other than a check, there is ordinarily no duty on the drawee to accept the draft or to make payment if it has not been accepted. Therefore, the drawee is not liable to the drawer when an unaccepted draft is not paid.

Even if the normal printed form supplied by the bank is not used, the bank must pay a proper order by a depositor. The bank must honor any written document that contains the substance of a normal printed check.

A divorced man making his last alimony payment wrote a check on a T-shirt to send a message to his ex-wife that she was taking "the shirt off his back." She did not care for the technique, but the T-shirt check was valid.

The liability of the drawee bank for improperly refusing to pay a check only runs in favor of the drawer. Even if the holder of the check or the payee may be harmed when the bank refuses to pay the check, a holder or payee has no right to sue the bank. However, the holder has a right of action against the person from whom the check was received. This right of action is based on the original obligation, which was not discharged because the check was not paid.

A check that is presented more than six months after its date is commonly called a **stale check**. A bank that acts in good faith may pay it. However, unless the check is certified, the bank is not required to pay it.

Stopping Payment. Drawers have the power of stopping payment of checks. After a check is issued, a drawer can notify the drawee bank not to pay it when presented for payment. This is a useful procedure when a check is lost or mislaid. A duplicate check can be written, and to make sure that the payee does not receive payment twice or that an improper person does not receive payment on the first check, payment on the first check can be stopped. Likewise, if payment is made by check and the payee defaults on the contract, payment on the check can be stopped, assuming that the payee has not cashed it.

A stop-payment order may be written or oral. The bank is bound by an oral stop-payment order only for 14 calendar days unless confirmed in writing within that time. A written order is effective for no more than six months unless renewed in writing.

Unless a valid limitation exists on its liability, the bank is liable for the loss the depositor sustains when the bank makes payment on a check after receiving proper notice to stop payment. However, the depositor has the burden of proving the loss sustained.

Stale Check
Check presented more than six months after its date

PREVIEW CASE REVISITED

Facts: Decatur Auto Center sent a $30,500 check drawn on its account in Wachovia Bank to Northside Sales & Leasing to be cashed when Northside got title to a Mercedes Decatur wanted. Instead, Northside deposited the check in its account at Colonial Bank, and Colonial immediately paid $30,500 into Northside's account. The check bounced. Decatur paid for the Mercedes another way. However, Colonial kept the check and asked Wachovia almost daily over several months whether there were funds in Decatur's account to pay it. When Colonial learned there were sufficient funds, it sent Gregory Cade to a Wachovia branch where he met Decatur's president, Raimi Sanuse. Sanuse told Cade Northside had been paid for the Mercedes and put a stop-payment order on the check. Wachovia processed and charged Decatur for the stop order, but paid the check to Colonial and would not reimburse Decatur. Decatur sued Wachovia.

Outcome: Wachovia had to reimburse Decatur.

—*Decatur Auto Center v. Wachovia Bank, N.A.*, 583 S.E.2d 6 (Ga.)

A depositor who stops payment without a valid reason may be liable to the payee. Also, the depositor is liable for stopping payment with respect to any holder in due course or other party having the rights of a holder in due course unless payment is stopped for a reason that may be asserted against such a holder as a defense. The fact that the bank refuses to make payment because of the drawer's instruction does not make the case any different from any other instance in which the drawee refuses to pay, and the legal consequences of imposing liability on the drawer are the same.

When the depositor makes use of a means of communication such as the telegraph to give a stop-payment notice, the bank is not liable if the notice is delayed in reaching the bank and the bank makes payment before receiving the notice. The depositor can, however, sue the telegraph company if negligence on its part can be shown.

A payee who wants to avoid the potential of payment being stopped may require a certified check of the buyer or a cashier's check from the buyer's bank because neither the buyer nor the buyer's bank can stop payment to the payee on such checks.

Payment After Depositor's Death. Usually a check is ineffective after the drawer dies. However, until the bank knows of the death and has had a reasonable opportunity to act, the bank's agency is not revoked. A bank may even continue to pay or certify a depositor's checks for 10 days unless a person claiming an interest in the estate orders it to stop.

Bank Customer's Responsibility

Although a bank has several duties to its customers, customers also have some important responsibilities. They must examine monthly bank statements and notify the bank "with reasonable promptness" of any forged signatures. If a customer fails to do this and the bank suffers loss as a result, the customer will be liable for the loss. "Reasonable promptness" is not defined, but the UCC provides that a customer who does not report an unauthorized signature or alteration within one year may not assert them against the bank. If there is a series of forgeries by the same person, the customer must discover and report the first forged check to the bank within the time prescribed by agreement between the customer and bank. If no such time is prescribed, it must be within 30 days of receiving the bank statement.

QUESTIONS

1. Explain who the original parties to a promissory note are.
2. For what can the maker of a note be held accountable?
3. What is the difference among a bond, a collateral note, a real estate mortgage note, a debenture, and a certificate of deposit?
4. What is the difference between a sight draft and a time draft?
5. What is a trade acceptance?
6. How is a proper presentment for acceptance made?
7. When the drawee accepts a draft, what admissions are made concerning the drawer?
8. What is the difference between a check and a draft?

9. Who may have a check certified?

10. To what does the payee of a voucher check agree by indorsement?

11. To whom is a bank liable for improperly refusing to pay a check?

12. How may a drawer stop payment on a check?

CASE PROBLEMS

LO ❸

1. M&O insulation was hired by Quality Insulation to install some insulation. Quality had a line of credit through a promissory note with Harris Bank Naperville. Quality had not complied with is payment schedule, so Harris declared the loan in default and immediately due and payable. On September 23, Quality paid M&O by check for $76,000 which M&O deposited in its bank. On September 24, Harris placed an administrative hold or "freeze" on Quality's account. The same day, M&O's $76,000 check was presented for payment. On the 25th, Quality's account had sufficient funds to pay the check, but Harris returned it for insufficient funds. Harris subsequently honored checks totaling $23,700 on the account. M&O sued Harris. Harris claimed it had never accepted the check. Had it?

LO ❹

2. On August 26, Lottie McGuire asked Bank One of Louisiana to sell $200,000 worth of funds from her investment account and transfer the money to her checking account. McGuire was told it would take two or three days to make the transfer. The same day, McGuire gave Timothy Looney a $200,000 check dated August 26 in order to buy some bonds. McGuire told Looney not to deposit the check until August 28. Looney immediately deposited the check. Looney's bank presented the check to Bank One on August 27, and Bank One paid it even though it overdrew McGuire's checking account by $188,000. Bank One sent McGuire an overdraft notice on August 28 which she received on August 30. Looney used the money for himself and went to prison. McGuire sued Bank One. Who should win and why?

LO ❷

3. Frances Ford agreed to buy land from Wayne and Nadine Hagel by making a down payment and paying $375 a month. The contract gave the Hagels the right to declare a forfeiture effective in 91 days if Ford missed a payment. Ford missed three payments, and the Hagels notified her of forfeiture. The notice required Ford to pay all delinquencies by February 10 with $250 of it in cash. On February 10, Ford tendered a cashier's check for $1,800 and a personal check for $1,033.32. The Hagels refused them and recorded forfeiture. They were not entitled to declare forfeiture if Ford's personal check had been good on February 10. Ford sued to set aside the forfeiture. Mrs. Hagel testified that she refused the checks because she had "contacted the plaintiff's bank personally and determined that the [personal] check would not clear." Decide the case.

LO ❶

4. To finance the purchase of a bank, Mike Moody, George Krumme, and others executed as comakers two promissory notes in the amount of $8.17 million. Moody received a 19½ percent interest in a company that owned the bank. When a payment came due on the note, Moody could not pay his share, so the other comakers paid it. The other comakers sued Moody. What was Moody's responsibility on the note?

LO ❹

5. Several weeks after a depositor's death, Chase Manhattan Bank paid 12 checks on the deceased depositor's account. The depositor's signature on the checks had been forged. The estate sued Chase. Chase sued the estate's attorneys. The attorneys had advised Chase of the depositor's death and gave it a copy of the death certificate and a court order to examine his safe deposit box three weeks before Chase paid any of the forged checks. Of these parties, is any liable?

6. Chrysler Credit Corp. contracted with Fitter Jeep-Eagle, a dealer, to finance car sales. Chrysler supplied Fitter with form drafts to use. Chrysler was the drawee on the draft. Fitter was to be the drawer, and Fitter's bank would be the payee. The contract allowed Chrysler to deny payment on drafts if Fitter was in default on the contract. Fitter deposited three drafts in First National Bank and Trust Co. of McAlester, and First gave Fitter immediate credit for them. Chrysler dishonored the drafts. First sued Chrysler. Was Chrysler liable on the drafts?   LO ❷, ❸

7. Randall Stowell opened a checking account with Cloquet Co-op Credit Union, and he signed an agreement that required him to notify Cloquet of any errors in his account statement within 20 days of its mailing. Robert Nelson moved into a cabin, the mailbox for which was next to Stowell's mailbox. The boxes were a half-mile from Stowell's house. For nine months after stealing some of Stowell's checks, Nelson forged Stowell's signature and cashed his checks. To hide the forgeries, Nelson also stole all the mail sent to Stowell from Cloquet. Stowell realized he had not received account statements from Cloquet, but when he called Cloquet and it sent duplicate statements, Nelson would steal them from the mailbox. Finally, Stowell got a phone call from Finlayson State Bank at Barnum telling him a check written to Nelson had bounced and the thefts were discovered. Stowell sued Cloquet to recover the $22,000 paid on the forged checks. Should he recover? Explain.   LO ❹

8. When Timothy Holloway was six years old, Rountree Crisp purchased a $20,000 certificate of deposit payable to "Timothy Holloway, by Rountree Crisp, Agent" from Wachovia Bank. After Crisp's death, Wachovia paid the proceeds of the CD to Marcia Coleman, Crisp's daughter and Timothy's mother, and Louise Crisp, Crisp's widow and Timothy's grandmother. They had indorsed the CD "Timothy Holloway by Estate of George Crisp, Marcia Coleman, Adminx., Louise Crisp, Adminx." Coleman put the proceeds into another CD in the name of Timothy Holloway, by Marcia Coleman. Wachovia subsequently issued a check for the CD with the same payee. After Timothy became an adult he sued Wachovia. Should Wachovia be held liable?   LO ❶

Negotiation and Discharge

LEARNING OBJECTIVES

❶ Discuss how to negotiate by indorsement, and identify the different types of indorsements.

❷ Describe the liabilities of an indorser.

❸ Explain how negotiable instruments may be discharged.

PREVIEW CASE

→ Checks were made payable to "San Francisco Plumbing, Inc./Danco, Inc." San Francisco presented the checks to Commerce Bank and received payment after indorsing them and forging Danco's signature. Danco sued the bank for paying the instruments with a forged Danco indorsement. When there are multiple payees, who must indorse an instrument? What does the virgule (/) mean?

LO ❶
Indorsements

Indorsement
Signature of holder on back of instrument with any directions or limitations

Negotiation involves the transfer of a negotiable instrument in such a way that the transferee becomes the holder of the instrument. Bearer instruments may be negotiated by delivery. Delivery effectively vests ownership in the transferee. Thus the transferee becomes the holder.

An instrument payable to "order" can be negotiated only by authorized indorsement and delivery. An **indorsement** is a signature on the back of an instrument (usually the holder's) along with any directions or limitations regarding use of or liability for the instrument. Indorsing or transferring a negotiable instrument creates certain liabilities, depending on the nature of the indorsement or transfer.

Although an indorsement is not required for negotiation of bearer paper, a transferee may require it because this adds the liability of the new indorser to the paper and thus makes it a better credit risk. It also preserves a written chronological record of all negotiations.

COURT CASE

Facts: After Thornton Ring failed to pay the property tax on his real estate, the town of Freeport sent him a notice that it was going to foreclose unless he paid by March 7. In January, Ring presented a check, for $11,347.09 to the town. Advest, Inc. had issued the check, and Thornton Ring was the payee. On the back of the check was written: "Payable to town of Freeport, Property Taxes, 2 Main St." With the check was a letter signed by Ring that stated, "I have paid $11,347.09 of real estate taxes and request . . . action to redeem the . . . property."

The town sued to confirm its title to the property.

Outcome: Because the check was payable to Ring, it needed Ring's indorsement for the town to get payment on it. His signature was not on the check itself, and the letter accompanying the check did not serve as a valid indorsement because it was not affixed to the check.

—*Town of Freeport v. Ring,*
727 A.2d 901 (Me.)

PLACE OF INDORSEMENT

Banks require that an indorsement on a check be on the back and within 1½ inches of the trailing edge. The **trailing edge** is the left side of a check when looking at it from the front (see Illustration 23–1). If the indorser's signature appears elsewhere and it cannot be determined in what capacity the signature was made, it will be considered an indorsement. In any event, an indorsement must be on the actual instrument to be indorsed or on a paper firmly attached to the instrument. An **allonge** is a paper securely attached to an instrument. For example, a paper stapled to an instrument is securely affixed. The Uniform Commercial Code (UCC) states that such a paper is part of the instrument. If a party does not wish to be liable as an indorser, the instrument can be assigned by a written assignment on a separate piece of paper.

Trailing Edge
Left side of front of check

Allonge
Paper so firmly attached to instrument as to be part of it

ILLUSTRATION 23–1 Indorsed Check Folded to Show the Position of the Indorsement

Occasionally, the name of the payee or indorsee of an instrument is misspelled. If a paycheck intended for, and delivered to, Janice F. Smith is made out to "Janice K. Smith" through clerical error, Janice F. Smith may ask her employer for a new check properly made out to her or she may keep the check and indorse in any of the following ways:

1. Janice K. Smith
2. Janice F. Smith
3. Janice K. Smith, Janice F. Smith (If she intends to receive value for the check, the person to whom it is negotiated may require her to sign both names)

However, if Janice F. Smith obtains a check made payable to, and intended for, Janice K. Smith, it would be illegal for Janice F. to indorse it and receive payment for it. Only when the check is actually intended for Janice F. Smith may she make a corrective indorsement.

It is not always necessary to correct an irregularity in the name of a party to an instrument. An irregularity does not necessarily destroy negotiability. Only if it is shown that different people were actually identified by the different names is the irregularity significant. If the different names stand for the same person, the irregularity need not be considered. It has been held that a note was correctly negotiated when indorsed "Greenlaw & Sons by George M. Greenlaw," although it was payable to "Greenlaw & Sons Roofing & Siding Co." Nothing indicates that the two enterprises were not the same firm.

MULTIPLE PAYEES

Frequently, negotiable instruments are made payable to more than one person. Whether the instrument must be indorsed by more than one of them depends on the exact language used in naming them on the instrument.

If the parties are named using the word *and* between their names, then it is payable jointly and all of them must indorse the instrument in order to negotiate it. For example, if the instrument reads, "Pay to the order of Mary and John Doe," then both Mary and John must indorse the instrument. Neither can negotiate the instrument alone.

If the word *or* is used between the names of the parties, then the instrument is payable in the alternative and only one needs to indorse the instrument in order to negotiate it. When an instrument reads, "Pay to the order of Hank or Nancy Florio," either Hank or Nancy can indorse and negotiate the instrument.

PREVIEW CASE REVISITED

Facts: Checks were made payable to "San Francisco Plumbing, Inc./Danco, Inc." San Francisco presented the checks to Commerce Bank and received payment after indorsing them and forging Danco's signature. Danco sued the bank for paying the instruments with a forged Danco indorsement.

Outcome: The court held that the virgule (/) meant "or." Because the checks only needed the indorsement of either San Francisco or Danco and they contained the valid indorsement of San Francisco, the payment was proper.

—*Danco, Inc. v. Commerce Bank/Shore*, 675 A.2d 663 (N.J. Super. A.D.)

Normally, if the instrument is not clear as to whether it is payable jointly or alternatively, it will be construed to be payable in the alternative.

KINDS OF INDORSEMENTS

Four types of indorsements include:

1. Blank indorsements
2. Special indorsements
3. Qualified indorsements
4. Restrictive indorsements

Blank Indorsements

As the name indicates, a **blank indorsement** is one having no words other than the name of the indorser (see Illustration 23–2). If the instrument is bearer paper, it remains bearer paper when a blank indorsement is made. Thus, the new holder may pass good title to another holder without indorsing the instrument. The one primarily liable on the instrument is bound to pay the person who presents it for payment on the date due, even if the person is a thief or other unauthorized party.

> **Blank Indorsement**
> *Indorsement consisting of signature of indorser*

If the instrument is order paper, a blank indorsement converts it to bearer paper; if thereafter indorsed to someone's order, it becomes order paper again. Converting the instruments to order paper can minimize risks involved in handling instruments originally payable to bearer or indorsed in blank.

Special Indorsements

A **special indorsement** designates the particular person to whom payment should be made (see Illustration 23–2). After making such an indorsement, the paper is order paper, whether or not it was originally so payable or was originally payable to bearer. The holder must indorse it before it can be further negotiated. Of course, the holder may indorse the instrument in blank, which makes it bearer paper. Each holder has the power to decide to make either a blank or a special indorsement.

> **Special Indorsement**
> *Indorsement that designates particular person to whom payment is to be made*

An indorsee by a blank indorsement may convert it to a special indorsement by writing the words "pay to the order of [indorsee]" above the indorser's signature.

ILLUSTRATION 23–2 Blank Indorsement and Special Indorsement

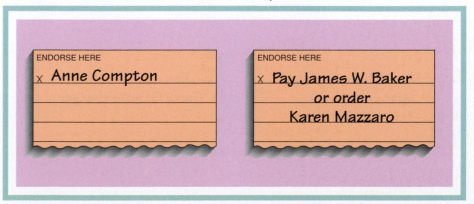

ENDORSE HERE
X Anne Compton

ENDORSE HERE
X Pay James W. Baker
or order
Karen Mazzaro

Such an instrument cannot now be negotiated except by indorsement and delivery. This in no way alters the contract between the indorser and the indorsee.

Qualified Indorsements

Qualified Indorsement
Indorsement that limits liability of indorser

A **qualified indorsement** has the effect of qualifying, thus limiting, the liability of the indorser. This type of indorsement is usually used when the payee of an instrument is merely collecting the funds for another. For example, if an agent receives checks in payment of the principal's claims but the checks are made payable to the agent personally, the agent can and should elect to use a qualified indorsement to protect from liability. There is no reason for the agent to risk personal liability when the checks are the principal's. The agent does this merely by adding to either a blank or special type of indorsement the words *without recourse* immediately before the signature (see Illustration 23–3). This releases the agent from liability for payment if the instrument remains unpaid because of insolvency or mere refusal to pay.

A qualified indorser still warrants that the signatures on the instrument are genuine, that the indorser has good title to the instrument, that the instrument has not been altered, that no defenses are good against the indorser, and that the indorser has no knowledge of insolvency proceedings with respect to the maker, acceptor, or drawer (as was mentioned in Chapter 22). An indorser may avoid these warranties as well by indorsing the instrument "without recourse or warranties."

Restrictive Indorsements

Restrictive Indorsement
Indorsement that restricts use of instrument

A **restrictive indorsement** is an indorsement that attempts to prevent the use of the instrument for anything except the stated use (see Illustration 23–3). The indorsement may state that the indorsee holds the paper for a special purpose or as an agent or trustee for another or it may impose a condition that must occur before payment. Such an indorsement does not prohibit further negotiation of the instrument.

Depository Bank
Bank receiving check for deposit

Conditional indorsements are ineffective with respect to anyone other than the indorser and indorsee. As against a holder in due course, it is immaterial whether the indorsee has in fact recognized the restrictions. A bank receiving a check for deposit is called a **depository bank**. A depository bank receiving a check with a restrictive indorsement, such as "for deposit" or "for collection," must honor the restriction.

ILLUSTRATION 23–3   Qualified Indorsement and Restrictive Indorsement

COURT CASE

Facts: The assistant comptroller of Interior Crafts, Inc., Todd Leparski, took customers' checks payable to Interior and indorsed them "Interior Crafts—for deposit only." He deposited the checks in Pan American Bank's ATM with instructions to deposit them in his account at Marquette Bank. Pan American did not have any idea who owned the Marquette account. In four months, he stole more than $500,000, until Marquette notified Interior that Leparski was depositing checks in his account payable to Interior.

Interior sued, and Pan American alleged it was not a depository bank, so it did not have to honor the restrictive indorsement.

Outcome: The court stated that Pan American was the first bank to take the checks, so it was a depository bank. As a depository bank it was required to apply the funds consistently with the restrictive indorsement.

—*Interior Crafts, Inc. v. Leparski,* **2006 WL 1980108 (Ill. App.)**

LIABILITY OF INDORSER

By indorsing a negotiable instrument, a person can become secondarily liable for payment of the face amount and responsible for certain warranties.

LO **2**
Indorser liabilities

Liabilities for Payment of Instrument

By making an indorsement, an indorser, with the exception of a qualified indorser, agrees to pay any subsequent holder the face amount of the instrument if the holder presents the instrument to the primary party when due and the primary party refuses to pay. The holder must then give the indorser in question notice of such default. This notice may be given orally or it may be given by any other means, but it must be given before midnight of the third full business day after the day on which the default occurs.

Warranties of the Indorser

Chapter 24 lists the warranties of all transferors. They differ from liability for the face of the paper in that they are not subject to the requirements of presentment and notice. The distinction is also important for purposes of limiting liability; an indorsement "without recourse" destroys only the liability of the indorser for the face of the instrument. It does not affect warranties. Thus, the warranty liability of a qualified indorser is the same as that of an unqualified indorser. An indorsement "without warranties" or a combined "without recourse or warranties" is required to exclude warranty liability.

OBLIGATION OF NEGOTIATOR OF BEARER PAPER

Bearer paper need not be indorsed when negotiated. Mere delivery passes title. One who negotiates a bearer instrument by delivery alone does not guarantee payment, but is liable to the immediate transferee as a warrantor of the genuineness of the instrument, of title to it, of the capacity of prior parties, and of its validity. These warranties are the same as those made by an unqualified indorser, except that the warranties of the unqualified indorser extend to all subsequent holders, not just to the immediate purchaser. But because negotiable instruments are not legal tender, no one is under any obligation to accept bearer paper without an indorsement. By requiring an indorsement even though it is not necessary to pass title, the holder is gaining protection by requiring the one who wishes to negotiate it to assume all the obligations of an indorser.

DISCHARGE OF THE OBLIGATION

LO ❸
Discharge of negotiable instruments

Cancellation
Act that indicates intention to destroy validity of an instrument

Renunciation
Unilateral act of holder giving up rights in the instrument or against a party to it

Negotiable instruments may be discharged by payment, by cancellation, or by renunciation. Payment at or after the date of the maturity of the instrument by the party primarily liable constitutes proper payment. **Cancellation** consists of any act that indicates the intention to destroy the validity of the instrument. A cancellation made unintentionally, without authorization, or by mistake is not effective. A holder of several negotiable instruments might intend to cancel one on its payment and inadvertently cancel an unpaid one. This does not discharge the unpaid instrument. **Renunciation** is a unilateral act of a holder of an instrument, usually without consideration, whereby the holder gives up rights on the instrument or against one or more parties to the instrument.

The obligations of the parties may be discharged in other ways, just as in the case of a simple contract. For example, parties will no longer be held liable on instruments if their debts have been discharged in bankruptcy or if there has been the necessary lapse of time provided by a statute of limitations.

A negotiable instrument may be lost or accidentally destroyed. This does not discharge the obligation. A party obligated to pay an instrument has a right to demand its return if possible. If this cannot be done, then the payor has a right to demand security from the holder adequate to protect the payor from having to pay the instrument a second time. The holder usually posts an indemnity bond. This is an agreement by a bonding company to assume the risk of the payor's having to pay a second time.

QUESTIONS

1. What is an indorsement?
2. May an indorsement ever be required for negotiation of bearer paper?
3. Where must an indorsement be placed?
4. When may a person make an indorsement correcting the name of the payee on a check?
5. When there are multiple payees on an instrument, how can one know whether all must indorse or only one need indorse the instrument to negotiate it?
6. Name four kinds of indorsements, and give an example of the proper use of each one.
7. If a check is indorsed "without recourse," is the indorser absolved from all liability on the instrument?
8. How may a negotiable instrument be discharged?
9. What is a depository bank?
10. What liability do all indorsers except qualified indorsers make for payment of the instrument?

CASE PROBLEMS

1. Chester Crow signed a promissory note for $21,500 payable "to the order of THE FIRST NATIONAL BANK OF SHREVEPORT or BEARER." Eleven years later, Credit Recoveries, Inc. sued Crow, alleging he owed $7,200 on the note. At that time, the back of the note had an undated indorsement, "PAY TO THE ORDER OF CREDIT RECOVERIES, INC. WITHOUT RECOURSE, REPRESENTATION OR WARRANTY OF ANY KIND. PREMIER BANK, NATIONAL ASSOCIATION." Premier Bank was a successor to First National. Crow alleged Credit did not have the right to enforce the note. Did it? Explain your answer.

LO ❶

2. James and Wylene Neely borrowed $28,500 from North Carolina Federal Savings & Loan Association and executed a promissory note for that amount. GE Capital Mortgage Services became the holder of the note. When the Neelys owed almost $25,000, GE erroneously credited $24,000 to their account and sent them a letter saying only $980 would pay off their debt. They immediately sent the required amount although they knew they owed much more. GE marked the note "Paid and Satisfied" and sent it to the Neelys. When GE realized its error it insisted the Neelys continue making payments. They refused, saying the note was void as a result of the mistaken cancellation. Can GE recover against them?

LO ❸

3. When Bottom Line Productions, Inc. borrowed $725,000 from Consumers United Insurance Co., Andre Bustamante, the vice president of Bottom Line, signed the back of the note without reference to his corporate position. Above his signature was language stating that, "The undersigned . . . waive [notice provisions] without prejudice to their liability as endorsers of this note." Bottom Line defaulted on the note and Consumers sued Bustamante as an indorser. Should he be held to indorser liability?

LO ❷

4. On a check payable to "Rick Knight-Simplot Soil Builders," Knight indorsed his name and forged Simplot's. He deposited the check in his account at Yakima Federal Savings & Loan. Simplot sued Yakima for improperly paying the check on a forged indorsement. Had Yakima improperly paid the check on a forged indorsement?

LO ❶

5. Home Center Supply of Maryland, Inc. owed CertainTeed Corp. $100,000, which was delinquent, so Home Center executed a note for $42,000. Joseph DelPo, Home Center's president, personally indorsed the note. Home Center made five payments and then defaulted, so CertainTeed sued Home Center and DelPo as an indorser. CertainTeed had presented the note to Home Center, which could not pay. What, if any, liability does DelPo have?

LO ❷

6. Curtis McClusky, then Mary Ann McClusky's husband, got a loan from the SBA to start a grocery business. The SBA required the McCluskys to put $75,000 of their own money into the business. They borrowed $75,000 from Frank Gardner and mortgaged a farm Mary Ann owned as security. They signed a note payable to Gardner's sons, Francis and Thomas. When the SBA loan was made, the McCluskys produced that note and a note from the business to them for $75,000. The McCluskys later divorced and Mary Ann found the note, which had the word "paid" written across its face, in the basement of their house. She assumed the note had been paid and sued the Gardners to clear the title to her farm. Did the fact that the note had been marked paid constitute cancellation and thus discharge of it?

LO ❸

LO ❶

7. First Texas Realty Corp. executed a promissory note to Canyon Lake Bank. The note was on an $8\frac{1}{2} \times 14$-inch piece of paper printed on both sides except an area of 2×4 inches on the back. After transfers, an indorsement filled the entire 2×4-inch area. Subsequent indorsements were written on an $8\frac{1}{2} \times 11$-inch piece of paper stapled to the note. Southwestern Resolution Corp., the final purchaser, sued First Texas on the note. When Southwestern produced the note and allonge at the trial, they were taped together and both had several staple holes in them. The note and allonge had been separated several times for photocopying. Southwestern could recover if it was the holder of the note, and it was a holder if all the indorsements were written on the note or on a paper affixed to it. Should the court rule that Southwestern can recover?

Liabilities of Parties and Holders in Due Course

LEARNING OBJECTIVES

❶ Summarize the rules for primary and secondary liability.

❷ Explain the procedures for an agent to use when executing a negotiable instrument.

❸ Define holder in due course and holder through a holder in due course.

❹ Discuss the special rules for holders of consumer paper.

PREVIEW CASE

➡ First National Bank of Chicago sent a form/notice to Muhamad Mustafa that his certificate of deposit (CD) was maturing. The bank received the form apparently signed by Mustafa with instructions to close the CD account. First mailed a cashier's check for $158,000 payable to Mustafa at his address. Michael Mustafa, Muhamad's nephew who shared his address, deposited the check in his account at MidAmerica Federal Savings Bank. The check was indorsed by Michael and also bore the purported signature of Muhamad. Michael lost all the money gambling at a riverboat casino. When Muhamad later tried to redeem the CD, First issued a replacement check and sued MidAmerica for breach of warranty. What warranties does a bank that accepts and pays a check make? Why does the bank make these warranties?

The Uniform Commercial Code (UCC) imposes liability on parties to negotiable instruments depending on the nature of the paper; the role of the party as maker, acceptor, indorser, or transferor; and the satisfaction of certain requirements of conduct by the holder of the instrument. Two basic categories of liability incidental to negotiable instruments include (1) the liability created by what is written on the face of the paper (contractual liability), and (2) the liability for certain warranties regarding the instrument.

LIABILITY FOR THE FACE OF THE PAPER

LO ❶
Primary and secondary
liability

Parties whose signatures do not appear on negotiable instruments are not normally liable for their payment. A signature can be any name, including a trade or assumed name, and may be handwritten, typed, or printed. It can even be a word or logo in place of a signature. For those whose signatures do appear, two types of contractual liability exist regarding the order or promise written on the face of the instrument: primary liability and secondary liability.

Primary Liability

Primary Liability
*Liability without
conditions for
commercial paper
that is due*

A person with **primary liability** may be called on to carry out the specific terms indicated on the paper. Of course, the paper must be due, but the holder of a negotiable instrument need meet no other conditions prior to the demand being made upon one primarily liable. The two parties who ordinarily have the potential of primary liability on negotiable instruments include makers of notes and acceptors of drafts.

The maker of a note is primarily liable and may be called on for payment. The maker has intended this by the unconditional promise to pay. Such a promise to pay contrasts sharply with the terms used by drawers of drafts who order drawees to pay.

The drawer of a draft does not expect to be called on for payment; the drawer expects that payment will be made by the drawee. However, it would be unreasonable to expect that the drawee could be made liable by a mere order of another party, the drawer. Understandably then, the drawee of a draft who has not signed the instrument has no liability on it. Only when a drawee accepts a draft by writing "accepted" and signing it does the drawee have liability on the instrument. By acceptance the drawee in effect says, "I promise to pay . . ." This acceptance renders the drawee primarily liable just as the maker of a note is primarily liable.

Secondary Liability

Indorsers and drawers are the parties whose liability on negotiable instruments is ordinarily secondary.

Secondary Liability
*Liability for a negotiable
instrument that has
been presented,
dishonored, and notice
of dishonor given*

When the conditions of **secondary liability** have been met, a holder may require payment by any of the indorsers who have not limited their liability by the type of indorsement used or by the drawer. Except for drawers of checks or banks that have accepted a draft, who do not need notice of dishonor, three conditions must be met for a party to be held secondarily liable:

1. The instrument must be properly presented for payment. *or acceptance*
2. The instrument must be dishonored.
3. Notice of the dishonor must be given to the party who is to be held secondarily liable.

Presentment
*Demand for acceptance
or payment*

Presentment. Presentment is the demand for acceptance or payment made on the maker, acceptor, drawee, or other payor of commercial paper. In order for indorsers to remain secondarily liable, the instrument must be properly presented. This means that the instrument should be presented to the correct person, in a proper and timely manner.

Presentment of instruments that state a specified date for payment should be made on that date. Other instruments must be presented for payment within a reasonable time after a party becomes liable on the instrument. The nature of the instrument, existing commercial usage, and the partial facts of the case determine what length of time is reasonable. The UCC specifies that for drawers on uncertified checks, a presentment within 30 days after the date of the check or the date it was issued, whichever is later, is presumed to be reasonable. As to indorsers, the UCC specifies presentment within seven days of the indorsement is presumed to be reasonable.

If presentment is delayed, drawers and makers of the instruments payable at a bank may no longer have funds in the bank to cover the instruments if the bank fails. If the bank failure occurs and the holder has delayed presentment for more than 30 days, drawers may be excused from liability on the basis that no proper presentment was made. To be so excused, the drawers must make a written assignment of their rights against the bank, to the extent of the funds lost, to the holders of the paper.

To reflect the fact that many banking transactions can be and are conducted by means of electronic devices, the UCC provides that presentment can be made electronically. The actual instrument need not be physically presented. Presentment takes place when a presentment notice is received. With electronic presentment, the banks involved have to have an agreement providing for presentment by electronic means. This agreement will specify what happens to the actual instrument—which bank holds it or if it follows the presentment notice to the drawee bank.

Proper presentment is not a condition to secondary liability on a note when the maker has died or has been declared insolvent. A draft does not require presentment if the drawee or acceptor has died or gone into insolvency proceedings. Commercial paper may contain terms specifying that the indorsers and the drawer agree to waive their rights to the condition of presentment. Furthermore, the holder is excused from the requirement of presentment if, after diligent effort, the drawee of a draft or the maker of a note cannot be located.

Finally, if the secondary party knows that the draft or note will not be paid or has no reason to believe that the paper will be honored, presentment is excused.

Dishonor. The UCC states that **dishonor** occurs when a presentment is made and a due acceptance or payment is refused or cannot be obtained within the prescribed time. This occurs when, for example, a bank returns a check to the holder stamped "insufficient funds" or "account closed." Return of a check lacking a proper indorsement does not constitute dishonor.

Dishonor
Presentment made, but acceptance or payment not made

Notice of Dishonor. A holder desiring to press secondary liability on an indorser or certain drawers must inform that party of the dishonor. Notice of dishonor must be conveyed promptly to these parties who are secondarily liable. The UCC requires that a bank give notice of dishonor to those it wishes to hold liable by midnight of the next banking day following the day on which it receives notice of dishonor. All other holders must give notice within 30 days following the day on which notice of dishonor is received. In order to avoid unduly burdening holders, the UCC provides that notice may be given by any commercially reasonable means. If by mail, proof of mailing conclusively satisfies the requirement that notice be given.

When a check is deposited into a bank account, the check can be from that bank or any other bank. When the drawee is a different bank, it needs to be returned to that bank for payment from the drawer's account. There is a system of clearinghouses that transfers checks from the banks in which they are deposited—depositary banks—to the drawee banks, called payor banks. Each bank in the clearinghouse system must give notice of dishonor in the prescribed time—by midnight of the next banking day following the day on which the check is received.

Generally, notice of dishonor does not need to be in any special form. However, if the dishonored instrument is drawn or payable outside the United States, notice of dishonor may be certified by a public official authorized to do so. This certificate of dishonor is known as **protest**.

Protest
Certification of notice of dishonor by authorized official

Delay or failure to give notice of dishonor is excused in most cases where timely presentment would not have been required. Basically, this occurs when notice has been waived; when notice was attempted with due diligence but was unsuccessful; or if the party to be notified had no reason to believe that the instrument would be honored, for example, because of death or insolvency.

COURT CASE

Facts: Prendergast & Associates, Inc. executed a promissory note to Fred Shearer & Sons, Inc. for $360,000. Patrick Prendergast signed the note on behalf of Associates as managing director, and he signed the note a second time. The note was due on September 30. On September 27, Prendergast asked for an extension of a year to pay the note. On September 28, Associates refused and demanded the note be paid on time. On the 29th, Prendergast confirmed that Associates did not have the money to pay the note. It was not paid when due, so Shearer sued Prendergast as an indorser. He alleged he was not liable because Shearer had not given him notice of dishonor.

Outcome: The court held that Shearer did not have to give Prendergast notice of dishonor because he admitted that Associates could not pay the note.

—*Fred Shearer & Sons, Inc. v. Prendergast*, 955 P.2d 324 (Ore. App.)

Guarantors

Indorsers can escalate their liability to primary status by indorsing an instrument "Payment guaranteed." These words indicate that the indorser agrees to pay the instrument if it is not paid when due. The holder does not need to seek payment from anyone else first.

If the transferor indorses the instrument with the words "Collection guaranteed," secondary liability is preserved. However, the contingencies that must be met by the holder in order to hold this type of guarantor liable change from presentment, dishonor, and notice of dishonor to obtaining against the maker or acceptor a judgment that cannot be satisfied.

People usually act as guarantors in order to increase the security of commercial paper. Frequently, if someone liable has a poor credit rating, the instrument could not be negotiated without having an additional party sign as a guarantor of the instrument.

Unauthorized Signatures

Normally, an unauthorized signature does not bind the person whose name is used. The signature is a forgery. However, there are two exceptions: (1) when the person whose name is signed ratifies the signature and (2) when the negligence of the person whose name is signed has contributed to the forgery.

When the forged signature is an indorsement, the loss usually falls on the first person to take the instrument after the forgery. That is one reason why banks ask for identification and even thumbprints before cashing a check for someone. Courts make the assumption that the person who deals with the forger is in the best position to prevent the loss.

There are exceptions to this rule usually involving dishonest employees. One occurs when someone signs an instrument on behalf of the maker or drawer, but intends the payee to have no interest in the instrument. For example, suppose Fazone, an employee of Gilbert Chemical, makes out Gilbert's checks to suppliers but does not intend the suppliers to receive the checks. Fazone then indorses and deposits the checks in his own account. Fazone is embezzling from Gilbert, but the unauthorized indorsements are effective.

COURT CASE

Facts: Western Iowa Farms Co. authorized Leonard and Mike Russell to write checks on Western's bank account. The Russells purchased livestock with Western checks and then sold the livestock to another buyer. When paid by the buyer, the Russells would pay Western the amount of its check. However, the Russells wrote checks totaling $275,000 to payees who did not know of the checks. The Russells forged the payees' indorsements, wrote "for deposit only," and deposited them in accounts at First Savings Bank.

Western sued First Savings for accepting the checks with forged indorsements. First Savings argued that the indorsements were effective because the Russells did not intend the payees to have any interest in the checks.

Outcome: This case falls into the exception to the normal rule regarding a loss on a forged indorsement. First Savings was not liable.

—*In re Western Iowa Farms Co.,*
135 F.3d 1257 (8th Cir.)

An additional exception occurs when an employer entrusts an employee with responsibility with respect to an instrument and the employee makes a fraudulent indorsement on the instrument in the name of the payee. As long as the person who takes the instrument does so in good faith, the indorsement is effective as the indorsement of the person to whom the instrument is payable. Responsibility with respect to an instrument means the authority, for example, to sign or indorse instruments, to control disposition of instruments in the name of the employer, or to prepare or process instruments for issuance in the name of the employer.

LIABILITY FOR WARRANTIES

Contractual liability requires a signature on the paper. However, transferring negotiable instruments creates warranty liability. Every transferor of commercial paper warrants the existence of certain facts. Unless specifically excluded, these warranties are automatically charged to every transferor of commercial paper. Note that a person can be liable as a warrantor even if the person's signature or name does not appear on the instrument, as, for example, when a person negotiates bearer paper by delivery alone.

The UCC specifies that each transferor who receives consideration and does not specifically limit liability makes a warranty that:

1. The transferor is entitled to enforce the instrument.
2. All signatures are genuine or authorized.
3. The instrument has not been altered.
4. The instrument is not subject to a defense or claim of any party that can be asserted against the transferor (explained in Chapter 25).
5. The transferor has no knowledge of any insolvency proceedings instituted with respect to the maker, acceptor, or drawer of an unaccepted draft.

PREVIEW CASE REVISITED

Facts: First National Bank of Chicago sent a form/notice to Muhamad Mustafa that his certificate of deposit (CD) was maturing. The bank received the form apparently signed by Mustafa with instructions to close the CD account. First mailed a cashier's check for $158,000 payable to Mustafa at his address. Michael Mustafa, Muhamad's nephew who shared his address, deposited the check in his account at MidAmerica Federal Savings Bank. The check was indorsed by Michael and also bore the purported signature of Muhamad. Michael lost all the money gambling at a riverboat casino. When Muhamad later tried to redeem the CD, First issued a replacement check and sued MidAmerica for breach of warranty.

Outcome: Because a bank that accepts and pays a check warrants the validity of the indorsements to subsequent transferees, the court held that MidAmerica, the bank that accepted the check with the forged indorsement, breached its warranties to First.

—First Natl. Bank v. MidAmerica Fed. Savings, 707 N.E.2d 673 (Ill. App.)

Liability of Agents

LO ❷
Agent liability

An agent may sign a negotiable instrument, and the principal, not the agent, will be bound. If the agent, authorized by the principal, signs the instrument, "John Smith, Principal, by Jane Doe, Agent," or more simply, "John Smith by Jane Doe," the principal will be bound, but the agent will not be bound by the terms of the instrument.

The agent, in these cases, has signed the instruments, and has (1) indicated a representative capacity, and (2) identified the person represented. If both of these two disclosures are not made, the agent appears to have signed the instruments as a personal obligation, and the agent will be personally liable on them.

In addition to giving both disclosures and not being bound or giving neither and being bound, an agent could sign an instrument and give just one of these disclosures. There are two ways of doing this.

1. The agent could sign the instrument in such a way that the principal was named, but it was not shown that the agent was acting merely as an agent. If the agent signed "John Smith" and immediately below that "Jane Doe," the agent and the principal would both be bound. The agent would be bound because she did not indicate that she was an agent, and the other party to the instrument might have relied on the signature of the agent as an individual.

2. The agent could sign the instrument in such a way that the principal was not named, but it would be clear that the agent signed as an agent. Such a case would occur if the agent signed "Jane Doe, Agent." In this situation, only the agent would be bound by the instrument, since it would not be evident from the face of the instrument who the principal might be.

However, in these last two examples, there is ambiguity about the agent's status. When a party to the instrument sues for payment, parol evidence may be introduced to prove the agency. So if the parties to the instrument knew that John Smith was the principal and Jane Doe was merely an agent, then only the principal would be bound on the instrument.

In both (1) and (2), a **holder in due course** without knowledge that the agent was not supposed to be liable can enforce liability against the agent. However, if a holder in due course is not involved, the revision states that the undisclosed

Holder in Due Course
Holder for value and in good faith with no knowledge of dishonor, defenses, or claims, or that paper is overdue

COURT CASE

Facts: Kurt and Todd Schumacher were the payees of notes signed by Donald Tabor. Above Tabor's signature was written "DBK Consultants, Inc.," and below it, "Donald R. Tabor." Tabor was the president, sole owner, and employee of DBK. There was no indication in the note that Tabor signed in other than his personal capacity. DBK was not mentioned in the body of the notes nor had it authorized the loans. The money loaned was used for the Talmadge Fitness Center, a business unrelated to DBK. The

Schumachers argued Tabor, not DBK, was liable on the notes.

Outcome: The notes were ambiguous with respect to Tabor's liability because the name DBK appeared above the signature line, and Tabor's signature was not qualified by his position in DBK. Therefore; the court said evidence of the parties' intent was admissible. That intent was that Tabor was personally liable on the notes.

—In re Tabor, **232 B.R. 85 (N.D. Ohio)**

principal is liable. In addition, an agent who can prove that the original parties did not intend the agent to be liable will not be liable.

COURT CASE

Facts: Attorney Eliot Disner's clients, Irvin and Dorothea Kipnes, owed $100,100 on a settlement with Sidney and Lynne Cohen. The payment was due March 9. The Kipneses gave Disner checks totaling $100,100. Disner deposited them in his client trust account on the 9th. After the Kipneses' bank said that the account could cover the $100,100, Disner wrote a trust account check for $100,100 to the Cohens' attorney. The Kipneses stopped payment

on their checks to Disner, so the trust account check bounced. The Kipneses filed for bankruptcy, so the Cohens sued Disner.

Outcome: The court held that Disner was not liable since he was merely an agent for transferring money from his clients to the payees.

—Cohen v. Disner, **42 Cal. Rptr. 2d 782 (Cal. App.)**

There is a special rule for checks signed by agents. If an agent signs a check in a representative capacity without indicating that capacity, but the check is on the principal's account and the principal is identified, the agent is not liable. Almost all checks today are personalized to identify the individual on whose account the check is drawn. Therefore, the agent does not deceive anyone by signing such a check.

In the case of a corporation or other organization, the authorized agent should sign above or below the corporation or organization's name and indicate the position held after the signature. For example, Edward Rush, the president of Acme Industries, should sign:

ACME INDUSTRIES
By Edward Rush, President

If the instrument were signed this way, Acme Industries, not Edward Rush, would be bound.

If an individual signs an instrument as an agent, "John Smith, Principal, by Jane Doe, Agent," but the agent is not authorized to sign for the principal, the principal would not be bound. It would be as if the agent, Jane Doe, had forged John Smith's signature. However, the agent who made the unauthorized signature would be bound. This protects innocent parties to the instrument who would not be able to enforce their rights against anyone if the unauthorized agent was not bound.

HOLDERS IN DUE COURSE

Negotiable instruments have an important advantage over ordinary contracts. Remote parties can be given immunity against many of the defenses available against simple contracts. To enjoy this immunity, the holder of a negotiable instrument must be a holder in due course, or an innocent purchaser. The terms *holder in due course* and *innocent purchaser* describe the holder of a negotiable instrument who has obtained it under these conditions:

1. The holder must take the instrument in good faith and for value.
2. The holder must have no notice the instrument is overdue or has been dishonored.
3. At the time the instrument is negotiated, the holder must have had no notice of any defense against or claim to the instrument.

For Value and in Good Faith

The law of negotiable instruments is concerned only with persons who give something for the paper. Thus, to attain the specially favored status of being a holder in due course, the holder must give value for the paper. Conversely, one who does not do so, such as a niece receiving a Christmas check from an uncle, cannot be a holder in due course. A mere promise does not constitute value.

The requirement that value be given in order to be a holder in due course does not mean that one must pay full value for a negotiable instrument. Thus, a person who purchases a negotiable contract at a discount can qualify as a holder in due course. The law states that it must be taken "for value and in good faith." Good faith means honesty in fact and the observance of reasonable commercial standards of fair dealing.

COURT CASE

Facts: James Camp contracted to perform some services for Shawn Sheth by October 15, so Sheth delivered a check for $1,300 to Camp but postdated it to October 15. Camp negotiated the check to Buckeye Check Cashing, Inc. on October 13. Afraid that Camp was not going to perform, Sheth ordered his bank to stop payment on the check on October 14. Buckeye deposited the check with its bank on October 14 thinking it would reach Sheth's bank on October 15. It was dishonored, so Buckeye sued Sheth.

Outcome: The court stated that receiving a postdated check should put a check cashing business on notice that the check might not be good. Buckeye did not act in a commercially reasonable manner, so it did not take the check in good faith.

—*Buckeye Check Cashing, Inc. v. Camp,*
825 N.E.2d 644 (Ohio App.)

If the instrument is offered at an exorbitant discount, that fact may be evidence that the purchaser did not buy it in good faith. It is the lack of good faith that destroys one's status as a holder in due course, not the amount of the discount. If the payee of a negotiable instrument for $3,000 offered to transfer it for a consideration of $2,900, and the purchaser had no other reason to suspect any infirmity in the instrument, the purchaser can qualify as a holder in due course. The instrument was taken in good faith. If, on the other hand, the holder had offered to discount the note by $1,000, the purchaser could not take it in good faith because it should be suspected that there is some serious problem with the contract because of the large discount.

Often a purchaser pays for an instrument in cash and other property. An inflated value placed on the property taken in payment could conceal a discount large enough to destroy good faith. The test always is: Were there any circumstances that should have warned a prudent person that the instrument was not genuine and in all respects what it purported to be? If there were, the purchaser did not take it in good faith.

If the holder is notified of a problem with the instrument or a defect in the title of the transferor before the full purchase price has been paid, the holder will be a holder in due course to the extent of the amount paid before notification.

No Knowledge That Instrument Is Past Due or Dishonored

One who takes an instrument known to be past due cannot be an innocent purchaser. However, a purchaser of demand paper on which demand for payment has been made and refused is still a holder in due course if the purchaser had no notice of the demand. A purchaser who has reason to know that any part of the principal is overdue, that an **uncured default** exists in payment of an instrument in the same series, or that acceleration of the instrument has been made has notice that the instrument is overdue. A note dated and payable in a fixed number of days or months shows on its face whether or not it is past due.

Uncured Default
Not all payments on instrument fully made and not all made by due date

COURT CASE

Facts: Lionel and Maureen Bolduc executed notes to BankEast secured by a mortgage on condominiums. When the Bolducs had difficulty paying the notes, they executed an agreement with the bank that allowed them to put off paying the notes and granted BankEast "blanket" second mortgages on their home and other land. The Bolducs later defaulted on the notes and the holder foreclosed on the condominiums, but the sale did not pay off the notes. After the foreclosure the holder transferred the deficiency on the notes to Beal Bank. Beal tried to foreclose on the Bolduc's home and the other land. The Bolducs raised a defense that could not be raised against a holder in due course.

Outcome: Because Beal Bank became a holder after foreclosure on the condominiums, it knew the notes had been dishonored and could not be a holder in due course.

—Bolduc v. Beal Bank, SSB,
994 F. Supp. 82 (D. N.H.)

An instrument transferred on the date of maturity is not past due but would be overdue on the next day. An instrument payable on demand is due within a reasonable time after issuance. For checks drawn and payable in the United States, 30 days is presumed to be a reasonable time.

No Knowledge of Any Defense or Claim to the Instrument

Fiduciary
A person in relationship of trust and confidence

When one takes a negotiable instrument by negotiation, to obtain the rights of an innocent purchaser there must be no knowledge of any defense against or claim adverse to the instrument. Knowledge of a claim may be inferred if, for example, the holder knows that a **fiduciary** has negotiated an instrument in payment of a personal debt. A fiduciary is a person in a relationship of trust and confidence such as a trustee. As between the original parties to a negotiable instrument, any act, such as fraud, duress, mistake, or illegality that would make a contract either void or voidable, will have the same effect on a negotiable instrument. However, as will be seen in the next chapter, many of these defenses are not effective if the instrument is negotiated to an innocent purchaser.

Knowledge of other potential irregularities does not destroy holder in due course status. Knowing that an instrument has been antedated or postdated, was incomplete and has been completed, that default has been made in the payment of interest, or that it was issued or negotiated in return for an executory promise or accompanied by a separate agreement, does not give a holder notice of a defense or claim.

HOLDER THROUGH A HOLDER IN DUE COURSE

Holder Through a Holder in Due Course
Holder subsequent to holder in due course

The first holder in due course brings into operation all the protections that the law has placed around negotiable instruments. When these protections once accrue, they are not easily lost. Consequently, a subsequent holder, known as a **holder through a holder in due course**, may benefit from them even though not a holder in due course. For example, Doerhoff, without consideration, gives Bryce a negotiable note due in 60 days. Before maturity, Bryce indorses it to Cordell under conditions that make Cordell a holder in due course. Thereafter, Cordell transfers the note to Otke for no consideration. Otke is not a holder in due course, as she did not give any consideration for the note. But if Otke is not a party to any wrongdoing or illegality affecting this instrument, she acquires all the rights of a holder in due course. This is true because Cordell had these rights, and when Cordell transferred the note to Otke, he transferred all of his rights, which included his holder in due course rights.

HOLDERS OF CONSUMER PAPER

LO ❹
Holders of consumer paper

Consumer Goods or Services
Goods or services primarily for personal, family, or household use

Setoff
A claim by the party being sued against the party suing

The UCC rules regarding the status of a holder in due course have been modified for holders of negotiable instruments given for consumer goods or services. **Consumer goods or services** are defined as goods or services for use primarily for personal, family, or household purposes. The changes resulted from both amendment to the UCC by the states—which means that the rules vary somewhat from state to state—and the adoption of a Federal Trade Commission (FTC) rule.

Generally, the rights of the holder of consumer paper are subject to all claims, defenses, and setoffs of the original purchaser or debtor arising from the consumer transaction. A **setoff** is a claim a party being sued makes against the party suing. In the case of consumer sales, the FTC rule requires that consumer credit contracts contain specified language in bold print indicating that holders of the contracts are subject to all claims and defenses the debtor could assert against the seller. It means that no subsequent holder can be a holder in due course. The language is:

NOTICE

ANY HOLDER OF THIS CONSUMER CREDIT CONTRACT IS SUBJECT TO ALL CLAIMS AND DEFENSES WHICH THE DEBTOR COULD ASSERT AGAINST THE SELLER OF GOODS OR SERVICES OBTAINED PURSUANT HERETO OR WITH THE PROCEEDS HEREOF. RECOVERY HEREUNDER BY THE DEBTOR SHALL NOT EXCEED AMOUNTS PAID BY THE DEBTOR HEREUNDER.

The state laws generally make holder in due course rules inapplicable to consumer sales or limit the cutoff of consumer rights to a specified number of days after notification of assignment.

Normally these rights of the debtor are available only when the loan was arranged by the seller or lessor of the goods or was made directly by the seller or lessor. The state laws do not apply to credit card sales on a credit card issued by someone other than the seller. However, federal law allows a credit card holder to refuse to pay credit card issuers in some cases when an earnest effort at returning the goods is made or a chance to correct a problem is given the seller.

Modifying or abolishing the special status of a holder in due course for consumer goods prevents frauds frequently practiced on consumers by unscrupulous businesspeople. Such individuals would sell shoddy merchandise on credit and immediately negotiate the instrument of credit to a bank or finance company. When the consumer discovered the defects in the goods, payment could not be avoided, because the new holder of the commercial paper had purchased it without knowledge of the potential defenses and was therefore a holder in due course. Furthermore, the seller who had frequently left the jurisdiction or gone bankrupt was unavailable to be sued. Thus, the consumer would be unable to assert a defense or rescind the transaction against either the seller or the holder. The modifications based on changes to the UCC and adoption of the FTC rule were enacted to remedy this problem. A consumer who purchases goods that are not delivered or worthless can avoid paying more and recover what has been paid.

COURT CASE

Facts: Fred and Cathi Beemus bought a car and service contract from MacKay-Swift, Inc. They financed the purchase by means of an installment contract. Primus Automotive Financial Services, Inc. was the assignee of the installment contract that included the language required by the FTC rule for consumer goods. The Beemuses sued Primus alleging that MacKay had charged amounts under the installment contract that violated the law. They further alleged that under the FTC rule, Primus was liable for all claims they could bring against MacKay.

Outcome: The FTC rule allows consumer-debtors to assert against assignees all claims for recovery they have against the sellers if the contracts had not been assigned.

—*Beemus v. Interstate Natl. Dealer Servs., Inc.,* 823 A.2d 979 (Pa. Super.)

Allowing the consumer to have such rights against a holder who would otherwise be a holder in due course is designed to protect consumers who usually do not have knowledge of negotiable instrument laws. Normally a bank or finance company, which may buy many instruments from the seller, can more easily ascertain whether the seller is reliable than individual consumers can.

QUESTIONS

1. What are the factors that determine whether the UCC imposes liability on parties to negotiable instruments?

2. What conditions need to be met in order to require a person with primary liability to carry out the terms indicated on the paper?

3. What is required for a proper presentment?

4. According to the UCC, when must notice of dishonor be given?

5. How can indorsers escalate their liability to primary status?

6. What are the two exceptions to the rule that an unauthorized signature does not bind the person whose name is used?

7. What warranties does a transferor of commercial paper make?

8. What two things must an agent do in order to escape personal liability?

9. List the conditions that a person must meet to become a holder in due course.

10. What does the term "good faith" mean?

11. Is an instrument transferred on the date of maturity past due? Explain.

12. What is the effect of the modification of UCC rules regarding the status of a holder in due course when a negotiable instrument has been given for consumer goods or services?

CASE PROBLEMS

LO ❶

1. Kenneth Wulf's job for Auto-Owners Insurance Co. was to decide whether Auto-Owners would pursue a claim. If so, he was to put a note in the file. When a check was received, clerical staff attached it to the file and gave the file to Wulf. He was to note receipt of the check in the file, complete a transmittal form, and return the check to the clerical staff. No record was kept of checks received nor of pending claims. Wulf opened an account at Bank One in the name, "Auto Owners Insurance." Wulf would work on a claim but not note anything in the file. When a check arrived, the clerical staff would attach it to the file and give it to Wulf. He would take the check; indorse it with a stamp he had made that said "Auto Owners Insurance Deposit Only" and deposit it in his Bank One account. The checks were payable to "Auto-Owners Insurance," "Auto-Owners Insurance Company," and "Auto-Owners Insurance Co." When the embezzlement was discovered, Auto-Owners sued Bank One. Was Bank One liable?

LO ❷

2. Alan H. Potamkin loaned The Classic Touch, Inc. $200,000. A promissory note prepared by Classic was signed by Suzanne De Maria and the corporation's name was typed under her name. Classic paid only $75,000, so Potamkin sued the corporation and De Maria. Is De Maria liable?

3. Dan Lofing bought a grand piano from the Steinway dealer, Sherman Clay. Part of the purchase price was a note for $19,650, which included the FTC language limiting holder in due course rights. Music Acceptance Corp. (MAC) purchased the note from Clay. Lofing began to have serious problems with the piano, which Clay tried to fix many times, but after two years the piano was unplayable. Lofing stopped making payments on the note, and MAC sued for the balance due. Lofing sued MAC and Clay. The jury awarded Lofing damages against Clay for breach of contract and MAC damages against Lofing on the note. Lofing appealed, saying that the FTC language meant that if he had a claim or defense against Clay, MAC would be subject to the same claim or defense. How should the case be decided?   LO ❹

4. On January 3, DeSimone Auto, Inc. issued a check to Bruce Rickett for a car. As frequently happens the first few days of a year, DeSimone inadvertently dated the check with the prior year. Two days later, Rickett deposited the check in Commerce Bank. DeSimone and Rickett had agreed the check would not be cashed if the car were damaged. The car was damaged, so DeSimone stopped payment on the check and told Rickett to return it. Rickett had already gotten the funds from it. Commerce sued DeSimone and Rickett when the check was not paid, but Rickett could not be found. Commerce alleged it was a holder in due course. DeSimone argued it was not since the incorrect date put Commerce on notice the check could be overdue. Discuss whether a check should be overdue when incorrectly dated early in the year but actually negotiated within a few days of its issuance.   LO ❸

5. On a Friday, Tonia Campbell tried to cash a $17,000 check drawn on a Citibank account at a Citibank. When told that Citibank did not cash such a large check and that the fastest way to get the money was to open a Citibank account, Campbell opened a Citibank savings account with the check. On Saturday she tried to make a withdrawal from the account at an ATM. She was told she had insufficient funds. Saturday and Sunday were not business days for Citibank. On Monday she was told there was a "block" on her account, but later that day she had access to her money. She sued Citibank for wrongful dishonor and late payment—after the midnight deadline. Should Citibank be liable on either charge?   LO ❶

6. Janet Hollandsworth, an accountant for Dalton & Marberry, P.C., embezzled $130,000 by taking appropriately signed Dalton & Marberry checks payable to NationsBank and having the bank issue blank cashier's checks. Dalton & Marberry sued NationsBank for failing to inquire whether Hollandsworth was authorized to do this. The bank alleged it was a holder in due course and was therefore not liable for negligence. Was NationsBank a holder in due course?   LO ❸

7. George Avery sent a letter to Jim Whitworth. Printed on the stationery was the name of Avery's employer, V & L Manufacturing Co., and the words "George Avery, President." The letter stated, "This is your note for $45,000.00, secured individually and by our Company . . . " Avery had signed the letter. V & L did not pay the entire $45,000, so Whitworth sued Avery. Avery said the stationery showed V & L was the debtor and he signed only in a representative capacity. Must Avery pay?   LO ❷

8. Eugene Perez hired Perma-Stone to install siding, new windows, screen doors, and vents at his house. To finance the improvements, Perez signed a promissory note and retail improvement contract containing the FTC required language. Perma-Stone sold the note to Briercroft Service Corp. Several   LO ❹ months later, the siding started to fall off the house, the new windows fell apart, the doors would not shut, and it was found that the sewer vents stopped in the attic instead of going through the roof. Perez stopped paying on the note. In the resulting lawsuit, Briercroft said Perez was entitled only to a refund of the money he had paid but not to cancellation of the note. How should the court rule?

LO ❸   **9.** M-H Enterprises and Michael Holmes requested a loan from Brookwood National Bank to buy some real estate. To get the loan, Brookwood required M-H and Holmes to buy a title insurance policy on the property naming Brookwood as beneficiary. M-H and Holmes bought the property, signed a note to Brookwood, and gave it a mortgage. They also bought a title policy from American Title Insurance Co. with Brookwood as insured. A year later, a prior mortgage on the property, which American had failed to notice, was foreclosed. M-H and Holmes told Brookwood they would make no more payments on the note and asked it to file a claim with American. American learned this and paid the claim, so Brookwood assigned its note and mortgage to American. It sued M-H and Holmes for the balance on the note. To win, American had to be a holder in due course. Was it?

LO ❶   **10.** Litchfield Co. of South Carolina, Inc. issued a check for $13,000 drawn on Bankers Trust of South Carolina to Jensen Farley Pictures, Inc. on September 9. On September 16, Farley deposited the check in First American Bank of Virginia, and the same day, Litchfield gave Bankers a stop-payment order. On September 19, Farley withdrew almost all the money, and two days later, Bankers returned the check marked "payment stopped" to First American. Farley could not repay the amount withdrawn, and on December 19, First American demanded payment from Litchfield. When sued by First American, which was admittedly a holder in due course, Litchfield argued that it was discharged because First American had not given timely notice of dishonor. Was Litchfield discharged?

Defenses

LEARNING OBJECTIVES

1 State the chief advantage of being a holder in due course of a negotiable instrument.

2 Distinguish between limited and universal defenses to holders.

3 Explain the nature of hybrid defenses and list them.

PREVIEW CASE

James and Marie Estepp wanted to get a loan from United Bank & Trust Co. of Maryland. United required an additional signature by an owner of real estate. James brought Marvin Schaeffer to the bank, saying he needed Schaeffer, whose wife had died, to sign a character reference. Estepp supervised Schaeffer at work and had helped Schaeffer make funeral arrangements. Schaeffer had a learning disability and could not read or write. The bank officer handling the transaction did not explain to Schaeffer that he was assuming a financial responsibility. Schaeffer signed the note. The Estepps defaulted, so United sued Schaeffer. Did Schaeffer have an effective defense? What did the Estepps tell Schaeffer he needed to sign? Was this true?

When the holder of commercial paper is refused payment, a lawsuit may be brought. Chapter 24 discussed the parties liable for the payment of the face of the paper. What defenses can the defendant being sued raise successfully? This question does not arise until it has first been determined that the plaintiff is actually the holder of the paper and that the defendant is a person who would ordinarily have liability for payment of the face of the paper. Assuming that those two questions have been decided in favor of the plaintiff, the remaining question concerns whether this defendant has a particular defense that may be raised.

Assume that there are four successive indorsers, and the holder who comes at the end of these four indorsers sues the first indorser. Can the first indorser raise against the holder a defense that the first indorser has against the second indorser? For example, can the defense be raised that the first indorser was induced by fraud to make the indorsement?

LO **1**
Advantage of being
holder in due course

Limited Defense
*Defense that cannot be
used against holder in
due course*

Universal Defense
*Defense against any
holder*

More commonly, the situation will arise in which the remote holder sues the drawer of a check. The drawer then defends on the ground that the check had been given in payment for goods or services that the drawer never got, did not work, or were not satisfactory. Can the drawer now raise against the remote holder the defense that the drawer has against the payee of the check, namely, the defense of failure of consideration? The answer to this depends on the nature of the defendant's defense against the person with whom the dealings were made and the character of the holder. If the defense is a **limited defense** and the remote holder is a holder in due course, the defendant cannot raise such a defense. This is the chief advantage of being a holder in due course of a negotiable instrument. If the defense is a **universal defense** or the holder is an ordinary holder, the defendant may raise that defense.

CLASSIFICATION OF DEFENSES

Certain defenses are limited to being raised against ordinary holders and cannot be raised against holders in due course. Limited defenses include:

1. Ordinary contract defenses
2. Fraud that induced the execution of the instrument
3. Conditional delivery
4. Improper completion
5. Payment or part payment
6. Nondelivery
7. Theft

Limited Defenses

LO **2**
Limited versus
universal defenses

A significant number of defenses cannot be raised against a holder in due course or a holder through a holder in due course. Limited defenses, also called *personal defenses,* must be distinguished from universal ones.

Ordinary Contract Defenses. In general, the defenses available in a dispute over a contract may be raised only against holders who do not qualify as holders in due course. Accordingly, if a holder in due course holds the instrument, the defense of failure of consideration is not effective when raised by the maker who alleges that no consideration was received for the paper. In an action on an ordinary contract, the promisor may defend on the ground that no consideration existed for the promise; or that if consideration did exist in the form of a counterpromise, the promise was never performed; or that the consideration was illegal. Thus, if Smith agreed to paint Jones's house but did not do it properly, Jones would have a right of action against Smith for breach of contract, or Jones could refuse to pay Smith the price agreed upon. If Smith assigned the right to payment, Jones would be able to raise against the assignee the defenses available against Smith.

However, if Jones paid Smith by check before the work was completed, and the check was negotiated to a holder in due course, Jones could not defend on the ground of failure of consideration. The check would have to be paid. Jones's only right of action would be against Smith for the loss.

Fraud that Induced the Execution of the Instrument. When a person knows a commercial paper is being executed and knows its essential terms but is

COURT CASE

Facts: Louis Politis contracted to have Sverdrup Corp. build three buildings for him. After construction was completed and Politis had not paid, Politis signed a demand note for the amount owed Sverdrup. When Politis did not pay the note, Sverdrup sued. Politis alleged lack of consideration since he got nothing at the time he executed the note.

Outcome: The court pointed out that consideration for a negotiable instrument can be a previous debt. Sverdrup had given consideration.

—Sverdrup Corp. v. Politis,
888 S.W.2d 753 (Mo. App.)

persuaded or induced to execute it because of false representations or statements, this is not a defense against a holder in due course. For example, if Randolph persuades Drucker to buy a car because of false statements made by Randolph about the car, and Drucker gives Randolph a note for it that is later negotiated to a holder in due course, Drucker cannot defend on the ground that Randolph lied about the car. Drucker will have to pay the note and seek any recovery from Randolph.

Conditional Delivery. As against a holder in due course, an individual who would be liable on the instrument cannot show that the instrument, absolute on its face, was delivered subject to an unperformed condition or that it was delivered for a specific purpose but was not used for it. If Sims makes out a check for Byers and delivers it to Richter with instructions not to deliver it until Byers delivers certain goods, but Richter delivers it to Byers, who then negotiates it to a holder in due course, Sims will have to pay on the check.

COURT CASE

Facts: Glenn and Gloria Wall signed a contract to buy and operate a restaurant from Lewis and Janet Scott. The contract provided that it was void if the Walls could not negotiate a three-year lease for the restaurant's current location. The Walls had not negotiated such a lease by the closing date, but the Scotts orally promised to release them from the transaction if the lease could not be negotiated. The sale took place, and the Walls signed a note for $45,000.

The Walls could not negotiate an acceptable lease and defaulted on the note. The Scotts sued for payment on the note.

Outcome: Because the Scotts were not holders in due course, the defense of conditional delivery was valid against them.

—Scott v. Wall, **777 P.2d 581 (Wash. App.)**

Improper Completion. If any term in a negotiable instrument is left blank, for example, the payee or the amount, and the drawer then delivers the instrument to another to complete it, the drawer cannot raise the defense of improper completion against a holder in due course. In this case, the holder in due course may require payment from the drawer.

Payment or Part Payment. On payment of a negotiable instrument, the party making the payment should demand the surrender of the instrument. If not surrendered, the instrument may be further negotiated, and a later holder in due course would be able to demand payment successfully. A receipt is not adequate as proof of payment, because the subsequent holder in due course would have no notice of the receipt from the instrument, whereas surrender of the instrument would clearly prevent further negotiation.

If only partial payment is made, a holder would not and should not be expected to surrender the instrument. In such a case, the person making the payment should note the payment on the instrument, thereby giving notice of the partial payment to any subsequent transferee.

Nondelivery. Normally, a negotiable instrument fully or partially completed but not delivered to the payee is not collectible by the payee. However, if a holder in due course holds the instrument, payment of it may be required. For example, if one person makes out a note to another person and that other person takes the note from the maker's desk without the maker's permission and negotiates the note to an innocent purchaser, or holder in due course, the holder in due course would be entitled to recover the amount of the note against the maker. This applies in spite of the nondelivery of the note.

Theft. A thief may not normally pass good title; however, an exception occurs when the thief conveys an instrument to a holder in due course. Such a purchaser will be able to enforce the obligation in spite of the previous theft of the paper. The thief or any ordinary holder cannot require payment of stolen paper.

Universal Defenses

Those defenses thought to be so important that they are preserved even against a holder in due course are called universal or *real*. Universal defenses can be raised regardless of who is being sued or who is suing. Thus, they can be raised against the holder in due course as well as an ordinary holder. The more common universal defenses include:

1. Minority
2. Forgery
3. Fraud as to the nature of the instrument or its essential terms
4. Discharge in bankruptcy proceedings

Minority. The fact that the defendant is a minor capable of avoiding agreements under contract laws is a defense that may be raised against any holder.

Forgery. Except in cases where the defendant's negligence made the forgery possible, forgery may be raised successfully against any holder. However, a forged signature operates as the signature of the forger in favor of a holder in due course.

Fraud as to the Nature of the Instrument and Its Essential Terms. The defense that one was induced to sign an instrument when one did not know that it was in fact commercial paper is available against any holder. For example, an illiterate person told that a note is a receipt and thereby induced to sign it may successfully raise this defense against any holder. The defense is not available, however, to competent individuals who negligently fail to read or give reasonable attention to the details of the documents they sign.

Discharge in Bankruptcy Proceedings. Even holders in due course are subject to the defense that a discharge in bankruptcy has been granted.

PREVIEW CASE REVISITED

Facts: James and Marie Estepp wanted to get a loan from United Bank & Trust Co. of Maryland. United required an additional signature by an owner of real estate. James brought Marvin Schaeffer to the bank, saying he needed Schaeffer, whose wife had died, to sign a character reference. Estepp supervised Schaeffer at work and had helped Schaeffer make funeral arrangements. Schaeffer had a learning disability and could not read or write. The bank officer handling the transaction did not explain to Schaeffer that he was assuming a financial responsibility. Schaeffer signed the note. The Estepps defaulted, so United sued Schaeffer.

Outcome: The court found fraud existed as to the nature and essential terms of the note.

—*Schaeffer v. United Bank & Trust Co. of Maryland*, 360 A.2d 461 (Md. Ct. Spec. App.)

Hybrid Defenses

Several defenses may be either universal or limited depending on the circumstances of a case. These include:

LO 3
Hybrid Defenses

1. Duress
2. Incapacity other than minority
3. Illegality
4. Alteration

Duress. Whether or not duress is a valid defense against a holder in due course depends on whether the effect of such duress under the state law makes a contract void or voidable. When the duress nullifies a contract, the defense is universal. When the duress merely makes the contract voidable at the option of the victim of the duress, the defense is limited.

Incapacity Other Than Minority. In cases of incapacity other than minority, if the effect of the incapacity makes the instrument void, a nullity, the defense is universal. If the effect of the incapacity does not make the instrument a nullity, the defense is limited.

Illegality. The fact that the law makes certain transactions illegal gives rise to a defense against an ordinary holder. Such a defense would be unavailable against a holder in due course unless the law making the transaction illegal also specifies that instruments based on such transactions are unenforceable.

Alteration. The UCC defines an **alteration** as "an unauthorized change in an instrument that purports to modify in any respect the obligation of a party, or . . . an unauthorized addition . . . to an incomplete instrument." When an alteration is fraudulently made, the party whose obligation is affected by the alteration is discharged. A payor bank or a drawee who pays a fraudulently altered instrument, or a person who takes it for value in good faith and with no notice of the alteration, may enforce the instrument according to its original terms or to its terms as completed.

Alteration
Unauthorized change or completion of negotiable instrument to modify obligation of a party

COURT CASE

Facts: William and Janet Westervelt executed a note to Gateway Financial Service for a loan secured by a mortgage on their house. Gateway required the Westervelts to obtain credit life insurance. The premium was deducted from the loan but never sent to the insurance company. The state's Secondary Mortgage Loan Act (the act) governed the transaction. The act prohibited requiring credit life insurance and provided that "any obligation . . . shall be void and unenforceable unless . . . executed in full compliance with the provisions of this act."

Gateway sold the note to Security Pacific Finance Corp. The Westervelts sued Gateway and Security to have the note declared void and unenforceable.

Outcome: The court held that the UCC provision subjecting a holder in due course to a defense of illegality that made the obligation a "nullity" applied here.

— *Westervelt v. Gateway Financial Serv.,*
464 A.2d 1203 (N.J. Super. Ch.)

COURT CASE

Facts: Carolyn Hartsock sold a payment of $60,096 she was due to Singer Asset Finance Company, LLC, and the payor sent the payment to Singer's post office box. Singer never received the check. At some point, it was altered to be payable to Ann McCardy, who indorsed it and deposited it in her account at Rich's Employees Credit Union. The drawee, CoreStates Bank of Delaware, N.A. paid the check. McCardy withdrew the money from her account and disappeared. On the front of the check, the fonts for the payee's name and address differed from

the amount of the check. Examining the area of the payee's name and address showed a "whiteout" or "rub-off" and a slight fade in the check's blue background. Rich's alleged it was a holder in due course.

Outcome: The court held that a holder in due course could not take an instrument that was clearly irregular on its face.

— *Hartsock v. Rich's Employees Credit Union,*
632 S.E.2d 476 (Ga. App.)

MISCELLANEOUS MATTERS

In addition to the defenses described earlier, remember that every lawsuit presents certain standard problems. Any defendant may, under appropriate circumstances, raise the defense that the suit is not brought in the proper court, that no service of process existed, or that the statute of limitations has run and bars the suit. Any defendant in a suit on a negotiable instrument can claim that the instrument is not negotiable; that the plaintiff is not the holder; and that the defendant is not a party liable for payment of the paper. If the holder claims that the defendant is secondarily liable for the payment of the face of the paper, the defendant also may show that the paper had not been properly presented to the primary party and that proper notice of default had not been given to the secondary party.

QUESTIONS

1. What must be determined before it can be ascertained what defenses the party sued for payment of a negotiable instrument can successfully raise against the holder?

2. Explain when the defense of failure of consideration is effective in a suit against the maker of a promissory note.

3. How effective are defenses that would be available in a contract dispute when a negotiable instrument is involved?

4. When is there fraud in the execution of an instrument?

5. Why is a receipt not adequate as proof of payment of a negotiable instrument?

6. May a thief convey good title to an instrument?

7. When forgery can be successfully raised against any holder of a negotiable instrument, does this mean that no one is liable on the instrument?

8. When does fraud as to the nature of the instrument and its essential terms occur?

9. When is duress a valid defense against a holder in due course?

10. Give three examples of defenses that the defendant in any lawsuit might successfully raise.

CASE PROBLEMS

1. Attorney John Rorem was to receive a fee of one-third of any recovery for representing Dora Coblentz and her children in a lawsuit. He settled the suit for $167,500 and the court calculated Coblentz's recovery at $131,500, the children's at $36,000 and Rorem's fee at $51,000. The court then entered an order prescribing a gross recovery for Coblentz of $131,500 with a net recovery of $80,500 and recovery of $36,000 for the children less $6,000 in attorneys' fees. Rorem transmitted $80,742 to Coblentz but believed she should receive $4,802 more, so he executed a promissory note to her for $4,802. Coblentz demanded immediate payment of the note and sued on it. Rorem alleged there was no consideration for the note. What kind of defense did he assert and could it be effective against Coblentz?   LO 2

2. Raejean and Robert Stotler bought a lot from SilverCreek Development Co. They signed a promissory note in payment. SilverCreek assigned the note to Geibank Industrial Bank. SilverCreek went bankrupt, and the Stotlers defaulted on the note. In the ensuing lawsuit, the Stotlers alleged that they were induced to buy the lot and sign the note on the basis of false representations that SilverCreek would develop the surrounding property with condominiums, a golf course, and a Western theme park. The court said Geibank was a holder in due course. Are the Stotlers' allegations good against Geibank?   LO 1

3. National Union Fire Insurance Company of Pittsburg, PA, issued securities but failed to register them as federal securities law required. Shashi Pachnanda had signed a promissory note in exchange for some of the securities. Violation of the securities law made obligations for the securities voidable. When the promissory note was not paid, National Union sued Pachnanda alleging it was a holder in due course. Pachnanda raised the defense that the securities were illegal. Was this defense good?   LO 3

4. James Roemer and James Featherstonhaugh established R & F, a professional corporation for the practice of law. Later Roemer signed a loan agreement for R & F to Chemical Bank secured by a promissory note. Featherstonhaugh resigned from R & F, and eight months later Three Feathers, Inc., a small   LO 2

corporation owned by Featherstonhaugh and his wife, bought R & F's note from Chemical. Three Feathers promptly declared R & F in default on the note and sued. Roemer defended saying Featherstonhaugh had fraudulently induced him to sign the agreement. Should this defense be valid against Three Feathers?

LO ③

5. A group organized Evergreen Valley Nurseries Limited Partnership to acquire and raise nursery stock. One of the organizers purchased nursery stock for $4.2 million and two months later sold 91 percent of it to Evergreen for $10.4 million. Evergreen financed this purchase by offering limited partnership units, which Roland Algrant and others purchased for $70,000 cash and $80,000 in promissory notes. After an IRS investigation, Evergreen admitted in writing that it had overvalued the nursery stock. Algrant and the other limited partners obtained a copy of the writing on October 11. More than two years later, on November 16, they sued the organizers of Evergreen asking the court to declare that the promissory notes could not be enforced. The statute of limitations for an action based on fraud or deceit was two years. Can the notes be enforced?

LO ①

6. Troy Garrison Sr. sued his son, Troy Jr., and daughter-in-law, Erika Garrison, on a note they had signed in the amount of $96,000. Erika alleged that she had never received any money from Troy Sr. She stated it had been given to Troy Jr. as a gift and they had only signed the note so Troy Sr. would have it for tax purposes. What defense did Erika allege? Discuss its effectiveness against various types of holders.

LO ②

7. Marjorie Jones gave her son, Glenn Davis, $90,000, which he used to buy and repair a house Lynne Phillips and her siblings had inherited. Several months later, Davis had a lawyer draw up a note that he and Phillips signed, but it was not delivered to Jones. Davis paid only $2,000 to Jones. After Phillips filed for divorce from Davis, Jones sued her for payment of the note. Does Phillips have a valid defense to Jones's suit?

Ethics in Practice

You have learned about the benefits the law gives to a holder in due course in order to promote business transactions. Such a holder is given immunity against many potential defenses. Consider the ethical implications of this. Is it ethical that the obligee on a negotiable instrument is unable to raise otherwise valid defenses simply because the holder meets the requirements of being a holder in due course?

Summary Cases

NEGOTIABLE INSTRUMENTS

1. GreenPoint Credit, LLC had a security interest in a mobile home owned by Rosetta Lunsford. The home was destroyed by fire, and Lunsford's insurer, Kentucky Farm Bureau Mutual Insurance Co. issued a check payable to Lunsford and GreenPoint. Lunsford indorsed the check and presented it to Tri-County National Bank for payment. Tri-County negotiated the check without GreenPoint's indorsement. GreenPoint sued Tri-County. Was Tri-County liable to GreenPoint? [*Tri-County Nat. Bank v. GreenPoint Credit, LLC*, 190 S.W.3d 360 (Ky. App.)]

2. Marie Hunt had executed a promissory note to Robert Rice in the amount of $35,000 secured by a mortgage on her home. Invest Co. paid Rice $25,000 for the note and then sold it to NationsCredit Financial Services Corp. for $27,000. Hunt did not pay off the face of the note so NationsCredit sued her. She alleged she only received $23,300 from Rice so she only repaid that amount. She alleged there was a failure of consideration for any further amount. Should NationsCredit recover? [*Hunt v. NationsCredit Financial Services Corp.*, 902 So.2d 75 (Ala. Civ. App.)]

3. After Faith Bursey filed for divorce from Arthur, a flood damaged their vacation home. They signed a proof of loss with their insurance company and the company issued checks totaling $72,000 to "Bursey, Arthur J. & Faith R." Arthur opened an account in CFX Bank in his name and Faith Robin Bursey, his daughter. He deposited the checks in this account. Only Arthur indorsed the checks. After Arthur and his daughter pledged this account for a loan on which he defaulted, CFX used the account to satisfy the loan. Faith Bursey sued CFX alleging it did not act in good faith in accepting the checks without her indorsement. Should Faith recover? [*Bursey v. CFX Bank*, 756 A.2d 1001 (N.H.)]

4. Getty Petroleum Corp. sold gasoline and products through dealer-owner stations. When a station customer paid with a credit card, the credit card company paid Getty, which then issued a check payable to the dealer for the sales. Getty did not intend many of the checks for the payees since it voided them and credited the amount toward the dealers' future gasoline purchases. Lorna Lewis had the job of voiding the checks. She stole 130 checks, forged indorsements of the dealers, and sent the checks to American Express to pay her credit card debt. After Getty discovered Lewis's theft, it sued American Express. Should American Express bear the loss as a result of the forged indorsements? [*Getty Petroleum Corp. v. American Exp.*, 660 N.Y.S.2d 689 (N.Y. Ct. App.)]

5. James Spolyar was a general partner of Plantation Oaks, a limited partnership. Spolyar met with Jerry Lutz and told him Plantation needed to sell one to three

partnership units to purchase an apartment complex. He promised to buy back any units Lutz purchased. Four days later Lutz received documents including a note that recited that it constituted part of Lutz's purchase price of units in Plantation. Lutz signed the note, which stated a promise to pay and listed a schedule of payments totaling $69,308. Lutz returned the note to Spolyar, who indorsed it to European American Bank in return for a loan and a guarantee from Northwestern National Insurance Co. However, after the promise to pay $69,308 someone had handwritten a caret (^) and the words "per unit" and below the payment schedule "$69,308 × 3 units = $207,924." Lutz did not pay the note. Northwestern paid European the amount for three units and then sued Lutz. How much, if anything, must Lutz pay? [*Northwestern Nat. Ins. Co. of Milwaukee v. Lutz,* 71 F. 3d 671 (7th Cir.)]

6. Dallas County State Bank sold a personal money order on a forged check. It then stopped payment on the money order and refused to accept and pay it when Northpark National Bank of Dallas presented it. The money order had a check-writing imprint, "Dallas County State Bank," as well as the name of the bank printed on it. Northpark sued for payment. Dallas alleged it was not liable on the money order since its signature did not appear on it. Was it liable? [*Interfirst Bank Carrollton v. Northpark National Bank of Dallas,* 671 S.W.2d 100 (Tex. Ct. App.)]

7. George Weast borrowed $140,000 from State National Bank of Maryland (SNB), and his wife, Ruth, cosigned for him. This debt later was in default, so George indorsed and delivered some notes made by Francis and Josephine Arnold and Randall Co. to the order of SNB. Payments were made on these notes for several years before default. Ruth and George got divorced. When Ruth paid off the amount owed on their debt, SNB indorsed the notes of the Arnolds and Randall to Ruth. She sued them for payment on the notes. They alleged she was subject to a defense regarding the transaction that gave rise to the notes. Ruth claimed to be a holder through a holder in due course, so the defense would not be valid against her. Was Ruth a holder through a holder in due course when the notes had been indorsed to her after default? [*Weast v. Arnold,* 474 A.2d 904 (Md.)]

8. Public Relations Enterprises, Inc. paid Melco Products Corp. for goods by means of personal money orders purchased from Nassau Trust Co. and Republic National Bank of New York. When Melco presented them for payment, the banks dishonored them on the ground that Public had stopped payment. Melco sued the banks for payment, alleging that the banks had no right to stop payment on the personal money orders. Did they? [*Melco Products Corp. v. Public Relations Enterprises, Inc.,* 460 N.Y.S.2d 466 (N.Y. Sup. Ct.)]

9. Blas Garcia told Arthur and Lucy Casarez he was a representative of Albuquerque Fence Co., so they contracted with the company to build a home for them. Blas introduced them to Cecil Garcia, who said he would make a loan for the home. The Garcias were in no way affiliated with Albuquerque. Cecil got a $25,000 loan from Rio Grande Valley Bank in the form of a cashier's check. The Casarezes signed a note, and Cecil indorsed the check: "Pay to the order of Lucy N. Casarez, Cecil Garcia." Lucy indorsed it: "Pay to the order of Albuquerque Fence Co., Lucy N. Casarez." She handed the check to Blas, who indorsed the check: "Alb. Fence Co." Cecil signed his own name under that and presented the check to Rio Grande in return for $5,000 and four cashier's checks for $5,000. The Casarezes sued

Rio Grande, alleging the words "Pay to the order of Albuquerque Fence Co." constituted a special indorsement and the check could be negotiated only by indorsement by an authorized official of the company. Was this a valid assertion? [*Casarez v. Garcia*, 660 P.2d 598 (N.M. Ct. App.)]

10. South Carolina Insurance Co. issued a draft to Kevlin Owens drawn on the account of Seibels, Bruce Group at South Carolina National Bank. Owens negotiated the draft to First National Bank of Denham Springs, which paid him the entire amount and delivered it to South Carolina National Bank. The insurance company alleged fraud in Owens's claim and issued a stop payment order. South Carolina National Bank did not honor the draft. The draft stated it was payable as follows: "Upon acceptance, pay to the order of Kevlin Owens." South Carolina Insurance Co. was a wholly owned subsidiary of Seibels, Bruce Group. Therefore, South Carolina was both drawer and drawee. First National sued South Carolina for payment. South Carolina said the words "upon acceptance" made the draft conditional and therefore the draft was not negotiable; First National was not a holder in due course; and the defense of fraud could be raised. Was the draft conditional? [*First National Bank of Denham Springs v. South Carolina Insurance Co.*, 432 So.2d 417 (La. Ct. App.)]

11. Omega Electronics, Inc., executed a promissory note to the order of State Bank of Fisk. Two officers of the corporation signed on the front and five individuals signed on the back. The note stated: "We, the makers, . . . endorsers and guarantors of this note, hereby severally waive presentment for payment, notice of nonpayment, protest, and notice of protest." When the note was not paid, the bank sued the individuals. They alleged they were not liable because they had not been given notice of dishonor and protest. Were they liable? [*State Bank of Fisk v. Omega Electronics, Inc.*, 634 S.W.2d 234 (Mo. Ct. App.)]

Agency and Employment

Employees and employers have rights and duties to each other. Many are covered in the chapters in this part. There are many sources of information on and assistance in maintaining employee/employer rights, including the Department of Labor, and the U.S. Equal Employment Opportunity Office. In addition to state employment offices, the DOL's *America's Career InfoNet* is a resource for jobs, and its Web site is at http://www.acinet.org

Nature and Creation of an Agency

LEARNING OBJECTIVES

1 Explain the nature of an agency and identify the parties involved.

2 Describe the different classifications of agents and the corresponding authority of each.

3 Discuss how an agency is usually created.

4 Distinguish between an agency and independent contractor or employer-employee relationships.

PREVIEW CASE

Because he did not want his daughter to inherit his home, George Pittman executed a power of attorney giving his wife, Rose, authority to make real property transactions "including the power to transfer the real estate known as the homeplace that I inherited from my mother." At George's directions, Rose executed a deed to the homeplace on behalf of George to Dessie Gaskill and Alice Durham. Gaskill and Durham paid George nothing. After George died, his daughter sued them claiming Rose did not have express authority to make a gift of the real estate since the law does not favor the power to make a gift. What does the word *transfer* mean? What was George's purpose in executing the power of attorney?

LO 1
Nature of agency

Principal
Person who appoints another to contract with third parties

When one party, known as a **principal**, appoints another party, known as an **agent**, to enter into contracts with third parties in the name of the principal, a contract of agency is formed. By this definition every contract that an agent negotiates involves at least three parties—the principal, the agent, and the third party. It is this making of contracts with third persons on behalf of the principal that distinguishes an agency from other employment relationships. The principal, the agent, or the third party may be an individual, a partnership, or a corporation.

IMPORTANCE OF AGENCY

Because of the magnitude and complexity of industries, business owners must delegate many of the important details pertaining to business transactions to agents. The general principles of law pertaining to contracts govern the relation creating this delegation of powers.

Even in the performance of routine matters by individuals, agents are necessary in order to bring one person into a business contractual relationship with other persons. Thus, a farmer who sends an employee to town to have a piece of machinery repaired gives the employee the authority to enter into a contract that binds the farmer to the agreement.

Agent
Person appointed to contract on behalf of another

WHAT POWERS MAY BE DELEGATED TO AN AGENT?

As a general rule, people may do through agents all of those things that they could otherwise do themselves. However, the courts will not permit certain acts of a personal nature to be delegated to others. Some of these acts that may not be performed by an agent include voting in a public election, executing a will, or serving on a jury.

What one may not lawfully do may not be done through another. Thus, no person can authorize an agent to commit a crime, to publish a libelous statement, to perpetrate a fraud, or to do any other act judged illegal, immoral, or opposed to the welfare of society.

ETHICAL POINT
Would it be ethical for a person to try to do something that could not be done personally through an agent?

COURT CASE

Facts: Robert Miner, a prisoner serving a life sentence, applied to participate in a department of corrections family reunion program and claimed he was legally married. Under state law, a person serving a life sentence was considered civilly dead. Miner had executed a document appointing Michael Foster his agent for the purpose of entering into a proxy marriage, which Foster had done.

Outcome: The court held that Miner was not legally married. As a civilly dead person, he could not lawfully marry. Because he could not marry, Miner could not appoint an agent to enter into that relationship on his behalf.

—Miner v. New York State Dept. of Correctional Servs., 479 N.Y.S.2d 703 (N.Y. Sup. Ct.)

WHO MAY APPOINT AN AGENT?

All people legally competent to act for themselves may act through an agent. This rule is based upon the principle that whatever a person may do may be done through another. Hence, corporations and partnerships, as well as individuals, may appoint agents.

The contract by which a minor appoints an agent to act for the minor is normally voidable. Some states, however, find such contracts void, not voidable.

WHO MAY ACT AS AN AGENT?

Ordinarily, any person who has sufficient intelligence to carry out a principal's orders may be appointed to act as an agent. The law does not impose this requirement. It arises from the practical consideration of whether the principal wants to have the particular person act as agent. Corporations and partnerships may act as agents.

An agent cannot perform some types of transactions without meeting certain requirements. For example, in many states a real estate agent must possess certain definite qualifications and must, in addition, secure a license to act in this capacity. Failure to do this disqualifies a person to act as an agent in performing the duties of a real estate agent.

CLASSIFICATION OF AGENTS

LO ②
Agent classification and authority

Agents may be classified as:

1. General agents
2. Special agents

General Agents

General Agent
Agent authorized to carry out particular kind of business or all business at a place

A **general agent** is one authorized to carry out all the principal's business of a particular kind or all the principal's business at a particular place even though not all of one kind. Examples of general agents who perform all of the principal's business of a particular kind include a purchasing agent and a bank cashier. A general agent who transacts all of the principal's business at a particular place includes a manager in full charge of one branch of a chain of shoe stores. A general agent buys and sells merchandise, employs help, pays bills, collects accounts, and performs all other duties. Such an agent has a wide scope of authority and the power to act without express direction from the principal.

A general agent has considerable authority beyond that expressly stated in the contract of employment. In addition to express authority, a general agent has that authority that one in such a position customarily has.

Special Agents

Special Agent
Agent authorized to transact specific act or acts

A **special agent** is one authorized by a principal to transact some specific act or acts. Such an agent has limited powers that may be used only for a specific purpose. The authorization may cover just one act, such as buying a house; or it may cover a series of merely repetitive acts, such as selling admission tickets to a movie.

COURT CASE

Facts: Jo Ann Walter was a real estate agent and listed her home for sale with a multiple-listing service. Jerri Murphy, a real estate agent with Showcase, Inc., found a buyer. Walter then made an offer to Leila Kennedy, the listing agent for Juliet Blanchard, to buy Blanchard's home. Kennedy was an agent with Showcase and told Murphy about Walter's offer. Murphy made a better bid that Blanchard accepted. Walter sued alleging Murphy violated her duty as an agent.

Outcome: Murphy's agency was only to find a buyer for Walter's home. She was a special agent, and that agency had nothing to do with the sale of Blanchard's home.

—*Walter v. Murphy,*
573 N.E.2d 678 (Ohio App.)

ADDITIONAL TYPES OF AGENTS

There are several additional types of agents. Most of these are special agents, but because of the nature of their duties, their powers may exceed those of the ordinary special agent:

1. Factors
2. Factors *del credere*
3. Brokers
4. Attorneys in fact

Factors

A **factor** is one who receives possession of another's property for the purpose of sale on commission. Factors, also called *commission merchants,* may sell in the name of the principal, but normally they sell in the merchant's own name. When factors collect the sale price, they deduct the commission, or factorage, and remit the balance to the principal. The third party, as a rule, is aware that the dealings are with an agent by the nature of the business or by the name of the business. The term *commission merchant* usually appears on all stationery. Commission merchants have the power to bind the principal for the customary terms of sale for the types of business they are doing. In this regard, their powers are slightly greater than those of the ordinary special agent.

Factor
Bailee seeking to sell property on commission

Factors *del Credere*

A **factor** *del credere* is a commission merchant who sells on credit and guarantees to the principal that the purchase price will be paid by the purchaser or by the factor. This is a form of contract of guaranty, but the contract need not be in writing as required by the Statute of Frauds, as the agreement is a primary obligation of the factor.

Factor *del Credere*
Factor who sells on credit and guarantees price will be paid

Brokers

A **broker** is a special agent whose task is to bring the two contracting parties together. Unlike a factor, a broker does not have possession of the merchandise. In real estate and insurance, a broker normally acts as the agent of the buyer rather than the seller. If the job merely consists of finding a buyer or, sometimes, a seller, the broker has no authority to bind the principal on any contract.

Broker
Agent with job of bringing two contracting parties together

Attorneys in Fact

An **attorney in fact** is a general agent who has been appointed by a written authorization. The writing, intended to be shown to third persons, manifests that the agent has authority.

Attorney in Fact
General agent appointed by written authorization

EXTENT OF AUTHORITY

As a rule, a general agent has authority to transact several classes of acts: (1) those clearly within the scope of the express authority, (2) those customarily within such an agent's authority, and (3) those outside of express authority but that appear to third parties to be within the scope of the agent's authority.

Express authority is the authority specifically delegated to the agent by the agreement creating the agency. It amounts to the power to do whatever the agent is appointed to do.

Express Authority
Authority of agent stated in agreement creating agency

PREVIEW CASE REVISITED

Facts: Because he did not want his daughter to inherit his home, George Pittman executed a power of attorney giving his wife, Rose, authority to make real property transactions "including the power to transfer the real estate known as the homeplace that I inherited from my mother." At George's directions, Rose executed a deed to the homeplace on behalf of George to Dessie Gaskill and Alice Durham. Gaskill and Durham paid George nothing. After George died, his daughter sued them claiming Rose did not have express authority to make a gift of the real estate because the law does not favor the power to make a gift.

Outcome: The court held that the word *transfer* included conveying by sale, gift, or other means, so Rose had the express authority to make the gift of the homeplace.

—*Whitford v. Gaskill*, 480 S.E.2d 690 (N.C.)

Implied Authority
Agent's authority to do things in order to carry out express authority

Customary Authority
Authority agent possesses by custom

Apparent Authority
Authority agent believed to have because of principal's behavior

Frequently, in order to carry out the purposes of the agency, the agent must have the authority to do things not specifically enumerated in the agreement. This authority is called **implied authority**. An agent appointed to manage a retail shoe store, for example, has implied authority to purchase shoes from wholesalers in order to have a stock to sell.

Authority to act on behalf of another arises when by custom such agents ordinarily possess such powers. This is sometimes called **customary authority**.

In addition, without regard to custom, the principal may have behaved in a way or made statements that caused the third person to believe that the agent has the authority. This is called **apparent authority**. For example, the Pardalos Insurance Company might advertise, "For all your insurance problems see your local Pardalos Insurance agent." This would give the local Pardalos Insurance Company agent apparent authority to arrange any insurance matters, even though the agents did not actually have such authority or had been told that certain kinds of cases had to be referred to the home office.

COURT CASE

Facts: On the premises of a Mobil Mini Mart gas station leased under a franchise agreement to Alan Berman, an employee of Berman attacked and beat up Jeremy Bransford. Mobil owned the station and required Berman to use Mobil symbols and sell Mobil products. Bransford sued Mobil alleging it had an apparent agency relationship with Berman.

Outcome: The court held that mere use of franchise logos does not indicate Mobil has apparent control over the operation of Berman's business.

—*Mobil Oil Corp. v. Bransford*, 648 So. 2d 119 (Fla.)

As to innocent third parties, the powers of a general agent may be far more extensive than those actually granted by the principal. Limitations on an agent's authority do not bind a third party who has no knowledge of them, but they do bind a third party who knows of them.

In every case, the person who would benefit by the existence of authority on the part of the alleged agent has the burden of proving the existence of authority. If a person appears to be the agent of another for the purpose of selling the car of that other person, for example, the prospective purchaser must seek assurance from the principal as to the agent's authority. Once the third party has learned the actual scope of an agent's express authority from the principal, the agent has no greater authority than the principal's actions and statements indicate, together with such customary authority as would attach.

CREATION OF AN AGENCY

Usually any one of the following may create the relationship of **agency**:

1. Appointment
2. Ratification
3. Estoppel
4. Necessity

Appointment

The usual way of creating an agency is by the statement of the principal to the agent. In most cases the contract may be oral or written, formal or informal. In some instances, however, the appointment must be made in a particular form. The contract appointing an agent must be in writing if the agency is created to transfer title to real estate. Also, to extend an agent's authority beyond one year from the date of the contract, the Statute of Frauds requires the contract to be in writing. The appointment of an agent to execute a formal contract, such as a bond, requires a formal contract of appointment.

A written instrument indicating the appointment of an agent is known as a *warrant* or **power of attorney**. To record a power of attorney, it must also be acknowledged before a notary public or other officer authorized to take acknowledgments. Illustration 26–1 shows an ordinary form of power of attorney.

Ratification

Ratification is the approval by one person of the unauthorized act of another done in the former's name. An assumed agent who purported to act as an agent without actual or apparent authority may have committed the unauthorized act, or it may have been done by a real agent who exceeded actual and apparent authority. Such an act does not bind the supposed principal in such a case unless and until it is ratified. Ratification relates back to the date of the act done by the assumed agent. Hence, ratifying the act puts the assumed agent in the same position as if there had been authority to do the act at the time the act was done.

A valid ratification requires:

1. The one who assumed the authority of an agent must have made it known to the third person that he or she was acting on behalf of the party who attempts to ratify the act.
2. The one attempting to ratify must have been capable of authorizing the act at the time the act was done. Some jurisdictions apply this rule to corporations so that a corporation formed subsequent to the time of the act cannot ratify an act of a promoter. Other states have ignored this requirement in regard to ratification of the acts of corporate promoters.
3. The one attempting to ratify must be capable of authorizing the act at the time approval of the act is given.
4. The one attempting to ratify must have knowledge of all material facts.

LO **3**
How agency is created

Agency
Contract under which one party is authorized to contract for another

Power of Attorney
Writing appointing an agent

Ratification
Approval of unauthorized act

ILLUSTRATION 26–1 Power of Attorney

Know All Men by These Presents:

That I, Amelia Clermont

of Portland

County of Multnomah   *, State of* Oregon

have made, constituted and appointed, and by these presents do make, constitute and

appoint James Turner

of Vancouver

County of Clark   *, State of* Washington

my true and lawful attorney   *in fact, for me and in my name, place and stead,*

to manage, operate, and let my rental properties in the City of Vancouver, County of Clark, State of Washington

giving and granting unto my said attorney full power and authority to do and perform all and every act and thing whatsoever requisite and necessary to be done in and about the premises, as fully to all intents and purposes as I might or could do, if personally present, with full power of substitution and revocation; hereby ratifying and confirming all that my said attorney——or his   *substitute——shall lawfully do, or cause to be done, by virtue hereof.*

In Witness Whereof, I have hereunto set my hand this tenth   *day of* July   *, 20 --*

Amelia Clermont

Signed and acknowledged in presence of:

Samuel Adamick

Teresa Romano

5. The one attempting to ratify must approve the entire act.
6. The ratified act must be legal, although the person whose name was forged may ratify a forgery on commercial paper.
7. The ratification must be made before the third party has withdrawn from the transaction.

Estoppel

Agency by Estoppel
Agency arising when person leads another to believe third party is agent

Agency by estoppel arises when a person by words or conduct leads another person to believe that a third party is an agent or has the authority to do particular acts. The principal who has made representations is bound to the extent of those representations for the purpose of preventing an injustice to parties who have been misled by the acts or the conduct of the principal.

Necessity

The relationship of agency may be created by necessity. Parents must support their minor children. If they fail to provide their children with necessaries, the parents' credit may be pledged for the children, even against the parents' will. Agency by necessity also may arise from some unforeseen emergency. Thus, the driver of a bus operating between distant cities may pledge the owner's credit in order to have needed repairs made and may have the cost charged to the owner.

COURT CASE

Facts: Rush Creek Solutions, Inc. contracted to supply Ute Mountain Ute Tribe with computer software and support. The tribe's chief financial officer (CFO) who was authorized to enter into contracts for the tribe signed the contract on behalf of the tribe. In the contract, the tribe waived objection to being sued on the contract in any state or federal court with jurisdiction over Littleton, CO. Rush and the tribe carried out their respective responsibilities under the contract to provide computer support and pay for that support for 18 months. Then the tribe failed to make payments, and Rush sued. The tribe alleged the CFO did not have the authority to waive objection to being sued in state or federal court.

Outcome: The court held the CFO had the agency by estoppel. The tribe accepted the contract for eighteen months and failed to complain about its provisions.

—*Rush Creek Solutions, Inc. v. Ute Mountain Ute Tribe*, 107 P.3d 402 (Colo. App.)

OTHER EMPLOYMENT RELATIONSHIPS

Two types of employment relationships differ from agency relationships:

1. Independent contractor
2. Employer and employee, originally referred to in law as master and servant

LO 4
Distinguish independent contractor

Independent Contractor

An **independent contractor** is one who contracts to perform some tasks for a fixed fee. The other contracting party does not control an independent contractor as to the means by which the contractor performs except to the extent that the contract sets forth requirements to be followed. The independent contractor is merely held responsible for the proper performance of the contract. Because one who contracts with an independent contractor has much less control over the performance of the work, the contract does not create either a principal-agent relationship or an employer-employee relationship. The most usual type of independent contractor relationship is in the building trades.

Independent Contractor
One who contracts to do jobs and is controlled only by contract as to how performed

Employer and Employee

An employee performs work for an employer. The employer controls the employee both as to the work to be done and the manner in which it is done. One contracting with an independent contractor does not have such control. The degree of control that the employer or principal exercises over the employee or agent and the authority the agent has to bind the principal to contracts constitute the main differences between an employee and an agent.

There are many reasons why a contract of employment must not be confused with a contract of an independent contractor. An employer may be held liable for any injuries employees negligently cause to third parties. This is not true for injuries caused by independent contractors. Second, employers must comply with laws relative to their employees. Employers must, for example, withhold social security taxes on employees' wages, pay a payroll tax for unemployment compensation, withhold federal income taxes, and, when properly demanded, bargain with their employees collectively. None of these laws apply when one contracts with independent contractors. Independent contractors are the employers of those employed by them to perform the contract.

QUESTIONS

1. When is a contract of agency formed?
2. Why is agency so important to business?
3. What acts can be delegated to an agent?
4. Who is eligible to appoint an agent?
5. Who may act as an agent?
6. Does a general agent or a special agent have more authority? Explain.
7. What is the difference between a factor and a broker?
8. What is an agent's implied authority?
9. When must the contract appointing an agent be in writing?
10. How does an independent contractor relationship differ from an agent?

CASE PROBLEMS

LO ❷
1. Patrick Castegnaro was an agent of Associated Insurance Agencies and on its behalf was authorized to bind coverage for Aetna Casualty and Surety Company. He failed to process renewals and submitted forged cancellation notices to Aetna for six clients of Associated. The clients, who thought they still had insurance with Aetna, submitted premium checks to Castegnaro. He cashed the checks. Aetna provided retroactive insurance for the clients and sued Associated. In the lawsuit that followed, the court had to decide whether even though Associated was unaware of Castegnaro's scheme, it was liable for his fraud. Was it?

LO ❹
2. Ash Grove Cement Company hired Electric Company of Omaha (ECO) to relocate a cable tray. ECO gained access to the tray from the flat roof of Ash Grove's building and controlled the work. While walking backward and carrying cable, Darryl Didier, an employee of ECO, fell off the roof 20 feet onto a concrete surface. He sued Ash Grove. Should he recover?

LO ❸
3. North American Specialty Insurance Co. (NAS) underwrote construction bonds. Brunson Bonding and Insurance Agency was an agent for NAS, and Reid Methvin was an employee of Brunson. The agency agreement between NAS and Brunson required NAS to give prior approval before a construction bond was issued. Methvin issued bonds without prior approval from NAS. After NAS learned about the unauthorized bonds, it accepted and kept the premiums from Brunson. When a number of the unauthorized bonds resulted in defaults, causing NAS to pay out claims on them, NAS sued Methvin, Brunson, and Brunson's insurer. The defendants argued that acceptance of the premiums by NAS constituted ratification of Methvin's unauthorized acts. Did it?

LO ❷
4. To find vendors and alternates for its TV program, QVC held trade shows. It hired Network Trade Associates (NTA) to work with the Illinois Department of Commerce and Community Affairs (DCCA). Roberta Janis, the DCCA employee responsible for the QVC project, sent vendors a QVC solicitation packet that included a product information sheet. The sheet stated, "An authorized QVC Purchase Order is the only valid contract." It also asked the

lead-time needed to fill a $10,000 wholesale order. On its sheet, Bethany Pharmacal, maker of a skin lotion, answered, "on hand." QVC representatives at the show told vendors that, if selected, QVC would send a purchase order and they should not to do anything until hearing directly from QVC. After the show, NTA sent Janis a list of the vendors and alternates and told her not to contact any of them until QVC had. Janis thought QVC had notified them and sent identical congratulatory letters to them asking that a sticky note with the word "Alternate" be attached to the alternates' letters. Bethany, chosen an alternate, received the letter without the sticky and spent $100,000 to buy more lotion. It then sued QVC for breach of contract arguing that Janis was its apparent agent and her letter formed a binding contact. Did QVC create the appearance that Janis was its agent?

5. Bob Dunn Ford, Inc., with Robert C. Dunn as the president, leased Ford and Jaguar cars. Wachovia Bank would buy the leases from Bob Dunn. Occasionally Robert C. Dunn would personally guarantee payment of the leases. However, he told two Wachovia vice presidents that he did not want to engage in any more transactions that allowed recourse against him and that only he personally could execute guaranties. He formed a new corporation, Bob Dunn Jaguar, to lease Jaguars. Mel Blackwell was the general manager of Dunn Jaguar. George and Lilly McKeathen leased a new Jaguar, and the lease application was sent to Wachovia. A Wachovia employee, Charles Patterson, phoned Blackwell and said Dunn Jaguar would have to guarantee the lease payments. Joe Parker, vice president of Dunn Ford, signed the guaranty and indicated he was vice president of Dunn Jaguar. Wachovia paid Dunn Leasing $39,000 for the lease. Three years later, the McKeathens defaulted on the lease, and Robert C. Dunn was told Parker had executed the guaranty. Robert C. Dunn immediately repudiated the guaranty. The bank sued Dunn Jaguar on the guaranty. Can it recover on the basis of agency by ratification? LO ❸

6. Charged with a crime, Carl Rosati hired an attorney, John Cicilline. Before hiring Cicilline, Kenneth Kuzman, Rosati's former coach, volunteered his services to Rosati's parents. Cicilline asked Kuzman to help with the investigation. At Cicilline's request, Kuzman interviewed witnesses, discussed matters with Rosati at the prison, and helped a private investigator Cicilline hired. The indictment against Rosati was dismissed, and two other people were indicted. Kuzman was told to appear for a deposition. Rosati sued to prevent Kuzman from disclosing information privileged under the attorney-client privilege. Was Kuzman acting as Cicilline's agent when he worked on Rosati's case? LO ❶

7. George Tapp signed a durable power of attorney to Nancy Wabner. It granted Wabner the power "to cash any certificates of deposit which I own or to change and redesignate the ownership thereof." Tapp told her to collect the funds from his bank accounts and CDs and put them in a bank account with her as joint owner with right of survivorship. Wabner did as Tapp directed, and Tapp died. Under Tapp's will, two church organizations received one-quarter of his estate. If Wabner's actions were proper, most of Tapp's estate remained in the joint account and passed automatically to her. The church organizations sued Wabner alleging she did not have the express authority to make gifts to herself. Did she have that authority? LO ❷

8. Something bit Rhea Sampson on the arm. The arm got swollen, so she went to the Southeast Baptist Hospital emergency room. Signs posted in the emergency LO ❸

room stated emergency room doctors were independent contractors. They, not the hospital, billed patients. Dr. Susan Howle, an emergency room physician, diagnosed the bite as an allergic reaction and prescribed accordingly. Sampson's arm got worse, and she returned to the emergency room. Another emergency room physician, Dr. Mark Zakula, gave her pain medication and told her to continue Dr. Howle's treatment. Fourteen hours later, she went to another hospital that admitted her in septic shock. The proper treatment was administered to save her life. Sampson sued Howle, Zakula, and Southeast alleging the doctors were ostensible agents of the hospital. Were they?

Operation and Termination of an Agency

LEARNING OBJECTIVES

1 Specify the duties an agent owes the principal and the principal owes the agent.

2 Describe an agent's and principal's liabilities to third parties.

3 State how an agency may be terminated, either by the parties or by operation of law.

PREVIEW CASE

John Kennon, doing business as Kennon Adjustment Co., was hired by Commercial Standard Insurance Co. to investigate a workers' compensation claim. They made no agreement as to the amount to be paid Kennon. After an award was made to the claimant, Kennon submitted a bill for more than three times the amount of the award. Commercial refused to pay the bill, saying that it was too high. Kennon sued. In the absence of an agreement for compensation, how much, if anything, must be paid to an agent? Do you think Commercial expected such a high bill?

In a contract of agency, the law imposes on the agent certain duties to the principal not set out in the contract. Likewise, the relationship of agency creates duties and obligations that the principal owes to an agent even though they are not specifically enumerated in the contract. In turn, the agency relationship imposes on both principal and agent certain duties and obligations to third parties. An examination of these duties and obligations will reveal the importance of the relationship of agent and principal as well as the necessity for each party in the relationship to be fully cognizant of the rights and duties that exist.

AGENT'S DUTIES TO PRINCIPAL

An agent owes the following important duties to the principal:

1. Loyalty and good faith
2. Obedience

LO **1**
Duties of agents
and principals

3. Reasonable skill and diligence
4. Accounting
5. Information

Loyalty and Good Faith

The relationship of principal and agent is fiduciary in nature; thus, the principal must be able to trust the agent to perform the duties according to contract. The relationship of agent and principal calls for a higher degree of faith and trust than do most contractual relationships. For this reason, the law imposes on agents the duty of loyalty and good faith and deprives them of their right to compensation, reimbursement, and indemnification when they prove disloyal to their principal or act in bad faith. Agents must promote the interests of the principal to the utmost of their ability.

Loyalty and *good faith* are abstract terms. Thus, the courts have wide latitude in interpreting what acts constitute bad faith or a breach of loyalty. Such acts as secretly owning an interest in a firm that competes with the principal, disclosing confidential information, selling to or buying from the agent without the knowledge of the principal, and acting simultaneously as the agent of a competitor constitute acts that the courts have held to be breaches of good faith. An agent who acts in bad faith not only may be discharged, but the principal also may recover any damages that have been sustained. Also, the principal may recover any profits the agent has made while acting in bad faith even though the act did not damage the principal.

COURT CASE

Facts: George Ferrara executed a will leaving his estate to the Salvation Army. Six months later, he was hospitalized and his nephew, Dominick Ferrara, visited him. A month later George executed a form power of attorney appointing Dominick attorney-in-fact. One of the provisions specifically permitted Dominick to make gifts to relatives of not more than $10,000 per year. A typewritten addition authorized him to make unlimited gifts to himself. Three weeks later, George died. Dominick had transferred $820,000 of George's assets to himself. State law provided that an attorney-in-fact authorized to make gifts of $10,000 a year or less had to do

so only for purposes reasonably in the principal's "best interest." The Salvation Army found out about George's will and a lawsuit ensued.

Outcome: The court said that the best interest requirement was consistent with the attorney-in-fact's duty of the utmost loyalty and good faith. That requirement also applied to the unlimited gift provision, and the gifts to Dominick did not meet the best interest requirement.

—*In re Estate of Ferrara*, 852 N.E.2d 138 (N.Y.)

Obedience

An agent may have two types of instructions from the principal: one routine and the other discretionary. The agent must carry out all routine instructions to the letter as long as compliance would not defeat the purpose of the agency, be illegal, or perpetrate a fraud on others. An instruction not to accept any payments made by check illustrates a routine instruction. An agent incurs liability for any losses caused by disobeying these instructions. There is no justification for disobeying such instructions under any conditions.

Agents must use the best judgment of which they are capable regarding discretionary instructions. For example, an agent instructed to accept checks incurs no liability for a bad check when in the agent's judgment the drawer of the check is solvent and reliable. If an agent accepts a check that the agent has reason to believe is bad, the agent incurs liability for any loss that the principal sustains by reason of this act.

Reasonable Skill and Diligence

One who acts as an agent must possess the skill required to perform the duties and must be diligent in performing the skill. An implied warranty exists that the agent has such skill and will exercise such diligence. Any breach of this warranty subjects the agent to a liability for damages for the loss by reason of the breach.

Because it is assumed that agents are appointed in reliance on their individual skills, talents, and judgment, agents may not generally appoint subagents. This, of course, is not true if the agency agreement provides for the appointment of subagents, if the work delegated is merely clerical, or if the type of agency is one in which it is customarily assumed that subagents would be appointed. Whenever appointing subagents, the agent must use skill and diligence in appointing competent subagents and remains liable to the principal for their breach of good faith or lack of skill.

Accounting

The duties of an agent include keeping a record of all money transactions pertaining to the agency. An accounting must be made to the principal for any of the principal's money and property that may come into the agent's possession. Money should be deposited in a bank in the name of the principal, preferably in a bank other than that in which the agent keeps personal funds. If the deposit is made in the name of the agent, any loss caused by the failure of the bank will fall on the agent. Personal property of the principal must be kept separate from property of the agent.

Information

Agents have a duty to keep principals informed of all facts pertinent to the agency that may enable the principals to protect their interests. In consequence, an agent cannot enforce a principal's promise to pay a bonus to the agent for information secured by the agent in the performance of agency duties because the principal was entitled to the information as a result of the agency. The promise was therefore not supported by consideration.

PRINCIPAL'S DUTIES TO AGENT

The principal has four important duties in respect to the agent:

1. Compensation
2. Reimbursement
3. Indemnification
4. Abidance by the terms of the contract

Compensation

The contract of agency determines the compensation due an agent. As in most other contracts, this provision may be either express or implied. If the amount is clearly and expressly stated, disputes seldom arise. When an agency agreement does not state the amount of compensation, the agent may obtain reasonable or customary compensation for the services provided. In the absence of customary rates of compensation, the court will fix a reasonable rate according to the character of the services rendered. Frequently, the parties set the compensation on a contingent basis, such as a percentage of the selling price, provided a sale occurs. In such a case, the agent cannot collect compensation from the principal unless a sale actually occurs.

PREVIEW CASE REVISITED

Facts: Commercial Standard Insurance Co. hired John Kennon, doing business as Kennon Adjustment Co., to investigate a workers' compensation claim. They made no agreement as to the amount to be paid Kennon. After the claimant received an award, Kennon submitted a bill for more than three times the amount of the award. Commercial refused to pay the bill, saying that it was too high. Kennon sued.

Outcome: The court held that in the absence of an agreement for compensation, an implied promise arises for a principal to pay a reasonable amount for such services rendered in the location where they were furnished.

—*Kennon v. Commercial Standard Ins. Co.*, 376 S.W.2d 703 (Tenn. Ct. App.)

Reimbursement

The principal must reimburse an agent for any expenses incurred or disbursements the agent makes from personal funds as a necessary part of the agency. If, for example, an agent had to pay from personal funds a $100 truck repair bill before a trip on behalf of the principal could be continued, the agent would be entitled to reimbursement. If, on the other hand, the agent had to pay a $50 fine for speeding, the principal would not be required to reimburse this expense. Any expense incurred as a result of an agent's unlawful act must be borne by the agent.

Indemnification

A contractual payment made by the agent for the principal is an expense of the principal. If the agent makes the payment not by reason of a contract but as a result of a loss or damage due to an accident, the principal must indemnify the agent. The principal must reimburse expenses and indemnify for losses and damages. If the principal directs the agent to sell goods in the stockroom that already belong to the principal's customer, that customer can sue both the principal and the agent. If the agent must pay the customer damages, the agent can in turn sue the principal for giving the instructions that caused the loss.

Abidance by the Terms of the Contract

The principal must abide by the terms of the contract in all respects, including any implied compliance. Thus, the agent must be employed for the period stated in the contract unless justification exists for terminating the contract at an earlier date. If the cooperation or participation of the principal is required in order to enable the agent to perform duties under the agency agreement, the principal must cooperate or participate to the extent required by the contract. For example, if an agent sells by sample and receives a commission on all sales, the agent must be furnished samples, and the opportunity to earn the fee or commission must be given.

AGENT'S LIABILITIES TO THIRD PARTIES

Ordinarily, whenever an agent performs duties, the principal is bound but not the agent. In relations with third parties, however, an agent may be personally liable on contracts and for wrongs in several ways:

LO 2
Agent's and principal's liabilities to third parties

1. Agents who contract in their own names and do not disclose the names of the principals become liable to the same extent as though they were the principals. For this reason, agents who sign contracts in their own names will be held liable. The proper way for an agent to sign so as to bind only the principal is to sign "principal, by agent." A signing of the principal's name alone will likewise protect the agent, although the third person may require the placing of the agent's name under the name of the principal so that at a later date it can be determined which agent had obtained the contract.

COURT CASE

Facts: Tim Redlinger, an employee of Jay Duran Associates, Inc., expressed concern to Jay Duran, the majority stockholder, that he did not have a retirement plan. Duran signed a letter on company letterhead that stated: "I, Jay Duran, promise to purchase an insurance policy on myself for $50,000 with Tim Redlinger as sole beneficiary." Beneath the text of the letter appeared:

JAY DURAN ASSOCIATES, INC.
[signed] Jay Duran
Jay Duran

Duran died without having set up a retirement plan or purchasing a life insurance policy.

Redlinger made a claim against Duran's estate. He claimed that because only Duran could take out insurance on his life and chose the beneficiary, Duran had obligated himself personally.

Outcome: The court said because Duran personally was the only person who could do what was promised in the letter, he, the agent of the company, had agreed to be personally bound for the insurance.

—*In re Estate of Duran,*
692 A.2d 176 (Pa. Super.)

2. Agents may make themselves personally liable to third parties by an express agreement to be responsible. This express agreement may be demonstrated if it is the only logical or legal interpretation of the contract.

3. People who assume to act for others but actually have no authority, or who exceed or materially depart from the authority they were given, incur personal liability to those with whom they do business. The latter situation may arise when overzealous agents affect what they may think is a desirable contract.

4. An agent incurs personal liability for fraud or any other wrongdoing, whether caused by disobedience, carelessness, or malice, or whether committed on the order of the principal.

PRINCIPAL'S DUTIES AND LIABILITIES TO THIRD PARTIES

The principal ordinarily has liability to third parties for contracts made within the actual or the apparent scope of an agent's authority.

When the agent enters into an unauthorized contract not within the apparent scope of authority, the principal is not bound unless the contract is subsequently ratified. The test of when an agent has apparent authority is whether, on the basis of the conduct of the principal, a reasonable person would believe that the agent had the authority to make the particular contract. If such a person would, the contract binds the principal. For example, if the manager of a furniture store sells a suite of furniture on credit contrary to the authority granted, the principal must fulfill the contract with the third party, provided the third party did not know of the limitation on the agent's authority. The agent has liability to the principal for any loss sustained.

The principal, as well as the agent, has liability for an injury to the person or the property of a third party caused by the negligence or the wrongful act of the agent in the course of employment. When the agent steps aside from the business of the principal and commits a wrong or injury to another, the principal is not liable for an unratified act.

TERMINATION OF AN AGENCY BY ACTS OF THE PARTIES

LO 3
How to terminate an agency

An agency may be terminated by acts of the parties by:

1. Original agreement
2. Subsequent agreement
3. Revocation
4. Renunciation by the agent

Original Agreement

The contract creating the agency may specify a date for the termination of the agency. In that event, the agency automatically terminates on that date. Most special agencies, such as a special agency to sell an automobile, terminate because their purpose has been accomplished.

Subsequent Agreement

An agreement between the principal and the agent may terminate an agency at any time.

Revocation

The principal may revoke the agent's authority at any time, thereby terminating the agency. The principal may terminate the agency by notifying the agent of the termination or by taking actions that are inconsistent with the continuation of the agency.

One must distinguish between the right to terminate the agency and the power to do so. The principal has the right to terminate the agency any time the agent

COURT CASE

Facts: Francis Gagnon executed a power of attorney in favor of his daughter, Joan Coombs. He specifically empowered Joan "to sell any of my real estate" and "to add property to . . . any trust of which I am the grantor or beneficiary." A few months later, Gagnon executed a document revoking the power of attorney but did not tell Joan. Gagnon found someone who wanted to buy his house, and they signed an agreement to sell. Gagnon told Joan about this sales agreement. Without telling Gagnon, Joan set up a trust with herself as trustee having total control of the trust without court approval and Gagnon as beneficiary.

Under authority of the power of attorney, Joan conveyed Gagnon's house to herself as trustee. When Joan refused to return his house, Gagnon sued her.

Outcome: The court found for Gagnon, holding that Joan should have realized he had revoked her authority to sell the home when she found out he had contracted to sell it.

—*Gagnon v. Coombs*,
654 N.E.2d 54 (Mass. App. Ct.)

breaches any material part of the contract of employment. If the agent, for example, fails to account for all money collected for the principal, the agent may be discharged, and the principal incurs no liability for breach of contract. The principal, on the other hand, has the power, with one exception, to revoke the agent's authority at any time. Under these circumstances, however, the principal becomes liable to the agent for any damage sustained by reason of an unjustifiable discharge. This is the agent's sole remedy. The agent cannot insist on the right to continue to act as an agent, even though nothing has been done to justify a termination before the end of the contract period.

The only exception to this rule that the principal has the power to terminate the agency occurs in the case of an **agency coupled with an interest**. Interest may take one of two forms: (1) interest in the authority and (2) interest in the subject matter. An agent has interest in the authority when authorized to act as an agent in collecting funds for the principal with an agreement not to remit the collections to the principal but to apply them on a debt owed to the agent by the principal. In the second case, the agent has a lien on the property of the principal as security for a debt and is appointed as agent to sell the property and apply the proceeds to the debt.

Agency Coupled with an Interest
Agency in which agent has financial stake in performance of agency because of having given consideration to principal

Renunciation

Like the principal, the agent has the power to renounce the agency at any time. An agent who abandons the agency without cause before fulfillment of the contract incurs liability to the principal for all losses due to the unjustified abandonment.

TERMINATION BY OPERATION OF LAW

An agency also may be terminated by operation of law. This may occur because of:

1. Subsequent illegality
2. Death or incapacity
3. Destruction
4. Bankruptcy
5. Dissolution
6. War

Subsequent Illegality

Subsequent illegality of the subject matter of the agency terminates the agency.

Death or Incapacity

Death or incapacity of either the principal or agent normally terminates the agency. For example, when the agent permanently loses the power of speech so that the principal's business cannot be performed, the agency automatically terminates.

Durable Power of Attorney
Appointment of agency that survives incapacity of principal

An exception to the rule of termination by incapacity has been enacted by states that provide for durable powers of attorney. A **durable power of attorney** is a written appointment of agency designed to be effective even though the principal is incapacitated. Such a power of attorney may allow an agent to make health-care decisions for the principal such as admission to a hospital or nursing home, authorization of a medical procedure, or insertion of a feeding tube. It may also direct the attorney in fact to withhold certain, specified medical treatments or procedures.

Destruction

Destruction of the subject matter, such as the destruction by fire of a house to be sold by the agent, terminates the agency.

Bankruptcy

Bankruptcy of the principal terminates the agency. In most cases, bankruptcy of the agent does not terminate the agency.

Dissolution

Dissolution
Termination of corporation's operation except activities needed for liquidation

Dissolution of a corporation terminates an agency in which the corporation is a party. This is similar to death, as dissolution of a corporation is a complete termination of operation except for the activities necessary for liquidation.

War

When the country of the principal and that of the agent are at war against each other, the agent's authority usually terminates or at least lapses until peace occurs. A war that makes performance impossible terminates the agency.

NOTICE OF TERMINATION

When principals terminate agencies, they must give notice to third parties with whom the agents have previously transacted business and who would be likely to deal with them as an agent. If such notice is not given, the principal might still be bound on any future contracts the agent negotiates. Notice can be given by sending written notice to the third parties in any way feasible. How the notice is given does not matter so long as the parties learn of the termination. Notice given to an agent constitutes notice to the principal.

COURT CASE

Facts: Shortly after Science and Engineering Associates, Inc. (SEA) employed Jerry Riehl as a part-time consultant for its clients, Stanton Keck and John Bevan asked him to supply consulting services for a venture, later incorporated as American Seamount Corp., involving incineration of hazardous wastes. He subsequently signed an agreement with Seamount not to disclose confidential information or compete with the project. When SEA told Riehl, as SEA's agent, to stop working with Seamount, Riehl told Seamount, but said he would work in his personal capacity. After Seamount laid Riehl off, he tried to sell the incineration project for himself. Seamount sued Riehl and SEA alleging Riehl was SEA's agent when he signed the agreement and then broke it.

Outcome: The court stated that once a third party has notice of the revocation of an agent's authority, the principal (SEA) was not liable for the agent's postrevocation acts.

—American Seamount Corp. v. Science and Engineering Assocs., Inc.,
812 P.2d 505 (Wash. App.)

When operation of law terminates an agency, notice need not be given either to the agent or to third parties.

QUESTIONS

1. What are the legal consequences if an agent acts in bad faith or proves disloyal to the principal?
2. Give two examples of the type of acts courts have held to be breaches of good faith by an agent.
3. What is an agent's liability for disobeying a routine instruction?
4. What implied warranty is there regarding the skill and diligence an agent will exercise?
5. May an agent enforce a principal's promise to pay a bonus to the agent for information secured by the agent in the performance of agency duties?
6. How should an agent handle deposits of the principal's money?
7. When are agents personally liable?
8. What is the test of when an agent has apparent authority?
9. When does a principal have the power to revoke an agent's authority?
10. Explain how notice of termination of an agency can be given.

CASE PROBLEMS

1. On September 21, under a power of attorney from Nell Pickett, Harold Johnson contracted for her to sell 181 acres of land to Bruce Kirkland. The sale was to close on December 15. Pickett died after the contract was executed but before the sale was completed. By the terms of her will, the land was to go to Kenneth and Betty Pearl Van Etten while most of the rest of her estate went to nieces and nephews, including Johnson. Kirkland asked the court to require the executor to carry out the contract. Was the contract for sale voided by Pickett's death because the contract was executed under a power of attorney?   LO ③

LO **1**

2. Jacques Levy and his wife, Leonie Levy, each executed documents making their spouse, their grandson, Russell Levy, and their lawyer, Charles Rosen, their attorneys-in-fact. The documents authorized only Rosen to make gifts to their respective spouse and their descendants. A year later, Rosen discovered an order transferring $40,000 in the Levy's securities to an account in the names of Russell Levy and Elizabeth Ballew. He recovered the securities and an audit of the Levy's accounts showed $550,000 went to Russell and Elizabeth. The Levys sued Russell for recovery of the money plus interest. Decide the case.

LO **2**

3. The Sonenberg Co. managed apartment complexes and had Redi-Floors, Inc. install carpet in several apartments. The apartments were actually owned by Manor Associates Limited Partnership. No signs on the apartment property disclosed the name of the apartment complex's owner, and no one with Sonenberg informed Redi-Floors who owned the property. Some bills for the carpeting were not paid, and Redi-Floors sued Sonenberg as well as Manor. The trial judge dismissed the suit with regard to Sonenberg. Redi-Floors appealed this decision saying Sonenberg was liable as an agent for an undisclosed principal. Was it?

LO **1**

4. Contracting with Adam and Susan Sokoloff, Harriman Estates Development Corp. agreed to furnish an architectural plan for their new house. Harriman contracted with Frederick Ercolino, an architect, who drew up the plans. Unknown to the Sokoloffs, that contract stated the plans could not be used unless they hired Harriman to build the house. Although the Sokoloffs paid Harriman in full, Harriman refused to provide them with the plans unless they hired it to build the house. The Sokoloffs sued alleging that Harriman was their agent in procuring the plans from Ercolino. Must Harriman give them the plans?

LO **3**

5. Steven Kaldi contracted to sell insurance on behalf of Farmers Insurance Exchange. The contract provided that either the agent or Farmers could terminate it with three months' notice. If Farmers terminated the agreement, Kaldi could request a review of the termination by a review board. Fifteen years later, Farmers gave notice of termination. Kaldi requested a review, and the review board approved the termination. Kaldi sued Farmers, alleging it did not have the right to terminate the agency. Did it?

LO **1**

6. Lerner Corp. had an agreement to act as the exclusive leasing and management agent for an apartment complex. Three Winthrop Properties, Inc. acted as the agent for the owners. The management agreement permitted the owner to terminate " . . . at anytime from and after the last day of the . . . month in which occurs the 10th anniversary of the date of this agreement [January 31]." The termination date could not be earlier than 90 days after written notice of termination. On October 17, Three Winthrop gave notice of termination as of January 31. Lerner claimed notice could not be given until January 31 and termination could not be until 90 days after that. Three Winthrop filed suit, but by the time the court tried the case, Lerner had continued to manage and take management fees from rental proceeds for the 90 days after January 31. Had Lerner acted in good faith?

LO **2**

7. Nancy Imhof hired attorney Richard French to represent her in a lawsuit after her husband died in a plane crash. French contacted Donald Sommer by phone and hired him to investigate the crash and testify. Sommer sent French his fee schedule, and French sent him a letter verifying their discussion and giving documents to review and a check as a retainer. French signed the letter.

Sommer rendered services in excess of $18,000 but was not paid, so he sued French. French said he was only acting as an agent for Imhof. Should the court hold French personally liable?

8. Needing money, Barbara Barlow "pawned" the title to her car with Quik Pawn Shop. EFS, Inc. owned Quik Pawn. Frank Evans was president and Charlotte Evans was secretary of EFS. No advertisements or documents Barlow received disclosed EFS's existence or ownership of Quik Pawn. Barlow claimed the terms of the pawn violated the Truth in Lending Act and sued EFS and the Evanses. She claimed the Evanses conducted a business and acted as agents of Quik Pawn without disclosing their principal and therefore should be personally liable. Should the Evanses be liable as agents for an undisclosed principal?

LO ❶

Employer and Employee Relations

LEARNING OBJECTIVES

1 Recognize how the relationship of employer and employee arises.

2 Identify the statutory modifications of an employer's defenses under the common law.

3 Describe the liability of an employer to third parties for acts of employees.

4 Name the duties an employee owes the employer.

PREVIEW CASE

While attending a contentious school board meeting in his capacity as superintendent of schools, Nathan Chesler suffered a heart attack that resulted in his death. Chesler's contract had not been renewed, and the meeting was the night before his contract expired. Although the meeting was expected to be short, it lasted one and a half hours. The meeting concerned a personnel problem, and the board members directed angry questions to Chesler about the way he handled it and criticized his recommendation. The board asked Chesler to leave the room. When he returned, the chairman stated the board would not take action on Chesler's recommendation. Chesler gasped, fell back in his chair, and died. His doctor said the stress at the meeting was a significant contributing factor to the attack. His widow sought workers' compensation. Was attendance at the board meeting part of Chesler's job? Was the stress that brought on the heart attack related to Chesler's job?

Over a period of many decades, the common law developed rules governing the relationship between an employer and employees. These rules have been greatly modified by statute. However, in every state remnants of the common law still apply. Many of the common-law rules dealing with safe working conditions and other aspects of the employment contract have been retained in labor legislation. These laws do not cover all employees. In every state, a small number of employees still have their rights and duties determined largely by common-law rules. This chapter deals with the common law and statutory modifications of it as they relate to employers and employees. However, the law regarding employers and employees varies significantly from state to state.

CREATION OF EMPLOYER AND EMPLOYEE RELATIONSHIP

The relationship of employer and employee arises only from a contract of employment, either express or implied. The common law allowed employers the right to hire whom they pleased and employees the right to freely choose their employers. The relationship of employer and employee could not be imposed on either the purported employer or employee without consent. One who voluntarily performs the duties of an employee cannot by that act subject the employer to the liability of an employer. But the relationship may be implied by conduct that demonstrates that the parties agree that one is the employer and the other the employee.

LO ❶
Employer-employee
relationship

Length of Contract

An employee discharged without cause may recover wages due up to the end of the contract period from the employer. However, when creating an employer-employee relationship, seldom does either party mention the length of the contract period. In some jurisdictions, the terms of compensation determine the contract period. In such jurisdictions, the length of time used in specifying the compensation constitutes the employment period, and an employee may be discharged at the end of that time without further liability. For example, an employee paid by the hour may be discharged without liability at the end of any hour. An employee paid by the week or by the month, as are many office employees, has a term of employment of one week or one month, as the case may be. For monthly paid employees, the term of employment may depend upon the way the employer specifies the compensation. A stated salary of $27,500 a year gives a one-year term of employment, even though the employer pays once a month. In other jurisdictions, employment at a set amount per week, month, or year does not constitute employment for any definite period but amounts to an indefinite hiring.

Many employer-employee situations have an indefinite length for the contract, and either the employer or the employee may terminate the employment for any reason or for no reason at any time. This situation is called **employment at will**.

Employment at Will
Employment terminable by employer or employee for any reason

C O U R T C A S E

Facts: Dan's Foods, Inc. distributed an employee handbook that stated, "Your employment at Dan's is at will and may be terminated without cause or prior notice by either you or Dan's." James Ryan, a pharmacist employed by Dan's, read the handbook and signed a form stating he had received and read it. Dan's received many customer complaints about Ryan, and after the management repeatedly counseled and warned him about the complaints, Dan's fired him. Ryan sued.

Outcome: Ryan was an at-will employee and could be fired at any time.

—*Ryan v. Dan's Food Stores, Inc.,* **972 P.2d 395 (Utah)**

However, as a result of labor legislation, union or other employment contracts, employee handbooks, or other exceptions that have developed to employment at will, many employees have significant job security. They may not be discharged except for good cause. As in the case of an employee discharged without cause who is employed for a specified period, such an employee may sue the employer for money damages. In some cases, the employee may also sue to be restored to the job.

Determination of Contract Terms

Employer-employee contracts frequently do not state terms other than the compensation. Terms are determined by law, custom, employee handbooks, and possibly by union contracts. If the employer publishes a handbook stating contract terms, the employer will usually be bound by those terms as long as the employee had a reasonable opportunity to learn them. In some cases, courts have held that statements in the employer's written policy manual constitute terms of employer-employee contracts.

Union Contracts

Formerly, the employer contracted individually with each employee. However, as the union movement developed and collective bargaining became commonplace, employers began agreeing with unions to provisions of employment that applied to large numbers of employees. The signed contract between them embodied this agreement between the employer and the union. As an agent of the employees, the union speaks and contracts for all the employees collectively. As a general rule, the employer still makes a contract individually with each employee, but the union contract binds the employer to recognize certain scales of union wages, hours of work, job classifications, and related matters.

DUTIES AND LIABILITIES OF THE EMPLOYER

Under the common law, the employer had five well-defined duties:

1. Duty to exercise care
2. Duty to provide a reasonably safe place to work
3. Duty to provide safe tools and appliances
4. Duty to provide competent and sufficient employees for the task
5. Duty to instruct employees with reference to the dangerous nature of employment

Duty to Exercise Care

This rule imposes liability on employers if their negligence causes harm to an employee. Employers have exercised proper care when they have done what a reasonable person would have done under the circumstances to avoid harm.

Duty to Provide a Reasonably Safe Place to Work

The employer must furnish every employee with a reasonably safe place to work. What constitutes a safe place depends on the nature of the work. Most states have statutes modifying the common law for hazardous industries.

Duty to Provide Safe Tools and Appliances

The tools an employer furnishes employees must be safe. This rule also applies to machinery and appliances.

Duty to Provide Competent and Sufficient Employees for the Task

Both the number of employees and their skill and experience affect the hazardous nature of many jobs. The employer has liability for all injuries to employees directly caused by either an insufficient number of workers or the lack of skill of some of the workers.

Duty to Instruct Employees

In all positions that use machinery, chemicals, electric appliances, and other production instruments, there are many hazards. The law requires the employer to give that degree of instruction to a new employee that a reasonable person would give under the circumstances to avoid reasonably foreseeable harm that could result from a failure to give such instructions.

COMMON-LAW DEFENSES OF THE EMPLOYER

Under the common law, when an injured employee sues the employer, the employer could raise the following defenses:

1. The employee's contributory negligence
2. The act of a fellow servant
3. A risk assumed by the employee

Contributory Negligence Rule

The contributory negligence rule states that an employer can escape liability for breach of duty if it can be established that the employee's own negligence contributed to the accident. An employee who could have avoided the injury by the exercise of due diligence has no right to collect damages from the employer.

The Fellow-Servant Rule

The fellow-servant rule allows an employer to avoid liability by proving the injury was caused by a fellow servant. A **fellow servant** is an employee who has the same status as another worker and works with that employee. This rule has been abrogated or so severely limited that it very rarely has any significance now.

Fellow Servant
Employee with same status and working with another worker

Assumption-of-Risk Rule

Every type of employment in industry has some normal risks. The assumption-of-risk rule states that employees assume these normal risks by voluntarily accepting employment. Therefore, if the injury results from the hazardous nature of the job, the employer cannot be held liable.

STATUTORY MODIFICATION OF COMMON LAW

The rules of the common law have been greatly altered by the enactment of laws modifying an employer's defenses when sued by an employee, laws providing for workers' compensation, and the Occupational Safety and Health Act.

LO ❷
Statutory modification of employer's defenses

Modification of Common-Law Defenses

Statutes have modified the defenses that an employer may use when an employee sues for damages. For example, the Federal Employers' Liability Act and the Federal Safety Appliance Act apply to common carriers engaged in interstate commerce. A plaintiff suing under these laws must still bring an action in court and prove negligence by the employer or other employees. However, winning the case is easier because of limits on the employer's defenses. An employer has liability even if the employee is contributorily negligent. However, such negligence may reduce the amount of damages. Many states also have modified the common-law defenses of employers of employees engaged in hazardous types of work.

Workers' Compensation

Every state has adopted workers' compensation statutes that apply to certain industries or businesses. These statutes allow an employee, or certain relatives of a deceased employee, to recover damages for injury to or death of the employee. They may recover whenever the injury arose within the course of the employee's work from a risk involved in that work. An injured party receives compensation without regard to whether the employer or the employee was negligent. Generally no compensation results for a willfully self-inflicted injury or an injury sustained while intoxicated. However, the employer has the burden of proving the injury was intentional and self-inflicted. The law limits the amount of recovery and sets it in accordance with a prescribed schedule.

PREVIEW CASE REVISITED

Facts: While attending a contentious school board meeting in his capacity as superintendent of schools, Nathan Chesler suffered a heart attack that resulted in his death. Chesler's contract had not been renewed, and the meeting was the night before his contract expired. Although the meeting was expected to be short, it lasted one and a half hours. The meeting concerned a personnel problem, and the board members directed angry questions to Chesler about the way he handled it and criticized his recommendation. The board asked Chesler to leave the room. When he returned, the chairman stated the board would not take action on Chesler's recommendation. Chesler gasped, fell back in his chair, and died. His doctor said the stress at the meeting was a significant contributing factor to the attack. His widow sought workers' compensation.
Outcome: The court held that a physical injury caused by work-related stress was a compensable injury. The widow was awarded death benefits.

—*Chesler v. City of Derby*, 899 A.2d 624 (Conn. App.)

Workers' compensation laws generally allow recovery for accident-inflicted injuries and occupational diseases. Some states limit compensation for occupational diseases to those specified by name in the statute. These diseases include silicosis, lead poisoning, or injury to health from radioactivity. Other states compensate for any disease arising from the occupation.

Whether based on the common law or an employer's liability statute, damages actions are tried in court. Workers' compensation proceedings differ because a special administrative agency or workers' compensation board hears them. However, either party may appeal the agency or board decision to the appropriate court of law.

Workers' compensation statutes do not bar an employee from suing another employee for the injury.

Occupational Safety and Health Act

In 1970, the federal government enacted the Williams-Steiger Occupational Safety and Health Act to ensure safe and healthful working conditions. This federal law applies to every employer engaged in a business affecting interstate commerce except governments. The Occupational Safety and Health Administration (OSHA) administers the act and issues standards with which employers and employees must comply. In order to ensure compliance with the standards, OSHA carries out job-site inspections. Employers must maintain detailed records of work-related deaths, injuries, and illnesses. The act provides fines for violations, including penalties of up to $1,000 per day for failure to correct violations within the allotted time.

LIABILITIES OF THE EMPLOYER TO THIRD PARTIES

An employer has liability under certain circumstances for injuries that employees cause to third parties. The theory of *respondeat superior* imposes liability on an employer for torts caused by employees. The employer is liable for personal injury as well as property damage.

LO ❸
Employer's liability

Respondeat Superior
Theory imposing liability on employers for torts of employees

To be liable, the employee must have committed the injury in the course of employment. An employee, who, without any direction from the employer, injures a third party and causes injury not as a result of the employment, has personal liability, but the employer does not. The employer has liability, however, if it ordered the act that caused the injury or had knowledge of the act and assented to it. The employer also has liability for the torts of employees caused by the employer's negligence in not enforcing safe working procedures; not providing safe equipment, such as trucks; or not employing competent employees. In rare cases, the employer is liable for intentional torts when the conduct constitutes a risk attributable to the employer's business.

COURT CASE

Facts: Wendell Taylor drove a Capital Transportation Corp. (CTC) bus. His supervisor told him he would have to drive an extra run. After he picked up some passengers, he pulled the bus to the side of the road because he was so angry he became teary eyed. While parked, Thomas Menson, a CTC route supervisor, asked him if there was something wrong with the bus. Taylor said the bus was okay but he wanted to know why he had to drive another run. Menson told him to just drive the bus. There was an incident that resulted in Menson getting two bones in his foot broken as well as a knee and shoulder injury. Menson sued CTC alleging that as Taylor's employer, it was liable for his actions.

Outcome: The court said that Taylor's action was employment-rooted. It resulted from an interchange regarding work, between employees, during work hours and in the work environment. CTC was liable.

—*Menson v. Taylor*, 849 So.2d 836 (La. App.)

EMPLOYEE'S DUTIES TO THE EMPLOYER

LO ❹
Duties of employee

The employee owes certain duties to the employer. Failure to comply with these duties may result in discharge. An employee's duties include:

1. Job performance
2. Business confidentiality
3. Granting of right to use inventions

Job Performance

The duties required by the job must be performed faithfully and honestly and to advance the employer's interests. In skilled positions, the worker must perform the task with ordinary skill.

Business Confidentiality

An employee has a duty of confidentiality regarding certain business matters. Trade secrets or other confidential business information must not be revealed.

C O U R T   C A S E

Facts: Royal Carbo Corp. employed Laurie McDonnell, Angel Ayala, and Anthony Lupo Jr. While so employed, McDonnell, Ayala, and Lupo organized a competing corporation and used Royal's trade secrets to secretly undersell Royal's customers. Royal sued the three, and they argued they should be paid up to the time Royal fired them.

Outcome: The court held that McDonnell, Ayala, and Lupo forfeited their right to compensation, and Royal was entitled to recover damages from them.

—*Royal Carbo Corp. v. Flameguard, Inc.,*
645 N.Y.S.2d 18 (A.D.)

Inventions

In the absence of an express or implied agreement to the contrary, inventions belong to the employee who devised them, even though the time and property of the employer were used in their discovery, provided that the employee was not employed for the express purpose of inventing the things or the processes that were discovered.

If the invention is discovered during working hours and with the employer's material and equipment, the employer has the right to use the invention without charge in the operation of the business. If the employee has obtained a patent for the invention, the employer must be granted a nonexclusive license to use the invention without the payment of royalty. This **shop right** of the employer does not give the right to make and sell machines that embody the employee's invention; it only entitles the employer to use the invention in the operation of the plant.

When an employer employs a person to secure certain results from experiments to be conducted by that employee, the courts hold that the inventions equitably belong to the employer. Courts base this result on a trust relation or an implied agreement to make an assignment.

In any case, an employee may expressly agree that inventions made during employment will be the property of the employer. Such contracts must be clear and

Shop Right
Employer's right to use employee's invention without payment of royalty

specific, or else courts normally rule against the employer. The employee may also agree to assign to the employer inventions made after the term of employment.

FEDERAL SOCIAL SECURITY ACT

The federal Social Security Act has four major provisions:

1. Old-age and survivors' insurance
2. Assistance to persons in financial need
3. Unemployment compensation
4. Disability and Medicare benefits

Old-Age and Survivors' Insurance

The Social Security Act provides payments to the dependents of covered workers who die before the age of retirement. This part constitutes the survivors' benefits. If workers live to a specified age and retire, they and their spouses draw retirement benefits. This part constitutes the old-age benefits. Both parts are called insurance because they constitute risks that could be insured against by life insurance companies. The survivors' insurance covers the risk of the breadwinner's dying and leaving dependents without a source of income. Old-age benefits cover the risk of outliving one's savings after retirement.

Who Is Covered? The old-age and survivors' insurance provisions of the Social Security Act cover practically everyone. Employees in state and local governments, including public school teachers, may be brought under the coverage of the act by means of agreements between the state and the federal government.

This provision of the act also covers farmers, professional people (such as lawyers), and self-employed businesspeople. The act does not cover certain types of work of close relatives, such as a parent for a child, work by a child under 21 for parents, and employment of a spouse by a spouse.

Eligibility for Retirement Benefits. To be eligible for retirement benefits, one must meet these requirements:

1. Be fully insured (40 quarters or the equivalent of 10 years) at the time of retirement.
2. Be 62 years of age or older.
3. Apply for retirement benefits after reaching the age of retirement. To be entitled to the maximum retirement benefits, one must wait until at least age 65 to apply for them.

Eligibility for Survivors' Benefits. The family of a worker who dies while fully insured or currently insured at the time of death has a right to survivors' benefits. Currently insured means the person had worked at least six quarters in the 13-quarter period ending with death.

Assistance to Persons in Financial Need

People over 65 who have financial need may be eligible for federal supplemental security income payments. These monthly payments go to blind or disabled people in financial need. No one contributes specifically to this system based only on need.

Unemployment Compensation

In handling unemployment compensation, the federal government cooperates with the states, which set up their own rules, approved by the federal government, for the payment of unemployment benefits. The states, not the federal government, make payments of unemployment compensation.

The unemployment compensation laws of the various states differ, although they tend to follow a common pattern. They all provide for raising funds by levies on employers. The federal government pays the cost of running the programs.

State unemployment compensation laws apply in general to workers in commerce and industry. Agricultural workers, domestic servants, government employees, and employees of nonprofit organizations formed and operated exclusively for religious, charitable, literary, educational, scientific, or humane purposes may not be included.

To be eligible for benefits, a worker generally must meet the following requirements:

1. Be available for work and registered at an unemployment office
2. Have been employed for a certain length of time within a specified period in an employment covered by the law
3. Be capable of working
4. Not have refused reasonably suitable employment
4. Not be self-employed
6. Not be out of work because of a strike or a lockout still in progress or because of voluntarily leaving a job without cause
7. Have served the required waiting period

Disability and Medicare Benefits

The government makes monthly cash benefits, called *disability insurance benefits*, to disabled persons under the age of 65 and their families. A disabled person is someone unable to engage in any substantial gainful activity because of a medically determinable physical or mental impairment expected to end in death or that has lasted or will last continually for 12 months.

Medicare is insurance designed to help pay a large portion of personal health-care costs. Virtually everyone age 65 and over may be covered by this contributory hospital and medical insurance plan. The program covers only specified services.

Taxation to Finance the Plan

To pay the life insurance and the annuity insurance benefits of the Social Security Act, both the employer and the employee pay a payroll tax (FICA) of an equal percentage of all income earned in any one year up to a specified maximum. The maximum income and the rate may be changed at any session of Congress. A payroll tax finances the unemployment compensation part of the act. In most states, the employer bears this entire tax. The assistance to persons in need is paid for by general taxation. No specific tax is levied to meet these payments. Disability and Medicare benefits are funded from a combination of four sources: FICA, a Medicare tax on people who are not covered by the old-age and survivors' insurance, premiums paid by the people covered, and the general federal revenue.

QUESTIONS

1. How does the relationship of employer and employee arise?

2. How may the terms of compensation determine the period of an employment contract, and what does this mean to employers?

3. What job security has labor legislation, union or other employment contracts, employee handbooks, or other exceptions to at-will employment given employees?

4. If an employment contract does not state any terms other than the compensation, how are the other terms determined?

5. What type of instruction does the law require an employer to give a new employee?

6. How does the defense of contributory negligence help an employer?

7. How has the statutory modification of an employer's common-law defenses made it easier for an employee to win a case?

8. May an employee recover workers' compensation for an intentional, self-inflicted injury? Explain.

9. When is an employer liable for injuries that employees cause to third parties?

10. When there is no agreement regarding inventions, to whom do they belong when made by an employee?

CASE PROBLEMS

1. ReadyLink Healthcare recruited and hired nurses and assigned them to its customer health-care providers who requested nurses. ReadyLink spent a great deal of time and money developing a database of nurses and its health-care providers. The information was used to hire nurses and service customers. ReadyLink hired Jerome Cotton as a nurse-recruiting agent but fired him for stealing confidential information. Police found confidential information in his possession and videotapes showed him sneaking into the office at night and copying confidential information. ReadyLink sued Cotton. Does it have a cause of action against him?   LO ❹

2. Sygma Network, Inc. hired Gladys Antonio as an accountant. In December, Antonio went to Zimbabwe on vacation. She was scheduled to return on December 31 which was the beginning of the accounting department's busy "quarter close" week. She called the accounting supervisor on December 29 and 31 saying she was delayed but promised to keep her updated. Getting no further communication from Antonio, Sygma terminated her on January 4. Sygma's employee handbook stated Antonio was an at-will employee and "[t]he contents of the SYGMA handbook do not constitute an express or implied contract of employment." It also said, "the handbook is non-binding and is not intended to create, nor to be construed as a contract." Antonio sued Sygma for breach of covenant based on the employee handbook. Can she recover?   LO ❶

3. While Ainsley Blair sat in the office of the New Laundromat that Percival Bailey owned, Bailey's son shot him. There was no indication that Blair knew Bailey's son. Blair came to the Laundromat two days a week, changing money for   LO ❷

customers, cleaning the machines, and mopping floors. He had a key for the office where Bailey kept the money to make change. Blair alleged he was paid $100 a week and filed for workers' compensation. Should Blair receive workers' compensation?

LO ❶

4. Carlisle Corp. owned and operated Wendy's restaurant franchises. John Stephens was an area manager with responsibility for six of them. Henrietta Bradford, the manager of one of the restaurants, complained of sexual harassment by Stephens to John Hughes, the CEO of Carlisle. Hughes told Stephens to change his conduct and told him he could be fired for sexual harassment. Sometime later Hughes received a similar complaint involving Stephens at another of the restaurants. Hughes fired him. Stephens sued for wrongful discharge claiming Carlisle's company handbook created an employment contract. The employee handbook stated, " . . . either the employee or the employer is privileged to terminate the employee." Should Carlisle be liable for firing Stephens?

LO ❸

5. A tenant of the Kings Arms Apartments, Kimberly Jackman awoke to see a man standing in her hallway. He stated he was the maintenance man, sat down next to Jackman, and started rubbing her thigh. She pleaded for him to leave, and he did so. Jackman called the police and later sued the owner of the Kings Arms. Was the maintenance man's employer liable for his assault on Jackman?

LO ❹

6. J.B. Hunt Transport Services, Inc. hired Thomas Hostetler and Vincent McLoughlin to build a new division that turned out to be successful for the company. When hired, Hostetler and McLoughlin had signed an agreement stating that Hunt's methods, operations, marketing, and the like constituted confidential information. Several years later, they resigned to take jobs with Cardinal Freight Carriers. Hunt sued Hostetler and McLoughlin. Did they have a duty to keep Hunt's information confidential?

LO ❶

7. Obstetricians & Gynecologists, P.C. offered Julie Goff-Hamel a full-time job, and Goff-Hamel accepted with employment starting October 4. Goff-Hamel resigned her current job. On October 3, Obstetricians' personnel consultant told Goff-Hamel not to report to work the next day. The wife of a part owner of Obstetricians opposed her employment. Goff-Hamel sued for breach of contract. Had Obstetricians breached the employment contract?

Employees' Rights

LEARNING OBJECTIVES

1 List the bases in federal law on which an employer may not discriminate against employees.

2 Explain the restrictions on employers in requiring invasive or offensive testing of employees and job applicants.

3 Discuss three significant protections given to employees by federal or state law, municipal ordinance, or employer regulation.

PREVIEW CASE

→ Wal-Mart employed Melanie Satterfield as a cashier. She had missed work without reason on May 28, May 29, and June 3. On June 16, she did not report to work and had her mother take a note to Wal-Mart saying she had pain in her side. Satterfield did not have a telephone but drove to a pay phone to call her doctor. She did not call Wal-Mart and did not work on June 17–20. She contacted Wal-Mart on June 28 after she found out her health insurance had been cancelled, and the manager told her she had been fired. Satterfield sued Wal-Mart for violation of the Family and Medical Leave Act (FMLA). What is the purpose of the FMLA? Does saying a person has side pain give notice of a serious illness?

M any federal and state laws, municipal ordinances, and court decisions grant specific rights to employees. However, not all laws apply to all employees. State laws, court decisions, and ordinances vary. Some rights extend to all or almost all employees, whereas others may extend only to those in specified industries. The law is constantly extending rights to cover ever-larger numbers of workers. Some of these rights include rights against discrimination on specified bases, the right not to be subjected to certain invasive or offensive tests, and various protections such as for taking leave, receiving notification of plant closing, and being protected from secondhand smoke.

DISCRIMINATION

LO ❶
Bases for protection
from discrimination

Federal laws protect employees from discrimination on a number of grounds. Some laws prohibit discrimination on only one basis, whereas others protect on many bases. These laws include the Civil Rights Act of 1964, the Equal Pay Act, the Age Discrimination in Employment Act, and the Americans with Disabilities Act.

Civil Rights Act of 1964

The most important law governing employment discrimination and also harassment on the basis of race, color, religion, sex, and national origin is Title VII of the federal Civil Rights Act of 1964. The act applies to every employer engaged in an industry affecting interstate commerce who has 15 or more employees and to labor unions with 15 or more members. It does not apply to the U.S. government (except the Congress) or to certain private membership clubs exempt from federal taxation.

This law makes it an unlawful employment practice for an employer to fail to hire, to discharge, or to in any way discriminate against anyone with respect to the terms, conditions, or privileges of employment because of the individual's race, color, religion, sex, or national origin. (Discrimination because of sex includes discrimination because of pregnancy, childbirth, or related medical conditions.) The employer also may not adversely affect an employee's status because of one of these factors. In addition, it is an unlawful employment practice for an employment agency or a labor organization to discriminate, classify, limit, or segregate individuals in any way on any one of these bases.

When a person sues under Title VII, the discrimination is usually claimed on either of two theories. These theories are disparate treatment and disparate impact.

Disparate Treatment
Intentional discrimination against a particular individual

Protected Class
Group protected by antidiscrimination laws

Disparate Treatment. In a discrimination case on the ground of **disparate treatment** in employment, the plaintiff alleges that the discrimination was against the plaintiff alone and was because of the plaintiff's membership in a protected class. A **protected class** is any group given protection by antidiscrimination laws, such as groups based on race, color, religion, sex, or national origin and protected by Title VII. Disparate treatment is basically intentionally different treatment. That is, women are treated differently than men, blacks are treated differently than whites, and people of one religion are treated differently than people of another religion, solely because of their sex, race, or religion, respectively. The plaintiff must show that the employer acted with the intention of discriminating. Plaintiffs make a case by showing direct evidence of discrimination or by showing four essential elements:

1. They belong to one of the protected classes.
2. They were qualified for the job or performed their job well.
3. They suffered an adverse employment action.
4. A person not in the protected class got the job or did not suffer the adverse action.

These elements vary slightly depending on the plaintiff's situation—that is, whether the plaintiff applied for a job or had a job. But once plaintiffs prove the four elements, employers must offer a nondiscriminatory reason for their actions.

If such reasons can be offered, plaintiffs must then show that the adverse treatment was because of their membership in one of the protected classes—that the employer intended to discriminate.

COURT CASE

Facts: Target Corporation hired Billeigh Riser Jr., who was black, as an Executive Team Lead In Training (ETL-IT). Three other ETL's who were white but not trainees worked Riser's shift. Riser was on probation the first 90 days on the job. At the end of 90 days, Riser was fired for poor job performance. He had a low number of "pulls" (pieces of stock replenished to store shelves), did not conduct "huddles" (nightly staff meetings), and did not answer overhead phone calls. Riser sued claiming he was fired because of his race.

Outcome: The court pointed out that Target had a legitimate, nondiscriminatory reason for Riser's discharge. There was no reasonable inference that race was a determining factor in his termination.

—*Riser v. Target Corp.,*
458 F.3d 817 (8th Cir.)

Disparate Impact. To prove a discrimination claim based on **disparate impact**, an employee must show that an action taken by the employer that appears fair, nonetheless negatively and disproportionally affects a protected class of employees. An important difference between this theory and disparate treatment is that no intent to discriminate need be shown for disparate impact. The action complained of could be a testing policy, an application procedure, a job qualification, or any other employment practice whose adverse effect on employees is significantly greater on the members of a protected class than on employees that are not in that class.

Sexual Harassment. Courts have held that the Title VII prohibition against discrimination on the basis of sex protects an employee against an employer who engages in or allows unwelcome sexual advances that create a **hostile work environment**. A hostile work environment exists when harassing conduct alters the terms or conditions of employment, creating an abusive work atmosphere, and it is based on the victim's membership in a protected class. Economic harm does not necessarily have to be proved. An employer can be liable for harassment by coworkers if the employer knows about the harassment and does not take prompt and appropriate corrective action. However, proper and corrective action by an employer after learning of harassment is an effective defense to a sexual harassment lawsuit.

In order to prove that the work environment was hostile, an alleged victim of sexual harassment must show that the environment was one that an objectively reasonable person would find abusive. This means that any reasonable employee would find the environment abusive. Such a requirement protects employers from overly sensitive employees who, for example, might feel that one isolated comment from a coworker created an abusive environment. In addition, victims themselves must find the environment abusive. A victim who is less sensitive than reasonable employees would probably have to have a more abusive work environment before a claim of sexual harassment would be upheld. If both of these requirements are met, the victim need not show psychological injury—the hostile work environment alone is actionable.

Disparate Impact
Fair policy disproportionately affecting protected class

Hostile Work Environment
Alteration of terms or conditions of employment by harassment

C O U R T   C A S E

Facts: Sgt. Justo Cruz told Officer Blanca Valentín-Almeyda she had nice eyes, pretty hair, great legs, and looked beautiful in the morning. He drove by Valentín's house several times a day and honked his horn. Cruz became upset with her because she did not greet him with a kiss on the cheek. Valentín rebuffed Cruz and tried to complain to the police commissioner, but he had her meet with Lt. Juan Vélez, an investigator. Vélez told Valentín it was her fault because she had Cruz "bedazzled." She was assigned double shifts and given the worst job assignment. Cruz constantly tried to be near her at work and approached her at the mall. He left a note under her windshield wiper saying she was his. When she went to the station house to file a grievance, Cruz, Officer David Ferrer, and Vélez gave her three warning letters about her job performance. She transferred to the state police station, but the commissioner, Cruz, and Ferrer came once or twice a week and the visits made her too uncomfortable to work. She sued for sexual harassment.

Outcome: The court found that there was ample evidence of a hostile work environment.

—*Valentín-Almeyda v. Municipality Of Aguadilla*, 447 F.3d 85 (1st Cir.)

Although many types of actions are prohibited under Title VII, to be actionable, the victim must be affected because of membership in a protected class. Behavior could discriminate or create an abusive work atmosphere, but only that behavior based on the victim's membership in a protected class is actionable. For example, a person could be teased about living in a high-rise apartment, having short hair, long hair, a pierced nose, driving a particular type of car, having freckles, or being tall. Even if they are insensitive or designed to humiliate, as long as a court does not find the comments are based on membership in a protected class, they are not actionable under Title VII.

Successful plaintiffs in Title VII cases are entitled to a remedy that would put them in the same position they would have been in if the discrimination had not occurred. This might include some kind of corrective action by employers, posting of notices about sensitivity training, reinstatement, promotion, payment of lost benefits, and attorneys' fees. If the discrimination is intentional, the plaintiff may recover punitive damages.

The act established the Equal Employment Opportunity Commission (EEOC), which hears complaints alleging violations of this and other laws. Individuals may file the complaints or the EEOC itself may issue charges. If the EEOC verifies the charge, it must seek by conference, conciliation, and persuasion to stop the violation. If this fails, the EEOC may bring an action in federal court. If the EEOC finds no basis for a violation, the employee may still sue the employer in court; however, the employee has the burden of hiring a lawyer and pursuing the case.

Equal Pay Act

Recognizing that women were frequently discriminated against in the workplace by being paid less than men were paid for the same work, the federal government enacted the Equal Pay Act of 1963. As an amendment to the Fair Labor Standards Act (discussed in detail in Chapter 30), the law applies to employers covered by that act. The Equal Pay Act requires that employers pay men and women equal pay for equal work. The law prohibits employers from discriminating on the basis of sex by paying employees at a rate less than the rate at which employees of the opposite sex are paid for equal work. To be equal work, the jobs must be performed under similar working conditions and require equivalent skill, effort, and responsibility.

An employer is not required to pay employees at the same rate if the payments are made on the basis of:

1. A seniority system
2. A merit system
3. Quantity or quality of production
4. A differential resulting from any factor other than sex

COURT CASE

Facts: Nebraska Public Power District employed Lynda Hunt as a general clerk in the district office where Jerry Craft was district supervisor. To save money when Craft retired, Bill Lofquest, the district office manager, asked Hunt assume some of Craft's duties and responsibilities. Lofquest promised to change her job title and increase her pay. Hunt agreed. She performed the bulk of Craft's duties and ran the office in addition to her clerical job. Hunt was making much less money than Craft had made. When she did not receive any additional pay, she complained about it and was fired. She sued alleging violation of the Equal Pay Act.

Outcome: The court held there was a violation of the Equal Pay Act.

—*Hunt v. Nebraska Public Power Dist.,* **282 F.3d 1021 (8th Cir.)**

In addition to its application to employers, the Equal Pay Act also prohibits labor unions from making or attempting to make employers discriminate against an employee on the basis of sex. Although the law was intended to help women, it is written in such a way that it requires equal pay for equal work and neither men nor women may be preferred.

Age Discrimination in Employment Act

In order to protect persons age 40 or over from employment discrimination, the federal government enacted the Age Discrimination in Employment Act (ADEA). This statute prohibits arbitrary age discrimination by employment agencies, employers, or labor unions against persons age 40 or above. Employers are prohibited from firing or failing to hire persons in this age group, and they may not limit, segregate, or classify their employees so as to discriminate against persons in this age group solely because of their age. The firing can be an actual termination or a constructive discharge.

The ADEA does not prevent an employer from ever considering an employee's age or age-related criteria. It prohibits arbitrary discrimination, which occurs when age is considered despite its complete irrelevance to the decision being made. The law allows age discrimination when age is a true occupational qualification, such as the rule that commercial pilots cannot be more than 60 years old. In this case, the age limit is related to very significant safety considerations affecting the lives of millions of people. Company seniority systems are also permitted, even though they may have an impact on employees based on their ages.

COURT CASE

Facts: When he was 62 years old, Daniel Kirsch's employer, Fleet Street, Ltd., changed the compensation for his sales position from a commission that had given him $80,000–$100,000 a year to a salary of $60,000 plus 2 percent on sales over $2 million. Three years before, all of the road sales representatives had been fired. They were all over 50. The sales manager, who was a company officer, told Kirsch that he should watch out because all around him were young people. When a new employee inquired why the company did not expect Kirsch to be employed much longer, the sales manager said the company wanted "younger blood." Shortly thereafter, Fleet reduced Kirsch's salary to $26,000. Kirsch sued Fleet alleging constructive termination based on his age in violation of the ADEA.

Outcome: The court said the reduction in compensation to $26,000 constituted a condition so grim that it could have compelled Kirsch to resign, thus constituting constructive discharge. The court further said age was a factor in the discharge in violation of the ADEA.

—*Kirsch v. Fleet Street, Ltd.,*
148 F.3d 149 (2d Cir.)

An employee who wishes to pursue an ADEA claim must file a claim with the EEOC within 180 days of the occurrence of the adverse employer action. If the EEOC does not find the claim valid, the employee may bring a court action against the employer. A successful employee could recover back pay, lost benefits, future pay (called *front pay*), and, at the discretion of the court, attorneys' fees. In addition, the court could order reinstatement, promotion, or, for an individual denied a job, hiring. If violation of the ADEA was willful, liquidated damages equal to the back-pay award is automatically awarded.

This law excludes from the definition of employee persons elected to state or local office and persons appointed at the policy-making level.

Americans with Disabilities Act

The Americans with Disabilities Act of 1990 (ADA), which applies to employers of 15 or more employees, prohibits employment discrimination against qualified people with disabilities. An employer may not discriminate because of the disability in job application, hiring, advancement, or firing. For the purposes of the ADA, a disability requires two elements:

1. A physical or mental impairment
2. A substantial limitation of one or more major life activities

COURT CASE

Facts: Jamie Lowe worked for Angelo's Italian Foods and did purchasing and inventory control. She presented her supervisor with a letter from her doctor indicating Lowe had a neurological problem and could not carry anything heavier than 15 pounds and could only carry things up to 15 pounds occasionally. She was fired that day. Later diagnosed with multiple sclerosis, for which there is no known cure, she sued Angelo's, alleging the termination violated the ADA.

Outcome: The court said that lifting was a major life activity, so that if Lowe's impairment substantially limited her ability to lift, she was disabled under the ADA.

—*Lowe v. Angelo's Italian Foods, Inc.,*
87 F.3d 1170 (10th Cir.)

It is not enough simply to have impairment and be unable to perform one specific job. The impairment must significantly limit a major life activity such as being unable to perform a class or broad range of jobs. A "major life activity" includes such actions as speaking, seeing, hearing, breathing, caring for oneself, walking, performing manual tasks, working, sitting, lifting, reaching, and standing.

To determine whether other impairments constitute a major life activity, courts consider the type and severity of the impairment, the duration of the impairment, and any permanent or long-term impact of the impairment. Thus, temporary, short-term, or nonchronic impairments with no long-term impact are not *disabilities*. Such impairments include broken bones, flu, sprains, appendicitis, and concussions. In addition, specifically excluded from the definition of a disability are compulsive gambling, kleptomania, pyromania, sexual behavior disorders, and current illegal drug users and alcoholics.

COURT CASE

Facts: Ingalls Shipbuilding hired Tamela Dutcher as a welder and assigned her to a job that required climbing 40 feet to reach her work. Dutcher had had a serious injury to her arm so she requested transfer to the fab shop because her bad arm made climbing difficult. Ingalls denied the transfer because of insufficient seniority. After a month of work, she obtained a transfer to the fab shop and worked until laid off. When recalled for a preemployment physical, she told the doctor she needed a job that did not require climbing. The doctor gave her that job restriction, and Ingalls told her it did not then have a job with no climbing. Shortly thereafter, every welder in Dutcher's job classification was laid off. Dutcher sued Ingalls, asserting it violated the ADA by refusing to reinstate her in her job in the fab shop when called back.

Outcome: The court said her work in the fab shop showed she could work as a welder; she just could not work in a job requiring a lot of climbing. Therefore she was not significantly restricted in her ability to perform a class of jobs and did not have a disability protected by the ADA.

—*Dutcher v. Ingalls Shipbuilding*, **53 F.3d 723 (5th Cir.)**

In addition, a person who has a history of an impairment that limits a major life activity, or is thought to have such impairment, is eligible for the benefits of the ADA. Thus, an employee can obtain the benefits of the ADA not because of actual impairment, but because the employee is treated by the employer as having a limiting impairment.

Once a job applicant or employee has been identified as disabled according to the law, it must be determined if the individual with a disability is otherwise qualified for a particular job. If qualified, employers are required by the ADA to make "reasonable accommodations" to allow the disabled person to perform the essential functions of the job. The reasonable accommodation might include rescheduling employees, raising the height of desks to accommodate wheelchairs, acquiring equipment, or hiring a reader or sign language interpreter. An employer does not have to accommodate a disabled person if the accommodation would impose an undue hardship on the business. Violation of the ADA allows a qualified employee to recovery, such as reinstatement, back pay, compensatory damages, punitive damages, and attorneys' fees.

TESTING

LO ❷
Restrictions on
employee testing

In order to make sure businesses run properly, protect employees, protect company property from employee misuse, and weed out applicants for employment who might not be the best employees, many businesses have tried to institute various testing programs. These include polygraph testing, drug testing, and AIDS testing. The right of employers to use such tests, either on a preemployment basis or on a random or mandatory basis after employment, has been limited by statute as well as by the courts.

Polygraph Testing

As lie detector tests appeared to become more reliable, increasing numbers of employers began using them, both as a tool to find out which employees had violated workplace rules and to screen applicants for employment. As a result of perceived injustices, both because of an intrusion on employees' rights and because of the debate about the reliability of such tests, the right to use these tests has been limited by statute. In 1988, the federal government enacted the Employee Polygraph Protection Act (EPPA). A **polygraph** is another word for a lie detector.

Polygraph
Lie detector

The EPPA limits the use of lie detector devices for preemployment screening or random testing of employees by employers engaged in interstate commerce. An employer may not retaliate against an employee who refuses to take a polygraph test and may not use the test results as the exclusive basis for an employment decision adverse to an employee who took a test. Private employers may not use polygraphs unless:

1. The employer is investigating a specific incident of economic loss, such as theft or industrial espionage or sabotage.
2. The employer provides security services.
3. The employer manufactures, distributes, or dispenses drugs.

An employer may use a polygraph as part of an ongoing investigation if the employee tested had access to the subject of the investigation and the employer has a reasonable suspicion of the employee's involvement. Before a polygraph test may be administered, the employee must be given written notice stating the specific economic loss, that the employee had access to the property that is the basis of the investigation, and giving a description of the employer's reasonable suspicion of the employee's involvement.

If an employer violates the EPPA, an employee or job applicant may sue the employer for the job, reinstatement, promotion, lost wages and benefits, or even punitive damages.

Except for the U.S. Congress, the law does not prohibit federal, state, and local governments from subjecting their employees to polygraphs.

AIDS Testing

With the spread of the AIDS virus, employees have been concerned about contamination from afflicted coworkers. At the same time, workers with the virus have been concerned that they could be stigmatized and even lose their jobs. Because the test for AIDS is a blood test, the test is an invasive procedure, and there are some limits to what an employer can require on constitutional grounds. The

Fourth Amendment to the Constitution prohibits "unreasonable search and seizure," and courts have held that requiring a blood test for AIDS is a search and seizure; therefore, it must be reasonable. To determine whether a search is reasonable, the court balances the intrusion the testing would cause on the constitutional rights of the person to be tested with the interests said to justify the intrusion.

Drug Testing

There has been concern about the ability of employees in certain jobs to properly do their jobs while under the influence of drugs. This concern has resulted in private employers and several federal administrative agencies requiring drug testing of employees or prospective employees. The Supreme Court has recognized three government interests that justify random drug testing. These are: (1) maintaining the integrity of employees in their essential mission, (2) promoting public safety, and (3) protecting sensitive information. For example, Customs Service employees seeking transfers or promotions to sensitive positions, and railroad workers involved in major railroad accidents or who violate certain safety rules are tested for drug use. Courts have upheld random drug testing for employees in order to promote safety.

Of course, because at-will employees can be discharged at any time, employers are free to terminate such employees who refuse drug testing even when their jobs cannot be held to involve public safety.

DNA Testing

As DNA testing has become more reliable it is possible employers might require it of employees for two reasons:

1. To make employment decisions to exclude persons with a genetic "defect"— a greater risk for certain diseases
2. For identification purposes

Many states have laws barring employers from discriminating against employees and prospective employees on the basis of their genetic makeup. These laws prohibit using genetic information when making hiring, promotion, or salary decisions. Victims of genetic discrimination normally can sue their employers for damages. It is likely that more states and the federal government will enact such legislation.

Employees in states that do not have such laws have sued employers for using DNA test results alleging violation of the ADA, the constitutional prohibition on illegal searches and seizures, and Title VII of the Civil Rights Act. Employers should be very careful to ascertain their legal rights before using DNA tests in making hiring, promotion, or salary decisions.

As a reliable method of identifying people, DNA samples could be useful in a number of areas. The military (an employer) takes DNA samples of all personnel to use in identifying remains. The states and the federal government have passed laws setting up DNA databases to use in solving crimes. All states require at least some convicted felons to submit DNA samples to their databases. The courts have almost uniformly upheld the legality of requiring DNA samples from criminals.

Facts: Felons in Wisconsin sued challenging the law that required all persons convicted of felonies to submit a DNA sample for a data bank. The prisoners alleged that requiring the DNA sample was an unconstitutional search and seizure prohibited by the Fourth Amendment.

Outcome: The court stated that the state's interest in getting reliable DNA identification evidence in the database to use in solving crimes was more important than the limited privacy interests of the prisoners. The DNA samples were required.

—*Green v. Berge,* 354 F.3d 675 (7th Cir.)

Many employers who need to be sure their employees are law-abiding, such as those providing security services or dealing with large sums of cash, might want to have prospective employees provide a DNA sample to make sure they are not convicted felons. Just as the military wants to have DNA samples to help in identifying remains, employers of employees involved in hazardous occupations such as firefighters, pilots, and demolition workers would have an interest in having DNA samples for identification.

PROTECTIONS

LO ❸
Protections for employees

In addition to rights against discrimination on various bases and against certain kinds of invasive or offensive testing, employees have been accorded a variety of protections. These include protection of their jobs when a family necessity or medical condition requires a leave, notification of plant closings, and protection from secondhand cigarette smoke.

Family and Medical Leave

In order to allow employees the right to take leaves when family circumstances or illnesses require it, the federal government enacted the Family and Medical Leave Act (FMLA). This law allows an employee to take an unpaid leave of up to 12 workweeks in a 12-month period on the following occasions:

1. Because of the birth, adoption, or foster care of the employee's child
2. To care for the employee's spouse, child, or parent with a serious health condition
3. Because of a serious health condition that makes the employee unable to perform the job

The law applies to public and private employers who have 50 or more full- or part-time employees for 20 weeks during the year. It gives leave rights to employees who have worked for the employer for at least 12 months and a total of 1,250 hours.

Although the FMLA gives workers the right to take leave, it is important to note that this leave is unpaid. Workers also may be required by their employers to use accrued paid vacation, personal, medical, or sick leave toward any part of the leave provided by the FMLA. If the leave is for the birth, adoption, or placement of a foster child, the leave must be taken within the first 12 months of the event. Unless the leave is not foreseeable, employees must give 30 days' notice of a leave request.

A "serious health condition" for which leave may be requested is an illness, injury, impairment, or physical or mental condition that requires inpatient care or continuing medical treatment. Its purpose is to provide leave for the more exceptional and presumably time-consuming events. The care given to another includes psychological as well as physical care.

The benefit provided by the FMLA is that after taking the leave and returning to work, employees have to be given back their previous positions. If this is not possible, the employer must put them in an equivalent job in terms of pay, benefits, and the other terms and conditions of employment.

PREVIEW CASE REVISITED

Facts: Wal-Mart employed Melanie Satterfield as a cashier. She had missed work without reason on May 28, May 29, and June 3. On June 16, she did not report to work and had her mother take a note to Wal-Mart saying she had pain in her side. Satterfield did not have a telephone but drove to a pay phone to call her doctor. She did not call Wal-Mart and did not work on June 17–20. She contacted Wal-Mart on June 28 after she found out her health insurance had been cancelled, and the manager told her she had been fired. Satterfield sued Wal-Mart for violation of the FMLA.

Outcome: The court held that telling her employer she had a pain in her side was "inconsistent with the purposes of the FMLA." It did not advise Wal-Mart that her condition might qualify for FMLA protection, so the court held for Wal-Mart.

—Satterfield v. Wal-Mart Stores, Inc., **135 F.3d 973 (5th Cir.)**

Plant Closing Notification

Under the provisions of the federal Worker Adjustment and Retraining Notification Act (WARN), a business that employs 100 or more employees must give 60 days' written notice of a plant closing or mass layoff. A mass layoff is defined by the act as a decrease in the workforce at a single site of employment that results in an "employment loss" during a 30-day period for:

1. Thirty-three percent of the full-time employees (at a minimum of 50 employees)
2. At least 500 full-time employees

An employment loss is a termination that is not a discharge for cause, a voluntary departure, or a retirement.

The written notice must be given to workers expected to experience some loss of employment, or their union representative, and to specified government officials. Workers in this instance include managers and supervisors. WARN does not require the full 60 days' notice if the plant closing or mass layoff occurs as a result of an unforeseeable business event, a natural disaster, a labor dispute (a lockout or permanent replacement of strikers), the completion of a project by employees who knew the employment was temporary, or certain relocations when employees are offered transfers.

COURT CASE

Facts: Uno-Ven Co. operated an oil refinery under a collective bargaining agreement with the International Oil, Chemical & Atomic Workers, Local 7-517. Uno-Ven was a partnership between VPHI Midwest and Unocal. Unocal wanted to get out of the oil refining business, so Uno-Ven was dissolved. VPHI transferred its interest in Uno-Ven to PDV Midwest Refining, which got the refinery upon the dissolution. PDV hired Citgo Petroleum Corp. to run it. Uno-Ven notified its 377 refinery workers they were terminated, but at the same time Citgo offered to hire them. Citgo rehired 367 of them at the same pay with no break in their work. The union sued alleging that the transaction violated WARN because there was no advance notice.

Outcome: Although the transfer of the business caused a technical termination of employment, Citgo's rehiring resulted in no "employment loss" except to 10 employees. The termination of 10 employees was not a "mass layoff."

—*International Oil, Chem. & Atomic Workers, Local 7-517 v. Uno-Ven Co.,* 170 F.3d 779 (7th Cir.)

In case of a violation of WARN, an employee may sue the employer for back pay for each day of violation as well as benefits under the employer's employee benefit plan. Courts have the discretion to allow the successful party in such lawsuits to recover their reasonable attorneys' fees.

Smoking

The disclosure of the damaging effects of breathing secondhand smoke has resulted in a desire by many nonsmoking employees to work in smoke-free environments. The right of employees to be protected from secondhand cigarette smoke is protected in a variety of ways.

Some employers have taken the initiative by prohibiting or restricting smoking at their workplaces. In addition, a number of states and municipalities have enacted restrictive smoking legislation. This legislation varies greatly. No state law totally bans smoking at all job sites. Some laws merely require employers to formulate and publicize a written policy about smoking in the workplace. Others require employers to designate smoking and nonsmoking areas. Nearly all of the laws have exceptions to the smoking ban that allow smoking in private offices. In spite of these exceptions, a very large percentage of employers have some kind of smoking restrictions in effect.

OTHER SOURCES OF RIGHTS

There are many other rights granted to employees, particularly through federal laws, which apply to large numbers of workers. These laws include the Rehabilitation Act and the Pregnancy Discrimination Act. The rights granted by these two laws are similar to those granted by statutes mentioned in this chapter.

QUESTIONS

1. What is an unlawful employment practice for an employer under the Civil Rights Act of 1964?

2. Explain the two theories under which discrimination under Title VII is usually claimed.

3. What should an employer who learns of sexual harassment by workers do?

4. What remedies are successful plaintiffs in Title VII cases entitled to?

5. What is it that the Equal Pay Act prohibits?

6. Does the Age Discrimination in Employment Act prevent employers from ever considering an employee's age or age-related criteria?

7. Under the ADA, what might an employer have to do to make reasonable accommodations to allow a disabled person to perform the essential functions of a job?

8. When may an employer use a polygraph as part of an ongoing investigation?

9. How do courts determine whether AIDS testing is reasonable under the Fourth Amendment?

10. What government interests justify random drug testing?

11. What is the benefit provided by the FMLA?

12. For purposes of WARN, what is a mass layoff?

CASE PROBLEMS

1. Burlington Resources Oil and Gas Company employed Paul Pippin as a senior engineer when Burlington began a reduction in force (RIF). Burlington sought to retain employees whose past performance reports and skill sets matched Burlington's future needs. Burlington fired Pippin who was 51 years old. Fourteen out of nineteen employees fired in the RIF were over 40. In the ranking before his firing Pippin ranked last among 13 senior engineers. In previous rankings, he was in or near the bottom half of his peers. Pippin sued Burlington, claiming age discrimination. Was this age discrimination?   LO ❶

2. Drummond Co., Inc. employed union members Gary Watson and Cloy Owens. Drummond suspected they had stolen from it and suspended them. The union asked that they be allowed to take a lie detector test. Watson and Owens were told they could be immediately reinstated by taking the polygraph test or opt to have their cases arbitrated. They both chose arbitration. The arbitrators upheld their dismissals. They sued Drummond alleging violation of the EPPA. Should they recover?   LO ❸

3. Info Pro Group Inc. employed Brandi M. Dearth as administrative assistant to Richard L. Collins, president, director, and sole shareholder. Info Pro fired Dearth who then claimed sexual harassment by Collins. Once Info Pro was informed of the alleged sexual harassment, its legal counsel immediately conducted an investigation. Info Pro's employee handbook stated that an employee subject to harassment or hostile conduct should immediately notify a supervisor or the Human Resources Department. Dearth sued Info Pro for sexual harassment. Decide the case.   LO ❶

LO ③   **4.** While working for Jaguar of Troy, Jeffrey Perry applied for leave for the summer under the FMLA in order to take care of his son, Victor. Victor had learning disabilities, attention deficit disorder, and attention deficit hyperactivity disorder. Although Victor took medication and visited a doctor every six months, he could feed and dress himself. He rode the bus to and from school, played video games, watched TV, played with neighborhood children, rode his bike, and swam. Two weeks after taking the leave, Jaguar informed Perry his leave was not considered to be under the FMLA. At the end of the summer Perry, inquired about his job and Jaguar told him it was filled and there were no other jobs available. Perry sued, claiming Jaguar violated the FMLA by failing to permit him to return to his job. Did it?

LO ②   **5.** Louis Aguilera, a member of the East Chicago Fire Department, was randomly tested for drugs. The test was positive for cocaine. Aguilera chose to participate in a drug rehabilitation program. Ten months later he was given a follow-up drug test. He again tested positive for cocaine and was fired. Aguilera sued claiming the follow-up test violated his Fourth Amendment rights against warrantless searches. Was the second test a violation of Aguilera's rights?

LO ①   **6.** James Whitlock worked for Mac-Gray, Inc. After he was diagnosed with attention deficit hyperactivity disorder (ADHD), he was allowed to build partitions around his workspace and use a radio to block background noise. Whitlock performed his work and taught himself to use Mac-Gray's new computer system. He worked for a while but frequently called in sick and finally stopped working after his doctor said he was totally disabled. Whitlock, alleging he was disabled from working, sued Mac-Gray for workplace discrimination and violation of the ADA. Should he recover?

LO ③   **7.** In a three-month period, 562 employees of McDonnell Douglas Corp. were laid off. None of them received the 60-day notice provided by the WARN Act. Of the 562, 50 were part-time employees, 32 were rehired within six months, and 31 elected early retirement instead of being laid off. Leonard Rifkin and others sued the company, alleging a violation of the WARN Act. McDonnell Douglas argued that both the employees rehired within six months and those who chose early retirement did not experience an employment loss as defined by WARN. One-third of the total employees was much more than 562. Did McDonnell Douglas violate the WARN Act?

LO ①   **8.** Albertson's, Inc. hired Hallie Kirkingburg as a truck driver. The doctor who examined his eyes erroneously certified that his eyesight met the Department of Transportation's (DOT) standards. A year later, Kirkingburg took a leave of absence after an injury, and Albertson's required a physical before he returned to work. This time, the doctor told Kirkingburg that his eyesight did not meet basic DOT standards. He applied for a waiver, but Albertson's fired him because he did not meet the standard. Kirkingburg sued Albertson's alleging the firing violated the ADA. Albertson's alleged that if Kirkingburg was disabled he was not a "qualified" person with a disability because Albertson's only required the minimum eyesight standards. Was Kirkingburg "qualified"?

LO ①   **9.** Monica Kindred worked as a school bus driver for the Northome/Indus. School District No. 363. The district reconfigured some school bus routes to eliminate a 180-mile route, the East Route, and eliminate the need to pay the driver, who had always been a male, a premium. The district assigned Kindred a 122-mile route that included part of the former East Route. Kindred asked for premium pay, but because she could complete the route in the time limit specified by a union/district agreement the district denied her request. Another female driver asked for premium pay and the district granted her request because her route exceeded the time limit. Kindred sued the district for violation of the Equal Pay Act. Did the refusal to pay Kindred premium pay violate the act?

10. Employed by Olsten Corp., Mary Ann Luciano had had consistently excellent performance reviews. Olsten's CEO offered to match the salary another company offered her and gave her a written promise to review her performance in a year, promoting her to vice president if her performance was acceptable. Several male Olsten vice presidents and Luciano's supervisor formulated a new job description for Luciano, which would be the basis of that performance review. They designed a job description to ensure unsatisfactory performance. Nine months later, the CEO left. Luciano got a new supervisor, Gordon Bingham, and increased job responsibilities. Luciano never got the promised review. Two years later, Bingham said her position was being eliminated, and she was fired. Luciano's responsibilities were given to two males, one currently employed and the other newly hired. Luciano was not given an opportunity to apply for either position or any other Olsten position. Olsten had promoted male employees with poor performance records to senior management and created new positions for male employees whose positions were eliminated. Luciano sued, alleging gender discrimination. Is Olsten liable?

LO ❶

Labor Legislation

LEARNING OBJECTIVES

1 Discuss the objectives and coverage of the Fair Labor Standards Act.

2 State the five major provisions of the Labor Management Relations Act.

3 Name the three major provisions of the Labor-Management Reporting and Disclosure Act.

PREVIEW CASE

Tim Schermerhorn and other members of Local 100, Transport Workers Union of America tried to enter meetings of groups of members of the local in order to hand out flyers or raise issues of concern to the union. Local 100's executive committee enacted a policy limiting attendance at meetings only to members of the particular smaller group of the union that was meeting unless the meeting participants voted to invite another member to speak on a specified subject at a subsequent meeting (the attendance policy). The executive committee also enacted a policy that distribution of flyers was to be by placing them on a table outside a meeting; members had to request that an officer place the flyers on the table; and a union officer could refuse to place flyers unrelated to operation of the local (the flyer distribution policy). Schermerhorn and others sued the union, claiming that the attendance and flyer distribution policies violated the Labor-Management Reporting and Disclosure Act. Did it? What was the real purpose behind the policies?

Since 1930, the federal government has enacted more laws dealing with industrial relations than had been enacted during the prior history of the republic. Although the scope of a course in business law does not include all of these laws together with court interpretations, some basic knowledge of them is valuable. This chapter covers the Fair Labor Standards Act, the Labor Management Relations Act, and the Labor-Management Reporting and Disclosure Act.

THE FAIR LABOR STANDARDS ACT

The federal Fair Labor Standards Act (FLSA) had two major objectives. The first objective placed a floor, regardless of economic conditions, under wages of employees engaged in interstate commerce (trade among or between states). The second objective discouraged a long workweek and thus spread employment. Setting a minimum wage accomplished the first objective. By successive amendments, this wage increased to a rate of $5.15 per hour. Employers are allowed to pay a lower hourly wage to disabled workers, full-time students, and new employees under age 20 during the first 90 days of employment. Requiring employers to maintain adequate records and pay time and a half for all hours worked over 40 achieved the second objective. An employer may work employees, other than children, any number of hours a week if the employer pays the overtime wage.

LO ❶
Objectives and coverage of FLSA

COURT CASE

Facts: Thomas Stewart owned a business that repaired broken shipping pallets. He paid pallet builders a piece-rate of 50 each for the first 100 pallets repaired each day. The builders recorded the number of pallets repaired each day and reported that to Stewart. Stewart recorded the builders' tardiness and absences but did not keep records of their time worked. Joseph Petty was a pallet builder and had keys to open up the business. Stewart occasionally allowed Petty to work on a weekend, and other weekends he found Petty at the shop and told him to go home. However, when Stewart found pallets Petty had repaired during the weekend, he paid Petty for the work. Petty was paid the piece-rate for most of his hours. He did not receive any overtime pay.

The secretary of labor sued Stewart alleging he violated the FLSA requirements of record keeping and overtime.

Outcome: Because Stewart had failed to keep proper time records, the secretary of labor estimated them by assuming the number of pallets Petty repaired per hour. That number times 50 was used as his hourly wage. The secretary took Petty's weekly earnings and divided by the estimated hourly wage to determine the number of hours worked. Stewart had to pay Petty 1½ times his estimated hourly wage for all the estimated overtime hours plus an equal amount for damages.

—*Reich v. Stewart*, 121 F.3d 400 (8th Cir.)

Exclusions from the Act

The FLSA does not cover the following:

1. Employees working for firms engaged in intrastate commerce (trade within a state). This results from the constitutional provision giving Congress power to regulate interstate, not intrastate, commerce.

2. Employees working for firms engaged in interstate commerce but in a business excluded from the act, such as agriculture.

3. Employees in certain positions, such as executives, administrators, and outside salespeople.

4. The workweek provisions do not apply to employees in that part of the transportation industry over which the Interstate Commerce Commission has control, to any employee engaged in the canning of fish, and to persons who are employed as outside buyers of poultry, eggs, cream, or milk in their natural state.

Child Labor Provisions

The FLSA forbids "oppressive child labor." It prohibits or severely limits the employment of children less than 16 years of age. This rule does not apply to certain agricultural employment, to parents or guardians employing their children or wards, to children employed as actors, or to certain types of employment specified by the secretary of labor as being exempted by the regulations. Youth between the ages of 16 and 18 are not permitted to work in industries declared by the secretary of labor to be particularly hazardous to health.

Contingent Wages

Many types of employment call for the payment of wages on a commission basis or on a piece-rate basis. Many salespeople receive a commission on their sales rather than a salary. For employees covered by the act, if commissions earned in any one week are less than the minimum wages for the hours worked, the employer must add to the commission enough to bring the total earnings to the minimum wage. The same applies to employees being paid on a piece-rate basis. The act allows these types of incentive wages, but they cannot be used to evade the minimum-wage provisions of the act.

THE NATIONAL LABOR RELATIONS ACT AND THE LABOR MANAGEMENT RELATIONS ACT

The National Labor Relations Act of 1935 (NLRA, known as the *Wagner Act*), expanded by the federal Labor Management Relations Act of 1947 (LMRA), also known as the *Taft-Hartley Act*, sought to create bargaining equality between employers and employees by permitting union activity. Specifically, it did this by attacking the denial of some employers of the right of employees to organize and the refusal to accept collective bargaining. **Collective bargaining** is the process by which employers and unions negotiate and agree on the terms of employment for the employees. These terms are then spelled out in a written contract. Collective bargaining requires that the employer recognize and bargain with the representative the employees select. The employees' representative is typically a union. The act also sought to eliminate certain forms of conduct from the scene of labor negotiations and employment by condemning them as unfair practices.

Collective Bargaining
Process by which employer and union negotiate and agree on terms of employment

The NLRA excludes agricultural laborers and domestic servants, individuals employed by a parent or spouse, and independent contractors from its definition of *employees*. Thus, they are not covered by the act. Included are all employers engaged in interstate commerce except:

1. The railroad industry, covered by the Railway Labor Act of 1947
2. Supervisory employees, who are considered part of management
3. Governments or political subdivisions of governments

LO ❷
Provisions of LMRA

The Labor Management Relations Act has the following five major provisions:

1. Continuation of the National Labor Relations Board (NLRB) created by the National Labor Relations Act
2. A declaration as to the rights of employees

COURT CASE

Facts: The Hardin County Board of Education hired Charles Strasburger as an industrial arts teacher, athletic director, and basketball coach. After Strasburger disciplined a basketball player, the player's father won a seat on the school board. The school board learned that Strasburger had been convicted of criminal trespass and disorderly conduct. It suspended him with pay from coaching and as athletic director without giving him notice or a hearing. After an investigation, the board reinstated Strasburger. At the end of the year, the board terminated him saying it needed to save money and he did not have enough students to justify his teaching position. Strasburger sued the union under the LMRA for inadequate representation in his grievance against the board.

Outcome: The court stated that the act excluded political subdivisions from the definition of *employer*. Because the school board was a political subdivision, it was not an employer and Strasburger was not covered by the act.

—*Strasburger v. Board of Education,*
143 F.3d 351 (7th Cir.)

---

3. A declaration as to the rights of employers
4. A prohibition of employers' unfair labor practices
5. A prohibition of unfair union practices

The National Labor Relations Board

The Labor Management Relations Act provides a continuation of the NLRB of five members appointed by the president and confirmed by the Senate. This board hears and, using subpoena power, conducts investigations of complaints of employer and union unfair labor practices. If the board finds that an unfair practice exists, it has the power to seek an injunction to stop the practice. When a strike threatens national health or safety, the president may appoint a five-person board of inquiry and on the basis of their findings may apply to the federal court for an injunction that will postpone the strike for 80 days. The NLRB supervises elections to determine the bargaining representative for the employees within each bargaining unit. In case of dispute, the NLRB determines the size and nature of the bargaining unit.

In addition to appointing the NLRB, the president appoints and the Senate confirms a general counsel. This general counsel has complete independence from the board in prosecuting complaint cases but in most other matters acts as the chief legal advisor to the board.

Declaration as to the Rights of Employees

The Labor Management Relations Act sets forth the following rights of employees:

1. To organize
2. To bargain collectively through their own chosen agents
3. To engage in concerted action; that is, **strike**, for their mutual aid and protection
4. To join or not to join a union unless a majority of all workers vote for a **union shop** and the employer agrees thereto

Strike
Temporary, concerted action of workers to withhold their services from employer

Union Shop
Work setting in which all employees must be union members

Declaration as to the Rights of Employers

The Labor Management Relations Act gives the employer many important rights:

1. To petition for an investigation when questioning the union's right to speak for the employees
2. To refuse to bargain collectively with supervisory employees
3. To institute charges of unfair labor practices by the unions before the board
4. To sue unions for breaches of the union contract whether the breach is done in the name of the union or as an individual union member
5. To plead with workers to refrain from joining the union provided the employer uses no threats of reprisal or promises of benefits

Prohibition of Employers' Unfair Labor Practices

The chief acts prohibited as unfair practices by employers comprise:

1. Interfering in the employees' exercise of the rights granted by the act.
2. Refusing to bargain collectively with employees when they have legally selected a representative.
3. Dominating or interfering with the formation or administration of any labor organization or contributing financial support to it.
4. Discriminating against or favoring an employee in any way because of membership or lack of membership in the union. An employee may be fired for nonmembership in a union when the union has a valid union shop contract.

COURT CASE

Facts: An electrical contractor, 3-E Co., hired Charles Campbell and then Elliot Tonken, a union member, to work full-time on a project. The foreman, Paul Werner, noticed Campbell talking to Tonken during a break. Werner asked Campbell if Tonken was talking about the union, and Campbell said he was. Werner said he did not like Tonken talking about the union at the project and that Tonken would be one of the first laid off when there was a lay-off. Werner showed Campbell a notebook with the names of the first employees who would be laid off. Tonken's name was first. Werner also asked Tonken if he belonged to the union and if he was there to cause trouble. A month later, Tonken was laid off. The International Brotherhood of Electrical Workers alleged an unfair labor practice.

Outcome: The court held that Werner's actions interfered with and coerced employees in the exercise of the right to organize.

—3-E Co., Inc. v. N.L.R.B., 26 F.3d 1 (1st Cir.)

5. Discriminating against an employee who has filed charges against the employer under the act.

When the NLRB finds the employer guilty of any of these acts, it usually issues a "cease and desist order." If the cease and desist order does not prove effective, an injunction may be obtained.

Prohibition of Unfair Union Practices

The Labor Management Relations Act lists seven specific acts that unions and their leaders may not engage in:

1. Coercion or restraint of workers in the exercise of their rights under the act.

2. Picketing an employer to force bargaining with an uncertified union (one that has not been elected to represent the employees).

3. Refusal to bargain collectively with the employer.

4. Charging excessive initiation fees and discriminatory dues and fees of any kind.

5. Barring a worker from the union for any reason except the nonpayment of dues.

6. Secondary boycotts or strikes in violation of law or the contract, although certain exceptions are made in the construction and garment industries. A **secondary boycott** is an attempt by employees to cause a third party to stop dealing with the employer. The third party would normally be a customer or supplier of the employer. A strike and picketing are the most common ways to carry out a secondary boycott.

7. Attempts to exact payment from employers for services not rendered.

Secondary Boycott
Attempt by employees to stop third party dealing with employer

THE LABOR-MANAGEMENT REPORTING AND DISCLOSURE ACT

In 1959, Congress passed the Labor-Management Reporting and Disclosure Act (LMRDA), also called the *Landrum-Griffin Act*. The purpose of this act was to protect union members from improper conduct by union officials. The act contains a bill of rights for union members, it classifies additional actions as unfair labor practices, and it requires unions operating in interstate commerce and their officers and employers to file detailed public reports.

LO **3**
Provisions of LMRDA

Bill of Rights

The bill of rights provisions of the LMRDA guarantee union members the right to meet with other union members, to express any views or opinions at the union meetings, and to express views on candidates for union office or business before the meeting.

Additional Unfair Labor Practices

In addition to the unfair labor practices outlawed by the Labor Management Relations Act, the Labor-Management Reporting and Disclosure Act declares the following acts unfair labor practices:

1. Picketing by employees in order to extort money and for recognition when another union is the legally recognized bargaining agent, and there is no question regarding union representation.

2. To close loopholes, an expanded range of activities defined as secondary boycotts, except in the garment industry.

Hot Cargo Agreement
Agreement employer will not use nonunion materials

3. "Hot cargo agreements," except in the construction and garment industries. A **hot cargo agreement** is an agreement between a union and an employer that the employer will not use nonunion materials.

PREVIEW CASE REVISITED

Facts: Tim Schermerhorn and other members of Local 100, Transport Workers Union of America tried to enter meetings of groups of members of the local in order to hand out flyers or raise issues of concern to the union. Local 100's executive committee enacted a policy limiting attendance at meetings only to members of the particular smaller group of the union that was meeting unless the meeting participants voted to invite another member to speak on a specified subject at a subsequent meeting (the attendance policy). The executive committee also enacted a policy that distribution of flyers was to be by placing them on a table outside a meeting; members had to request that an officer place the flyers on the table; and a union officer could refuse to place flyers unrelated to operation of the local (the flyer distribution policy). Schermerhorn and others sued the union, claiming that the attendance and flyer distribution policies violated the Labor-Management Reporting and Disclosure Act.

Outcome: The court held that the policies violated the law and issued an injunction prohibiting the union from enforcing them.

—*Schermerhorn v. Local 100, Transport Workers Union*, 91 F.3d 316 (2d Cir.)

Reporting Requirements

The very detailed reporting requirements of the LMRDA require unions to file copies of their bylaws and constitutions in addition to reports listing the name and title of each officer; the fees and dues required of members; and the membership qualifications, restrictions, benefits, and the like. A listing of assets and liabilities, receipts, and disbursements must be reported in such detail as is necessary to accurately disclose a union's financial condition and operations. Officials of the

COURT CASE

Facts: The secretary of labor promulgated regulations requiring unions with gross annual receipts in excess of $250,000 to itemize their general receipts and disbursements of $5,000 or more. They were required to specify the name, address, purpose, date, and amount of each transaction. Unions also were required to identify vendors and other entities that received union receipts and disbursements of $5,000 or more. Finally they were required to itemize all accounts receivable and payable at the end of the year of $5,000 or more. The AFL-CIO sued alleging the regulations exceeded the secretary's authority under the LMRDA.

Outcome: The court held the secretary could require the more detailed reports.

—*American Federation of Labor and Congress of Indus. Organizations v. Chao*, 409 F.3d 377 (D.C.)

union must sign the union reports and the information contained in them must be made available to the union members.

The officials of the union must each file a report indicating any financial interest in or benefit they have received from any employer whose employees the union represents. They must also report whether they have received any object of value from an employer.

In addition to the requirement of annual reports by the union and its officials, employers must file annual reports listing any expenditures made to influence anyone regarding union organizational or bargaining activities. Everyone involved in labor-persuader activities must disclose certain information. As public information, these reports must be available to anyone who requests them.

The act also contains a number of additional provisions aimed at making unions more democratic and at protecting union funds from embezzlement and misappropriation.

QUESTIONS

1. May employers subject to the Fair Labor Standards Act ever pay employees less than the minimum wage?

2. How does the Fair Labor Standards Act discourage a long workweek?

3. Does the FLSA prohibit all employment of children under the age of 16 years?

4. What workers are not covered by the National Labor Relations Act of 1935?

5. What does the National Labor Relations Board do?

6. What four rights does the Labor Management Relations Act give employees?

7. Under what circumstances may an employer plead with workers not to join a union?

8. **a.** If an employer refuses to bargain collectively with employees, is this an unfair labor practice?

   b. Name some unfair labor practices by employers.

9. What are the three main provisions of the Labor-Management Reporting and Disclosure Act?

10. How detailed must the union reports listing assets and liabilities, receipts and disbursements be?

CASE PROBLEMS

1. Spectacor Management Group (SMG) managed the Atlantic City Convention Center. It agreed with the South Jersey Regional Council of Carpenters, Local 623 that the installation, assembly, and dismantling of temporary trade shows at the center would be subcontracted only to companies that hired Local 623 members. A subcontractor, Atlantic Exposition Services, Inc. (AES), used its own employees rather than members of Local 623. SMG demanded that AES use Local 623 members or leave the convention center. AES filed charges against AES and Local 623. Did they engage in an unfair labor practice under the LMRA?

LO **2**

LO ③   **2.** Edward Fire, president of the International Union of Electronic, Electrical, Salaried, Machine and Furniture Workers, AFL-CIO (IUE), proposed transferring money from IUE's strike insurance fund to its general fund to reduce IUE's operating deficit. Ron Gilvin, as secretary-treasurer, sent letters to IUE local presidents and members characterizing the proposal as a "raid" on the strike fund, a "reckless change" in the union's financial structure, and an effort to give Fire "dictatorial powers." Gilvin wrote a congressional subcommittee investigating union corruption that three IUE checks totaling $163,000 had been issued without an identifiable union purpose. The executive board was severely critical of Gilvin's letters and suspended him. Gilvin lost a recall election and his job as secretary-treasurer. He sued the IUE, Fire, and the board alleging violation of the LMRDA. Was there any possible violation?

LO ①   **3.** Corrections Corp. of America operated private correctional institutions in Puerto Rico. Union General de Trabajadores de Puerto Rico was certified as the bargaining representative of all the clerical workers, food service workers, lab technicians, social penal workers, and maintenance workers at the institutions. The union asked Corrections to bargain with it. Corrections refused to recognize the union as the bargaining agent of the employees or bargain with it, arguing that it was not subject to the NLRA. It said there was an implied exclusion of guards from the act. Is the company subject to the NLRA?

LO ②   **4.** Local 217, Hotel and Restaurant Employees and Bartenders Union, AFL-CIO was the certified bargaining representative of employees of the Waterbury Sheraton Hotel. New Castle LLC bought the hotel and Waterbury Hotel Management ran it. For jobs in the bargaining unit, Waterbury hired 65 employees, 20 of whom had worked there previously. Sixty-two prior employees, including all the members of the union's negotiating committee, were interviewed but rejected for jobs. The banquet manager told a former employee, hired as a temporary worker and denied permanent employment, "I'm sorry, but we were told not to hire any of the old people back." A student hired asked if there was a union and the accounting director said, "No, there is no union here, the word 'union' has been wiped clear of this place." The union filed unfair labor practice charges alleging Waterbury discriminated against prospective employees because of union membership. Should the NLRB find an unfair labor practice?

LO ③   **5.** Eugene Ruocchio served as treasurer of Local 60 of the United Transportation Union (UTU). In a letter to the union vice chairperson, Ruocchio mistakenly stated that a check received to replace one incorrectly made out to the secretary instead of the local had been for a "drastically reduced" amount. The secretary was the wife of the local's general chairperson, and after the letter was read at a union meeting, Ruocchio was removed from office. Ruocchio sued for money damages alleging the local and its general chairperson violated his free speech rights under the LMRDA. Before the case was tried, the international president reinstated Ruocchio. The trial court dismissed Ruocchio's suit because of his reinstatement. Should he be able to pursue his suit?

LO ①   **6.** Pine Lodge Nursing and Rehabilitation Center sent a letter addressed to the union representing its employees offering a wage increase. Shortly after sending the letter, Pine Lodge posted a copy of it near the employee time clock so employees could read it. The union allowed the offer to expire, and Pine

Lodge sent another offer to the union. Pine Lodge copied this offer to its employees after sending it to the union. The union charged Pine Lodge had violated the NLRA by dealing directly with its employees, thus refusing "to bargain collectively with the representatives" of the employees. Was the publication of the letters to the employees after sending them to the union a refusal to bargain with the union?

Ethics in Practice

Although employers are legally prohibited from hiring, promoting, and firing employees for reasons based on race, creed, color, national origin, and sex, and they may not discriminate against persons over the age of 40 or with a disability, there are still a number of grounds on which employers may discriminate against employees. For example, they could legally discriminate on the basis of height, weight (as long as it was not held to be a disability), attractiveness, right- or left-handedness, and so on. Although employers may legally discriminate on such a basis, do you think it is ethical for them do to so?

Summary Cases

AGENCY AND EMPLOYMENT

1. Jose Mendoza contracted with John Rast as a commission merchant to market Mendoza's pomegranate crop. He harvested and delivered the crop to Rast. When Mendoza got information and documents reporting grades, quality, weights, sales, receipts, and expenses, he noticed some sales were significantly below market price. He alleged Rast pretended to sell the pomegranates but really reconsigned the product to subagents who accepted the fruit without setting a designated price. Rast then used false and misleading documents to hide the amount due Mendoza. He sued alleging violation of fiduciary duty by Rast and the subagents. Did Mendoza allege a violation of duties owed him by the subagents? [*Mendoza v. Rast Produce Co., Inc.*, 45 Cal.Rptr. 3d 525 (Cal. App.)]

2. American Medical Response, Inc. (AMR) had facilities in 35 states including Bridgeport, Connecticut. The International Association of EMTs and Paramedics, SEIU/NAGE, AFL-CIO (Union) began an organizing campaign at AMR's Bridgeport facility. Subsequently, AMR's Bridgeport management had a series of employee meetings and announced it would form "action teams" at all its nonunion facilities. The teams would include supervisory and rank-and-file employees to develop improvements on a range of issues including employee safety and cash incentive awards. AMR said employees would be paid extra for serving on the teams. It set up action teams at all its nonunion facilities. The Union charged that offering to pay employees for participating in the action teams violated the NLRA. The NLRB issued a subpoena to AMR requesting documents relating to its implementation and operation of action teams at its other nonunion facilities. When AMR did not comply with the subpoena the NLRB asked a court to order it to produce the documents. Should the court so order? [*N.L.R.B. v. American Medical Response, Inc.*, 438 F.3d 188 (2nd Cir.)]

3. After creating a supermarket promotional game, Leo Weber & Associates contracted to implement it with four Winn Dixie (W/D) stores. The contract stated each party was an independent contractor. Weber asked George Vickerman to do artwork and other materials for the game. Vickerman hired Process Posters, Inc. (PPI) to manufacture some game materials and told PPI to bill Weber. Weber was the main contact with W/D. Vickerman's contact with W/D was pursuant to the contract between Weber and W/D. After completion of the game, W/D paid Weber who paid Vickerman and gave PPI checks totaling $149,000. Several months later, PPI tried to cash the checks, but Weber's account had been closed. PPI sued W/D for payment, alleging Vickerman was W/D's agent; therefore, W/D was liable when PPI, hired by Vickerman, was not paid. Was Vickerman W/D's agent? [*Process Posters, Inc. v. Winn Dixie Stores, Inc.,* 587 S.E.2d 211 (Ga. App.)]

4. Police officer Lori Ann Molloy heard an officer, Robert Sabetta, complain about being suspended for improper use of force. He said he should have killed, or should kill the people who had complained. A month later, he shot and killed three teenage boys and wounded another. Some of the victims had filed the brutality complaints. The Rhode Island state police asked Molloy some general questions about Sabetta, and she did not volunteer what he had said. During his murder trial, the state police received a "tip" that Molloy had relevant information. When questioned, she disclosed his comments, but the police believed she knew more. They told Molloy's chief, Wesley Blanchard, she was refusing to cooperate. She insisted she had disclosed everything, but Blanchard suspended her. He did not give her the hearing she requested under the Officers' Bill of Rights. In about 12 cases against male officers, Blanchard had granted such rights. He did not even suspend some of the male officers suspected of highly questionable behavior. Molloy sued Blanchard and the town for sex discrimination. Who should win and why? [*Molloy v. Blanchard,* 115 F.3d 86 (1st Cir.)]

5. The Aroostook County Regional Ophthalmology Center (ACROC) had an office policy manual, which at the end of a discussion of patient confidentiality stated, "No office business is a matter for discussion with spouses, families, or friends." It also stated, "It is totally unacceptable for an employee to discuss any grievances within earshot of patients." Four ACROC employees, within earshot of patients, expressed dissatisfaction and exasperation over the inconvenience caused by sudden changes in work schedules and complained that work schedules often were changed. They were fired. They filed a complaint alleging that enforcing the policies was an unfair labor practice. Was it? [*Aroostook County v. N.L.R.B.,* 81 F.3d 209 (D.C. Cir.)]

6. Cathy Jackson consented to sell five lots and to have her husband, Mark, show the property. Mark met with Larry McSweeney to look at the property. The next day Mark was showing the property to someone else, and McSweeney appeared at the property. After Mark came over to him, McSweeney tried to give him a check for $4,000. Mark told McSweeney he could not take the check because he was showing the property to someone else. McSweeney folded the check and stuck it in Mark's shirt pocket. McSweeney left and returned with a friend. Mark asked if McSweeney had already contracted to resell the property and told him he wanted McSweeney to take the check back. Mark said they did not have a deal and gave back the check. When sued by McSweeney, the Jacksons alleged Mark was not the agent of Cathy simply because they were married so he could not have made a binding agreement to sell without her. Was Mark Cathy's agent? [*McSweeney v. Jackson,* 691 N.E.2d 303 (Ohio App.)]

7. Employed by Arneson Products, Inc., Sidney Sanders was diagnosed with cancer. He had surgery during a leave from October 26 to December 2. He then worked part-time, but on December 18 he was diagnosed as suffering a psychological reaction to the cancer. His doctor told him to take time off and estimated he could return to work on March 1. In March, Sanders's doctor said he could return to work on April 5. Arneson paid Sanders's full salary until April 5, but refused to allow him to return to work. Sanders sued Arneson, alleging a violation of the ADA. Arneson claimed Sanders's temporary

psychologial impairment was not a disability under the ADA. Was it an ADA disability? [*Sanders v. Arneson Products, Inc.,* 91 F.3d 1351 (9th Cir.)]

8. Willie Ray Burwell browsed through the Giant Genie food store. He went to the checkout line and paid the cashier the total for his groceries. When Burwell picked up his bags of groceries and started to leave the store, the manager blocked his path and accused him of stealing two cartons of cigarettes. The manager grabbed Burwell's arm and pulled him toward the store office. After searching Burwell's bags and patting him down, the manager found no cigarettes. Burwell sued Giant Genie for false imprisonment and assault and battery. Should the actions of the manager be imputed to Giant Genie? [*Burwell v. Giant Genie Corp.,* 446 S.E.2d 126 (N.C. App.)]

9. Someone stole a guitar, two drum machines, and a receiver from Thomas Martin's home. Martin suspected Christopher DiGiulio, who had repaired electronic equipment at the house and two days prior to the burglary had asked for more work. Eager to recover his guitar, Martin asked DiGiulio to help him find it and said he would pay for its return. The next day DiGiulio told Martin he had found it and could get it for $350, but asked Martin to write a note authorizing him to get it. The note Martin signed said, "I have empowered Chris DiGiulio to recover . . . [the guitar] . . . he is not to be held responsible or liable to prosecution in the theft." Martin gave him the money. DiGiulio went to an electronics business where he got the guitar. He had sold it to the owner for $65. When he returned the guitar, the police arrested him for trafficking in stolen property. DiGiulio claimed he was merely acting as Martin's agent. Was there a valid agency? [*State v. DiGiulio,* 835 P.2d 488 (Ariz. App. Div.)]

10. While employed as a professor of food science and microbiology at the University of North Carolina, Marvin Speck, with the assistance of Stanley Gilliland, professor of food science, developed a new procedure by which lactobacillus acidophilus could be added to milk without causing a sour taste. Both were employed to teach and do research on the use of high temperature for pasteurization and sterilization of foods. It was in the course of this research that the new procedure was developed. The process was discovered at the university, and resources provided for their research by the university made it possible for them to discover it. They sued the university to share in the royalties from the commercial use of the process. Are they entitled to payment? [*Speck v. North Carolina Dairy Foundation,* 319 S.E.2d 139 (N.C.)]

Business Organization

Introduction to Business Organization

LEARNING OBJECTIVES

1. Discuss the nature of a sole proprietorship including its main advantages and disadvantages.
2. Explain the purposes of a partnership and various types of partnerships and partners.
3. Give two reasons why the corporate form of business organization is important.

PREVIEW CASE

Wayne Long, Sergio Lopez, and Don Bannister formed Wood Relo, a general partnership. Long signed a lease agreement between Wood Relo and IKON for office equipment for the partnership. Six months later, the partnership fell apart and closed its office because it could not continue its trucking business. IKON repossessed the equipment and demanded past due and accelerated future lease payments, plus interest, costs, and attorneys fees in excess of $16,000. IKON sued and Long settled for $9,000. Long then notified Lopez and Bannister of the settlement, claiming they were jointly and severally liable. Did Long have authority to settle partnership debts? Was the equipment part of the business? What powers do partners have?

An individual who is contemplating starting a business has a choice of several common types of business organizations. The number of owners, the formality in setting up the business, and the potential for personal liability are important factors that help distinguish the three most widely used types of business organization: sole proprietorship, partnership, and corporation.

Sole Proprietorship
Business owned and carried on by one person

Proprietor
Owner of sole proprietorship

SOLE PROPRIETORSHIP

A **sole proprietorship** is a business owned and carried on by one person called the **proprietor**. A sole proprietorship, the simplest and most common form of business, has a unique nature different from other businesses. It also has significant advantages and disadvantages as a result of the fact that one individual owns and runs it.

Nature

The proprietor directly owns the business. This means that the proprietor owns every asset of the business including the equipment, inventory, and real estate just as personal assets are owned. Although owned and run by one person, the business may have any number of employees and agents. However, the proprietor has ultimate responsibility for business decisions.

To start a sole proprietorship, an individual need only begin doing business. The law does not require any formalities to begin and operate this form of business. A license may be needed for the particular type of business undertaken. However, the type of business imposes this requirement, not the form of business organization. (See Illustration 31–1 for a sample Application for Employer Identification Number form.)

It is equally easy to end a sole proprietorship. The proprietor simply stops doing business. Because the proprietor directly owns all the business assets, the proprietor need not dispose of them in order to go out of business. A sole proprietorship normally ends at the death of the proprietor. Such a business may be willed to another, but the proprietor has no assurance the business will be continued.

LO ❶
Nature of sole proprietorship

Advantages

The sole proprietorship form of business has two major advantages:

1. Flexible management
2. Ease of organization

Flexible Management. As the sole owner, the proprietor has significant flexibility in managing the business. Other people do not have to be consulted before business decisions may be made. The proprietor has full control and the freedom to operate the business in any way desired.

Ease of Organization. Because an individual need do nothing but start doing business, the sole proprietorship is the simplest type of business to organize. The law imposes no notice, permission, agreement, or understanding for its existence. If the proprietor intends to operate the business under an assumed name, a state law will normally require registration of the name with the appropriate state official. These laws are called **fictitious name registration statutes**. In registering a fictitious name, the business must disclose the names and addresses of the owners of the business and the business's purpose. This allows anyone who wishes to sue the business to know whom to sue. A business operated under the proprietor's name, and that does not imply additional owners, does not have to be registered.

Fictitious Name Registration Statute
Law requiring operator of business under assumed name to register with state

Disadvantages

The most significant disadvantage of the sole proprietorship form of business is the **unlimited liability** of the owner for the debts of the business. Unlimited liability means that business debts are payable from personal, as well as business, assets. If the business does not have enough assets to pay business debts, business creditors may also take the proprietor's personal assets. The sole proprietor's financial risk cannot be limited to the investment in the business.

In addition to unlimited liability, a sole proprietorship has additional disadvantages of limited management ability and capital. Because only one person runs a sole proprietorship, the management ability of the proprietor limits the

Unlimited Liability
Business debts payable from personal assets

ILLUSTRATION 31–1 Application for Employer Identification Number   U.S. Internal Revenue Service
(http://www.irs.gov)

Form **SS-4**
(Rev. April 2000)
Department of the Treasury
Internal Revenue Service

Application for Employer Identification Number
(For use by employers, corporations, partnerships, trusts, estates, churches, government agencies, certain individuals, and others. See instructions.)
▶ Keep a copy for your records.

EIN

OMB No. 1545-0003

SAMPLE

Please type or print clearly.

1 Name of applicant (legal name) (see instructions)

2 Trade name of business (if different from name on line 1)

3 Executor, trustee, "care of" name

4a Mailing address (street address) (room, apt., or suite no.)

5a Business address (if different from address on lines 4a and 4b)

4b City, state, and ZIP code

5b City, state, and ZIP code

6 County and state where principal business is located

7 Name of principal officer, general partner, grantor, owner, or trustor—SSN or ITIN may be required (see instructions) ▶

8a Type of entity (Check only one box.) (see instructions)
Caution: *If applicant is a limited liability company, see the instructions for line 8a.*

☐ Sole proprietor (SSN) _____
☐ Partnership
☐ REMIC
☐ State/local government
☐ Church or church-controlled organization
☐ Other nonprofit organization (specify) ▶ _____
☐ Other (specify) ▶

☐ Personal service corp.
☐ National Guard
☐ Farmers' cooperative

☐ Estate (SSN of decedent) _____
☐ Plan administrator (SSN) _____
☐ Other corporation (specify) ▶ _____
☐ Trust
☐ Federal government/military
(enter GEN if applicable) _____

8b If a corporation, name the state or foreign country (if applicable) where incorporated

State

Foreign country

9 Reason for applying (Check only one box.) (see instructions)
☐ Started new business (specify type) ▶_____
☐ Hired employees (Check the box and see line 12.)
☐ Created a pension plan (specify type) ▶
☐ Banking purpose (specify purpose) ▶ _____
☐ Changed type of organization (specify new type) ▶ _____
☐ Purchased going business
☐ Created a trust (specify type) ▶ _____
☐ Other (specify) ▶

10 Date business started or acquired (month, day, year) (see instructions)

11 Closing month of accounting year (see instructions)

12 First date wages or annuities were paid or will be paid (month, day, year). **Note:** *If applicant is a withholding agent, enter date income will first be paid to nonresident alien. (month, day, year)* . . . . ▶

13 Highest number of employees expected in the next 12 months. **Note:** *If the applicant does not expect to have any employees during the period, enter -0-. (see instructions)* . . . . ▶

Nonagricultural	Agricultural	Household

14 Principal activity (see instructions) ▶

15 Is the principal business activity manufacturing? . . . . ☐ Yes ☐ No
If "Yes," principal product and raw material used ▶

16 To whom are most of the products or services sold? Please check one box.   ☐ Business (wholesale)
☐ Public (retail)   ☐ Other (specify) ▶   ☐ N/A

17a Has the applicant ever applied for an employer identification number for this or any other business? . . . . ☐ Yes ☐ No
Note: *If "Yes," please complete lines 17b and 17c.*

17b If you checked "Yes" on line 17a, give applicant's legal name and trade name shown on prior application, if different from line 1 or 2 above.
Legal name ▶   Trade name ▶

17c Approximate date when and city and state where the application was filed. Enter previous employer identification number if known.
Approximate date when filed (mo., day, year) | City and state where filed | Previous EIN

Under penalties of perjury, I declare that I have examined this application, and to the best of my knowledge and belief, it is true, correct, and complete.

Business telephone number (include area code)
( )

Fax telephone number (include area code)
( )

Name and title (Please type or print clearly.) ▶

Signature ▶

Date ▶

Note: *Do not write below this line. For official use only.*

Please leave blank ▶

Geo.	Ind.	Class	Size	Reason for applying

For Privacy Act and Paperwork Reduction Act Notice, see page 4.   Cat. No. 16055N   Form **SS-4** (Rev. 4-2000)

business. The business also has only whatever capital the proprietor has or can raise. This may limit the size of the business.

A sole proprietor has liability for the activities of the business because the proprietor is the sole manager of the business. The proprietor is in a sense the business. The responsibility for all business decisions rests with the proprietor. A sole proprietor may not only be liable in damages for torts committed by the business but also criminally liable for crimes.

PARTNERSHIP

A **partnership** is a voluntary association of two or more people who have combined their money, property, or labor and skill, or a combination of these, for the purpose of carrying on as co-owners some lawful business for profit. The agreement of individuals to organize a partnership and run a business forms this type of organization. The individuals who have formed a partnership and constitute its members are called **partners**. They act as agents for the partnership.

The partnership must be formed for the purpose of operating a lawful business. The attempt to form a partnership to operate an unlawful business does not result in a partnership. Furthermore, a partnership may not be formed for the purpose of conducting a lawful business in an illegal manner.

A hunting club, a sewing circle, a trade union, a chamber of commerce, or any other nonprofit association cannot be treated as a partnership because the purpose of a partnership must be to conduct a trade, business, or profession for profit.

Classification

Several different kinds of partnerships exist depending on the liabilities of the partners and the business carried out. Partnerships may be classified as follows:

1. Ordinary or general partnerships
2. Limited partnerships
3. Trading and nontrading partnerships

Ordinary or General Partnerships. An **ordinary** or **general partnership** forms when two or more people voluntarily contract to pool their capital and skill to conduct some business undertaking for profit. An ordinary partnership results in no limitations on a partner's rights, duties, or liabilities. The Uniform Partnership Act governs this type of business organization in most states.[1] This act aims to bring about uniformity in the partnership laws of the states.

Limited Partnerships. A **limited partnership** is one in which one or more partners have their liability for the firm's debts limited to the amount of their investment. This type of partnership cannot operate under either the common law or the Uniform Partnership Act. However, all states now permit limited partnerships. Most do so because of passage of the Uniform Limited Partnership Act or the Revised Uniform Limited Partnership Act. A limited partnership cannot be formed without a specific state statute prescribing the conditions under which it can operate. If the limited partnership does not comply strictly with the enabling statute, courts hold it to be an ordinary partnership.

LO ❷
Purposes of partnerships

Partnership
Association of two or more people to carry on business for profit

Partner
Member of a partnership

Ordinary or **General Partnership**
Partnership with no limitation on rights and duties of partners

Limited Partnership
Partnership with partner whose liability is limited to capital contribution

---

[1] The Uniform Partnership Act has been adopted in all states except Louisiana.

PREVIEW CASE REVISITED

Facts: Wayne Long, Sergio Lopez, and Don Bannister formed Wood Relo, a general partnership. Long signed a lease agreement between Wood Relo and IKON for office equipment for the partnership. Six months later, the partnership fell apart and closed its office because it could not continue its trucking business. IKON repossessed the equipment and demanded past due and accelerated future lease payments, plus interest, costs, and attorneys fees in excess of $16,000. IKON sued and Long settled for $9,000. Long then notified Lopez and Bannister of the settlement, claiming they were jointly and severally liable.

Outcome: As an agent of a general partnership, Long had the right to negotiate a settlement with IKON.

—*Long v. Lopez*, 115 S.W.3d 221 (Tex. App.)

Trading Partnership
One engaged in buying and selling

Nontrading Partnership
One devoted to professional services

Trading and Nontrading Partnerships. A **trading partnership** is one engaged in buying and selling merchandise. A **nontrading partnership** is one devoted to providing services, such as accounting, medicine, law, and similar professional services. The distinction matters because the members of a nontrading partnership usually have considerably less apparent authority than the partners in a trading partnership. For example, one partner in a nontrading partnership cannot borrow money in the name of the firm and bind the firm. One dealing with a nontrading partnership must exercise more responsibility in ascertaining the actual authority of the partners to bind the firm than a person dealing with a trading partnership.

Who May Be Partners? As a contractually based entity, any person competent to make a contract has the competence to be a partner. A minor may become a partner to the same extent to which the minor may make a contract about any other matter. The law holds such contracts voidable, but a minor acting as the agent of the other partner or partners can bind the partnership on contracts within the scope of the partnership business. A minor partner also incurs the liabilities of the partnership. The states disagree as to whether a minor who withdraws from a partnership can withdraw the entire contribution originally made or whether a proportion of any losses must first be deducted.

ETHICAL POINT

Do you think it would be ethical for a minor to be able to withdraw the entire contribution orginally made or should losses first be deducted?

Kinds of Partners

The members of a partnership may be classified as follows:

1. General partner
2. Silent partner
3. Secret partner
4. Dormant partner
5. Nominal partner

General Partner
Partner actively and openly engaged in business

General Partner. A **general partner** is one actively and openly engaged in the business and held out to everyone as a partner. Such a partner has unlimited liability in respect to the partnership debts. A general partner appears to the public as a full-fledged partner, assumes all the risks of the partnership, and does not have any limitations of rights. This is the usual type of partner.

COURT CASE

Facts: A limited partnership, the Quinn-L Baton Rouge Partnership, was formed to build an apartment complex. The Quinn-L Corp. was a general partner. Thomas R. Elkins was a limited partner. The corporation became the managing general partner. When the project proved to be more expensive than anticipated, the corporation loaned substantial money to the partnership. After construction was completed, the corporation was removed as managing general partner and replaced by Elkins. Three years later, the corporation had received no payments on its loan. It sued the partnership and the partners.

Outcome: The court said that, having become the managing general partner, Elkins had the unlimited liability of a general partner.

—*Quinn-L Corp. v. Elkins,*
519 So. 2d 1164 (La. App.)

Silent Partner. A **silent partner** is one who, although possibly known to the public as a partner, takes no active part in the management of the business. In return for investing in the partnership capital, such a partner has a right as a partner only to share in the profits in the ratio agreed on. Why would a person invest money but take no active part in the management? A person would do this because such a partner gains limited liability and no share of the losses beyond the capital contribution. People frequently refer to this type of partner as a **limited partner** when known to the public as a partner.

Secret Partner. An active partner who attempts to conceal that fact from the public is a **secret partner**. Such a partner tries to escape the unlimited liability of a general partner but at the same time takes an active part in the management of the business. Should the public learn of such a partner's relationship to the firm, however, unlimited liability cannot be escaped. Secret partners differ from silent partners in that secret partners: (1) are unknown to the public and (2) take an active part in the management of the business. Secret partners may feign the status of employees or may work elsewhere, but they meet frequently with the other partners to discuss management problems.

Dormant Partner. A **dormant partner** (sometimes referred to as a **sleeping partner**) usually combines the characteristics of both the secret and the silent partner. A dormant partner is usually unknown to the public as a partner and takes no part in the management of the business of the firm. When known to the public as a partner, a dormant partner has liability for the debts of the firm to the same extent as a general partner. In return for limited liability so far as the other partners can provide it, a dormant partner forgoes the right to participate in the management of the firm. In addition, such a partner may agree to limit income to a reasonable return on investment, as no services are contributed.

Nominal Partner. **Nominal partners** hold themselves out as partners or permit others to do so. In fact, however, they are not partners, as they do not share in the management of the business or in the profits; but in some instances they may be held liable as a partner.

Silent Partner
Partner who takes no part in firm

Limited Partner
Partner who takes no active part in management and whom the public knows as a partner

Secret Partner
Partner active but unknown to public

Dormant or **Sleeping Partner**
Partner unknown to public with no part in management

Nominal Partner
Person who pretends to be a partner

Advantages of the Partnership

By the operation of a partnership instead of a proprietorship, capital and skill may be increased, labor may be made more efficient, the ratio of expenses per dollar of business may be reduced, and management may be improved. Not all of these advantages will accrue to every partnership, but the prospect of greater profits by reason of them leads to the formation of a partnership.

Disadvantages of the Partnership

A partnership has the following disadvantages:

1. The unlimited personal liability of each partner for the debts of the partnership
2. The relative instability of the business because of the danger of dissolution by reason of the death or withdrawal of one of the partners
3. The divided authority among the partners, which may lead to disharmony

Organizations Similar to Partnerships

Some business organizations resemble partnerships. However, they differ from them. These include joint-stock companies, joint ventures, and limited liability companies.

Joint-Stock Company
Entity that issues shares of stock, but investors have unlimited liability

Joint-Stock Companies. A **joint-stock company** resembles a partnership, but shares of stock, as in a corporation, indicate ownership. The ownership of these shares may be transferred without dissolving the association. Thus, one of the chief disadvantages of the general partnership is overcome. Shareholders in a joint-stock company do not have the authority to act for the firm. The joint stock-holders have liability, jointly and severally, for the debts of the firm while members. For this reason, joint-stock companies do not offer the safeguards of a corporation. Some states permit joint-stock companies to operate by special statutes authorizing them, or in some states, without statute, as common-law associations.

Joint Venture
Business relationship similar to partnership, except existing for single transaction only

Joint Ventures. A **joint venture** is a business relationship in which two or more persons combine their labor or property for a single undertaking and share profits and losses equally or as otherwise agreed. For example, two friends enter into an agreement to get the rights to cut timber from a certain area and market the lumber. A joint venture resembles a partnership in many respects. The primary difference is that a joint venture exists for a single transaction, although its completion may take several years. A partnership generally constitutes a continuing business.

Limited Liability Company
Partnership-type organization but with limited liability

Limited Liability Companies. Some states have enacted statutes providing for the formation of a business organization run like a partnership but without the disadvantage of unlimited liability. This is a **limited liability company** or LLC. The owners, who also run the LLC, are called members. The initial members sign an operating agreement or articles of organization, the contract that governs the operations of the LLC. This contract must be filed with the appropriate state office. Most states require two members for an LLC, which may be formed for any legal business purpose.

LO ❸
Importance of corporate form

Corporation
Association of people created by law into an entity

CORPORATIONS

The Supreme Court described a **corporation** as "an association of individuals united for some common purpose, and permitted by law to use a common name and to change its members without dissolution of the association." The law creates a corporation—it does not exist merely by agreement of private individuals.

COURT CASE

Facts: PGI, Inc., which marketed and produced exhibits, and Rathe Productions, Inc., which produced museum displays, submitted a joint proposal to the Smithsonian Institute and managed and produced "America's Smithsonian Exposition"—a traveling museum. By letter, the Smithsonian later chose PGI/Rathe to undertake a market study for $250,000 of the feasibility of producing a self-sustaining international exposition. The letter stated, "This letter serves to formally notify Rathe/PGI that it has been chosen.... This letter also authorizes Rathe/PGI . . . as the exclusive producer." The letter repeatedly referred to the companies as Rathe/PGI and was signed "ACCEPTED AND AGREED" by agents of PGI and Rathe. The proposal they had submitted was titled, "A Joint Venture Report by Rathe/PGI." After both jobs were completed, the parties disagreed about how much the Smithsonian would pay for them. PGI and Rathe decided Rathe should negotiate with the Smithsonian for both. Rathe settled for $250,000 but did not notify PGI. Six months later, PGI learned of the settlement and demanded a distribution from Rathe. Rathe refused, so PGI sued alleging a joint venture and therefore Rathe owed it payment.

Outcome: A joint venture exists when two or more parties engage in a special combination for the purpose of profit in a specific business undertaking, Because PGI and Rathe combined to profit on the Smithsonian's projects, they were engaged in a joint venture. Rathe had to pay PGI.

—PGI, Inc. v. Rathe Productions, Inc.,
576 S.E.2d 438 (Va.)

It comes into existence by the state's issuing a charter. A corporation may be organized for any lawful purpose, whether pleasure or profit.

The law recognizes a corporation as an *entity*, something that has a distinct existence separate and apart from the existence of its individual members. The law views a corporation as an artificial person substituted for the natural persons responsible for its formation who manage and control its affairs. When a corporation makes a contract, the contract is made by and in the name of this legal entity, the corporation, not by and in the name of the individual members. It has almost all the rights and powers of an individual. It can sue and be sued, it can be fined for violating the law, and it has recourse to the Constitution to protect its liberties.

Importance of Corporations

There are two major reasons why the corporation has such importance as a form of business organization. Corporations allow:

1. Pooling of capital from many investors
2. Limited liability

Pooling of Capital. The rapid expansion of industry from small shops to giant enterprises required large amounts of capital. Few people had enough money of their own to build a railroad or a great steel mill, and people hesitated to form partnerships with any but trusted acquaintances. In addition, even though four or five people did form a partnership, insufficient capital was still a major problem. Such a business needed hundreds or even thousands of people, each with a few hundred or a few thousand dollars, to pool their capital for concerted undertakings. The corporate form of business provided the necessary capital from any number of investors.

Limited Liability
Capital contribution is maximum loss

Limited Liability. Incorporation is attractive to businesspersons as a means of obtaining **limited liability**. Limited liability means that the maximum amount an investor can lose equals that person's actual investment in the business. Suppose that three people with $20,000 each form a partnership with capital of $60,000. Each partner risks losing not only this $20,000 but also almost everything else owned, because of personal liability for all partnership debts. If a corporation is formed and each investor contributes $20,000, this amount is the maximum that can be lost, as an investor has no liability for corporate debts beyond the investment. Many businesses that formerly would have been organized as either a partnership or a sole proprietorship are today corporations in order to have the benefit of limited liability. The partners or the sole proprietor simply owns all, or virtually all, the stock of the corporation.

COURT CASE

Facts: As the president of Laurence J. Rice, Inc., Laurence Rice signed a contract by which Rice, Inc. was to construct a building for JoAnne Von Zwehl. Laurence Rice was a stockholder in Rice, Inc. Von Zwehl later sued for breach of the contract and sued Laurence Rice personally. Rice asked the court to dismiss the suit because he had never acted or implied that he acted in his individual capacity.

Outcome: The court said that as a stockholder, Rice could not be personally liable for the actions of the corporation.

—*431 Conklin Corp. v. Rice*, 580 N.Y.S.2d 475 (Sup. Ct., App. Div.)

Piercing the Corporate Veil
Ignoring the corporate entity

Piercing the Corporate Veil. Courts will, however, ignore the corporate entity under exceptional circumstances. When courts do, they say they are piercing the corporate veil. This can occur if one individual or a few individuals own all the stock of a corporation and ignore the corporate entity. Ignoring the corporate entity might be shown by such actions as an insolvent corporation loaning money to the stockholder, by commingling corporate and personal funds, and by having corporate assets go to the stockholder rather than the corporation. Instead of avoiding the disadvantage of unlimited liability of a sole proprietorship and a partnership, a corporate investor can thus be held personally liable.

COURT CASE

Facts: Allen and Sandra Lorenz leased land to David Read. The lease stated that if Read defaulted the Lorenzes could give notice to cure the default within 30 days. If the default was not cured, the Lorenzes could enter the property and terminate the lease. On December 23, the Lorenzes served Read a notice of default for unpaid rent and profits. On January 17, Read orally assigned the lease to Beltio, Ltd., a corporation owned by Arthur and Barbara Struble, and they signed a written assignment on January 20. On January 23, 31 days after serving notice of default, the Lorenzes entered the property and declared the lease terminated. The secretary of state issued the certificate of incorporation for Beltio on January 30. Arthur conducted Beltio's business through his sole proprietorship and mingled corporate and noncorporate funds. Barbara was secretary of Beltio, but knew and did basically nothing with respect to Beltio's business affairs. The Lorenzes sued Arthur personally.

Outcome: The court found that because Arthur ran the corporation as his sole proprietorship, commingled funds, and had no functional corporate secretary, he had personal liability on the lease.

—*Lorenz v. Beltio, Ltd.*, 963 P.2d 488 (Nev.)

Disadvantage of Corporations

In a sole proprietorship, the investor completely manages the business. In a partnership, each investor has an equal voice in the management of the business. The main disadvantage of a corporation is that the people who own or control a majority of the voting stock have not merely a dominant voice in management but the sole voice. If there are 15 stockholders, but one owns 51 percent of the voting stock, this stockholder is free to run the corporation as desired. The stockholder who owns the majority of the voting stock has the ability to dominate the board of directors and therefore the corporate officers. People who invest their savings in a business in the hope of becoming "their own boss" will not find the corporate type of business organization the most desirable unless they can control a majority of the voting stock.

QUESTIONS

1. What are the three important factors that help distinguish sole proprietorships, partnerships, and corporations?

2. Explain how an individual starts a sole proprietorship.

3. What are the advantages and the most serious disadvantage of a sole proprietorship?

4. How is a partnership formed?

5. Can a limited partnership be formed just as easily as a sole proprietorship or ordinary partnership?

6. May anyone be a partner?

7. What is one advantage a joint-stock company has over a partnership?

8. What is a limited liability company?

9. Explain the two reasons for the importance of the corporate form of business organization.

10. When will a court pierce the corporate veil?

CASE PROBLEMS

1. When limited partnership Parsons Hill Partnership built its low-income housing, it was advised by the state that the water at the units contained unsafe levels of Perchloroethylene (PCE). The department of health assigned the water "no drink" status and asked the partnership to advise the tenants. The tenants were not told the status of the water. Fourteen years later, a tenant inadvertently found out that the water at Parsons Hill was contaminated with PCE. Eight tenant families sued Parsons Hill and Yvonne Rooney, the general partner of Parsons. Does Rooney have any liability for Parsons Hill's actions?   **LO ❷**

2. Carol Gonzalez was the sole proprietor of Castaways Family Diner, and her mother, Phyllis Foust, and husband, Ricardo Gonzalez, ran it. Carol did not supervise them or regulate the way in which they worked or ran the diner. They received regular paychecks. Cyndee Smith, a former part-time waitress at Castaways, sued Carol and Castaways for Civil Rights Act violations. The act   **LO ❶**

only applies to businesses that employ at least 15 individuals for at least 20 weeks in a calendar year. It applied to Castaways only if Ricardo or Foust were employees. Were either of them employees?

LO ❸ 3. Jim and Sheila Haff were the only shareholders and officers of J.A. Haff & Sons, Inc., which over a decade bought items from Cosgrove Distributors, Inc. Cosgrove's bills were made out to J.A. Haff & Sons, Inc. The Haff trucks that picked up goods were so labeled as were correspondence and checks sent to Cosgrove. J.A. Haff held annual shareholder meetings and kept corporate accounts separate from Jim and Sheila. J.A. Haff closed owing Cosgrove $9,000, and Cosgrove sued Jim and Sheila personally for the money. Should the court pierce the corporate veil and find the shareholders liable?

LO ❷ 4. The original limited partners of Kanawha Trace Development Partners (KTDP) consisted of Jeffrey Rawn and John Thornton. Thornton withdrew as a limited partner but returned three years later. Although Thornton was not a limited partner, KTDP contracted with William Sloan to do some construction work on KTDP's condominium project. KTDP did not pay Sloan, and he sued Thornton alleging Thornton had signed a guaranty contract on behalf of KTDP and therefore had personal liability for KTDP's debt as a limited partner in control of KTDP. Prior to the lawsuit Sloan had never met or dealt with Thornton. Should Thornton be personally liable?

LO ❸ 5. Robert and Glenn Scott owned Scott Brothers, Inc., although it issued no stock certificates, which operated video rental stores. It contracted with Danny Warren to loan it video cassette players to rent to customers. Rental revenues and replacement costs of any lost equipment were to be shared 50/50. Warren placed 544 machines in 25 stores not knowing that Scott Development, Inc. or Scott Entertainment, Inc. owned some of the stores. Three years later, Scott Brothers refused to make rental payments, so Warren took back his machines, but 311 were missing. The corporations were insolvent but loaned money to Glenn, who did not repay the loans. He had run the three corporations as one entity using the same bookkeeping and management. He sold their assets, and $55,000 of the proceeds went directly to him personally. Scott Brothers refused to pay replacement costs for the missing machines. Warren sued Glenn Scott. Should he be personally liable?

LO ❷ 6. A general partnership, Bamco 18, guarantied payment of a $4.5 million note by Hospitality Associates payable to United States Trust Co. When Hospitality defaulted on the note, U.S. Trust sued Bamco and all its individual partners to recover on the guaranty. Are the individual partners liable on Bamco's debt?

Creation and Operation of a Partnership

LEARNING OBJECTIVES

1 Describe how a partnership is created.

2 Specify the duties the law imposes on partners.

3 Identify the rights and liabilities every partner has.

4 Explain how partnership profits and losses are shared.

PREVIEW CASE

→ The only partners in the trusts and estates department of Breed, Abbott & Morgan (BAM), Charles Gibbs and Robert Sheehan announced on June 19 that they were leaving to join Chadbourne & Parke (C&P). Shortly after Gibbs and Sheehan left, four other members of the trusts and estates department, two attorneys, an accountant, and a paralegal, accepted jobs with C&P. In April, Sheehan had prepared a memo listing the personnel in his department at BAM and giving their annual billable hours, the rates at which BAM billed them to clients, their salaries and bonuses, and other information. While still partners at BAM, Sheehan and Gibbs had sent the memo to C&P to help recruit some of the personnel. Was the information in the memo public information? Would BAM have wanted it to be secret? On whose benefit were Sheehan and Gibbs acting? Was their behavior beneficial to their partnership?

A partnership is formed as a result of a contract, written or oral, express or implied, just as all other business commitments result from a contract. The parties to the contract must give the utmost fidelity in all relationships with the other partners. If any partner fails in this duty, the other partners have several legal remedies to redress the wrong.

PARTNERSHIP AGREEMENTS

The partnership agreement must meet the five requirements of a valid contract as set out in Chapter 5. A partnership also may be created when two or more parties who do not have a written agreement act in such a way as to lead third parties to believe that a partnership exists.

Written Agreement

LO ❶
How partnership is
created

The partners ordinarily need not have a written agreement providing for the formation of a partnership. However, having an agreement in writing might help avoid some disputes over rights and duties. If the parties choose to put their agreement in writing, in the absence of a statute to the contrary, the writing need not be in a particular form. The written partnership agreement is commonly known as the **articles of partnership**. Articles of partnership vary according to the needs of the particular situation, but ordinarily they should contain the following:

Articles of Partnership
*Written partnership
agreement*

1. Date
2. Names of the partners
3. Nature and duration of the business
4. Name and location of the business
5. Individual contributions of the partners
6. Sharing of profits, losses, and responsibilities
7. Keeping of accounts
8. Duties of the partners
9. Amounts of withdrawals of money
10. Unusual restraints upon the partners
11. Provisions for dissolution and division of assets
12. Signatures of partners

Implied Agreement

A partnership arises whenever the persons in question enter into an agreement that satisfies the definition of a partnership. Thus, three persons who agree to contribute property and money to the running of a business as co-owners for the purpose of making a profit, even though they do not in fact call themselves partners, have formed a partnership. Conversely, the mere fact that persons say "we are partners now" does not establish a partnership if the elements of the definition of a partnership are not satisfied.

In many instances, the death of witnesses or the destruction of records makes proof of exactly what happened impossible. Because of this, the Uniform Partnership Act provides that proof that a person received a share of profits is *prima facie* evidence of a partnership. This means that in the absence of other evidence, it should be held that a partnership existed. This *prima facie* **evidence** can be overcome, and the conclusion then reached that no partnership existed, by showing that the share of profits received represented wages or payment of a debt, interest on a loan, rent, or the purchase price of a business or goods.

Prima Facie
On the face of it

Prima Facie Evidence
*Evidence sufficient on
its face, if
uncontradicted*

Partnership by Estoppel

The conduct of persons who in fact are not partners could be such as to mislead other persons into thinking they are partners. The situation resembles that in which a person misleads others into thinking that someone is an authorized agent. In a case of a false impression of a partnership, the law will frequently hold that the apparent partners are estopped from denying that a partnership exists; otherwise, third persons will be harmed by their conduct.

COURT   CASE

Facts: Brent Chastain and Douglas Hillme decided to share the work, profit, losses, and expenses in a cabinet making business "50/50." Both contributed money, tools, and equipment. They named the business "C & H Custom Cabinets" based on their last names and opened a checking account allowing each to issue checks in that name. They obtained business cards and yellow pages advertising for C & H with both their names and phone numbers in them. They drew a flat, equal amount of pay each week. Hillme made cabinets and Chastain did bookkeeping, arranged installations, and ran errands. The first year each claimed half the business expenses and reported half the income on his income tax return. Later, Hillme was secretly removed from the checking account. With business funds, they purchased a cargo trailer and pickup truck with both personally signing the note for the trailer but unknown to Hillme both were titled in Chastain's name. Chastain wanted to build a new shop building, but Hillme objected, so Chastain built one with his own money. They eventually disagreed over running the business, and Hillme sued alleging they had a partnership.

Outcome: The court said the combination of facts showed an intention by Chastain and Hillme to form a partnership.

—Hillme v. Chastain,
75 S.W.3d 315 (Mo. App.)

COURT   CASE

Facts: Under a written agreement, Carmen Allen and Sandy Newsome engaged in business using the name Newsome Carpets. Allen agreed to invest $5,000 and Newsome agreed to invest an equal value of carpet stock, fixtures, and equipment. Newsome also agreed to supply purchasing power, and John Robertson agreed to supply credit backing. The parties agreed to divide profits 50 percent to Newsome, 40 percent to Allen, and 10 percent to Robertson. Eight months later Allen and Newsome signed a partnership agreement that referred to each as *partners* with a 50 percent interest. Allen did share in profits from the business, gave business advice, and signed documents as a general partner of Newsome Carpets. Orders Distributing Co. sued Allen and Newsome as partners for carpet stock delivered to Newsome Carpets. Allen claimed she was not a partner.

Outcome: The court found Allen and Newsome acted like partners; thus, even if they were not, Allen was estopped to deny it.

—Orders Distributing v. Newsome Carpets,
418 S.E.2d 550 (S.C.)

PARTNERSHIP FIRM NAME

The law does not require a firm name for a partnership, but it makes identification convenient. The firm may adopt any name that does not violate the rights of others or the law. The partnership name may be changed at will by agreement. In some states, the name of a person not a member of the firm or the words *and Company,* unless the term indicates an additional partner(s), may not be used. Many states permit the use of fictitious or trade names but require the firm to register under the fictitious name registration statutes (see Chapter 31).

A partnership may sue or be sued either in the firm name or in the names of the partners. Under the Uniform Partnership Act, any partnership property, whether real or personal, may be owned either in the names of the partners or in the name of the firm. To hold partnership property in the names of the partners, the owner should convey the property to the partners d/b/a (doing business as) the partnership.

PARTNER'S INTEREST IN PARTNERSHIP PROPERTY

Tenancy in Partnership
Ownership of partner in partnership property

In a **tenancy in partnership** (also called *owner in partnership*), each partner owns and can sell only a pro rata interest in the partnership as an entity. The purchaser of one partner's share cannot demand acceptance as a partner by the other partners. The purchaser acquires only the right to receive the share of profits the partner would have received. A surviving partner does not get full ownership on the death of the other partner, as is the case in joint tenancy. One partner may not freely sell an interest in partnership property. The personal creditors of one partner cannot force the sale of specific pieces of partnership property to satisfy personal debts, nor can they force the sale of a fractional part of specific assets. The personal creditors of one partner can ask a court to order that payments due the debtor partner from the partnership be made to the creditors. They also can force the sale of a debtor partner's interest in the partnership.

DUTIES OF PARTNERS

LO ❷
Partner's duties

Five common duties that one partner owes to the others include:

1. Duty to exercise loyalty and good faith
2. Duty to work for the partnership
3. Duty to abide by majority vote
4. Duty to keep records
5. Duty to inform

Exercise Loyalty and Good Faith

Partners owe each other and the firm the utmost loyalty and good faith. As an agent of the firm, each partner has a fiduciary duty to the firm, so strict fidelity to the interests of the firm must be observed at all times. No partner may take advantage of the copartners. Any personal profits earned directly as a result of one's connection with the partnership must be considered profits of the firm. If the personal interest or advantage of the partner conflicts with the advantage of the partnership, the partner has a duty to put the firm's interest above personal advantage. This duty lasts as long as the enterprise exists.

The partnership contract must be observed scrupulously. Each partner has the power to do irreparable damage to the copartners by betraying their trust. For this reason, the law holds each partner to the utmost fidelity to the partnership agreement. Any violation of this agreement gives the other partners at least two rights: First, they can sue the offending partner for any loss resulting from the failure to abide by the partnership agreement; second, they may elect also to ask a court to decree a dissolution of the partnership. A trivial breach of the partnership agreement will not justify dissolution, however.

Work for the Partnership

Unless provided otherwise in the partnership agreement, each partner has a duty to work on behalf of the partnership. In working for the partnership, partners must use reasonable care and skill in conducting the firm's business. Each partner

PREVIEW CASE REVISITED

Facts: The only partners in the trusts and estates department of Breed, Abbott & Morgan (BAM), Charles Gibbs and Robert Sheehan announced on June 19 that they were leaving to join Chadbourne & Parke (C&P). Shortly after Gibbs and Sheehan left, four other members of the trusts and estates department, two attorneys, an accountant, and a paralegal, accepted jobs with C&P. Several months before, Sheehan had prepared a memo listing the personnel in his department at BAM and giving their annual billable hours, the rates at which BAM billed them to clients, their salaries and bonuses, and other information. While still partners at BAM, Sheehan and Gibbs had sent the memo to C&P to help recruit some of the personnel. A lawsuit resulted and BAM alleged Sheehan and Gibbs had breached their duty of loyalty and good faith.

Outcome: The court said disclosure of confidential BAM data to another firm to help it recruit BAM personnel was a breach of the partners' duty of loyalty to their current partners at BAM.

—*Gibbs v. Breed, Abbott & Morgan,* 710 N.Y.S.2d 578 (N.Y. App. Div.)

has liability for partnership debts, but a partner must reimburse any loss resulting to the firm because of the partner's failure to use adequate care and skill in transacting business. If the partnership supplies expert services, such as accounting or engineering services, then each partner must perform these services in a manner that will free the firm from liability for damages for improper services. However, honest mistakes and errors of judgment do not render a partner liable individually nor the partnership liable collectively.

COURT CASE

Facts: Dr. Donald Schwartz prescribed Poly-vi-flor for a child, Daniel Keech. The doctor instructed the parents to use the tablet form of Poly-vi-flor. When Keech tried to swallow a tablet, he suddenly choked on it and could not breathe. He suffered massive brain damage. The parents sued Schwartz, his medical partnership, and his partner, Joan Magee, for failure to use adequate care and skill as physicians.

Outcome: The court removed Magee as a party, saying that she did not have personal liability. Any liability Magee had resulted from her participation in the partnership.

—*Keech v. Mead Johnson and Co.,* 580 A.2d 1374 (Pa. Super. Ct.)

Abide by Majority Vote

A partnership operates on the basis of a majority vote. Unless the partnership agreement provides otherwise, the majority of the partners bind the firm on any ordinary matters in the scope of the partnership business. A decision involving a basic change in the character of the enterprise or the partnership agreement requires the unanimous consent of the partners. Therefore, the majority rule does not apply to such actions as an assignment for the benefit of creditors, disposition of the firm's goodwill, actions that would make carrying on the firm's business impossible, confession of a judgment, or the submission of a firm claim to arbitration.

Keep Records

Each partner must keep such records of partnership transactions as required for an adequate accounting. If the partnership agreement provides for the type of records to be kept, a partner fulfills this duty when such records are kept, even though they may not be fully adequate. Because each partner must account to the partnership for all business transactions, including purchases, sales, commission payments, and receipts, this accounting should be based on written records.

Inform

Each partner has the duty to inform the other partners about matters relating to the partnership. On demand, true and full information of all things affecting the partnership must be rendered to any partner or the legal representative of any deceased partner or partner under legal disability.

COURT CASE

Facts: Academy Investors, a general partnership of E.A. Brim, James Williams, David McAllister, and Harry Green, owned land it wanted to develop. Green owned 35 percent of the partnership and was the "lead developer." B.W.M. Investments, a general partnership consisting of Brim, Williams, and McAllister, had loaned Academy money to purchase the land. McAllister notified Green that he was in arrears on B.W.M.'s loan to Academy. Without notifying Green and with partnership funds, the other three partners had the land appraised at $273,000 not including an old building on it. The three issued a "capital call" to pay off the loan.

Green could not pay his $33,600 share. The three voted to sell Academy's assets, and Green dissented. They voted three to one to sell the assets to B.W.M. at the appraised value. Green said that the land was worth more. Without notifying Green, Academy transferred the land to B.W.M. Green's appraiser set the value of the land at $877,600. Green sued.

Outcome: The three partners breached their duty to inform Green of partnership activities.

—*Green v. McAllister,*
14 P.3d 795 (Wash. App.)

LO ❸
Rights and liabilities of partners

RIGHTS OF PARTNERS

Every partner, in the absence of an agreement to the contrary, has five well-defined rights:

1. Right to participate in management
2. Right to inspect the books at all times
3. Right of contribution
4. Right to withdraw advances
5. Right to withdraw profits

Participate in Management

In the absence of a contract limiting these rights, each partner has the right by law to participate equally with the others in the management of the partnership business. The exercise of this right often leads to disharmony. It is a prime advantage, however, because the investor maintains control over the investment. The right of each partner to a voice in management does not mean a dominant voice. With respect to most management decisions, regardless of importance, the majority vote of the individual partners is controlling.

COURT CASE

Facts: The Eastville Realty Co. was a general partnership whose members were Robert Posner and a trust managed by his brother, S. Paul Posner. The partnership agreement specified that Robert was the managing partner. The only asset of the partnership was an apartment building. For tax reasons, Robert wanted the building sold in a likekind exchange, whereas Paul wanted a cash sale. Years of litigation resulted in which it was alleged that Paul was interfering by trying to participate in the management of the partnership.

Outcome: Because the partnership was a general one, both partners had the right to participate in its management.

—Krulwich v. Posner, **738 N.Y.S.2d 315 (N.Y. App. Div.)**

Inspect the Books

Each partner must keep a clear record of all transactions performed for the firm. The firm's books must be available to all partners, and each partner must explain on request the significance of any record made that is not clear. All checks written must show the purpose for which they are written. There may be no business secrets among the partners.

Contribution

A partner who pays a firm debt or liability from personal funds has a right to contribution from each of the other partners.

The Uniform Partnership Act states that "the partnership must indemnify every partner in respect of payments made and personal liabilities reasonably incurred by him in the ordinary and proper conduct of its business or for the preservation of its business or property." The partner has no right, however, to indemnity or reimbursement when (1) acting in bad faith, (2) negligently causing the necessity for payment, or (3) previously agreeing to bear the expense alone.

COURT CASE

Facts: After David Rosenbaum bought some real estate, he and Steve Beilgard executed a partnership agreement to improve and develop the property. They began building a house and took out a loan to complete it. When they finished the house, Beilgard wanted to buy it. While waiting for a loan to finance the purchase, Beilgard and his wife moved into the house. Beilgard made the loan payments. Several months later, Beilgard had not concluded the purchase and, without telling him, Rosenbaum sold the house to another couple. While living in the house, Beilgard had upgraded the appliances. He sued for reimbursement of the appliance upgrades.

Outcome: The court stated that a partner is entitled to reimbursement for money advanced to the partnership that was used in the scope of the partnership business.

—B & R Builders v. Beilgard, **915 P.2d 1195 (Wyo.)**

Withdraw Advances

A partner has no right to withdraw any part of the original investment without the consent of the other partners. One partner, however, who makes additional advances in the form of a loan, has a right to withdraw this loan at any time after the due date. Also, a partner has a right to interest on a loan unless there is an agreement to the contrary. A partner has no right to interest on the capital account. Therefore, the firm should keep each partner's capital account separate from that partner's loan account.

Withdraw Profits

Each partner has the right to withdraw a share of the profits from the partnership at such time as specified by the partnership agreement. Withdrawal of profits could be by express authorization by vote of the majority of the partners in the absence of a controlling provision in the partnership agreement.

LIABILITIES OF PARTNERS

A partner's liabilities include the following:

1. Liability for contracts
2. Liability for torts
3. Liability for crimes

Contracts

Every member of a general partnership has individual personal liability for all the enforceable debts of the firm. A partner who incurs a liability in the name of the firm but acted beyond both actual and apparent authority has personal liability. The firm has no liability for such unauthorized acts. The firm also has no liability for illegal contracts made by any member of the firm, since everyone is charged with knowledge of what is illegal. Thus, if a partner in a wholesale liquor firm contracted to sell an individual a case of whiskey, the contract would not be binding on the firm in a state where individual sales are illegal for wholesalers.

Torts

A partnership has liability for the torts committed by a partner in the course of partnership business and in furtherance of partnership interests. When such liability occurs, the responsible partner has liability for indemnifying the partnership for any loss it sustains. The partnership does not have liability for deeds committed by one partner outside the course of partnership business and for the acting partner's own purposes, unless the deeds have been authorized or ratified by the partnership.

In addition to the partnership's liability, a partner has liability for the torts of another partner committed in the course of partnership business. This rule applies to negligent as well as intentional acts, such as embezzlement of funds, even if the innocent partner has no knowledge of the acts.

Crimes

Courts will not imply criminal liability. In order to be liable for a crime, an individual partner must somehow have agreed to or have participated in the crime.

The individual partners cannot be punished if they are free of personal guilt. However, the partnership has liability for any penalty incurred by the act of a partner in the ordinary course of business. *In the ordinary course of business* means while the partner acts as a partner in the business and in the promotion of partnership interests. The partnership has liability to the same extent as the acting partner. Thus, the criminal acts of one partner can justify a fine levied on partnership assets. The partnership can be guilty of a crime even if no individual is convicted of the crime.

COURT CASE

Facts: Beehive Ltd. Partnership was convicted of forging a power of attorney and two other crimes involving the power of attorney. Walter Burks, Kathleen Patton, and others were general partners of Beehive. Burks and Patton were acquitted of the same offenses for which Beehive was convicted. Beehive argued that it could not be guilty of a crime that required an individual to act when the individuals charged were found innocent.

Outcome: The court pointed out that any number of people working on behalf of the partnership, not just the partners, could have committed the acts for which the partnership was found guilty.

—*State v. Beehive Ltd. Partnership,*
627 N.E.2d 592 (Ohio App.)

NATURE OF PARTNERSHIP LIABILITIES

The partners have joint liability on all partnership contractual liabilities unless the contract stipulates otherwise. They have joint and several liability on all tort liabilities. For joint liabilities, the partners must be sued jointly. If the firm does not have adequate assets to pay the debts or liabilities of the firm, the general partners, of course, have individual liability for the full amount of debts or liabilities. If all the partners but one are insolvent, the remaining solvent partner must pay all the debts even though the judgment is against all of them. The partner who pays the debt has a right of contribution from the other partners but as a practical matter, may be unable to collect from the other partners.

Withdrawing partners have liability for all partnership debts incurred up to the time they withdraw unless the creditors expressly release these partners from liability. Under the Uniform Partnership Act, incoming partners have liability for

COURT CASE

Facts: The general partnership Popkin, Stern, Heifitz, Lurie, Sheehan, Reby, & Chervitz executed a lease for office space with 8182 Maryland Associates, Ltd. in a building to be constructed. Richard Sheehan and all 13 general partners personally signed the lease. Before occupying the office space, Sheehan withdrew from the partnership and its name was shortened to Popkin & Stern. Five years after moving in, Popkin & Stern defaulted on the lease, and 8182 Maryland sued all the partners for past due and future rent. Sheehan argued he was not liable on the lease because he withdrew from the partnership before the lease commenced and before any breach.

Outcome: The court held that Sheehan was liable on the lease.

—*8182 Maryland Associates, Ltd. Partnership
v. Sheehan,* **14 S.W.3d 576 (Mo.)**

all debts as fully as if they had been partners when the debt was incurred, except that this liability for old debts is limited to their investment in the partnership. Withdrawing partners may contract with incoming partners to pay all old debts, but this does not bind creditors.

AUTHORITY OF A PARTNER

A partner has authority expressly given by the partnership agreement, by the partnership, and by law. By virtue of the existence of the partnership, each partner has the authority to enter into binding contracts on behalf of the partnership, as long as they are within the scope of the partnership business. Thus, each partner can, and often does, act as an agent of the partnership. This right can be limited by agreement as long as there is notice given of the limitation.

In addition, a partner has all powers that it is customary for partners to exercise in that kind of business in that particular community. As in the case of an agent, any limitation on the authority the partner would customarily possess does not bind a third person unless made known. The firm, however, has a right to indemnity from the partner who causes the firm loss through violation of the limitation placed on the authority.

Customary or Implied Authority

Each partner in an ordinary trading partnership has the following customary or implied authority:

1. To compromise and release a claim against a third party
2. To receive payments and give receipts in the name of the firm
3. To employ or to discharge agents and employees whose services are needed in the transaction of the partnership business
4. To draw and indorse checks, to make notes, and to accept drafts
5. To insure the property of the partnership, to cancel insurance policies, or to give proof of loss and to collect the proceeds
6. To buy goods on credit or to sell goods in the regular course of business

SHARING OF PROFITS AND LOSSES

LO ④
Partnership profits and losses

The partnership agreement usually specifies the basis on which the profits and the losses are to be shared. This proportion cannot be changed by a majority of the members of the firm. If the partnership agreement does not fix the ratio of sharing the profits and the losses, they will be shared equally, not in proportion to the contribution to the capital. If designated partners fix the ratio, it must be done fairly and in good faith. In the absence of a provision in the partnership agreement to the contrary, the majority of the partners may order a division of the profits at any time.

QUESTIONS

1. Must a partnership have a written agreement providing for its formation? Explain.
2. How can a person overcome *prima facie* evidence of a partnership?

3. Under the Uniform Partnership Act, is partnership property owned in the name of the partnership or in the names of the partners?

4. What can personal creditors of one partner do to try to collect the partner's debt from the partnership?

5. If a partner violates the partnership agreement, what rights do the other partners have?

6. Must each partner work on behalf of the partnership?

7. What type of agreement is required to decide to make a basic change in the character of a partnership or its agreement? Give two examples of such decisions.

8. When the partnership agreement does not authorize withdrawal of profits from the partnership, how can such authorization be obtained?

9. Will courts imply criminal liability to an individual partner?

10. What liability does a withdrawing partner have for partnership debts?

CASE PROBLEMS

1. Consolidated Equities Corporation (CEC) and John Hancock Mutual Insurance Company owned Accolades Apartments Joint Venture (AAJV). AAJV publicly filed a "statement of partnership." Fulton County condemned real estate owned by AAJV, and the proceeds amounted to $200,000. Coyote Portfolio, LLC, which held a judgment lien against CEC, and some lienholders claimed the condemnation proceeds. Ownership of the proceeds depended on whether AAJV was a partnership. Was it?   **LO ❶**

2. Laurence Kelly and Stephen MacKenzie had an option to buy a parking lot. MacKenzie gave Kelly's financial statement to Russell Glidden, the principal of QAD Investors, Inc. The three met frequently, and on behalf of QAD, Glidden invested $20,000. The money was put into an account Kelly controlled. MacKenzie signed a note that recited Kelly and MacKenzie promised to pay $20,000 secured by their interests in the parking lot. There was a signature line for Kelly, but he did not sign. MacKenzie made two or three payments, but Kelly made all other payments out of an account he controlled. The payments became late. Glidden reminded Kelly of the arrearages and indicated he looked to Kelly for payment. Kelly made more payments, but after the payments stopped, QAD sued Kelly. Kelly claimed he was not liable because he had not signed the note, had not authorized MacKenzie to sign it, it was not in the partnership name and not in the ordinary course of partnership business. Was Kelly liable?   **LO ❸**

3. A partner in the law firm Fordham & Starrett, Ian Starr withdrew from the partnership at the end of his second year. The partnership agreement provided that the founding partners had the authority to determine each partner's share of the firm's profits. Starr had been hesitant to join the firm because he did not expect to be able to get a lot of clients for the firm, but one of the founding partners had assured him that business origination would not be significant in allocating profits. The first year in business, the founding partners had divided the profits equally among the partners. After Starr's withdrawal, the founding partners allocated 6.3 percent of the profits to him. The other four partners divided the remainder. In making the allocation, the founding   **LO ❹**

partners did not take into consideration any of the firm's accounts receivable or work in process even though Starr had produced billable dollar amounts of 15 percent of the total for all partners. Was the profit allocation proper?

LO ❷

4. Linda Crouse hired the law firm of Brobeck, Phleger, & Harrison (BPH) to represent her in selling a partnership interest. David Boatwright was the BPH attorney responsible. She sold her interest for a promissory note of $7.25 million. Boatwright did not deliver the note to Crouse. Boatwright left BPH and became a partner at Page, Polin, Busch, & Boatwright (PPB&B). More than a year after the sale, Crouse told Boatwright that she did not have the note. When BPH transferred Crouse's file to Boatwright at PPB&B it did not include the note. Boatwright negotiated a restructuring of the note by which Crouse would receive $6.25 million cash and a $1 million note for the $7.25 million note. The parties scheduled this restructuring to take place in six months. During this time Boatwright made no effort to find the $7.25 million note. The restructuring did not go through as scheduled because Boatwright could not produce the note. When Crouse sued Boatwright and the two law firms, BPH sued Boatwright for indemnity. Boatwright claimed that BPH's suit violated its duty of loyalty and good faith. Did it?

LO ❶

5. Ronnel Parker owned companies Cap Care Group, Inc. and PWPP Partners, which had made attempts to purchase a building. Fearing the seller would be skeptical of any more offers from them, their realtor suggested they purchase the property with someone else. Parker met with Wayne McDonald, owner of C & M Investments, and told McDonald of the offers. They discussed forming a partnership to purchase, renovate, and manage the property. McDonald agreed it was a good investment and said he could renovate more cheaply. While McDonald negotiated on the purchase, PWPP gave McDonald checks totaling $10,000 as its share of an earnest money deposit on the property. McDonald contracted to purchase the property, deposited PWPP's checks in his account, and applied the $10,000 to a $20,000 earnest money deposit since he did not have $20,000. McDonald continued to meet with Parker's employees to discuss the details of the purchase and development plans. McDonald bought the property only in the name of C & M. Cap Care and PWPP sued after McDonald refused to put the property in the partnership. Had McDonald entered into a partnership with Cap Care and PWPP?

LO ❸

6. Stephen Jones, Daniel Fern, and three others were partners in a law firm. Kansallis Finance, Ltd. obtained an opinion letter from Jones issued on the law firm's letterhead. It contained several intentional misrepresentations concerning a proposed transaction and was part of a conspiracy by Jones and others (but not any of his law partners) to defraud Kansallis. Jones was convicted of fraud, but Kansallis was unable to recover its loss from Jones or the other conspirators. Kansallis sued Jones's law partners alleging Jones had authority to issue the letter, thus they were liable for the damage caused by it when issued on the partnership letterhead and within the scope of its business. How should the court rule on the liability of Jones's partners?

LO ❶, ❹

7. When appointed to a judgeship, Joel Aurnou withdrew from the Greenspan & Aurnou law firm partnership. He sued for an accounting of his share of the firm's assets at his withdrawal. A month before Aurnou's withdrawal, a case had been settled entitling the firm to a contingent fee of $200,000 payable in four equal, annual installments. Should Aurnou recover anything from the contingent fee?

8. Bernard Peskin and Earl Deutsch were partners in a law firm until Peskin withdrew. The partnership agreement obligated each partner to "devote his entire time" to the partnership business. Each accounted to the partnership for earnings not specifically related to legal work, such as fees for serving as a master in chancery and salary as a state legislator. After his withdrawal, Peskin happened to find out that Deutsch had filed income tax returns showing income from "legal fees," which had not been reported to the partnership. Peskin sued Deutsch to require him to account for sums received during the partnership existence that had not been reported. Should Deutsch be required to account for these sums?

LO ❷

Dissolution of a Partnership

LEARNING OBJECTIVES

1. List the methods the partners may use to dissolve a partnership.
2. Discuss the reasons why a court may order dissolution of a partnership.
3. Identify those events that result in dissolution of a partnership by operation of law.
4. Explain who should be notified of a partnership's dissolution.

PREVIEW CASE

Alexander Bertolla (Andy) owned 47 percent of a farming partnership and his aunt, Mary, and her son, Michael Bill, owned the other 53 percent. Andy and Mary were the managing partners but, contrary to the partnership agreement, Andy managed with complete disregard for Mary. He signed promissory notes, paid bonuses to employees during losing years, put the partnership into new business ventures, and hired people—all without consulting the other partners. As a result, the partnership lost money for four years in a row. Mary and Michael voted their 53 percent to dissolve the partnership, but Andy continued to make large purchases. Was it misconduct for Andy to operate the partnership without Mary? Was his action harmful to the partnership? Is it appropriate for a partner or partners to engage in conduct detrimental to the partnership?

Dissolution of a Partnership
Change in relation of partners by elimination of one

Winding Up
Taking care of outstanding obligations and distributing remaining assets

The change in the relation of the partners caused by any partner's ceasing to be associated in the carrying on of the business is called **dissolution of a partnership**. The withdrawal of one member of a going partnership historically dissolved the partnership relation, and the partnership could not thereafter do any new business. The partnership continued to exist for the limited purpose of **winding up** or cleaning up its outstanding obligations and business affairs and distributing its remaining assets to creditors and partners. After the partnership completed this process, it was deemed terminated and went out of existence. However, if a partner wrongfully withdrew, the remaining partners could continue the business. The Revised Uniform Partnership Act somewhat modified these rules.

DISSOLUTION BY ACTS OF THE PARTIES

Acts of the partners that dissolve a partnership include:

LO **1**
Dissolution by partners

1. Agreement
2. Withdrawal or alienation
3. Expulsion

Agreement

At the time they form the partnership agreement, the partners may fix the time when the partnership relation will cease. Unless they renew or amend the agreement, the partnership is dissolved on the agreed date. If no date for the dissolution is fixed at the time the partnership is formed, the partners may by mutual agreement dissolve the partnership at any time. Even when a definite date is fixed in the original agreement, the partners may dissolve the partnership prior to that time. In this case, the subsequent decision to dissolve the partnership does not bind the partnership unless all the partners consent to the dissolution.

Sometimes the parties do not fix a date for dissolving the partnership, but the agreement sets forth a particular purpose of the partnership, such as the construction of a specified building. In this event, the partnership is dissolved as soon as the purpose has been achieved.

Withdrawal or Alienation

The withdrawal of one partner at any time and for any reason unless wrongful historically dissolved the partnership. There is no prescribed form for withdrawal. A partner can withdraw merely by informing the other partners of the withdrawal. In a partnership for a definite term, any partner has the power, but not the right, to withdraw at any time. A withdrawing partner has liability for any loss sustained by the other partners because of the withdrawal. If the partnership agreement does not set a dissolution date, a partner may withdraw at will without liability. After creditors are paid, the withdrawing partner is entitled to receive capital, undistributed profits, and repayment of any loans to the partnership.

If the partnership agreement or a subsequent agreement sets a dissolution date, the withdrawing partner breaches the contract by withdrawing prior to the agreed date. When a partner withdraws in violation of agreement, the withdrawal is wrongful and damages suffered by the firm may be deducted from that partner's distributive share of the assets of the partnership.

Similar to withdrawal, the sale of a partner's interest either by a voluntary sale or an involuntary sale to satisfy personal creditors does not of itself dissolve the partnership. But the purchaser does not become a partner by purchase, as the remaining partners cannot be compelled to accept as a partner anyone who might be *persona non grata* to them. The buying partner has a right to the capital and profits of the withdrawing partner but not a right to participate in the management.

Expulsion

The partnership agreement may, and should, contain a clause providing for the expulsion of a member, especially if the partnership has more than two members. This clause should spell out clearly the acts for which a member may be expelled and the method of settlement for such a partner's interest. A partnership may not expell a partner for self-gain. The partnership agreement should also set forth that the remaining partners agree to continue the business upon expulsion of a partner; otherwise, it might be necessary to wind up the partnership business and distribute all the assets to the creditors and partners, thereby terminating the partnership's existence.

C O U R T   C A S E

Facts: In accordance with a clause in the partnership agreement, the executive committee of a large law firm expelled a partner, Philip Heller. Heller had produced little more than half the expected billable hours a year for the firm. The firm lost a potential client because Heller made a proposal to it that differed from a proposal made by another partner Heller knew was working with the prospective client. Heller also wrote an off-color letter to the executive vice president of Bank of America, one of the firm's most important clients. A few days later, Heller sent an off-color story to him. The bank called the firm to indicate it would use another firm if such mailings did not stop. A member of the firm's executive committee told Heller not to send anything more to the bank, not even an apology. Heller sent an apology and the firm expelled him. Heller sued the firm.

Outcome: The court held that Heller's expulsion was not for self-gain and therefore was valid.

—Heller v. Pillsbury Madison & Sutro,
58 Cal. Rptr. 2d 336 (Cal. App.)

DISSOLUTION BY COURT DECREE

LO **2**
Court-ordered
dissolution

Under certain circumstances a court may issue a decree dissolving a partnership. The chief reasons justifying such a decree include:

1. Insanity of a partner
2. Incapacity
3. Misconduct
4. Futility

Insanity of a Partner

A partner may obtain a decree of dissolution when a court declares another partner insane or of unsound mind.

Incapacity of a Partner

If a partner develops an incapacity that makes it impossible for that partner to perform the services to the partnership that the partnership agreement contemplated, a petition may be filed to terminate the partnership on that ground. A member of an accounting firm who goes blind would probably be incapacitated to the extent of justifying dissolution. The court, not the partners, must be the judge in each case as to whether or not the partnership should be dissolved. As a rule, the incapacity must be permanent, not temporary, to justify a court decree dissolving the partnership. A temporary inability of one partner to perform duties constitutes one of the risks that the other partners assumed when they formed the partnership.

A question may arise as to whether an illness or other condition causing a partner's inability to perform duties is temporary or not. The safest procedure is for the remaining partners to seek a court order determining the matter.

Misconduct

If one member of a partnership engages in misconduct prejudicial to the successful continuance of the business, the court may, on proper application, decree a dissolution of the partnership. Such misconduct includes habitual drunkenness, dishonesty, persistent violation of the partnership agreement, irreconcilable discord among the partners as to major matters, and abandonment of the business by a partner.

PREVIEW CASE REVISITED

Facts: Alexander Bertolla (Andy) owned 47 percent of a farming partnership and his aunt, Mary, and her son, Michael Bill, owned the other 53 percent. Andy and Mary were the managing partners but, contrary to the partnership agreement, Andy managed with complete disregard for Mary. He signed promissory notes, paid bonuses to employees during losing years, put the partnership into new business ventures, and hired people—all without consulting the other partners. As a result, the partnership lost money for four years in a row. Mary and Michael voted their 53 percent to dissolve the partnership, but Andy continued to make large purchases. They sued for dissolution based on Andy's misconduct.

Outcome: Because the law permitted dissolution of a partnership for a partner's persistently breaching the partnership agreement, the court dissolved the partnership.

—*Bertolla v. Bill*, 774 So. 2d 497 (Ala.)

Futility

All business partnerships are conducted for the purpose of making a profit. If this objective clearly cannot be achieved, the court may decree dissolution. One partner cannot compel the other members to assume continued losses after the success of the business becomes highly improbable and further operation appears futile. A temporarily unprofitable operation does not justify dissolution. A court will issue a decree of dissolution only when the objective reasonably appears impossible to attain.

DISSOLUTION BY OPERATION OF LAW

Under certain well-defined circumstances, a partnership will be dissolved by operation of law; that is to say, it will be dissolved immediately on the happening of the specified event. No decree of the court is necessary to dissolve the partnership. The most common examples include:

LO ❸
Events resulting in dissolution by operation of law

1. Death
2. Bankruptcy
3. Illegality

Death

The death of one member of a partnership automatically dissolves the partnership unless the agreement provides it shall not be dissolved. A representative of the deceased may act to protect the interest of the heirs but cannot act as a partner. This is true even when the partnership agreement provides that the partnership is not to be dissolved by the death of a member. The representative receives the deceased partner's share of the partnership's profits.

The partnership agreement can provide for an orderly process of dissolution upon the death of a member. Thus, a provision that the surviving partners shall have 12 months in which to liquidate the firm and pay the deceased partner's share to the heirs is binding.

Bankruptcy

Persons who have their debts discharged in bankruptcy no longer have responsibility for paying most of their debts, including those connected with the partnership. This destroys the unlimited liability of the partner that could otherwise exist, and the partner is not a good credit risk. Because of this, the law regards bankruptcy of a partner as automatically terminating the partnership. The trustee in bankruptcy has the right to assume control of the debtor partner's share of the partnership business, but the trustee does not become a partner. The trustee merely stands in the place of the partner to see that the creditors' interests are protected.

The bankruptcy of the partnership also terminates the partnership. The partnership cannot continue doing business when in the course of the bankruptcy proceeding all of its assets have been distributed to pay its creditors.

Illegality

Some types of business are legal when undertaken, but because of a change in the law, they later become illegal. If a partnership is formed to conduct a lawful business and later this type of business becomes illegal, the partnership is automatically dissolved. A law restricting operating an insurance underwriting business to corporations dissolves a partnership formed for this purpose.

EFFECTS OF DISSOLUTION

Historically dissolution terminated the right of the partnership to exist unless there was an agreement to the contrary and had to be followed by the winding up of the business. Existing contracts could be performed. New contracts could not be made, except for minor contracts that were reasonably necessary for completion of existing contracts in a commercially reasonable manner. If part of the assets of the firm were goods in process, and additional raw materials had to be purchased before the goods in process could be converted into finished goods, these raw materials could be purchased.

The Revised Uniform Partnership Act mitigated these rules so that unless otherwise provided in the partnership agreement, a partnership may be continued when a partner departs if the remaining partners decide to buy out the departing partner's share. The power to buy out a departing partner does not even have to be expressly included in the partnership agreement. The remaining partners simply have to choose to buy out the departing partner.

After dissolution, a third person making a contract with the partnership stands in much the same position as a person dealing with an agent whose authority has been revoked by the principal. If the transaction relates to winding up the business, the transaction is authorized and binds the partnership and all partners just as though dissolution had not occurred. If the contract constitutes new business, it is not authorized, and the liability of the partnership and of the individual contracting partner depends on whether notice of dissolution has been properly given. Dissolution does not relieve the partners of their duties to each other. These duties remain until they wind up the business.

NOTICE OF DISSOLUTION

When a partnership is dissolved, creditors and other third parties who have done business with the old firm may not know the change. For the protection of these third parties, the law requires that when dissolution is caused by an act of the parties, third persons who have done business with the firm must be given notice of the dissolution. If notice is not given, every member of the old firm may be held liable for the acts of the former partners that are committed within the scope of the business.

LO ❹
Notification of dissolution

A partnership usually gives notice to customers and creditors by mail. It is sufficient to give the general public notice by publication, such as in a newspaper. When a new partnership or corporation has been organized to continue the business after dissolution and termination of the original partnership, the notice of dissolution will also set forth this information as a matter of advertising. If the name of the dissolved partnership included the name of a withdrawing partner, this name should be removed from the firm name on all stationery so that the firm will no longer be liable for the contracts or torts of that person.

Because a partnership exists as a result of the agreement of the parties to jointly operate a business, if one partner no longer agrees to operate the business, courts have held dissolution of the partnership occurs. However, courts have required the partner who no longer wishes to operate the business to notify the other partners. Until such notice is given, the partnership will be held to continue.

Notice of dissolution is usually not deemed necessary:

1. When the partnership was dissolved by the operation of law
2. When the partnership was dissolved by a judicial decree
3. When a dormant or a secret partner retires

DISTRIBUTION OF ASSETS

After the dissolution of a partnership, the partners share in the assets remaining after payment of the debts to creditors. The distribution of the remaining assets among the partners is usually made in the following order:

1. Partners who have advanced money to the firm or have incurred liabilities in its behalf are entitled to reimbursement.

2. Each partner is next entitled to the return of the capital that was contributed to the partnership.

3. Remaining assets are distributed equally, unless a provision in the partnership contract specifies an unequal distribution.

When a firm sustains a loss, the partners will share the loss equally, unless the partnership agreement provides to the contrary.

QUESTIONS

1. What is the dissolution of a partnership?
2. When may partners fix the time the partnership relation will cease?
3. What are the consequences to a partner who withdraws prior the term specified in the partnership agreement?
4. What should the expulsion clause of a partnership agreement contain?
5. Does the temporary incapacity of a partner justify a court decree dissolving the partnership?
6. Explain when a court will decree dissolution of a partnership for misconduct.
7. Does the death of a partner always dissolve a partnership?
8. Does the trustee in bankruptcy of a partner become a partner?
9. After dissolution of a partnership, what is the position of a third person making a contact with the partnership?
10. What is the potential liability if notice of dissolution is not given to third persons who have done business with the partnership?

CASE PROBLEMS

LO ❹ 1. Notre Dame Properties (NDP), a general partnership of Maurice Bourgeois and Dennis Proulx, owned property on Laval Street on which Maurice's wife, Irene, held a second mortgage of $120,000. Maurice and Dennis signed a $4,000,000 note to a bank to purchase other real estate for NDP. The bank sued Maurice and Dennis when payments were overdue. Dennis settled by assigning his one-half interest in NDP. Later, Maurice and Dennis's relationship soured, and Maurice stopped participating in NDP. Dennis filed documents with the state withdrawing Maurice as a partner, but they both continued to equally share the profits from the Laval Street property. Maurice finally settled the bank's suit by executing another note and assigning his one-half interest in NDP. Then Irene sued Maurice and Dennis to collect on her second mortgage. Irene received a $60,000 note from Dennis, and Maurice transferred his interest in NDP to Dennis. A lawsuit ensued, and the court had to decide if and when NDP was dissolved. Was it dissolved and, if so, when?

LO ❶ 2. Richard Fischer and his son, Todd Fischer, formed a partnership, T & D Enterprises, with the purpose of "purchasing, leasing, and selling of real estate at 8415 U.S. 42, Florence, Kentucky." On the death of a partner, the surviving partner had to purchase the deceased partner's interest for $50,000. T & D bought the property, and subsequently Richard learned he was terminally ill. His share of the partnership was worth $200,000, but if he died a partner, Todd would buy it for $50,000. Richard's lawyer wrote Todd that Richard was exercising his right to dissolve the partnership because no definite term or particular undertaking had been specified. Richard died and his widow, Todd's stepmother, sued alleging Richard had dissolved the partnership prior to his death. Had he?

3. The Gast & Peters (G&P) partnership composed of attorneys William Gast and Paul Peters merged with Schmid, Mooney & Frederick (SM&F). The merger agreement required pending contingent fee cases to be valued by G&P and SM&F on the date of merger with percentages of the fees apportioned between the firms. The percentages of the fees would become "vested" in G&P and SM&F. When Gast and Peters left SM&F, two cases, *Yager* and *Stenson,* had not been concluded. Gast worked on *Yager* with his new firm, Gast, Ratz & Gutierrez (GR&G), and received a fee of $97,892. According to the merger agreement, 60 percent of the fee, or $58,735, was to go to G&P and 40 percent to SM&F. But Gast and GR&G paid only 24 percent, $23,494, to G&P. Peters kept the *Stenson* file when he left SM&F. G&P was entitled to 88.75 percent, or $74,032, of the Stenson fee, and SM&F issued a check for that amount to G&P. Peters deposited the check in a G&P account and told Gast since they each shared equally in G&P, he was taking 50 percent, or $37,016. Peters said he was withholding $17,620 from Gast's 50 percent share because Peters had been underpaid by that amount from the *Yager* fees. Gast sued saying he was entitled to the $17,620. Peters alleged dissolution of G&P had not relieved Gast of his obligation to properly account for profits of the firm, which he did not do when disbursing the *Yager* fees. Who is correct? **LO ❸**

4. Albert Heyward with Frank Norris, John Popp, Scott Strohecker, and William Taylor formed a partnership to buy a ministorage facility. The facility started losing money the next year, and the following year each partner had to contribute money to fund the losses in the percentage of his ownership interest. The next year the facility was offered for sale. A year later Heyward told the other partners he could not put in any more money and was withdrawing from the partnership. The other partners sent Heyward a letter saying, "Pursuant to Article VIII of the . . . partnership agreement, enclosed herewith is a copy of our election to continue the partnership business." Article VIII stated, "The death, insanity, bankruptcy, or withdrawal from the partnership of any partner . . . shall dissolve the partnership unless . . . the remaining partners shall elect to continue the partnership business . . . by notice . . . to each partner." They then sued Heyward. Had Heyward withdrawn from the partnership? **LO ❶**

5. Joseph Creel, Arnold Lilly, and Roy Altizer formed a partnership. Their agreement stated that at termination "the assets, liabilities, and income . . . shall be ascertained: [and] the remaining . . . profits will be distributed." It also provided that "Upon the death . . . of a partner, his share will go to his estate." Without telling Lilly and Altizer, Creel changed the account so only he had the right to sign partnership checks. Creel died and the court appointed Mrs. Creel to handle his estate. Lilly and Altizer conducted an inventory and had a statement of assets, liabilities, and income prepared. They asked Mrs. Creel to release the funds in the partnership account so they could pay debts and wind up the partnership affairs. When she refused, they sued her. She claimed the partnership assets had to be liquidated. Did they? **LO ❸**

6. A partner in the Washington, D.C., office of Butler & Binion, Collette Bohatch received internal firm reports about billing. The reports made her concerned that John McDonald, the managing partner of the office, engaged in overbilling **LO ❶**

of Pennzoil, the office's major client. Bohatch told Louis Paine, the firm's managing partner, who said he would investigate. Two days later, Bohatch repeated her concerns to Paine and two other members of the firm's management committee. They investigated Bohatch's concerns. Pennzoil's contact with the firm said Pennzoil had no complaint with the bills. Paine told Bohatch the investigation uncovered no basis for her complaints and the firm expelled her. She sued alleging that although the partnership agreement provided for expulsion, she should not be expelled for reporting possible overbilling. Could the firm expel her without liability?

LO ❷   7. FBI Foods, Ltd. and Green Apple Partnership formed a joint venture, Granny Apple Associates, to grow apples in South Carolina for 50 years. Green was to handle day-to-day administration while FBI was exclusively responsible for marketing the fruit. Granny bought land and planted apple trees. For several years, there was no crop. The first crop yielded only two truckloads, which FBI sold to wholesalers on consignment. Green alleged that this marketing violated the marketing agreement and that FBI did not remit the proceeds promptly. Green notified FBI that the marketing agreement was terminated for material breach. FBI denied the breach. When the next apple crop was ready for packing, FBI told the farm the packing standard to follow. Boxes packed to the standard were sold to chain stores, the most desirable market. But farm personnel lowered the standard. The chains rejected that fruit and the venture had to sell it on consignment for much lower prices. Green claimed these consignment sales violated the agreement. Green sued for dissolution of the venture, alleging that it was economically nonviable. Based on testimony of its expert that assumed higher costs than actually experienced, it argued that the venture had a negative value and could not operate at a profit for two more years. FBI's expert used actual costs and a realistic discount rate to find a positive value for the venture. Using partnership principles, should the venture be dissolved for futility?

Nature of a Corporation

LEARNING OBJECTIVES

❶ List the different classifications and kinds of corporations.

❷ Discuss how a corporation is formed and potential promoter liability.

❸ Name the types of powers a corporation has and the significance of *ultra vires* contracts.

PREVIEW CASE

→ Coosa Valley Electric Cooperative, Inc., a not-for-profit corporation formed to provide electric service to its members, incorporated Coosa Valley Propane Services, Inc. Coosa Propane bought all the stock of DeKalb County LP Gas Co., Inc. Coosa Electric, Coosa Propane, and DeKalb then chose the same officers and directors. A group of propane dealers sued the companies, alleging Coosa Electric did not have the authority to operate a propane business. Coosa Electric argued the propane dealers had no right to contest the power of Coosa Electric to acquire DeKalb's stock. One of the propane dealers, Suburban Gas, was a member of Coosa Electric. What does it mean to be a member of a not-for-profit corporation? What powers does a member have?

Corporations have become a widely used form of business organization. No matter what the size of a business, a corporation may be formed to run it. Because of the variety of uses to which corporations may be put, there are different types of corporations. They are also classified by the state of incorporation because, as an entity of the state, its laws of incorporation govern them.

CLASSIFICATION BY PURPOSE

Corporations may be classified according to their purpose or function as public or private.

LO ❶
Types of corporations

Public Corporations

A **public corporation** is one formed to carry out some governmental function. Examples of public corporations include a city, a state university, and a public

Public Corporation
One formed for governmental function

hospital. The powers and functions of public corporations may be much greater than those of private corporations conducted for profit. Public corporations may, for example, have the power to levy taxes, impose fines, and condemn property. Public corporations are created by the state primarily for the purpose of facilitating the administration of governmental functions.

Some public bodies, such as school boards, boards of county commissioners, and similar bodies, are not true public corporations but have many similar powers. Such powers include the right to sue and be sued; the power to own, buy, and sell property; and the power to sign other contracts as an entity. These bodies are called **quasi public corporations**, *quasi* meaning "as if" or "in the nature of."

Quasi Public Corporation
Public body with powers similar to corporations

Private Corporations

Private corporations are those formed by private individuals to perform some nongovernmental function. They in turn include:

1. Not-for-profit corporations
2. Profit corporations

Private Corporation
One formed to do nongovernmental function

Not-for-Profit Corporations. A **not-for-profit corporation** is one formed by private individuals for some charitable, educational, religious, social, or fraternal purpose. This corporation is not organized for profit; does not distribute income or profits to members, officers, or directors; and usually does not issue stock. As a legal entity like any other corporation, it can sue and be sued as a corporation, buy and sell property, and otherwise operate as any other corporation. A person acquires membership in a not-for-profit corporation by agreement between the charter members in the beginning and between the present members and new members thereafter.

Not-for-Profit Corporation
One formed by private individuals for charitable, educational, religious, social, or fraternal purpose

PREVIEW CASE REVISITED

Facts: Coosa Valley Electric Cooperative, Inc., a not-for-profit corporation formed to provide electric service to its members, incorporated Coosa Valley Propane Services, Inc. Coosa Propane bought all the stock of DeKalb County LP Gas Co., Inc. Coosa Electric, Coosa Propane, and DeKalb then chose the same officers and directors. A group of propane dealers sued the companies alleging Coosa Electric did not have the authority to operate a propane business. Coosa Electric argued the propane dealers had no right to contest the power of Coosa Electric to acquire DeKalb's stock. One of the propane dealers, Suburban Gas, was a member of Coosa Electric.
Outcome: The court held that as a member of the not-for-profit corporation, Suburban Gas had the right to challenge Coosa's acts as illegal.

—*DeKalb County LP Gas Co. v. Suburban Gas*, 729 So. 2d 270 (Ala.)

Profit Corporations. A **profit corporation** is one organized to run a business and earn money. In terms of number and importance, **stock corporations** organized for profit constitute the chief type. Certificates called *shares of stock* represent ownership in a stock corporation. The number of shares of stock owned and the charter and the bylaws of the corporation determine the extent of one's rights and liabilities.

Profit Corporation
One organized to run a business and earn money

A profit corporation that has a very small number of people who own stock in it is called a **close corporation** or a **closely held corporation**. Because of the small number of stockholders, they normally expect to be and are active in the management of the business.

Many close corporations choose to be designated Subchapter S corporations for federal income tax purposes. Unlike other corporations, a Subchapter S corporation files only an information tax return. It does not pay corporate income tax. The owners report the profit of the corporation as income on their personal income tax returns. This results in tax savings. The corporation's profits are not taxed twice—once when shown on a corporate tax return and a second time when shown as income from the corporation to the owners on their personal tax returns.

CLASSIFICATION BY STATE OF INCORPORATION

Corporations may be classified depending on where they were incorporated. A corporation is a **domestic corporation** in the state where it received its initial charter; it is a **foreign corporation** in all other states. If incorporated in another country, a corporation may be referred to as an **alien corporation**. The corporation can operate as a foreign corporation in any other state it chooses as long as it complies with the registration or other requirements of the other state.

FORMATION OF A CORPORATION

One who acts as the **promoter** usually takes the initial steps of forming a corporation. A corporation can be organized in any state the promoter chooses. A lot of preliminary work must be done before the corporation comes into existence. The incorporation papers must be prepared, a registration statement may need to be drawn up and filed with the Securities and Exchange Commission (SEC) and the appropriate state officials, the stock must be sold, and many contracts must be entered into for the benefit of the proposed corporation. Filing with the SEC is not required in the case of smaller corporations.

Minor defects in the formation of a corporation may generally be ignored. In some instances; however, the defect is of a sufficiently serious character that the attorney general of the state that approved the articles of incorporation of the corporation may obtain the cancellation or revocation of such articles. In other cases, the formation of the corporation is so defective that the existence of a corporation is ignored, and the persons organizing the corporation are held liable as partners or joint venturers.

LIABILITY ON PROMOTER'S CONTRACTS AND EXPENSES

The corporation does not automatically become a party to contracts made by the promoter. After it is incorporated, a corporation will ordinarily approve or adopt the contracts made by the promoter. The approval may be either express or by the corporation's conduct. Once approved, such contracts bind the corporation, and it may sue on them.

The promoter may avoid personal liability on contracts made for the benefit of the corporation by including a provision in the contract that the promoter incurs no personal liability if the corporation does or does not adopt the contract. In the

---

Stock Corporation
One in which ownership is represented by stock

Close or **Closely Held Corporation**
One with very small number of shareholders

Domestic Corporation
One chartered in the state

Foreign Corporation
One chartered in another state

Alien Corporation
One chartered in another country

LO ❷
Formation of corporation and liability

Promoter
One who takes initial steps to form corporation

ETHICAL POINT

Regardless of the law on the subject, do you think it is ethical for a promoter to be able to be relieved of liability on contracts made for the benefit of the corporation?

absence of such a provision, the promoter may have liability. Courts look at whether the other contracting party knew the corporation was not yet in existence. The wording of the contract is also very significant in determining whether it binds the promoter either pending the formation of the corporation or after it has come into existence.

COURT CASE

Facts: When Manzar Zuberi entered into a lease of a warehouse owned by Steven and Janis Gimbert, he signed the lease "ATM MANU-FACTURING, INC. BY: Manzar Zuberi Its: Pres/CEO." Unfortunately, ATM Manufacturing, Inc. never was a corporation. In his manufacturing in the building, Zuberi used hydrochloric acid that the Gimberts claimed severely damaged the premises. They sued Zuberi personally for the damage.

Outcome: Because Zuberi purported to act on behalf of a corporation, although there was no incorporation, he was liable for damages caused while he acted for the nonexistent corporation.

—*Zuberi v. Gimbert*, 496 S.E.2d 741 (Ga. App.)

Along with the adoption of the promoter's contracts, the corporation may or may not pay the expenses of the promoter in organization of the corporation. After the corporation comes into existence, it customarily reimburses the promoter for all necessary expenses in forming the corporation. This may be done by a resolution passed by the board of directors.

ISSUANCE OF STOCK

Subscriber
One who agrees to buy stock in proposed corporation

When a new corporation is about to be formed, agreements to buy its stock will generally be made in advance of actual incorporation. In such a case the purchase agreement or subscription to stock by a prospective stockholder or investor, called a **subscriber**, constitutes merely an offer to buy. In most jurisdictions this offer may be revoked any time prior to acceptance. As the offeree, the corporation cannot accept the subscription until the state issues its charter. If an existing corporation sells stock, it can accept all subscriptions immediately and make them binding contracts. If the promoter is to be paid by means of a stock option, the corporation can make such a contract with the promoter before any services are performed. Most state laws provide that a minimum amount of stock must be sold and paid for before the corporation can begin operations.

Once a valid subscription agreement is signed, the subscriber has rights in the corporation even if the stock certificates have not been received or issued.

COURT CASE

Facts: At the organization of Delta Medical Electronics, Inc. (DME), Richard Pfeifer subscribed to shares of its stock. It was agreed that Pfeifer would give DME a promissory note and stock pledge agreement as payment for his shares. DME did not ask for the note and agreement and Pfeifer never gave it. Sometime later, DME sold its main assets at a significant profit, filed articles of dissolution, and transferred its remaining assets to the trustee of the DME Liquidating Trust. Pfeifer had died, so his wife, Edna, sued for a share of DME's assets.

Outcome: The court agreed that as a subscriber, Richard had the rights and obligations of a stockholder even if he had not paid for his shares unless the subscription had been lawfully revoked.

—*Pfeifer v. DME Liquidating, Inc.*, 753 P.2d 1389 (Ore. App.)

ARTICLES OF INCORPORATION

The written document setting forth the facts prescribed by law for issuance of a certificate of incorporation or a charter and asserting that the corporation has complied with legal requirements is the **articles of incorporation**. Once approved by the state, the articles determine the authority of the corporation. This document constitutes a contract between the corporation and the state. So long as the corporation complies with the terms of the contract, the state cannot alter the articles in any material way without obtaining the consent of the stockholders. The articles include such information as the name of the corporation, the names of the people forming the corporation (the **incorporators**), and the amount and types of stock the corporation has authorization to issue. The incorporators elect a board of directors and begin business, which constitutes acceptance of the charter and binds all parties.

Articles of Incorporation
Document stating facts about corporation required by law

Incorporators
People initially forming a corporation

POWERS OF A CORPORATION

A corporation has three types of powers: express, incidental, and implied.

LO ❸
Types of powers

Express Powers

The statute or code under which a corporation is formed and, to a lesser degree, the corporation's articles of incorporation determine its express powers. In a few instances, the state constitution sets forth the powers of a corporation. The statutes limit a corporation's powers to what they grant, and a corporation may not do what statutes prohibit.

Incidental Powers

Certain powers always incidental to a corporation's express powers or essential to its existence as a corporation include but are not limited to:

1. Have a corporate name
2. Have a continuous existence
3. Have property rights
4. Make bylaws and regulations
5. Engage in legal actions
6. Have a corporate seal

Corporate Name. A corporation must have a corporate name. The members may select any name they wish, provided that it does not violate the statutes or that another firm or corporation within the state does not use it. Many of the states have statutes regulating corporate names. For example, statutes may require the name to end with *Corporation* or to be followed by the word *Incorporated*, an abbreviation thereof, or other indication of corporate status.

Continuous Existence. The existence of the corporation continues for the period for which the state grants the charter. This feature of a corporation makes this form of organization valuable. The death of a stockholder does not dissolve the organization. Sometimes people refer to this characteristic as *perpetual*, or *continuous*, *succession*.

Property Rights. A corporation has the right to buy, sell, and hold property necessary in its functioning as a corporation and not foreign to its purpose.

Bylaws
*Rules enacted by
directors to govern
corporation's conduct*

Bylaws and Regulations. The organization needs rules and regulations to govern it and to determine its future conduct. They must conform to the statutes and must not be contrary to public policy. The corporation's board of directors adopts these rules, called the corporation **bylaws**.

Legal Actions. Long considered incidental to corporate existence is the corporation's power to sue in its own name. Because a corporation may be composed of hundreds or thousands of stockholders, it would be a cumbersome, if not impossible, task to secure the consent of all the stockholders each time a corporation needed to bring a suit. A corporation may likewise be sued in the corporate name. In some states a corporation may represent itself in low-level trial courts by an officer/shareholder who is not an attorney, just as a person who is not an attorney may represent himself.

Corporate Seal. A corporation has the incidental power to have and to own a seal. Normally, a corporation need not use a seal except (1) in executing written instruments that require the use of a seal when executed by natural individuals, or (2) in carrying out transactions for which special statutory requirements require the use of the seal.

Implied Powers

In addition to incidental or express powers conferred on all corporations, a corporation has the implied power to do all acts reasonably necessary for carrying out the purpose for which the corporation was formed. A corporation may borrow money and contract debts if such acts are necessary for the transaction of the corporate business. It may make, indorse, and accept negotiable instruments. It has the power to acquire and convey property and to mortgage or lease its property in case such transactions are necessary for carrying on its business. Corporation codes as a rule expressly list the various implied powers described above so that they constitute express powers.

ULTRA VIRES CONTRACTS

***Ultra Vires* Contract**
*Contract exceeding
corporation's powers*

Any contract entered into by a corporation that goes beyond its powers is called an *ultra vires* **contract**. As between the parties to the contract, the corporation and the third person, the contract generally binds them. However, a stockholder may bring an action to prevent the corporation from entering into such a contract or to recover damages from the directors or officers who have caused loss to the corporation by such contracts. In extreme cases, the attorney general of a state may obtain a court order revoking the articles of incorporation of the corporation for frequent or serious improper acts that make it proper to impose such an extreme penalty.

COURT CASE

Facts: West Daniels Land Association was incorporated to hold, own, and manage grazing land for the livestock owned by its shareholders. In order to generate revenue for the association, the board of directors voted to advertise the property for lease to the highest bidder. It leased all the association's land to a nonshareholder. Ray Okelberry, a shareholder, sued.

Outcome: The court said that by leasing all its land to a nonshareholder, the association acted contrary to the limited purpose for which it was incorporated, as expressed in the articles of incorporation.

—*Okelberry v. West Daniels Land Ass'n*,
120 P.3d 34 (Utah)

QUESTIONS

1. What is the purpose of public corporations?
2. How does a person acquire membership in a not-for-profit corporation?
3. How does using the designation Subchapter S result in tax savings?
4. In what states may a corporation operate as a foreign corporation?
5. Is a corporation automatically a party to contracts made by promoters?
6. What is a corporation's articles of incorporation and what is their importance?
7. What determines what the express powers of a corporation are?
8. What potential penalties are there for a corporation that enters into an *ultra vires* contract?

CASE PROBLEMS

1. James Blaszak started Consumers Land Title Agency, Inc., a corporation. The articles of incorporation were filed on December 27. On December 12, Consumers entered into an agency agreement with Commonwealth Land Title Company. At the space for signatures, the agreement had Consumers' name followed by Blaszak's signature and beneath his signature were the words "By James L. Blaszak." Several years later, Commonwealth terminated the agreement because Blaszak failed to properly report and remit fees. Blaszak filed for bankruptcy, and Commonwealth alleged Blaszak was personally liable under the agreement. Was he?   LO ❷

2. Isaiah 61:1, Inc.'s certificate of incorporation stated its purpose was "to provide shelter, companionship, and a place of sharing and caring, meals, clothing referrals and all other feasible services for ex-offenders." Isaiah acquired property and renovated it as a licensed rooming house. The state paid it on the basis of occupancy to rehabilitate and counsel inmates completing their sentences. Employed residents were required to pay weekly "rent" of $10 to $80. The city assessed taxes on the property, and Isaiah claimed it was tax exempt. In the lawsuit that followed, the city claimed Isaiah's providing housing was *ultra vires*. Was it?   LO ❸

3. Lennox Hill Hospital employed radiologists Frank Purnell and Carmel Donovan along with 10 others. The 12 doctors agreed to form a corporation to employ them to provide radiology services at the hospital. They were to be equal shareholders of the corporation, and 10 of them contributed $3,000 to start it. Lewis Rothman, who paid only $100, signed the certificate of incorporation that listed each of the 12 doctors as shareholders. He had all the corporation's stock issued to him. Purnell and Donovan demanded the right to inspect the corporation's records, but Rothman refused saying they were not shareholders. Were they shareholders?   LO ❷

4. WillieAnn Madison incorporated Cherokee Children & Family Services, Inc. (CCFS) as a nonprofit public benefit corporation and was its executive director. CCFS was to provide childcare brokerage services to low-income families. The corporation had no members. Its income was almost exclusively state and federal grants. CCFS paid for travel to Hawaii, personal travel the next year, and a trip to London—all by Madison and several of her relatives. Madison was regularly paid bonuses of 50 percent of her salary. She bought a building   LO ❶, ❸

and leased it to CCFS (signing on behalf of CCFS) for five years at an annual rent of $49,932. During the first year the lease was renegotiated at a retroactive annual rent of $72,000. Prior to expiration, the lease was renegotiated again to reflect leasing 20,000 square feet, although the building had only 9,700 square feet, at an annual rent of $210,000. The next year three members of the board of directors approved the payment of "prorated back rent" for the contract period. This was $210,000 rent times five, minus what CCFS had paid in rent to Madison. This amounted to $437,000 and was paid to Madison's company. The state attorney general sued to dissolve CCFS saying it had abandoned its public purpose and had become devoted to private gain. Should it be dissolved?

LO ❷   **5.** Roy Lathan signed a contract on behalf of Royal Development and Management Corp. with Guardian 50/50 Fund V, Ltd. By the contract, Guardian agreed to sell Royal 23 lots on a closing date set by North Carolina National Bank (NCNB). NCNB set the date, but Guardian had not removed construction debris as required, so Royal refused to close. Guardian sued Royal and Lathan for breach of contract. Lathan contended he should not be personally liable because he did not know when he signed the contract that Royal had not been incorporated. Lathan signed the articles of incorporation three days after executing the contract. Should Lathan have personal liability on the contract?

LO ❶   **6.** An earthquake damaged the Oak Park Calabasas condominium complex. The homeowners' association, a nonprofit corporation, contracted with ECC Construction, Inc. to repair the common areas and individual units. None of the individual condominium owners signed the contract. After ECC completed the repairs there was a dispute about how much was due it. ECC sued the association and the 300 condominium owners for breach of contract. The condominium owners alleged they were not parties to the contract. Are they liable on the contract entered into by the association?

LO ❸   **7.** Renaissance Enterprises, Inc., a corporation with only Mr. and Mrs. Malcolm Babb as shareholders, was a party to a lawsuit in an appellate court. Malcolm, who was not an attorney, had represented Renaissance. Does a corporation have the power to represent itself in court by a shareholder/officer who is not an attorney?

LO ❷   **8.** Claud Koch and Don Czeschin resolved to form a corporation called Quality Aloe Vera Labs, Inc., and it was incorporated on June 3. However, on April 25, knowing Quality was not yet incorporated, Thoeni Aloe Vera agreed to sell aloe vera leaves to Quality. The agreement recited it was between Quality and Thoeni and Czeschin signed it, "Quality Aloe Vera Labs, Inc. by Don Czeschin." Quality ordered and paid for 10 shipments of leaves through August. Then Quality ordered 10 more shipments but did not pay for them and went into bankruptcy. Thoeni sued Koch and Czeschin alleging they were liable as promoters because the contract was signed before the corporation was incorporated. Should Koch and Czeschin be personally liable?

Ownership of a Corporation

LEARNING OBJECTIVES

1 Define capital stock.

2 List the various types of stock and stock rights.

3 Explain what dividends are and how they may be paid.

4 Name the various laws regulating the sale of securities, exchanges, and brokers.

PREVIEW CASE

Charles Huttoe wanted to increase the value of Software of Excellence Inc.'s (SOE's) shares. He controlled millions of issued shares. A trader agreed to manipulate the price of the stock. As a part of the scheme, William Calvo, the sole managing member of Diversified Corporate Consulting Group, negotiated and signed a contract to supply consulting services for SOE in return for 10 percent of SOE's outstanding stock. The trader bid the price of SOE stock up through market distortions. Buyers were duped into believing there was a real demand for the stock. Calvo signed documents that opened a Diversified brokerage account into which the SOE shares were deposited; he signed stock transfer authorization and stock powers for sales or transfers of stock out of Diversified's brokerage account; and he received proceeds through Diversified from the sale of 1,345,000 shares of SOE stock. They were all unregistered. The SEC sued Calvo alleging he sold unregistered securities. Why was Diversified hired? What part did Calvo play in the transaction?

The **capital stock** of the corporation is the declared money value of its outstanding stock. The owners subscribe and pay for this stock. Generally, not all the stock a corporation may issue need be subscribed and paid for before the corporation begins operation. After a corporation is formed, the board of directors authorizes the sale of stock. The amount of capital stock authorized in the charter cannot be altered without the consent of the state and a majority of the stockholders. The capital stock is divided into units called **shares**.

LO **1**
Capital stock

Capital Stock
Declared value of outstanding stocks

Share
Unit of stock

Shareholder or
Stockholder
Person who owns stock

OWNERSHIP

A person achieves ownership in a stock corporation by acquiring title to one or more shares of stock. Owners are known as **shareholders** or **stockholders**. A person may obtain shares of stock by subscription either before or after organization of the corporation, or shares may be obtained in other ways, such as by gift or purchase from another shareholder.

STOCK CERTIFICATE

The amount of ownership (the number of shares owned) may but need not be evidenced by a stock certificate. A certificate is not the actual stock, just written evidence of ownership of stock. If there is a certificate, it shows on its face the number of shares represented, the par value of each share if the stock has a par value, and the signatures of the officers. The fact that a person is named on the certificate, either by issuance or endorsement, and has possession of it is *prima facie* evidence that the person is the owner of the certificate.

COURT CASE

Facts: When Bertha Vicknair formed Albany Wrought Iron Manufacturing, Inc., two stock certificates, each for 250 shares, were issued—one to Vicknair and the other to her daughter, Deborah. Vicknair later consulted with her lawyer about transferring her stock to Deborah. Vicknair endorsed her stock certificate before a witness, gave it to her lawyer, and the secretary recorded the alleged transfer on the corporate ledger for the lawyer. After a court declared Vicknair incompetent and appointed another daughter, Diana, to care for her affairs, Deborah alleged she owned Vicknair's shares.

Outcome: Because Deborah never had possession of the endorsed certificate, she was not the owner of the stock.

—*In re Interdiction of Vicknair,*
822 So. 2d 46 (La. App.)

TRANSFER OF STOCK

A stock certificate indicates the manner in which the stock may be transferred to another party. The owner may use a blank form on the back of the certificate in making a transfer. The signature of the previous owner gives the new holder full possession and the right to exchange the certificate for another made out by the corporation to the new owner. Whenever an owner transfers stock, the new owner should have the certificate exchanged for a new one showing the correct name so that the corporation's books will show the correct stockholders' names. Stockholders who are not registered do not have the rights and privileges of a stockholder and will not receive any profits of the corporation.

If a broker holds the stock and certificates have not been issued, the broker can transfer the stock at the written direction of the owner. Under the Uniform Stock Transfer Act, the unregistered holder of stock has a right to the distribution that represents a return of capital. As under common law, the unregistered holder has no right to any distribution that represents a share of the profits.

CLASSES OF STOCK

Stock is divided into many classes. The articles of incorporation and the laws under which the corporation is organized determine the classes. The two principal classes of stock are:

LO ❷
Types of stock and rights

1. Common stock
2. Preferred stock

Common Stock

Common stock is the simplest form of stock and the normal type of stock issued. The owners of common stock control the corporation because they may vote for members of the board of directors. The board in turn hires the individuals who manage and operate the corporation. Unless selected as a director or appointed as an officer, a stockholder has no voice in the running of the corporation beyond the annual vote for the board of directors. Common stockholders have the right to a share of the assets of a corporation on dissolution.

Common Stock
Stock that entitles owner to vote

Preferred Stock

Preferred stock differs from common stock in that the holder of this stock has some sort of special advantage or preference. In return for a preference, the preferred stockholders usually give up two rights common stockholders retain—the right to vote in stockholders' meetings and the right to participate in profits beyond the percentage fixed in the stock certificate.

The preference granted may pertain to the division of dividends, to the division of assets on dissolution, or to both of these. Most often, the preference relates both to dividends and assets. Calling particular stock preferred does not tell what preference the holder has. The stock certificate will indicate the type of preference, although the certificate of incorporation governs the exact rights of preferred shareholders. Preferred stock may be:

Preferred Stock
Stock giving special advantage

1. Preferred as to assets
2. Preferred as to dividends
3. Participating
4. Nonparticipating

Preferred as to Assets.
Stock preferred as to assets gives the holder an advantage only in the event of liquidation. Preferred stockholders receive their proportionate share of the corporation's assets prior to any share going to common shareholders.

Preferred as to Dividends.
Stock preferred as to dividends means the preferred stockholders receive a dividend before any common stockholders receive one. Preferred stock usually states the percentage it receives. Once this percentage has been paid to preferred stockholders, any money remaining may be paid as a dividend to holders of common stock. This right to preference as to dividends may be cumulative or noncumulative.

Cumulative preferred stock is preferred stock on which all dividends must be paid before the common stock receives any dividend. These dividends on cumulative preferred stock must be paid even for years in which the corporation did not earn an adequate profit to pay the stated dividend.

Cumulative Preferred Stock
Stock on which all dividends must be paid before common dividends

Noncumulative Preferred Stock
Stock on which current dividends must be paid before common dividends

Noncumulative preferred stock is preferred stock on which dividends have to be paid only for the current year before common stock dividends are paid. Thus, dividends do not have to be paid for years in which the corporation does not make a profit or even for years in which the directors simply do not declare a dividend.

The difference between cumulative and noncumulative preferred stock can be significant if the corporation operates at a loss in any given year or group of years. For example, a corporation that has $1 million outstanding common stock and $1 million outstanding 7 percent preferred stock operates at a loss for two years and then earns 21 percent net profit the third year. Noncumulative preferred stock would be entitled to only one dividend of 7 percent. The common stock is entitled to the remaining 14 percent. Cumulative preferred stock would be entitled to three preferences of 7 percent, or 21 percent in all, before the common stock is entitled to any dividend. If the company earned a net profit each year equal to only 7 percent on the preferred stock, and the preferred stock was noncumulative, the directors could pass the dividend the first year and declare a 7 percent dividend on both the common and the preferred stocks for the second year. Because the common stockholders elect the directors, the common stockholders could easily elect directors who would act in ways to help them as much as possible. For that reason, the law provides that preferred stock be cumulative unless specifically stated to be noncumulative. All this can occur, however, only when the corporation earns a profit but fails to declare a dividend. Unless the stock certificate expressly states that it is cumulative, the preference does not cumulate in the years during which the corporation operated at a loss.

Participating Preferred Stock
Stock that shares with common stock in extra dividends

Participating. Shareholders with **participating preferred stock** are entitled to share equally with the common shareholders in any further distribution of dividends made after the common shareholders have received dividends equal to those that the preferred shareholders have received by virtue of their stated preference. Thus, 7 percent participating preferred stock may pay considerably more than 7 percent annually. If the preferred stock is to participate, this right must be expressly stated on the stock certificate and in the articles of incorporation. It can participate only according to the terms of the articles of incorporation. The articles may provide that the preferred stock shall participate equally with the common stock. On the other hand the articles may provide, for example, that the preferred stock is entitled to an additional 1 percent for each additional 5 percent the common stock receives.

Nonparticipating Preferred Stock
Stock on which maximum dividend is stated percentage

Nonparticipating. **Nonparticipating preferred stock** is stock on which the maximum dividend is the percentage stated on the stock. If it is 7 percent nonparticipating preferred, for example, 7 percent annually would be the maximum to which the preferred stockholders would be entitled no matter how much the corporation earned. The law presumes stock is nonparticipating in the absence of a provision to the contrary in the articles of incorporation.

KINDS OF STOCK

In addition to the two classes of stock, stock comes in several different kinds. These include par-value stock, no-par-value stock, treasury stock, and watered stock.

Par-Value Stock

Par-Value Stock
Stock with assigned face value

Stock to which a face value, such as $25, $50, or $100, has been assigned and that has this value printed on the stock is **par-value stock**. Preferred stock usually has a par value. The law requires that when a corporation issues par-value stock in return for payment in money, property, or services, the par value of the stock must be equal in value to the money, property, or services. This relates only to the price at which the corporation may issue the stock to an original subscriber. It has no effect on the price paid between a shareholder and a buyer thereafter. The price a buyer pays a shareholder ordinarily equals the market price, which may be more or less than the par value. If a corporation sells par value stock at a discount, the purchaser incurs liability to subsequent creditors of the corporation for the discount.

No-Par-Value Stock

Stock to which no face value has been assigned is **no-par-value stock**. A corporation may issue no-par-value stock at any price, although some states do set a minimum price, such as $5, for which it can be issued. Common stock may be either par, value or no-par-value stock.

No-Par-Value Stock
Stock without face value

Treasury Stock

If a corporation purchases stock that it has sold, this reacquired stock is referred to as **treasury stock**. When a corporation first offers stock for sale, less sales resistance may be encountered if the prospective purchaser can be assured that the corporation will repurchase the stock on request. Treasury stock also may be reacquired by gift. The reacquired stock may be sold at any price fixed by the directors. Until the corporation resells it, no dividends can be paid on it nor can it be voted.

Treasury Stock
Stock reacquired by a corporation

COURT CASE

Facts: Ampco-Pittsburgh Corp. attempted to buy all Buffalo Forge Co. stock at $25 a share. Buffalo resisted the acquisition and contracted to merge with Ogden Corp. By the contract, Ogden bought 425,000 shares of Buffalo treasury stock for $32.75 per share. Ogden also obtained an option to buy 143,400 more treasury shares. A bidding war between Ampco and Ogden ended with Ampco offering $37.50 per share. Ogden tendered its 425,000 shares of Buffalo stock, but Ampco refused to buy them.

Ampco also refused to allow Ogden to exercise its option to buy the additional 143,400 treasury shares. Ampco sued for rescission of the treasury stock sale and option, claiming Buffalo's directors had breached their duty by selling the treasury stock at too low a price.

Outcome: The court held that Buffalo could sell the treasury shares at any price it wanted.

—Buffalo Forge Co. v. Ogden Corp.,
555 F. Supp. 892 (W.D.N.Y.)

Watered Stock

Stock issued as fully paid up, but paid with property of inflated values, is said to be **watered stock**. If someone conveys real estate actually worth $40,000 for stock having a par value of $100,000, the stock is watered to the extent of $60,000. Watering stock may be prohibited outright, but in any case it cannot be used to defraud creditors. In the event of insolvency, the creditors may sue the original recipients of watered stock for the difference between the par value and the actual purchase price. This may not be true, of course, if the creditors knew the stock was watered. Although creditors are allowed these rights, most state statutes do not prohibit the watering of stock by corporations other than public utility companies.

Watered Stock
Stock paid for with property of inflated value

If a person pays for stock with overvalued real estate, the extent of the watering should be determinable with reasonable accuracy. However, if a person pays in the form of patents, trademarks, blueprints, or other similar assets, the extent of the watering may be difficult to determine because the value of such assets might be extremely difficult to determine.

STOCK OPTIONS

Stock Option
Right to purchase shares at set price

A **stock option** is a contract entered into between a corporation and an individual. The contract gives the individual the option for a stated period of time to purchase a prescribed number of shares of stock in the corporation at a given price. If a new corporation sells stock to the public at $2 a share, the individual having the option must also pay $2 but may be given 2, 5, or even 10 years in which to exercise the option. If the corporation succeeds, and the price of the stock goes up, the individual will of course want to exercise the option and buy at the low option price and then resell at the higher market price. If the corporation fails, the option does not have to be exercised. Existing corporations may give officials of the corporation an option to purchase a given number of shares of stock in lieu of a salary increase. If the market price of the stock rises, an official may make a capital gain by buying the stock, holding it for the required time, and selling it. The income tax on a capital gain may be considerably less than that on other income. This type of compensation may be more attractive to top management officials than a straight increase in salary, enabling a corporation to retain their services at a lower cost than with a salary increase. If the corporation makes stock available to all the corporation's employees, the option price may be less than the fair market value.

DIVIDENDS

LO ❸
Dividends and how paid

Dividend
Profits of a corporation allocated to stockholders

The profits of a corporation belong to the corporation until the directors set them aside for distribution to the stockholders by declaring a **dividend**. Dividends may be paid in cash, stock, or other property.

A cash dividend usually can be paid only out of retained earnings with two exceptions. A cash dividend may be paid out of donated or paid-in surplus. Also, for corporations with depleting assets, such as coal mines, oil companies, lumber companies, and similar industries, cash dividends may be paid out of capital.

C O U R T C A S E

Facts: GM Sub Corp. bought up 87.4 percent of Liggett Group, Inc.'s common stock. Gabelli & Company, Inc. Profit Sharing Plan, which owned 800 shares of Liggett, did not sell its shares to GM. The majority of Liggett stockholders approved a merger of GM and Liggett. The merger became effective on August 7, and the Liggett stock was bought out. Liggett had historically paid quarterly dividends. That year, the March and June dividends were paid, but no dividend was declared or paid Liggett stockholders for the third quarter, which in the past had been declared in July with an August record date and September payment. Gabelli sued Liggett and GM to compel the declaration and payment of a third-quarter dividend.

Outcome: The court said a minority shareholder (Gabelli) could not force the payment of a dividend without a showing of fraud or gross abuse of discretion by the board of directors. Because there was no such showing, no dividend could be compelled.

—*Gabelli & Co. v. Liggett Group,*
479 A.2d 276 (Del.)

Stock dividends may be in the corporation's own stock or in stock the corporation owns in another corporation. When in the corporation's own stock, they are usually declared out of retained earnings, but they can be paid out of other surplus accounts. A stock dividend of the corporation's own stock cannot be declared if the corporation has no surplus of any kind. Dividends also may be paid in the form of property that the corporation manufactures, but this seldom happens.

The declaration of a dividend on either common or preferred stock depends almost entirely on the discretion of the directors. The directors, however, must act reasonably and in good faith. This means minority stockholders can ask the court to require a corporation to declare a dividend out of surplus profits only when they clearly have a right to a dividend.

Once the directors declare a cash dividend, it cannot later be rescinded. It becomes a liability of the corporation the minute the directors declare it. A stock dividend, on the other hand, may be rescinded at any time prior to the issuance and delivery of the stock.

LAWS REGULATING STOCK SALES

In order to protect investors in corporations, a number of laws have been enacted. These laws seek to prevent fraudulent activities and protect investors from loss as a result of stockbrokers becoming insolvent.

LO ❹
Laws regulating securities sales, exchanges, brokers

Blue-Sky Laws

The purpose of so-called **blue-sky laws** is to prevent fraud through the sale of worthless stocks and bonds. State blue-sky laws apply only to intrastate transactions.

These security laws vary from state to state. Some prescribe criminal penalties for engaging in prohibited transactions. Others require that dealers be licensed and that a state commission approve sales of securities before a corporation offers them to the public.

Blue-Sky Laws
State laws to prevent sale of worthless stock

Securities Act of 1933

Because the state blue-sky laws apply only to intrastate sales of securities, in 1933 Congress passed the federal Securities Act to regulate the sale of securities in interstate commerce. Anyone offering a new issue of securities for sale to the public must register it with the SEC and issue a **prospectus**, which is a document containing specified information about the stock offering and the corporation, including the information contained in the registration statement. An issuer includes a person in control of a corporation such as an officer, director, or controlling shareholder. The SEC may exempt securities if it is not necessary to protect investors because of the small amount involved; however, every issuance of securities more than $5 million must be registered. The act does not regulate the sale or purchase of securities after the corporation has properly issued them.

In addition to filing the registration statement with the SEC, a corporation must furnish a prospectus to each purchaser of the securities. Full information must be given relative to the financial structure of the corporation. This information must include the types of stock to be issued; types of securities outstanding, if any; the terms of the sale; bonus and profit-sharing arrangements; options to be created in regard to the securities; and any other data the SEC may require.

The company, its principal officers, and a majority of the board of directors must sign the registration statement. If either the registration statement or the prospectus contains misstatements or omissions, the SEC will not permit the

Prospectus
Document giving specified information about a corporation

PREVIEW CASE REVISITED

Facts: Charles Huttoe wanted to increase the value of Software of Excellence Inc.'s (SOE's) shares. He controlled millions of issued shares. A trader agreed to manipulate the price of the stock. As a part of the scheme, William Calvo, the sole managing member of Diversified Corporate Consulting Group negotiated and signed a contract to supply consulting services for SOE in return for 10 percent of SOE's outstanding stock. The trader bid the price of SOE stock up through market distortions. Buyers were duped into believing there was a real demand for the stock. Calvo signed documents that opened a Diversified brokerage account into which the SOE shares were deposited; he signed stock transfer authorization and stock powers for sales or transfers of stock out of Diversified's brokerage account; and he received proceeds through Diversified from the sale of 1,345,000 shares of SOE stock. They were all unregistered. The SEC sued Calvo alleging he sold unregistered securities.

Outcome: The court held that Calvo illegally sold unregistered securities.

—SEC v. Calvo, **378 F.3d 1211 (11th Cir.)**

corporation to offer the securities for sale. If the corporation sells them before the SEC ascertains the falsity of the information, an investor may rescind the contract and sue for damages any individual who signed the registration statement. Any failure to comply with the law also subjects the responsible corporate officials to criminal prosecution.

Securities Exchange Act of 1934

The security exchanges and over-the-counter markets constitute the chief markets for the sale of securities after the initial offerings. In 1934 Congress passed the Securities Exchange Act to regulate such transactions. The act requires the registration of stock exchanges, brokers, and dealers of securities traded in interstate commerce and SEC-regulated, publicly held corporations. The law also requires regulated corporations to make periodic disclosure statements regarding corporate organization and financial structure.

Under rule-making authority of the Securities Exchange Act, the SEC has declared it unlawful for any broker, dealer, or exchange to use the mails, interstate commerce, or any exchange facility to knowingly make an untrue statement of a material fact or engage in any other act that would defraud or deceive a person in the purchase or sale of any security. This provision applies to sellers as well as buyers.

Insider
Officer, director, or owner of more than 10 percent of stock

The act requires certain disclosures of trading by **insiders**—officers, directors, and owners of more than 10 percent of any class of securities of the corporation. The corporation or its stockholders suing on behalf of the corporation may recover any profits made by an insider in connection with the purchase and sale of the corporation's securities within a six-month period. Such profits are called **short-swing profits**.

Short-Swing Profits
Profits made by insider buying and selling corporation's stock in six months

A 1975 amendment to this act attempts to foster competition among securities brokers by reducing regulation of the brokerage industry.

Securities Investor Protection Act of 1970

In order to protect investors when the stockbroker or investment house with which they do business has severe financial difficulty that threatens financial loss to the customers, Congress passed the Securities Investor Protection Act of 1970. This federal law requires generally that all registered brokers and dealers and the members of a national securities exchange contribute a portion of their gross revenue from the securities business to a fund regulated by the Securities Investor Protection Corporation (SIPC).

The SIPC is a not-for-profit corporation whose members are the contributors to the fund. If the SIPC determines that any of its members has failed or is in danger of failing to meet its obligations to its customers and finds any one of five other specified indications of its being in financial difficulty, the SIPC may apply to the appropriate court for a decree adjudicating the customers of such member in need of the protection provided by the act. If the court finds the requisite financial problems, it will appoint a trustee for liquidation of the SIPC member. The SIPC fund may be used to pay certain customers' claims, up to $500,000 for each customer.

QUESTIONS

1. What must a corporation do to alter the amount of capital stock authorized?

2. Why should the new owner of stock have the certificate exchanged for a new one showing the correct name?

3. What preference might be granted to preferred stockholders?

4. Explain what it means for stock to be preferred as to dividends.

5. What does it mean if stock is 7 percent nonparticipating?

6. What liability does a purchaser of par-stock from a corporation at less than par-value risk?

7. Is it always possible to easily determine whether stock has been watered? Explain.

8. Why would corporate officials prefer a stock option to a salary increase?

9. Discuss the difference in the ability of a corporation to rescind a cash dividend and a stock dividend.

10. Why must insiders of a corporation disclose their trading?

CASE PROBLEMS

1. Richard Rosso died owning shares of Strata Real Estate Corp. The actual certificates and other documents relating to Strata had been destroyed in a flood, and Richard had thrown all he papers out. His wife, Sandra, said the shares were owned by Richard and her jointly and therefore were not part of his estate. Linda, Richard's daughter from a previous marriage, sued alleging the shares had been owned by Richard alone. Under his will she was entitled to one-sixth of his estate. She argued that even if the shares had been owned jointly and destroyed, Richard's disposal of them destroyed that joint ownership. Did Richard's disposal of the certificates alter the ownership of the stock?   LO ❶

2. When Ford Holdings, Inc. (Holdings) merged with Ford Holdings Capital Corp., Holdings's preferred stock was cashed out. The preferred stockholders received the liquidation value of their stock plus a "merger premium" called for in the certificate creating the preferred stock, plus any accumulated and   LO ❷

unpaid dividends. The certificate stated this was to be paid, "and no more in exchange for such shares." Holders of preferred stock sued claiming they were entitled to the "fair value" of their shares, an amount greater than the amount Holdings had paid. Are they?

LO ❸

3. Henry Reget owned 19 of the 1,811 outstanding shares of Astronautics Corp. of America. He filed suit asking the court to order payment of dividends. The company had never paid a dividend. The corporation acquired significant profits, but the board of directors decided that it would be better off reinvesting its profits in research, development, acquisition of other companies and their assets, and profit sharing for its employees. Can Reget compel payment of a dividend?

LO ❹

4. Arthur Gustafson contracted to sell his stock in Alloyd, Inc. to Wind Point Partners II, LP through Alloyd Holdings, a corporation Wind Point owned. Holdings was to pay $18,709,000 for the stock plus $2 million to reflect the estimated increase in Alloyd's net worth since its most recent financial statements. The agreement recited assurances by Gustafson that the financial statements "present fairly . . . the Company's financial condition" and provided for adjustment of the $2 million figure if the year-end audit showed a difference between actual and estimated increase in net worth. The audit showed the increase was less than estimated and the buyer was entitled to recover $815,000. However, Wind Point sued for rescission of the contract, alleging that the assurances in the contract were false, the contract was a prospectus, and therefore under the Securities Act of 1933, Wind Point was allowed to rescind the contract. Gustafson alleged that a prospectus was a solicitation to the public to purchase stock from the issuer. Was the contract a prospectus?

LO ❷

5. Drever Partners, Inc. employed Allen Stephenson. The two executed an agreement with Maxwell Drever, the majority shareholder, by which Drever Partners sold Stephenson 500 shares of its stock. The agreement provided that if Stephenson left Drever's employ then within 90 days, Drever had the right and duty to repurchase the shares at their fair market value. Later the parties agreed to terminate Stephenson's employment and value the shares as of May 1 of that year. They could not agree on the shares' value by May 1, and Stephenson filed suit. Drever alleged that Stephenson had ceased to be a shareholder. Was Stephenson a shareholder or were the 500 shares treasury stock?

LO ❹

6. Prince Alwaleed Bin Talal Bin Abdulaziz Al Saud entered into an agreement with Citicorp by which Alwaleed became the owner of 5,900 shares of Citicorp nonvoting convertible preferred stock. Under the agreement, Alwaleed promised he would not become the owner of more than 10 percent of Citicorp common stock for five years. Before five years had passed, Lawrence Levner, a stockholder of Citicorp, sued Alwaleed, alleging that he had violated the Securities Exchange Act of 1934 by engaging in a shortswing purchase and sale while he owned more than 10 percent of Citicorp's common stock. In order to have owned more than 10 percent of the common stock, Alwaleed would have to have been considered as owning the common stock into which his preferred stock could be converted. Was the law violated?

Management and Dissolution of a Corporation

LEARNING OBJECTIVES

❶ Discuss how a corporation is managed and controlled by the stockholders.

❷ Identify the rights of stockholders.

❸ Specify the responsibilities and powers of directors and officers.

❹ Describe how a corporation is combined or dissolved.

PREVIEW CASE

➡️ Independent of her position as the president of Northeast Harbor Golf Club, a corporation, Nancy Harris learned that real estate surrounded on three sides by the club was for sale. The land was adjacent to three of the club's golf holes. The club's board of directors had discussed the possibility of buying and developing land adjacent to the club but did not have the money to do so. Harris bought the property and disclosed her purchase to the club's board of directors. What responsibility does an officer have to a corporation? Would there have been any question about Nancy's purchase if the club's board had not indicated an interest in buying land adjacent to the club?

As an artificial being, existing only in contemplation of law, a corporation can perform business transactions only through actual persons, acting as agents. The directors as a group act as both fiduciaries and agents. To the corporation, they are trustees and have responsibility for breaches of trust. To third parties, directors as a group constitute agents of the corporation.

The board of directors selects the chief agents of the corporation, such as the president, the vice president, the treasurer, and other officers, who perform the managerial functions. The board of directors is primarily a policy-making body. The chief executives in turn appoint subagents for all the administrative functions of the corporation. These subagents constitute agents of the corporation, however, not of the appointing executives.

LO ❶
Management and control of corporations

The directors and officers manage the corporation. Because the stockholders elect the board of directors, they indirectly control it. However, neither the individual directors nor a stockholder, merely by reason of membership in the corporation, can act as an agent or exercise any managerial function.

Even a stockholder who owns 49 percent of the common stock of a corporation has no more right to work or take a direct part in running the corporation than another stockholder or even a stranger would have. In contrast, a person who owns even 1 percent of a partnership has just as much right to work for the partnership and to participate in its management as any other partner.

STOCKHOLDERS' MEETINGS

In order to make the will of the majority binding, the stockholders must act at a duly convened and properly conducted stockholders' meeting.

A corporation usually holds a regular meeting such as its annual meeting at the place and time specified in the articles of incorporation or in the bylaws; notice of the meeting is ordinarily not required (see Illustration 36–1). The directors of the corporation or, in some instances, a particular officer or a specified number of stockholders, may call a special meeting. The corporation must give notice specifying the subjects to be discussed for a special meeting.

ILLUSTRATION 36–1 Notice of a Stockholders' Meeting

WATERS, MELLEN AND COMPANY
900 West Lake Avenue
Cincinnati, Ohio 45227

NOTICE OF ANNUAL MEETING OF STOCKHOLDERS
August 22, 20–

The Annual Meeting of Stockholders of Waters, Mellen and Company, a Delaware corporation, will be held in the Auditorium, Building C, at the headquarters of the Company, 900 West Lake Avenue, Cincinnati, Ohio, on Wednesday, August 22, 20– at 10:00 A.M. for the following purposes:

1. To elect a Board of thirteen Directors of the Company;

2. To consider and vote upon the ratification of the appointment of Arthur Andrews & Co. as independent public accountants for the Company for the fiscal year May 1, 20– through April 30, 20– and

3. To transact such other business as may properly come before the meeting or any adjournment thereof.

The Accompanying Proxy Statement provides additional information relating to the above matters.

The Board of Directors has fixed the close of business on Friday, July 6, 20– as the record date for the determination of stockholders entitled to notice of and to vote at this meeting or any adjournment thereof. The stock transfer books will not be closed.

Please sign and mail the accompanying proxy in the envelope provided. If you attend this meeting and vote in person, the proxy will not be used.

By order of the Board of Directors.

RICHARD P. ROBERTS

Secretary

July 18, 20–

IMPORTANT—You can help in the preparation for the meeting by mailing your proxy promptly.

Meetings of the stockholders theoretically act as a check on the board of directors. Corporations must have one annually. If the directors do not carry out the will of the stockholders, they can elect a new board that will carry out the stockholders' wishes. In the absence of fraud or bad faith on the part of the directors, this procedure constitutes the only legal means by which the investors can exercise any control over their investment.

Quorum

A stockholders' meeting, in order to be valid, requires the presence of a **quorum**, or a minimum number of shares that must be represented in order that business may be lawfully transacted. At common law, a quorum consisted of the stockholders actually assembled at a properly convened meeting. A majority of the votes cast by those present expressed the will of the stockholders. Statutes, bylaws, or the articles of incorporation now ordinarily require that a majority of the outstanding stock be represented at the stockholders' meeting in order to constitute a quorum. This representation may be either in person or by proxy.

Quorum
Minimum number of shares required to be represented to transact business

COURT CASE

Facts: P.M. Place Stores Co. offered to buy 67 percent of its issued and outstanding stock from shareholders, announcing it would allow employees to buy the stock for 28¢ per share down and a promissory note for the rest. Phillip Place and three other stockholders (Phillip et al.) who owned 20,748 shares (27 percent) sued to prevent this, but lost in the trial court. The board bought the stock and then sold it to the employees. The board called a special meeting of stockholders to elect a new board. Phillip et al. did not attend. At the next annual meeting a new board was elected, but Phillip et al. again did not attend. The appellate court held that the sale of stock to employees for promissory notes was illegal. The board rescinded the sales to employees and reported the stock as treasury stock. The corporation then transferred that stock back to the former owners. Phillip et al. sued to rescind the transfer of the stock back to the former owners and alleged that the boards elected since the special meeting were illegally constituted. If the treasury stock was not returned to the former owners, Phillip et al. owned 90 percent of the outstanding stock, and their absence from the shareholders meetings meant there had not been a quorum. Thus, the board that returned the stock to former shareholders was not validly elected.

Outcome: The annual meeting Phillip et al. did not attend, at which a board was elected that authorized the treasury stock transfer to the former owners, did not have the required quorum of stockholders.

—Place v. P.M. Place Stores Co., 950 S.W.2d 862 (Mo. App.)

Voting

The right of a stockholder to vote is the most important right, because only in this way can the stockholder exercise any control over investment in the corporation. Only stockholders shown by the stockholders' record book have a right to vote. A person who purchases stock from an individual does not have the right to vote until the corporation makes the transfer on its books. Subscribers who have not fully paid for their stock, as a rule, may not vote. State corporation laws control the right to vote. Voting and nonvoting common stock may be issued if the law permits.

LO **2**
Stockholders' rights

Two major classes of elections are held during stockholders' meetings in which the stockholders vote. They include the annual election of directors and the elections to approve or disapprove some corporate acts that only the stockholders can authorize. Examples of some of these acts are consolidating with another corporation, dissolving, increasing the capital stock, and changing the number of directors.

Giving Minority Stockholders a Voice. Each stockholder normally has one vote for each share of common stock owned. In the election of a board of directors, the candidates receiving a majority of the votes of stock actually voting win. In corporations with 500,000 stockholders, control of 10 percent of the stock often suffices to control the election. In all cases, the owners of 51 percent of the stock can elect all the directors. This leaves the minority stockholders without any representation on the board of directors. To alleviate this situation, two legal devices exist that may give the minority stockholders a voice, but not a controlling voice, on the board of directors. These devices are:

1. Cumulative voting
2. Voting trusts

Cumulative Voting
Stockholder has votes equal to shares owned times number of directors to be elected

Some state statutes provide that in the election of directors, a stockholder may cast as many votes in the aggregate equal to the number of shares owned multiplied by the number of directors to be elected. This method of voting is called **cumulative voting**. Thus, if a stockholder owns 10 shares and 10 directors are to be elected, 100 votes may be cast. All 100 votes may be cast for one director. As a result, under this plan of voting, the minority stockholders may have some representation on the board of directors, although still a minority.

Voting Trust
Device whereby stock is transferred to trustee to vote it

Under a voting trust, stockholders give up their voting privileges by transferring their stock to a trustee and receiving in return **voting trust** certificates. This is not primarily a device to give the minority stockholders a voice on the board of directors; but it does do that, and often in large corporations it gives them a controlling voice. Twenty percent of the stock always voted as a unit has more effect than individual voting. State laws frequently impose limitations on voting trusts, as by limiting the number of years that they may run.

Proxy
Person authorized to vote for another; written authorization to vote for another

Absentee Voting. Under the common law, only stockholders who were present in person were permitted to vote. Under the statutory law, the articles of incorporation, or the bylaws, stockholders who do not wish to attend a meeting and vote in person may authorize another to vote their stock for them. The person authorized to vote for another is known as a **proxy**. The written authorization to vote is also called a proxy (see Illustration 36–2). Corporations send proxy forms to shareholders; the law does not require any special form for a proxy.

As a rule, a stockholder may revoke a proxy at any time. If a stockholder should sign more than one proxy for the same stockholders' meeting, the proxy having the later date would be effective. A proxy may be good in some states for only a limited period of time. If the stockholder attends the stockholders' meeting in person, this acts as a revocation of the proxy.

The management of a corporation may legally solicit proxies for candidates selected by the board of directors. However, the incumbent board must disclose the proposals fairly by disclosing all material facts. A fact is material if there is a substantial likelihood a reasonable shareholder would find it important in deciding how to vote. Proxies secured by means of misleading or fraudulent representations to stockholders will be disqualified.

Proxy Wars

Stockholders dissatisfied with the policies of the present board of directors can try to elect a new board. Electing a new board is often a difficult or impossible task. If one or even several people own a majority of the voting stock, the objecting

ILLUSTRATION 36–2 Proxy

WATERS, MELLEN AND COMPANY

PROXY
ANNUAL MEETING AUGUST 22, 20–

KNOW ALL MEN BY THESE PRESENTS, That the undersigned shareholder of WATERS, MELLEN AND COMPANY hereby constitutes and appoints O. W. PRESCOTT, A. B. BROWN, and GEORGE CONNARS, and each of them, the true and lawful proxies of the undersigned, with several power of substitution and revocation, for and in the name of the undersigned, to attend the annual meeting of shareholders of said Company, to be held at the Main Office of the Company, 900 West Lake Avenue, Cincinnati, Ohio, on Thursday, August 22, 20–, at 10:00 o'clock A.M., Standard Time, and any and all adjournments of said meeting, receipt of the notice of which meeting, stating the purposes thereof, together with Proxy Statement, being hereby acknowledged by the undersigned, and to vote for the election of a Board of thirteen directors for the Company, to vote upon the ratification of the appointment of Arthur Andrews & Co. as independent public accountants for the fiscal year May 1, 20– through April 30, 20– and to vote as they or he may deem proper upon all other matters that may lawfully come before said meeting or any adjournment thereof.

Signed the _____**1st**_____ day of March, 20–

_____**Wanda Klimecki**_____

COURT CASE

Facts: A property settlement agreement signed by Jack Lewis and Cecilia, his former wife, granted Cecilia 175,000 shares of Health Concepts IV, Inc. titled in her name and 175,000 shares titled in Jack's name. However, the agreement granted Jack the voting rights to all those shares. The agreement required Cecilia to execute a proxy designating Jack as the person authorized to vote the stock. At a stockholders' meeting, Jack voted Cecilia's 175,000 shares under the authority of the settlement agreement since she had not executed a formal proxy. A stockholder sued for a determination of whether Jack could validly vote Cecilia's shares.

Outcome: The court said he could because a proxy need only appoint someone to vote the shares and have the signature of the stockholder.

—*Lobato v. Health Concepts IV, Inc.*,
606 A.2d 1343 (Del. Ch.)

stockholders cannot obtain a majority of the voting stock to ensure success. If the voting stock is widely held and no group owns a majority of the voting stock, then the objecting stockholders at least have a chance to elect a new board. To do this, this dissatisfied group must control a majority of the stock represented at a stockholders' meeting. To ensure success, the leaders of the group will obtain proxies from stockholders who cannot attend the stockholders' meeting in person. The current board members will also attempt to secure proxies. This is known as a **proxy war**. The present board of directors may in most instances pay the cost of this solicitation from corporate funds. The "outsiders" generally must bear the cost of the proxy war out of their personal funds. If there are one million shareholders, the cost of soliciting their proxies is enormous. For this reason, proxy wars seldom happen.

Proxy War
Attempt by competing sides to secure majority of stockholders' votes

RIGHTS OF STOCKHOLDERS

The stockholders of a corporation enjoy several important rights and privileges. Three of these rights that have already been discussed include the following:

1. A stockholder has the right to receive a properly executed certificate as evidence of ownership of shares of stock.

2. A stockholder has the right to attend corporate meetings and to vote unless this right is denied by express agreement, the articles of incorporation, or statutory provisions.

3. A stockholder has the right to receive a proportionate share of the profits when profits are distributed as dividends.

In addition, each stockholder has the following rights:

4. The right to sell and transfer shares of stock.

5. The right, when the corporation issues new stock, to subscribe for new shares in proportion to the shares the stockholder owns. For example, a stockholder who owns 10 percent of the original capital stock has a right to buy 10 percent of the shares added to the stock. If this were not true, stockholders could be deprived of their proportionate share in the accumulated surplus of the company. This is known as a **preemptive right**. Only stockholders have the right to vote to increase the capital stock.

Preemptive Right
Right to purchase new shares in proportion to shares owned

6. The right to inspect the corporate books and to have the corporate books inspected by an attorney or an accountant. This right is not absolute, as most states have laws restricting the right. These laws tend to be drawn to protect the corporation from indiscriminate inspection, not to hamper a stockholder who has a proper purpose for the inspection.

COURT CASE

Facts: David Lang and others were members of a nonprofit corporation, Western Provider's Physician Organization, Inc. (WPPO). During an investment review, they requested WPPO corporate documents from the secretary of state. They discovered WPPO had not filed annual reports and was not in good standing as a corporation. They requested an inspection of WPPO books and records. WPPO turned over some requested documents but resisted an unlimited inspection. Lang asked the court to compel WPPO to allow review of all corporate documents. WPPO contended Lang had not met his burden of proving a "proper purpose" for an inspection.

Outcome: The court held that members must disclose their purpose for inspecting corporate books, but this purpose is presumed proper. The inspection was allowed.

—*Lang v. Western Providers Physician Organization, Inc.,* 688 N.W.2d 403 (S.D.)

7. The right, when the corporation is dissolved, to share pro rata in the assets that remain after all the obligations of the company have been paid. In the case of certain preferred stock, the shareholders may have a preference in the distribution of the corporate assets on liquidation.

DIRECTORS

LO ❸
Responsibilities and powers of directors and officers

A board of directors elected by the stockholders manages every corporation. Laws normally require every board to consist of at least three members; but if the number exceeds three, the articles of incorporation and the bylaws of the corporation fix the number, together with qualifications and manner of election.

The directors, unlike the stockholders, cannot vote by proxy, nor can they make corporate decisions as individual directors. All decisions must be made collectively and in a called meeting of the board.

The functions of the directors can be classified as:

1. Powers
2. Duties

Powers

Law, the articles of incorporation, and the bylaws limit the powers of the board of directors. The directors have the power to manage and direct the corporation. They may do any legal act reasonably necessary to achieve the purpose of the corporation so long as this power is not expressly limited. They may elect and appoint officers and agents to act for the corporation, or they may delegate authority to any number of its members to so act. If a director obtains knowledge of something while acting in the course of employment and in the scope of authority with the corporation, the corporation is charged with this knowledge.

Duties

The directors have the duty of establishing policies that will achieve the purpose of the corporation, selecting executives to carry out these policies and supervising these executives to see that they efficiently execute the policies. They must act in person in exercising all discretionary power. The directors may delegate ministerial and routine duties to subagents, but the duty of determining all major corporate policies, except those reserved to the stockholders, must be assumed by the board of directors.

OFFICERS

In addition to selecting and removing the officers of a corporation, the board of directors authorizes them to act on behalf of the corporation in carrying out the board's policies. As agents of the corporation, the principles of agency apply to the officers' relationship with the corporation and define many of their rights and obligations.

PREVIEW CASE REVISITED

Facts: Independent of her position as the president of Northeast Harbor Golf Club, a corporation, Nancy Harris learned that real estate surrounded on three sides by the club was for sale. The land was adjacent to three of the club's golf holes. The club's board of directors had discussed the possibility of buying and developing land adjacent to the club but did not have the money to do so. Harris bought the property and disclosed her purchase to the club's board of directors. The club later sued Harris for usurping an opportunity that belonged to the club.
Outcome: The court said that because the club was interested in purchasing land adjacent to it and developing it, Harris's purchase of such land did constitute usurping a corporate opportunity. Harris would be liable for breaching her fiduciary duty to the club.

—*Northeast Harbor Golf Club v. Harris*, **725 A.2d 1018 (Me.)**

State statutes may specify a few of the officers that corporations must have. The corporation's bylaws will specify what additional officers the corporation must have and the duties of each officer. A corporation commonly has a president, vice president, secretary, and treasurer. In small corporations, some of these offices may be combined. Additional officers may be assistant secretaries or treasurers, additional vice presidents, and a chief executive officer (CEO). The CEO is frequently the president or the chairman of the board of directors. The board of directors creates or deletes some positions.

LIABILITIES OF DIRECTORS AND OFFICERS

Although directors and officers of all corporations have potential liability for actions taken as a result of their positions with the corporation, directors and officers of publicly held corporations are subject to additional potential liabilities. This is because such individuals have a responsibility to perhaps hundreds of thousands of investors, both small and large. If the actions of directors or officers lead to the financial collapse of huge corporations, there can be a serious impact on enormous numbers of people. The responsibility for protecting investors in publicly held corporations has led to laws providing serious penalties for officers, directors, and even employees or those under contract with corporations who misuse corporate funds or mislead the public about the financial condition of the corporation. The most recent legislation relating to this is the Sarbanes-Oxley Act. Directors and officers of a corporation face the potential of personal liability for actions taken on behalf of the corporation as well as actions taken for personal gain. They can be liable if the corporation suffers losses or simply if the action is wrongful.

Director Liability

Corporate Losses. As fiduciaries of the corporation, directors incur liability for losses when they are caused by bad faith and by negligence. They do not incur liability for losses when they act with due diligence and reasonably sound judgment. Directors make countless errors of judgment annually in operating a complex business organization. Only when losses are caused by errors resulting from negligence or a breach of good faith can a director be held personally liable.

The test of whether the directors failed to exercise due care depends on whether they exercised the care that a reasonably prudent person would have exercised under the circumstances. If they did that, they were not negligent and do not incur liability for the loss that follows.

The test of whether directors acted in bad faith is whether they acted in a way that conflicted with the interests of the corporation. The corporate directors have a duty of loyalty to the corporation similar to the duty of loyalty an agent has to a principal, or a partner has to the partnership and the other partners.

Wrongful Actions. Directors may be held liable for some acts without evidence of negligence or bad faith, either because the act is illegal or bad faith is presumed. Paying dividends out of capital and *ultra vires* acts constitute illegal acts. Loaning corporate funds to officers and directors constitutes an act to which the court will impute bad faith.

The members of the board of directors incur civil and criminal liability for their corporate actions. This means that a director does not get any immunity or protection from the legal consequences of actions taken. Because of this, individual directors who do not agree with action taken by the other directors must be careful to protect themselves by having the minutes of the meeting of the directors show that they dissented from the board's action. Otherwise stated, every director present at a board meeting is conclusively presumed to have assented to the action taken unless the director takes positive action to overcome this presumption. If the directors present who dissent have a record of their dissent entered in the minutes of the meeting, then they cannot be held liable for the acts of the majority.

Officer Liability

A corporate officer or agent who commits a tort or crime incurs personal liability even when the act was done for the corporation in a corporate capacity. In this case, both the corporation and the individual could be jointly liable. Only personal liability is imposed when the acts are detrimental to the corporation and outside the scope of the officer's authority. Thus, an officer has liability when actions are improper or unjustified such as when based on spite toward the injured party. Federal law even imposes liability on officers and agents for aiding and abetting lower-ranking employees in the commission of crimes. Specific statutes may impose liability on officers if they have a duty to ensure violations do not occur and to seek out and remedy violations that do occur. Corporate officers and agents are not personally liable for acts in which they do not participate, authorize, consent to, or direct.

Sarbanes-Oxley. The financial collapse of corporations such as Enron and WorldCom led to the demand for stronger federal laws imposing liability on corporate officers and directors. The Sarbanes-Oxley Act does so by requiring greater financial disclosure and by putting the responsibility for that disclosure on the CEOs and chief financial officers (CFOs) of corporations. It also requires attorneys and accountants to report evidence of certain law violations to the corporation's chief in-house lawyer or CEO. If they do not respond appropriately, the matter must be reported to the corporation's board of directors or audit board.

The law penalizes individuals who alter, destroy, or conceal records to obstruct an investigation and increases the penalties for certifying reports that do not comply with legal requirements.

The law also makes protection for informants stronger. People who expose wrongdoing in an organization are called **whistleblowers**. Often corporate whistleblowers may face loss of their jobs. Sarbanes-Oxley penalizes anyone who takes action harmful to a person who truthfully reports information about the commission or possible commission of a federal crime to a law enforcement officer.

Whistleblower
Person who exposes wrongdoing in an organization

CORPORATE COMBINATIONS

When two corporations wish to combine, they frequently do so by means of a **merger** or a **consolidation**. A merger of two corporations occurs when they combine so that one survives and the other ceases to exist. One absorbs the other. A consolidation occurs when two corporations combine to form a new corporation. Both of the two previous corporations disappear.

It has become a rather common practice recently for a corporation to try to take over another corporation. The acquiring corporation can do this by making a formal tender offer, an offer to buy stock in the target corporation at a set price. Because attempts at takeovers usually cause the price of the stock of the target company to rise, the acquiring corporation may try to obtain the amount of stock it wants in its target through the purchase of large blocks of the target's stock. The purchase of a large amount of stock cannot be kept quiet for long, however, because the Securities Exchange Act requires any person who acquires 5 percent of any class of stock to file a schedule reporting the acquisition within 10 days.

LO ④
Combination and dissolution

Merger
One corporation absorbed by another

Consolidation
Combining two corporations to form a new one

DISSOLUTION

A corporation may terminate its existence by paying all its debts, distributing all remaining assets to the stockholders, and surrendering its articles of incorporation. The corporation then ceases to exist and completes its dissolution. This action may be voluntary on the part of the stockholders, or it may be involuntary by action of the court or state. The state may ask for dissolution for any one of the following reasons:

1. Forfeiture or abuse of the corporate charter
2. Violation of the state laws
3. Fraud in the procurement of the charter
4. In some states, failure to pay specified taxes for a specified number of years

A foreign corporation that has been granted authority to do business in a state may have its authority revoked for similar reasons.

When a corporation dissolves, its existence is terminated for all purposes except to wind up its business. It cannot sue, transfer property, or form contracts except for the purpose of converting its assets into cash and distributing the cash to creditors and stockholders. Similarly, a foreign corporation whose authority to do business in the state has been revoked may not sue, transfer property, or form contracts until its authority has been reinstated.

In the event that assets cannot cover the corporation's debts, the stockholders do not incur personal liability. This is one of the chief advantages to business owners of a corporation over a sole proprietorship or partnership. It is an advantage from the stockholders' standpoint, but a disadvantage from the creditors' standpoint.

QUESTIONS

1. How do the stockholders of a corporation control it?
2. In what way do stockholders meetings act as a check on the board of directors?
3. What is normally a quorum and how is it determined?
4. What is a stockholder's most important right and why?
5. Explain the two legal devices that may give minority stockholders a voice on the board of directors.
6. What happens if a stockholder signs more than one proxy?
7. What right does a stockholder have to inspect corporate books and records?
8. What is the test of whether directors exercised due care when making corporate decisions?
9. What is the difference between a merger and a consolidation?
10. When a corporation dissolves, what may it still do?

CASE PROBLEMS

LO **4**

1. The Baptist Convention of the State of Georgia (GBC) had the authority to name the board of trustees (Board) of Shorter College, a not-for-profit corporation. As a result, GBC assumed the status of a "member" of the College. A conflict arose as to GBC's exercise of its authority under the charter to fill two

vacancies on the Board. GBC rejected candidates proposed by the College and named two new trustees who lacked the prior approval of the school. The College refused to recognize the new trustees. Calling it a dissolution, the "old" Board approved a transfer of all assets of the school, including its name, for no consideration to the Shorter College Foundation. A lawsuit resulted, and the validity of the dissolution had to be determined. Was the college dissolved?

2. Jo Ellen Hensley owned 70 percent and Don A. Poole owned 30 percent of Gold Rush Tax Services, Inc. Jo Ellen was president and the sole director. She owned the building from which Gold Rush operated. Poole visited the office while Jo Ellen was away. He noticed bank statements indicating that Jo Ellen was receiving payroll checks from Gold Rush. Poole sued Jo Ellen for breach of fiduciary duty, waste, and misappropriation of corporate assets. At trial, experts testified that Jo Ellen received rent from Gold Rush in excess of the market rate for the building she owned and was paid more than she was worth to the business. Should Poole recover?   LO ❸

3. When TVG Network entered into a license agreement with Youbet.com, TVG received the right to purchase enough Youbet common stock to own 51 percent. Youbet was required "to use its best efforts" to allow TVG to designate directors to Youbet's board based on TVG's stock ownership. Youbet agreed not to "avoid or seek to avoid the observance or performance of any of the terms . . . hereunder . . . or take any act which is inconsistent with the rights granted to" TVG. Youbet hired a consulting firm to help develop a strategy regarding TVG's potential 51 percent ownership. In numerous meetings and documents a strategy to discourage TVG purchasing 51 percent by staggering the terms of the board and requiring a super majority of stockholders to change the bylaws was discussed. The Youbet board set an annual meeting to make these changes to the bylaws. It sent out proxy notices. These notices stated that the changes were to promote continuity and stability. They did not mention TVG or its potential 51 percent ownership. TVG sued alleging the proxy notices were misleading and the board breached its duty to fully and fairly disclose material information to the stockholders. Did TVG state a good case?   LO ❷

4. After the board of managers of Dag Hammarskjold Tower Condominium notified the unit owners of major work needed on the building, and that special assessments would be levied and common charges increased by 20 percent, a group of unit owners requested an annual meeting to elect members of the board. There had been no election for many years. The unit owners put up a slate of candidates (Pro Slate) and solicited proxies. The vote inspectors at the annual meeting announced there was a quorum and the Pro Slate had won. The board had previously adopted a resolution that required all proxies to be notarized. Corporate proxies had to include an opinion by a New York attorney that the entity was property organized and in good standing; the identity of all directors, managers, or officers; and a certified copy of the board resolution authorizing the proxy. The board said that there was not a quorum, as proxies had to be disallowed because a candidate for the board had notarized them, and proxies submitted by corporate unit owners had defects in attorney letters, board resolutions, and certifications. The bylaws of the condominium only required the proxies to be in writing, signed, and dated. Was there a quorum?   LO ❶

5. James Tooley was a shareholder of Robinson Springs Corp. (RSC). When Tooley asked to examine RSC's books and records to value his share and determine the financial status and health of the corporation, RSC denied the request.   LO ❷

Tooley sued to require RSC to make the records available for his inspection. Did Tooley have a proper purpose for inspection so that the records had to be made available?

LO ④

6. Health Care Facilities, Inc. (HCF) bought the real estate, nursing home license, all the equipment, patient medical records, and facility name of Crestview Manor Nursing Home II, Inc. All other assets of Crestview were expressly excluded from the purchase. HCF was a self-insured employer for workers' compensation purposes. HCF notified the state Bureau of Workers' Compensation (BWC) of the purchase and asked it to add Crestview to its self-insurance coverage. The BWC refused saying that HCF had merged with Crestview by buying so much of its business. Had HCF merged with Crestview?

LO ③

7. Angelique Stahl was chairman of the board and later chief executive officer, while W. George Allen and Ross Beckerman were directors of Broward Federal Savings and Loan Association. Broward had a growth strategy of paying high interest rates to attract depositors. To do so it had to reinvest the deposits in high-yield assets like commercial real estate loans. It made a large number of risky loans. Federal regulators found deficiencies in its loan underwriting and made Broward execute an agreement promising to take steps to eliminate the weaknesses. Broward made six loans that violated the agreement; it became insolvent and lost about $30 million on the six loans. The federal agency that insured Broward sued Allen, Beckerman, and Stahl. What standard of liability was applicable to the directors in this case?

Ethics in Practice

Suppose that an employee of a business finds some papers in a newspaper left on the subway. Miraculously the papers are a report written by an employee of a competitor with some really helpful ideas for a report the employee has been asked to write. Would it be ethical for the employee to "borrow" the ideas in the found report and use them? Would it make any difference if the person who had written the report had intended to discard it?

Summary Cases

BUSINESS ORGANIZATION

1. East Park Limited Partnership signed a $9 million note. Before the note was due, Joseph Della Ratta, the general partner issued a "capital call" to try to squeeze out some of the limited partners. He informed them East Park could not pay the note, so they would have to pay their proportionate shares of the balance. He said he would try to refinance the note but did not. Some partners said they were withdrawing from East Park before the loan due date. Della Ratta responded they would forfeit their interests in East Park if they did not pay and accelerated the capital call to a date prior to the limited partners' withdrawal date. The withdrawing partners sued. Must they pay the capital call or lose their interests in East Park? [*Della Ratta v. Larkin*, 856 A.2d 643 (Md.)]

2. Charles Grimes and his wife owned 9.9 percent of Alteon, Inc.'s stock. Kenneth Moch, the Chief Executive Officer of Alteon, told Grimes that Alteon needed additional funds and was considering a private placement stock offering. Grimes told Moch that he would buy 10 percent of any such offering. According to Grimes, Moch orally promised that he would offer Grimes 10 percent of the offering. Subsequently, Alteon publicly announced a private placement offering. It did not allow Grimes to participate in this private placement. Grimes sued Alteon. Should Grimes recover? [*Grimes v. Alton, Inc.*, 804 A.2d 256 (Del. Supr.)]

3. The board of directors of Dime Bancorp, Inc. solicited proxies in favor of five sitting directors prior to the annual meeting. North Fork Bancorporation, Inc., a shareholder, solicited proxies against them. Both sets of proxy cards contained a general authorization of the holder to vote all the shares held and then allowed stockholders to vote "for" the election of the five candidates or vote to "withhold authority" for the election of them. The votes were 23,800,000 in favor and 55,200,000 withheld. The bylaws required the affirmative vote of a majority of the voting power present at the meeting. Dime claimed the proxies marked "withhold authority" did not give voting power at all so they did not count as "voting power present." By this reasoning, the five had been elected, basically unanimously. North Fork claimed that the shareholders who marked "withhold authority" gave instructions to the proxy holders to take action, so these proxies should be counted as "voting power present." Should the proxies be counted as "voting power present?" [*North Fork Bancorp., Inc. v. Toal*, 825 A.2d 860 (Del. Ch.)]

4. The owner of Central Plains, Joe Skeith, suggested to David Tate of C.J. Tate & Sons, that Tate work with Central Plains on a job and they would share the profits. They both supplied equipment at the site: Tate provided the bonding,

hired the workers and did all the payroll paperwork. Skeith supervised on the job, set the working hours, and arranged for housing and transportation. Both obtained workers' compensation insurance. Tate hired Dennis Hickson, who usually worked for Central. One day after being paid, Hickson and his coworker roommate, L, went to dinner and then a club. L got aggressive toward other patrons, so Skeith asked Hickson and another to take L to his motel room. When Hickson later returned, L and a woman were in the room. L and the woman left. Hickson went to sleep but let L in when he returned. The next thing Hickson remembered was waking to find L attacking him. Hickson was stabbed. Hickson filed a workers' compensation claim against Central, and Central moved to add Tate, alleging Tate was Hickson's employer. Tate alleged Hickson was an employee of a joint venture of Central and Tate. Who was Hickson's employer? [*Central Plains Const. v. Hickson*, 959 P.2d 998 (Okla. Civ. App.)]

5. Amos Welder purchased, as an equal partner, an interest in an accounting firm. His partner, William Green, was the accountant and trustee for a major client who paid the firm about $80,000 in fees annually. Unknown to Welder, from those fees Green annually received $5,000 as a trust management fee. Green increased this fee to $45,000; Welder found out and objected. Green paid all the fees back to the firm, gave Welder a $27,500 check, and told him the partnership was over. Welder sued. Had Green breached his duty of good faith to Welder? [*Welder v. Green*, 985 S.W.2d 170 (Tex. App.)]

6. Jerold Murphy and three others were the incorporators and original stockholders of Country House, Inc. For nine years they all worked as full-time employees of Country House and were paid wages. Twice they were paid "bonuses" that were authorized when fiscal reports indicated sufficient corporate earnings. Murphy terminated his employment but kept his stock. Then Country House paid stockholder-employee bonuses in addition to their wages. No dividends were ever paid. Murphy brought suit, alleging the bonuses were really dividends and, as a stockholder, money was due him, too. Were the payments dividends? [*Murphy v. Country House, Inc.*, 349 N.W. 2d 289 (Minn. Ct. App.)]

7. Darden, Doman & Stafford Associates (DDS), a partnership, executed a renovation contract with "Building Design and Development, Inc. (in formation), John A. Goodman, President." DDS knew the corporation was not in existence, but Goodman had told them he would form a corporation to limit his personal liability. The work was to be completed by October 15, and disputes were to be settled by arbitration. The first check in payment for the work was made out to "Building Design and Development Inc.—John Goodman." Goodman crossed out his name and indorsed it "Bldg. Design & Dev. Inc., John A. Goodman, Pres." and told DDS to make payments only to the corporation. The work was not finished by October 15, and DDS claimed it was of poor quality. A corporate license for Building Design and Development, Inc. was issued on November 2. DDS served a demand for arbitration and named the corporation and Goodman. DDS testified it never agreed to make the contract only with the corporation; therefore, Goodman should be a party to the arbitration. Should he? [*Goodman v. Darden, Doman & Stafford Associates*, 670 P. 2d 648 (Wash.)]

8. The Timely Investment Club (TIC), a partnership, was formed to educate the partners in investing and allow them to invest on a regular basis. The

partnership agreement provided that when partners withdrew, TIC was required to redeem units of ownership of the withdrawing partners from the funds available. Eight partners withdrew. Was the partnership dissolved by their withdrawal? [*Cagnolatti v. Guinn,* 189 Cal. Rptr. 151 (Cal. Ct. App.)]

9. Paul Wright and John Termeer were partners in an auto repair business. Interstate Motors, Inc. brought in a car for repairs. Wright accepted the car and then drove it to Houston and into a lake, causing significant damage. Is Termeer liable for Wright's negligence? [*Termeer v. Interstate Motors, Inc.,* 634 S.W. 2d 12 (Tex. Ct. App.)]

10. United Electronics Co. (UE) borrowed money from Factors and Note Buyers and pledged stock it owned in Frost Controls Corp. UE defaulted on the loan, so Factors foreclosed. Factors offered the stock for sale publicly and then bought it itself. Frost's president, Arthur Thomson, started a new company, which bought Frost's assets. UE sued Thomson and his new company. To win the lawsuit, UE had to have owned the Frost stock when Frost's assets were sold. To establish that it owned the stock at that time, UE tried to show the foreclosure sale was invalid because Factors, trying to sell the Frost stock, was an "underwriter" as defined in the Securities Act. UE alleged that Factors, with a view to the distribution of the securities, sold the stock for UE, which controlled Frost. Because the Frost stock was unregistered, it alleged the public foreclosure sale violated the Securities Act. Did the sale violate the Securities Act? [*A.D.M. Corp. v. Thomson,* 707 F. 2d 25 (1st Cir.)]

11. Bernard Susman and members of the Asher family were partners in a real estate business. They had a dispute concerning whether the partnership was to develop a portion of the property or whether it was to be sold to a developer. Their dispute became so heated the Ashers told Susman he was no longer a partner, changed the partnership tax returns to show Susman's interest was zero, kept him out of partnership business, refused to give him information concerning the business, and refused to account for expenses of the partnership. Susman sued for breach of the partnership agreement. Were the breaches serious enough to order dissolution? [*Susman v. Venture,* 449 N.E. 2d 143 (Ill. App. Ct.)]

Risk-Bearing Devices

Both the federal and state governments regulate insurance companies. While some state laws apply to bankruptcy, the actual procedure is a federally regulated one. All of these issues are covered in the following chapters.

State Web sites are excellent resources for specific information on state insurance, bankruptcy, and other related laws. Some state sites, such as Tennessee's, have easy ways to get to insurance information, while others will require a search through a list of state agencies. Try out Tennessee's Web site at http://www.state.tn.us/commerce

Principles of Insurance

LEARNING OBJECTIVES

1 Identify important terms used in insurance.

2 Explain who may obtain insurance.

3 List the five aspects of the law of contracts that have special significance for insurance contracts.

PREVIEW CASE

Shortly after purchasing a pharmaceutical manufacturing plant, Rohm and Haas Co. (R&H) found out arsenic waste from the manufacturing had been dumped on the property. When neighboring residents' wells disclosed high levels of lead, R&H supplied them with bottled water and paid medical bills. R&H faced liability under the Clean Streams Law, and its legal department was concerned with the potential liability. The company considered the situation a grave emergency. R&H had excess liability insurance coverage (insurance above a set amount to supplement the primary liability insurance) with Continental Casualty Co. It added the new plant to this insurance coverage and over the years, as it became aware of the extent of the problem, increased the coverage. R&H kept dumping arsenic waste, but cooperated with government agencies to correct the problem, and kept the situation private. It sold the plant, but after the Superfund law was passed, making all present and former owners liable for polluted facilities, the EPA told R&H it was strictly liable for cleanup costs. More than 20 years after insuring the plant with Continental, R&H said it was asserting a claim for $21 million in cleanup costs. Was there concealment? What type of information must be withheld to constitute concealment?

I nsurance provides a fund of money when a loss covered by the policy occurs. Life is full of unfavorable financial contingencies. Not every financial peril in life can be shifted by insurance, but many of the most common perils can. **Insurance** is a contract whereby a party transfers a risk of financial loss to the risk bearer, the insurance company, for a fee.

Every insurance contract specifies the particular risk being transferred. The name that identifies the policy does not control either the coverage or protection

Insurance
Contract that transfers risk of financial loss for a fee

of the policy. For example, a particular contract may carry the name "Personal Accident Insurance Policy," but this name may not clearly indicate the risk being assumed by the insurance company. A reading of the contract may reveal that the company will pay only if an accident occurs while the insured is actually attending a public school. In such a case, in spite of the broad title of the policy, the premium paid covers only the described protection against a financial loss due to an accident, not the loss due to any accident. The contract determines the risk covered, and it binds the parties.

TERMS USED IN INSURANCE

The company agreeing to compensate a person for a certain loss is known as the **insurer**, or sometimes as the underwriter. The person protected against the loss is known as the **insured**, or the policyholder. In life insurance the person who will receive the benefits or the proceeds of the policy is known as the **beneficiary**. In most states the insured may make anyone the beneficiary.

Whenever a person purchases any kind of insurance, a contract is formed with the insurance company. The written contract is commonly called a **policy**. The maximum amount that the insurer agrees to pay in case of a loss is known as the **face** of the policy, and the consideration the insured pays for the protection is called the **premium**.

The danger of a loss of, or injury to, property, life, or anything else, is called a **risk** or **peril**; when the danger may be covered by insurance, it is known as the insurable risk. Factors such as fire, floods, and sleet, which contribute to the uncertainty, are called **hazards**.

An insurance company assumes the risks caused by normal hazards. The insured must not do anything to increase the risk. Negligence by the insured constitutes a normal hazard. Gross negligence indicating a criminal intent does not. With regard to the risk, when a loss occurs, the insured must use all due diligence to minimize it. However, the insured has no responsibility for an increased risk over which the insured has no control or knowledge. For example, the insured must remove household effects from a burning building or keep a car involved in an accident from being vandalized if it can be done safely.

LO ❶
Important terms

Insurer
Company writing insurance

Insured
Person protected against loss

Beneficiary
Person who receives proceeds of life insurance

Policy
Written contract of insurance

Face
Maximum insurer pays for loss

Premium
Consideration paid by insured

Risk or **Peril**
Danger of loss

Hazards
Factors that contribute to uncertainty

COURT CASE

Facts: Darnasai Hamin owned a house on which Auto-Owners Insurance Company had issued a homeowners' policy. Hamin's sister, Vermica Grant, aged 15, and their mother also lived in the house. During a fight, Grant stated she would see that "nobody lived in the house." The house was severely damaged in a fire. Grant started the fire by pouring gasoline in the basement and lighting a piece of paper. There was an intentional loss exclusion in the policy that denied coverage for any loss "caused . . . by . . . [a]n action by any insured committed with the intent to cause a loss." The policy defined insured as "you, your relatives; and any other person under the age of 21 residing with you who is in your care or the care of a relative." Auto-Owners asked a court to declare the exclusion barred Hamin's claim.

Outcome: Grant's action was a hazard Auto-Owners had excluded, so the court held there was no coverage.

—*Auto-Owners Ins. Co. v. Hamin,*
629 S.E.2d 683 (S.C. App.)

Rider
Addition to insurance policy that modifies, extends, or limits base contract

A **rider** on an insurance policy is a clause or even a whole contract added to another contract to modify, extend, or limit the base contract. A rider must be clearly incorporated in, attached to, or referred to in the policy so that there is no doubt the parties wanted it to become a part of the policy.

Frequently, an individual needs insurance coverage immediately, or before an insurer can issue a formal policy. Insurance agents customarily have the authority to issue a **binder,** or a temporary contract of insurance, until the company investigates the risk and issues a formal policy.

Binder
Temporary contract of insurance

TYPES OF INSURANCE COMPANIES

There are two major types of insurance companies:

1. Stock companies
2. Mutual companies

Stock Companies

Stock Insurance Company
Corporation of stockholder investors

A **stock insurance company** is a corporation for which the original investment was made by stockholders and whose board of directors conducts its business. As in all other corporations, the stockholders elect the board of directors and receive the profits as dividends. Unlike other corporations, insurance companies must place a major portion of their original capital in a reserve account so claims can be paid. As business volume increases, companies must increase the reserve by setting aside part of the premiums into this account.

Mutual Companies

Mutual Insurance Company
Company of policyholder investors

Assessment Mutual Company
Mutual insurance company in which losses are shared by policyholders

In a **mutual insurance company** the policyholders are the members and owners and correspond to the stockholders in a stock company. In these companies, the policyholders are both the insurer and the insured, but the corporation constitutes a separate legal entity. A person who purchases a $10,000 fire insurance policy in a mutual company that has $10 million of insurance in force owns $1/_{1,000}$ of the company and is entitled to share the profits in this ratio. Losses also may have to be shared in the same ratio in an **assessment mutual company**. A policyholder is not subject to assessment where the policy makes no provision for it. In a stock company, policyholders never share the losses.

WHO MAY BE INSURED

LO ❷
Insureds

To contract for a policy of insurance, an individual must be competent to contract. Insurance does not constitute a necessary; thus, a minor who wishes to disaffirm is not bound on insurance contracts. A minor who disaffirms a contract may demand the return of any money. Because insurance contracts provide protection only, this cannot be returned. Some states hold that because of this a minor can demand only the unearned premium for the unexpired portion of the policy. A few states have passed laws preventing minors from disaffirming some insurance contracts by reason of minority.

Insurable Interest
Interest in nonoccurrence of risk insured against

To become a policyholder, one must have an insurable interest. An **insurable interest** means that the policyholder has an interest in the nonoccurrence of the risk insured against, usually because there would be financial loss. The insurance contract is in its entirety an agreement to assume a specified risk. If the insured has no interest to protect, there can be no assumption of risk, and hence no insurance. The law covering insurable interest is different for life insurance and for property insurance.

Life Insurance

The insured has an insurable interest in his or her life. When people insure another's life, however, and make themselves or someone else the beneficiary, they must have an insurable interest in the life of the insured at the time the policy is taken out. That interest normally does not need to exist at the time of the death of the insured. However, if a court finds that there is no longer an insurable interest, and that the interest of the beneficiary is adverse to that of the insured, the policy could be invalidated.

A person has an insurable interest in the life of another when such a relationship exists between them that a reasonable expectation of benefit will be derived from the continued existence of the other person. The relationships most frequently giving rise to an insurable interest are those between parents and children, husband and wife, partner and copartner, and a creditor in the life of the debtor to the extent of the debt. There are numerous other relationships that give rise to an insurable interest. With the exception of a creditor, if the insurable interest exists, the amount of insurance is irrelevant.

COURT CASE

Facts: Clifford Burns, Terrence McKeon, and James D'Agosto formed Sound Propeller Services, Inc. They were stockholders, and in accordance with a stockholders agreement, they each procured life insurance policies on the lives of the others. Each policy named the remaining two stockholders as beneficiaries. The named beneficiaries of each policy were each the owners of that policy. Later Burns and McKeon terminated D'Agosto and purchased his stock. Six months later, D'Agosto died. Burns and McKeon said they had an insurable interest in D'Agosto's life when the policy was issued and the subsequent events did not end their right to the insurance proceeds.

Outcome: The court said the relevant time for purposes of determining an insurable interest in a person's life is when the insurance contract is made. Burns and McKeon could collect.

—*In re Estate of D'Agosto*, **139 P.3d 1125 (Wash. App. Div.)**

Property Insurance

One must have an insurable interest in the property at the time the policy is issued and at the time of the loss to be able to collect on a property insurance policy. Ownership is, of course, the clearest type of insurable interest, but there are many other types of insurable interest. Insurable interest occurs when the insured would suffer a monetary loss by the destruction of the property. Common types of insurable interest other than ownership include:

1. The mortgagee has an insurable interest in the property mortgaged to the extent of the mortgage.

2. The seller has an insurable interest in property sold on the installment plan when the seller retains a security interest in it as security for the unpaid purchase price.

3. A bailee has an insurable interest in the property bailed to the extent of possible loss. The bailee has a potential loss from two sources. Compensation as provided for in the contract of bailment might be lost. Second, the bailee may be held legally liable to the owner if the bailee's negligence or the negligence of the bailee's employees causes the loss.

4. A partner has an insurable interest in the property owned by the firm to the extent of the possible loss.

5. A tenant has an insurable interest in property to the extent of the loss that would be suffered by damage to or destruction of the property.

A change in title or possession of the insured property may destroy the insurable interest, which in turn may void the contract, because insurable interest must exist at the time of the loss.

COURT CASE

Facts: Fire totally destroyed Gaylon and Tammy Foote's home, which Farm Bureau Mutual Insurance Co. insured. The Foots sued Farm Bureau when it claimed they did not have an insurable interest in the home. Title to the home was in Gaylon's parents' names because when purchased, Gaylon and Tammy were divorced and trying to reconcile. Gaylon and Tammy had lived in the home several years and built a garage and a two-story addition. They had made all mortgage, insurance, and tax payments.

Outcome: The court said Gaylon and Tammy had a substantial economic interest in safeguarding the home and would definitely endure loss as a result of its destruction. Thus, they had an insurable interest.

—Farm Bureau Mut. Ins. Co. v. Foote,
14 S.W.3d 512 (Ark.)

SOME LEGAL ASPECTS OF THE INSURANCE CONTRACT

LO ③
Contract law specially applicable to insurance

The laws applicable to contracts in general apply to insurance contracts. Five aspects of the law, however, have special significance for insurance contracts:

1. Concealment
2. Representation
3. Warranty
4. Subrogation
5. Estoppel

Concealment

Concealment
Willful failure to disclose pertinent information

An insurer must rely on the information supplied by the insured. This places the responsibility of supplying all information pertinent to the risk on the insured. A willful failure to disclose this pertinent information is known as **concealment**. To affect the contract the concealed facts must be material; this means they must relate to matters that would affect the insurer's decision to insure the insured and the determination of the premium rate. Also, the concealment must be willful. The willful concealment of a material fact in most states renders the contract voidable.

PREVIEW CASE REVISITED

Facts: Shortly after purchasing a pharmaceutical manufacturing plant, Rohm and Haas Co. (R&H) found out arsenic waste from the manufacturing had been dumped on the property. When neighboring residents' wells disclosed high levels of lead, R&H supplied them with bottled water and paid medical bills. R&H faced liability under the Clean Streams Law, and its legal department was concerned with the potential liability. The company considered the situation a grave emergency. R&H had excess liability insurance coverage (insurance above a set amount to supplement the primary liability insurance) with Continental Casualty Co. It added the new plant to this insurance coverage and over the years, as it became aware of the extent of the problem, increased the coverage. R&H kept dumping arsenic waste, but cooperated with government agencies to correct the problem, and kept the situation private. It sold the plant, but after the Superfund law was passed, making all present and former owners liable for polluted facilities, the EPA told R&H it was strictly liable for cleanup costs. More than 20 years after insuring the plant with Continental, R&H said it was asserting a claim for $21 million in cleanup costs.

Outcome: The court held that R&H concealed a material fact from Continental.

*—Rohm and Haas Co. v. Continental Casualty Co., **781 A.2d 1172 (Pa.)***

The rule of concealment does not apply with equal stringency to all types of insurance contracts. In the case of property insurance, where the agent has an opportunity to inspect the property, the insurance company waives the right to void the contract. Concealment arises in ocean marine insurance whenever the insured withholds pertinent information, even if there is no intent to defraud.

Representation

An oral or written misstatement of a material fact by the insured prior to the finalization of the contract is called a **false representation**. If the insured makes a false representation, the insurer may avoid the contract of insurance. This results whether or not the insured made the misstatement purposely.

False Representation
Misstatement of material fact

COURT CASE

Facts: Thomas Foster obtained a fire insurance policy from Auto-Owners Insurance Co. on a house. Fire later damaged the house. The application of the insurance included a request to "List all losses for past 5 years at this . . . location." Although Foster had incurred several fire losses, the box "None" was checked. If Auto-Owners had known about the previous losses it would not have issued the policy. Foster claimed he had supplied the insurance agent who filled out the application with the truth and therefore, although he had signed the application, he had made no misrepresentation.

Outcome: The court stated that because he had signed the application, Foster was responsible for the misrepresentation.

—Foster v. Auto-Owners Ins. Co.,
703 N.E.2d 657 (Ind.)

Some insurance applications require the applicant to state that the answers to questions in the application are made "to the best of the applicant's knowledge and belief" or in similar language. If the policy uses such language, and the applicant has answered truthfully, the fact that the applicant is unaware of the truth will not invalidate the contract.

Insurance policies now usually provide that if the age of the insured is misstated, the policy will not be voided; however, the face amount paid on the policy "shall be that sum which the premium paid would have provided for had the age been correctly stated."

Warranty

Warranty
Statement of insured that relates to risk and appears in contract

A **warranty** is a statement or promise of the insured that relates to the risk and appears in the contract or another document incorporated in the contract. Untrue statements or unfulfilled promises permit the insurer to declare the policy void.

Warranties differ from representations in several ways. The insurance company includes warranties in the actual contract of insurance or incorporates them in it by reference. Representations are merely collateral or independent, such as oral statements or written statements appearing in the application for insurance or other writing separate from the actual contract of insurance.

Also, in order to void the contract of insurance, the false representations must concern a material fact, whereas the warranties may concern any fact or be any promise. A representation need only be substantially correct, whereas a warranty must be absolutely true or strictly performed.

Several states have enacted legislation that eliminates any distinction between warranties and representations and does not require a showing of materiality for a warranty or that the insured intended to defraud. In these states, a breached warranty does not void the policy. Even in states without such statutes, courts are reluctant to find policies invalid and will construe warranties as representations whenever possible and interpret warranties strictly against the insurer so as to favor the insured.

Subrogation

Subrogation
Right of insurer to assume rights of insured

In insurance, **subrogation** is the right of the insurer under certain circumstances to assume the legal rights of, or to "step into the shoes" of, the insured. Subrogation particularly applies to some types of automobile insurance. If the insurer pays a claim to the insured, under the law of subrogation the insurer has a right to any claims that the insured had because of the loss. For example, A has a collision insurance policy on a car. B negligently damages the car. The insurance company will pay A but then has the right to sue B to be repaid.

Estoppel

Estoppel
One party leads the second to a false conclusion the second party relies on; the second party would be harmed if the first party were later allowed to show the conclusion was false

Neither party to an insurance contract may claim the benefit of a violation of the contract by the other party. Each party is **estopped**, or prevented, from claiming the benefit of such violation. An estoppel can arise whenever a party, by statements or actions, leads the second party to a conclusion, even if false, on which the second party relies. If the second party would be harmed if the first party were later allowed to show that the conclusion was not true, there is an estoppel. For example, if an insurer gives the insured a premium receipt, the insurance company would lead the insured to the conclusion that the premium had been paid. The insurer would be estopped from later asserting that the insured had not paid the premium in accordance with the terms of the policy.

COURT CASE

Facts: Jacqueline Matthews purchased a Dodge van with financing from Chrysler Financial Corp. (CFC). Matthews never had a driver's license, but she bought the van because her husband had bad credit. After they separated, she kept the van. Matthews let her sister, Annette Foster, use the van as long as she drove Matthews when she needed a ride. Foster had insured the van under a policy she and her husband already had on another vehicle. When Matthews went through a bankruptcy proceed-

ing, CFC claimed there was no insurance on the van because the Fosters did not have an insurable interest in it. The Fosters had been completely open with their insurance company about their interest, such as it was, in the van.

Outcome: Because the Fosters had told their insurance company about the van's situation, the company would be estopped from questioning the adequacy of their interest in the van.

—*In re Matthews*, 229 B.R. 324 (E.D. Pa.)

QUESTIONS

1. How can a person know what risk is covered by insurance?

2. What risks does an insurance company assume when a loss occurs, and what risks does it not assume?

3. Can a person ever obtain insurance coverage immediately?

4. How do insurance companies differ from other corporations regarding their reserves?

5. **a.** When must a person have an insurable interest for life insurance purposes?

   b. Give three examples of relationships giving rise to an insurable interest for life insurance.

6. **a.** When must a person have an insurable interest for property insurance purposes?

   b. Give three examples of persons who have an insurable interest in property.

7. Explain how the rule of concealment does not apply equally to all types of insurance contracts.

8. If the age of an insured is misstated, will the policy of insurance be voided?

9. How has the strictness of the rule regarding warranties in insurance policies been mitigated?

10. When can an estoppel arise?

CASE PROBLEMS

LO **2**

1. In his capacity as attorney-in-fact for his mother, Michael F. Cassadei executed a deed purporting to convey her home from his mother to himself. He later obtained a homeowners' insurance policy from Nationwide Mutual Fire Insurance Co. on the property. However, based on a deed executed by Cassadei's mother prior to his deed, Cassadei's sister claimed title to the property and sued to quiet title. The court declared Cassadei's deed void and recognized his sister as the rightful owner of the property. The property was vandalized and sustained significant damage, prompting Cassadei to file a claim with Nationwide. Should it have to pay the claim?

LO **3**

2. Between approximately 7:45 P.M. and 9:30 P.M., bartenders at Big Jim's Tavern served four Long Island Ice Teas to Alan Wickliff. Shortly after leaving Big Jim's, Wickliff drove his vehicle into a car driven by William Roland Stine, who died as a result. At the time, Wickliff was intoxicated and had a blood alcohol level of .21. Property-Owners Insurance had issued a Commercial General Liability Policy to Big Jim's that was in force and effect. The policy excluded bodily injury for which Big Jim's was liable by reason of causing or contributing to the intoxication of any person or furnishing alcoholic beverages to a person under the influence of alcohol. Property-Owners asked a court to rule the policy provided no coverage for Wickliff's death. Was Property-Owners correct?

LO **3**

3. Edward Lawson and Kenneth Wheeler formed a law partnership in New Jersey, although Wheeler was not licensed there. Wheeler acted as an attorney for several real estate transactions in New Jersey. He opened and maintained the firm's bank accounts and ledgers. He distributed most, if not all, the real estate closing checks. Lawson found out Wheeler had been illegally transferring money from client accounts to other client's accounts and the firm's business account to pay expenses. Lawson joined Wheeler in a check "kiting" conspiracy, continuing to transfer money from various accounts to pay other clients, business expenses, and Lawson personally. Wheeler applied for professional liability insurance. When he filled out the application, he answered this question in the negative: "is any attorney in your firm aware of . . . [a]ny acts, error or omissions in professional services that may reasonably be expected to be the basis of a professional liability claim?" He signed a warranty asserting that the application was accurate. Certain Underwriters for Lloyd's of London issued a policy. After being sued by several title insurance companies for failing to pay money due parties in real estate transactions, the insurance company denied coverage. Did the company have a right to cancel the coverage?

LO **2**

4. Federal Home Loan Mortgage held a mortgage on a home owned by Bobby and Josie Wright. The Wrights put a second mortgage on the home in favor of Citizens Bank and Trust. Assurance Company of America issued a property insurance policy on the home. Federal foreclosed on the home, and the sheriff sold it at auction to Citizens. Citizens sent a check for its bid to the sheriff's department, but the sheriff's department did not immediately complete processing the sheriff's sale and held Citizens' check until after fire destroyed the home. When asked to pay for the destruction of the home, Assurance claimed the Wrights did not have an insurable interest. Did they?

LO **3**

5. The application for a home health-care benefits policy with Life & Health Insurance Company of America listed nine medical conditions and asked, "Have you or your spouse within the past 5 years had or been told you have the following." Next to "kidney failure" and "chronic obstructive lung disease" Harold Green checked the "no" box. Green signed the application that stated, "The answers given by me are full, true and complete to the best of my knowledge and belief." Life issued the policy. A year later, Green made a claim. Life discovered Green suffered from chronic renal failure and chronic obstructive pulmonary disease, although his physician had merely told Green he had "some sluggish kidneys" and "a little bronchitis." Life rescinded the policy based on material misrepresentations in the application, and Green sued alleging he answered honestly. May Life rescind the policy?

6. Barbara Garnes had two Bose speakers stolen from her. Her insurance company paid her for the loss. The thief pawned the speakers at King's Pawn Shop, owned by Jerry King. The police seized them as evidence. In court proceedings to determine to whom the speakers should go, King argued he purchased them in good faith and had a right to them against everyone but the true owner—Garnes. Having paid Garnes, the insurance company claimed it was entitled to subrogation and could assert Garnes's superior rights to the speakers. Who should get the speakers?   LO ❸

7. Hazel loaned Bean $120,000, and the note required Bean to maintain a life insurance policy on his life, with Hazel the beneficiary in an amount not less than the remaining balance due on the note. Bean changed the beneficiary on a $200,000 life insurance policy he owned naming Hazel the beneficiary of $120,000. Bean made payments on the note and paid all the premiums on the life insurance policy. Bean died owing $80,000 on the note. When the insurance company paid Hazel $120,000, Bean's estate sued for the $40,000 that exceeded the balance due on the note. Because a creditor has an insurable interest in the life of the debtor only to the amount of the debt, the estate argued Hazel could only be paid $80,000. Whose insurable interest is relevant here, and what impact does that have on naming Hazel the beneficiary of $120,000?   LO ❷

8. Kimberly and Walter Goodwin applied for a life insurance policy on Walter from Investors Life Insurance Co. through its agent, Charles Toomey. Toomey asked the Goodwins questions from the application and filled out the form. One question asked, "Within the past two years have you had your driver's license suspended or had two or more moving violations or accidents?" Toomey checked the box indicating "no." Kimberly knew Walter's license had been suspended three months previously and that he had two moving violations as well as two accidents within two years. The Goodwins signed the application, which stated they had read it and given complete and true answers. Investors issued the policy. Eight months later, Walter died from massive head trauma received in an accident while racing at 70 MPH in a 35 MPH zone. Investors found out about Walter's driving record and refused to pay, claiming false representation. Should Investors have to pay?   LO ❸

Types of Insurance

LEARNING OBJECTIVES

1 Explain the nature of life insurance and its normal limitations.

2 Define property insurance.

3 Identify the types of coverage afforded by automobile insurance.

PREVIEW CASE

The decree divorcing Michael Stone and Joan Thomas provided that Joan was to remain the beneficiary on one-half of the life insurance provided by Michael's employer so long as he remained obligated by the decree to provide child or spousal support to Joan. After Michael married Wendy, he designated her as the beneficiary for his $250,000 life insurance policy. Michael died owing child support of $62. Wendy argued that because the divorce decree required Michael to designate Joan a beneficiary as security for his child support obligation, and he had only one child support payment in the net amount of $62 remaining, Joan was only entitled to $62 in proceeds from the insurance policy. Was Michael required to obey the divorce decree? What would Joan have received if Michael had owed $5,000?

Insurance companies provide many types of policies to help people protect against financial loss. Three types of policies that most people purchase include:

1. Life insurance
2. Property insurance
3. Automobile insurance

LIFE INSURANCE

LO 1
Nature of life insurance

Life insurance is a contract by which the insurer agrees to pay a specified sum or sums of money to a beneficiary upon the death of the insured. An insured generally obtains life insurance to protect the beneficiary from financial hardship resulting from the death of the insured.

Types of Life Insurance Contracts

The most important types of life insurance policies include:

1. Term insurance
2. Endowment insurance
3. Whole life insurance
4. Combinations

Term Insurance

Term insurance contracts are those whereby the company assumes for a specified period of time the risk of the death of the insured. The term may be for only 1 year; or it may be for 5, 10, or even 50 years. The term must be stated in the policy.

Many variations of term policies exist. In short-term policies, such as five years, the insured might have the option of renewing it for another equal term without a physical examination. This is called **renewable term insurance**. The cost is higher for each renewal period. In nonrenewable term insurance, the insured does not have the right to renew unless the company consents.

Term policies also may be either level term or decreasing term. In level term contracts, the face of the policy is written in units of $1,000. The face amount remains the same during the entire term of the policy. In decreasing term contracts, the length of time the proceeds are collected or the face amount decreases over the life of the policy. The policy may be written in multiples of an amount of monthly income. For example, a person age 20 could purchase a decreasing term policy of 50 units, or $500 a month, covering a period of 600 months, or 50 years. If the insured dies the first month after purchasing the policy, the beneficiary would draw $500 a month for 600 months or $300,000 ultimately. If the insured dies at the end of 25 years, the beneficiary would draw $500 a month for 300 months or $150,000 ultimately. Some decreasing term insurance is paid in a lump sum rather than periodically.

All term policies have one thing in common—they are pure life insurance. They shift the specific risk of loss as a result of death and nothing more.

Endowment Insurance

An **endowment insurance** policy is decreasing term insurance plus a savings account. Part of the premium pays for the insurance, and the remainder earns interest so that at the end of the term the savings will equal the face amount of the policy. If the insured dies during the term of the policy, the beneficiary will collect the face. If the insured is still living at the end of the term, the insurance company pays the face to the insured or a designated beneficiary.

Whole Life Insurance

All life insurance contracts are either term insurance or endowment insurance. A whole life insurance policy is one that continues, assuming the premium is paid, until age 100 or death, whichever occurs first. If the insured is still living at age 100, the face of the policy is collected as an endowment. A whole life policy might correctly be defined as endowment insurance at age 100.

Life Insurance
Contract of insurer to pay money on death of insured

Term Insurance
Contract whereby insurer assumes risk of death of insured for specified time

Renewable Term Insurance
Term insurance renewable without physical examination

Endowment Insurance
Decreasing term insurance plus savings account

Combinations

The three basic life insurance contracts—term, endowment, and whole life—can be combined in an almost endless variety of combinations to create slightly different contracts. In the case of universal life insurance, any premiums paid that exceed the current cost of term insurance are put into a fund and earn interest. The fund can be withdrawn by the owner or paid to the beneficiary at the death of the insured. The Family Income Policy, for example, is merely a straight life policy with a 20-year decreasing term policy attached as a rider.

Insurers frequently add several other riders to life insurance policies for an added premium. The disability income rider may be attached to any policy and pays an income to an insured who becomes disabled. A rider requiring the insurer to make a greater payment, customarily twice the ordinary amount when death is caused by accidental means, is called a **double indemnity rider**.

Double Indemnity Rider
Policy requiring insurer to pay twice ordinary face amount if death is accidental

Limitation on Risks in Life Insurance Contracts

Two common limitations on the risk covered by life insurance include: (1) suicide and (2) death from war activity.

Suicide

Life insurance policies commonly refuse payment when death occurs from suicide. Other suicide clauses stipulate that the company will not pay if the suicide occurs within two years from the date of the policy.

COURT CASE

Facts: Before her death, Fister left messages with friends indicating her intention to end her life. She asked friends to assist her in either performing the task or finding someone who would. Fister told Lawrence Goldman that her death could not appear to be a suicide because her life insurance policies would exclude coverage. To make it appear that she was murdered, she asked Goldman to hold a shotgun to her head while she pulled the trigger. Fister had tied a string to the shotgun trigger housing. She attempted to pull the string, but the shotgun did not discharge. She kept pulling and then yelled at Larry to help her. Goldman pulled the trigger. He pled guilty to voluntary manslaughter. Allstate Life Insurance Company had issued life insurance policies on Fister's life within two years of her death. Each policy excluded coverage if Fister died by suicide within that time.

Outcome: The court said that Fister did not commit suicide because she did not take her own life; rather, another person, exercising his own free will, was ultimately responsible for her death.

— *Fister ex rel. Estate of Fister v. Allstate Life Ins. Co.*, 783 A.2d 194 (Md.)

Death from War Activity

A so-called war clause provides that if the insured dies as a consequence of war activity the company will not pay. If a member of the armed forces dies a natural death, the company must pay. In order to refuse payment, the insurance company has the burden of proving war activity caused the death.

Payment of Premiums

If the premiums are not paid when due, and the policy so provides, it either will lapse automatically or may be declared forfeited at the option of the insurer. The policy or a statute of the state may provide that after a certain number of premiums have been paid, an unpaid premium results in the issuance of a smaller, paid-up policy for the same term. By the payment of an additional premium, the insured may generally obtain a policy containing a waiver of premiums that becomes effective if the insured becomes disabled. When disability occurs, the insured does not have to pay premiums for the period of time during which the disability exists.

Grace Period

The law requires life insurance companies to provide a **grace period** of 30 or 31 days in every life insurance policy. This grace period gives the insured 30 or 31 days from the due date of the premium in which to pay it without the policy's lapsing. Without this provision, if the insured paid the premium one day late, the policy either might lapse or be forfeited by the insured. The insured might be able to obtain a reinstatement of the policy but might be required to pass a new physical examination. To buy a new policy, the insured might have to pass a physical examination and would have to pay a higher rate for the current age.

Grace Period
30- or 31-day period in which late premium may be paid without policy lapsing

Incontestability

Life insurance policies are incontestable after a certain period of time, usually one or two years. After that time, the insurance company usually cannot contest the validity of a claim on any ground except nonpayment of premiums.

Change of Beneficiary

Life insurance policies ordinarily reserve to the insured the right to change the beneficiary at will. Policies also permit the insured to name successive beneficiaries so that if the first beneficiary should die before the insured, the proceeds would pass to the second named or contingent beneficiary.

PREVIEW CASE REVISITED

Facts: The decree divorcing Michael Stone and Joan Thomas provided that Joan was to remain the beneficiary on one-half of the life insurance provided by Michael's employer so long as he remained obligated by the decree to provide child or spousal support to Joan. After Michael married Wendy, he designated her as the beneficiary for all of his $250,000 life insurance policy. Michael died owing child support of $62. Wendy argued that because the divorce decree required Michael to designate Joan a beneficiary as security for his child support obligation, and he had only one child support payment in the net amount of $62 remaining, Joan was only entitled to $62 in proceeds from the insurance policy.
Outcome: The court stated it was bound to follow the divorce decree. It held the designation of Joan as beneficiary was not limited to the amount of life insurance proceeds to which she was entitled, or to the amount of unpaid support. The designation limited only the period of time during which she was entitled to be named a beneficiary.

—*Thomas v. Stone*, 711 N.W.2d 199 (N.D.)

Courts uphold divorce decrees or separation agreements fixing beneficiaries of insurance policies. Later attempts by the insured to change a beneficiary required by a court order do not succeed.

Assignment of the Policy

The policy of insurance may be assigned (or the rights in the policy may be transferred to another) by the insured. The assignment may be either absolute or as collateral security for a loan that the insured obtains from the assignee, such as a bank.

A beneficiary also may make an assignment; however, the assignee of the beneficiary is subject to the disadvantage that the insured may change beneficiaries. If the assignment is made after the insured has died, the assignment is an ordinary assignment of an existing money claim.

Annuity Insurance

Annuity Insurance
Contract that pays monthly income to insured while alive

An **annuity insurance** contract pays the insured a monthly income from a specified age, generally age 65, until death. It is a risk entirely unrelated to the risk assumed in a life insurance contract, even though life insurance companies sell both contracts. Someone has defined life insurance as shifting the risk of dying too soon and annuity insurance as shifting the risk of living too long, or outliving one's savings. An individual age 65 who has $50,000 and a life expectancy of 72 years could use up the $50,000 over the expected seven additional years of life by using approximately $600 a month for living expenses. However, if the individual lives for more than seven years, there would be no money left. An annuity insurance policy could be purchased for $50,000, and the monthly income would be guaranteed no matter how long the insured lives. If the annuity contract calls for the monthly payments to continue until the second of two insureds dies, it is called a **joint and survivor annuity**. Couples who wish to extend their savings as long as either one is still living frequently use this type of annuity.

Joint and Survivor Annuity
Annuity paid until second of two people die

PROPERTY INSURANCE

LO ❷
Property insurance

Property Insurance
Contract by which insurer pays for damage to property

Property insurance is a contract whereby the insurer, in return for a premium, agrees to reimburse the insured for loss or damage to specified property caused by the hazard covered. A contract of property insurance is one of indemnity or compensation for loss that protects the policyholder from actual loss.

If a building actually worth $40,000 is insured for $45,000, the extra premiums that were paid for the last $5,000 worth of coverage do not provide any benefit for the insured. The actual value, $40,000, is the maximum that can be collected in case of total loss. On the other hand, if a building is insured for only $20,000 and is totally destroyed, the insurance company has to pay only $20,000. The maximum amount paid for total loss of property is the lesser of the face of the policy or the value of the property.

Losses Related to Fire

Hostile Fire
Fire out of its normal place

Friendly Fire
Fire contained where intended

Normally, fire insurance covers damage to property caused only by hostile fires. A **hostile fire** is defined as one out of its normal place, whereas a **friendly fire** is one contained in the place where it is intended to be. Scorching, searing, singeing, smoke, and similar damages from a friendly fire are not covered under a fire policy. For a fire policy to cover damage, normally an actual fire must occur. The policy does not cover loss caused by heat without fire. However, in one case the court held that soybeans were damaged by fire when there were hot spots in the beans that "glowed like charcoal and were orange" and there was an odor of smoke.

COURT CASE

Facts: Gleason Corp. owned a metal building leased to Missouri Fabricated Products (MFP). MFP made metal lawn and garden wheels in the building using a process that required the use of a degreaser—a large vat partially filled with liquid trichloroethane (TCE). Electrical coils in the bottom would warm the TCE, causing it to boil, evaporate, and create a vapor in the top of the vat. A pipe of cold water around the top caused the TCE to condense and fall back into the vat. An employee came by after the plant had closed and found some lights left on. He went into the building, found it "smoky," and called the fire department. The "smoke" was vapor from the vat that was not turned off when the cold water was. The firemen saw no flame, charring, or smoke stains. Gleason sought recovery for damage to the building from the vapor under its fire insurance policy.

Outcome: The loss was not covered under the fire policy.

—*U.S. Fidelity & Guaranty Co. v. First State Bank & Trust Co.*, 125 F.3d 680 (8th Cir.)

Fire insurance also does not cover economic loss that results from a fire. A hostile fire may cause many losses other than to the property insured, yet the fire policy on the building and contents alone will not cover these losses. An example is the loss of profits while the building is being restored. This loss can be covered by a special policy called **business interruption insurance**. If one leases property on a long-term, favorable lease and the lease is cancelled because of fire damage to the building, the tenant may have to pay a higher rent in new quarters. This increased rent loss can be covered by a **leasehold interest insurance** policy but not by a fire policy.

The typical fire policy may also cover the risks of loss by windstorm, explosion, smoke damage from a friendly fire, falling aircraft, water damage, riot and civil commotion, and many others. Each of these additional risks must be added to the fire policy by means of riders. This is commonly known as extended coverage.

Business Interruption Insurance
Insurance covering loss of profits while business building is repaired

Leasehold Interest Insurance
Covers cost of higher rent when leased building is damaged

The Property Insurance Policy

The property insurance policy will state a maximum amount that will be paid by the insurer. When only a maximum is stated, the policy is called an **open policy**, and in the event of partial or total loss, the insured must prove the actual loss that has been sustained. The policy may be a **valued policy**, in which case, instead of stating a maximum amount, it fixes values for the insured items of property. Once a policyholder shows a covered total destruction of the property, the insurer pays the total value. If only a partial loss occurs, the insured under a valued policy must still prove the amount of loss, which amount cannot exceed the stated value of the property.

Insurance policies also may be specific, blanket, or floating. A specific policy applies to one item only, such as one house. A blanket policy covers many items of the same kind in different places or different kinds of property in the same place, such as a building, fixtures, and merchandise in a single location. **Floating policies** are used for trucks, theatrical costumes, circus paraphernalia, and similar items that are not kept in a fixed location. A floating policy is also desirable for

Open Policy
Policy that requires insured to prove loss sustained

Valued Policy
Policy that fixes values for insured items

Floating Policy
Coverage no matter where property is located

items that may be sent out for cleaning, such as rugs or clothes, and articles of jewelry and clothes that may be worn while traveling. An insurance policy on household effects covers for loss only at the named location. The purpose of the floating policy is to cover the loss no matter where the property is located at the time of the loss.

Most people who own their homes obtain **homeowners' insurance**. A homeowners' policy protects the house and also its contents from almost every peril. It covers damage from such perils as fire, wind, lightning, hail, and theft. It also covers liability of the homeowner in case someone suffers injury on the property. A tenant can obtain similar insurance that protects the tenant's personal property but not the building itself.

Another type of insurance policy of particular interest to merchants is the **Reporting Form for Merchandise Inventory**. This policy permits the merchant to report periodically, usually once a month, the amount of inventory on hand. This enables the merchant to carry full coverage at all times and still not be grossly overinsured during periods when inventory is low.

Homeowners' Policy
Coverage of many perils plus liability for owners living in their houses

Reporting Form for Merchandise Inventory
Policy allowing periodic reporting of inventory on hand to vary coverage amount

DESCRIPTION OF THE PROPERTY

All property and its location must be described with reasonable accuracy in order to identify the property and to inform the insurer of the nature of the risk involved. It is not accurate to describe a house with asphalt brick siding as brick. Personal property should be so described that in the event of loss, its value can be determined. The general description "living room furniture" may make it difficult to establish the value and the number of items. A complete inventory should be kept. If this is done, such description as "household furniture" in the policy is adequate.

Because the location of the property affects the risk, it must be specified. If personal property used in a brick house on a broad paved street is moved to a frame house on an out-of-the-way dirt road, the risk from fire may be increased considerably. To retain coverage, express permission must always be obtained from the insurer when property is moved except under a floating policy. Most homeowners' policies sold today continue coverage at a new location for several days together with coverage during the moving trip. If a loss occurs during the specified period, the company must pay, even though it received no notice of the changed location.

COINSURANCE

Coinsurance
Insured recovers in ratio of insurance to amount of insurance required

Under the principle of **coinsurance**, the insured recovers on a loss in the same ratio as the insurance bears to the amount of insurance that the company requires. Many policies contain an 80 percent coinsurance clause. This clause means the insured may carry any amount of insurance up to the value of the property, but the company will not pay the full amount of a partial loss unless insurance is carried for at least 80 percent of the value of the property. If a building is worth $50,000 and the insured buys a policy for $20,000, the company under the 80 percent coinsurance clause will pay only half of the damage and never more than $20,000. The 80 percent clause requires the insured to carry $40,000, or 80 percent of $50,000, to be fully protected from a partial loss. Because only half of this amount is carried, only half of the damage can be collected.

The coinsurance clause may be some percentage other than 80 percent. In burglary insurance, it may be as low as 5 or 10 percent. On rare occasions, it is as high as 100 percent in fire insurance.

REPAIRS AND REPLACEMENTS

Most insurance contracts give the insurer the option of paying the amount of loss or repairing or replacing the property. The amount the insurance company will pay for a loss will vary depending on whether market value or replacement cost is used to measure the amount of loss. If market value is used, the insurance company will pay whatever the value of the property was immediately before the loss. If the property has been used for several years, the market value could be much less than the cost to replace the property. If replacement value is used, the insurance company will pay what the cost is to procure another item as identical to the insured item as possible. Even if the item is older and shows wear and tear, it will be replaced with a new one. For example, suppose fire damages Alphonse's 15-year-old furniture, for which he paid $5,000. Alphonse has raised four children, so the furniture has seen a lot of use and has not always had the best treatment. The market value of his much-used, 15-year-old furniture would probably be very little, say $500. If Alphonse has an insurance policy that pays only market value, he would recover only $500. If the policy pays replacement cost it could easily cost $5,000 or more to replace the furniture. The amount paid by the insurance company can thus vary dramatically depending on whether market value or replacement cost is the measure. Which measure is used will depend on the policy.

When the property is repaired or replaced, materials of like kind and quality must be used. The work must be completed within a reasonable time. When the insurance company has the choice of repair or replacement, the insurer seldom exercises the option to replace. The insurer also may have the option of taking the property at an agreed valuation and then paying the insured the full value of the damaged property.

DEFENSE AND NOTICE OF LAWSUITS

Under a **defense clause** found in property insurance policies that protect the insured from liability to others injured on the property or by the property, the insurer agrees to defend the insured against any claim for damages. This means that if the insured is sued, the insurance company supplies a lawyer to defend the suit. For example, under a normal homeowners' policy, the homeowner is protected not only against damage to the property but also from liability to anyone injured on the property. If someone who slips on ice at the door sues the homeowner, the insurance company will supply a lawyer to defend the suit. This saves the insured the cost of hiring an attorney.

Defense Clause
Policy clause in which insurer agrees to defend insured against damage claims

C O U R T   C A S E

Facts: Arc Electrical Construction Co. employed Edward Holmes on a construction project for which Arc was a subcontractor for Tishman Construction Corp. Holmes was injured on the job and sued Tishman and Morgan Guaranty and Trust Co., the owner of the property. Tishman and Morgan sued Northbrook Property and Casualty Company, which had issued an insurance policy, claiming Northbrook was obligated to defend them. Once Holmes sued Tishman and Morgan, they did not notify Northbrook of the suit for 10 months.

Outcome: The court held that the unexcused delay of 10 months in notifying Northbrook of Holmes's suit released Northbrook from its duty to defend the suit.

— Holmes v. Morgan Guaranty & Trust Co. of N.Y.,
636 N.Y.S.2d 778 (App. Div.)

In the event of an injury to a third party or an accident in the case of automobile insurance, the policyholder has the duty to give the insurer written notice and proof of loss regarding the damages. The notice must identify the insured and give such information as the names and address of injured persons, the owner of any damaged property, witnesses, and the time, place, and detailed circumstances of the incident. This notice must be given within a reasonable time.

If a claim or a suit is brought against the insured, every demand, notice, or summons received must immediately be forwarded to the insurance company. The insured must give the fullest cooperation to the insurer, who normally has the right to settle out of court any claims or lawsuits as it deems best.

AUTOMOBILE INSURANCE

LO ❸
Auto insurance coverage

Automobile insurance is a special type of property insurance and includes two major classes of insurance: physical damage insurance (including fire, theft, and collision) and public liability insurance (including bodily injury and property damage). To understand the law, one must know what specific risk the insurance carrier assumes and the terms of the policy covering that specific risk. The term *automobile insurance* refers to insurance that the insured obtains to cover a car and the injuries that the insured and other members of the family may sustain. The term also refers to liability insurance, which protects the insured from claims that third persons may make for injuries to them or damage to their property caused by the insured.

Physical Damage Insurance

Physical Damage Insurance
Insurance for damage to car itself

As the name implies, **physical damage insurance** covers the risks of injury or damage to the car itself. It includes:

1. Fire insurance
2. Theft insurance
3. Collision insurance
4. Comprehensive coverage

Fire Insurance

Much of the law of property insurance discussed in the preceding pages applies to automobile insurance. The fire policy covers loss to a car damaged or destroyed by the burning of any conveyance on which the car is being transported, such as a barge, boat, or train. Fire insurance can be obtained separately but is normally included in comprehensive coverage.

Theft Insurance

Theft
Taking another's property without consent

Conversion
Obtaining possession of property and converting it to own use

Robbery
Taking property by force

Theft is taking another's property without the owner's consent with the intent to wrongfully deprive the owner of the property. Automobile theft insurance either by law or by contract normally covers a wide range of losses. Obtaining possession of a car and converting it to one's own use to the exclusion of or inconsistent with the rights of the owner is known as **conversion**. Taking another's car by force or threat of force is known as **robbery**. In some states, the automobile theft policy must cover all these losses. The policy itself may define theft broadly enough to cover theft, conversion, and robbery. Unless the policy is broadened either by law or by the wording of the policy, a theft policy covers only the wrongful deprivation of the car without claim of right.

COURT CASE

Facts: Rachel Collier arranged with her neighbor, Rick Tinley, to trade her Nissan, insured by State Farm Mutual Automobile Insurance Co., for a Lincoln. Tinley told her to sign the power of attorney on the Nissan title, pay him $480 down and $5,000 additional. The Nissan was to be sold to pay off its loan and the rest applied to the purchase of the Lincoln. She made one payment of $2,500, but when the papers on the Lincoln arrived, Collier's husband thought they were not right and called the police. The Lincoln and other cars in Tinley's driveway were stolen. Collier's Nissan was gone and the Lincoln was taken too. Her insurance policy excluded "loss . . . due to: . . . conversion, [or] embezzlement . . . by any person who has the vehicle due to any . . . sales agreement." Collier sued State Farm.

Outcome: Because theft by conversion or embezzlement by a person who had the car due to a sales agreement was not covered, State Farm did not have to pay Collier.

—Collier v. State Farm Mut. Automobile Ins. Co., **549 S.E.2d 810 (Ga. App.)**

Automobile theft insurance usually covers pilferage of any parts of the car but not articles or clothes left in the car. It also covers any damage done to the car either by theft or attempted theft. It does not cover loss of use of the car unless the policy specifically provides for this loss.

Collision Insurance

The standard collision policy covers all damage to the car caused by a collision or upset. A collision occurs whenever an object strikes the insured car or the car strikes an object. Both objects need not be automobiles nor be moving. Frequently, collision policies require the collision to be "accidental." A court held that a rolling rock that crashed into a parked car constituted a collision. Likewise, there was a collision when a horse kicked the door of the insured automobile. However, no collision occurs when the colliding object consists of a natural phenomenon, such as rain or hail. If the language of an insurance policy can be given two different, reasonable interpretations, the interpretation most helpful to the insured is used.

Practically all collision policies void or suspend coverage if a car hauls a trailer unless insurance of the same kind carried on the car is placed on the trailer. The question of interpretation then arises as to what constitutes a "trailer." A small boat trailer and a small two-wheel trailer generally are not considered trailers, but horse or cattle trailers are.

If a car has collision insurance but not fire insurance, the policy will, in most states, pay both the fire loss and the collision loss occurring in the same wreck so long as the fire ensues after collision and is a direct result of it.

Most collision insurance policies have a **deductible clause**. A deductible clause provides that the insurance company will pay for damages to the car in excess of a specified amount. The specified amount, called the *deductible*, is usually $100 to $250. The insured must pay this amount. Suppose a collision results in $850 in damages to a car covered by $250 deductible collision insurance. The insured must pay the first $250 and the insurance company pays the remainder—$600. Policies without any deductible clause have extremely high rates. It is much cheaper for the insured to assume some of the risk.

An insurance company may pay the insured a claim for collision damage caused by someone else's negligence. If so, under the law of subrogation the company has the right to sue this other party to the collision for the damages.

Deductible Clause
Insurance provision whereby insured pays damage up to specified amount; company pays excess up to policy limits

Comprehensive Coverage

Insurance companies will write automobile insurance covering almost every conceivable risk to a car, such as windstorm, earthquake, flood, strike, spray from trees, malicious mischief, submersion in water, acid from the battery, riot, glass breakage, hail, and falling aircraft. A comprehensive policy may include all of these risks plus fire and theft. A **comprehensive policy** covers only the hazards enumerated in the policy, and collision is normally excluded.

Comprehensive Policy
Insurance covering large number of miscellaneous risks

Public Liability Insurance

The second major division of automobile insurance, **public liability insurance** protects third persons from bodily injury and property damage.

Public Liability Insurance
Insurance designed to protect third persons from bodily injury and property damage

Bodily Injury Insurance

Bodily injury insurance covers the risk of bodily injury to the insured's passengers, pedestrians, or the occupants of another car. The insurance company obligates itself to pay any sum not exceeding the limit fixed in the policy for which the insured may be personally liable. If the insured has no liability for damages, the insurance company has no liability except the duty of defending the insured in court actions brought by injured persons. This type of insurance does not cover any injury to the person or the property of the insured.

Coverage under an automobile liability policy is usually written as 10/20/5, 25/50/10, 100/300/15, or similar combinations. The first number indicates that the company will pay $10,000, $25,000, or $100,000, respectively, to any one person for bodily injury in any one accident. The middle number fixes the maximum amount the company will pay for bodily injury to more than one person in any one accident. The third figure sets the limit the company will pay for property damage. This usually is the damage to the other person's car but may include damage to any property belonging to someone other than the insured.

A bodily injury insurance policy does not cover accidents occurring while an underage person drives the car. It may not cover accidents occurring while the car is rented or leased unless specifically covered, while the car is used to carry passengers for a consideration, while the car is used for any purpose other than that named in the policy, or while it is used outside the United States and Canada. Some policies exclude accidents while the car is being used for towing a trailer or any other vehicle used as a trailer. These are the ordinary exclusions. Policies may have additional exclusions of various kinds.

The insured may not settle claims or incur expenses other than those for immediate medical help. As in the case of property insurance, the insurer has a duty to defend any lawsuits and the insured must give prompt notice of any claims or suits. In the event that the insurance company pays a loss, it is subrogated to any rights that the insured has against others because of such losses.

Property Damage Insurance

In automobile property damage insurance, the insurer agrees to pay, on behalf of the insured, all sums the insured may be legally obligated to pay for damages arising out of the ownership, maintenance, or use of the automobile. The liability of the insurer, however, is limited as stated in the policy.

The policy usually provides that the insurer will not be liable in the event that the car is being operated, maintained, or used by any person in violation of any

COURT ⚖ CASE

Facts: Continental Western Insurance Co. insured Leo Deprez's car. Deprez was seriously injured when an oncoming car driven by Susan Sedelmeier spun out of control and hit his car. He sued Sedelmeier but later dismissed the suit. Deprez did not notify Continental of the suit or the accident until four years later when he sought payment under one of the provisions of his policy. The statute of limitations had run on any claims against Sedelmeier. Continental refused to pay on the ground he had breached the contract provisions which required him to promptly notify it of an accident or any lawsuit. Deprez sued Continental.

Outcome: The court pointed out that the policy required prompt notice of any accident or lawsuit. Deprez failed to notify Continental of either and it could otherwise have intervened in the lawsuit to protect its interests. Judgment was for Continental.

—Deprez v. Continental Western Ins. Co.,
584 N.W.2d 805 (Neb.)

state or federal law as to age or occupation. The insurer has no liability for damage to property owned by, leased to, transported by, or in charge of the insured.

Medical Payments and Uninsured Motorist Insurance

In addition to physical damage and public liability insurance, there is insurance that covers injury to the insured or passengers in the insured's car. Medical payments cover bodily injury and are paid regardless of other insurance. Uninsured motorist coverage protects the insured when injury results from the negligence of another driver who does not have liability insurance.

Recovery Even When at Fault

Normally the injured party must prove the driver of the insured car was negligent or at fault before the insurer becomes liable. Frequently, both drivers are negligent. Formerly, if the driver who sues negligently contributed even slightly to the accident, no recovery could be had. This harsh rule has been replaced in most states by the **last clear chance rule**. This rule states that if one driver is negligent but the other driver had one last clear chance to avoid hitting the negligent driver and did not take it, the driver who had the last clear chance is liable.

In a number of states, **comparative negligence** statutes also have modified the harshness of the common-law rule as to contributory negligence. These statutes provide that the contributory negligence of the plaintiff reduces the recovery but does not completely bar recovery from a negligent defendant. That means the court balances the negligence of each party against that of the other. Suppose that Roemer and Griffero have an automobile accident and both were negligent. It is determined that the damage to Roemer's car was caused 60 percent by Griffero and 40 percent by Roemer's own negligence. If the total damage to Roemer's car is $2,500, Griffero will have to pay 60 percent or $1,500.

Some states have established **no-fault insurance**. Under this plan, insurance companies pay for injuries suffered by their insureds no matter who has responsibility for negligence. States use this no-fault plan for a limited amount of damages. Above this amount, the fault rules apply. The purpose of no-fault insurance is to make sure that injured parties are compensated promptly and reduce the number of lawsuits. It is assumed that it is faster and easier to collect from your own insurance company than from the insurance company of the other driver.

Last Clear Chance
Negligent driver recovers if other driver had one last clear chance to avoid injury

Comparative Negligence
Contributory negligence reduces but does not bar recovery

No-Fault Insurance
Insurance companies pay for their insureds' injuries regardless of fault

Required Insurance

People with poor driving records might find it difficult or impossible to obtain mandatory automobile insurance. When the law requires a person to carry insurance in order to be permitted to drive but no insurance company will sell a policy, a state agency will assign this driver to an insurance company. The company must issue the policy under the "assigned risk" rule. States require all insurance companies to accept the drivers assigned in this manner.

QUESTIONS

1. What is it that all term life insurance policies have in common?
2. What is a double indemnity rider?
3. What is the benefit of a grace period?
4. May a beneficiary assign a life insurance policy? Explain.
5. What is the maximum amount an insurer will pay for total loss of property?
6. Why must property and its location be described accurately?
7. What is the duty of the insured under a defense clause of an insurance policy?
8. What losses does automobile theft insurance usually cover as well as wrongful deprivation of the car without claim of right?
9. Give three examples of when a bodily injury insurance policy might not cover an accident.
10. Under what theories or programs may the injured party recover even when at fault?

CASE PROBLEMS

LO ❷

1. Robert Sartno worked for Frankie's Pizzeria and Restaurant cleaning the restaurant, preparing food, and delivering pizza. He was paid by the hour, regardless of his duties. Pizza delivery was free, but Sartno was permitted to keep any tips he received. Sartno left to deliver pizzas. He did not see Michele Hebal while crossing behind his car. The car rolled backward, hitting Hebal. Sartno did not habitually use his personal vehicle to deliver pizza. He insured his vehicle through Prudential Property and Casualty Insurance Company. The policy contained a cars for hire exclusionary provision that stated: "We will not pay for bodily injury . . . caused by anyone using a car covered under this part to carry people or property for a fee." Hebal sued Sartno. Prudential alleged Sartno carried property for a fee because his deliveries occurred during the course of his employment, for which he received wages; therefore, the exclusion applied. Did Sartno carry "property for a fee"?

LO ❶

2. After being diagnosed with terminal lung cancer, Albert Lauer applied for life insurance with American Family Life Insurance Co. He did not disclose the diagnosis or that he had been treated with chemotherapy. Lauer paid the first premium on March 26, and American issued a conditional receipt. The receipt supplied temporary life insurance that ended at the earlier of 120 days, or the date a policy was issued. American issued the policy on April 12. Lauer died two years and two days after the date of the conditional receipt, but before two years after issuance of the policy. The policy's incontestability clause stated the

company would not contest its validity after it had been in force "for two years from . . . the [i]ssue [d]ate . . . " Lauer's wife, Marilyn, submitted a claim under the policy, and American denied it because of Lauer's misrepresentation of his health. Marilyn argued that the two-year period began the date the company issued the conditional receipt. Did it?

3. Jones, Walker, Waechter, Poitevent, Carrere & Denegre, L.L.P. stored business personal property with Records Storage & Services, Inc. (RSSI). RSSI stored it in a warehouse located at 900 Atlantic Street. The property was damaged. Certain Underwriters at Lloyd's London was the commercial property insurer of RSSI. The Lloyd's policy stated that for contents or personal property to be considered covered property, a limit of insurance had to be shown on the Declaration page of the policy. The only coverage relating to 900 Atlantic St. was (1) for the building itself and (2) for business income. The Declaration page of the Lloyd's policy did not reflect any coverage for contents or the personal property of others. Jones sued Lloyd's. Was Lloyd's liable? LO ❷

4. Kelly Strode ran over Dianna Silcox while driving a pickup truck and fled the scene of the accident. The police were able to identify Strode as the driver, and Silcox learned his identity also. She notified Strode's insurer, Utica Mutual Insurance Co., a year after the accident. She then sued Strode and obtained a $60,000 default judgment. Again, she informed Utica of the judgment. The insurer sued Silcox and Strode asking the court to order that it had no duty under the insurance policy because the policy required prompt notice of accidents. Did the insurer have any responsibility under the policy? LO ❸

5. Standard Life Insurance Co. of Indiana insured Michael Tedrow's life. He became despondent when his marriage broke up, and he left a suicide note. Then he started his pickup's engine in his enclosed garage. He apparently changed his mind about committing suicide because he was found overcome by carbon monoxide in the house near the front door. The medical examiner ruled Tedrow's death a suicide, so Standard denied the beneficiary's claim for death benefits because the policy excluded suicide within two years from issue. Did Tedrow die by suicide? LO ❷

6. David and Kimberly Hall bought automobile insurance including collision coverage from Acadia Insurance Co. An accident caused damage to their vehicle. The Halls claimed payment for repair work and the diminution in the value of the vehicle for having been repaired. The insurance policy limited liability to the lesser of the value of the damaged vehicle or the amount needed to repair it. Acadia paid the Halls for the repair work only, and the Halls sued arguing that "repair" included supplying what was lost—the value of the vehicle. Are the Halls entitled to more than the repair costs? LO ❷, ❸

7. Guardian Pearl Street Garage Corp. leased a portion of a building from ZKZ Associates LP. Guardian carried a liability insurance policy with CNA Insurance Co., which also covered ZKZ for liability "arising out of the ownership, maintenance and use of that part of the described premises which is leased" to Guardian. A pedestrian tripped and fell on the sidewalk used for access in and out of Guardian's garage and sued ZKZ. Did CNA have a duty to defend the suit? LO ❶

Security Devices

LEARNING OBJECTIVES

1. State the general nature of contracts of guaranty or suretyship.
2. Identify ways contracts of guaranty and suretyship are discharged.
3. Discuss the rights of the parties in a secured credit sale.
4. Discuss the rights of the seller and buyer in a secured credit sale.

PREVIEW CASE

Jackie L. Eley owned a pickup truck purchased through a loan from Mid/East Acceptance Corporation of N.C., Inc. Eley missed two consecutive payments, and Mid/East arranged for repossession with Carolina Repossessions. At approximately 4:00 A.M., Roger Pinkham of Carolina arrived at Eley's home and began to hitch her pickup to his tow truck. Eley heard him and explained she was not contesting the repossession but that she was concerned about the 130 watermelons in the truck bed. The truck also contained a coat, an ice chest, and some children's toys. Eley asked to unload her melons and other personal property. Pinkham refused. Eley called Mid/East's office at 8:00 A.M. and spoke to an employee who denied knowledge of the truck. Eley filed a complaint alleging conversion. Did Mid/East have a right to the melons and other personal property? Had Eley had an opportunity to recover her personal property?

This chapter discusses two types of security devices: (1) guaranty and suretyship contracts and (2) secured credit sales.

GUARANTY AND SURETYSHIP

A contract of guaranty or suretyship is an agreement whereby one party promises to be responsible for the debt, default, or obligation of another. Such contracts generally arise when one person assumes responsibility for the extension of credit to another, as in buying merchandise on credit or in borrowing money from a bank.

LO 1
Nature of guaranty and suretyship

A person entrusted with the money of another, such as a cashier, a bank teller, or a county treasurer, may be required to have someone guarantee the faithful performance of the duties. This contract of suretyship is commonly referred to as a **fidelity bond**.

In recent years, **bonding companies** have taken over most of the business of guaranteeing the employer against losses caused by dishonest employees. These bonding companies are paid sureties, which means they receive money for entering into the suretyship. The bonding company's obligation arises from its written contract with the employer. This contract of indemnity details the conditions under which the surety will be liable.

Parties

A contract of guaranty or of suretyship involves three parties. The party who undertakes to be responsible for another is the **guarantor**, or the **surety**; the party to whom the guaranty is given is the **creditor**; and the party who has primary liability is the principal debtor, or simply the **principal**. Because these three parties are distinct and have differing rights and obligations, it is important to identify exactly what role a party has in a guaranty or suretyship arrangement.

Fidelity Bond
Suretyship for someone who handles another's money

Bonding Company
Paid surety

Guarantor or **Surety**
Party who agrees to be responsible for obligation of another

Creditor
Party who receives guaranty

Principal
Party primarily liable

COURT CASE

Facts: As the trustees of Hopping Brook Trust, James Flett and John Arno signed a promissory note for $4 million. A mortgage on land owned by the trust secured payment of the note. Flett and Arno each also signed a personal guaranty of the trust's debt up to $1 million. The guaranties included a clear waiver of "presentment and demand for payment and protest of nonpayment." The trust defaulted on the note and it was taken over by the FDIC. The FDIC foreclosed on the mortgage without any notice to Flett and Arno. When the mortgage sale did not pay off the note, the FDIC sued Flett and

Arno for the deficiency. They alleged that they were not really guarantors but the primary obligors or principals and as such the FDIC had to give them notice of the foreclosure.

Outcome: The court stated that the waivers in the guaranties would be unnecessary if Flett and Arno were the principals instead of guarantors; therefore, they were guarantors, not principals and the FDIC did not have to give them notice of foreclosure.

—*FDIC v. Hopping Brook Trust*,
117 F.3d 639 (1st Cir.)

Distinctions

The words *surety* and *guarantor* are often used interchangeably, and they have many similarities. Some states have abolished any distinction between them. However, in other states, their legal usages differ. In a contract of suretyship, the surety has liability coextensive with that of the principal debtor. The surety has direct and primary responsibility for the debt or obligation just like the primary debtor. The surety's obligation, then, is identical with the debtor's.

A guarantor's obligation is secondary to that of the principal debtor. As a secondary obligation, the guaranty agreement may not even be executed at the same time or in the same instrument as the principal obligation. The guarantor's promise to pay comes into effect only in the event the principal defaults. The guarantor's obligation does not arise simultaneously with the principal's. The obligation depends on the happening of another event, namely, the failure of the principal to pay.

For the most part, the law of suretyship applies with equal force to both paid sureties and accommodation sureties. A bail bondsman is a paid surety. An accommodation surety agrees to be a surety as a favor to the principal. A parent who cosigns a note for a teenager constitutes an accommodation surety. In some instances, the contract of a paid surety will be interpreted strictly. Thus, in the case of acts claimed to discharge the surety, courts sometimes require paid sureties to prove that they have actually been harmed by the conduct of the principal before allowing recovery.

Importance of Making a Distinction

In states that recognize a difference between guarantors and sureties, the distinctions involve three aspects:

1. Form
2. Notice of default
3. Remedy

Form. All the essential elements of a contract must be present in both contracts of guaranty and contracts of suretyship. However, a contract of guaranty must be in writing (see Illustration 39–1), whereas most contracts of suretyship may normally be oral.

ILLUSTRATION 39–1 A Letter of Guaranty

WATERS, MELLEN AND COMPANY
900 West Lake Avenue
Cincinnati, Ohio 45227

May 16, 20–

Ms. Norma Rae
201 E. Fifth Street
Campton, KY 41301

Dear Ms. Rae

In consideration of the letting of the premises located at 861 South Street, this city, to Mr. William H. Prost for a period of two years from date, I hereby guarantee the punctual payment of the rent and the faithful performance of the covenants of the lease.

Very truly yours

Orvinne L. Meyer
Vice-President, Personnel

The Uniform Commercial Code (UCC) provides: "The promise to answer for the debt, default, or obligation of another must be in writing and be signed by the party to be charged or by his authorized agent." This provision should apply to a promise that creates a secondary obligation, which means an obligation of guaranty, not to a promise that creates a primary obligation or suretyship.

Notice of Default. A creditor need not notify sureties—parties primarily liable for the debt—if the principal defaults. On the other hand, the creditor must notify guarantors. In some states, failure to give notice does not of itself discharge the guarantyship. A guarantor damaged by the failure to receive notice may offset the amount of the damage against the claim of the creditor.

Remedy. In the case of suretyship, the surety assumes an original obligation. The surety must pay. Sureties have liability as fully and under the same conditions as if the debt were theirs from the beginning. The rule is different in many contracts of guaranty. In a conditional guaranty, the guarantor has liability only if the other party cannot pay.

For example, Arnold writes, "Let Brewer have a suit; if he cannot pay you, I will." This guaranty depends on Brewer's ability to pay. Therefore, the seller must make all reasonable efforts to collect from Brewer before collecting from Arnold. If Arnold had written, "Let Brewer have this suit, and I will pay you," an original obligation would have been created for which Arnold would have been personally liable. Therefore, Arnold would be deemed a surety if the understanding was that Arnold was to pay for the suit.

Rights of the Surety and the Guarantor

A guarantor and a surety have the following rights:

1. Indemnity
2. Subrogation
3. Contribution
4. Exoneration

Indemnity. A guarantor or surety who pays the debt or the obligation of the principal has the right to be reimbursed by the principal, known as the right of **indemnity**. The guarantor or the surety may be induced to pay the debt when it becomes due to avoid the accumulation of interest and other costs on the debt.

Subrogation. When the guarantor or the surety pays the debt of the principal, the law automatically assigns the claim of the creditor to the guarantor or surety. The payment also entitles the guarantor or surety to all property, liens, or securities that were held by the creditor to secure the payment of the debt. This right of subrogation does not arise until the creditor has been paid in full, but it does arise if the surety or the guarantor has paid a part of the debt and the principal has paid the remainder.

Contribution. Two or more persons jointly liable for the debt, default, or obligation of a certain person are **coguarantors** or **cosureties**. Guarantors or sureties who have paid more than their proportionate share of the debt are entitled to recover from the other guarantors or sureties the amount in excess of their pro rata share of the loss. This is the right of **contribution**. It does not arise until the surety or the guarantor has paid the debts of the principal in full or has otherwise settled the debt.

Indemnity
Right of guarantor to be reimbursed by principal

Coguarantors or **Cosureties**
Two or more people jointly liable for another's obligation

Contribution
Right of coguarantor to recover excess of proportionate share of debt from other coguarantor(s)

COURT CASE

Facts: Preferred Capital (PC) managed Lakeview Tower Apartments and had a liability insurance policy with American Equity Insurance Co. (AE). Under its management contract, PC also had to be named as an insured in the Travelers Casualty & Surety Co. insurance policy covering the building. A tenant at Lakeview, Alonzo Henry, sued PC after he was injured jumping out of his window to escape from an intruder. Travelers defended the lawsuit, but AE refused to participate. Travelers settled with Henry and then sued AE for contribution of half the costs of defense and settlement. Travelers argued that because both insurance companies were equally liable it should only have to pay half the costs.

Outcome: Since both insurance companies insured the same risk, Travelers was entitled to contribution from AE.

—*Travelers Casualty & Surety Co. v. American Equity Ins. Co.,* 113 Cal. Rptr. 2d 613 (Cal. App.)

Exoneration
Guarantor's right to have creditor compel payment of debt

Exoneration. A surety or guarantor may call on the creditor to proceed to compel the payment of the debt; otherwise the surety or guarantor will be released. This is the right of **exoneration**. The creditor may delay in pressing the debtor to pay because of the security of the suretyship. A creditor who fails to compel payment when due releases the surety in cases in which the debtor can pay. The surety then has no uncertainty concerning potential liability.

Discharge of a Surety or a Guarantor

LO 2
Discharge of guaranty or suretyship

The usual methods of discharging any obligation, including performance, voluntary agreement, and bankruptcy of the surety or guarantor, discharge both a surety and a guarantor. However, some additional acts that will discharge the surety or the guarantor include:

1. Extension of time
2. Alteration of the terms of the contract
3. Loss or return of collateral by the creditor

Extension of Time. If the creditor extends the time of the debt without the consent of the surety or the guarantor and for a consideration, the surety or the guarantor is discharged from further liability.

Alteration of the Terms of the Contract. A material alteration of the contract by the creditor without the surety's or guarantor's consent discharges the surety or guarantor. In most states, the change must be prejudicial to the surety or the guarantor. A reduction in the interest rate has been held not to discharge the surety, whereas a change in the place of payment has been held to be an act justifying a discharge of the surety. A material change in a contract constitutes substituting a new contract for the old. The surety guaranteed the payment of the old contract, not the new one.

Creditor's Loss or Return of Collateral. If the creditor through negligence loses or damages collateral security given to secure the debt, a surety or a guarantor is discharged. The return of any collateral security to the debtor also discharges a surety or guarantor. Collateral must be held for the benefit of the surety until the debtor pays the debt in full.

COURT CASE

Facts: Dee Keip and Fina Shubert guaranteed a lease entered into by their closely held corporation with Elva Mangold, the owner of the leased property. The corporation and Mangold renewed the lease and added a provision that gave Mangold an unqualified right to end the lease if the corporation-tenant made an unauthorized commercial use of the property. When the corporation defaulted on the renewed lease, Mangold sued Keip and Shubert under their guaranty.

Outcome: The court said that adding the provision in the renewed lease was a material change and released the guarantors.

—*Mangold v. Keip*, 679 N.Y.S.2d 240

SECURED CREDIT SALES

When someone other than the buyer finances goods (a credit purchase is made), a convenient way to protect creditors from loss is to allow them to have an interest in the goods. When sellers retain the right to repossess the items sold if the buyers breach the sales contracts, the transactions are **secured credit sales**. In such cases, the buyers obtain possession of the items, and the risk of loss passes to them. Article 9 of the UCC governs secured credit sales. A security interest cannot attach or become enforceable until the buyer and seller agree it shall attach, the seller gives value, and the buyer has the right to possess or use the item.

LO ③
Rights in secured credit sales

Secured Credit Sale
Sale in which seller retains right to repossess goods upon default

Security Agreement

A creditor may not enforce a security interest unless the buyer has signed a security agreement. The **security agreement** is a written agreement, signed by the buyer, that describes the collateral, or the item sold, and usually contains the terms of payment and names of the parties.

Security Agreement
Written agreement signed by buyer that creditor has a security interest in collateral

COURT CASE

Facts: Dianna Meade orally agreed to sell Carson Thacker mining equipment and supplies. Meade provided the items with the understanding that title would pass to Thacker only as he paid for them, and any items not paid for would be returned to Meade. Thacker used the items while mining property leased from Richardson. Thacker and Richardson's agreement allowed Thacker to remove all personal property, except items belonging to Richardson, within 30 days of termination of the agreement. All personal property remaining after 30 days became the property of Richardson. When Thacker's operation failed, he left items on the site and did not make demand for them for 60 days. Richardson did not release them. Meade and Thacker sued him.

Outcome: The court found that Meade's attempted reservation of title, pending payment, was the attempted reservation of a security interest. However, she had not complied with Article 9 of the UCC.

—*Meade v. Richardson Fuel, Inc.*,
166 S.W.3d 55 (Ky. App.)

Rights of the Seller

The rights of the seller, referred to as the secured party under the security agreement, may be transferred to a third person by assignment. In any sale, the buyer

LO ④
Rights of buyer and seller

may have claims or defenses against the seller. In the case of consumer sales, the Federal Trade Commission requires the seller to include in the agreement a notice that any holder of the agreement is subject to all claims and defenses that the buyer could assert against the seller. Thus, an assignee would be subject to any claims or defenses. This protection for the buyer applies only to consumer transactions.

Rights of the Buyer

The buyer, also called the debtor, has the right to transfer the collateral and require a determination of the amount owed.

Transfer of Collateral. Even though there is a security interest in the collateral, the debtor may transfer the collateral to others. Such a transfer will usually be subject to the security interest.

Determination of Amount Owed. A buyer who wishes may sign a statement indicating the amount of unpaid indebtedness believed to be owed as of a specified date and send it to the seller with the request that the statement be approved or corrected and returned.

Perfection of Security Interest

When the rights of the seller to the collateral are superior to those of third persons, the seller has a **perfected security interest**. The use to which the buyer puts collateral at the time of perfection of the security interest determines how the creditor perfects a security interest.

Inventory and Equipment. Articles purchased with the intention of reselling or leasing them are called **inventory**. **Equipment** consists of goods used or purchased for use in a business, including farming or a profession. In order to have a perfected security interest in inventory or equipment, the seller must usually file a financing statement in the appropriate public office. However, filing need not be made when the law requires a security interest to be noted on the document of title to the goods, such as in the case of noting a lien on a title to a motor vehicle. Buyers of inventory sold in the regular course of business and for value acquire title free of the security interest. For example, any time a customer goes into a store, buys, and pays for a TV, the customer obtains the TV free of any security interest. Any time an item subject to a security interest is sold at the direction of the secured party, the buyer takes it free of the security interest.

A **financing statement** is a writing signed by the debtor and the secured party that contains the address of the secured party, the mailing address of the debtor, and a statement indicating the types of or describing the collateral. A copy of the security agreement may serve as a financing statement if it contains the required items.

Fixtures. Personal property attached to buildings or real estate is called a **fixture**. A creditor perfects a security interest in fixtures by filing the financing statement in the office where a mortgage on the real estate involved would be filed or recorded. This is normally the recorder's office in the county where the real estate is located.

Consumer Goods. **Consumer goods** are items used or bought primarily for personal, family, or household purposes. A security interest in consumer goods is perfected as soon as it attaches and without filing in most cases. It is not perfected, however, against a buyer who purchases the item without knowledge of the security

---

Perfected Security Interest
Seller's right to collateral that is superior to third party's right

Inventory
Articles purchased with intention of reselling or leasing

Equipment
Goods for use in business

Financing Statement
Writing with signatures and addresses of debtor and secured party and description of collateral

Fixture
Personal property attached to real estate

Consumer Goods
Items purchased for personal, family, or household purposes

COURT CASE

Facts: When Contract Carpets (CC) sold a building to Interstate Land Corp., CC agreed to pay the balance due under a security agreement on an electronic sign on the property. The sign was 50 feet high and supported by pillars embedded in concrete. CC did not pay the balance, but continued to make monthly payments. It later refinanced this agreement to reduce the payments and signed a new conditional sales agreement with Young Electric Sign Co. (Yesco), the seller. Yesco filed a financing statement with the state Division of Corporations. After checking the county property records for encumbrances, William and Gwendolyn Webb bought the property and Interstate executed a deed stating there were no encumbrances. Two years later, CC again refinanced its balance, and Yesco again filed a financing statement with the state. CC then defaulted. Yesco discovered the Webbs owned the property and demanded they pay the $26,100 due on the sign. Without contacting Interstate, the Webbs paid off the sign and then sued Interstate saying Yesco's interest in the sign had been an encumbrance on the property. Although the sign had been personal property when sold, both parties agreed it became a permanent fixture on the property when it was installed.

Outcome: In order to perfect a security interest in a fixture, the financing statement must be filed with the county recorder where the property is located. Because Yesco did not comply with this requirement, its security interest in the sign was not protected against anyone but CC. There was no encumbrance on the property, so Interstate was not liable.

—*Webb v. Interstate Land Corp.,*
920 P.2d 1187 (Utah)

interest for value and for the buyer's own personal, family, or household use. The secured party can be protected against such a buyer only by filing a financing statement. However, as in the case of inventory and equipment, listing the secured party as the lienholder on a motor vehicle certificate of title is the way a security interest in a motor vehicle used for personal, family, or household purposes is perfected.

Duration of Filing. Perfection of a security interest by filing a financing statement lasts for five years. However, creditors may file a continuation statement that continues the effectiveness of the filing for five more years. Succeeding continuation statements may be filed, each of which lasts five years.

If a continuation statement is not filed, the effectiveness of a filing statement lapses at the end of five years. The security interest is then unperfected even against a purchaser of the goods before the lapse.

EFFECT OF DEFAULT

Under the UCC, the seller has certain rights if the buyer fails to pay according to the terms of the security agreement or otherwise breaches the contract. These rights include repossession and resale. The buyer has the rights to redemption and an accounting.

Repossession. When the buyer has the right to possession of the collateral before making full payment and the buyer breaches the purchase contract, the seller may repossess, or take back, the collateral. If it can be done without a breach of the peace, the repossession may be made without any judicial proceedings. In any case, judicial action may be sought. The seller may retain the collateral in satisfaction of the debt unless the debtor, after being notified, objects. Any personal property in the repossessed collateral must be returned to the debtor.

PREVIEW CASE REVISITED

Facts: Jackie L. Eley owned a pickup truck purchased through a loan from Mid/East Acceptance Corporation of N.C., Inc. Eley missed two consecutive payments, and Mid/East arranged for repossession with Carolina Repossessions. At approximately 4:00 A.M., Roger Pinkham of Carolina arrived at Eley's home and began to hitch her pickup to his tow truck. Eley heard him and explained she was not contesting the repossession, but that she was concerned about the 130 watermelons in the truck bed. The truck also contained a coat, an ice chest, and some children's toys. Eley asked to unload her melons and other personal property. Pinkham refused. Eley called Mid/East's office at 8:00 A.M. and spoke to an employee who denied knowledge of the truck. Eley filed a complaint alleging conversion.

Outcome: The court said Mid/East assumed and exercised the right of ownership over Eley's watermelons without her permission, to the exclusion of her own rightful ownership interest. Eley recovered damages and attorney's fees.

—MBank El Paso, N.A. v. Sanchez, 836 S.W.2d 151 (Tex.)

Resale. After default, the seller may sell the collateral. A public or private sale may be used, and any manner, time, place, and terms may be used as long as the disposition is commercially reasonable and done in good faith. Advance notice of the sale must be given to the debtor unless the goods are perishable. If the buyer has paid 60 percent or more of the cash price of the goods, the seller must resell the goods within 90 days after possession of them unless the buyer, after default, has signed a statement waiving the right to require resale. The purpose of this requirement is to cause a sale before the goods decline in value.

Redemption. At any time prior to the sale or the contracting to sell of the collateral, the buyer may redeem it by paying the amount owed and the expenses reasonably incurred by the seller in retaking and holding the collateral and preparing for the sale. This includes, if provided in the agreement, reasonable attorney's fees and legal expenses.

Accounting. After the sale of the collateral, the creditor must apply payments in the following order: the expenses of retaking and selling the collateral, the amount owed on the security interest, and all amounts owed on any subordinate security interests. The seller must pay any surplus remaining to the buyer. The buyer has liability for any deficiency.

QUESTIONS

1. Who are the parties to a contract of guaranty or suretyship?
2. Does the law apply with equal force to both paid sureties and accommodation sureties?
3. What requirements are there with respect to form for contracts of guaranty and contracts of suretyship?
4. Must a creditor notify sureties and guarantors if the principal defaults?
5. What right does a guarantor have against the principal by virtue of having paid the debt?

6. What is the impact on a surety when a creditor fails to compel payment when due?

7. Why does a material alteration in the terms of the contract by the creditor without the surety's or guarantor's consent discharge the surety or guarantor?

8. When there is a consumer sale under a security agreement, what does the Federal Trade Commission require in the agreement?

9. Why would a seller in a secured credit sale want to have a perfected security interest?

10. How may a buyer in a secured credit sale redeem the property after default?

CASE PROBLEMS

1. Valley Bank and Trust Company provided financing to an automobile dealership to purchase cars. Valley had a security interest in the dealership's motor vehicle inventory and its proceeds. Valley perfected this interest by filing a financing statement with the secretary of state. Holyoke Community Federal Credit Union provided funding for three vehicles to customers of the dealership and filed security agreements to perfect its security interest in the vehicles. Valley discovered that the dealership sold those vehicles without remitting the proceeds to it. A lawsuit between Valley and Holyoke ensued. Whose security interest was superior? LO 4

2. J.R. Simplot Company sold chemicals and fertilizer on credit to Bountiful Valley Produce, Inc. (BVP). Simplot maintained annual security agreements with BVP. It filed a UCC financing statement with the Utah Department of Commerce, Division of Corporations and Commercial Code, Central Filing System, the proper place for filing agricultural liens. The financing statement stated Simplot retained a security interest in BVP's onion crops and their proceeds. Sales King International, Inc. sold BVP's crops, collecting the proceeds and retaining amounts to cover commissions and expenses. Claiming a security interest in all BVP's crops and proceeds from their sale, Sales King filed a financing statement with the county recorder two years after Simplot's filing. From one onion crop, Sales King retained $96,597 for advances it made to BVP giving Simplot nothing. Simplot sued. Who was entitled to the proceeds? LO 3, 4

3. After Union Indemnity Insurance Co. became insolvent, 43 West 61st Street Associates (Associates) filed a claim against the company. Union had issued a performance bond covering the performance of LSR Electrical Construction Co. (LSR). Associates alleged that LSR defaulted in its performance under a construction contract, and in November Associates had Luis Electrical Contracting Corp. (Luis) complete the work. Evidence showed that both LSR and Luis had the same address; there was no paper trail documenting a default by LSR; Associates paid LSR after its alleged default in May; and Luis was involved in the work in May. If LSR had not defaulted, substituting Luis for the work was a material alteration of the contract that Union bonded. Should the claim be disallowed? LO 2

4. George Bumila agreed to loan Keiser Homes of Maine, Inc. $300,000. Keiser executed a $300,000 promissory note, which permitted assignment to Bumila, and Bumila gave Keiser two checks. One check was a bank check and the other was from Pine Hill Estates Pension Plan and Trust. Edward Luck, Dorothy Luck, LO 1

Robert Cross, Samuel Deegan, and Hanya Kandlis, all shareholders and directors of Keiser Homes, signed guaranties to George Bumila of all obligations of Keiser created by the $300,000 note. When Keiser's first payment was made to Bumila, he returned the check and asked that subsequent checks be made out to Pine Hill. Keiser's president executed a note payable to Pine Hill and Bumila returned the first note to Keiser. When Keiser later defaulted on the note, Bumila sued the guarantors who alleged a material alteration of the obligation that discharged them. Was there a material alteration?

LO ❸, ❹

5. While living in Kansas, Roger Moddelmog bought a pickup truck on which Boeing Wichita Credit Union (BWCU) held a security interest. The state of Kansas issued a certificate of title for the truck listing BWCU as a lienholder. Moddelmog then moved to Colorado and, without BWCU's knowledge, surrendered the Kansas title to apply for a Colorado title. A Colorado title was issued which, for unknown reasons, did not include the BWCU lien. Moddelmog then moved back to Kansas and applied for a new Kansas title. This title also did not show BWCU's lien. When Moddelmog went through bankruptcy, BWCU claimed it had a perfected lien on the truck. Did it?

LO ❶

6. Richard Gold, Richard Oshana, and Jonah Jacob as general partners of Northeast Glen Limited Partnership executed two promissory notes secured by a mortgage on commercial real estate to Shawmut Bank. At the same time, each of them executed personal guaranties agreeing to pay all existing and future debts of Northeast. After Northeast defaulted on the notes, the holder sued Gold, Oshana, and Jacob under their guaranties. The real estate was sold at a foreclosure sale without giving notice to Gold, Oshana, and Jacob. The law required that notice be given to primary obligors before foreclosure, but not to guarantors. Gold, Oshana, and Jacob claimed the guaranties were the same as the notes and therefore they were primary obligors and entitled to notice. Were the guaranties the same as the notes?

LO ❸, ❹

7. Vinod and Surekha Vashi leased a telephone system. The lease created a security interest. When the Vashis defaulted, General Electric Capital Corp. (GECC), the secured party, took possession of the equipment. GECC notified the Vashis it would sell the collateral, but GECC could not sell it because it was worthless. GECC obtained a deficiency judgment that gave the Vashis no credit for the equipment kept by GECC. The Vashis argued a court could not enter a deficiency judgment if GECC kept the collateral. Should the appellate court affirm the deficiency judgment?

Bankruptcy

LEARNING OBJECTIVES

1 Identify the purposes for bankruptcy and who may file for it.

2 Describe the procedures in a bankruptcy case.

3 Explain the effect of a discharge of indebtedness.

PREVIEW CASE

As family farmers, Bobby and Millie Graven filed a voluntary petition under Chapter 12 of the Bankruptcy Code. By means of multiple transactions, the Gravens transferred almost all their property to closely held corporations controlled by Bobby. The bankruptcy trustee found the transactions fraudulent and asked the court to convert the case to a Chapter 7 case. The Gravens objected and stated the court could not convert the case to Chapter 7 without their consent because the law did not permit the filing of an involuntary Chapter 7 petition against farmers. Who brought the case to the attention of the bankruptcy court? Why do you think the code does not permit filing an involuntary Chapter 7 petition against farmers?

Bankruptcy is a judicial declaration as to a person's (the debtor's) financial condition. The federal bankruptcy law has two very definite purposes: to give the debtor a new start and to give creditors an equal chance in the collection of their claims.

An honest debtor, hopelessly insolvent, may be tempted to cease trying even to earn a living. By permitting an insolvent debtor to give up all assets with a few exceptions and thereby get forgiveness of the debts, at least a new start can be made. The court determines what it deems an equitable settlement under the circumstances; and when these conditions are fully met, the debtor may resume full control of any business.

It is unfair to permit some unsecured creditors to get paid in full by an insolvent person while others receive nothing. By appointing a trustee to take over the debtor's property and pay each creditor in proportion to a claim, the trustee seeks to achieve a more equitable settlement. This arrangement promotes equity, wastes fewer assets, and costs less money than for each creditor to separately sue the debtor.

LO **1**
Bankruptcy, purposes and eligibility

WHO CAN FILE A PETITION OF BANKRUPTCY?

Today, any person who lives in, or has a residence, place of business, or property in the United States can be a debtor under the Bankruptcy Code except banks, insurance companies, savings and loan associations, and some municipalities. Rehabilitation proceedings may be instituted against all of these exempted institutions except municipalities, but the proceedings may not be filed under the Bankruptcy Code.

There are several chapters under the code, and only specified persons may be debtors under the various chapters. They have different impacts on debtors as to what property is taken, how long the bankruptcy supervision lasts, and who runs the debtor's business. Also, Chapter 7, providing for liquidation, applies to any person; Chapter 9 applies to municipalities; Chapter 11, providing for reorganization, applies to any person; Chapter 12 applies to farmers; and Chapter 13 applies to individuals with regular income.

KINDS OF DEBTORS

There are two kinds of debtors:

1. Voluntary
2. Involuntary

Voluntary Debtors

Anyone, except the institutions listed previously, may file a voluntary petition with the bankruptcy court under one of the four chapters of the code. A husband and wife may file a petition for a joint case.

Involuntary Debtors

Under certain conditions one may be forced into involuntary bankruptcy. Generally, if a debtor has 12 or more creditors, three must join the petition for involuntary bankruptcy. If a debtor has fewer than 12 creditors, one may sign. The creditors who sign must have aggregate claims amounting to $10,000 in excess of any collateral held as security. The claims may not be contingent or subject to a valid dispute. Involuntary petitions may not be filed under Chapters 9 or 13 or against farmers and charitable corporations. However, the court can, without the debtor's agreement, convert a voluntary filing to a filing under another section of the bankruptcy law that could not be filed involuntarily.

A court will enter an order for relief on the filing of an involuntary bankruptcy petition if either of the following two situations exists:

1. The debtor does not pay debts as they become due.
2. A custodian of the debtor's assets was established within 120 days preceding the filing of the involuntary petition.

Bankruptcy law uses the same procedure in liquidating the estate whether under a voluntary bankruptcy proceeding or an involuntary one. The filing of a petition automatically stays, or prevents, the filing or continuation of proceedings against the debtor that could have been begun or were to recover a claim against the debtor that arose before the bankruptcy petition.

PREVIEW CASE REVISITED

Facts: As family farmers, Bobby and Millie Graven filed a voluntary petition under Chapter 12 of the Bankruptcy Code. By means of multiple transactions, the Gravens transferred almost all their property to closely held corporations controlled by Bobby. The bankruptcy trustee found the transactions fraudulent and asked the court to convert the case to a Chapter 7 case. The Gravens objected and stated the court could not convert the case to Chapter 7 without their consent because the law did not permit the filing of an involuntary Chapter 7 petition against farmers. **Outcome:** The court pointed out that the code prohibited the *commencement* of an involuntary Chapter 7 petition against farmers. It did not prohibit the conversion of a voluntarily commenced Chapter 12 case into a Chapter 7 case.

—*In re Graven*, 196 Bankr. Rep. 506 (W.D. Mo.)

REQUIRED COUNSELING

Before debtors may file for bankruptcy, they must complete a 90-minute credit counseling session in the six months prior to filing. The counseling must be done by a credit counselor approved by the U.S. trustee's office. The U.S. trustee administers the bankruptcy procedures and enforces bankruptcy laws.

The counseling is to help debtors understand whether bankruptcy is necessary or whether a repayment plan is workable. Debtors do not have to agree with repayment plans proposed by credit counselors. However, any proposed plan must be submitted to the bankruptcy court in addition to a certificate attesting to completion of the counseling if a debtor wants to go ahead and file for bankruptcy.

In addition to prefiling credit counseling, after the bankruptcy case is done, a debtor must receive additional counseling on personal financial management. Debtors must provide proof of this counseling in order to get their debts excused.

PROCEDURE IN A CHAPTER 7 CASE

LO **2**
Procedures in bankruptcy cases

After filing a petition in bankruptcy, creditors must be notified and a meeting of them called. These creditors elect a trustee who takes over all the assets of the debtor. The trustee also steps into the shoes of the debtor and collects all debts due the debtor, preserves all physical assets, sues all delinquent creditors of the estate, and finally distributes all money realized from these actions according to a definite priority that will be discussed later in this chapter. The debtor is left with only that property the law exempts from liquidation.

NONLIQUIDATION PLANS

The bankruptcy laws provide special arrangements that do not result in liquidation and distribution of the debtor's assets. These are business reorganization and Chapter 13 plans.

Business Reorganization

Bankruptcy proceedings under Chapter 7 result in the liquidation and distribution of the assets of an enterprise. Under Chapter 11, the Bankruptcy Code provides a special rehabilitation system designed for businesses so that they may be reorganized rather than liquidated. Although designed for businesses, the language of Chapter 11 allows individuals not engaged in business to request relief.

Reorganization proceedings may be voluntary or involuntary. Normally, the debtor will be allowed to continue to run the business; however, a disinterested trustee may be appointed to run the business in cases of mismanagement or in the interest of creditors. The debtor running its business has the first right, for 120 days, to propose a rehabilitation plan indicating how much and how creditors will be paid. The court will confirm a plan that does not discriminate; is fair, equitable, and feasible; has been proposed and accepted in good faith; and all the payments made or proposed are found to be reasonable.

Cram Down
Reorganization plan imposed by court in spite of creditors' objections

The court can impose a reorganization plan even if a class of creditors objects to the plan. This is called a **cram down**. A cram down cannot be imposed if dissenting unsecured creditors are not paid in full or the holder of a claim with less priority receives some property on account of a claim or interest. If no acceptable plan of reorganization can be worked out, the business may have to be liquidated under Chapter 7.

Chapter 13 Plans

If the debtor is an individual, a Chapter 13 plan may be worked out. This chapter attempts to achieve for an individual an alternative to liquidation just as Chapter 11 does not liquidate businesses. An individual with a regular income, except a stock or commodity broker, who has unsecured debts of less than $100,000 and secured debts of less than $350,000 may in good faith file a petition under Chapter 13. This chapter is voluntary for the debtor.

Under Chapter 13, the debtor is put under a plan lasting up to five years, under which all disposable income is used to make payments on the debtor's debts. Not all debts may be fully paid and a majority of creditors can impose a settlement plan upon a dissenting minority. The debtor is as fully released from debts as under Chapter 7 of the Bankruptcy Code. These arrangements help prevent the hardship of an immediate liquidation of all the debtor's assets. These plans benefit the creditors because they are likely, in the long run, to receive a greater percentage of the money owed them. The plan may not pay unsecured creditors less than the amount they would receive under a Chapter 7 liquidation.

ELIGIBILITY RESTRICTIONS FOR CHAPTER 7

In order to file under Chapter 7, debtors must compare what the law defines as their "current monthly income" to the median income of families of their size in their state. However, the law defines "current monthly income" to be a debtor's average income over the previous six months before filing. Thus, if a debtor has recently lost a job, "current monthly income" could be much more than actual income by the time of filing for bankruptcy.

If "current monthly income" is the same as or less than the median income, a debtor may file under Chapter 7. If "current monthly income" is greater than the median, a debtor must pass a means test, which can be somewhat complicated, in order to file under Chapter 7.

Debtors are allowed to prove that they face "special circumstances" by which they were forced into bankruptcy by a crisis beyond their control. For example, the U.S. trustee has classified a major hurricane as a "special circumstance," making its victims more likely to be allowed to file under Chapter 7.

EXEMPT PROPERTY

The federal bankruptcy law lists property that will not be used to pay debts. In addition, each state has laws exempting property from seizure for the payment of debts. The debtor has a choice between federal or state exemptions unless state law specifies state exemptions must be used. The debtor must have lived in a state for two years before filing in order to use that state's exemptions. Otherwise, the exemptions of the state where the debtor previously lived must be used.

The most common types of property excluded include a limited interest in a residence and vehicle, household effects, tools of the trade, such as a carpenter's tools or a dentist's equipment, and similar items within reasonable limits. The debtor also may exclude unmatured life insurance contracts owned other than credit life insurance. Most states specifically exempt all necessary wearing apparel for the debtor and members of the family, such items as the family Bible, and all pictures of the members of the family even though some of these may be portraits of some value. Many of the federal exemptions set a limit on the value of items that may be excluded.

INCLUDED PROPERTY

The law includes some property acquired by the debtor after the bankruptcy proceedings have been instituted in the debtor's estate and uses it for the payment of creditors. This includes property acquired by inheritance, divorce, or as a beneficiary of life insurance within 180 days after the date of filing.

COURT CASE

Facts: When Martin Johnson went through bankruptcy, the court found the monthly payments he received from the Tunica Biloxi Tribe of Louisiana were part of the bankruptcy estate. The payments represented a part of the profits of the Grand Casino Avoyelles paid to persons born into the tribe and were paid for their lifetimes. No services were performed to receive the money.

Outcome: The monthly payments were part of Johnson's estate and available for payment to his creditors.

—*Johnson v. Cottonport Bank*, 259 Bankr. Rep. 125 (La.)

If the debtor transfers property, normally within 90 days preceding the filing of the bankruptcy petition, to one creditor with the intent to prefer one creditor over another, and the debtor is insolvent, the transfer may be set aside and the property included in the debtor's estate. Such a transfer that is disallowed is called a **preference**. If the creditor is a relative, a transfer made up to a year before the filing can be a preference.

Preference
Disallowed transfer to a creditor

DEBTOR'S DUTIES DURING BANKRUPTCY

The debtor must cooperate fully with the trustee. When requested, the debtor must attend creditors' meetings and must furnish all relevant evidence about debts due. The debtor must file with the trustee a schedule of all assets and all liabilities. This schedule must be in sufficient detail so that the trustee can list the secured creditors, the partially secured creditors, and the unsecured creditors.

Failure of the debtor to cooperate with the trustee and to obey all orders of the trustee not only may prevent discharge from bankruptcy but may also subject the debtor to criminal prosecution for contempt of court.

PROOF OF CLAIMS

All unsecured creditors must present proof of their claims to the court. The court sets a deadline for filing proof of claims, but they generally must be filed within 90 days after the date for the first meeting of creditors.

COURT CASE

Facts: Billy J. Harris and Dorothy E. Harris filed a Chapter 13 petition. About a month before the deadline, Three Rivers Federal Credit Union filed a proof of claim. Because of a secretarial error, the claim was prepared with the caption (heading) of a case Billy had filed that had been dismissed a month before the current case was filed. The claim was then electronically filed under the incorrect case number. Nine months later, the Credit Union realized its error and filed a proof of claim in the proper case. It asked the court to treat the claim as if it had been originally filed in the proper case.

Outcome: The court held that it did not have the power to allow a late-filed claim outside of narrow exceptions that did not apply in this case.

—*In re Harris*, 341 B.R. 660 (Ind.)

RECLAMATIONS

Frequently, at the time that the court discharges debts, the debtor has possession of property owned by others. This property takes the form of consigned or bailed goods, or property held as security for a loan. The true owner of the property is not technically a creditor of the debtor in bankruptcy. The owner should file a reclamation claim for the specific property so that it may be returned.

A person in possession of a check drawn by the debtor may or may not be able to get it paid depending on the circumstances. If the check is an uncertified check, the holder is a mere creditor of the debtor and cannot have it cashed. This occurs because a check is not an assignment of the money on deposit, and the creditor merely holds the unpaid claim the debtor intended the check to discharge. If the check has been certified, the creditor has the obligation of the drawee bank on the check, which may be asserted in preference to proceeding upon the claim against the drawer of the check.

TYPES OF CLAIMS

Claims of a debtor in bankruptcy may be classified as fully secured claims, partially secured claims, and unsecured claims.

Fully secured creditors may have their claims satisfied in full from the proceeds of the assets that were used for security. If these assets sell for more than enough to satisfy the secured debts, the remainder of the proceeds must be surrendered to the trustee in bankruptcy of the debtor.

Partially secured creditors have a lien on some assets but not enough to satisfy the debts in full. The proceeds of the security held by a partially secured creditor are used to pay that claim; and, to the extent any portion of a debt remains unpaid, the creditor has a claim as an unsecured creditor for the balance.

Unsecured claims are those for which creditors have no lien on specific assets.

PRIORITY OF CLAIMS

The claim with the highest priority is that for the administrative expenses of the bankruptcy proceedings (such as filing fees paid by creditors in involuntary proceedings and expenses of creditors in recovering property transferred or concealed by the debtor). Additional priority claims include debts incurred after the filing of an involuntary petition and before an order of relief or appointment of a trustee; wage claims not exceeding $2,000 for any one wage earner, provided the wages were earned not more than three months prior to bankruptcy proceedings; fringe benefits for employees; claims by individuals who have deposited money with the debtor for undelivered personal, family, or household goods; and tax claims.

DISCHARGE OF INDEBTEDNESS

If the debtor cooperates fully with the court and the trustee in bankruptcy and meets all other requirements for discharge of indebtedness, the discharge will be granted. To be discharged, the debtor must not hide any assets or attempt to wrongfully transfer them out of the reach of creditors. A discharge voids any liability of the debtor on discharged debts and prevents any actions for collection of such debts.

LO **3**
Effect of discharge

COURT CASE

Facts: August Perez filed a voluntary petition for relief under Chapter 7. Hibernia National Bank, to which Perez owed a considerable sum, contended the court should deny Perez a discharge. It alleged Perez failed to explain a loss of assets from Perez's distribution of tax refunds between himself and his wife. Under an agreement signed prior to their marriage, 85 percent of the tax refunds should have gone to August.

However, he had divided them equally between himself and his wife because, he said, "She's on this check here, . . . so she's entitled to half." The tax refunds amounted to $300,000.

Outcome: The court found evidence of intent to defraud creditors and denied the discharge.

—*Matter of Perez,* **954 F.2d 1026 (5th Cir.)**

DEBTS NOT DISCHARGED

Certain obligations cannot be avoided by bankruptcy. The most important of these claims include:

1. Claims for alimony and child support
2. All taxes incurred within three years
3. Debts owed by reasons of embezzlement
4. Debts due on a judgment for intentional injury to others, such as a judgment obtained for assault and battery
5. Wages earned within three months of the bankruptcy proceedings
6. Debts incurred by means of fraud
7. Educational loans

Under some other circumstances, bankruptcy does not discharge certain debts, but the list above includes the most common ones.

QUESTIONS

1. Why is a trustee appointed in a bankruptcy case?
2. What are the impacts on debtors of the various bankruptcy chapters?
3. What are the two bases for entering an order for relief on an involuntary bankruptcy petition?
4. What procedure may be followed rather than liquidating a business that cannot pay its debts as they are due?
5. Is there a restriction on a debtor's income in order to file under Chapter 7? Explain.
6. Are there any restrictions on a debtor's use of state law exemptions?
7. What happens if the debtor has made a preference?
8. If the debtor holds bailed property, must this property be included in the debtor's estate to pay creditors?
9. What happens when the claims of a secured creditor are satisfied in full from the proceeds of the secured assets?
10. What claim is given the highest priority in bankruptcy proceedings?

CASE PROBLEMS

LO ❸

1. Paul O. Palumbo was indebted to Millbury National Bank on a promissory note and guaranties. He and his wife, Nanci, owned their home jointly. They transferred the house to just Nanci for nominal consideration, and a year later she filed under Chapter 7. Several creditors objected to her attempt to exempt the house from the payment of her debts. Before the court allowed her exemption, Paul also filed under Chapter 7. Nanci received a discharge. Millbury alleged that Paul concealed the house transfer and therefore should be denied a discharge. Millbury said Paul never notified the bank of the transfer, even though he was obligated to do so. He also misrepresented that he owned the house after the transfer. Did Paul conceal the house transfer?

LO ❷

2. Danny Lee Carr received a notice of foreclosure on his principal residence. He filed a Chapter 13 bankruptcy petition. The court dismissed that case because Carr had failed to obtain prepetition, budget and credit counseling services. Carr obtained the requisite credit counseling services and nine days after the dismissal filed a second Chapter 13 case. Carr listed his monthly gross income as $13,708 and his monthly expenditures as $12,025. That left Carr's monthly disposable income of $1,683 and his proposed monthly plan payment was also $1,683. Carr testified that he had the financial ability to make his plan payments in the future. No party objected to Carr pursuing Chapter 13. Did the fact that Carr had filed two bankruptcy cases within one year show he acted in bad faith?

LO ❶

3. In its involuntary Chapter 7 petition against James Lee, Crossroads Real Estate, Inc., joined by William Seach, alleged that Lee had fewer than 12 creditors; therefore, just the two of them could compel the bankruptcy. Lee claimed to have 31 creditors. Most of them were investors who agreed to buy stock in Lee County Development, L.C., a limited liability company. Lee had agreed to repurchase their stock and had executed promissory notes reflecting his indebtedness if the stocks became worthless, which they did. Had enough creditors filed to prosecute the involuntary case?

4. Albert Bethea hired Robert J. Adams & Associates, a law firm, to prepare his
bankruptcy petition and handle his case. The legal fee would be paid over
time with some payments made before the petition was filed and some afterward. Adams handled the case; the court ordered Bethea discharged; and the
case was closed. When Adams continued to collect the unpaid installments
on the fee, Bethea hired a new lawyer and sued alleging the installments constituted a debt discharged by the bankruptcy. Was the legal fee a debt discharged by the bankruptcy?

LO ❸

5. Prior to filing a petition under Chapter 7 of the bankruptcy law, Andrew
McElroy owed his parents about $15,000. Six months before filing he re-
ceived $15,000 in settlement of a personal injury claim and paid $10,000 to
his parents. The bankruptcy trustee claimed the payment was a preferential
transfer. Was the $10,000 payment a preference?

LO ❷

6. Lavurne Unruh, who operated a family farm as a sole proprietorship, filed for
reorganization under Chapter 11. Under his plan he would operate the farm
and 2 percent would be paid on unsecured creditors' claims. Unruh would keep
his assets subject to secured claims and when they were paid, he would own
the assets free of all claims. The unsecured creditors rejected the plan, and
Unruh requested a cram down. Unruh could not obtain a cram down if he
received "property" because the unsecured creditors were not to be fully paid.
Did the fact that the plan would allow Unruh to retain ownership of all his
assets allow him to retain "property"?

LO ❷

7. Under a Chapter 13 plan for the payment of Curtis Hudson's debts, a percentage of his future wages were to be paid to the plan's trustee to distribute to his
creditors. The U.S. Postal Service employed Hudson, and the court ordered it to
withhold part of his wages and pay them to the trustee. The Postal Service complied with the order, but charged a $50 fee to cover its costs in processing the
order. A year later, the court issued a second order adjusting the amount to be
withheld, and the Postal Service charged another $50 fee. Hudson charged that
the fees violated the automatic stay of proceedings against his property. Were
the charging of the fees acts to obtain property of the debtor's estate?

LO ❶

8. Harold Younger's ex-wife filed an involuntary Chapter 7 bankruptcy petition
with Younger as the debtor. The U.S. marshal arrested Younger to compel his
attendance at an examination as to location of marital assets. At the examination, Younger refused to testify, citing the Fifth Amendment to the Constitution. The judge granted him immunity and ordered him to testify. Younger
refused again. What do you think will happen now?

LO ❷

Ethics in Practice

The normal rule is that life insurance policies are incontestable after a specified period of time, usually one or two years. This means that the insurance company cannot contest the validity of the policy for any reason
except nonpayment of premiums. Is this a rule that encourages people to
take out insurance policies and hide facts from the insurance company
until the policies are incontestable? Although hiding a fact that would
otherwise invalidate an insurance policy might not end up invalidating the
policy, is it ethical? What is the reason for this rule?

Summary Cases

RISK-BEARING DEVICES

1. When fire destroyed their home, Frances and Charles Roland, husband and wife, were both named insureds under their fire insurance policy issued by Georgia Farm Bureau Mutual Insurance Co. (GFB). Both had lived in the home until Frances moved out, five months before the fire. Charles had continued to live in the home. They were divorced after the fire. The policy stated that the home was "the only premises where the named insured or spouse maintains a residence." GFB refused to pay Frances' claim under the policy because she had not lived in the home at the time of the fire. Should GFB have to pay Frances? [*Roland v. Georgia Farm Bureau Mut. Ins. Co.,* 462 S.E.2d 623 (Ga.)]

2. Central Bank made a car loan to Lorraine Turner. Central was acquired by Mercantile Bank, which was acquired by Firstar Bank, N.A. Turner then received the title to her car along with written confirmation her loan was paid. Ten days later, Turner discovered that her car was missing. The police informed her Shamrock Recovery Service, Inc., acting on orders of Firstar, had seized her car. Turner went to Shamrock and displayed the documents confirming payment of her loan and release of Firstar's lien. Shamrock said Firstar claimed she still owed $300. Turner's attorney ultimately succeeded in convincing Firstar to release her car. Turner had to go to Shamrock's impound lot but found her laptop computer, discs containing computer software, and a digital camera that she had left in the car were missing. For two years Turner's lawyer attempted to secure their return. Firstar made no substantive response to Turner's inquiries and demand so she sued. Is Firstar liable for an illegal repossession? [*Turner v. Firstar Bank, N.A.,* 845 N.E.2d 816 (Ill. App.)]

3. Sheila Kercher sued for dissolution of her marriage, and on November 3, the court issued an order restraining her husband "from transferring . . . or in any way disposing of any property except in the usual course of business or for the necessities of life." He had a term life insurance policy on which Sheila was the beneficiary and which gave him the right to change the beneficiary. On November 11, he changed the beneficiary to his mother, Helen Tallent, and on December 11, he committed suicide. Should Kercher or Tallent receive the proceeds of the life insurance? [*Metropolitan Life Insurance Co. v. Tallent,* 445 N.E.2d 990 (Ind.)]

4. Evelyn Vlastos carried a fire insurance policy on her building. The policy included a section labeled Endorsement No. 4 that was incorporated into the policy and stated: "Warranted that the third floor is occupied as Janitor's residence." The building was destroyed by fire, and the insurers refused to pay on the policy, charging breach of warranty. Vlastos sued the insurers alleging

there was no proof the provision in Endorsement No. 4 was a warranty, implying it was a representation. Which was it, and what difference would it make? [*Vlastos v. Sumitomo Marine & Fire Insurance Co. (Europe) Ltd.,* 707 F.2d 775 (3d Cir.)]

5. Merrimack Mutual Fire Insurance Co. issued a fire insurance policy to James and Loree Stewart as owners. There was a mortgage clause requiring payment on loss to Portland Savings Bank as mortgagee. The clause provided: "The mortgagee . . . shall notify this Company of any change of ownership . . . or increase of hazard . . . " Portland later foreclosed on the property, and after the Stewarts' redemption period expired, it became the owner. It did not notify Merrimack of the foreclosure and its ownership before there was a fire loss. Merrimack denied coverage because Portland had not notified it of the change in ownership. Was Merrimack liable under the policy? [*Hartford Fire Insurance Co. v. Merrimack Mutual Fire Insurance Co.,* 457 A.2d 410 (Me.)]

6. In one year Oral F. Sekendur filed two Chapter 13 petitions within days of adverse decisions in nonbankruptcy cases. They were dismissed because Sekendur failed to report all his assets. He was ordered to pay one opposing parties attorney's fees, and minutes before a hearing to consider sanctions for his failure to comply with that order, he filed another Chapter 13 petition. He never paid the filing fee. Sekendur admitted he had no income and there was no change in circumstances following dismissal of his earlier Chapter 13 cases. He was warned that his Chapter 13 case might be dismissed for having been filed in bad faith, so he moved to convert his case to a Chapter 7 case. On its own motion, the court moved to consider dismissal for Sekendur's failure to pay filing fees. Sekendur did not show up at the hearing. The court dismissed the case for unreasonable delay prejudicial to creditors—that the case was filed in bad faith. Did Sekendur file in bad faith? [*In re Sekendur,* 334 B.R. 609 (Ill.)]

7. A car driven by James Hilton struck a parked trash truck that extended onto the travel lane of the highway. Two people in the Hilton car received severe head lacerations, and the car was considerably damaged. Joe Blakeney owned the truck and carried insurance with Safeco Insurance Co. of America. At the scene, Blakeney saw the damage and injury, was issued a traffic summons, and was told by a police officer to file an accident report within 10 days. Seven weeks later, an attorney for the Hiltons wrote the insurance agent who had written the Safeco policy and advised him of the accident. He prepared an accident report form and sent it to Safeco. Its policy stated: "written notice . . . with respect to the time, place and circumstances . . . and the names and address of the injured and of available witnesses, shall be given by or for the insured to the company . . . as soon as practicable." Blakeney never notified anyone. Safeco denied coverage. Was it liable? [*Liberty Mutual Insurance Co. v. Safeco Insurance Co.,* 288 S.E.2d 469 (Va.)]

8. Huey Stewart had a homeowner's policy issued by Louisiana Farm Bureau Mutual Insurance Co. on his mobile home. After the policy was in force, the original roof of the mobile home leaked, so Stewart nailed boards to the old roof decking, put in insulation, and put a new roof over the insulation. High winds damaged the roof Stewart had built on top of the original mobile home roof. The policy stated it did not cover "awnings, . . . shelters, cabanas, porches, completely enclosed additions, carports, or other structures and equipment . . . not part of the mobile home when purchased new." Farm Bureau denied coverage of the new roof, and Stewart sued. Should damage to

the new roof be covered? [*Stewart v. Louisiana Farm Bur. Mut. Ins. Co.*, 420 So.2d 1217 (La. App.)]

9. Devers Auto Sales financed its inventory with Thrift, Inc., which perfected its security interest in the inventory by filing a financing statement with the secretary of state in accordance with Article 9 of the UCC. The statement included a security interest in after-acquired inventory. A.D.E., Inc., agreed to sell three cars to Devers and gave it possession of them but not the titles. Thrift gave Devers the money for the cars, and Devers gave checks to A.D.E., but the checks were dishonored. Thrift took possession of Devers's inventory and demanded the titles from A.D.E. A.D.E. demanded the three cars. Did Thrift have a perfected security interest in the cars? [*Thrift, Inc. v. A.D.E., Inc.*, 454 N.E.2d 878 (Ind. Ct. App.)]

10. Robert McCloskey obtained a life insurance policy from New York Life Insurance Co. The medical questionnaire asked, "Have you ever consulted a physician or . . . had or been treated for . . . heart attack . . . or any other disorder of the heart or blood vessels . . . or diabetes?" McCloskey answered no. He in fact had diabetes and had had a heart attack. A paramedical examination had revealed he was overweight, so the policy New York issued required a higher premium than was standard. Within a month of the issuance of the policy, McCloskey died. New York refused to pay on the policy, alleging misrepresentation. Was there misrepresentation? [*McCloskey v. New York Life Insurance Co.*, 436 A.2d 690 (Pa. Sup. Ct.)]

Real Property

This section on real property includes not only real estate—land, buildings, and houses—but also wills and trusts. Laws about these issues can be very complex. Transferring, buying, and selling real property involves the legalities of contracts, mortgages, deeds, titles, and many other items. Even being a landlord or tenant has legal responsibilities. In addition, the transfer of real property to your heirs can be a complicated matter involving many legal issues, discussed in Chapter 45. If you're curious, CourtTV's Web site contains wills of famous people.

http://www.hud.gov
http://www.courttv.com/legaldocs/
newsmakers/wills

Nature of Real Property

LEARNING OBJECTIVES

1 Define real property, and explain the rules about vegetation, running water, and fixtures.

2 Name the types of multiple ownership of property.

3 List the estates and other interests in real property.

4 Identify methods of acquisition exclusive to real property.

PREVIEW CASE

→ Walter Rogers, Ronald Rogers, and their corporation, Rogers Brothers, Inc., won a judgment against Charles Rogers in a federal bankruptcy court for not complying with his fiduciary responsibilities. They then secured a separate judgment on a different ground against Eleanor Rogers, Charles Rogers's wife, in a state trial court. Charles and Eleanor owned real estate as tenants by the entireties, and the judgment creditors asked the court to sell the real estate to satisfy the judgments. What does it mean to be a tenant by the entireties? What are the reasons for using this type of multiple ownership?

LO 1
Real property rules

Real Property
Land and permanent attachments to land

Real property consists of land, including the actual soil, and all permanent attachments to the land, such as fences, walls, other additions and improvements, timber, and other growing things. It also includes minerals under the soil and the waters on it.

DISTINGUISHING REAL PROPERTY

Through court interpretations we have accumulated a definite set of rules to guide us in identifying real property and distinguishing it from personal property. The most important of these rules pertains to the following specific items of property:

1. Vegetation—trees and perennial crops

2. Waters—rivers and streams

3. Fixtures

Trees and Perennial Crops

Vegetation may be real or personal property. Trees growing on the land, orchards, vineyards, and perennial crops, such as clovers, grasses, and others not planted annually and cultivated, are classified as real property until severed from the land. Annual crops and severed vegetation are personal property. When a person sells land, questions sometimes arise as to whether or not a particular item belongs to the land or constitutes personal property. The parties should agree before completing the sale just how to classify the item.

Rivers and Streams

If a nonnavigable river flows through property, the person who owns the property owns the riverbed but not the water that flows over the bed. The water cannot be impounded or diverted to the property owner's own use in such a way as to deprive any neighbors of its use. If the river or the stream forms the boundary line, then the owner on each side of the river owns the land to the middle of the riverbed.

   In most states where navigable rivers form the boundary, the owner of the adjoining land owns the land only to the low-water mark.

Fixtures

Personal property attached to land or a building that becomes a part of it is known as a **fixture**. To determine whether or not personal property has become real estate, one or more of the following questions may be asked by a court:

Fixture
Personal property so securely attached to real estate that it becomes part of the real estate

1. How securely is it attached? If the personal property has become a part of the real estate and lost its identity, such as the boards or bricks making up a house wall, it constitutes a fixture. If it is so securely attached that it cannot be removed without damaging the real property to which it is attached, such as windows or light switches, then it also ceases to be personal property.

2. What was the intention of the one installing the personal property? No matter what one's intention, the personal property becomes real property if it cannot be removed without damaging the property. But, if it is loosely attached and the person installing the fixture indicates the intention to make the fixture real property, then this intention controls. Refrigerators have been held to be real property when apartments were rented unfurnished but

COURT CASE

Facts: When Marc and Deborah Gauze bought a manufactured home, Green Tree Acceptance, Inc. had a security interest in the mobile home. The Gauzes owned a lot in Hazel Park, zoned for single-family residences, on which they built a concrete foundation and put the home on it. The home had a porch; connections to gas, electric, sewer, and water lines; and was surrounded by a fence on three sides. The law assessed the mobile home for tax purposes as part of the real estate. The Gauzes did not pay their real estate taxes. Equivest Financial bought the real estate by paying the unpaid taxes and sold it to Ottaco, Inc. Ottaco sued to quiet title to the property in itself.

Outcome: The mobile home became a fixture, and title to it passed to Ottaco.

—*Ottaco, Inc. v. Gauze*, 574 N.W.2d 393 (Mich. App.)

contained refrigerators. In determining intention, courts frequently consider the purpose of the attachment and who did the attaching.

a. What is the purpose of attachment? The purpose for which the fixture is to be used may show the intention of the one annexing it.

b. Who attached the item? If the owner of a building installs personal property to the building, this usually indicates the intention to make it a permanent addition to the real property. If a tenant makes the same improvements, the court presumes that the tenant intended to keep the fixture as personal property unless a contrary intention can be shown.

MULTIPLE OWNERSHIP

LO ②
Multiple property ownership

One person can own property, or more than one person can own property. When more than one person owns land, each person has the right to use and possess it. The most common ways real property can be owned by more than one person include:

1. Tenancy in common
2. Joint tenancy
3. Tenancy by the entirety
4. Community property

Tenancy in Common

Tenancy in Common
Multiple ownership in which, at death, one owner's share passes as will directs or to heirs

A **tenancy in common** occurs when two or more persons own property and when one dies that owner's interest in the property passes to a person named in the deceased's will or, if no will exists, to the deceased's heirs. In this type of ownership, the other owner or owners have no automatic right to the deceased's share of the property. Each owner determines who gets the share of the property at his or her death. A tenant in common has the right not only to determine who becomes the owner of the fractional share on death but also to convey the property while alive. The property may be given away or sold. The new owner then becomes a tenant in common with the remaining owner or owners.

The owners of property held as a tenancy in common each own an undivided fractional share of the property. For example, if two people equally own a piece of land, each tenant owns an undivided one-half interest in the land. Three people who own land equally each own an undivided one-third interest in the land. This means they do not own a specific portion of the land, but own a one-third interest in the entire piece of land. They thus have an interest in the entire property, but only to the extent of their percentage interest.

The property does not have to be owned equally. Two people could own a piece of property as tenants in common, and one could own a one-third interest and the other could own a two-thirds interest.

When more than one person takes title to property, the law presumes they hold the property as tenants in common. Thus, when the type of ownership is not clearly spelled out, it will be held a tenancy in common.

Joint Tenancy

Joint Tenancy
Multiple ownership in which, at death of one, that share passes to remaining owners

A **joint tenancy** exists when two or more persons own property and on the death of one, the remaining owners own the entire property free of any interest of the

COURT CASE

Facts: Theodore Beck and Harold Burbach owned a tract of land as tenants in common. Burbach transferred his interest to his wife, Bridgett Burbach. Later, Sussex County Municipal Utilities Authority (SCMUA) secured a default judgment against Harold and Bridgett. SCMUA directed the sheriff to sell Bridgett's interest in the tract. Although notice of the sale was sent to Bridgett and Harold, none was sent to Beck, and SCMUA bought the property at the sale for a small sum. When Beck found out about the sale, he notified SCMUA of his ownership interest and alleged the sale was void because the law required all owners of record to be notified, and he had not been.

Outcome: The court held that because the title of each tenant in common is subject to the possessory right to the whole property of every other cotenant, each tenant in common is a record owner of the property. Beck had to be notified.

—Burbach v. Sussex County Mun. Utilities Authority, **723 A.2d 137 (N.J. Super. A.D.)**

deceased. This means that a joint owner does not have the power to determine who owns the property at death. The remaining joint owner or owners automatically own the entire property. This automatic ownership of the entire property by the surviving owners is called the **right of survivorship**.

As in the case of a tenancy in common, each joint owner owns an undivided interest in the property. No joint owner owns a specific portion of the property.

The law does not favor the creation of a joint tenancy so there must be a clear intention to create one. The language normally used conveys the property "to X and Y as joint tenants with right of survivorship."

Right of Survivorship
Automatic ownership of property by survivors

COURT CASE

Facts: Lou Hill with his daughter, Louanne, executed a new signature card for his bank account at Garfield County Bank. They both signed the card that described the account as a "joint account, with right of survivorship." After Lou died, his son, Phil, alleged the account was part of Lou's estate, whereas Louanne said that by right of survivorship the funds belonged to her.

Outcome: The court said that because the signature card expressly stated the account was a joint tenancy with right of survivorship and both Lou and Louanne had signed it, a joint tenancy had been created. At Lou's death, the account became the sole property of Louanne.

—In re Estate of Hill, **931 P.2d 1320 (Mont.)**

A joint tenancy can be destroyed by one joint tenant selling or giving that tenant's interest to another person. The new owner becomes a tenant in common of the interest conveyed. If there are three or more joint tenants and one sells his or her interest, the new owner is a tenant in common and the remaining, original joint tenants remain joint tenants as between themselves.

A joint tenancy also can be destroyed by one joint tenant suing for a division of the property, called a suit for **partition**. Any joint tenant may sue for partition.

Because a joint tenant's interest in the property disappears at the joint tenant's death, a joint tenant cannot dispose of such an interest by will. If a joint tenant purports to dispose of an interest in jointly held property by will, the will has no effect with regard to such property.

Partition
Suit to divide joint tenancy

Tenancy by the Entirety

Tenancy by the Entirety
Co-ownership by husband and wife with right of survivorship

Similar to a joint tenancy, a **tenancy by the entirety** can exist only between a husband and wife. At the death of one, the other becomes the sole owner of the property. Almost half of the states recognize this form of ownership. This type of tenancy is popular with married couples because most want the survivor to have title to the property and to get it without any court proceedings. Many couples also like this type of ownership because the creditors of just the husband or just the wife cannot claim the property. To have a claim against the property, a creditor must be a creditor of both spouses.

PREVIEW CASE REVISITED

 Facts: Walter Rogers, Ronald Rogers, and their corporation, Rogers Brothers, Inc., won a judgment against Charles Rogers in a federal bankruptcy court for not complying with his fiduciary responsibilities. They then secured a separate judgment on a different ground against Eleanor Rogers, Charles Rogers's wife, in a state trial court. Charles and Eleanor owned real estate as tenants by the entireties, and the judgment creditors asked the court to sell the real estate to satisfy the judgments.

Outcome: The court stated that the two separate judgments did not impose joint liability on Charles and Eleanor, so the judgment creditors could not force the sale of the real estate held as tenants by the entireties.

—Rogers v. Rogers, 512 S.E.2d 821 (Va.)

ETHICAL POINT

Is it really ethical for a married couple to own property in a tenancy by the entirety if the creditors of just one of the spouses cannot claim the property?

A joint tenancy differs in other ways from a tenancy by the entirety. In the case of property held as a tenancy by the entirety, neither the husband nor the wife alone may sell or otherwise dispose of it. Both the husband and the wife must join in any conveyance of the property. A divorce changes the husband and wife from tenants by the entirety to tenants in common with respect to the property.

Community Property

Community Property
Property acquired during marriage owned separately and equally by both spouses

Nine states, mostly in the West, recognize a form of ownership called **community property**. Community property is a type of ownership reserved for married couples, such that both spouses own a separate and equal share of the property no matter how titled. In these states, unless the parties agree that it shall be separate property, property acquired by a husband and wife during their marriage constitutes community property. This is normally important if a couple divorces. In that case, each owns one-half of the property acquired during the marriage. Property owned by one spouse prior to the marriage normally is that spouse's separate property and not community property.

ESTATES IN PROPERTY

LO ③
Interests in property

Estate
Interest in property

An **estate** is the nature and extent of interest that a person has in real or personal property. The estate that a person has in property may be:

1. A fee simple estate
2. A life estate

COURT CASE

Facts: Before Linda Thomas and Paul Pace married, Thomas owned an A.G. Edwards investment account (172 account). Because they lived in a community property state, 23 days after they married, Thomas instructed A.G. Edwards to "sweep" all dividends, interest, and income from the 172 account monthly and place the income in a new account (204 account). Three years later, Thomas set up the Linda Ruth Thomas Management Trust as the donor, trustee, and sole beneficiary to segregate her separate property. The 172 account was transferred into the Management Trust, and A.G. Edwards continued to "sweep" all dividends, interest, and income from that account into the 204 account. After Thomas filed for divorce, Pace claimed the Management Trust was community property.

Outcome: The court said that income earned during the marriage from the 172 account and later the Management Trust was community property; however, that income was never commingled with Thomas's separate property. The Management Trust was not community property.

—*Pace v. Pace*, **160 S.W.3d 706 (Tex. App.)**

Fee Simple Estate

A **fee simple estate** is the largest and most complete right that one may possess in property. A fee simple owner of property, whether real or personal, has the right to possess the property forever. The owner of a fee simple estate may also sell, lease, or otherwise dispose of the property permanently or temporarily. At the death of such an owner, the property will pass to the persons provided for in the owner's will or, if no will exists, to the heirs at law.

A fee simple owner of land has the right to the surface of the land, the air above the land "all the way to heaven," and the subsoil beneath the surface all the way to the center of the earth. The courts have held, however, that the right to the air above the land is not absolute. An individual cannot prevent an airplane from flying over the land unless it flies too low. It is possible for a person to own the surface of the land only and not the minerals, oil, gas, and other valuable property under the topsoil. A person also may own the soil but not the timber.

Fee Simple Estate
Largest, most complete right in property

Life Estate

One may have an estate in property by which the property is owned for a lifetime, known as a **life estate**. The person owning for the lifetime is called a **life tenant**. At the death of the life tenant, the title passes as directed by the original owner. The title may revert, or go back, to the grantor, the one who conveyed the life estate to the deceased. In this case, the interest of the grantor is called a **reversion**. Alternatively, the property may go to someone other than the grantor. Such an interest is called a **remainder**.

The life tenant has the exclusive right to use the property and may exclude the holder of the reversion or remainder during the life tenant's lifetime. However, although the life tenant has exclusive use of the property, there is a duty on the life tenant to exercise ordinary care to preserve the property and commit no acts that would harm the remainder interest permanently.

Life Estate
Estate for duration of a person's life

Life Tenant
Person owning property for a lifetime

Reversion
Interest of grantor in life estate that returns to grantor on death of life tenant

Remainder
Interest in life estate that goes to someone other than grantor on death of life tenant

OTHER INTERESTS IN REAL PROPERTY

Although not classified as estates, other interests a person may have in real property exist. Two common ones are easements and licenses.

Easement
An interest in land for nonexclusive or intermittent use

An **easement** is a right to use land, such as a right-of-way across another's land or the use of another's driveway. An easement does not give an exclusive right to possession, but a right of permanent, intermittent use. It is classified as an interest in land and created by deed or by adverse use for a period of time set by statute. An easement may be granted that is not transferable; that is, only the specific person to whom it is granted can use it. Another type of easement transfers to any subsequent owner of the real estate to which the easement is granted. Such an easement is said to "run with the land."

COURT CASE

Facts: Herman and Jeanette Brown sold Marygaele Jaffe part of a tract of land that did not have direct access to a public road. The deed granted three easements including the use with others of the "main driveway, running in a generally southwesterly direction between South Ferry Road and the . . . residence." Two other easements were defined by measurements to the hundredth of a foot. Later, Neda Young and her husband acquired the Brown's tract. They began construction of a large house, swimming pool, and tennis court. Jaffe had given oral consent to the changes including moving the driveway; however, she died before construction began. The Youngs had the driveway moved, but it still ran "in a generally southwesterly direction between South Ferry Road and the . . . residence" and overlapped the original drive at some points. Roger Lewis obtained title to

Jaffe's property and said he would agree to relocate the driveway if landscaping and other improvements were made. The Youngs agreed to do so when the house was completed. Several months later, Lewis demanded that the improvements be made in 10 days or he would move the driveway back at Young's expense despite destruction of the tennis court. Lewis sued to determine his rights concerning the easement.

Outcome: The court held that the indefinite description of the right of way, particularly when two other easements were described so precisely, indicated an intention to allow the landowner to relocate the driveway. Because the relocation did not impair Lewis's use of the driveway, the court approved Young's relocation.

—*Lewis v. Young*, 682 N.Y.S.2d 657 (N.Y.)

License
Right to do certain acts on land

A **license** is a right to do certain acts on the land but not a right to stay in possession of the land. It constitutes a personal right to use property for a specific purpose. A licensor normally may terminate a license at will.

COURT CASE

Facts: Lake Shore Park was an area with 3,300 feet of frontage on Lake Winnipesaukee and contained 310 cottages and mobile homes. The LSP Association owned all the land in the park and used it as a social club for the owners of the 310 units. The unit owners had title to their structures, and could use, but did not own, any of the land or amenities, such as tennis courts, beach, and marina, in the park. In assessing real estate taxes, the town of Gilford assessed each unit owner $20,000 for the value of each unit and added what it called a site

amenity charge of $30,000 against each owner. The site amenity charge was a value the town alleged adhered to the units in the marketplace by virtue of their site. The unit owners protested the site amenity charges.

Outcome: The court held that the unit owners held a license in the Association's land and amenities. Because a license was not an interest in land, it was not a taxable interest in land.

—*LSP Assn. v. Town of Gilford*, 702 A.2d 795 (N.H.)

ACQUIRING REAL PROPERTY

Real property may be acquired in many of the same ways as personal property (Chapter 14). However, some ways exist in which real property, but not personal property, can be acquired. These include accretion and adverse possession.

LO ❹
Acquiring real property

Accretion

Accretion is the addition to land as a result of the gradual deposit by water of solids. It takes place most commonly when a stream, river, lake, or ocean constitutes the boundary line of property. Dirt deposited along the boundary is added to the property. In the case of a navigable river, if one's land extends to the low-water mark, title to some land may be acquired by the river's shifting its flow. This occurs slowly by the deposit of silt. Also, the accretion may be the result of dredging or channeling of the river. If the silt and sand are thrown up on the riverbank, thereby increasing the acreage of the land contiguous to the river, the added acreage belongs to the owner of the contiguous land.

Accretion
Addition to land by gradual water deposits

Adverse Possession

An individual may acquire title to real property by occupying the land owned by another for a period fixed by statute. This is known as **adverse possession** and basically means the original owner may no longer object to a trespass. The statutory period required varies from 7 years in some states to 21 in others. Occupancy must be continuous, open, hostile, visible, actual, and exclusive. It must be apparent enough to give the owner notice of trespass. In colonial times, this was known as "squatter's rights." To get title by adverse possession, one had to go one step further than the "squatter" did; this meant the adverse possession had to continue for the statutory period.

Adverse Possession
Acquiring title to land by occupying it for fixed period

COURT ⚖ CASE

Facts: When Damion DiFranco bought his home, there was a redwood fence surrounded on both sides by trees and shrubbery between his property and the property next door. Kathleen Buszkiewicz later bought the property next door. DiFranco made minor repairs on the fence. Twenty one years after DiFranco bought his property, a survey showed that the fence encroached on Buszkiewicz's property by 1.2 to 1.9 feet. The law set the statutory period for adverse possession at 21 years. Buszkiewicz sued for a declaration that the encroachment was illegal.

Outcome: The court found exclusive possession and open, notorious, continuous, and adverse use of the narrow strip of land for 21 years, so DiFranco acquired it by adverse possession.

—Buszkiewicz v. DiFranco,
746 N.E.2d 712 (Ohio App.)

Possession for the statutory period then gave clear title to all the land one's color of title described. **Color of title** is a person's apparent title. It usually arises, but does not have to, from some defective document purporting to be a deed or a will or even a gift.

Color of Title
One's apparent title

QUESTIONS

1. What is real property? Give three examples.
2. What questions are asked to determine if personal property has become a fixture?
3. What right to determine ownership does a tenant in common have of the interest that tenant owns?
4. Does a person who owns property in a joint tenancy determine who owns the property at death? Explain.
5. May a husband or wife alone transform a tenancy by the entirety into a tenancy in common by conveying to a third party?
6. When a couple living in a community property state divorce, how is their property divided?
7. Explain the difference between a fee simple estate and a life estate.
8. What right to use land does an easement give a person? Explain.
9. Explain how accretion most commonly occurs.
10. How must a person occupy another's land in order to acquire it by adverse possession?

CASE PROBLEMS

LO ❶

1. The town of Windham condemned real property owned by ATC Partnership. ATC claimed that located in the premises taken through the condemnation proceeding was personal property that Windham failed, neglected, and refused to return, and prevented ATC from removing it from the real estate. The property consisted of machinery and equipment previously used in the operation of a textile mill, the bulk of which was bolted to the realty. ATC conceded that at the time the pieces were installed, the mill owner intended them to be permanent accessions to the realty. ATC acquired the machinery by means of the deed by which it acquired the real property. The court had to decide whether the machinery was part of the real estate or personal property. What was it?

LO ❸

2. Michele Cody and her daughter, Paula Skoog, decided to combine their households. Skoog and her family moved into Cody's house, and Cody signed a deed conveying her house to Skoog but retaining a life estate. The deed stated Cody "shall have the full possession, use and benefit of said property, as well as the rents, revenues and profits thereof, for and during [her] natural life." After four years, Cody became very uncomfortable living in the home. Skoog tried to have her declared incompetent. When Cody moved out of the house, Skoog changed the locks and put Cody's remaining belongings in garbage sacks on the front porch. A lawsuit ensued. Who was entitled to possession of the house?

LO ❷

3. Kohl, Metzger, Spotts, P.A. obtained a judgment against Shelman Morse. Kohl tried to get a court to order that a bank account that Morse and his wife held as tenants by the entireties could be taken to pay off the judgment. The bank signature card specifically designated the account as being held as tenants by the entireties. Shelman signed almost all the checks issued on the account,

contributed the funds to it, and Mrs. Morse had a separate bank account. May Kohl obtain the funds in the account?

4. In 1940, Harve Wright and Aitchey Wright each paid $100 down on a $2,000 farm. Harve died two years later and his wife and minor children lived on the farm for six years with Aitchey and his family. Aitchey and his wife, Lorene, farmed the property, paid off the mortgage, made substantial improvements, and paid all the taxes. Aitchey conveyed 8.6 acres to the county and warranted he had the right to sell and transfer the land. He also gave easements for construction purposes. In the 70s Aitchey's siblings had the title investigated but were afraid to confront Aitchey with the allegation that he and Harve had owned the property in common. After Aitchey died, Lorene asked the court to declare she owned the whole property by adverse possession. Had Aitchey and Lorene possessed the property adversely to Aitchey's siblings?   LO ❹

5. Lucille Howe had a life estate in 750 acres of farmland and her children, Catherine Rowan and James Howe, held the remainder interests. James leased and farmed the property and made improvements, including constructing a well 1,169-feet deep on the southern part. After Lucille's death, James and Catherine owned the property as tenants in common, and James continued to lease Rowan's share. Ultimately, James became the owner of the northern half and Catherine the southern half, but James continued to farm the whole property. James executed a bill of sale purporting to convey well equipment located on Catherine's land to his daughter and son-in-law, Robin and Norman Riley. Catherine sued to establish her rights to the well and well equipment on her land alleging that the well was a fixture and a part of her real estate. Was it?   LO ❶

6. Earl and Madge Davis conveyed an easement over their property for an access road. The easement stated it was to "Fir Manufacturing Co., its successors and assigns, for and during such period of time as said Fir Manufacturing Co., shall have ownership of . . . timberlands from which it is necessary or convenient to haul logs . . . across said property." Fir later dissolved and it had no corporate successor. Michael and Beverly Hunnell acquired the Davises' land, and Roseburg Resources Co. acquired part of the land Fir had owned. Roseburg used the access road for logging and the Hunnells discovered Roseburg also charged others to use the road. The Hunnells sued Roseburg to prevent its use of the road. Roseburg claimed because it owned part of the land Fir had owned, the easement "ran with the land" and it now had the right to it. Does Roseburg have an easement over the Hunnell's land?   LO ❸

7. With her own funds Nina Zarins purchased a condominium. The deed was made to Zarins and Mara Teranis without mention of joint ownership with right of survivorship. Zarins was the only person who lived in the condominium, and she paid all the maintenance, taxes, and utilities. She mortgaged the property, and the mortgage showed Zarins and Teranis as mortgagors. Teranis filed for bankruptcy, and the trustee filed suit to sell the condominium to obtain Teranis's half-ownership. Zarins alleged she was to be the sole owner while alive and Teranis was to obtain ownership only after Zarins's death. Is half the value of the condominium available to pay Teranis's debts?   LO ❷

Transfer of Real Property

LEARNING OBJECTIVES

1 Describe the means by which title to real estate is transferred.

2 Explain the provisions normally contained in a deed.

3 Summarize the steps taken to safely and effectively transfer title to real property after a deed is signed.

PREVIEW CASE

Arthur Lynn made the highest bid for Janna Dodge's real estate at a sheriff's sale. The sheriff executed a deed to the property and delivered the deed to Lynn on April 5. The law gave Dodge one year to redeem the property from the sale. She formally sought to redeem the property on the following March 6. What did this deed convey to Lynn? Who had control of the property after Lynn received the sheriff's deed?

LO 1
Means of transferring real estate

Deed
Writing conveying title to real property

A sale constitutes the most common reason for transferring title to real estate. In the ordinary case, the parties sign a contract of sale, but the title is not transferred until the seller delivers a deed to the buyer. A **deed** is a writing, signed by the owner, conveying title to real property. One may, by means of a lease, transfer a leasehold title giving the rights to the use and possession of land for a limited period. The provisions of the deed or the lease determine the extent of the interest transferred.

Even when the owner makes a gift of real property, the transfer must be evidenced by a deed. As soon as the owner executes and delivers a deed, title vests fully in the donee. Acceptance by the donee is presumed.

DEEDS

Grantor
Person conveying property

The law sets forth the form that the deed must have, and this form must be observed. The parties to the deed include the **grantor**, or original owner, and the

grantee, or recipient. The two principal types of deeds are:

1. Quitclaim deeds
2. Warranty deeds

Quitclaim Deeds

A **quitclaim deed** is just what the name implies. The grantor gives up whatever interest he or she may have in the real property. However, the grantor makes no warranty that he or she has any claim to the property.

Grantee
Person receiving title to property

Quitclaim Deed
Deed that transfers whatever interest grantor has in property

---

COURT CASE

Facts: The city of Branson, Missouri, vacated Chestnut Street for the benefit of adjacent property owners. Josephine Madry owned property on both sides of the street. Without mentioning the vacated portion of the street, she deeded Lot 1, on the west side, to Belinda Ruddick's predecessor in title. She later deeded her lots on the east side to Security Bank and Trust Co. That deed purported to convey all "that part of Chestnut Street . . . heretofore vacated" that was west of the lots. The bank conveyed the lots and the east half of Chestnut Street adjacent to them to James and Mabel Bryan. Ten years later, the bank quitclaimed the west half of the vacated street to the Bryans.

Ruddick sued claiming she owned the west half of the vacated street. The Bryans claimed Madry's conveyance to Ruddick's predecessor in title did not convey the west half of Chestnut Street, and the quitclaim deed from the bank conveyed that half to them.

Outcome: Because the street was vacated for the benefit of the adjacent property owners, Madry's conveyance of Lot 1 also conveyed the adjoining (west) half of Chestnut Street. The bank's quitclaim deed to the Bryans conveyed nothing.

—Ruddick v. Bryan,
989 S.W.2d 202 (Mo. App.)

In the absence of a statute or an agreement between the parties requiring a warranty deed, a quitclaim deed may be used in making all conveyances of real property. A quitclaim deed transfers the grantor's full and complete interest as effectively as a warranty deed. When buying real property, however, one does not always want to buy merely the interest that the grantor has. A buyer wants to buy a perfect and complete interest so that the title cannot be questioned by anyone. A quitclaim deed conveys only the interest of the grantor and no more. It contains no warranty that the grantor has good title. In most real estate transactions, therefore, a quitclaim deed cannot be used because the contract will specify that a warranty deed must be delivered.

Warranty Deed

A **warranty deed** not only conveys the grantor's interest in the real property but, in addition, makes certain warranties or guarantees. The exact nature of the warranty or guarantee depends upon whether the deed is a general warranty or a special warranty deed. A **general warranty deed** (see Illustration 42–1) not only warrants that the grantor has good title to the real property but further warrants that the grantee "shall have quiet and peaceable possession, free from all encumbrances, and that the grantor will defend the grantee against all claims and demands from whomsoever made." This warranty, then, warrants that all prior

Warranty Deed
Deed with guarantees

General Warranty Deed
Warrants good title free from all claims

ILLUSTRATION 42–1 General Warranty Deed

WARRANTY DEED
Know All Men by These Presents:

That Donald C. Coson and Millicent M. Coson, his wife

of Butler County, Ohio

in consideration of the sum of Forty-five Thousand Dollars ($45,000)

to them *in hand paid by* Eugene F. Acknor, the grantee, the receipt of

which is hereby acknowledged,

do hereby **Grant, Bargain, Sell and Convey**

to the said Eugene F. Acknor

h *is heirs*

and assigns forever, the following described **Real Estate** *situated in the* City

of Hamilton *in the County of* Butler *and State of* Ohio

Lot No. 10, Section 14, Range 62, Randall Subdivision, being a portion of

the estate of Horace E. Cresswell and Alice B. Cresswell *and all the* **Estate,**

Right, Title and Interest *of the said grantors in and to said premises;* **To have and to**

hold *the same, with all the privileges and appurtenances thereunto belonging, to said grantee,* his

heirs and assigns forever. And the Said Donald C. Coson and Millicent M. Coson

do hereby **Covenant and Warrant** *that the title so conveyed is* **Clear, Free**

and Unencumbered, *and that* they will **Defend** *the same against all lawful claims of*

all persons whomsoever.

In Witness Whereof, *the said grantors have hereunto set* their *hands, this* first

day of December *in the year A.D. two-thousand and —*

Signed and acknowledged in presence of us:

Michael R. Wiser	Donald C. Coson
Antonia C. Patricelle	*Millicent M. Coson*

State of Ohio, Butler **County,** ss-

On this first *day of* December *A.D. 20* *, before me, a* Notary Public

in and for said County, personally came Donald C. Coson and Millicent M. Coson

the grantor in the foregoing deed, and

acknowledged the signing thereof to be their *voluntary act and deed.*

Witness *my official signature and seal on the day last mentioned.*

Sarah M. Evans

Sarah M. Evans
Notary Public, State of Ohio
My commission expires June 1, 20–

grantors had good title and that no defects exist in any prior grantor's title. The grantee does not have to assume any risks as the new owner of the property.

A **special warranty deed** warrants that the grantor has the right to sell the real property. The grantor makes no warranties of the genuineness of any prior grantor's title. Trustees and sheriffs who sell land at a foreclosure sale use this type of deed. Executors and administrators also use such a deed. These officials should not warrant anything other than that they have the legal right to sell whatever interest the owner has.

Special Warranty Deed
Warrants grantor has right to convey property

When a builder sells a new house, most courts now impose an implied warranty of fitness not found in the deed. The warranty amounts to a promise that the builder designed and constructed the house in a workmanlike manner, suitable for habitation by the buyer.

PROVISIONS IN A DEED

Unless statutes provide otherwise, a deed usually has the following provisions:

1. Parties
2. Consideration
3. Covenants
4. Description
5. Signature
6. Acknowledgment

LO **2**
Deed provisions

Parties

The grantor and the grantee must be identified, usually by name, in the deed and the grantee must be a living or legal person. If the grantor is married, the grantor's name and that of a spouse should be written in the deed. If the grantor is unmarried, the word *single* or the phrase "a single person" should be used to indicate that status.

Consideration

The amount paid to the grantor for the property is the consideration. The payment may be in money or in money's worth. A deed usually includes a statement of the consideration, although the amount specified does not need to be the actual price paid. Some localities have a practice of indicating a nominal amount, such as one dollar, although a much larger sum was actually paid. The parties state a nominal amount as the consideration to keep the sale price from being a matter of public record.

Covenants

A **covenant** is a promise contained in a deed. There may be as many covenants as the grantor and the grantee wish to include. **Affirmative covenants** obligate the grantee to do something, such as agreeing to maintain a driveway used in common with adjoining property. In **negative covenants** the grantee agrees to refrain from doing something. Such covenants frequently appear in deeds for urban residential developments. The more common ones prohibit the grantee from using the property for business purposes and set forth the types of homes that can or cannot be built on the property. Most covenants are said to "run with the land," which means they basically attach to the property and thereby bind all future owners.

Covenant
Promise in a deed

Affirmative Covenant
Promise by grantee to do an act

Negative Covenant
Agreement by grantee not to do an act

Description

The property to be conveyed must be correctly described. Unless the law provides otherwise, any description that will clearly identify the property suffices. Ordinarily, however, the description used in the deed by which the present owner

COURT CASE

Facts: The Pine Haven development lots were subject to covenants and restrictions running with the land. They included, "[n]o mobile home . . . shall be used as a residence at any time." Jerry and Janet White agreed to purchase a Pine Haven lot contingent on allowing them to place a manufactured home on the lot. The developer agreed. The Whites closed on the lot and began moving a home onto the lot. Marvin J. Halls, a resident of Pine Haven, sued claiming that a manufactured home fell within the "mobile home" restriction. At the time that the Pine Haven covenants were drafted, there was no definition of "manufactured home" in state law. When such a definition was added, it was the same as the definition of "mobile home."

Outcome: The court stated that because "manufactured home" had replaced the term "mobile home" the covenant allowed Halls to prevent having a manufactured home in the development.

—*Halls v. White*, 715 N.W.2d 577 (S.D.)

acquired the title should be used if correct. The description may be by lots and blocks if the property is in a city; or it may be by metes and bounds or section, range, and township if the property is in a rural area. If the description is indefinite, the grantor retains title.

COURT CASE

Facts: Lake Minnewaska Mountain Houses, Inc. (LMMH) contracted to convey land to the Nature Conservancy. LMMH employed Albin Rekis and allowed him to live in a house located on five acres of the land. LMMH called Rekis to the office to sign some documents, including an agreement providing:

1. LMMH would execute a deed to real property to Rekis. LMMH would record it prior to the conveyance to the Nature Conservancy.

2. Rekis would execute a deed of property to LMMH.

It would be recorded after the conveyance to the Nature Conservancy.

The parties executed the deeds. The deed Rekis signed contained no description of the property to be conveyed by the deed. Rekis later discovered that LMMH's contract with the Nature Conservancy excluded the five-acre parcel and stated LMMH agreed to convey that parcel to Rekis. He sued LMMH.

Outcome: The court held that because the deed Rekis signed had no description, it was void.

—*Rekis v. Lake Minnewaska Mountain Houses*, 573 N.Y.S.2d 331 (N.Y. App. Div.)

Signature

The grantor should sign the deed in the place provided for the signature. A married grantor must have the spouse also sign for the purpose of giving up the statutory right of the spouse. In some states, a witness or witnesses must attest the signatures. If the grantor cannot sign the deed, an agent, the grantor with assistance, or the grantor making a mark, may execute it as:

Maria Smith
Witness of the mark of   Henry   { His X Mark }   Finn
Henry Finn

Acknowledgment

The statutes normally require that the deed be formally acknowledged before a notary public or other officer authorized to take acknowledgments. The acknowledgment allows the deed to be recorded. After a deed has been recorded, it may be used as evidence in a court without further proof of its authenticity. Recording does not make a deed valid, but it helps give security of the title to the grantee.

The **acknowledgment** is a declaration made by the properly authorized officer, in the form provided for that purpose, that the grantor has acknowledged signing the instrument as a free act and deed. In some states, the grantor also must understand the nature and effect of the deed or be personally known to the acknowledging officer. The officer attests to these facts and affixes an official seal. The certificate provides evidence of these actions.

Acknowledgment
Declaration grantor has stated execution of instrument is free act

DELIVERY

A deed has no effect on the transfer of an interest in real property until it has been delivered. **Delivery** consists of the grantor intending to give up title, possession, and control over the property. So long as the grantor maintains control over the deed and reserves the right to demand its return before delivery of the deed to the grantee, there has been no legal delivery. If the grantor executes a deed and leaves it with an attorney to deliver to the grantee, there has been no delivery until the attorney delivers the deed to the grantee. Because the attorney is the agent of the grantor, the grantor has the right to demand that the agent return the deed. If the grantor, however, delivers the deed to the grantee's attorney or agent, then there has been an effective delivery because releasing control constitutes evidence of intent that title pass. Once the grantor makes delivery, title passes.

LO **3**
Steps taken after deed signed

Delivery
Giving up possession and control

PREVIEW CASE REVISITED

Facts: Arthur Lynn made the highest bid for Janna Dodge's real estate at a sheriff 's sale. The sheriff executed a deed to the property and delivered the deed to Lynn on April 5. The law gave Dodge one year to redeem the property from the sale. She formally sought to redeem the property on the following March 6.
Outcome: The court held that the sale of the property was effective on the date the deed was delivered, April 5, so Janna had exercised her right to redeem within one year after the sale.

—*Ex parte Lynn*, 727 So. 2d 90 (Ala.)

RECORDING

Statutes in every state require grantees to file their deeds with a public official in the county in which the land lies. Any other instrument affecting title to real property in the county also can be filed. These public records of land transactions give notice of title transfers to all, particularly potential subsequent purchasers.

A deed need not be recorded in order to complete one's title. Title passes on delivery of the deed. Recording the deed protects the grantee against a second sale by the grantor and against any liens that may attach to the property while still recorded in the grantor's name. Recording also raises the presumption of delivery of the deed.

When the recording official receives a deed for recording, the law ordinarily requires that the deed be stamped with the exact date and time the grantee leaves the deed for recording.

ABSTRACT OF TITLE

Abstract of Title
History of real estate

Before one buys real estate, an abstract of title may be prepared. An abstract company normally does this, but an attorney may also do it. The **abstract of title** gives a complete history of the real estate. It also shows whether or not there are any unpaid taxes and assessments, outstanding mortgages, unpaid judgments, or other unsatisfied liens of any type against the property. Once an abstracting company makes the abstract, an attorney normally examines the abstract to see if it reveals any flaws in the title.

TITLE INSURANCE

Some defects in the title to real estate cannot be detected by an abstract. Some of the most common of these defects are forgery of signatures in prior conveyances; claims by adverse possession; incompetency to contract by any prior party; fraud; duress; undue influence; defective wills; loss of real property by accretion; and errors by title examiners, tax officials, surveyors, and many other public officials. The owner of real estate can obtain a title insurance policy that will cover these defects. The policy may expressly exclude any possible defects that the insurance company does not wish to be covered by the policy. The insured pays one premium for coverage as long as the property is owned. The policy does not benefit a subsequent purchaser or a mortgagee.

QUESTIONS

1. How is title to real estate transferred in the case of a sale and in the case of a gift?
2. Why is a quitclaim deed not used for all transfers of real property?
3. What warranty do most courts now impose when a builder sells a new house?
4. Does a deed always recite the actual consideration paid?
5. What does it mean to say a covenant "runs with the land"?
6. What description would ordinarily be best to use in a deed to describe the property conveyed?
7. What is an acknowledgment, and why is it necessary?
8. Does title to real property pass at the time a deed is recorded? Explain.
9. What is an abstract of title, and what is its significance when transferring real estate?
10. Explain who is benefited by title insurance.

CASE PROBLEMS

LO ❶

1. The Fulton County Sheriff conducted a tax sale of certain real property and conveyed the property to a third party. A tax deed subsequently was issued to that party documenting the sale. After the taxes and costs of sale were paid,

the excess was deposited with the sheriff's department. Two years after the sale, the delinquent taxpayer executed a quitclaim deed to Georgia Lien Services. The quitclaim deed stated: "The purpose of this quitclaim deed is to give the grantee all the rights, entitlements, and obligations that grantor may have in the property." Georgia Lien Services applied for the excess funds from the sheriff's department. The sheriff refused. Is Georgia Lien entitled to the money by virtue of the quitclaim deed?

2. Weaver and G. E. Jordan executed a warranty deed of 50 acres to Daniel and Pearline Dallinga. The deed contained restrictive covenants prohibiting commercial enterprise or enterprise of any kind on the property. There were several subsequent conveyances of the property until Jeremiah 29:11, Inc. became the owner. None of these conveyances referenced the restrictions of the Jordans' deed. Jeremiah used the property as a leadership training center for pastors and leaders of nonprofit corporations and as a Boy Scout camp. Ernest Douglas and Leslie Seifert owned adjacent property formerly owned by the Jordans and alleged Jeremiah's use violated the commercial enterprise restriction. Jeremiah alleged it was not limited by the Jordans' restrictions because they were not in subsequent deeds. Did the restrictive covenants apply to Jeremiah? **LO ➋**

3. Although unmarried, Mark Rausch and Michelle Devine lived together and had a daughter, Sydney. Devine cared for Sydney and all household paperwork and bills. Rausch provided their living expenses. Rausch, an attorney with experience in marital property law, asked lawyer friends to draft and acknowledge a quitclaim deed to Devine for his house in Anchorage. His friends recorded the deed, and Rausch apparently never thought about the deed. Devine did not have funds, and Rausch continued to pay the mortgage. Several years later, Devine sued to have Rausch vacate the house. Devine alleged the house was a gift from Rausch. Rausch asked the court to order that he owned it alleging the deed was never delivered to Devine. Who owns the house? **LO ➌**

4. HCM Restaurant, Inc. quitclaimed lot 434-2 to Bluff Head Corp. and reserved a parking easement for patrons of its marina. At the time, Bluff Head planned to buy lot 434-1, that HCM did not own. The reserved easement stated Bluff Head would determine the precise location of the easement but it would "be located on the premises conveyed herein [Lot 434-2] or Lot 434-1." Bluff Head never bought lot 434-1. Sakonnet Point Marina Association, Inc. (Sakonnet) acquired the marina from HCM and sued to enforce the easement. Bluff Head alleged that it had the right to select the location of the easement on either lot 434-2 or 434-1, and it selected lot 434-1. The owner of lot 434-1 sought an order that the quitclaim deed could not have created an easement, over lot 434-1 because HCM had not owned it. Does Sakonnet have an easement, and if so, over what property? **LO ➊**

5. A month after Alice Ramsey purchased a house, she became very ill and did not expect to live. She had several children living at home and decided that Allen Walters was an appropriate person to maintain her home for her children because she had no relatives. Ramsey executed a deed of the property to Walters and had it recorded even though she did not intend to give the home to Walters. She and her children continued to live in the house, and she made all the payments including the taxes. Twenty years later, Robert Johnson got a judgment against Walters as a result of an automobile accident, and the sheriff was going to seize the property to pay the judgment. Ramsey, who was still **LO ➌**

alive, sued to be declared the owner of the property. Had there been a valid delivery of the deed to Walters making him the owner of the property?

LO **2**   **6.** Lillian Julian and Joseph Corbridge, her brother, owned property as joint tenants. She quitclaimed her interest in the property to Corbridge. Before the deed was recorded, someone without Julian's knowledge added the name LaRetta Corbridge as a grantee to the deed. LaRetta was Joseph's wife. After the deed was recorded, LaRetta died. Seven years later, Joseph signed and recorded an affidavit stating that LaRetta was the same person named as grantee in the quitclaim deed. He also executed and recorded a quitclaim deed of the property to Julian and him as joint tenants. Then Joseph died. Carl, Leonard, and Arnold Petersen, LaRetta's children by a previous marriage, claimed an interest in the property. They alleged that Joseph owned the property after the initial deed from Julian and could and did validly convey part of his interest to LaRetta without Julian's consent. Did Joseph convey an interest to LaRetta by:

   a. Recording the quitclaim deed?

   b. The combination of the quitclaim deed and the affidavit?

   c. The affidavit alone?

LO **3**   **7.** Martha Wisdom executed a deed conveying certain real property to her son, Charles Smith. Wisdom put the deed in an envelope and asked Smith to hide the envelope with other papers in a wall heater in Wisdom's house, which he did. Wisdom had told Smith she had made a deed of the house to him. At a later time, when at Wisdom's home, Smith went through the papers and found the deed. After Wisdom died, Smith recorded the deed. Smith's sister, Mildred Cecil, filed a suit to have the deed set aside based on failure of Wisdom, the grantor, to deliver the deed. Should the court find a valid delivery?

Real Estate Mortgages

LEARNING OBJECTIVES

1 Define and discuss the effect of a mortgage.

2 List the duties and rights of a mortgagor.

3 Explain the rights of parties on foreclosure, sale, and assignment of the mortgage.

PREVIEW CASE

Dianna Deppe and her husband, Mark Schaefer, borrowed $55,000 from Schaefer's parents to buy their home. They signed a note for $55,000 and orally promised to execute a mortgage but made only one payment on the note. Several years later, they were divorced, and Deppe was given "all right, title, and interest, free and clear" of Schaefer to the home. The court ordered Deppe to take responsibility for all the debt on the home. A year later, Deppe filed for bankruptcy. Under state law, the full value of her home was exempt from payment of her debts. Schaefer's parents sued her, alleging they held a mortgage on the home. Did they? What form must a mortgage be in?

A **mortgage** is an interest in real estate given to secure the payment of a debt. The mortgage does not constitute the debt itself but the security for the debt. If the debt is not paid the property may be sold to pay the debt. Land or any interest in land may be mortgaged. Land may be mortgaged separately from the improvements, or the improvements may be mortgaged apart from the land. A person who gives a mortgage as a security for a debt is a **mortgagor**. A person who holds a mortgage as security for a debt is a **mortgagee**.

The mortgagor normally retains possession of the property. In order for the mortgagee to obtain the benefit of the security, the mortgagee must take possession of the premises on default or sell the mortgaged property at a foreclosure sale. In some states, the mortgagee may not take possession of the property on default but may obtain the appointment of a receiver to collect the rents and income. If the sale of the property brings more than the debt and the costs, the mortgagor must be paid the balance.

LO 1
Effect of mortgage

Mortgage
Interest in real estate given to secure debt

Mortgagor
Person who gives mortgage

Mortgagee
Person who holds mortgage

THE MORTGAGE CONTRACT

A mortgage must be in writing. The contract, as a rule, must have the same form as a deed, which means it must be acknowledged. The mortgage, like all other contracts, sets forth the rights and the duties of the contracting parties (see Illustration 43–1). As a type of contract, mortgages are interpreted according to contract law rule.

PREVIEW CASE REVISITED

Facts: Dianna Deppe and her husband, Mark Schaefer, borrowed $55,000 from Schaefer's parents to buy their home. They signed a note for $55,000 and orally promised to execute a mortgage but made only one payment on the note. Several years later, they were divorced, and Deppe was given "all right, title, and interest, free and clear" of Schaefer to the home. The court ordered Deppe to take responsibility for all the debt on the home. A year later, Deppe filed for bankruptcy. Under state law, the full value of her home was exempt from payment of her debts. Schaefer's parents sued her, alleging they held a mortgage on the home.
Outcome: The court held that because Deppe and Schaefer had only made an oral promise to execute a mortgage and had not executed a written document, there could be no mortgage.

—In re Deppe, 215 Bankr. Rep. 743 (Minn.)

A mortgagor normally gives a mortgage to raise money for the purchase price of real estate, but it may be given for other reasons. One may borrow money for any reason and secure the loan by a mortgage. One may assume a contingent liability for another, such as becoming a surety, and receive a mortgage as security.

Lien
Encumbrance or claim against property

The effect of a mortgage is to be a lien against the mortgaged property. A **lien** is an encumbrance or claim against property. The lien of the mortgage attaches to the property described in the mortgage. A mortgage generally also provides that the lien attaches to additions thereafter made to the described property; for example, the lien of the mortgage attaches to personal property, which thereafter becomes a fixture. A clause purporting to make the security clause of a mortgage cover future debts will be valid if the parties intended it to cover future debts.

RECORDING

Depending upon the law of the state in which the land lies, the mortgage gives the mortgagee either a lien on the land or title to the land. The mortgagor's payment of the debt divests or destroys this title or lien. Recording the mortgage protects the mortgagee against subsequent creditors, since the public record normally constitutes notice to the whole world as to the mortgagee's rights. There may be both a first mortgage and subsequent, or junior, mortgages. The mortgage recorded first normally has preference. This is not true when actual notice of a prior mortgage exists. However, a purchase money mortgage has preference over other claims arising through the mortgagor. The mortgage is also recorded to notify subsequent purchasers that as much of the purchase price as is necessary to pay off the mortgage must be paid to the mortgagee. Recording must be proper, otherwise the purpose of the mortgagee providing notice to others cannot be accomplished.

ILLUSTRATION 43–1 Mortgage Contract

MORTGAGE
WITH <u>POWER OF SALE</u> (**Realty**)

KNOW ALL MEN BY THESE PRESENTS:

THAT   Walter A. Righetti   and
  Susan L. Righetti   husband and wife, GRANTORS, for and in consideration of the sum of
One Dollar ($1.00), to GRANTORS in hand paid, the receipt of which is hereby acknowledged, and in consideration of the
premises hereinafter set forth, do hereby grant, bargain, sell and convey unto Third National Bank of Russellville ,
GRANTEE, (Whether one or more) and unto GRANTEE'S ~~heirs~~ (Successors) and assigns forever, the following
property, situated in   Pope   County, Arkansas:
Lot 37 in GREENE HEIGHTS SUBDIVISION

TO HAVE AND TO HOLD the same unto the said GRANTEE, and unto GRANTEE's ~~heirs~~ (successors) and assigns
forever, with all appurtenances thereunto belonging; and all rents, income, and profits therefrom after any default herein.

We ~~[I]~~ hereby covenant with the said GRANTEE, GRANTEE's ~~heirs~~ (successors) and assigns, that said lands are
free and clear of all encumbrances and liens, and will forever warrant and defend the title to said property against all lawful claims. And, we, GRANTORS,   Walter A. Righetti and Susan L. Righetti   ,
for the consideration aforesaid do hereby release unto the said GRANTEE and unto GRANTEE's ~~heirs~~ (successors) and
assigns forever, all our rights and possibility of dower, curtesy and homestead in and to the said lands.

The sale is on the condition, that whereas, GRANTORS are justly indebted unto said GRANTEE in the sum of
Sixty Thousand and $^{00}/_{100}$ Dollars ($ 60,000.00   ), evidenced by   their
promissory note   dated   October 17   , 20 – , in the sum of $ 60,000.00 bearing interest from date
until due at the rate of 10 % per annum and thereafter until paid at the rate of 10 % per annum, payable as follows:
$ 545 per month, due and payable on the first day of the month, beginning November 1, 20 – and
continuing for 25 years.

This mortgage shall also be security for any other indebtedness of whatsoever kind that the GRANTEE or the
holders or owners of this mortgage may hold against GRANTORS by reason of future advances made hereunder, by
purchase or otherwise, to the time of the satisfaction of this mortgage.

In the event of default of payment of any part of said sum, with interest, or upon failure of GRANTORS to perform the agreements contained herein, the GRANTEE, GRANTEE's ~~heirs~~ (successors) and assigns, shall have the right
to declare the entire debt to due and payable; and

GRANTORS hereby covenant that they will keep all improvements insured against fire, with all other full coverage insurance, loss payable clause to holder and owner of this mortgage; that said improvements will be kept in a good
state of repair, and waste will neither be permitted nor committed; that all taxes of whatever nature, as well as assessments for improvements will be paid when due, and if not paid GRANTEE may pay same and shall have a prior lien
upon said property for repayment, with interest at the rate of 10% per annum; now,

THEREFORE, if GRANTORS shall pay all indebtedness secured hereby, with interest, at the times and in the manner aforesaid, and perform the agreements herein contained, then this conveyance shall be void. In case of nonpayment or
failure to perform the agreements herein contained, the said GRANTEE, GRANTEE's ~~heirs~~ (successors) and assigns, shall
have the right and power to take possession of the property herein conveyed and expel any occupant therefrom without
process of law; to collect rents and profits and apply same on unpaid indebtedness; and with or without possession to sell
said property at public sale, to the highest bidder for cash, (*or*   ),
at   the county courthouse   of   Pope   County,
Arkansas, public notice of the time, terms and place of sale having first been given twenty days by advertising in some
newspaper published in said County, by at least three insertions, or by notices posted in five public places in the County, at
which sale any of the parties hereto, their heirs (successors), or assigns may bid and purchase as any third person might do;
and GRANTORS hereby authorize the said GRANTEE, GRANTEE's ~~heirs~~ (successors), or assigns to convey said property
to anyone purchasing at said sale, and to convey an absolute title thereto, and the recitals of such conveyance shall be taken
as *prima facie* true. The proceeds of said sale shall be applied, first to the payment of all costs and expenses attending said
sale; second to the payment of all indebtedness secured hereby, with interest; and the remainder, if any, shall be paid to said
GRANTORS. GRANTORS hereby waive any and all rights of appraisement, sale, redemption, and homestead under the
laws of the State of Arkansas, and especially under the Act approved May 8, 1899, and acts amendatory thereof.

WITNESS our hand s and seal s this   17th   day of   October   , 20 –

  Walter A. Righetti   (seal)
  Susan L. Righetti   (seal)

(ACKNOWLEDGMENT BEFORE NOTARY FOLLOWS)

Facts: Burl Brunson borrowed $50,000 from Howard Savings Bank securing the loan by a mortgage on real estate. This mortgage was properly recorded but not properly indexed. (The index is the alphabetical listing of the names of the mortgagors.) Two years later, Brunson conveyed the property by deed to Jesus and Celeste Ijalba, and the Ijalbas executed a mortgage on the property to Chrysler First Financial Services Corp. This mortgage was properly recorded and indexed. Chicago Title Insurance Co. conducted a thorough title search and, finding no mortgage under Brunson's name, issued a title insurance policy on the property to Chrysler.

Six months later, Howard filed a foreclosure suit against Chrysler and Ijalba claiming its mortgage had priority.

Outcome: The court said the law requires recording to give notice to subsequent purchasers and encumbrancers of real estate. Because each county has thousands of record books, each with at least 1,000 pages, a mortgage cannot be duly recorded without being properly indexed. Howard's mortgage did not have priority over the one to Chrysler.

— *Howard Sav. Bank v. Brunson,*
582 A.2d 1305 (N.J. Super. Ct. Ch. Div.)

DUTIES OF THE MORTGAGOR

LO ❷
Duties and rights of mortgagor

The mortgagor assumes three definite duties and liabilities when placing a mortgage on real estate. These pertain to:

1. Interest and principal
2. Taxes, assessments, and insurance premiums
3. Security of the mortgagee

Interest and Principal

The mortgagor must make all payments of interest and principal as they become due. Most mortgages call for periodic payments, such as monthly, semiannually, or annually. These payments are used to pay all accrued interest to the date of payment, and the mortgagee applies the balance on the principal. Other mortgages call for periodic payment of interest and for the payment of the entire principal at one time. In either case, a failure to pay either the periodic payments of interest and principal or of interest only constitutes a default. A default gives the mortgagee the right to foreclose. Most mortgages contain a provision that if the mortgagor does not make an interest or principal payment when due or within a specified time after due, the mortgagee may declare the entire principal immediately due. This is known as an **acceleration clause**.

Acceleration Clause
Clause allowing entire principal to be due

If the mortgagor wishes to pay off the mortgage debt before the due date so as to save interest, that right must be reserved at the time the mortgage is given.

Taxes, Assessments, and Insurance Premiums

The mortgagor, who is the owner of the land regardless of the form of the mortgage, must continue to make such payments as would be expected of an owner of land. The mortgagor must pay taxes and assessments. If the mortgagor does not pay the taxes and assessments, the mortgagee may pay them and compel a reimbursement from the mortgagor. If the mortgage contract requires the mortgagor to pay these charges, a failure to pay them becomes a default.

The law does not require the mortgagor to keep the property insured nor to insure it for the benefit of the mortgagee. This duty can be imposed on the mortgagor by the mortgage contract. Both the mortgagor and the mortgagee have an insurable interest in the property to the extent of each one's interest or maximum loss.

Security of the Mortgagee

The mortgagor must do no act that will materially impair the security of the mortgagee. Cutting timber, tearing down buildings, and all acts that waste the assets impair the security and give the mortgagee the right to seek legal protection. Some state statutes provide that any one of these acts constitutes a default. This gives the mortgagee the right to foreclose. Other statutes provide only that the mortgagee may obtain an injunction in a court of equity enjoining any further impairment. Some states provide for the appointment of a receiver to prevent waste. Many state laws also make it a criminal offense to willfully impair the security of mortgaged property.

COURT CASE

Facts: After borrowing $1.2 million, Big "K" Development Corp. mortgaged a residential development as security. Five months later, Big "K" sold lot 40 of the development to Roddy and Martha McCaskill. The recorded deed included an easement "for . . . an unrestricted view from said Lot 40" over lots 21, 22, and 23. Some time later, Big "K" defaulted on its note, and Amstar/First Capital, Ltd. (Amstar), the mortgagee, sued to foreclose the mortgage. Amstar alleged its prior recorded mortgage had priority over the view easement.

Outcome: Because a mortgagor may do nothing that would prejudice the rights of the mortgagee, the view easement was subordinate to Amstar's mortgage.

—*Amstar/First Capital, Ltd. v. McQuade*, 856 S.W.2d 326 (Ark. App.)

RIGHTS OF THE MORTGAGOR

The mortgagor has several rights, including:

1. Possession of the property
2. Rents and profits
3. Cancellation of lien
4. Redemption
5. Sale of the property

Possession of the Property

As the owner of the property, the mortgagor usually has the right to retain possession of the mortgaged property. On default, the mortgagee usually may take possession to collect rents and profits and apply them to the mortgage debt in compliance with a duty as a fiduciary to the mortgagor. In some states, possession cannot be taken, but the appointment of a receiver to collect rents and profits may be obtained.

COURT CASE

Facts: After Thomas Tacon defaulted on his mortgage, Equity One, Inc., the mortgagee began foreclosure proceedings. The mortgage allowed Equity to enter to make repairs on default. Equity asked REO National to get a price for the property from a realtor. REO hired Century 21 to assess the exterior and verify the house was vacant. Debbie Muldoon, a Century 21 agent, took exterior photographs. She looked in the windows and found the house contained junk and debris but no beds or couches, the electric meter was not running, and the house appeared unoccupied. Equity authorized Muldoon to rekey the locks and enter to "winterize" the pipes and inspect the interior to determine its value. Muldoon found the house had been rekeyed, but the back door was open and the electricity on. She did not think anyone was living in the house that had no heat. Concerned about vandals, she had four items of furniture removed and relocked the door. She put the furniture into storage and notified Tacon that the property appeared to have been "ransacked." He got inside and discovered several items missing. He sued claiming Equity was not entitled to enter the property to secure it.

Outcome: The court held that Equity was entitled to enter the house to secure the premises and protect its interest in the property.

—Tacon v. Equity One, Inc.,
633 S.E.2d 599 (Ga. App.)

Rents and Profits

The mortgagor, as the owner of the property, has the right to rents and profits from the property. In the absence of an express agreement to the contrary, the mortgagor has the right to all rents and profits obtained from the mortgaged property. The mortgagor may retain the profits. This rule or any other rule may, of course, be superseded by a contract providing otherwise.

Cancellation of Lien

The mortgagor has the right to have the lien cancelled on final payment. As soon as the mortgagee receives the mortgage, it becomes a lien on the mortgaged real estate. The clerk in the recorder's office cancels a mortgage lien by entering a notation, usually on the margin, certifying that the debt has been paid and that the lien is cancelled. The mortgagee, not the mortgagor, must have this done. If the mortgagee does not, the mortgagor may institute court action to have this cloud removed from the title so that there may be a clear title.

Redemption

Redemption
Right to free property from lien of mortgage

The mortgagor has the right to free the mortgaged property from the lien of the mortgage after default, known as the right of **redemption**. Statutes in most states prescribe a specific time after the foreclosure and sale when this right may be exercised. In order to redeem the property, the mortgagor must pay the amount of the mortgage, the costs of the sale, and any amounts paid to protect the purchaser's interest in the property, such as taxes or insurance.

Usually only a person whose interests will be affected by foreclosure may exercise the right of redemption. This includes the executor or administrator and heirs of the mortgagor, and frequently a second mortgagee or junior lienholder.

Sale of the Property

The mortgagor has a right to sell the property on which a mortgage exists. The purchaser may agree to "assume the mortgage," which means to be primarily liable for its payment. "Assuming" the mortgage differs from buying the property "subject to the mortgage." In the first case, the buyer agrees to be liable for the mortgage obligation as fully as the original mortgagor. If the buyer takes the property "subject to the mortgage" and default occurs, the property may be lost, but no more.

A sale of the mortgaged property does not automatically release the original mortgagor whether the purchaser assumed the mortgage or bought it subject to the mortgage. The mortgagor remains fully liable in both cases.

To excuse the mortgagor from liability under a mortgage, a novation must take place. This can occur if the parties involved sign a written agreement releasing the mortgagor. Courts also have found novations if the mortgagee extends the time of payment for the purchaser of the property without the mortgagor's consent. Accepting an interest payment after the principal of the mortgage has become due constitutes an extension of the mortgage. If the mortgagee does this without the mortgagor's consent, a novation results and releases the mortgagor from all liability under the mortgage. However, the action of the mortgagee must amount to an extension of time of payment.

FORECLOSURE

If the mortgagor fails to pay the debt secured by the mortgage when it becomes due, or fails to perform any of the other terms set forth in the mortgage, the mortgagee has the right to foreclose for the purpose of collecting the debt. **Foreclosure** usually consists of a sale of the mortgaged property. Generally, an officer of the court makes the sale under an order of a court. The mortgagor must be properly notified of the foreclosure proceedings.

LO ❸
Foreclosure and assignment of rights

Foreclosure
Sale of mortgaged property to pay debt

COURT CASE

Facts: Principal Residential Mortgage, Inc. (PRM) began foreclosure proceedings on Zann Nash's home, and Nash participated in the proceedings. The proceedings were delayed when Nash filed a bankruptcy petition. After the bankruptcy case was dismissed, PRM scheduled the sheriff's sale of Nash's home, and had notice of the sale published in the newspaper. PRM did not mail notice of the sale to Nash or her lawyer. PRM bought the property at the sale. State law required that every written notice be served on each of the parties to a case. Nash did not learn of the sale until five months later.

Outcome: The court invalidated the foreclosure sale of Nash's home.

—*Principal Residential Mortgage, Inc. v. Nash,*
606 N.W.2d 120 (N.D.)

Foreclosure literally means "a legal proceeding to shut out all other claims." A first mortgage may not necessarily constitute a first claim on the proceeds of the sale. The cost of foreclosure and taxes always takes precedence over the first mortgage. People who furnish materials for the construction of a house and workers who work on it have a claim under what is known as a **mechanics' lien**. A mechanics' lien takes precedence over unrecorded mortgages. The law varies

Mechanics' Lien
Lien of people who have furnished materials or labor on property

somewhat among the states, but normally a mortgage recorded before a mechanics' lien attaches has priority. The foreclosure proceedings establish the existence of all prior claims and the order of their priority. Foreclosure proceedings are fixed by statute and therefore vary in different states.

If the proceeds of the sale of mortgaged property exceed the amount of the debt and the expenses of foreclosure, the surplus must be used to pay off any other liens such as second mortgages. Any money remaining belongs to the mortgagor.

If a deficiency results, however, the mortgagee may secure a deficiency judgment for this amount. In that case, the unpaid balance of the debt will be a claim against the mortgagor personally until it is paid.

When the mortgagor has given a mortgage for the purpose of purchasing the property, some states limit the amount of a deficiency judgment. The deficiency cannot be greater than the amount by which the debt exceeds either the fair market value or the selling price, whichever amount is smaller. This gives protection to the mortgagor from the mortgagee buying the property at foreclosure for a very low price. For example, suppose A mortgages property to B for $50,000, and the value of the property declines to $40,000. A defaults and B forecloses. B buys the property at foreclosure for $30,000.

	Fair Market Value	Selling Price
Amount of debt	$50,000	$50,000
Less amount "received"	40,000	30,000
Deficiency	$10,000	$20,000

B may obtain a deficiency judgment of $10,000 because it is the lesser of the two amounts.

ASSIGNMENT OF THE MORTGAGE

The rights of the mortgagee under the mortgage agreement may be assigned. The assignee, the purchaser, obtains no greater rights than the assignor had. To be protected, the assignee should require the assignor to produce an estoppel certificate signed by the mortgagor. This certificate should acknowledge that the mortgagor has no claims of any kind in connection with the mortgage. This would bar the mortgagor from subsequently claiming the right of offset.

The assignee of a mortgage should have this assignment recorded. In the event that the mortgagee assigns the mortgage to more than one party, the one who records an assignment first has preference. This can be important when the proceeds are not adequate to pay both assignees.

DEED OF TRUST

Deed of Trust
Deed that transfers property to trustee for benefit of creditor

Trustee
One who holds title to property for another

In a number of states, parties commonly use a deed of trust instead of a mortgage for securing a debt with real estate. A mortgage involves two parties, a debtor and a creditor. A **deed of trust** involves three parties. It conveys title to the property to a disinterested party, called a **trustee**. The trustee holds the property in trust for the benefit of the creditor. Most courts treat a deed of trust like a mortgage. If a default in payment occurs, the trustee forecloses on the property and applies the proceeds to the payment of the debt. The right to redeem under a deed of trust, when it exists, is similar to the right of redemption under a mortgage.

The advantage to the creditor in using a deed of trust instead of a mortgage is in the power held by the trustee. In the event that a mortgagor defaults in the payments, the mortgagee who holds an ordinary mortgage can foreclose. In most states, however, the mortgagee must go into court and have a judicial foreclosure in order to have the mortgaged property sold to satisfy the debt. A trustee of a deed of trust may sell the mortgaged property at public auction if the debtor defaults. No time-consuming court foreclosure proceedings are necessary. Hence, the property can be sold more quickly at a trustee's sale.

MORTGAGE INSURANCE

Private companies and several agencies of the federal government insure or guarantee mortgages against default by the mortgagor. The insurance lasts for the term of the mortgage. The government agrees to pay in case of default by the mortgagor in order to make it easier for some people to obtain a mortgage. The most frequently used government programs are those administered by the Federal Housing Administration (FHA) and the Veterans Administration (VA).

FHA-insured mortgages require a smaller downpayment than conventional mortgages. Anyone who meets the financial qualifications may obtain an FHA loan. Because FHA mortgages are insured, the interest rate is slightly less than for a conventional mortgage. The FHA sets a maximum amount that may be mortgaged. The FHA bases this amount on the average sale price in the area for a home. The mortgagor pays premiums for this mortgage insurance.

The VA guarantees mortgages for people who have served on active duty in the armed forces for a minimum period of time. The mortgage must be on owner-occupied property. The VA charges the mortgagor a percentage of the loan amount for its guarantee. It sets the interest rate charged. As a benefit to veterans, it sets this rate less than the market rate for conventional loans. A VA mortgage may be for up to 100 percent of the value of the real estate. This means that no downpayment is required. The maximum loan amount is $144,000.

QUESTIONS

1. How does a mortgage obtain the benefit of the security of a mortgage?

2. Explain the purpose for which a mortgagor may execute a mortgage.

3. Why does recording a mortgage protect a mortgage against subsequent creditors?

4. What right does an acceleration clause in a mortgage give the mortgagee?

5. What payments must a mortgagor make in addition to payments of interest and principal?

6. Who has the right to possess mortgaged property?

7. What must a mortgagor do to redeem property after default?

8. What happens if a foreclosure does not completely pay off a mortgage?

9. What should the assignee of a mortgage do to be protected from possible claims by the mortgagor?

10. What is a deed of trust, and how is it used?

CASE PROBLEMS

LO **3**

1. An unknown person stole Aurora Lepe's identity and bought real estate in her name. The identity thief obtained a loan secured by a mortgage on the property. The mortgage was subsequently foreclosed and the property sold. Following payment of the first and second mortgages, there were surplus funds, presumably because the property value had increased. As the mortgagor of record, Lepe was notified of the surplus. The law required that any excess after foreclosure be paid to the mortgagor. Lepe claimed the surplus because the unknown wrongdoer had fraudulently used her name and Social Security number to obtain funding to purchase the property. Should Lepe be paid the excess?

LO **2**

2. Lora Hubbel purchased real estate at a sheriff's sale foreclosing a mortgage. She secured insurance and paid two months' premiums. Eight days after the sale, Dacotah Bank (Dacotah), as a junior lienholder on the property, delivered a notice of redemption and a check for the purchase price plus interest to the sheriff. The sheriff served Hubbel with the notice of redemption, but she disputed the amount of the check because it did not cover her insurance payment. Meanwhile, Hubbel paid real estate taxes and continued to pay insurance premiums, but did not notify Dacotah of these additional expenses. Dacotah delivered a supplemental notice of redemption to Hubbel and to the sheriff with an additional check covering the insurance premiums. Both Hubbel and Dacotah claimed they were entitled to a sheriff's deed to the property. Had Dacotah complied with redempton requirements?

LO **1**

3. When James Townsend and his mother, Donna Townsend, bought real property as joint tenants with right of survivorship, Donna executed a mortgage on the property. James was not a party to the mortgage. After Donna died five years later, no payments were made on the mortgage. Chase Manhattan Mortgage Corp., the holder of the mortgage, foreclosed on the property. James sued to have the foreclosure set aside arguing that since Donna's interest in the property ended at her death, the mortgage ended at her death. Should the foreclosure be put aside?

LO **3**

4. Angela Lutz mortgaged real property to Alligriff Mortgage Corporation, Inc. Alligriff assigned the mortgage to Huntington Mortgage Company. The mortgage and assignment were recorded. Lutz died, and John Wead was appointed administrator of her estate. GMAC believed it acquired the mortgage as part of a bulk transaction with Huntington and sued for foreclosure because the mortgage was in default. The court dismissed GMAC's action because GMAC did not prove it had received an assignment from Huntington. Wead asked the probate court for permission to sell the real estate. Huntington then assigned the mortgage to GMAC, and GMAC recorded the assignment. Wead alleged GMAC's mortgage was invalid because recording of the assignment was untimely. Was GMAC's mortgage valid?

LO **2**

5. Michael and Drue Gisvold defaulted on their home mortgage and GMAC, the holder, began foreclosure proceedings. Several sales were held or attempted at which Randall Cudd and Jim Claycomb were the high bidders, but the Gisvolds prevented or delayed the sales or court confirmation of sales by filing bankruptcy petitions or objections. At the confirmation hearing of the second sale the court agreed to allow the Gisvolds until January 17 to redeem

the property or the confirmation would be effective January 18. Cudd and Claycomb then had 10 days to pay the purchase price. Three hours before the redemption time expired Michael filed another bankruptcy petition. A week after the bankruptcy petition was dismissed, the Gisvolds paid the amount due on the mortgage. Had they redeemed the property in time?

6. New Panorama Development Corp. bought a tract of land from Robert Simpson and executed a mortgage for $654,000 covering only lot 126 of the land. New Panorama created lot 130, mostly from part of lot 126 but also with some of the unmortgaged acreage. The mortgage allowed for release of portions of the mortgaged property upon payment of $752,100 "divided by the total number of subdivided . . . lots." Lot 130 was ultimately sold to Caryn Woods. There was default on the mortgage and foreclosure. Woods sued alleging the mortgage was ambiguous. She asked the court to set a price based on acreage at which the portion of her lot taken from lot 126 could be released from the mortgage. What rules should the court use in interpreting the mortgage?   LO ❶

7. Crossroads, Inc. mortgaged land to First Interstate Bank of Texas to secure payment of a $3 million debt. The state condemned the land for a highway. A condemnation award of more than $6 million was made, and the state and Crossroads objected to it, but the state deposited the $6 million with the court. Crossroads and the bank moved to withdraw the $6 million. Because no one objected, Crossroads got the money and paid its debt to the bank. The state and Crossroads finally agreed on a $3.5 million value for the property, and the court ordered Crossroads to pay back the $2.5 million excess. Crossroads could not repay the excess, so the state alleged the bank was liable for it. State law provided that when an award paid exceeded the finally determined value of the property "the court shall order the property owner to return the excess." The state alleged that a mortgagee was the owner of mortgaged property; therefore, the bank had to pay the $2.5 million. Decide the case.   LO ❷

8. Victor Paulos, Dan Lamountt, and Stanley Stephen formed Westridge Court Joint Venture to build an apartment complex. Westridge borrowed $1.9 million secured by a deed of trust on the complex's property to finance construction. After construction, Paulos, Lamountt, and Stephen did not like the occupancy rate and sold the project to DFAI. DFAI defaulted on the loan, and the mortgagee foreclosed. The mortgagee made the only bid at the foreclosure sale and purchased the project for $957,000. The court entered a deficiency judgment against DFAI for the difference—the difference between the debt and the price bid at the foreclosure sale. Discuss the rights of the parties depending on whether or not the state has a law regarding the sufficiency of the sale price at a foreclosure.   LO ❸

Landlord and Tenant

LEARNING OBJECTIVES

1 Explain the nature and formation of the landlord/tenant relationship.

2 Name the various types of tenancies.

3 List the rights and duties of tenants and landlords.

4 Explain how a lease may be terminated.

PREVIEW CASE

David Clark leased 13 acres of vacant property to American Pipe Threading. American built three buildings on the property and one on property owned by the Whiteheads that it had no right to use. Clark acquired American's assets and leased the Whiteheads' property for one year at $1,200 a month. The lease provided that if Clark held over after termination of the lease the rent would be $1,500. At the end of the lease term, Clark held over and paid $1,500 a month for three months. He then gave notice of termination, but he did not remove all his property, including large trucks and trash, from the Whitehead property for several years. When sued for rent for the holdover period, Clark claimed he was a trespasser and not a holdover tenant. How is a tenancy terminated? Who has the right to determine the character of relief available to a landlord when a tenant holds over?

LO 1
Nature and formation of relationship

Landlord or **Lessor**
Owner of leased property

Tenant or **Lessee**
Possessor of leased property

A contract whereby one person agrees to lease land or a building to another creates the relationship of landlord and tenant. Such an agreement does not require special words or acts for creation unless the lease lasts for more than a year, in which case it must be in writing. The tenant's temporary possession of the premises and payment of rent for its use constitute the chief characteristics that determine the relationship of landlord and tenant. The landlord may retake possession of the property at the end of the lease period.

The owner of the leased property is known as the **landlord**, or **lessor**. The person given possession of the leased property is the **tenant**, or **lessee**. The contract or agreement between the landlord and tenant is called a **lease** (see Illustration 44–1).

ILLUSTRATION 44–1 Lease

RENTAL AGREEMENT

1. Parties:

_____*Richard T. Mowbray, Cincinnati, OH*_____(Owner) and _____*Edward J. and Doris L. Caldwell,*
*Cincinnati, OH*_____(Tenant) hereby agree as follows:

2. Premises:
Owner rents to Tenant and Tenant rents from Owner for residential use only, the premises located at:
_____*2669 Russell Road, Cincinnati, OH 45299* together with the following furnishings, appliances, and fixtures:
_____*stove, refrigerator, dishwasher, washer, and dryer* on the following terms:

3. Term:
This agreement shall begin on _____*May 1, 2007*_____ and shall continue from that date
_____A) on a month-to-month basis. This agreement will continue for successive terms of one month each until
either owner or tenant terminate the tenancy by giving the other thirty (30) days written notice of an intention
to terminate the tenancy. In the event such notice is given, tenant agrees to pay all rent up to and including the
notice period.
X B) for a period of _____*12*_____ months, expiring on _____*April 30, 2008*_____ .

4. Rent:
Tenant shall pay Owner rent of _____*$775*_____ per month. Rent for each month is payable in advance on or before
the first day of the month for which the rent is due. Rent shall be paid by personal check, money order, or cashier's
check only, to the order of _____*Mowbray Apartments*_____ (Cash shall not be accepted).

5. Security Deposit:
Tenant shall deposit _____*$400*_____ with Owner as security. Owner may use all or any part of this security
deposit to remedy defaults in the payment of rent, to repair damage to the premises, to clean the premises, or for
any other purpose allowed by law. This deposit shall be refunded to Tenant within three weeks (21 days) after
vacating said apartment, if the following conditions have been satisfied:
a) Proper notice of termination has been given;
b) There is no default in the payment of rent and/or late charges;
c) The premises are left in clean, orderly condition, including the cleaning of carpets, refrigerator, stove,
oven, etc.
d) There has been no damage to premises, equipment, or furnishings; and
e) All other terms and conditions of this agreement have been satisfied.
In the event Owner incurs expenses to remedy any default in this agreement, including but not limited to the
above conditions, the cost may be deducted from the Security Deposit. If Owners' expenses exceed said deposit,
Tenant shall be liable for excesses.

6. Utilities:
Tenant shall pay all utility charges related to his/her occupancy of the premises except *trash collection services.*

7. Late Charges:
Tenant shall pay Owner a late charge of_____*$100*_____ if rent is not received by Owner by 5:00 p.m. on the fifth
day of the month for which it is due.

8. Habitability:
Tenant has examined the entire interior and exterior of the premises and acknowledges that the entire premises
are in good, clean condition. Tenant, to the best of his/her ability, has examined all furnishings, appliances, and

ILLUSTRATION 44–1 (*Continued*)

fixtures on the premises including plumbing, heating and electrical appliances, and fixtures and acknowledges that these items are in good working order with the following exceptions:

_____ Tenant shall immediately give Owner written notice upon discovery of any damage, defects, or dangerous conditions on or about the premises, including plumbing, heating and electrical appliances, and fixtures.

9. Disturbances:
Tenant shall not use the premises for any unlawful purpose, violate any law or ordinance, commit waste, or create a nuisance on or about the premises or permit such acts to occur. It shall be presumed that three disturbance complaints from other tenants in the building or occupants of nearby buildings during any consecutive sixty-day period shall constitute an irremediable breach of this agreement and Owner shall have the right to immediately terminate the tenancy.

10. Right of Entry:
Upon reasonable notice, Owner may enter the premises during reasonable hours for the purpose of making repairs, alterations, decorations or improvements, to supply services, to show the premises to others, or for any other purpose allowed by law. In an emergency, Owner may enter the premises at any time without prior notice to Tenant for the purpose of taking such action as is necessary to alleviate the emergency.

11. Smoke Detectors:
The premises are equipped with a smoke detection device(s), and Tenant shall be responsible for reporting any problems, maintenance, or repairs to Owner. Replacing batteries is the responsibility of the Tenant.

12. Termination of Tenancy:
A thirty-day notice of termination may be given by either Tenant or Owner at any time during the month and tenancy does not have to terminate at the end of the calendar month. Rent shall be due and payable up to and including the date of termination. When the thirty-day notice is given by Tenant, it may not be revoked or modified without written approval of the Owner. As a condition for the full refund of all of the security deposit Tenant shall do the following: a) completely vacate the premises, including any storage or other areas of the general premises which Tenant may be occupying or in which Tenant may have personal property stored; b) deliver all keys and other personal property furnished to Tenant during the term of this Agreement; c) and leave Tenant's forwarding address. Tenant shall cooperate in allowing the Manager to show Tenant's apartment at any reasonable time during this thirty-day period.

Tenant's and Co-Signer's Certificate and Acknowledgement of Receipt:

I hereby certify that I have read all provisions of this agreement, that I understand them, that I agree to abide by them, and that I acknowledge receipt of a copy of this agreement and all attachment to it.

April 18, 2007   *Edward J. Caldwell*
Date   Tenant

April 18, 2007   *Doris L. Caldwell*
Date   Tenant

April 18, 2007   *Richard T. Mowbray*
Date   Owner/Agent

The amount that the tenant agrees to pay the landlord for the possession of the leased property is called the **rent**.

A tenant differs from a lodger or roomer in that the former has the exclusive legal possession of the property, whereas the latter has merely the right to use the premises subject to the control and supervision of the owner.

Lease
Contract between landlord and tenant

Rent
Amount paid landlord for possession of property

THE LEASE

The lease may be oral or written, express or implied, formal or simple, subject, however, to the general statutory requirement that a lease of land for a term longer than one year must be in writing to be enforceable. If a dispute arises between the tenant and the landlord over their rights and duties, the court will look to the terms of the lease and the general body of landlord and tenant law to determine the decision.

In order to avoid disputes, a lease should be in writing and should cover all terms of the contract. The parties should include such items as a clear identification of the property, the time and place of payment of rent, the notice required to vacate, the duration or the nature of the tenancy, and any specific provision desired by either party, such as the right of the landlord to show the property to prospective purchasers or an agreement requiring the landlord to redecorate.

COURT CASE

Facts: Russell Ratliff rented a house to Johnny and Mary Gorman. The Gormans became delinquent in their rent to Ratliff, and he asked them to vacate the house. The written lease provided that if the Gormans did not pay any rent when due, Ratliff "may, if desired, take immediate possession . . . removing and storing at the expense of said lessees all property contained therein." Relying on such provisions in the lease, Ratliff entered the house in the Gormans' absence, removed all their personal property, and put it in storage. State law provided that "carrying away the goods of the party in possession . . ." constituted the offense of forcible entry and detainer. The Gormans sued Ratliff.

Outcome: The court said that although the lease gave Ratliff the authority to take possession of the Gormans' property, state law invalidated that portion of the lease.

—*Gorman v. Ratliff*, 712 S.W.2d 888 (Ark.)

TYPES OF TENANCIES

Four separate and distinct classes of tenancies exist, each of which has some rule of law governing it that does not apply to any other type of tenancy. The four classes of tenancies are:

LO ❷
Tenancy types

1. Tenancy for years
2. Tenancy from year to year
3. Tenancy at will
4. Tenancy at sufferance

Tenancy for Years

A **tenancy for years** is a tenancy for a definite period of time, whether it is 1 month, 1 year, or 99 years. The lease fixes the termination date. However, by law most states limit the length of time a lease may last. A lease for a time greater than the

Tenancy for Years
Tenancy for any definite period

statutory limit is void. The payment of the rent may be by the month even when a tenancy for a specified number of years exists. No notice to terminate the tenancy need be given by either party when the lease fixes the termination date. Most leases provide that they will continue to run on a year-to-year basis after the termination date, unless the tenant gives notice to the landlord not less than a specified number of days before the termination date that the tenant intends to leave on that date.

Tenancy from Year to Year

Tenancy from Year to Year
Tenancy for indefinite period with yearly rent

A tenancy for an indefinite period of time with rent set at a yearly amount is known as a **tenancy from year to year**. Under such a tenancy, a tenant merely pays the rent periodically, and the lease lasts until proper notice of termination has been given. A tenancy of this kind also may be by the month or any other period agreed on. If by the month, it is called a *tenancy from month to month*. The length of the tenancy is usually determined by the nature of the rent stated or paid, although there could be a tenancy from year to year with the rent paid quarterly or monthly.

Notice to terminate this type of tenancy must exactly follow the state law governing it. Notice must normally be in writing. In a tenancy from month to month, the law usually requires notice 30 days before a rent due date.

Tenancy at Will

Tenancy at Will
Tenancy for uncertain period

A **tenancy at will** exists when the tenant has possession of the property for an uncertain period. Either the tenant or the landlord can terminate the tenancy at will, because both must agree to the tenancy. This tenancy, unlike any of the others, automatically terminates on the death of the tenant or the landlord, if the tenant attempts to assign the tenancy, or if the landlord sells the property.

Tenancy at Sufferance

Tenancy at Sufferance
Holdover tenant without landlord's permission

When a tenant holds over the tenancy after the expiration of the lease without permission of the landlord, a **tenancy at sufferance** exists until the landlord elects to treat the tenant as a trespasser or as a tenant. The landlord may treat the tenant as a trespasser, sue for damages, and have the tenant removed by legal proceedings. If the landlord prefers, payment of the rent due for another period may be accepted, and thus the tenant's possession may be recognized as rightful.

PREVIEW CASE REVISITED

Facts: David Clark leased 13 acres of vacant property to American Pipe Threading. American built three buildings on the property and one on property owned by the Whiteheads that it had no right to use. Clark acquired American's assets and leased the Whiteheads' property for one year at $1,200 a month. The lease provided that if Clark held over after termination of the lease the rent would be $1,500. At the end of the lease term, Clark held over and paid $1,500 a month for three months. He then gave notice of termination, but he did not remove all his property, including large trucks and trash, from the Whitehead property for several years. When sued for rent for the holdover period, Clark claimed he was a trespasser and not a holdover tenant.

Outcome: The court pointed out that a landlord has the option of treating a lessee in possession after expiration of a lease as a trespasser or as a holdover tenant.

—*Clark v. Whitehead*, 874 S.W.2d 282 (Ct. App. Tex.)

RIGHTS OF THE TENANT

A lease gives the tenant certain rights, as follows:

1. Right to possession
2. Right to use the premises
3. Right to assign or sublease

LO 3
Tenant and landlord rights and duties

Right to Possession

By signing the lease, the landlord warrants the right to lease the premises and that the tenant shall have possession during the period of the lease. During the term of the lease, tenants have the same right to exclusive possession of the premises as if they owned the property. If someone questions the owner's right to lease the property, the landlord must defend the tenant's right to exclusive possession. Failure of the landlord to give possession on time or to protect the tenant's rights subjects the landlord to liability for damages.

A nuisance that disturbs the tenant's quiet enjoyment of the property often causes disputes between landlords and tenants. Courts have held that failure to remove dead rats from the wall, failure to stop disorderly conduct on the part of other tenants, and frequent and unnecessary entrances on the property by the landlord or agents constitute acts that destroy the tenant's right to quiet enjoyment and constitute a breach of warranty on the part of the landlord.

If the nuisance existed at the time the tenant leased the property and the tenant knew of its existence, the right to complain would be deemed to have been waived. Also, if the landlord has no control over the nuisance, the tenant cannot avoid the contract even though the nuisance arose subsequent to the signing of the lease. If the landlord fails or refuses to abate a nuisance over which the landlord has control, the tenant not only may terminate the lease but also may sue for damages. In other cases, the tenant may seek an injunction compelling the landlord to abate a nuisance.

Right to Use the Premises

Unless the lease expressly restricts this right, the tenant has the right to use the premises in any way consistent with the nature of the property. A dwelling cannot be converted into a machine shop, nor can a clothing store be converted into a restaurant. Damage to leased property other than that which results from ordinary wear and tear is not permissible. In the case of farming land, the tenant may cut wood for personal use but not to sell.

Right to Assign or Sublease

If the tenant transfers all interest in the lease to another party who agrees to comply with its terms, including the payment of the rent to the landlord, there is an **assignment**. In an assignment, the assignee pays the rent directly to the landlord. An assignment must include the entire premises. In a **sublease**, the tenant transfers the premises for a period less than the term of the lease or transfers only a part of the premises. The tenant usually collects the rent from the subtenant and pays the landlord. Ordinarily a written lease prohibits assigning or subleasing the premises unless the lessor gives written consent thereto first. Residential leases commonly restrict the use of the premises to the tenant and the immediate family or to a certain number of persons. Unless the lease expressly prohibits both assignment and subleasing, either may be done. If the lease prohibits only subleasing, then the lease may be assigned.

Assignment
Transfer to another of tenant's rights

Sublease
Transfer of less than a tenant's full rights under a lease

Joint occupancy closely relates to subleasing. A provision in the lease prohibiting subleasing does not forbid a contract for a joint occupancy. In joint occupancy, the tenant does not give up exclusive control of any part of the premises. The tenant merely permits another party to jointly occupy all or a part of the premises.

DUTIES OF THE TENANT

The lease imposes certain duties upon the tenant:

1. To pay rent
2. To protect and preserve the premises

To Pay Rent

The tenant's primary duty is to pay the rent. This payment must be made in money unless the contract provides otherwise, such as a share of the crops. The rent is not due until the end of the term, but leases almost universally provide for rent in advance.

Landlords commonly appoint an agent for the purpose of collecting the rent. The death of the principal automatically terminates such a principal-agent relationship. Any rent paid to the agent after this termination and not remitted to the proper party must be paid again.

If the tenant fails to pay rent on time, the landlord may terminate the lease and order the tenant to vacate, or the landlord may permit the tenant to continue occupancy and sue for the rent. However, even if the landlord forces the tenant to vacate the property, the tenant is still liable for the agreed rent. Under the common law, the landlord could seize and hold any personal property found on the premises. This right has been either curtailed or abolished by statute.

To Protect and Preserve the Premises

Traditionally, a tenant had to make repairs on the premises. This was because a tenant had a duty to keep the leased property in as good condition as the landlord had it when the lease began. Some states have enacted statutes requiring the landlord to make repairs. Other states find a warranty of habitability, which makes the landlord responsible for keeping the premises livable. Some statutes even give tenants a form of self-help. The tenant must notify the landlord of needed repairs. If the landlord does not make the repairs, the tenant may fix things and deduct the cost from the rent. Tenants, however, must repair damage caused by their negligence. In states in which statutes have not altered the traditional responsibility, tenants must repair damage except reasonable wear and tear and damage by the elements.

COURT CASE

Facts: Priscilla Tucker rented an apartment in a building owned by 64 West 108th St. Corp. (64 West). A fire in the apartment injured Priscilla and David Tucker. A working smoke detector had been installed in the apartment about 10 years prior to the fire. The Tuckers sued 64 West for their injuries and alleged 64 West's employees had removed the smoke detector.

Outcome: In this state, the tenant was totally responsible for the maintenance, repair, and replacement of the smoke detector. The landlord was not liable for the Tuckers' injuries.

—*Tucker v. 64 West 108th St. Corp.,*
768 N.Y.S.2d 460 (N.Y. App. Div.)

RIGHTS OF THE LANDLORD

The landlord has three definite rights under the lease:

1. To regain possession
2. To enter upon the property to preserve it
3. To assign rights

To Regain Possession

On termination of the lease, the landlord has the right to regain peaceable possession of the premises. If the tenant refuses this possession, the most common remedy is to bring an **action of ejectment** in a court of law. On the successful completion of this suit, the sheriff will forcibly remove the tenant and any property.

Action of Ejectment
Action to have sheriff remove tenant

When the landlord repossesses leased property, all permanent improvements and fixtures may be retained. Courts determine whether or not the improvements have become a part of the real estate. If they have, they cannot be removed.

To Enter on the Property to Preserve It

The landlord has a right to enter on the property to preserve it. Extensive renovations that interfere with the tenant's peaceable occupancy cannot be made. If the roof blows off or becomes leaky, the landlord may repair it or put on a new roof. This occasion cannot be used to add another story. A landlord who enters the property without permission may be treated as a stranger. A landlord has no right to enter the premises to show the property to prospective purchasers or tenants unless the lease reserves this right.

To Assign Rights

The landlord has the right to assign the rights under the lease to a third party. The tenant cannot avoid any duties and obligations by reason of the assignment of the lease. Like all other assignments, the assignment does not release the assignor from the contract without the consent of the tenant. If, for example, the tenant suffers injury because of a concealed but defective water main cover and the landlord knew of this condition, the landlord has liability even though rights under the lease were assigned before the injury.

DUTIES OF THE LANDLORD

The lease imposes certain duties on the landlord:

1. To pay taxes and assessments
2. To protect the tenant from concealed defects
3. To mitigate damages on abandonment by the tenant

To Pay Taxes and Assessments

Although the tenant occupies and uses the premises, the landlord must pay all taxes and special assessments. Sometimes the lease provides that the tenant shall pay the taxes. In such event, the tenant has no liability for special assessments for sidewalks, street paving, and other improvements.

To Protect the Tenant from Concealed Defects

The landlord has liability to the tenant if the tenant suffers injury by concealed defects that were known or should have been reasonably known to the landlord at the time of giving the tenant possession of the premises. Such defects might be contamination from contagious germs; concealed, unfilled wells; and rotten timbers in the dwelling. The tenant bears the risk of injury caused by apparent defects or defects reasonably discoverable on inspection at the time that the tenant enters into possession. Most cities and many states have tenement laws that require the landlord to keep all rental property habitable and provided with adequate fire escapes. The question of the habitability of the property relates to major defects in the structure. Any damage caused by a failure to observe these laws may subject the landlord to liability for damages.

To Mitigate Damages Upon Abandonment by the Tenant

Unless the landlord accepts the abandonment, a tenant who abandons leased property before the end of the lease term still has an obligation to pay the rent due through the end of the term. Under the common law, the landlord could do nothing and sue the tenant for the unpaid rent. However, in most states the landlord now has a duty to take reasonable steps to mitigate the tenant's damages by attempting to secure a new tenant. If a new tenant occupies the premises, the landlord's damage from the first tenant abandoning the property equals the difference between the rent the original tenant had to pay and the rent the new tenant pays. In this way, the original tenant's obligation amounts to less than the original rent called for by the lease and the new tenant's payments mitigate the landlord's damage due from the original tenant.

COURT CASE

Facts: CMCB Enterprises, Inc. owned property leased to Bocci's Foods, Inc., which was owned and operated by William Ferguson and Craig Camozzi. Ferguson and Camozzi signed personal guaranties of the lease requiring CMCB to attempt to mitigate damages prior to proceeding on the guaranties. They started Duggan's Grill on the property. When the rent was not paid, CMCB sent Ferguson and Camozzi a demand for payment of rent or possession so CMCB could try to re-rent the property. Before the property was vacated, CMCB asked a real estate broker to look for a replacement tenant. The broker contacted other restaurant owners, advertised the property in the newspaper, sent out e-mails, distributed a brochure to potential tenants, and posted a "for lease" sign. When CMCB sued, Ferguson and Camozzi alleged CMCB had not attempted to mitigate its damages before suit.

Outcome: The court found CMCB had adequately attempted to mitigate its damages.

—*CMCB Enterprises, Inc. v. Ferguson,*
114 P.3d 90 (Colo. App.)

TERMINATION OF THE LEASE

LO ❹
Lease termination

A lease for a fixed time automatically terminates on the expiration of that period. The death of either party does not ordinarily affect the lease. If the leased property consists of rooms or apartments in a building and fire or any other accidental cause destroys them, the lease terminates without liability on the part of the tenant. In the case of leases of entire buildings, serious problems arise if fire, tornado, or any other cause destroys the property. Under the common law, the tenant had to continue to pay rent even though the property was destroyed. Some states retain this rule; other states have modified it. A landlord who has a 10-year lease on a $100,000 building destroyed by fire one year after signing the lease would not be inclined to rebuild if fully covered by fire insurance. The landlord would find it more profitable to invest the $100,000 and continue to collect the rent. To prevent this, statutes may provide that if the landlord refuses to restore the property, the lease terminates. The lease itself may contain a cancellation clause. If it does not, the tenant can carry fire insurance for the amount of possible loss. Even when the lease will thus terminate, the tenant will probably wish to carry fire insurance for personal property and, if the premises are used for a business purpose, may carry insurance to indemnify for business interruption or loss of business income.

The landlord may agree to the voluntary surrender of the possession of the premises before the lease expires. This terminates the lease. However, an abandonment of the premises without the consent of the landlord does not constitute a termination of the lease, but a breach of contract.

If the lease runs from year to year or from month to month, the party wishing to terminate it must generally give the other party a written notice of this intention (see Illustrations 44–2 and 44–3). Statutes prescribe the time and the manner of giving notice; they also may specify other particulars, such as the grounds for a termination of the tenancy.

If either party fails to give proper notice, the other party may continue the tenancy for another period.

Eviction

Tenants sometimes refuse to give up possession of the property after the expiration of the lease or fail to comply with requirements of the lease or laws. In such

ILLUSTRATION 44–2 Landlord's Notice to Leave the Premises

NOTICE TO LEAVE THE PREMISES

To Mr. C. Harold Whitmore

You will please take notice that I want you to leave the premises you now occupy, and which you have rented of me , situated and described as follows:

Suite 4
Lakeview Apartment
Lake Shore Drive at Overview Street

in Cleveland County of Cuyahoga and State of Ohio

Your compliance with this Notice July 31

will prevent legal measures being taken by me to obtain possession of the same, agreeably to law.

Yours respectfully,
H. L. Simpson
May 1   20 –

ILLUSTRATION 44–3 Tenant's Notice That the Tenant Is Leaving the Premises

January 2, 20 –

Mr. George A. Hardwick
1719 Glenview Road
St. Louis, Missouri 65337

Dear Mr. Hardwick

This is to notify you that on March 31, 20 –, I intend to vacate the premises now leased from you and located at 1292 Clarendon Road, St. Louis, Missouri. In accordance with the terms of our written lease, this letter constitutes notice of the termination of said lease as of March 31, 20 –.

Sincerely,

John N. Richter

JOHN N. RICHTER

Eviction
Expulsion of tenant from leased property

Forcible Entry and Detainer Action
Summary action by landlord to regain possession

a case, a landlord may seek an **eviction** of the tenant. Eviction is the expulsion of the tenant from the leased property. The laws of the states vary, but all have some form of summary eviction law. The summary action brought by the landlord is called a **forcible entry and detainer action**. The tenant has a right to written notice and a court hearing. However, the court will set an early date, usually 7 to 15 days after notification of the tenant, for the trial. If the landlord wins, law enforcement officers may enforce the eviction in a few days. The proceedings permit quick recovery of real property by the one legally entitled to it.

IMPROVEMENTS

Trade Fixtures
Fixtures used in business

Tenants frequently make improvements during the life of the lease. Many disputes arise as to the tenant's right to take these improvements after the lease is terminated. Courts must determine whether an improvement has become a fixture, which must be left on the land, or whether it remains personal property. If the improvements are **trade fixtures**, or fixtures used in business, and can be removed without substantial injury to the leased property, the tenant may remove them. If a farm tenant builds a fence in the normal way, the fence is a fixture, and the tenant has no right to remove it on leaving. A poultry house built in the usual way is a fixture and cannot be removed. In a similar case, a tenant built the poultry house on sledlike runners. When ready to leave, the tenant had the poultry house hauled away and took it when vacating. The court held the shed had not become a fixture but remained personal property.

Unless prohibited by law, one may freely contract away rights or may waive them, so the parties may agree as to how to treat fixtures. In one case, a tenant built a permanent frame house on leased property with the landlord's agreement that the house could be moved at the end of the lease. The landlord was bound by this contract.

DISCRIMINATION

Federal law prohibits landlords from discriminating against tenants or proposed tenants because of race, color, religion, sex, familial status, or national origin. The term *familial status* refers to whether the tenant has children. Additionally, some states and even municipalities prohibit discrimination based on such aspects as physical or mental handicaps, age, or marital status.

QUESTIONS

1. What is the difference between a tenant and a lodger or roomer?
2. What determines the decision of a court when there is a dispute between a tenant and a landlord over their rights and duties?
3. How is the length of a tenancy from year to year determined?
4. What causes the automatic termination of a tenancy at will?
5. Under what circumstances is a tenant unable to terminate a lease because of a nuisance?
6. **a.** If a hurricane breaks all the windows in a dwelling, must the tenant replace these windows?
   b. If leased property is destroyed by fire, must the tenant continue to pay rent?
7. From what defects does a landlord have a liability to the tenant?
8. Explain the duty of a landlord to mitigate damages.
9. If the tenant moves out of leased premises before expiration of the lease, is the lease terminated?
10. If a tenant refuses to give up possession after the expiration of a lease, what may the landlord do?

CASE PROBLEMS

1. Samuel Oliva leased Amtech Reliable Elevator Company an office. Before the end of the term, Oliva sent a rider stating all terms of a new lease period would be the same as the original lease except the monthly rent was to be $3,864 the first extra year, $4,057 the next, and $4,260 the third. It gave Amtech an option for three more years after that at $4,473, $4,696, and then $4,931. Amtech signed the rider and paid the prescribed rent for three years. Amtech then paid $4,473 for 12 months and after assigning the lease to Otis Elevator Company, Amtech started paying $4,696, the rent for the second year of the option period. Four months later, Otis notified Oliva the lease had expired at the end of the first three extra years and it was a month-to-month tenant. It gave notice it was vacating in a month. The lease said that any holding over with the landlord's consent would be a tenancy from month to

LO **1**, **2**

month at the final year's rent. Oliva sued for rent for the remaining option period. Should he recover it?

LO ❹

2. Agnes Randall leased a home from Lakota Community Homes (LCH), a federally subsidized cooperative. Her son, Daryl Mesteth, age 20, lived with Randall. Mesteth was arrested for minor consumption of alcohol, and Randall admitted Mesteth had an alcohol abuse history. He was found to have a pipe, alleged by a police officer to smell strongly of burnt marijuana. He was charged with possession of drug paraphernalia. Federal regulations provided criminal activity or alcohol abuse by a household member as grounds for termination of a tenancy in a federally subsidized residence. LCH brought a forcible entry and detainer action against Randall. Can LCH evict Randall?

LO ❸

3. Lemstone, Inc., a Christian bookstore, leased store space for a term of 10 years in a shopping mall owned by Frenchtown Square Partnership (Frenchtown). Another tenant in the mall was Alpha Gifts (Alpha). About nine years into Lemstone's lease, Alpha started to sell items similar or identical to items sold by Lemstone. Lemstone alleged that the competition from Alpha decreased its profits so much that it could not pay the rent required by the lease. About six months before the expiration of the lease, Lemstone closed and abandoned its store. Lemstone paid no more rent, and Frenchtown did not relet the store. Frenchtown sued Lemstone for the unpaid rent, and Lemstone alleged that Frenchtown failed to mitigate its damages. Discuss Lemstone's argument.

LO ❶

4. Thomas Guastello, as landlord leased a building, site improvements, and seven acres of land to Kroger Limited Partnership I. The building was in the location and dimensions shown in Exhibit B, the site plan. Exhibit B, incorporated into the lease, showed an enclosed building of 80,160 square feet. The site plan showed an area near the building labeled "garden shop" not included in the 80,160 square foot building. The lease permitted Kroger at its expense to construct additional buildings on any portion of the leased premises; however, structural changes required Guastello's consent. Such consent would not be withheld if the structural integrity of the building would not be impaired. Kroger demolished the "garden shop" and built a post office facility. Guastello objected. In the ensuing lawsuit, he alleged that his consent for demolition of the garden shop was necessary. Was it?

LO ❷

5. Cross Timbers owned property mortgaged to AgriBank FCB to secure payment of a note. Cross Timbers defaulted on the note and AgriBank foreclosed on the mortgage, buying the property at the foreclosure sale. Cross Timbers and AgriBank engaged in negotiations regarding the redemption or lease of the property by Cross Timbers, but no agreement was reached. Cross Timbers had remained in possession during the nine months of negotiations, but never paid rent. AgriBank sued for possession. Cross Timbers alleged that it had a tenancy at will, and therefore AgriBank had to give it 60 days' notice of termination. Did a tenancy at will exist?

LO ❸

6. Geraldine McAllister was a tenant in property owned by the Boston Housing Authority. Ice had accumulated on the outside stairs of the property from snow and cold weather. After McAllister slipped and fell on the ice, she sued alleging a breach of the warranty of habitability. Was the natural accumulation of ice and snow a breach of the warranty of habitability?

Wills, Inheritances, and Trusts

LEARNING OBJECTIVES

❶ Describe a will, its characteristics, and the limitations on disposition of property.

❷ Explain the normal formalities required for executing the various types of wills.

❸ Name the ways in which a will may be changed or revoked.

❹ Discuss the requirements for probate and administration.

❺ Recognize a trust and the parties to a trust.

PREVIEW CASE

→ When Lloyd Maquar executed his will, he was physically unable to sign his name. He signed each page with an "X" or similar mark. His will contained the statement: "The testator . . . has declared that he knows how to sign his name, but is unable to sign it because of physical infirmity and so has affixed his mark." The will left his estate to his wife, Denise Ott, and nothing to his daughter, Nia Maquar. State law provided that "the formalities prescribed for the execution of a testament must be observed or the testament is absolutely null." Nia alleged that because Lloyd did not declare to the witnesses that he was able "to see and read" but unable to sign, as required by law, the will was invalid. Therefore, she alleged Lloyd had no valid will, and she was heir to his estate. What do you think the purposes of the state laws providing that wills executed without proper formalities were null and that a physically incapacitated testator had to declare the ability "to see and read" were? Is it important that a will clearly show the intent of a testator? What did Lloyd want to have happen to his estate?

T itle to all property, both real and personal, may be transferred by a will. A **will** is an instrument prepared in the form prescribed by law that provides for the disposition of a person's property and takes effect after death. The property left by a person who has died is called the **estate**.

The person making the will is called a **testator** (**testatrix** if a woman). Testators do not have to meet as high a standard of capacity to make a will as a person does in

LO ❶
Will characteristics

Will
Document providing disposition of property after death

Estate
Property left by a deceased

Testator (Testatrix)
Person making a will

order to make a contract. They must have the mental capability at the time of making the will to know the natural objects of their bounty, understand the nature and extent of their property, understand that they are making a will, and have the ability to dispose of their property by means of a plan they have formulated. Even if they do not have the mental capacity to carry on a business or if they make unusual provisions in the will, this does not necessarily mean that they do not have the capacity to make a will. An insane person lacks sufficient capacity; however, an insane person who has intervals of sanity has capacity during sane intervals to make a will. Any person, other than a minor, of sound mind ordinarily has the competence to make a will. In a few states, under limited circumstances, minors can make a will.

COURT CASE

Facts: William and Alberta McQuady executed identical wills leaving everything to the survivor and upon the survivor's death to a cousin and Thomas Beavin, Alberta's brother. Alberta died, and her estate went to William. William was blind and hired Mary Bye as his housekeeper. Two months later, McQuady and Bye visited his lawyer, and McQuady executed a new will leaving all but $100 to Bye. She had a garage built on McQuady's property and kept her car—not McQuady's—in it. McQuady's cousin and Beavin had Beavin appointed as a limited guardian for McQuady who was diagnosed with Alzheimer's disease. A petition to allow McQuady to marry Bye was filed, and at a hearing, McQuady said Bye had misled him about the content of the petition. He stated he did not want to marry Bye

and was afraid of her. The judge denied the petition, and Bye was fired. McQuady then executed a will that reenacted the will he had executed with his wife. After McQuady died, Bye challenged the validity of the latest will alleging lack of testamentary capacity.

Outcome: The court stated that although McQuady suffered from Alzheimer's, he was presumed to have had a lucid interval when the will was executed. McQuady's testimony during the hearing on the marriage petition showed he could have lucid intervals and that at that time he had a total grasp of the circumstances. Bye had to show he lacked capacity, and she did not do that.

—*Bye v. Mattingly*, 975 S.W.2d 451 (Ky.)

LIMITATIONS ON DISPOSITION OF PROPERTY

The law places few restrictions on the right to dispose of property by will. However, some restrictions include:

Right to Take Against the Will
Spouse's right to share of estate provided by statute if will leaves smaller share

1. A spouse may elect to take that share of property that would have been received had the deceased died without leaving a will, or the share provided by statute, if the spouse's will does not leave as large a share, called the **right to take against the will**.

Most state laws now provide that when an individual dies without leaving a will, a spouse has the right to a set portion of all the property the deceased spouse owned at the time of death. The spouse's portion varies depending on the number of children or other heirs who survive. The surviving spouse in some states also may claim an interest in property conveyed by the deceased spouse during the marriage without the consent of the surviving spouse.

The right to take against the will can be barred by actions of the surviving spouse. If the surviving spouse commits acts that would have justified the deceased in securing a divorce, the surviving spouse generally cannot elect to take against the will.

Except for the cases of a surviving spouse electing to take against the will and in some cases of a subsequent marriage, birth, or adoption, the testator may exclude or disinherit any person from receiving any portion of the estate. If the testator gives the entire estate to someone else, all persons who would inherit in the absence of a will are excluded. The testator does not even have to mention in a will those persons disinherited except for disinherited children who must be mentioned to prove the testator did not forget them. A nominal sum does not have to be left to those disinherited.

2. One cannot control by will the distribution of property in perpetuity (for all time). The common-law rule against perpetuities requires that an interest in property must vest within 21 years after the death of persons living on the date the owner of the property creates the interest. When the interest is created by will, the date of death of the owner constitutes the date of creation.

TERMS COMMON TO WILLS

A number of terms may refer to individuals named or gifts given in a will. The one receiving a gift of real estate (the beneficiary) is called the **devisee**; the beneficiary of personal property is a **legatee**. A **devise** is real property given by will. A **bequest**, or a **legacy**, is a gift by will of personal property. The person named in a will as the one to administer the estate is an **executor** or **personal representative**. One who dies without having made a will is said to die **intestate**. A person appointed by a court to settle the affairs of an intestate is an **administrator** (man) or an **administratrix** (woman) or the **personal representative**.

DISTINGUISHING CHARACTERISTICS OF A WILL

A will has the following outstanding characteristics that distinguish it from many other legal instruments:

1. The courts construe a will with less technical strictness than a deed or any other kind of written document.

2. A will devising real property must be executed in conformity with the law of the state in which the property is situated. The law of the state in which the testator was domiciled (had permanent residence) at the time of death governs a will bequeathing personal property.

3. A will may be revoked at any time during the life of the testator.

FORMALITIES

All states prescribe formalities for wills. These formalities must be strictly followed. A will almost always must be in writing and signed by the testator.

A will written in the testator's own handwriting and dated need not be witnessed in a number of states. In almost all states, the will must be witnessed by at least two, and in some states three, disinterested witnesses regardless of how it is written. Usually, the witnesses and the testator must sign in the presence of each other. Many states also require the testator to inform the witnesses that the instrument being signed is the testator's will. This is called **publication**.

When the law requires subscribing witnesses, they must be available at the time of probate of the will to identify their signatures and the signature of the testator and to state that they were present when the testator signed the will. If the witnesses cannot be found, two persons must normally identify the signature of the testator on the will. They base their opinion regarding the testator's signature on their experience through prior correspondence or business records involving

Devisee
One receiving realty by will

Legatee
One receiving personal property by will

Devise
Realty left by will

Bequest or **Legacy**
Personal property left by will

Executor or **Personal Representative**
Person named in will to administer estate

Intestate
One who dies without a will

Administrator, Administratrix, or **Personal Representative**
Person appointed by court to administer estate of intestate

LO **2**
Will formalities

Publication
Testator's informing witnesses that document is will

PREVIEW CASE REVISITED

Facts: When Lloyd Maquar executed his will, he was physically unable to sign his name. He signed each page with an "X" or similar mark. His will contained the statement: "The testator . . . has declared that he knows how to sign his name, but is unable to sign it because of physical infirmity and so has affixed his mark." The will left his estate to his wife, Denise Ott, and nothing to his daughter, Nia Maquar. State law provided that "the formalities prescribed for the execution of a testament must be observed or the testament is absolutely null." Nia alleged that because Lloyd did not declare to the witnesses that he was able "to see and read" but unable to sign, as required by law, the will was invalid. Therefore, she alleged Lloyd had no valid will, and she was heir to his estate.

Outcome: Because the law required the formality of the testator who was unable to sign to declare the ability to see and read, and Lloyd did not, the will was void.

—In re Succession of Maquar, 849 So. 2d 773 (La. Ct. App.)

the testator's signature. A will executed in another jurisdiction is valid if correctly executed in the other jurisdiction. If a person's will is not drawn according to the legal requirements, the court may disregard it and the testator's estate may be disposed of in a manner entirely foreign to the testator's wishes.

SPECIAL TYPES OF WILLS

Under special circumstances, testators can make valid wills that are less formal than usual. Three special types of wills include:

1. Holographic wills
2. Nuncupative wills
3. Soldiers' and sailors' wills

Holographic Wills

Holographic Will
Will written out by testator

Holographic wills are written entirely in longhand by the testator. Some states make no distinction between holographic and other wills. In other states, variations of the general law of wills exist for holographic wills. In still other states, holographic wills may not be recognized.

COURT CASE

Facts: After Mark Lambert died in Montana, his mother, Charlotte Lambert, found a will in his papers completely handwritten and signed by Mark. He had titled the document "Last Will and Testament," and in it he stated that he declared the "instrument as and for my Last Will and Testament hereby expressly revoking any and all wills and codicils . . . heretofore made by me." In 11 pages, Mark detailed the distribution of his estate. The will named Charlotte executrix, and she offered it for probate in Montana. To be valid in Montana, a holographic will's material provisions had to be written and signed by the testator and the testator must have had testamentary intent—he must have intended the document would dispose of his property after death. Joshua Lambert, Mark's son, alleged the handwritten will was invalid in Montana.

Outcome: The court found that the document was a valid holographic will.

—In re Estate of Lambert,
333 Mont. 444 (Mont.)

Nuncupative Wills

Nuncupative wills are oral wills declared by the testator in the presence of witnesses. Usually such a will can only be made during the testator's last illness. A nuncupative will only applies to personal property, and sometimes only a limited value of personal property may be so disposed. The witnesses frequently must reduce the will to writing within a specified number of days, and they must agree as to how the deceased disposed of the property.

Nuncupative Will
Oral will made during last illness

Soldiers' and Sailors' Wills

Most states make special provision for members of the armed forces. They are allowed to make oral or written wills of personal property without complying with the formalities required of other wills. These wills are in force even after the testator returns to civilian life. They must be revoked in the same manner as other wills.

THE WORDING OF A WILL

Any words that convey the intention of the testator suffice (see Illustration 45–1). No matter how rough and ungrammatical the language may be, if the intention of the testator can be ascertained, the court will order that the provisions of the will be carried out. Because the court will order the terms of a will to be carried out exactly, the wording of the will should express the exact wishes of the testator.

REVOCATION

A will may be revoked at any time prior to the death of the testator. The revocation may take any one of several forms.

LO ❸
Will revocation and change

CODICILS

A **codicil** is a separate writing that modifies a will. Except for the part modified, the original will remains the same. A codicil must be executed with all the formalities of the original will.

Codicil
Writing that modifies a will

Destruction or Alteration

If the testator deliberately destroys a will, this constitutes a revocation. If the testator merely alters the will, this may or may not revoke it, depending on the nature and the extent of the alteration. If the testator merely obliterates a part of the will, in most states this does not revoke the will.

Marriage and Divorce

If a single person makes a will and later marries, the marriage may revoke the will in whole or in part, or the court may presume it is revoked unless made in contemplation of the marriage or unless it made provision for a future spouse. In some states, a marriage will not revoke a will completely, but only so that the spouse will get the estate that would have been received in the absence of a will. A divorce automatically revokes a will to the extent of the property left to the divorced spouse if the court orders a division of property; otherwise, a divorce usually in no way affects the will.

ILLUSTRATION 45–1 Will

WILL OF FRANK JOSEPH ROSE

I, Frank Joseph Rose, of the City of Chicago and State of Illinois, revoke all prior wills and codicils and declare that this is my will.

FIRST: If she survives me, I give to my beloved daughter, Anna Rose, now residing in Crestwood, Illinois, that certain piece of real estate, with all improvements thereon, situated at 341 Hudson Avenue, Crestwood, Illinois. If my daughter predeceases me, I give this real estate to my brother, James Earl Rose, now residing in Crestwood, Illinois.

SECOND: All the remainder and residue of my property I give to my beloved wife, Mary Ellen Rose, if, she survives me. If my wife predeceases me, I give the remainder and residue of my property to my daughter, Anna. If both my wife and my daughter predecease me, I give the remainder and residue of my property to my brother, James.

THIRD: I hereby nominate and appoint my wife, Mary Ellen Rose, executrix of this will. If my wife is unable or unwilling to act as executrix, I nominate and appoint my daughter, Anna, executrix. I direct that neither Mary Ellen nor Anna be required to give bond or security for the performance of duties as executrix.

IN WITNESS WHEREOF, I have subscribed my name this tenth day of October, in the year two thousand–.

Frank Joseph Rose
Frank Joseph Rose

We, the undersigned, certify that the foregoing instrument was, on the tenth day of October, signed and declared by Frank Joseph Rose to be his will, in the presence of us who, in his presence and in the presence of each other, have, at his request, hereunto signed our names as witnesses of the execution thereof, this tenth day of October, 20–.

Constance O. Moore	4316 Cottage Grove Avenue residing at Chicago, Illinois 60600
Sarah J. King	1313 East 63 Street residing at Chicago, Illinois 60600
Stewart S. Samuels	2611 Elm Street residing at Chicago, Illinois 60400

COURT CASE

Facts: Grady Miles made a will leaving his "friend," Georgia Hall, his car and a life interest in his home. Georgia had rejected numerous marriage proposals from Grady. More than a year later, Grady and Georgia married. Grady died seven months later without having changed his will. Georgia filed suit claiming the marriage revoked the will.

Outcome: The court said that although Grady did make some provision for Georgia in the will, he made no indication that the bequest was made in contemplation of marriage. In fact, Georgia had refused to marry him many times and it took more than a year for Grady to persuade her to marry him. The will, not having been made in contemplation of marriage, was revoked by the marriage.

—*Miles v. Miles*, 440 S.E.2d 882 (S.C.)

Execution of a Later Will

The execution of a later will automatically revokes a prior will if the terms of the second conflict with the first will. If the second will merely changes a few provisions in the first will and leaves the bulk of it intact, then a second revokes the first will only to the extent of such inconsistency.

After-Born Child

A child may be born or adopted after a person makes a will. If the original will does not provide for subsequent children or the testator makes no codicil to provide for the child, this revokes or partially revokes the will.

ABATEMENT AND ADEMPTION

An **abatement** occurs when a testator makes bequests of money in the will and the estate does not have enough money to pay the bequests. The legatees will receive a proportionate share of the bequests.

An **ademption** occurs when a testator makes a bequest of specific property and the estate does not have the property at death. In this case, the legatee gets nothing.

If a testator leaves $20,000 to his son John, $10,000 to his sister Mary, and a painting to his brother Adam, there could be both an abatement and an ademption. If the estate has only $15,000 in cash left after paying all debts, the cash gifts to John and Mary will abate. Each will receive a proportionate share, in this case 50 percent, or $10,000 and $5,000, respectively. If the testator had sold the painting, given it away, or someone had stolen, destroyed, or lost the painting before the death of the testator, Adam would get nothing. The bequest to him is adeemed because the property was not in the estate at the testator's death. He has no right to its cash value or any other substitute item of property.

Abatement
Proportionate reduction in monetary bequest because of insufficient funds

Ademption
Failure of bequest because property not in estate

COURT CASE

Facts: Bertha Matthews executed a will that bequeathed all her "corporate stocks, corporate bonds, and all municipal bonds owned by me at my death" to Mississippi Baptist Foundation (Baptist). Matthews later set up an investment account with Trustmark National Bank (Trustmark). As Matthews's bonds or securities matured or were called, she put the money in Trustmark mutual funds. David Gandy was appointed Matthews's conservator but made no changes in her investment plan. After Mathews's death, Gandy, as executor, presented the final accounting to Baptist, which refused to accept it claiming the Trustmark mutual funds as well as the stocks and bonds. Corporate stocks, bonds, and municipal bonds had gone from 40.5 percent of Matthews's estate when Gandy was appointed to 16 percent at final accounting.

Outcome: The court found that the bequest of corporate stocks, corporate bonds, and municipal bonds had been adeemed to the extent they had been sold during Matthews's lifetime.

—*Mississippi Baptist Found., Inc. v. Estate of Matthews*, 791 So. 2d 213 (Miss.)

PROBATE OF A WILL

When a testator dies leaving a will, the will must be probated. **Probate** is the court procedure that determines the validity of a will. The will normally names an executor to preserve and handle the estate during probate and distribute it to the

LO 4
Requirements for administration

Probate
Court procedure to determine validity of a will

rightful individuals. An executor has liability to legatees, creditors, and heirs for loss to the estate as a result of negligence, bad faith, or breach of trust and must comply with any instructions in the will. A will may expressly direct the executor to continue a business owned by the deceased. If the will does not so provide, an executor frequently can obtain permission of the appropriate court to continue the business. With but few exceptions, anyone may be appointed executor. The testator may excuse the executor from furnishing a bond that would be an expense to the estate. If the will does not name an executor, then on petition of one of the beneficiaries, the court will appoint an administrator.

If a person contests the will, the court must hear the contest to determine the validity of the will. A contest of the will differs from litigation over the meaning or interpretation to be given the will. If the contest alleges and proves fraud, undue influence, improper witnessing, mental incapacity of the testator, revocation of the will, or any other infirmity in the will affecting its legality, the court will find the will nullified. It will then distribute the property of the testator according to the law of descent described later in this chapter.

WHEN ADMINISTRATION IS UNNECESSARY

Of course, if an individual does not own any property at the time of death, no need for administration exists. Also, all property jointly owned with someone else who acquires the interest by right of survivorship does not require administration.

Some states have special statutes allowing the administration procedures to be shortened for very small estates. In many states, all of the persons interested in the estate, relatives and creditors, can agree on the share each one is to receive and can divide the estate without formal court proceedings.

TITLE BY DESCENT

When a person dies intestate, the property is distributed in accordance with the state law of descent. Every state has such a law. Although these laws vary slightly, on the whole they provide as follows: The property of the intestate goes to any children subject to the rights of the surviving spouse. If no spouse, children, or grandchildren survive, the father and mother, as the next of kin, receive the property. If no parents survive, the brothers and sisters become the next of kin, followed by grandparents, aunts and uncles, and so on. Some statutes permit any person related by blood to inherit when no nearer relative exists. Other statutes do not permit those beyond first cousins to inherit. In any case, if no proper person to inherit survives, the property passes to the state.

The administrator conveys title to real estate by means of an administrator's deed. When approved by the court, the grantee obtains good title to the property.

PER CAPITA AND *PER STIRPES* DISTRIBUTION

Per Capita
Per head

The lineal descendants of a decedent include the children and grandchildren. If all of the children were living at the time of an intestate's death, and the spouse was dead, the property would be distributed *per capita*, meaning per head, or equally to the children (see Illustration 45–2). If one child predeceased the intestate and

ILLUSTRATION 45–2 Per Capita Distribution

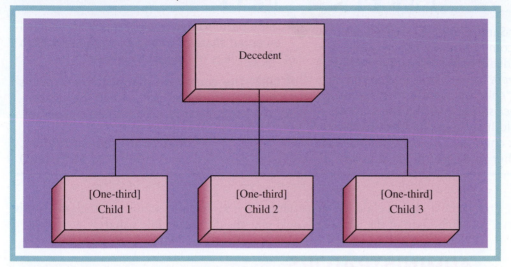

left two surviving children, then the property would be divided into equal parts on the basis of the number of children the intestate had. The dead child's part would then be divided into two equal parts with one of these parts going to each of the grandchildren. This divides the property **per stirpes** (see Illustration 45–3).

Per Stirpes
Distribution among heirs according to relationship to deceased

ILLUSTRATION 45–3 Per Stirpes Distribution

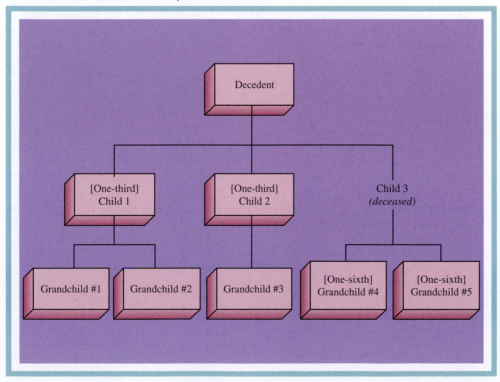

If the deceased child left no children or other lineal descendants, then the surviving children of the intestate would take the deceased child's share.

ADMINISTRATORS

For the most part, the duties and responsibilities of administrators resemble those of executors, with two significant differences. First, in the appointment of an administrator, some states have a clear order of priority. The surviving spouse has first priority, followed by children, grandchildren, parents, and brothers or sisters. Second, an administrator must in all cases execute a bond guaranteeing the faithful performance of the duties.

The prime duty of administrators is the same as that of executors—to preserve the estate and distribute it to the rightful parties. Administrators must act in good faith, with prudence, and within the powers conferred on them by law. If any part of the estate is a going business, with only a few exceptions the business must be liquidated. However, the administrator may obtain leave of court to continue the business for either a limited time or an indefinite time, depending largely on the wishes of those entitled to receive the estate. Third parties dealing with administrators, as well as executors, must know of limitations upon their authority.

TRUSTS

LO **5**
Trust and its parties

Trust
Contract by which one holds property for another

A **trust** is a form of contract by which one person or entity agrees to hold property for the benefit of another. Chapter 41, "Nature of Real Property," examined one way in which ownership of property may be divided between two owners. That chapter discussed the difference between a life estate, or income interest, and a remainder interest in property. This division in ownership separates the total ownership, or the fee simple estate, over time. The life tenant is the first owner, and the holder of the reversion or remainder is the second after the death of the life tenant.

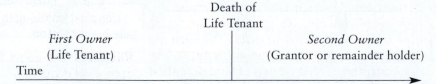

Death of
Life Tenant

First Owner
(Life Tenant)

Second Owner
(Grantor or remainder holder)

Time

Ownership of property in trust can be described as a division at the same time of two ownership interests—the legal ownership and the beneficial ownership. The legal owner of trust property is the person or entity who holds title to the property and who has the authority to control, or administer, the way in which the property is used. The legal owner of trust property is usually referred to as the **trustee**. If no trustee is specified, a court will appoint a trustee because there must be a person with title to the property.

The beneficial owner of trust property is entitled to the income, enjoyment, or benefits of the trust property. The beneficial owner is usually referred to as the trust **beneficiary**. The benefits of the property usually include income generated by property and the right to inhabit or use the property. In older documents, you might encounter the Latin words *cestui que trust*, meaning beneficiary. Both the trustee and the beneficiary have ownership interests in the property at the same time.

Trustee
Legal owner of trust property

Beneficiary
Person entitled to income or enjoyment of trust property

Owner 1 (Trustee—holds legal title)

Time $\longrightarrow$

Owner 2 (Beneficiary—enjoys use of property)

Creation of a Trust

Because a trust is a specific form of contract, the law of contracts generally applies to trusts. Since a contract may be oral or written, a trust may also be oral or written, subject to the Statute of Frauds. Of course, the more valuable the property subject to the trust contract, the more important it is that the trust be written. It is easier both to remember and to enforce the terms of a written trust than those of an oral trust.

The person who creates a trust is known as the **grantor**. Other words used to describe the grantor include **settlor** and **trustor**. A grantor must have the legal capacity to enter into a contract in order to create a trust. Normally, the grantor gives the trust property to the trustee and instructs the trustee how the property is to be used to benefit the beneficiary.

Grantor, Settlor, or Trustor
Creator of trust

It is not necessary that the grantor, trustee, and beneficiary all be different persons or entities. However, they cannot all be the same person. That is, property may be given to the grantor, as trustee, to hold for another beneficiary. Or a grantor may give property to another, as trustee, to hold for the benefit of the grantor. The legal and beneficial ownership must be separate; therefore, the trustee and beneficiary must be separate and distinct entities. Otherwise, the grantor has simply given the property to the trustee/beneficiary in fee simple.

Because a trust is a creature of the law of contracts, the grantor has almost limitless ability to place restrictions on or grant options to the trustee and beneficiary as to the use of the trust property. Nonetheless, the trustee must have some identifiable purpose for administering the trust.

COURT CASE

Facts: Luther Sutter signed a declaration of trust that named him trustee to hold the trust corpus for his benefit. He specified a successor trustee who was directed to divide the trust estate among named beneficiaries at his death. The estate consisted of nine parcels of land described in deeds attached to the declaration and listed on the schedule of assets of the trust estate. He specified which beneficiary was to receive each parcel of land. After Sutter's death, one of his grandchildren who received nothing under the trust challenged whether a trust had actually been created.

Outcome: The court found that Sutter had created a valid trust.

—*Sutter v. Sutter*, 43 S.W.3d 736 (Ark.)

Specific Types of Trusts

Several types of trusts are frequently used. These include:

1. Express trust
2. Resulting trust
3. Constructive trust
4. Blind trust
5. Testamentary trust

Express Trust. A trust that is created by a grantor clearly establishing a trust, whether oral or written, is sometimes referred to as an **express trust**. This designation helps distinguish express trusts from other types of trusts, some of which may be implied. However, no specific words are required to create an express trust. It must just be clear that the grantor intended to create a trust.

Express Trust
Trust clearly established as a trust

Resulting Trust. A **resulting trust** occurs when one person supplies the purchase price for property but has title issued in another person's name. This is sometimes called a **purchase money trust**. The theory of this type of trust is that unless the purchaser intended to make a gift, the one who pays for property should be the one to enjoy it and receive the benefits from it.

Resulting or **Purchase Money Trust**
Resulting trust created when person buys property but takes title in another's name

Constructive Trust. A **constructive trust** arises by operation of law when one acquires title to property to which he or she cannot in good conscience retain the beneficial interest. A constructive trust is most often declared by a court in cases of fraud but also arises in cases of bad faith, duress, coercion, undue influence, mistake, wrongdoing, or any other form of unconscionable conduct. Under these circumstances, a court will declare a constructive trust to prevent a wrongdoer from continuing to take advantage of the other party.

Constructive Trust
Trust created by court to correct a wrong

COURT CASE

Facts: Lexie-Leigh Shepler, Scott Thornock, and Michael Whalen were all creditors with judgments against Sanford Altberger and Orovi, Inc. During a legal proceeding, Whalen learned that Altberger's house, titled in the name of his wife, Judith Altberger, had been bought with a loan from P.C. Financial. Before any of the creditors' judgments had been recorded but when Altberger and Orovi owned them money, Altberger had transferred $353,000 from Orovi to pay off the loan. Whalen asked the court to find a constructive trust alleging Altberger had fraudulently caused Orovi to pay off the loan in order to defraud creditors.

Outcome: The court held that because of the fraud a constructive trust arose. Judith Altberger was considered to hold the property in trust for the creditors.

—*Shepler v. Whalen*, 119 P.3d 1084 (Colo.)

Blind Trust
Assets and administration of trust hidden from grantor

Blind Trust. A **blind trust** is most commonly used when the grantor, for some reason, does not want to know exactly what is in the trust, but wants to retain the benefit of the property. An example is when a government official with authority to regulate a certain industry gives management of property to a trustee, so that there will be no conflict between the official's personal financial interests and official government duties. Wealthy members of Congress frequently use blind trusts so they will not know exactly what securities they own. Then when they vote on legislation they cannot know whether their vote helps the companies in which they have a personal financial interest.

Testamentary Trust. A **testamentary trust** is a special form of express trust created by the will of a testator. Even though the trust will not actually be created until the death of the testator, it will become a valid trust at that time. The trustee may, but need not, be the same person or entity as the executor of the will. A trust created by a will is subject to the same rules as other trusts.

Consider, as an example, the will of Heinrich Heine, the famous 19th-century German poet. His will included the following provision for his wife: "I leave all my estate to my wife on the express condition that she remarry. I want at least one person to sincerely grieve my death." Does this language have the effect of placing the entire estate into a trust? Heine died in France, but if his will had been probated in the present-day United States, it is highly unlikely a court would enforce this provision because of the requirement that Heine's widow remarry. Instead, the property would most likely be distributed directly to Heine's widow, outright and free from trust.

Testamentary Trust
Trust created in will

QUESTIONS

1. At the time of making a will, what mental capacity must people have?

2. May a person by a will control the distribution of property for all time?

3. What happens if all the prescribed formalities are not followed in executing a will?

4. What are the limitations of nuncupative wills?

5. What are the ways in which a will may be revoked?

6. Do legatees receive anything when an abatement occurs?

7. **a.** What is the difference between distributing property per capita and per stirpes?

   b. When would a per stirpes distribution be required?

8. What is the prime duty of an administrator and how does it differ from that of an executor?

9. What ownership interests of property are divided by the establishment of a trust?

10. Under what circumstances do courts declare a constructive trust?

CASE PROBLEMS

1. Dr. Charles Wellshear designated his three adult children from his first marriage as the primary beneficiaries of the IRA he owned. When Charles died his widow, Virginia Wellshear who had been married to him for 20 years, also claimed the IRA. The IRA consisted of funds Charles had accumulated before his marriage to Virginia, after he married Virginia, and $77,000 contributed by Virginia shortly after their marriage. Was Virginia entitled to any of the IRA funds?

LO ❺

2. Ruth Dineen died intestate leaving her son, James Dineen and daughter, Marie Dineen as heirs. The heirs' relationship had been contentious and a lawyer, Richard LeBlanc, was appointed personal representative of Ruth's estate.

LO ❹

Richard owed the estate for loans secured by two mortgages. Richard alleged that the mortgages should be satisfied from the assets of the estate and interest should stop accruing on them. LeBlanc was concerned about Richard's propensity to litigate and thought the estate should keep enough liquid assets to cover any litigation costs. The probate court issued an order finding LeBlanc acted reasonably in allowing interest to accrue on the mortgages and not satisfying them with estate funds until final settlement of the estate. Richard appealed. Had LeBlanc acted properly?

LO ❸

3. Maria and W. R. Prestie married but divorced two years later. They maintained an amiable relationship. W. R. executed a will and the W. R. Prestie Living Trust. The will left everything to the trust and the beneficiary of the trust was W. R.'s son, Scott Prestie. Neither provided for his former wife, Maria. When diagnosed with macular degeneration, W. R. moved to Las Vegas and bought a condominium. Maria also moved to Las Vegas and, as W. R.'s sight worsened, she took him to the doctor, cooked for him, and cleaned his condo. W. R. amended his trust to give Maria a life estate in his condo when he died. Then W. R. and Maria remarried. State law presumed marriage revoked a will unless the spouse was provided for by the will or a marriage contract, or the deceased showed an intent not to provide for the spouse. When W. R. died, Maria alleged their marriage revoked his will. Did it?

LO ❺

4. While an employee of Oakwood Homes Corp. (Oakwood), Kevin Brogan embezzled $550,000. He used some of it as deposits with State Street Interiors (SSI). Brogan hired the law firm of Hicks, McDonald, Allen, & Noecher, L.L.P. (HMA&N) to defend him in embezzlement litigation and sue SSI for some of the embezzled funds deposited with it. Brogan had no money, so he agreed to pay HMA&N for both cases with any recovery from SSI. A $550,000 judgment was entered against Brogan for Oakwood. Oakwood moved to intervene in the suit against SSI, but the judge denied the motion because HMA&N said the money deposited with SSI was Oakwood's and any recovery would be transferred to Oakwood to apply to the $550,000 judgment. Brogan got a judgment for $27,000 against SSI. The judge ordered that HMA&N get $10,000 for its representation in the case and Oakwood get the rest. HMA&N alleged it was entitled to $9,300 more that Brogan owed it from the embezzlement case. Oakwood argued that the judge should impose a constructive trust and return the money to it. Should the court find a constructive trust?

LO ❹

5. Baltimore police shot and killed Betty Keat after she advanced on them brandishing a knife. Keat's will directed that her house be sold and the proceeds paid to Morgan State University (MSU). Keat's sister, Janet Beyer, was the personal representative. She hired Anton Keating to sue the officers who shot Keat and hired David Allen as attorney for the estate. Allen notified MSU's legal counsel of the bequest and that Keat's relatives were investigating her death. He said estate funds would be used for the investigation and any litigation. MSU's counsel replied that such costs should not take precedence over the bequest. No reply was received. Beyer sold Keat's house, and then paid Keating $30,000 from the estate without notifying MSU or obtaining approval from the court as required by law. A year later Keating requested $40,000. Several years after the sale of Keat's house MSU finally learned about it and petitioned for distribution of the funds. Had Beyer breached her duty as personal representative?

LO ❸

6. When Jerome Linet died, Louis Claps and Anthony Cioeta, named as copersonal representatives in Linet's will, applied to administer the estate. Harry and Rhonda Linet, the beneficiaries of the estate, objected. They produced a properly executed codicil that named Claps and Cioeta as copersonal representatives, but a line was drawn through Cioeta's name. In the margin next to it was the word "deleted," the date, and decedent's signature. There were no witnesses to this change. Claps and Cioeta alleged the original codicil, without the alteration, had to be enforced. Decide the case.

7. Stanley Bernatowicz attempted to sign his name to his will but had difficulty signing in spite of making several attempts. He was very ill and died several hours later. Bernatowicz's attorney told Sherry Callara, who was the named executrix and mother of a legatee under the will, that she could help Bernatowicz by steadying his hand. The attorney told Callara she could not sign the will for Bernatowicz or move his hand, and she assisted him in signing. After Bernatowicz's death, Natalie Mack contested the will alleging Callara had controlled Bernatowicz rather than assisted him. Had Bernatowicz signed the will?   LO ❷

8. John Gerard executed a will naming his sister-in-law, Eva Gerard, executrix and making provision for his wife of two years, Violet. Gerard had told numerous people he wanted to provide for Violet and leave her his house. Gerard had cancer and was taking medicine that interfered with mental processes and caused confusion and forgetfulness. He was depressed and unable to make up his mind. His acquaintance, Joyce Crabtree, took Gerard to the doctor leaving Violet in the waiting room while Crabtree accompanied Gerard to see the doctor. Gerard began living with Joyce and her husband who would not let anyone else talk with him. Two weeks after Gerard's first will, he executed a new one using a different lawyer and removing all mention of Violet. This will funded a trust that was amended several times. The final amendment made two days before Gerard's death was dictated to the lawyer by Joyce and put the Crabtrees in complete control of the trust eliminating Eva, Violet, and all other heirs. After Gerard's death Violet attacked the second will alleging he lacked testamentary capacity. Did he?   LO ❶

Ethics in Practice

Having learned that real property is conveyed by deed and that property that is owned by two persons as joint tenants with right of survivorship passes automatically to the survivor at the death of one owner, consider the following scenario:

After her husband dies, Rose Markovitz lives with her daughter, Sandy Olsen, and her family in Markovitz's house, and Olsen pays the real estate taxes for Markovitz. In order to permit Olsen to deduct the real estate taxes on her income tax return, Markovitz executes a quitclaim deed to the house to herself and Olsen as joint tenants with right of survivorship. Markovitz tells her five other children that she is quitclaiming the house to Olsen as joint tenant only to enable Olsen to deduct the taxes that she pays for Markovitz. After Markovitz dies, Olsen claims the house belongs to her alone by right of survivorship. Discuss the ethical considerations involved in this situation.

Summary Cases

PROPERTY

1. When she was 100 years old, Biddie L. Ware executed a will leaving her estate to her daughter, Almira Jane Howell. Howell had given the information about the will to a lawyer who drafted it. Howell drove Ware to a parking lot. A legal assistant gave Ware the will and described what it provided. The two witnesses, Rhonda Lawson and Sandra Harman, saw Ware sign it. Harman signed in Ware's presence. However, Lawson signed the will in the office. Ware never left the car. The will stated that the witnesses signed the will in the presence of the testatrix. After Ware's death, Howell filed the will for probate and relatives who were disinherited alleged Ware had not validly executed the will. Had she? [*Ware v. Howell,* 614 S.E.2d 464 (W.Va.)]

2. Peter and Suzanne Adams owned Lot 2 in a subdivision, and Albert and Sue Anderson owned adjoining Lot 3. The Adamses asked a court to declare they owned a disputed piece of property along their border with the Andersons. The piece was a portion of Lot 3 that was sold by Myers, a previous owner of Lot 3, to Oberbillig, then the owner of Lot 2. Oberbillig paid for the piece and had a lot line readjustment survey evidenced by a written Record of Survey describing the piece, signed by the two parties, and recorded. Both lots were then sold several times. The deeds to Lot 2 did not mention the Record of Survey. When the Adamses bought Lot 2, their deed conveyed Lot 2 "amended by record of survey recorded May 20, . . . as Instrument No. 8221580." Did the Record of Survey convey the piece of property? [*Adams v. Anderson,* 127 P.3d 111 (Idaho)]

3. Alma Rodowicz leased property to United Social and Mental Health Services, Inc. for ten years. The written lease allowed United to renew it only by notifying Rodowicz within six months of the expiration of the lease or any extension of it. Three days before the expiration, Rodowicz's attorney wrote United that the parties had come to an agreement that United could continue as a tenant at a reduced rent. United never responded but referred to the new lease as a month-to-month tenancy and paid the reduced rent for five years. United then notified Rodowicz it planned to renew the lease for five more years. Rodowicz demanded United vacate and pay an increased monthly rental until it vacated. United protested, but paid the increased rent and sued for enforcement of the lease. Had United renewed or extended the lease? [*United Social and Mental Health Services, Inc. v. Rodowicz,* 899 A.2d 85 (Conn. App.)]

4. Patricia Gifford executed a deed on January 13 to Beth Linnell as "[t]rustee of Droffig Family Trust." She executed a trust agreement titled "Droffig Family Trust" on January 16. Several years later, Gifford sued for a court declaration that the deed was void because the trust did not exist until three

days after she executed the deed. Therefore, she alleged the deed did not identify a valid grantee. Linnell claimed that because she was a person existing on January 13, the deed was valid. Was the deed effective? [*Gifford v. Linnell*, 579 S.E.2d 440 (N.C. App.)]

5. Frank Billotti owned two pieces of real estate as a joint tenant with right of survivorship with his wife, Carolyn. Frank murdered Carolyn and their daughters and was convicted of the murders. Frank conveyed the properties to his mother, Rose Billotti. State law stated that no one convicted of killing another could acquire any property from the person killed "by descent and distribution, or by will, . . . or otherwise." Carolyn's parents sued for the joint tenancy property. Did the words "or otherwise" in the statute include taking property under joint tenancy with right of survivorship? [*Lakatos v. Estate of Billotti*, 509 S.E.2d 594 (W.Va.)]

6. Honolulu Book Shops (HBS) leased real property from Hi Kai Investment. HBS assigned the lease to Aloha Futons, which defaulted in the payment of the rent. Hi Kai sued for summary possession of the property, past rent, and future rent under the lease. Aloha alleged that Hi Kai could get summary possession of the property or future rent, but not both. May Hi Kai get both possession of the property and future rent or is its remedy limited to only one? [*Hi Kai Inv., Ltd. v. Aloha Futons Beds & Waterbeds, Inc.*, 929 P.2d 88 (Hawaii)]

7. Dillie McIntyre sold a tract of land to Russell and Sally Scarbrough reserving a life estate in 1.2 acres on which her mobile home sat. The reservation required McIntyre to maintain the 1.2 acres and pay the real estate taxes on them. Several years later, McIntyre had failed to pay the prior three years' real estate taxes. The Scarbroughs sued to terminate the life estate alleging McIntyre was also not maintaining the property. Should the life estate be terminated? [*McIntyre v. Scarbrough*, 471 S.E.2d 199 (Ga.)]

Table of Cases

Glossary

A

Abandon Discard with no intention to reclaim

Abatement Proportionate reduction in monetary bequest because of insufficient funds

Abstract of Title History of real estate

Acceleration Clause Clause allowing entire principal to be due

Acceptance Assent of buyer to become owner of goods; assent to an offer resulting in a contract; drawee's signed agreement to pay draft

Acceptor Person who agrees to: pay a draft; receive goods; or assent to an offer

Accession Acquiring property by adding property of another to one's own

Accretion Addition to land by gradual water deposits

Acknowledgment Declaration grantor has stated execution of instrument is free act

Action of Ejectment Action to have sheriff remove tenant

Active Fraud Party engages in action that causes the fraud

Ademption Failure of bequest because property not in testator's estate

Administrative Agency Governmental board or commission with authority to regulate matters or implement laws

Administrator, Administratrix, or Personal Representative Person appointed by court to administer estate of intestate

Adverse Possession Acquiring title to land by occupying it for fixed period

Affirmative Covenant Promise by grantee of deed to do an act

Agency Contract under which one party is authorized to contract for another

Agency by Estoppel Agency arising when person leads another to believe third party is agent

Agency Coupled with an Interest Agency in which agent has financial stake in performance of agency because of having given consideration to principal

Agent Person appointed to contract on behalf of another

Alien Corporation One chartered in another country

Allonge Paper so firmly attached to instrument as to be part of it

Alteration Unauthorized change or completion of negotiable instrument to modify obligation of a party

Annual Percentage Rate (APR) Amount charged for loan as percentage of loan

Annuity Insurance Contract that pays monthly income to insured while alive

Anonymous Remailer Device that permits sending anonymous e-mail and software

Answer or Motion Written response of defendant to a complaint

Anticipatory Breach One party announces intention not to perform contract prior to time to perform

Antitrust Law Statute that seeks to promote competition among businesses

Apparent Authority Authority agent believed to have because of principal's behavior

Appellate Court Court that reviews decision of lower court

Articles of Incorporation Document stating facts about corporation required for issuance of charter

Articles of Partnership Written partnership agreement

Assessment Mutual Company Insurance company in which losses are shared by policyholders

Assignee Person to whom contract right is assigned

Assignment Conveyance of rights in a contract to a person not a party

Assignor Person making an assignment

Attorney in Fact General agent appointed by written authorization

Auction Oral sale of property to the highest bidder

Automated Teller Machine EFT terminal that performs routine banking services

B

Bad Check Check the drawee bank refuses to pay

Baggage Articles necessary for personal convenience while traveling

Bailee Person in possession of bailed property

Bailment Transfer of possession of personal property on condition property will be returned

Bailor Person who gives up possession of bailed property

Balloon Payment Payment more than twice the normal installment one

Bank Draft or Teller's Check Check drawn by one bank on another

Bearer Payee of instrument made payable to whomever is in possession

Bearer Paper Negotiable instrument payable to bearer

Beneficiary   Person who receives: Income or enjoyment of trust property; proceeds of life insurance; or property by will

Bequest or **Legacy**   Personal property left to person by will

Bidder   Person who makes offer at auction

Bilateral Contract   Contract consisting of mutual exchange of promises

Bill of Exchange   A draft

Bill of Lading   Receipt and contract between consignor and carrier

Bill of Rights   First ten amendments to U.S. Constitution

Bill of Sale   Written evidence of title to tangible personal property

Binder   Temporary contract of insurance

Blank Indorsement   Indorsement consisting of signature of indorser

Blind Trust   Assets and administration of trust hidden from grantor

Blue-Sky Laws   State laws to prevent sale of worthless stock

Boardinghouse Keeper   Person in business to supply accommodations to permanent lodgers

Bond   Sealed, written contract obligation with essentials of note

Bonding Company   Paid surety

Breach of Contract   Failure or refusal to perform contractual obligations

Broker   Agent with job of bringing two contracting parties together

Business Crimes   Crimes against business or committed by using a business

Business Interruption Insurance   Insurance covering loss of profits while business building is repaired

Business Law   Rules of conduct for the performance of business transactions

Business Tort   Tort caused by or involving a business

Bylaws   Rules enacted by directors to govern corporation's conduct

C

Cancellation   Act that indicates intention to destroy validity of an instrument

Capital Stock   Declared value of outstanding stock

Carrier   Transporter of goods, people, or both

Cashier's Check   Check drawn by bank on its funds in bank

Caveat Emptor   Let the buyer beware

Certificate of Deposit   Acknowledgment by bank of receipt of money with engagement to repay it

Certified Check   Check accepted by bank's writing "certified" on it

Check   Draft drawn on a bank and payable on demand

Check Truncation   Shortening check's trip from payee to drawer

Civil Law   Law dealing with enforcement or protection of private rights

Close or **Closely Held Corporation**   One with very small number of shareholders

Codicil   Writing that modifies a will

Coguarantors or **Cosureties**   Two or more people jointly liable for another's obligation

Coinsurance   Insured recovers in ratio of insurance to amount of insurance required

Collateral Note   Note secured by personal property

Collective Bargaining   Process by which employer and union negotiate and agree on terms of employment

Color of Title   One's apparent title

Commercial Paper or **Negotiable Instrument**   Writing drawn in special form that can be transferred as substitute for money or as instrument of credit

Commercial Unit   Quantity regarded as separate unit

Common Carrier   One that undertakes to transport without discrimination all who apply for service

Common Law   English custom recognized by courts as binding

Common Stock   Stock that entitles owner to vote

Communication   Telling something to third person

Community Property   Property acquired during marriage owned separately and equally by both spouses

Comparative Negligence   Contributory negligence reduces but does not bar recovery

Compensatory Damages   Amount equal to the loss sustained

Complaint or **Petition**   Written request to a court to settle a dispute

Composition of Creditors   When all of multiple creditors settle in full for a fraction of the amount owed

Comprehensive Policy   Insurance covering large number of miscellaneous risks

Computer Crime   Crime committed with involvement of computers

Computer Trespass   Unauthorized use of or access to a computer

Concealment   Willful failure to disclose pertinent information

Confusion   Inseparable mixing of goods of different owners

Confusion of Source   Representing goods or services as those of another

Consideration   What promisor requires as the price for a promise

Consignee   One to whom goods are shipped

Consignment   Transfer of possession of goods for purpose of sale

Consignor   One who ships by common carrier

Consolidation   Combining two corporations to form a new one

Constitution   Document that contains fundamental principles of a government

Constructive Bailment Bailment imposed when a person controls lost property

Constructive Notice Information or knowledge imputed by law

Constructive Trust Trust created by court to correct a wrong

Consumer Goods or **Services** Goods or services primarily for personal, family, or household use

Contract Legally enforceable agreement

Contract to Sell Agreement to transfer title to goods for a price

Contribution Right of coguarantor to recover excess of proportionate share of debt from other coguarantor(s)

Conversion Obtaining possession of property and converting it to own use

Convict Person found guilty by court of major criminal offense

Corporation Association of people created by law into an entity

Counteroffer Offeree's response that rejects offer by varying its terms

Coupon Bond Bond with detachable individual coupons representing interest payments

Court of Original General Jurisdiction Court of record in which case is first tried

Court of Record Court in which an official record of the proceedings is kept

Covenant Promise in a deed

Cram Down Reorganization plan imposed by court in spite of creditors' objections

Creation Bringing property into being

Creditor Party who receives guaranty

Creditor Beneficiary Person to whom promisee owes obligation, which is discharged if promisor performs

Crime Offense against society

Criminal Law Law dealing with offenses against society

Cumulative Preferred Stock Stock on which all dividends must be paid before common dividends

Cumulative Voting Stockholder has votes equal to shares owned times number of directors to be elected

Customary Authority Authority agent possesses by custom

D

Damages Sum of money a wrongdoer must pay to an injured party

Debenture Unsecured bond issued by a business

Debt Obligation to pay money

Deductible Clause Insurance provision whereby insured pays damage up to specified amount and company pays excess up to policy limits

Deed Writing conveying title to real property

Deed of Trust Deed that transfers property to trustee for benefit of creditor

Default Breach of contractual obligation

Defendant Person against whom a case is filed

Defense Clause Policy clause in which insurer agrees to defend insured against damage claims

Delegation Transfer of duties

Delivery Intentional transfer of possession and control of something

Depository Bank Bank receiving check for deposit

Destination Contract Seller liable until goods delivered to destination

Devise Realty left by will

Devisee One receiving realty by will

Disaffirmance Repudiation of a voidable contract

Discovery Means of obtaining information from other party before a trial

Dishonor Presentment made, but acceptance or payment not made

Disparate Impact Fair policy disproportionately affecting protected class

Disparate Treatment Intentional discrimination against a particular individual

Dissolution Termination of corporation's operation except activities needed for liquidation

Dissolution of a Partnership Change in relation of partners by elimination of one

Diversity Jurisdiction Federal jurisdiction based on parties being from different states

Dividend Profits of a corporation allocated to stockholders

Document of Title Document that shows ownership

Domestic Corporation One chartered in the state

Domestic Relations Court Court that handles divorce and related cases

Donee Person who receives a gift

Donee Beneficiary Third-party beneficiary for whom performance is a gift

Donor Person who makes a gift

Dormant or **Sleeping Partner** Partner unknown to public with no part in management

Double Indemnity Rider Policy requiring insurer to pay twice ordinary face amount if death is accidental

Draft or **Bill of Exchange** Written order by one person directing another to pay sum of money to third person

Drawee Person ordered to pay draft

Drawer Person who executes a draft

Durable Power of Attorney Appointment of agency that survives incapacity of principal

Duress Obtaining consent by means of a threat

E

Easement An interest in land for nonexclusive or intermittent use

Electronic Fund Transfer Fund transfer initiated electronically, telephonically, or by computer

Embezzlement Improper appropriation of property by entrustee

Employment at Will Employment terminable by employer or employee for any reason

Endowment Insurance   Decreasing term insurance plus savings account

Equipment   Goods for use in business

Equity   Justice system based on fairness; provides relief other than merely money damages

Estate   Interest in property; property left by a deceased

Estoppel   One party leads the second to a false conclusion the second party relies on; the second party would be harmed if the first party were later allowed to show the conclusion was false

Ethics   Principles that determine the morality of conduct, its motives, and its duties

Eviction   Expulsion of tenant from leased property

Executed Contract   Fully performed contract

Executor or **Personal Representative**   Person named in will to administer estate

Executory Contract   Contract not fully carried out

Existing Goods   Goods that are in being and owned by the seller

Exoneration   Guarantor's right to have creditor compel payment of debt

Express Authority   Authority of agent stated in agreement creating agency

Express Contract   Contract the terms of which are specified in words

Express Trust   Trust clearly established as a trust

Express Warranty   Statement of guarantee by seller

F

Face   Maximum insurer pays for loss

Factor   Bailee seeking to sell property on commission

Factor *del Credere*   Factor who sells on credit and guarantees price will be paid

False Representation   Misstatement of material fact

Federal Court of Appeals   Court that hears appeals in federal court system

Federal District Court   Trial court of federal court system

Fee Simple Estate   Largest, most complete right in property

Fellow Servant   Employee with same status and working with another worker

Felony   A more serious crime

Fictitious Name Registration Statute   Law requiring operator of business under assumed name to register with state

Fidelity Bond   Suretyship for someone who handles another's money

Fiduciary   A person in relationship of trust and confidence

Finance Charge   Total amount paid for credit

Financing Statement   Writing with signatures and addresses of debtor and secured party and description of collateral

Firm Offer   A merchant's signed, written offer to sell or purchase goods saying it will be held open

Fixture   Personal property so securely attached to real estate that it becomes part of the real estate

Floating Policy   Insurance coverage no matter where property is located

FOB (Free on Board)   Designated point to which seller bears risk and expense

Forbearance   Refraining from doing something

Forcible Entry and Detainer Action   Summary action by landlord to regain possession of leasehold

Foreclosure   Sale of mortgaged property to pay debt

Foreign Corporation   One chartered in another state

Formal Contract   Contract with special form or manner of creation

Fraud   Inducing another to contract as a result of an intentionally or recklessly false statement of a material fact

Fraud in the Execution   Party did not intend to enter into a contract but signed a document because of false statements

Fraud in the Inducement   Defrauded party intended to make a contract because of false statements regarding contract

Friendly Fire   Fire contained where intended

Full Warranty   Warranty with unlimited duration of implied warranties and agreement to remedy defects without charge

Fungible Goods   Goods of a homogeneous nature sold by weight or measure

Future Goods   Goods not both existing and identified

G

Gambling Contract   Agreement in which parties win or lose by chance

General Agent   Agent authorized to carry out particular kind of business or all business at a place

General Partner   Partner actively and openly engaged in business

General Warranty Deed   Warrants good title free from all claims

Gift   Transfer of ownership without consideration

Goods   Movable personal property

Grace Period   30- or 31-day period in which late premium may be paid without policy lapsing

Grantee   Person receiving title to property

Grantor   Person conveying property; in trusts also called settlor or trustor

Guarantor or **Surety**   Party who agrees to be responsible for obligation of another

Guest   Transient received by hotel for accommodations

H

Hacker   Unauthorized person who gains access to another's computer

Hazards   Factors that contribute to uncertainty

Holder　Person in possession of instrument payable to bearer or that person

Holder in Due Course　Holder for value and in good faith with no knowledge of dishonor, defenses, or claims, or that paper is overdue; acquires rights superior to original owner

Holder Through a Holder in Due Course　Holder subsequent to holder in due course

Holographic Will　Will written out by testator

Homeowners' Policy　Insurance for owners living in their houses with coverage of many perils and liability

Hostile Fire　Fire out of its normal place

Hostile Work Environment　Alteration of terms or conditions of employment by harassment

Hot Cargo Agreement　Agreement employer will not use nonunion materials

Hotelkeeper　One engaged in business of offering lodging to transients

I

Identified Goods　Goods picked to be delivered to the buyer

Implied Authority　Agent's authority to do things in order to carry out express authority

Implied Contract (Implied in Fact Contract)　Contract with major terms implied by the parties' conduct

Implied Warranty　Warranty imposed by law

Incidental Beneficiary　Person who unintentionally benefits from performance of contract

Incorporators　People initially forming a corporation

Incoterms　International commercial terms

Indemnity　Right of guarantor to be reimbursed by principal

Independent Contractor　One who contracts to do jobs and is controlled only by contract as to how performed

Indorsee　Named holder of indorsed negotiable instrument

Indorsement　Signature of holder on back of instrument with any directions or limitations

Indorser　Payee or holder who signs back of instrument

Inferior Court　Trial court that hears only cases involving minor offenses and disputes

Injunction　Court's permanent order forbidding an action

Injunctive Powers　Power to issue cease-and-desist orders

Injurious Falsehood, Commercial Disparagement, or **Trade Libel**　False statement of fact that degrades quality of another's goods or services

Inland Draft　Draft drawn and payable in the United States

Innocent Misrepresentation　False statement made in belief it is true

Insider　Officer, director, or owner of more than 10 percent of stock

Insurable Interest　Interest in nonoccurrence of risk insured against

Insurance　Contract that transfers risk of financial loss for a fee

Insured　Person protected against loss

Insurer　Company writing contract to compensate for loss specified in contact

Intangible Personal Property　Evidences of ownership of rights or value

Intellectual Property　Property produced by human innovation and creativity

Intestate　One who dies without a will

Inventory　Articles purchased with intention of reselling or leasing

Issue　First delivery of negotiable instrument by maker or drawer to give rights to another

J

Joint and Several Contract　Agreement by which two or more people are bound jointly and individually

Joint and Survivor Annuity　Contractual payments made until second of two people dies

Joint Contract　Agreement obligating or entitling two or more people together to performance

Joint-Stock Company　Entity that issues shares of stock, but investors have unlimited liability

Joint Tenancy　Multiple ownership in which, at death of one, deceased's share passes to remaining owners

Joint Venture　Business relationship similar to partnership, except existing only for single transaction

Judge, Justice of the Peace, Magistrate, or **Trial Justice**　Chief officer of court

Judicial Admission　Fact acknowledged in course of legal proceeding

Jurisdiction　Authority of a court to hear a case

Justice of the Peace or **Magistrate**　Chief officer of inferior court

Juvenile Court　Court that handles delinquent, dependent, and neglected children

L

Landlord or **Lessor**　Owner of leased property

Larceny　Taking property without consent of person in possession

Last Clear Chance　Negligent driver recovers if other driver had one last clear chance to avoid injury

Law　Governmental rule prescribing conduct and carrying a penalty for violation

Law Merchant　Rules applied by courts set up by merchants in early England

Lawyer or **Attorney**　Person licensed to represent others in court

Lease　Contract between landlord and tenant

Leasehold Interest Insurance　Covers cost of higher rent when leased building is damaged

Legal Rate　Interest rate applied when no rate specified

Legal Tender　Any form of lawful money

Legatee   One receiving personal property by will

License   Right to do certain acts on land

Lien   Encumbrance or claim against property

Life Estate   Estate for duration of a person's life

Life Insurance   Contract of insurer to pay money on death of insured

Life Tenant   Person owning property for a lifetime

Limited Defense   Defense ineffective against holder in due course

Limited Liability   Capital contribution is maximum loss

Limited Liability Company   Partnership-type organization but with limited liability

Limited Partner   Partner who takes no active part in management, whom the public knows as a partner, and whose liability is limited to capital contribution

Limited Partnership   Partnership with at least one limited partner

Limited Warranty   Written but not full warranty

Liquidated Damages   Sum fixed by contract for breach where actual damages are difficult to measure

Lost Property   Property unintentionally left with no intention to discard

M

Maker   Person who executes a note

Malpractice   Failure to perform with ability and care normally exercised by people in the profession

Marshal   Executive officer of federal court

Maximum Contract Rate   Highest legal rate of interest

Mechanics' Lien   Lien of people who have furnished materials or labor on property

Merchant   Person who deals in goods of the kind or by occupation is considered to have particular knowledge or skill regarding goods involved

Merger   One corporation absorbed by another

Minor   Person under the legal age to contract

Misdemeanor   A less serious crime

Misrepresentation   False statement of a material fact

Model   Replica of an article

Money Order   Instrument issued by business indicating payee may receive indicated amount

Mortgage   Interest in real estate given to secure debt

Mortgagee   Person who holds mortgage

Mortgagor   Person who gives mortgage

Movable Personal Property   All physical items except real estate

Mutual Insurance Company   Company of policyholder investors

Mutual Mistake   Mistake by both parties to a contract

N

Necessaries   Items required for living at a reasonable standard

Negative Covenant   Agreement by grantee not to do an act

Negligence   Failure to exercise reasonable care

Negotiability   Transferability

Negotiable Instrument   Document of payment, such as a check

Negotiation   Act of transferring ownership of negotiable instrument

No-Fault Insurance   Insurance companies pay for their insureds' injuries regardless of fault

Nominal Damages   Small amount awarded when there is technical breach but no injury

Nominal Partner   Person who pretends to be a partner

Noncumulative Preferred Stock   Stock on which current dividends must be paid before common dividends

Nonparticipating Preferred Stock   Stock on which maximum dividend is stated percentage

Nonresellable Goods   Specially made goods not easily sellable to others

Nontrading Partnership   One devoted to professional services

No-Par-Value Stock   Stock without face value

Not-for-Profit Corporation   One formed by private individuals for charitable, educational, religious, social, or fraternal purpose

Notice and Comment Rule Making   Enacting administrative rules by publishing the proposed rule and then the final rule without holding formal hearings

Novation   Termination of a contract and substitution of a new one with same terms but new party

Nuncupative Will   Oral will made during last illness

O

Offer   A proposal to make a contract

Offeree   Person to whom offer is made

Offeror   Person who makes an offer

Open Policy   Insurance contract that requires insured to prove loss sustained

Option   Binding promise to hold an offer open

Oral Contract   Contract with terms spoken

Order Bill of Lading   Contract allowing delivery of shipped goods to bearer

Order Paper   Negotiable instrument payable to order

Ordinance   Law enacted by a city

Ordinary or General Partnership   Partnership with no limitation on rights and duties of partners

P

Parol Evidence   Oral testimony

Parol Evidence Rule   Complete, written contract may not be modified by oral testimony unless evidence of fraud, accident, or mistake

Participating Preferred Stock   Stock that shares with common stock in extra dividends

Partition   Suit to divide joint tenancy

Partner   Member of a partnership

Partnership   Association of two or more people to carry on business for profit

Par-Value Stock   Stock with assigned face value

Passive Fraud   Failure to disclose information when there is duty to do so

Pawn   Tangible personal property left as security for a debt

Payee   Party to whom instrument is payable

Per Capita   Per head

Per Se **Violation**   Activity illegal regardless of its effect

Per Stirpes   Distribution among heirs according to relationship to deceased

Perfected Security Interest   Seller's right to collateral that is superior to third party's right

Personal Property   Movable property; interests less than complete ownership in land; or rights to money

Physical Damage Insurance   Insurance for damage to car itself

Piercing the Corporate Veil   Ignoring the corporate entity

Pirated Software   Software copied illegally

Plaintiff   Person who begins a civil lawsuit

Pledge   Intangible property serving as security for a debt

Point-of-Sale System   EFTs begun at retailers when customers pay for goods or services

Policy   Written contract of insurance

Polygraph   Lie detector

Postdated Check   Check drawn before its date

Power of Attorney   Writing appointing an agent

Preauthorized Credit   Automatic deposit of funds to account

Preauthorized Debit   Automatic deduction of bill payment from checking account

Precedent   Court decision that determines the decision in a subsequent, similar case

Preemptive Right   Right to purchase new shares in proportion to shares owned

Preference   Disallowed transfer to a creditor

Preferred Stock   Stock giving special advantage

Premium   Consideration paid by insured

Presentment   Demand for acceptance or payment

Price   Consideration in a sales contract

Prima Facie   On the face of it

Prima Facie **Evidence**   Evidence sufficient on its face, if uncontradicted

Primary Liability   Liability without conditions for negotiable instrument that is due

Principal   Party primarily liable; person who appoints another to contract with third parties

Private Carrier   Carrier that transports under special arrangements for a fee

Private Corporation   One formed to do nongovernmental function

Privity of Contract   Relationship between contracting parties

Probate   Court procedure to determine validity of a will

Probate Court   Court that handles estates

Procedural Law   Law specifying how actions are filed and what trial procedure to follow

Profit Corporation   One organized to run a business and earn money

Promissory Estoppel   Substitute for consideration when another acts in reliance on promisor's promise

Promissory Note   Unconditional written promise to pay sum of money to another

Promoter   One who takes initial steps to form corporation

Property   Anything that may be owned

Property Insurance   Contract by which insurer pays for damage to property

Proprietor   Owner of sole proprietorship

Prosecutor or **District Attorney**   Government employee who brings criminal actions

Prospectus   Document giving specified information about a corporation

Protected Class   Group protected by antidiscrimination laws

Protest   Certification of notice of dishonor by authorized official

Proxy   Person authorized to vote for another; written authorization to vote for another

Proxy War   Attempt by competing sides to secure majority of stockholders' votes

Public Corporation   One formed for governmental function

Public Liability Insurance   Insurance designed to protect third persons from bodily injury and property damage

Publication   Testator's informing witnesses that document is will

Punitive Damages   Amount paid to one party to punish the other

Purchase   Ownership by payment

Q

Qualified Indorsement   Indorsement that limits liability of indorser

Quasi Contract (Implied in Law Contract)   Imposition of rights and obligations by law without a contract

Quasi Public Corporation   Public body with powers similar to corporations

Quitclaim Deed   Deed that transfers whatever interest grantor has in property

Quorum   Minimum number of shares required to be represented to transact corporate business

R

Ratification   Approval of unauthorized act; adult indicating contract made while a minor is binding

Real Estate Mortgage Note   Note secured by mortgage on real property

Real Property   Land and permanent attachments to land

Receipt   Taking possession of goods

Recognizance   Obligation entered into before a court to do an act required by law

Redemption   Right to free property from lien of mortgage

Reformation   Judicial correction of a contract

Registered Bond   Bond payable to specific person, whose name is recorded by issuer

Remainder   Interest in life estate that goes to someone other than grantor on death of life tenant

Renewable Term Insurance   Term insurance renewable without physical examination

Rent   Amount paid landlord for possession of property

Renunciation   Unilateral act of holder giving up rights in the instrument or against a party to it

Reporting Form for Merchandise Inventory   Insurance policy allowing periodic reporting of inventory on hand to vary coverage amount

Rescind   Set aside or cancel

Respondeat Superior   Theory imposing liability on employers for torts of employees

Restraining Order   Court's temporary order forbidding an action

Restrictive Indorsement   Indorsement that restricts use of instrument

Resulting or **Purchase Money Trust**   Trust created when person buys property but takes title in another's name

Reversion   Interest of grantor in life estate that returns to grantor on death of life tenant

Rider   Addition to insurance policy that modifies, extends, or limits base contract

Right of Survivorship   Automatic ownership of property by survivors

Right to Take Against the Will   Spouse's right to share of estate provided by statute if will leaves smaller share

Risk or **Peril**   Danger of loss

Robbery   Taking property by force

Rogue Program   Software instructions that produce abnormal computer behavior

S

Sale   Transfer of title to goods for a price

Sale on Approval   Sale that is not completed until buyer approves goods

Sale or **Return**   Completed sale with right to return goods

Sample   Portion of whole mass of goods sold

Secondary Boycott   Attempt by employees to stop third party dealing with employer

Secondary Liability   Liability for a negotiable instrument that has been presented, dishonored, and notice of dishonor given

Secondary Meaning   Special meaning of a mark that distinguishes goods and warrants trademark protection

Secret Partner   Partner active but unknown to public

Secured Credit Sale   Sale in which seller retains right to repossess goods upon default

Security Agreement   Written agreement signed by buyer that creditor has a security interest in collateral

Setoff   A claim by the party being sued against the party suing

Several Contract   Two or more people individually agree to perform obligation

Share   Unit of stock

Shareholder or **Stockholder**   Person who owns stock

Sheriff   Court of record executive officer

Shipment Contract   Seller liable until goods delivered to carrier

Shop Right   Employer's right to use employee's invention without payment of royalty

Shoplifting   Taking unpurchased goods from store

Short-Swing Profits   Profits made by insider buying and selling corporation's stock within six months

Sight Draft   Draft payable on presentation by holder

Silent Partner   Partner who takes no part in firm

Simple Contract   Contract that is not formal

Sole Proprietorship   Business owned and carried on by one person

Special Agent   Agent authorized to transact specific act or acts

Special Federal Court   Federal trial court with limited jurisdiction

Special Indorsement   Indorsement that designates particular person to whom payment is to be made

Special Warranty Deed   Warrants grantor has right to convey real property

Specific Performance   Carrying out the terms of contract

Specific Policy   Insurance on only one item

Stale Check   Check presented more than six months after its date

Stare Decisis   Principle that a court decision controls the decision of a similar future case

State Court of Appeals   Intermediate appellate court

State Supreme Court   Highest court in most states

Statute   Law enacted by legislative bodies

Statute of Frauds   Law requiring certain contracts to be in writing

Statute of Limitations   Time within which right to sue must be exercised or lost

Stock Corporation   One in which ownership is represented by stock

Stock Insurance Company   Corporation of stockholder investors

Stock Option   Right to purchase shares at set price

Straight Bill of Lading   Contract requiring delivery of shipped goods to consignee only

Strict Tort Liability   Manufacturer of dangerous product liable without proof of negligence for dangerous product

Strike   Temporary, concerted action of workers to withhold their services from employer

Sublease   Transfer of less than a tenant's full rights under a lease

Subrogation   Right of insurer to assume rights of insured

Subscriber   One who agrees to buy stock in proposed corporation

Summons or **Process**   Notice of suit

Supreme Court of the United States   Highest court in the United States

T

Tangible Personal Property   Personal property that can be seen, touched, and possessed

Tenancy at Sufferance   Holdover tenant without landlord's permission

Tenancy at Will   Tenancy for uncertain period

Tenancy by the Entirety   Co-ownership by husband and wife with right of survivorship

Tenancy for Years   Tenancy for any definite period

Tenancy from Year to Year   Tenancy for indefinite period with yearly rent

Tenancy in Common   Multiple ownership in which, at death, deceased owner's share passes as will directs or to heirs

Tenancy in Partnership   Ownership of partner in partnership property

Tenant or **Lessee**   Possessor of leased property

Tender of Payment   Offer and ability to pay money owed

Tender of Performance   Offer to perform in satisfaction of terms of contract

Term Insurance   Contract whereby insurer assumes risk of death of insured for specified time

Testamentary Trust   Trust created in will

Testator (Testatrix)   Person making a will

Theft   Taking another's property without consent

Third-Party Beneficiary   Person not party to contract but whom parties intended to benefit

Time Draft   Draft payable certain number of days or months after date or presentation

Title   Ownership; evidence of ownership of property

Tort   Private wrong for which damages may be recovered

Tortfeasor   Person whose action causes injury

Trade Acceptance   Draft drawn by seller on purchaser of goods

Trade Fixtures   Fixtures used in business

Trademark   Word, symbol, device, or combination used to identify goods

Trademark or **Trade Name Dilution**   Lessening the capacity of trademark or name to distinguish goods

Trademark or **Trade Name Infringement**   Unauthorized use or imitation of another's mark or name

Trading Partnership   One engaged in buying and selling

Trailing Edge   Left side of front of check

Treasury Stock   Stock reacquired by a corporation

Trial Court   Court that conducts original trial of a case

Trust   Contract by which one holds property for another

Trustee   One who holds title to property for another

U

***Ultra Vires* Contract**   Contract exceeding corporation's powers

Uncured Default   Not all payments on instrument fully made by due date

Undue Influence   Person in special relationship causing another's action contrary to free will

Unenforceable Contract   Agreement that is not currently binding

Unfair Competition   Impression of product results in confusion regarding its origin

Unilateral Contract   Contract calling for an act in consideration for a promise

Unilateral Mistake   Mistake by one party to a contract

Union Shop   Work setting in which all employees must be union members

Unit Pricing   Price stated per unit of measurement

Universal Defense   Defense against any holder

Unjust Enrichment   One benefiting unfairly at another's expense

Unlimited Liability   Business debts payable from personal assets

Usury   Charging higher rate of interest than law allows

V

Valid Contract   Contract enforceable by law

Valued Policy   Policy that fixes values for insured items

Venue   Location where a case is to be tried

Verdict   Decision of a jury

Violation or **Infraction**   Offense less serious than a misdemeanor

Void   Of no legal effect

Voidable Contract   Enforceable agreement that may be set aside by one party

Voting Trust   Device whereby stock is transferred to trustee to vote it

Voucher Check   Check with voucher attached

W

Warehouse Receipt   Document of title issued by storage company for goods stored

Warranty   Assurance goods conform to a standard; statement of insured that relates to risk and is in contract

Warranty Deed   Deed with guarantees

Watered Stock   Stock paid for with property of inflated value

Whistleblower Person who exposes wrongdoing in an organization

Will Document providing disposition of property after death

Winding Up Taking care of outstanding obligations and distributing remaining assets of partnership

With Reserve Auction goods may be withdrawn after bidding starts

Without Reserve Auction goods may not be withdrawn after bidding starts

Wobbler An offense that can be either a felony or a misdemeanor

Writ of Certiorari Order to produce record of a case

Written Contract Contract with terms in writing

Index